MICHAEL CURTIZ

MICHAEL CURTIZ

A Life in Film

ALAN K. RODE

UNIVERSITY PRESS OF KENTUCKY

Published by the University Press of Kentucky,
scholarly publisher for the Commonwealth, serving Bellarmine University,
Berea College, Centre College of Kentucky, Eastern Kentucky University, The
Filson Historical Society, Georgetown College, Kentucky Historical Society,
Kentucky State University, Morehead State University, Murray State University,
Northern Kentucky University, Transylvania University, University of Kentucky,
University of Louisville, and Western Kentucky University.
All rights reserved.

Editorial and Sales Offices: The University Press of Kentucky
663 South Limestone Street, Lexington, Kentucky 40508-4008
www.kentuckypress.com

Library of Congress Cataloging-in-Publication Data

Names: Rode, Alan K., 1954– author.
Title: Michael Curtiz : a life in film / Alan K. Rode.
Description: | Includes bibliographical references and index.
Identifiers: LCCN 2017029778| ISBN 9780813173917 (hardcover : alk. paper) |
    ISBN 9780813173979 (pdf) | ISBN 9780813173962 (epub)
Subjects: LCSH: Curtiz, Michael, 1888–1962. | Motion picture producers and
    directors—United States—Biography.
Classification: LCC PN1998.3.C87 R65 2017 | DDC 791.4302/32092 [B] — dc23
LC record available at https://lccn.loc.gov/2017029778

This book is printed on acid-free paper meeting
the requirements of the American National Standard
for Permanence in Paper for Printed Library Materials.

Manufactured in the United States of America.

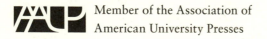 Member of the Association of
American University Presses

For Mom,
who first told me about Hollywood

Contents

Prologue

People began queuing up on Thursday afternoon, March 2, 1944, to secure a bleacher seat on Hollywood Boulevard for the sixteenth annual Academy Awards. Although the banquet to bestow the coveted statuettes had become an increasingly popular event, the Academy of Motion Picture Arts and Sciences had never produced anything on the scale of this evening's opus.

The local police couldn't handle the mass of fandom and photographers that spilled out in front of Grauman's Chinese Theatre. Louis B. Mayer, Hollywood's top mogul, donated the services of his studio police chief, Whitney Hendry, along with a contingent of Metro-Goldwyn-Mayer cops to provide crowd control.

Accustomed to the mundane routine of waving Mickey Rooney's convertible through the front gate at Culver City, MGM's finest couldn't distinguish some of the Hollywood luminaries from the surging hoi polloi. The resultant heavy-handed treatment didn't go over well. *Variety* reported the following day that "many of the stars found themselves pushed around by minions of the law and expressed their chagrin." Adding to the general confusion was the fact that no one had thought to assign valets to whisk away the long line of cars disgorging movie royalty curbside. George Jessel, America's toastmaster, nervously worked the red carpet amid a gaggle of late-arriving movie stars, including Humphrey Bogart and his wife, Mayo Methot, who struggled through the crush to enter the theater by the 8:00 p.m. start time.

What had been a self-congratulatory gathering for industry elites in the swank environs of the Ambassador or Biltmore hotels was being reinvented this night as the premier public event of the motion picture industry at Sid Grauman's 2,200-seat movie palace in the heart of Hollywood. With the war's outcome still in doubt, the sixteenth Academy Awards discarded the insular dining format for a ceremonial spectacle dedicated to the U.S. military.

The 1944 Academy Awards program opened with a U.S. Army–produced short film saluting Hollywood's mobilization to support the war. Susanna Foster, the star of Universal's 1943 version of *Phantom of the Opera,* sang the national anthem. The audience was thick with uniforms: Colonel and Mrs. Frank Capra, Colonel and Mrs. Darryl Zanuck, Captain and Mrs. Ronald Reagan, and so on, along with lesser mortals from all branches of the services. Jack Benny would host the second part of the ceremony—"I am here through the courtesy of Bob Hope's having a bad cold"—on a worldwide shortwave radio hookup broadcast to the U.S. Armed Forces. The Academy's president, Walter Wanger, intoned in the program: "The motion picture industry places above all other considerations service to our nation."

The nominated films in the different categories offered emblematic testimony to a world at war: *In Which We Serve, Five Graves to Cairo, Destination Tokyo, Sahara, So Proudly We Hail, This Is the Army, Hangmen Also Die!, This Land Is Mine, Crash Dive, Stand By for Action, Commandos Strike at Dawn, Corvette-K225,* and *Bombardier,* among others. Half of the ten Best Picture nominees were associated with the ongoing conflict; studio insiders and local bookies piled change on either *Casablanca* or the distinctly non-war-themed *Song of Bernadette* for Best Picture.

The evening's program picked up momentum after a series of technical awards were acknowledged by polite applause and brief expressions of gratitude by the winners. Greer Garson's embarrassing five-minute monologue after receiving the Best Actress Oscar for *Mrs. Miniver* the previous year eliminated any possibility of stem-winder acceptance speeches by tonight's winners. The director Mark Sandrich was tapped to present for Best Director. The nominees included some of the top film directors in Hollywood: Ernst Lubitsch for *Heaven Can Wait,* George Stevens for *The More the Merrier,* Henry King, the favorite for *The Song of Bernadette,* Clarence Brown for *The Human Comedy,* and Michael Curtiz for *Casablanca.*

Seated with the Warner Bros. contingent, Michael Curtiz appeared resigned to his fate. Even though his wife, Bess Meredyth, a charter member of the Academy, told him that tonight would finally be his turn, the veteran director believed he was snakebit when it came to the Oscars. Nominated as a write-in candidate for *Captain Blood* (1935), splitting the vote with *Four Daughters* and *Angels with Dirty Faces* (both 1938), and then narrowly missing with *Yankee Doodle Dandy* the previous year, Curtiz had never been recognized as Best Director. He reputedly summarized the dilemma in his mangled Hungarian-Anglo diction that made him the butt of countless jokes: "Always the bridesmaid and never the Mother."

Fatalism leavened by humor was Curtiz's cultural inheritance from his Magyar forebears. Throughout its long history, Hungary had endured an untold number of conquerors and privations, most recently being torn apart after World War I. The country also produced some of the twentieth century's most talented people, many of whom ended up in the movie business. An apocryphal anecdote recalled a sign posted on a Hollywood studio soundstage during the 1940s: "It's not enough to be Hungarian to make films. One must also have talent." Michael Curtiz assuredly met both these criteria. Though he realized that it was the work, not awards, that mattered, the lack of an Academy Award still rankled.

There had been the marginal recognition of his 1940 Oscar-winning short film *Sons of Liberty,* a Technicolor chronicle of Haym Salomon, the Jewish financier of the American Revolution. This project delighted his studio chief, Jack L. Warner, so much that he uncharacteristically gave Curtiz a three-thousand-dollar bonus. But a two-reeler wasn't a feature, and Mike Curtiz was about making prestige feature films. For nearly a decade after his arrival in Hollywood, he had directed every type of movie assigned to him at Warner Bros. Although most of his movies had been successful, he craved greater freedom to make his own pictures—but never at the risk of jeopardizing his current position. He had become deft at keeping his bosses happy. For those who labored under Curtiz, it was often a different story.

More than a few actors, along with an assortment of film crews, disliked working with him. His reputation for explosive temper tantrums, the difficulty communicating in English, and his perceived disregard for the well-being of others were notorious within the industry. During his first decade at Warner Bros., Curtiz's demonic work ethic approached savagery as he pushed casts and crews past the breaking point of twenty-hour days and seven-day weeks. More than any other studio director, Curtiz was, in a perverse way, responsible for the founding of the Screen Actors Guild in 1933. Yet he consistently turned out superbly crafted pictures within the compressed shooting schedules and strict budgets mandated at Warner Bros. People who aroused his ire included actors who were late or unprepared, production assistants who tattled to the front office, and sound mixers who caused retakes. Those on the set who wanted to break for the obligatory midday meal were derisively called "lunch-bums." Curtiz simply couldn't understand why anyone would want to eat when he was ready to make a movie. The mordant Peter Lorre provided pithy context when he remarked, "Curtiz eats pictures and excretes pictures."

Those who are artistically gifted often straddle the line between passion and obsession. Curtiz strode across this boundary in assuming the mantle of what can only be described as an incandescent mania for filmmaking. He cared only about the picture he was making; everything else, including nourishment, was secondary.

Despite his reputation, Curtiz was neither a raving hobgoblin nor a sadist. He could be charming and maintained warm friendships with many coworkers. The accolades he received didn't make for good copy, but they were as effusive as the horror stories from his detractors. Personal relationships, however, remained secondary to the task at hand. Getting it right in front of the camera always came first, no matter what. Hal Mohr, the pioneer cinematographer of *The Jazz Singer* who worked on Curtiz's early Warner Bros. films, offered a cogent summary of the director's dichotomy: "I enjoyed Mike very much; he was a brutal son-of-a-bitch. He had no consideration for anybody's feelings, but was a very kindly guy."

Curtiz's prowess as a wolfish, back-of-the-set Lothario was equally renowned by means of the Hollywood gossip circuit. His reputation for assignations with nubile extras and wannabe ingénues in dressing rooms and behind soundstage flats assumed legendary proportions. Industry insiders believed that Mike Curtiz lived only to fuck and direct movies . . . not in that order, of course.

Despite squabbles over assignments and the dead weight of studio micromanagement that acted as a brake on his energetic creativity, Curtiz remained steadfastly loyal to Harry and Jack Warner. Although the former Emmanuel Kaminer had risen from childhood poverty to untold prosperity, his devotion to Warner Bros. was so slavish that insiders wondered if there was something more than mere gratitude that bound him so completely to the studio in Burbank.

Curtiz eventually became more resolute in lobbying for quality projects while sidestepping many of the dog assignments. He became first among equals with *Captain Blood* and *The Charge of the Light Brigade* and ascended to become the top director on the Warner lot in 1938 with *The Adventures of Robin Hood, Four Daughters,* and *Angels with Dirty Faces.* These were followed in turn by *Dodge City, The Sea Hawk,* and *The Sea Wolf.* Then there was *Yankee Doodle Dandy,* the George M. Cohan bio-musical hit that made James Cagney into much more than a sneering gangster. On this night, Curtiz culminated the most successful eight-year run of any director in the history of American cinema with *Casablanca* and *This Is the Army,* the Irving

Berlin musical revue that was the biggest-grossing film of the year; the hyper-patriotic brothers Warner donated all the profits to the Army Emergency Relief Fund.

Hal B. Wallis was also in attendance at the Oscars, awaiting the evening's results for his productions of *Casablanca, Watch on the Rhine,* and *Air Force.* Wallis had overseen many of Curtiz's best films with the firm grip of a cold-blooded yet tasteful executive whose instincts were proved right far more often than wrong. The yin and yang of Warner Bros., the pair had risen together since their first meeting in 1926. That was the year when Curtiz arrived in Hollywood from Europe, and Wallis ascended from being the publicity minder of the studio's first major star, Rin Tin Tin. Their spectacular successes had melded their often-tumultuous relationship—particularly on the part of Wallis, with his vituperative production memos—into a close friendship.

Mark Sandrich opened the envelope with the name of the year's Best Director while remarking, "As a director, the element of surprise is much more than I can stand. . . . I know it before you do." Then the announcement: "*Casablanca,* Warner Bros., Michael Curtiz!" Again louder: "*CASABLANCA!*" Like nearly everyone else in Hollywood, Sandrich mispronounced Curtiz's surname "Cur-teeeze," rather than the correct "Cur-tezz." The applause swelled to an ovation as the winner purposefully strode onstage to accept his statuette, then moved forward to the CBS/KNX microphone to say a few words.

He offered his sincere appreciation along with a humorous dig: "Ladies and gentleman, three times I had the great honor to be nominated for this great award. Each time, very carefully I prepared a little speech . . . to express my gratitude to everyone who help me to this great honor. I never had the chance to deliver this speech. I never win. So I may condense all that I want to say. All the speeches for few word [*sic*]. I thank you. I am humbly grateful. Most of all, I am grateful for thirty-second time limit. I thank you."

Michael Curtiz and *Casablanca* were now bound together for the ages—but not in the same manner of his contemporaries and their classic films. If John Ford is joined at the hip to *How Green Was My Valley,* as Alfred Hitchcock is to *Shadow of a Doubt,* the historical underpinning of Mike Curtiz to *Casablanca* is akin to a remora attached to the underside of a cinematic whale shark. *Casablanca* evolved into a cultural phenomenon that would be embraced by succeeding generations to such an extent as to dwarf nearly every other film ever made. But there was more to the historical diminishment of Michael Curtiz than simply being marginalized by perhaps the most popular movie of all time.

Beginning in the late 1950s, a new generation of film critics and historians achieved cultural purchase by crafting a fresh perspective about the style and meaning of directors and direction. Analysis on directorial style became a litmus test established by the auteur school of cinema cognoscenti. Like a painter, a film director had to render his movies with a specific signature and achieve a thematic, repeatable style in order for his work to be contextually analyzed and properly appreciated. While this modern wave of critical writing enhanced the historical standing of Hitchcock, Ford, Capra, and Hawks, it diminished Michael Curtiz. Dismissed as a vocational mechanic of the studio system—"workhorse" was the standard descriptor—Curtiz was serially omitted from critical discussions about the seminal film directors of the twentieth century.

Receiving short shrift from the critics, many of Curtiz's credits were venerated by succeeding generations of moviegoers. It is a striking paradox: one of the most accomplished film directors became virtually anonymous while his films remain pillars of popular culture. No other director has had his work feted with such ritualistic permanence. Americans continue to celebrate each Yuletide with *White Christmas,* observe Independence Day with *Yankee Doodle Dandy,* and fall in love while watching *Casablanca. Captain Blood, The Adventures of Robin Hood, Angels with Dirty Faces, The Sea Hawk, Mildred Pierce, Life with Father,* and *The Breaking Point* endure as classic cinema. The work is revered, but what of the director?

Because he passed from the scene before the renaissance of appreciation for Hollywood golden-age filmmakers, Curtiz didn't burnish his reputation with contemporary chroniclers as some of his peers managed to do. There was no opportunity for him to relate anecdotes at retrospectives of his movies or participate in a filmed interview, although this probably wouldn't have happened even if he had lived longer. The directorial maestro might have been a colossus on the soundstage, but privately he was a reserved man who kept his personal life shrouded from public view. According to his youngest brother, Gabriel, Curtiz was "several entities in one." He also didn't feel the need to toot his own horn because his public image was so prominent.

During his career, Curtiz became one of Hollywood's most colorful legends. Over a half century after his death, he remains the anecdotal gift that keeps on giving. The Curtiz persona enshrined in show business lore begins with his aforementioned garbled Hungarian-English syntax that gave rise to more one-liners than Henny Youngman ever spouted. Intimates averred that Curtiz spoke five languages, all unintelligibly. His countless malapropisms were remembered, retold, and archived. The actor David Niven appropriated a Curtiz utterance from the set of *The Charge of the Light Brigade*—"Bring on the empty horses"—as the title of his best-selling memoir. The Hollywood columnist James Bacon believed that "most of the so-called Goldwynisms were the result of Sam Goldwyn's press agents following Mike Curtiz around." So much of what Curtiz said or was attributed to him became fodder for stories that his surname would be appropriated as a descriptive noun for anecdotal malapropisms: Curtizisms.

Although Curtiz manipulated his linguistic deficit into a valuable publicity attribute, he didn't feel his command of English was lacking compared to that of some of his countrymen. "Of all Hungarians what is famous, I speak the best goddamn English," he declared. Although many people claimed afterward that they didn't understand what Curtiz was saying, there was no doubt about his ability to somehow express exactly what he wanted to everyone who mattered on his movie sets. The actor Paul Henreid, dealing with Curtiz at his most harried during the filming of *Casablanca,* offered, "His command of English was excellent, but his pronunciation left something to be desired."

Little was known about this contradictory man during his days of fame in Hollywood that wasn't sourced from a studio press release or a calculated quote. Warner Bros. and other studio publicity departments spun several different versions of his early life and disclosed virtually nothing of a personal nature. Much of this opacity was due to Curtiz's being adamant till the day he died that nothing substantive be written about him. Few realized that he started out as a classically trained actor who virtually invented the film industry in his native Hungary. He ran a movie studio and directed scores of impressive films in Europe before coming to America. Practically no one knew anything about his formative years, his family, and his personal life. The films are his heritage, and that was exactly the way he wanted it. The movies of Michael Curtiz proved to be the most prolific of legacies.

Whole and in part, he directed 181 films, a staggering output that outstrips John Ford and exceeds the combined totals of George Cukor, Victor Fleming, and Howard Hawks.[1] More significant than the aggregate number of films is the protean nature of his work.

Curtiz was the anti-auteur. During his unprecedented tenure at Warner Bros., he helmed rousing adventures, Westerns, musicals, war movies, romances, historical dramas, horror films, tearjerkers, melodramas,
comedies, spectacles, and film noirs. No other director would become so
closely identified with a single movie studio: it is impossible to recount the
career of Michael Curtiz without relating much of the history of Warner
Bros. After finally moving on from the studio, Curtiz directed one of his
most enduringly popular films, *White Christmas,* followed by *The Egyptian,* one of the most controversial of the wide-screen Technicolor period
spectacles. Although the final part of his career has been written off as pedestrian, Curtiz directed several distinctive pictures, including *The Proud
Rebel* and *King Creole,* a noir-stained drama regarded as the best of Elvis
Presley's features.

Curtiz's extraordinary European period, from 1912 to 1926, has been
indifferently chronicled. Before setting foot in Hollywood, he completed
upward of seventy films, including epic spectacles such as *Sodom und Gomorrha* (1922) and *Die Sklavenkönigin* (The King's Slave or The Moon of
Israel, 1924), a rendition of the Exodus story so spectacular that Adolph
Zukor tied up the U.S. distribution rights in order to protect his studio's
investment in Cecil B. DeMille's *The Ten Commandments* (1923).

With such an overwhelming career yield, not every Curtiz film could
be an outstanding picture. Nor could any director imprint a distinctive
thematic signature throughout such an enormous and so varied a body
of work. The era of the studio system was defined more by each studio's
brand of films adorned by its stars rather than a directorial imprint. Warner Bros., perhaps the embodiment of this factory approach, cranked
out movies with conveyor-belt precision during the majority of Curtiz's
tenure.

Despite the vagaries of the studio system and Curtiz's reputation as
the Swiss Army knife of contract directors, there was no greater visual
poet of the cinematic medium. As he put it, "I don't see black-and-white
words in script when I read it. I see action." The sweep of his camera and
artistry of his compositions were Curtiz's John Hancock. He aptly summarized the tenuous balance between the creativity that distinguished his
work and the requisite commercial success that sustained his continued
ability to make movies: "I put all the art into my pictures that I think the
audience can stand."

Curtiz's work with actors was equally impressive. He directed ten different performers to Oscar-nominated performances in the widest variety

of roles imaginable. His reputation as a discoverer-nurturer of new talent was unparalleled. Errol Flynn, Doris Day, John Garfield, Alexis Smith, Ann Blyth, Lili Damita, Danny Thomas, and Walter Slezak were among those who made their debuts or were cast in their first significant roles by Curtiz.

Curtiz exercised control over his movies during his early Hungarian period and somewhat tenuously with his own production company at Warner Bros. in 1947–48. Attempting to portray him as a thematic auteur is a specious exercise, even though he frequently revisited similar material or methods that appealed to him. In much the way that Laurence Olivier mastered acting, he became a virtuoso of technique. In the end, Curtiz made so many movies that he ended up being taken for granted.

A cinematic pioneer, Curtiz made a seamless transition from the earliest hand-cranking cameras in silent films to directing the first sound feature at Warner Bros. in which the characters spoke their parts. He led the way in two- and three-color Technicolor productions, directed the first motion picture produced in VistaVision, and worked extensively in CinemaScope. When the camera had to remain stationary during the earliest days of sound, he insisted on moving his actors whenever possible. His tireless concentration was legendary. To successfully direct a film, he declared, "You should be a tiger on the camera, fighting for the success from the picture." His movies mirrored his life: an existence in perpetual motion.

An unquenchable appetite for a strenuous lifestyle sustained him. He would be directing a film while maintaining a relentless schedule of premieres, screenings, and related social events. He frequently entertained at his Canoga Park ranch, which included his stable of horses, a polo field, a skeet-shooting range, a photo lab, and the main house fit for a Scottish lord, all spread over a huge estate in the San Fernando Valley. After World War II he would relocate to a smaller, but just as sylvan, country setting in Encino that was closer to his professional home on the Warner Bros. soundstages. Despite these and other trappings of success, Curtiz remained the same obsessive dreamer from Budapest who slept a restless four hours or less every night. He was directing a film, planning to direct a film, or thinking about directing a film, usually all three. So long as he could continue to make motion pictures, Curtiz's life as a feast of work would continue unabated.

On the night that Michael Curtiz won the Academy Award for what would be his most enduring success, *Casablanca* won two more Oscars:

A quintet of *Casablanca* winners: a sleepy Michael Curtiz, Jack Warner (talking, as usual), Hal Wallis (with his Thalberg Award), one of the event's hosts, Jack Benny, and the screenwriter Howard Koch (author's collection).

Howard Koch and the Epstein Brothers for writing, and the big one: Best Picture of 1943.

Riding back to his ranch and clutching his wax-cast Oscar (a gold one would replace it after the war), however, Curtiz felt unsettled rather than content.

The 1944 Academy Awards should have been an unalloyed triumph for Hal Wallis, who received his second Irving Thalberg Memorial Award for distinguished production. Instead, when he stood up and headed for the stage to accept the Best Picture Oscar as the producer of *Casablanca*, Jack L. Warner ran up ahead of him and took the statuette from a startled Jack Benny. Still steaming over the incident four decades later, Wallis recalled feeling "humiliated and furious" about ceding public recognition for his deserved triumph to a mercurial mogul who had virtually nothing to do with the making of his movie.

It was the inevitable denouement of a schism between the pair of titans that began shortly after Wallis inked his exclusive independent production contract with Warner Bros. in January 1942. Jack Warner came to resent his producer's independence and was jealous of his spectacular successes. Wallis, whose appetite for personal publicity had expanded with his achievements, was galled to defer to a boss who interfered with the production of his pictures and, in his view, was not living up to his contractual obligations concerning access to talent and scripts. There was no doubt that Hal Wallis would soon be leaving Warner Bros.

As midnight approached on March 2, 1944, the rift between Wallis and Warner was an unresolved dilemma for Curtiz. The director was conflicted by his feelings of loyalty to both men while cannily assessing his future opportunities at the age of fifty-seven in a business where acclaim and prosperity were notoriously short-lived.

The director realized that the imbroglio represented both uncertainty and opportunity. But like a cat, Michael Curtiz had long before mastered the technique of always landing on his feet. From the first time he sipped a coffee at the Café New York in Budapest and mused about how he would tell stories with moving images, it had always been so.

1

A River Runs through It

Long before Budapest was a city, it was three villages. At the northern reaches of the Great Hungarian Plain, a trio of settlements were separated by the mighty Danube River. Buda and Obuda were on the west bank, and Pest on the east.

The region was originally settled by the Celts; the Romans established a frontier outpost by the Danube named Aquincum. Located on the Buda side of the river, the enclave was part of the imperial province of Lower Pannonia, serving as an early warning system against barbarian invaders of the empire. Succeeding conquerors, including the Huns of the fifth century, held sway, but the carousel of historical dominance continued to rotate as leaders died off or the next wave of aggressors swept down from the east.

The Magyars arrived in the ninth century and never left. These horsemen from the steppe, the descendants of Attila the Hun, established a bulwark of Western culture between Rome and Byzantium. The kingdom of Hungary prospered under a series of Arpadian kings until being nearly annihilated by Batu Khan's Mongol horde in 1242. A century and a half of subsequent rule by the Ottoman Turks partitioned the country into a perpetual battlefield that effectively protected Europe against further invasion. Although eventually dominated by the Germanic Habsburg Empire, Magyar-speaking descendants increasingly assimilated with Germans and Jews along with influxes of Romanians, Serbs, Slovaks, and Croats. By the middle of the nineteenth century, the Hungarians were flourishing, and the trio of cities straddling the Danube reflected this increased prosperity.

The *Ausgleich*, or Compromise, of 1867 dissolved the old Habsburg multinational empire that had endured for five centuries. The compromise was a grand bargain between the Germans of Austria-Bohemia and the Magyars of Hungary to formalize their joint hegemony over a diverse population. Both nations became theoretically equal under a single ruler who was crowned emperor of Austria and king of Hungary. Each nation-state had its own parliament and its own language: German for Austria and Magyar for Hungary. One was a citizen of Austria or Hungary, but all were subjects of the Germanic emperor-king.

The merger of Buda, Obuda, and Pest into Budapest in 1873 codified the new empire. It was the beginning of a golden age rivaling that of any other European city before World War I. A cosmopolitan metropolis of stunning vistas and modern urban planning and infrastructure, Budapest became the crown jewel of eastern Europe and was the largest port on the Danube. By 1900 Budapest had the first subway in Europe, a sophisticated municipal water system, and an electrical tram service; electric lights replaced gaslit street lamps throughout the city.

Thirteen years after Emperor Franz Joseph rode across the Chain Bridge to commemorate the unification of Budapest, Emmanuel Kaminer, later to rename himself Mihály Kertész, then Michael Kertész, and finally Michael Curtiz, was born on Christmas evening in 1886. Curtiz's correct birth date was historically elusive. His year of birth is recorded variously as 1888, 1889, and 1892 by different sources, and there is a death certificate with a birth date of December 25, 1887.

Curtiz fueled much of this uncertainty, first by falsifying the date of birth on his U.S. passport registration in 1934 and then fibbing about his age in press interviews and news articles. When his wife Bess Meredyth complained that her spouse's erroneous passport date gave the appearance that she was considerably older than he was (he was actually three years her senior), Curtiz shrugged and said, "Why don't you lie like I am?"

A birth certificate noting his name as Mano Kaminer records 9:00 p.m. on December 25, 1886, as the time and date of his birth. The certificate on file at the Jewish Community Archive in Budapest also includes the additional detail that Curtiz's circumcision was performed in January 1887 by Jakab Weinberger at 12 Gyár Street, located in the Seventh District, where the Kaminers lived. Other sources incorrectly identify Curtiz's given name as Miksa. This is actually a common Hungarian familial nickname that Curtiz was tagged with as a boy.

During Curtiz's tenure at Warner Bros., his father was sometimes identified in magazine articles and studio biographies as an architect and his mother as an opera singer or a dancer. In interviews, Curtiz occasionally referred to his father as a carpenter. Curtiz's father, Ignacz, was a painter and a bricklayer born in 1845 in Dalatyn, a Galician village in the foothills of the Carpathian Mountains (now part of Poland). He immigrated to Budapest in 1866. Curtiz's mother, named Aranka Nathan, was born in Delatyu, Poland, in 1862 and probably was a singer at one time.

Curtiz's boyhood home was an apartment building, 23 Szovetseg, in the Seventh District of Budapest, the Pest side of the city, three blocks from the square named for the nineteenth-century Hungarian actress Lujza Blaha. The Magyar Theater, later renamed the Hungarian National Theater, was 250 yards from his front door.

Few details survive about Curtiz's childhood. While it wasn't a nightmarish saga of Dickensian misery, life certainly wasn't easy. His father's employment was sporadic; it was said that he laid the brick walls outside St. Stephen's Basilica in Budapest. Late in life, Curtiz recalled from his childhood days "that many times we are hungry." The family would eventually include seven children: Michael was the oldest, followed by Regina (1889), Dezso (David, 1893), Margit (1897), Kornelia (1900), Lajos (1901), and the youngest, Gabor (Gabriel, 1904). There was an apartment building boom in Budapest near the end of the nineteenth century, and the Seventh District was the most crowded; many residences were adjudged as "foul-smelling, cramped warrens."

The Kaminers lived in a small apartment with a living room, two small bedrooms, and a tiny kitchen. Late in life, Curtiz recalled the poverty of his early days for a magazine interviewer: "I tell my brothers then, all my life I will work to keep from being that way. Sleeping with four kids in one room!" Such memories were the major impetus of Curtiz's obsessive work ethic.

Mano Kaminer was a robust youngster and an attention-getter. Although raised in a gritty urban environment, he did not become a street urchin. Instead, he evolved into a budding artist. His earliest professional association with the entertainment business consisted of selling candies and refreshments to theater patrons, especially at the Népszínház (Folk Theater), running beer, cigarettes, and flowers to the actors backstage, then ducking in to watch plays and operettas. With his exuberant personality, the youthful Kaminer was drawn to show business like a moth to a flame.

He completed gymnasium, or middle and high school, in 1904. It was an education that was equivalent or superior to any in Europe. The rigorous Budapest citywide curriculum mandated six years of Latin, three years of Greek, mathematics to the level of calculus, and a heavy load of Magyar literature and Hungarian history. It was a pressurized environment characterized by rote memorization, testing, recitation, intensive study, and more testing. The rigidity of his formative education burnished several aspects of his personality. On the positive side, his robust ego became balanced by a well-rounded intelligence. But he also developed a lifelong impatience that could give way to explosive frustration.

Curtiz aspired to be a professional actor. So, as the imperial government categorized acting as a vested profession akin to engineering or medicine, he had to attend the Royal Academy of Theater and Art in order to legally work as a contract performer. How Curtiz accrued the money to attend the academy became fodder for another recycled saga concerning his youthful employment.

The year-round circus at City Park in Budapest had a profound effect on him as a boy. He apparently spent a period during his early teen years performing with a circus as a pantomime actor, a strongman, or an acrobat. The director Byron Haskin observed Curtiz during the filming of *Black Fury* in 1935 scuttling up a tipple ladder "like a monkey, having been a circus acrobat." Another account had Curtiz performing as a teenage acrobat in something called "the Becket of Circus." Curtiz told Pete Martin in a 1947 interview with the *Saturday Evening Post* that he went on the road with a circus when he was seventeen, performing pantomime and juggling because "I was good athlete at school. Runner, jumper, like that." Curtiz remained a physically nimble man into his late middle age. On the set of *The Unsuspected* in 1947, he demonstrated an old circus trick by tossing a lighted match in the air and catching it by the unlighted end without extinguishing the flame. There was a fictitious claim that Curtiz was a member of the 1912 Olympic fencing team from Austria-Hungary that won four medals. Not coincidentally, this story was peddled at the time Curtiz directed *Jim Thorpe—All American* for Warner Bros. in 1951. Another version has him leaving home at the age of fourteen and joining a theatrical troupe in Székesfehérvár, a city in central Hungary, and touring the country for two years before applying for admission to the Royal Academy. Although the accuracy of these stories is uncertain, Curtiz's youthful employment not only alleviated the severity of his impoverishment but also taught him how to perform in front of an audience.

Being a Jew didn't damage his ambitions either. Under the long reign of Emperor Franz Joseph, Jews became semiassimilated as participative citizens. Fully one-fifth of Budapest's population of 733,000 was Jewish in 1900, and a Jew named Ferenc Heltai was elected mayor in 1912. Although the specter of anti-Semitism was omnipresent, it noticeably receded in Hungary during the first decade of the new century and did not bar entry to most occupations; in fact, Jews constituted the largest percentage of selected professional classes, particularly artists and writers. In greater Budapest, Curtiz was part of a modern generation of Jews who considered themselves Hungarians and strove to achieve their dreams in that dynamic metropolis at the dawning of a new age.

Many Jews in Budapest spoke Magyar rather than Yiddish. The future film director formally acknowledged his Hungarian pedigree and cloaked his heritage when, upon embarking on his acting career, he changed his surname from the Jewish Kaminer to the Magyar Kertész. It was a common practice. The noted playwright (and Curtiz's friend) Lajos Bálint boasted of his record of Magyarizing Jewish surnames for a plethora of Hungarian actors, including changing Mano Kaminer into Mihály Kertész.

Kertész's artistic sensibility was developed in Budapest during those heady years before World War I. The city had a tremendously robust intellectual and cultural life. The new main thoroughfare of Andrassy Avenue bisected its three-mile ring of boulevards. At 140 feet wide, Andrassy was the Hungarian Champs-Élysées, home of the Magyar Theater, the Royal Academy of Music (later renamed the Franz Liszt Academy of Music), and the Comic Opera. Along Nagymezo Utca there was glut of cabarets highlighted by the famous Orpheum Theater, which specialized in operettas, highly popular at that time. And throughout Budapest there was the great cultural integrator of Hungarian society: the coffeehouse.

Budapest's coffeehouses were an incubator of intellectual and artistic talent that shaped the new century. By the time of Kertész's bar mitzvah, there were approximately six hundred coffeehouses throughout the city. Each establishment possessed a unique identity, bearing little resemblance to the modern chains of efficient but identical coffee purveyors. In addition to doubling as full-service restaurants and islands of leisure for families of different classes, they served almost as professional clubs by providing services and entertainment while competing for customers. One could receive mail at one's coffeehouse, read multiple newspapers (there were twenty-two daily papers published in Budapest in 1900), write (pen, ink, and paper were provided upon request), discuss, debate, and think.

Foremost among the city's coffeehouses was the Café New York. It was an opulently appointed café ensconced in a lavish building on the

Elizabeth Ring in the Seventh District. Alajos Hauszmann, the chief architect of Buda Castle and many of the finest buildings in the city, designed the structure. Opening night in 1894 at the Café New York was consecrated by a celebrated event that will be forever associated with Hungarian show biz history. The story goes that on that night, around what would have been closing time, a tipsy group of artists strolled down to the Danube and ceremoniously consigned the front door key to the bottom of the river. From that moment on, the Café New York was officially open twenty-four hours a day, every day.

The interior of the Café New York, replete with faun statues, fancy chandeliers, and baroque decorations heavy with marble and gold, became the center of Budapest's literary and artistic life. The film director Andre de Toth recalled waiters attired in white tie and tails who "glided through the SRO crowds as if skating on ice."

One of the café's habitués from the post-Curtiz generation, de Toth later summed up the New York's unique atmosphere and clientele, which grew to include the distinguished nuclear physicists Edward Teller and Leo Szilard, as "the home of artists and fakers, literary geniuses and illiterates, apostles of peace and the future makers of the atomic and hydrogen bombs. In short, a full-blown nut house."

A co-owner of the Café New York was a former newspaper columnist, Vilmos Tarjan, a charming bon vivant and ferocious card player. He unhesitatingly supported his artist friends when they were financially down on their luck with gratis food and drink and interest-free loans. After a couple of decades, Tarjan's guest book resembled a who's who of show business: Fritz Lang, Dita Parlo, Rod La Rocque and his wife, Vilma Bánky, Sonja Henie, Annabella, Sydney Chaplin, Max Pallenberg, Josephine Baker, Thomas Mann, Danielle Darrieux, Helene Thimig (Mrs. Max Reinhardt), Lilian Harvey, Adolph Zukor, and Louis B. Mayer.

It is easy to romanticize the Café New York, with its talented artistic clientele and environment of creative bonhomie. As the film historian László Kriston put it, it was more about the practicality of insular relationships: "Everyone knew everyone, they all screwed the same chorus girls and got drunk together and worked and argued."

The interior had a definitive occupational pecking order. The table for film journalists who wrote for city's three cinema magazines was located on the second-floor balcony; many a film review and subtitles for a foreign film were scribed there over coffee and pastries. By 1913 the owners and operators of movie studios and cinemas, together with filmmakers and actors, congregated downstairs. The cinemas had shows scheduled every two hours till 10:00 p.m. After these wheeler-dealers scrutinized box-office figures, the card games would begin at midnight and continue into the wee hours. Budapest had 114 cinemas when Kertész began making films; the number of theaters and studios would swell during World War I, when most foreign films were embargoed or unavailable. By the war's end, in 1918, there were thirty-seven film companies operating in Budapest.

Kertész's contemporaries at the New York included a pair of close companions: Sandor Kellner, who grew up down the street from Kertész and would famously reinvent himself as Sir Alexander Korda, and Lehol Gabor, who became Gabriel Pascal, the producer who first brought the work of George Bernard Shaw to the screen. There was also the photographer André Kertész, the novelist and playwright Ferenc Molnár, the portly actor-comedian Jacob Gerö, later known to American audiences as the jowl-shaking S. Z. Sakall, and a National Theater actor named Béla Blaskó who billed himself Arisztid Olt. When Olt transitioned into films, he appropriated the name of his hometown of Lugos and changed his name to Bela Lugosi.

Although Thomas Edison's kinetoscope made its New York City debut in 1894, it was the Lumière brothers in France with their cinematograph projector who introduced the commercial possibilities of film in Europe. The Lumières presented a series of ten short films in Paris on December 28, 1895, at the Grand Café on the Boulevard des Capucines. In April 1896 the first screening of a Lumière film in Budapest occurred in the coffeehouse of the Hotel Royal on the Elizabeth Ring. Movies were also exhibited at the Urania Scientific Theater at City Park during Hungary's 1896 millennium celebration. These early venues went bankrupt, but movies continued to be exhibited in movable cinema tents at the City Park as well as in cafés in Budapest.

The influence of these early images on the young Kertész cannot be underestimated. As he wrote in a 1913 Budapest movie magazine article: "Who could have dared to assume a mere ten years ago in the tents of Varosliget [City Park], watching those flickery images on badly constructed wooden benches, that Edison's invention, the motion picture, would grow into such a grandiose enterprise."

Mihály Kertész had discovered a new method of artistic expression. He became determined to shape it into his own.

2

Actor to Director

Kertész graduated from the Royal Academy of Theater and Art in 1906. Located on Rakoczi Avenue in Budapest, the academy was a highly competitive institution that provided its students with detailed instruction on acting, set design, and related subjects. The curriculum was designed to winnow out those who were not exceptionally talented, supremely confident, and willing to work intensely.

The actor Victor Varconi remembered that every September, a line of "handsome men and pretty girls" queued up for blocks down Rakoczi Avenue to take the entrance examination, which amounted to a cold audition. Varconi attended the academy in 1909 and remembered performing for three judges—all members of the National Theater—who reviewed hundreds of auditions over three days. The instructors were among the most revered performers in Hungary: Ujházi Ede, Teréz Csillag, Gyula Gál, and the school's director, Sándor Somló.

It was the equivalent of actor commando training. The attrition rate was high. Kertész recalled the academic rigor in a 1947 interview: "I study three languages. I even study anatomy and makeup. There are examinations every three months. It is tough. There are a hundred eighty-two in the class. Sixteen get a diploma."

The young actor became particularly interested in direction. Unlike other students, he obsessively scrutinized the smallest details of a production's staging.

His initial experience as a contract actor was with a touring theatrical company known as Thalia. It led to engagements in plays at the municipal theaters in Pécs and in Szeged, the latter the third-largest city in the country. He achieved a coveted contractual assignment to the Magyar National Theater in 1910, yet he was still relegated to a minor role in the greater theatrical world of Budapest. He was not playing leading roles and

A 1910 postcard portrait of Mihály Kertész as a young actor at the Magyar National Theater (author's collection).

was billed below many of his contemporaries, including Bela Lugosi and Charles Puffy.

Despite being listed down in the cast of players, Kertész was frequently mentioned and quoted in the weekly magazine *Színházi Élet* (Theater Life). This was due primarily to the support of his cousin Sándor Incze, the magazine's founder and editor. Kertész's public visibility was also a byproduct of his robust ego. The young actor relentlessly exaggerated his accomplishments to advance his career. But he didn't permit conceit to cloud his professional judgment. By 1911 he'd begun to feel uncertain about his future as an actor. According to his friend Lajos Bálint, Kertész doubted his thespian abilities: "I do not believe [he said with total sincerity] that I can become a great actor. I lack something, and each time, I realize that I can only do a fraction of what I feel or imagine."

Kertész continued to perform in classical and modern theatrical dramas, but he inserted himself into directorial situations whenever possible. He developed a reputation for an innate visual sense when it came to arranging scenes and directing actors. He was also becoming aware of the inherent constraints of theater. He remarked to Bálint about the new medium that was capturing everyone's attention in the cafés: "I do not know what you think about films. I see some marvelous perspectives. It offers some possibilities that the limited dimensions of the theater will never be able to offer." Mór Ungerleider, owner of the Velence coffeehouse on Rakoczi Street, had been exploring the possibilities of film since the turn of the century. He screened movies in his café with his headwaiter, József Bécsi, acting as the projectionist; a sheet suspended from the ceiling was the screen. Bécsi would eventually become Hungary's first cinematographer and would shoot many films with Kertész. His boss had even bigger plans. In 1898 Ungerleider and a former circus acrobat named József Neumann founded Projectograph, the first Hungarian film company.

Ungerleider and Neumann established a public cinema—the Apollo—near their headquarters on the Ring to screen films for patrons. They dealt in cameras and projectors while importing and exhibiting foreign films. They also published the first cinema magazines that featured scholarly articles by directors, writers, and technicians. Projectograph produced and exhibited its own contemporary newsreels, Méliès brothers films, and productions from the burgeoning German and Danish film industries. Some of Projectograph's earliest productions included *Hare Hunting in the Plain, Arrival of the Bulgarian Ruler at Budapest,* and *Fire at the Kovald Factory.* Although these newsreels were brief, spectators flocked to see them. By 1912 there were 270 permanent cinemas doing business in Hungary, 92 of them located in greater Budapest. The Hungarian film scholar István Nemeskürty estimated Hungarian movie attendance at this time to be 1.5 million patrons per week. The sun had risen on what would become a golden age in Hungarian cinema.

Projectograph's initial feature film production, *Ma és holnap* (Today and Tomorrow), a moralistic warning about the societal evils of gambling and alcohol, was released in October 1912. Kertész played the supporting character Arisztid. His role was minor, but his contributions to the production were significant. He befriended the two young scenarists Imre Roboz and Iván Siklósi and made numerous suggestions that helped their story conform to the realities of the camera. *Today and Tomorrow* was the beginning of a long and mutually beneficial association between Kertész and Siklósi, who over many cups of Café New York coffee would collaborate on ten films during the next seven years.

Shortly before production, Kertész received a lucky break when the director, Raymond Pellerin, withdrew because of another commitment. Kertész's budding reputation and successful involvement with the script made him the obvious choice to step in. He later recalled his directorial debut with characteristic simplicity: "The producer signed a cameraman, but no director. A director was too expensive. The cameraman yelled for instructions for what to do. I said, 'I know stage direction. I help you.'"

Today and Tomorrow premiered on October 14, 1912. The following advertisement appeared in the weekly *Motion Picture News:*

The First Hungarian Dramatic Art Film.
Monday
October 14
will be a memorable day
in the history of Hungarian cinematography.
The first Hungarian film drama played by Hungarian actors,
in a Hungarian setting, with a Hungarian subject, will be
presented on that day.

Kertész was dissatisfied with the results of his first endeavor. He understood only the rudiments of camera technique and directing actors for film and was essentially making it up as he went along. He declared: "Neither I nor my technicians know enough. I am going to learn."

He threw himself into new movies for Projectograph: *Krausz Doktor a vérpadon* (Doctor Krausz on the Scaffold), *Hazasodik az uram* (My Husband Marries), and *Mozikirály* (Movie King). *Movie King* was actually a short film that was presented as part of an operetta. Referred to as a "sketch film,"[1] it was screened at the Kiraly Theater and featured Sári Fedák, one of the best-known Hungarian operetta stars of the day. Another sketch film that has until now has been omitted from the director's filmography is *Gyerünk csak!* (Come On!), shown during a folk opera revue in May 1913. These films were produced and released during the first half of 1913. Kertész was becoming much more than an interesting character actor who knew how to direct; he was a pioneer of the new medium that had become the talk of Budapest.

After four directorial credits, Kertész realized that further on-the-job training as a filmmaker in Budapest had limited benefit. In July 1913 he decided to travel to Denmark and visit Nordisk, then one of the most technically modern movie companies in the world. Hollywood was still a blip on the world's cinematic radar, whereas the Danish and Swedish film industries were more advanced. Although he told the Hungarian press that Nordisk had invited him, he had to convince Mór Ungerleider to finance the trip. A surviving account of Kertész's conversation with Ungerleider from the producer-composer István Radó indicates that this "internship" was an investment by Projectograph:

> Kertész, the discovery of the Ungerleiders, had accepted the invitation of Nordisk in 1912 for a lengthy internship. He had to tell Ungerleider that he was leaving. He called him from Café New York:
> "Mr. CEO, I quit. Effective immediately."
> "Come up to my office, we'll talk it over."
> "There's nothing to talk over. I'm off."
> "Where are you?"
> "At Café New York."
> "Hang on, I'm coming right over."
> Ten minutes later, he duly showed up.
> "Why do you want to quit?"
> "I'm going to Copenhagen to Nordisk. To study! When I come back I'll direct magnificent films for you!"
> "You think it works like that? What about the advance I gave you?! You owe it to me."
> Kertész was taken aback a bit. "But Mr. CEO, this is the biggest chance of my life! I don't care—to hell with the advance!"
> Ungerleider cracked up. While still laughing, he decided to give Kertész a little stipend for his trip.

Arriving during Nordisk's mammoth production of *Atlantis,* Kertész had to become an active participant. According to one account, he pretended to be a deaf-mute and applied for a job as an extra. He was hired, then fired within two weeks when it became evident that the twenty-five-year-old Hungarian didn't understand a word of Danish. His charade brought him to the attention of the principal director and Nordisk production chief, August Blom, who then hired him to play a supporting role in *Atlantis*.

In a less colorful but more plausible scenario, Kertész was initially kept at arm's length because he was a foreigner working for a potential competitor and Nordisk wanted to safeguard the patents on its equipment and related proprietary processes. Employing a persuasive combination of talent and chutzpah, Kertész convinced Blom not only to cast him in a supporting character role but also to let him assist with the direction of the film. He ended up becoming an assistant director on what was one of most ambitious films undertaken at that time.

In the movie Kertész is an instantly recognizable but dandier version of the forbidding countenance that would later stride the Warner Bros. soundstages. Dapper in a cutaway suit, he sports a thick head of parted hair.

Gerhart Hauptmann, the acclaimed German playwright and novelist, won the Nobel Prize for literature in 1912, the same year his novel *Atlantis* was published. At Blom's insistence, Nordisk paid 50,000 kroner (approximately $200,000 in today's dollars) for the screen rights to *Atlantis,* but the deal permitted Hauptmann to retain creative control over his semiautobiographical soap opera about the tragic marriage and unfulfilled love affairs of a dedicated biologist who embarks on a lengthy odyssey in search of happiness. The tragic sinking of an ocean liner after a collision at sea is a highlight of the story, but Hauptmann wasn't referring to the RMS *Titanic*'s sinking: the book's publication preceded that catastrophe by a month. The timing of the movie's release—more than a year after the *Titanic* cataclysm—was still too close for comfort in many places. *Atlantis* was banned in Sweden and Germany owing to, as Kertész put it, "bad memories."

Atlantis is one of the longest feature films of its time. It was critically acclaimed but never did make back its huge investment. Available in a superlative restoration, *Atlantis* remains a compelling epic of early cinema. The fascinating location photography in pre–World War I Berlin, Paris, and New York is complemented by the restrained simplicity of Blom's direction during a period when florid performances were the norm. Blom also filmed two endings—a conventional happy ending, and a tragic denouement in which the good doctor expires—because it was believed that the grimmer conclusion would play better in Russia.

Where *Atlantis* excels is in the staging of the shipboard sequences and the sinking of the *Roland*. Blom chartered the Norwegian steamship *C. F. Tietgen* and spent two days in the bay off Køge, Denmark, with cast and crew. The company included five hundred extras. Kertész assisted in the direction of these sequences. The entire experience left a permanent impression, as he recalled after returning to Budapest: "It took enormous financial expenditure and two months of grueling work to finish the film by late August, with 1,500 people working on it. One sequence resembles the catastrophic demise of the *Titanic*. For this scene, the company had bought a separate ship in order to play out the terrible visions of our imagination. . . . It's a frightful sight to see them fighting for their own survival, tossing each other into the sea and screaming for help."

By skillfully cutting from expertly filmed sequences of a miniature ship sinking to scenes shot aboard the actual ocean liner, then to extras flailing in the water and clinging to lifeboats, Blom created an illusion of maritime disaster that became a minor sensation. Kertész never forgot what he learned about the logistics and choreography of location filming during *Atlantis*. Depicting realism at all costs became his professional mantra. Actors, extras, and stunt people whose physical safety was often a directorial afterthought did not always share his enthusiasm.

After his Denmark sojourn, Kertész concluded that while he understood acting, it was a craft at which he would never excel. Like a violinist who prefers the conductor's baton, he could not be a mere participant. As he put it in a 1913 *Motion Picture News* article: "It is the director who makes the film happen in his humble ways. Building up the scenario invisibly, he brings it to success, he makes the actors famous—even the unknown ones—while he himself remains a no-name entity because in the row of the movie theater, the viewer cannot comprehend how a film is made. . . . The director's attention has to encompass even such tiny details because the ultimate responsibility rests on one man's shoulders: the director's."

Despite the decision to switch his vocation upon his return from Copenhagen, Kertész informed Budapest newspapers that he'd signed a contract with Nordisk to act in five films in 1915. It never happened, nor did an earlier directorial collaboration in Sweden with the legendary Victor Sjöström. (The latter has largely been discounted by reputable film historians, who ascertained that Sjöström never used an assistant on his films before the 1920s.)

Kertész continued to leverage every opportunity to increase his public visibility. When the Danish silent film star Valdemar Psilander visited

Budapest in 1914, Kertész treated it as a public relations coup. Psilander had a brief vogue as the most popular early silent star in Europe. Kertész gave the visiting luminary a guided tour of the city, accompanied by his editor cousin, who conducted an interview and brought along a crew of photographers. Sándor Incze published a special edition of his magazine featuring the Psilander visit and sold out all three thousand copies.

He directed several movies in rapid succession. *Az utolsó bohém* (The Last Bohemian), Budapest is the backdrop for a period farce about a millionaire's daughter. An aspiring thespian, she falls for an actor who was hired by her father to dissuade her from treading the boards.

Kertész remained dissatisfied; he wanted to make films characterized by action, romance, and adventure that did not resemble Hungarian stage productions. This transition would take somewhat longer than he hoped, but a notable effort in the interim was *Az aranyásó* (The Gold Digger), loosely adapted from a Bret Harte story about life in the nineteenth-century California gold camps. Although Harte witnessed much of what he wrote about in his short stories, it is doubtful that this tale could have been based on real-life experience. The lead character, Xarkrow, leaves the mythical Hungarian town of Fortanska and travels to the Sierra Nevada to seek his fortune. After striking it rich, he is hounded by a Barbary Coast femme fatale, down on her luck because a crooked financier stole her prized show dog. Xarkrow ends up saving the lady from a misdirected mine cart set ablaze, falls in love, and returns to Hungary with the lady and the loot to live happily ever after.

The esteemed scenarist and novelist Ferenc Molnár scripted this fantastical soap opera. Molnár, whose play *Liliom* would be adapted into the Rodgers and Hammerstein stage musical *Carousel* in 1945, was a bon vivant and womanizer (a wag might observe that he was simply a Hungarian heterosexual). It is probable that he outlined this quickie scenario for Kertész over coffee and dashed it off it in a couple of days. Molnár didn't take movies too seriously even after he immigrated to the United States in 1939. *The Gold Digger* was also an example of how filmmakers of the period routinely appropriated novels and stories produced in other countries without any consideration of copyright.

Contemporary critical observations of *The Gold Digger* and Kertész's other early films are not particularly insightful. What frequently passed for reviews in Hungarian trade papers and film magazines were simply unqualified endorsements written by the filmmakers and their friends. Even though there were twenty film companies in Hungary by 1914, it was not a cutthroat atmosphere. Competition did not extend to publicly denigrating one's colleague, particularly when one would probably be lunching with that colleague to discuss a new project.

During this period Kertész was trenchant about the practical aspects of what filmmakers needed to or should do to be successful. He harped on the notion that the director was *the* essential creative artist. His early magazine articles detailed the essence of the auteur theory a full five decades before *Cahiers du cinéma* and the film critic Andrew Sarris made it popular.

Kertész reneged on his self-imposed retirement from acting by appearing in *Az éjszaka rabja* (Captive of the Night), which he also directed and cowrote with his friend Iván Siklósi, and *A szökött katona* (The Escaped Soldier), adapted from a play by the famous Hungarian dramatist Ede Szigligeti. After these productions wrapped, an opportunity to direct movies outside Budapest materialized that would have a profound effect on Kertész's career.

3

Transylvanian Idyll

Jenő Janovics had been the director of the National Theater in Kolozsvár (now Cluj-Napoca, Romania) in Transylvania since 1905. Like Kertész, Janovics considered film a new art form, but he was an ardent believer in national literary productions aimed at traditional Hungarian audiences that would uplift popular culture. Even after his career had been truncated by professional jealousies, anti-Semitism, and nationalism (Transylvania was a province claimed by Hungary and Romania), Janovics remained faithful to his cinematic credo: "My firm belief was that the Hungarian film industry can only make a hit shooting national stories."

Janovics's initial foray into cinema was an adaptation of Ferenc Csepreghi's folk drama *The Yellow Foal*. The pioneering Pathé Company opened an office in Budapest in December 1912 and was actively seeking Hungarian scenarios to produce. After an August 1913 meeting in Paris with Janovics, Pathé agreed to provide the director Félix Vanyl with both a cameraman who would split duties with a Hungarian counterpart and the equipment to shoot the picture. Pathé would also handle postproduction and distribution. Janovics wrote the script and provided the actors from his theatrical company. The National Theater in Budapest selected the Transylvania locations. Although Vanyl didn't speak Hungarian, he insisted on providing rapid-fire direction in French to the company before each scene. Janovics scrambled to translate the director's words while adding his own instructions to the actors, and the latter proved essential. The actress Lili Hegyi remembered, "The boss [Janovics] wasn't a good actor, we all knew that, but he could show you how to play a scene in a way that it should be taught in acting schools. A few words, a few gestures, and he led the actor to the right path."

The Yellow Foal was the first Hungarian film to become an international hit: 137 prints were screened in forty countries. Its huge success more than compensated for the bad publicity caused by the accidental death of the actress Erzsi Imre during the production. Filmmaking in Transylvania was often a hazardous undertaking in these early days. Imre drowned during a sequence filmed on the Someş River. Her demise was witnessed by hundreds of onlookers along the riverbank who initially believed her frantic cries for help were part of the movie. (Janovics was charged with negligent homicide and subsequently acquitted.) At one point, Vanyl fainted, fell into the river, and had to be rescued. After Imre's death and Vanyl's near miss, Pathé refrained from financing any more of Janovics's productions. The fledgling film producer quickly set up a new distribution deal with Kino-Riport.

Janovics aspired to make his own films but needed an experienced director to realize his vision of building a national film industry in Hungary. Enter Kertész. It is not known where the two met in Budapest, possibly the Café New York, but more likely it was at the offices of Projectograph. The Budapest-based Projectograph would partner with Janovics to establish Proja Studios. Proja essentially was a business arrangement consisting of Janovics producing his own films in Transylvania; the editing and postproduction work were handled by Projectograph in Budapest.

It wouldn't have taken much effort to persuade Kertész to join up with Janovics. His relationship with Projectograph at the time was on a picture-by-picture basis. The insular world of Budapest show business was agog at the success of *The Yellow Foal,* and Kertész pounced at the opportunity to make films with Hungary's new cinematic wunderkind. He quickly agreed to terms and arrived in Kolozsvár in the early summer of 1914.

Kertész helmed three films that summer that were released in mid-1915. The delay was caused by the outbreak of World War I. Although Romania and Hungary were officially neutral, wartime uneasiness descended in August 1914, and people stayed home. After the initial shock wore off during the spring of 1915, the film business regained momentum.

The first collaboration between Janovics and Kertész, *A kölcsönkért csecsemők* (The Borrowed Babies), was a familial comedy inspired by the American scenarist Margaret Mayo's stage play *Baby Mine,* published in 1911 in Hungary under the title *The Stork.* It was filmed at an open-air set behind the Summer Theater and on the streets of Kolozsvár. Janovics recalled of it, "*The Borrowed Babies* adapted an American comedy but became a typically Hungarian film. . . . It was screened in the biggest cinema in Prague for six consecutive weeks. In those days, it was a phenomenal success!"

Jenő Janovics, Mihály Kertész, and the cinematographer József Bécsi during filming of *The Borrowed Babies* (1914) (courtesy of Photofest).

Their second venture was derived from the type of nationalist literary material that Janovics preferred. *A tolonc* (The Undesirable, or The Exile) was an adaptation of Ede Tóth's nineteenth-century Hungarian folk play that would resonate with national audiences. In 2008 a nitrate print of this title was discovered in the basement of the Hungarian Cultural Center in New York. The restored film provides a rare look at Kertész's early work in Hungary.

The film begins with a deathbed confession by an elderly man, who tells his daughter (Lili Berky) that she was actually adopted from his sister, who is in prison for murdering the girl's father. The daughter becomes a maid for a well-to-do middle-aged couple, falls for their virtuous landlord (Mihály Várkonyi, later Victor Varconi), is falsely accused of theft, and is banished to the provinces. There she meets up with her mother (Mari Jászai), who has been released from jail and is consumed with sorrow. After a taxing ordeal that concludes with the mother drinking poison, all is happily resolved as the daughter and the landlord are married in a classical Hungarian wedding ceremony replete with strolling musicians and extras in native costumes.

The Exile remains a time capsule for what it does and does not reveal about Kertész's evolving mise-en-scène. One contemporary critic remarked about the "poor visuals" as filmed by a fixed camera. The performances are overly theatrical, in keeping with the period and the actors' stage pedigrees. The most significant sequence is the wedding ceremony, for which Kertész used two hundred extras from the local populace. Although the camera was mounted on a tripod with limited rotation (this was before modular heads and dolly tracks), there is fluidity to the movement of the people relative to the background composition. As the wedding procession passes the camera into the courtyard of the church, the scene visually prefigures *The Adventures of Robin Hood* (1938). It is not a total stretch to conclude that the staging of a key sequence of one of Curtiz's most famous films—in which Prince John, Sir Guy of Gisbourne, and the Sheriff of Nottingham are seated at a long dais while knights of the realm, priests, and Robin's disguised Merry Men file elegantly into Nottingham Castle—had its genesis in the wedding procession at the conclusion of *The Exile*.

As an additional precursor of future events, Kertész was accused of disregarding the personal safety of one of his actors during the filming. The sixty-five-year-old Mari Jászai, grand dame of the Hungarian theater, reportedly broke a rib after falling off a wagon during one sequence. Jászai blamed Kertész for the accident. It quickly escalated into a public feud between the star and her director. After Jászai leaked her version to the newspapers, the director took umbrage in the paper *Ujság* on July 21, 1914:

> They throw money from the carriage, and she gazes at them in gratitude. As a director, I had the scene rehearsed twice, despite that it was unlikely that any incident would occur. It worked both times. Then I signaled shooting, and the scene went well until the carriage started to move. Mari Jászai stepped back and slipped on the wet grass. She fell backward and hit her back on a [wooden] sign on the roadside. It must have been pure coincidence, but as director the responsibility for its happening fell on me. I owe the truth to you in telling that I was most struck by what happened, but I inquired at the doctor, who later who told me that her injury will heal in a few days, and we cannot expect any serious complications. That makes her statement [to the press] about breaking her rib even more puzzling to me. She partied hard that night and the following day's evening in a company that included me, too, from 7 [p.m.] till midnight; we all sang, danced, and had great fun. That's the truth. Only in an angry moment could she accuse me [of causing a broken rib], seriously damaging my reputation as a director.

In full diva mode, Jászai (who had been Jenő Janovics's drama instructor at the National Academy during the previous century) fired back in *Ujság* the following day:

> No, dear Mr. Kertész! One can't twist the truth like that! Ten colleagues, all witnesses, can attest and tell you to your face that you had the carriage start earlier than it should have, and it pushed me back and pushed me to a stake nearly a meter away. If someone falls at one place, he doesn't fly a meter! Nevertheless, the following day I made myself available for filming, after which I could hardly get out of bed from pain. Your description of me partying is equivalent in accuracy to your description of my incident. I vehemently object to the tone of your statement because you offend not only me but the excellent doctors of the clinic as well. It was I, while suffering from terrible physical pain, who

kept the news of my incident and my misery from the papers, but it reached them nevertheless. No spinning of the truth, Mr. Kertész, I won't tolerate that.

The brouhaha validated the bromide about any type of publicity being good box office. *The Exile* was an instant hit inside Hungary and played well in Vienna and Berlin.

Bánk bán (Bánk the Regent) was the most significant of the trio of Transylvanian films directed by Kertész. A Shakespearean-flavored tale laden with revolt, seduction, and murder set in 1213 has King Andreas II away at war, and Queen Gertrudis susceptible to the intrigues of the regent Bánk, who seeks to take over Hungary. The drama, written as a five-act stage play by József Katona in 1815, spawned an acclaimed opera by Ferenc Erkel. Through numerous revivals, including movie and television productions, *Bánk bán* endures as the best-known literary classic derived from Hungary's ancient cultural heritage. In an attempt to maximize the box-office potential, Janovics delayed the release of the film a full year, until the summer of 1915, to coincide with the hundredth anniversary of Katona's play.

Bánk bán (1914) was the most ambitious production Kertész had yet undertaken. Instead of the familiar terra firma of Budapest, he shot complicated setups at the Economic Institute in Kolozsvár as well as an array of outdoor sequences. Some of the locations included the Kornis Castle in Szentbenedek and the town of Szamosújvár, where the director enlisted a large number of peasants to play soldiers. He staged a number of impressive sequences, including a scene of the king's army on the move across the Carpathian Mountains. Kertész thrived under the pressure of establishing order out of potential chaos in the rugged countryside of Transylvania.

He received his best notices to date for what was a major commercial success. Béla Zolnai, writing for the respected literary review *Nyugat,* waxed rhapsodic about the director's visual depiction. Although *Bánk bán* would be remade several times, no trace of Kertész's 1914 version survives.

His dashing star, Mihály Várkonyi (Victor Varconi), would be the prototype for another Kertész discovery named Errol Flynn. Like Flynn, he was so charismatically handsome that contemporary audiences were initially indifferent to his acting ability. Várkonyi appeared in eight of Kertész's Hungarian films, then followed the director to Vienna for three more movies before immigrating to the United States in 1924. Victor Varconi became a charter member of the Cecil B. DeMille stock company in Hollywood and transitioned to character parts after talkies exposed his thick Hungarian accent.

There was a profound conceptual divergence between Janovics and Kertész concerning the suitability of material. Kertész was not philosophically wedded to a single filmmaking approach. He viewed each of his movies on its own merits and was disinclined to embrace Janovics's obsession with cultural prestige and literary uplift.

The "Hungarian Hollywood" period in Transylvania concluded in 1920 after a run of seventy films. Janovics poured the money earned from his movies into the National Theater. His fortune evaporated over the next decade, and he resigned from his theater director post in 1930. Surviving the Holocaust, he returned to the city now called Cluj to lead the theater again at the age of seventy-three. In a brutish act, the Romanian government evicted Janovics and his acting company from the theater into the chill of the Transylvanian winter. The producer caught pneumonia and died on the same day that a revival of *Bánk bán* was scheduled to open.

On June 28, 1914, while Kertész was finishing *Bánk bán*, a radical Serbian nationalist assassinated Austria-Hungary's Archduke Franz Ferdinand in Sarajevo. The political murder of the heir to the throne of Emperor Franz Joseph and subsequent declaration of war by Austria-Hungary against Serbia triggered mobilization of the armies of European countries that were bound together by a Gordian knot of alliances. "The war to end all wars" would be unleashed by a cascade of strategic miscalculations by European countries guided by the divine right of crowned heads of state. Austria-Hungary was the least prepared of the belligerent Central Powers to initiate a war that they were certain to lose.

For Kertész, the outbreak of war forced the conclusion of his Transylvanian filmmaking idyll. He returned to Budapest and was called up to the Austro-Hungarian army in August 1914. He served as an artillery officer in the 24th Howitzer Regiment and was reportedly wounded at the Russian front, near Poland. After recovering, he served in Italy before being repatriated to Budapest permanently in the summer of 1915. Other sources indicate he was wounded more than once. The fragmentary accounts of his military service are anecdotal. No records of Kertész's Austro-Hungarian Army service could be located in the Hungarian Museum of Military Service.

Kertész was horrified by the sobering realities of barbed wire, machine guns, and concentrated shelling that slew men by the millions. Modern war bore no relationship to the flag-waving élan of Hungarian military history that he had studied in school. The wanton slaughter of a generation permanently altered his outlook. Years afterward, he recalled: "When we marched out in the mornings and passed the cemetery, I thought we are going to the barracks to prepare the raw material for the cemetery. One morning, we were ordered to the battlefield. After that many things happened: destruction, thousands forever silenced, crippled or sent to anonymous graves. Then came the collapse. Fate had spared me."

Improbably, it would be in the midst of the carnage of war that Kertész would experience the most creatively liberating period of his entire career.

4

Phönix Rising

His military service concluded by the summer of 1915, Kertész married and celebrated the arrival of a daughter soon afterward. But matrimony and fatherhood provided fleeting contentment for the workaholic director driven to recover his prewar prestige.

His bride was a seventeen-year-old ballerina named Ilonka Kováks, who later changed her name to Lucy Doraine for professional reasons. The scion of a well-to-do Protestant family in Budapest, she was beautiful and mercurial. The besotted Kertész had no intention of getting married, but then his much-younger paramour announced that she was pregnant. It was not uncommon for a well-to-do older man to marry a younger woman during the waning days of Habsburg imperialism, but an out-of-wedlock child would have been scandalous. Accordingly, the pair wed in a civil ceremony in Budapest in July. Their daughter, Katalin ("Kitty") Eva Ilonka Kertész, was born on November 25, 1915.

Kertész had precious little time to indulge in parenting. Lucy Doraine reportedly doted on herself. It was a less than idyllic situation for the offspring of two ambitious show business parents that would only grow worse. The baby was raised by a succession of nannies.

Kertész was scrambling to regain his stature as a film director after a year at war. He made a couple of sketch films in October 1915, *A paradicsom* (The Tomato) and *Akit ketten szeretnek* (One Who Is Loved by Two). The latter was the final film in which he did double duty as actor and director.

At the beginning of 1916, Kertész received an offer he couldn't refuse. Jenő Illés, a noted director and cinematographer, invited him to be principal director at the production company Kino-Riport, owned by János Frölich and Aladár Fodor. This timely career boost coincided with a wartime ban on the importation and exhibition of movies produced by

A young Lucy Doraine is depicted on one of a series of movie star collectible cards from a Spanish chocolate company (author's collection).

the Allies. This prohibition spurred the Hungarian film industry into an extraordinary period of expansion. Six new Hungarian film studios released their inaugural features in 1914 alone. Wartime production would peak with eighty-eight films released in 1917.

Kertész commented on the rise of wartime Hungarian cinema in the July 1916 edition of *Mozihét* (*Movie News*): "The program of our cinemas is beginning to be dominated by Hungarian pictures, which is a great proof of our industry boom. Although most of our films have not risen to the level of quality that either Nordisk or the famous American film factories achieved—and this objective criticism we must accept—yet, they cater to/satisfy the tastes of our audiences, and the reason for this is that in this war situation, the absence of film companies of enemy nations allowed Hungarian cinematography to gain foothold more easily than before."

Kertész directed seven features in 1916. For the most part, he dealt with contemporary social issues or was inspired by the writings of modern Hungarian authors. His initial Kino-Riport effort, *Makkhetes* (The 7th of Acorns), addresses the moral pitfall of gambling in a sorrowful tale that portrays the death of the main protagonist as the sole path to redemption. Salvation by sacrifice became a repetitive narrative. *A doktar úr* (Mister Doctor) and *Az ezüst kecske* (The Silver Goat; the alternative title is *A medikus,* The Medical Student) were adapted from a contemporary play by Ferenc Molnár and a novel by Sándor Bródy, respectively.

As Hungary's self-anointed expert on the new medium, Kertész expounded on the required attributes for directorial success in *Movie News:* "Good film directing requires not only effort, but expertise, routine knowledge of literature, and artistic taste. . . . The public's taste has been refined, and instead of empty and clichéd gestures, it expects things to come into motion in an elegant way. An effective director has to feel what the audience wants and what the moods of the time are." More than conceptual "large brushstrokes," Kertész insisted that directorial competence required both artistic and technical mastery:

> A film director has to know the scenario backward, be adept at turning a theme into a plot to make the action sweeping, yet condense it so that it will unfold in a concise, rapid manner so the viewer will not cease to be under its spell, not even for a second, which isn't the result of the dazzling effects of photography, but life itself presented in a serious, realistic form. He has to have the knowledge of how to shorten the action to prevent the scene from being boring; he has to set the focus of the image with the cinematographer, has to line up the camera, the wider his gestures should be and when he is nearer, his every move and facial expressions should be more subtle and discreet.

Kertész also expounded his philosophy of how film directors should work with actors: "To keep the drama in a consistent direction, it is required that the actors submit themselves to the director's interpretation, and even though the director might diminish the actors' merits, *a consistent direction and leadership is needed to make a successful film, a leadership that is solely in the director's hands* [emphasis added]."

The article captured the essentials of Kertész's philosophy: the director is the creative leader. His artistic modus operandi would be continually refined by situational experience, but sharing creative decisions on a movie set would be an accommodation that Kertész vehemently resisted.

During his prolific period in Hungary, Kertész's natural impatience became accentuated by frustration toward anyone who attempted to interpose recommendations about his work. This attribute would be sorely tested later on when he was forced to accommodate the demands of Darryl Zanuck, Hal Wallis, and Jack Warner. His view of actors—"a film actor in the hands of a film director is like a marionette puppet"—would also evolve after working with powerful Hollywood stars like James Cagney and Bette Davis. For the present, if he couldn't bully, persuade, or flatter the misguided, he'd resort to subterfuge—or, as a last resort, compromise—to retain his central vision.

His status as Hungary's foremost filmmaker was becoming unassailable. *A farkas* (The Wolf), released in January 1917, was another adaptation of Molnár. Kertész collaborated on the screenplay with Ladislaus Vajda, who was the director of the Hungarian Theater and also wrote for *Theater Life* magazine. The collaboration would flourish for nearly a decade and involve some of Kertész's most prominent European films.

Kertész followed this hit with *A fekete szivárvány* (The Black Rainbow), a Kino-Riport production financed by the Hungarian magnate Sándor Rudnyánszky that is similar to Warner's *The Man Who Played God* (1932), a George Arliss vehicle that costarred a young Bette Davis. *The Black Rainbow*'s uncharacteristically generous budget allowed Kertész to travel around Hungary with the equivalent of a second-unit team while acquiring new talent, including the cabaret singer Vilma Medgyaszay. The director reportedly became so involved in shooting exteriors that he forgot to eat. He did find time to cast his daughter, Kitty, in a bit part as an infant. Acclaim for this film emboldened him to declare that his artistic objective was to distance himself from traditional Hungarian themes and create a movie in true American style.

Rather than working on something that would reflect his stated desire for contemporary entertainment, Kertész pivoted to make a propaganda-style war documentary for the Hungarian Red Cross. *A magyar föld ereje* (The Power of the Hungarian Soil or The Strength of the Fatherland) supported the war while using professional actors—including his wife, Ilonka—to convey the humanistic aspects of the story.

The war began to sap the Hungarian economy, and films were increasingly produced on shoestring budgets. In October 1916 Kertész expounded about the situation in *Movie News:* "In the case of Hungarian filmmaking, the most important ingredient, capital, is only scarcely present, and even what we have isn't remotely close to what the Americans have. The fact that we can still produce first-rate pictures speaks highly of our artistic capabilities, willpower, and unwavering ambition."

Filmmaking during the Great War became a preparatory school for Kertész's future at thrift-conscious Warner Bros., where he was constantly hounded to economize. He mastered the nuances of working within the limitations of budget and schedule while always seeking greater autonomy and more money for his films. He inked a deal with the nascent studio Star-Film and directed *A Halálcsengő* (The Death Bells), the initial entry of a three-picture deal, but then left. Once again, he'd gotten a better offer—arguably the best of his entire career.

Declaration of war by the United States against the Central Powers on April 6, 1917, ended the exhibition of Hollywood-produced films in Austria-Hungary. Four days after Woodrow Wilson declared that America would make the world safe for democracy, Projectograph bought Kino-Riport studios, and the two companies became a single entity. From this merger Phönix-Film was born.

Phönix joined the existing Projectograph facilities and infrastructure with Kino's laboratories, fixed assets, and studios. Phönix-Film was capitalized to compete artistically and exported its films internationally. Kertész was appointed executive producer with artistic control over all productions. He now had complete freedom to shape his vision onscreen. Over the next two years, he would produce and direct eighteen films.

Kertész dove into preproduction at Phönix with a slate of eight features in 1917. Overseeing the writing team of Ladislaus Vajda and Iván Siklósi, he coordinated the production of several films simultaneously to take advantage of the availability of artists, sets, and locations.

His first production was *A kuruzsló* (The Charlatan), an adaptation of an acclaimed 1909 play by Imre Földes. It was an excellent choice by Kertész to jump-start his tenure at Phönix. In the story an adopted son, who is in love with his stepsister, attends medical school with his drunken foster brother. He is sent to prison after accepting the blame when his ne'er-do-well sibling kills a patient during an illegal operation. Released after three years, he finds his foster brother dead, assumes his identity, and becomes a world-class surgeon until his past inevitably catches up with him.

Kertész became so enamored with *The Charlatan* that he remade it twice. He shot the first remake as *Nameless* (1923) with Victor Varconi in Vienna for Sascha-Film. The third version was produced ten years later at Warner Bros. as *Alias the Doctor,* starring Richard Barthelmess.

The sole surviving feature from Kertész's tenure at Phönix evidences his growing skill as a director. *Az utolsó hajnal* (The Last Dawn) was produced in 1917. Vajda and Siklósi adapted Alfred Deutsch-German's novel to the screen as a fascinating brew of redemptive melodrama and comedy. A Dutch version of *The Last Dawn* was located and restored by the EYE Film Instituut Nederland in 2009. The original Phönix title *Life Is a Game: A Drama in Five Acts* does not adequately convey the exotic convolutions of this film.

Harry (Leopold Kramer) is the iconoclastic heir of the Kernetts, "a family prepared only to live well and die beautifully." His attempted suicide by jumping off the Chain Bridge in Budapest is prevented by Lord Harding (Eugen Balasso). Harding takes Harry under his wing, bucks him up, and makes him his personal secretary. Harry witnesses the love of Edward (Kálmán Ujj) for Hella (Klary Lotto), one of Harding's daughters, along with the bankruptcy of the kindly lord, who confesses to Harry about his embezzlement of his eccentric daughter Mary's inheritance. The bankrupt Harding must restore the money to Mary before she comes into her majority the following year, or marry off Hella to a rich colonel who will financially bail him out.

Harry concocts a bizarre scheme to rescue his benefactor and permit Hella to marry her true love. He buys insurance, makes Harding the beneficiary, and proposes to die at an opportune moment. Enjoying his last year on Earth, Harry vacations in India, where he meets and falls in love with an enchanting princess who is actually Mary; she is aware of Harry's plan and determined to thwart it. Another suitor, a mysterious Sikh doctor who trails Harry and Mary back to Budapest, vies for Mary's attention and is clearly up to no good.

In the denouement the Sikh reveals his actual identity as Edward, a scene so startling that it elicited an audible gasp from the audience at Le Giornate del Cinema Muto in Pordenone, Italy, where *The Last Dawn* was screened in October 2011. The film demonstrates the director's evolving ability to establish a rhythmic tempo with his actors that moves the story to an exciting conclusion rather than a disparate group of sequences bundled together with expositional descriptions. As Kertész put it, "An actor should not explain the scenes; the scenes should explain themselves." *The Last Dawn* demonstrated that Kertész had become more adroit at cutting, using dissolves, and transitioning from master shots to close-ups. Kertész was cognizant that Hungarian cinema had reached a developmental apex and was acutely aware of his pivotal role. He wrote in *Movie News,* "I am witnessing this revolutionary period of Hungarian cinema with great pleasure, a period that is driven by a few ambitious and expert individuals." Not surprisingly, Kertész viewed himself as the foremost expert individual.

But there was another Hungarian filmmaker whose star was ascending. Kertész's success at Phönix coincided with that of his young friend Sándor Kellner, the future Sir Alexander Korda. Korda and Miklós Pásztory bought Corvin Studios from Jenő Janovics in 1917. The difficulty of wartime communications was the reason Janovics gave the press for abandoning the movie business in Budapest and sticking with film production in his native Kolozsvár. The reality was that Korda could not work for Janovics—or for anyone other than himself. This trait was also one of the defining professional differences between him and Kertész. Korda required unhindered freedom to produce his own pictures. Able to endure almost any hardship save an inability to direct films, Kertész would surrender absolute control in order to work constantly. It was a key distinction that would result in Korda's becoming a knighted film mogul in England while Kertész was content to direct more films in Hollywood than almost anybody else. Although they remained friends, Korda and Kertész never collaborated on a major project. They knew each other too well. This absence of a professional partnership sustained their personal relationship until Korda's death in 1956.

Another notable Kertész 1917 production was *A vörös Sámson* (The Crimson Samson, based on the novella *The Bondsman* by the popular Victorian novelist Hall Caine.

The Crimson Samson proved memorable for the actor Tivadar Uray, who considered quitting acting in films after being exposed to Kertész's penchant for realism: "*The Crimson Samson* was a terrible job. They actually tied me down . . . then the Cossacks captured me and beat me up. I had to slide down from the edge of the cave in one scene. The ledge couldn't stand my weight and I fell right into the rocks. 'Carry on, you do it splendidly,' enthused Kertész. I could have screamed with pain, but the movie was silent!" In another scene, Uray was temporarily blinded by gunpowder and thrown to the ground in order to roll down a rock-strewn hill at a seventy-five-degree angle. There were no stuntmen at that time, particularly in a Kertész movie. Uray gutted it out and wryly recalled: "The film was full of pleasures. Of course, it turned into a big hit."

The disintegration of the old order in Austria-Hungary accelerated at the end of 1917. The Central Powers were losing the war. As strikes and protests became commonplace, there was a greater sense of urgency for the distraction provided by cinema. The film industry appeared immune to the dissolution of nearly everything else that was a part of daily life. Despite severe wartime material shortages, Phönix opened a new six-hundred-seat movie theater in Budapest.

Although Kertész elevated his regular screenwriter Iván Siklósi to head director at Phönix, he continued his punishing work schedule, simultaneously supervising twelve pictures in various stages of production. Heady with success, he couldn't have realized where his life behind the camera would shortly take him.

5

A Stirred-up Anthill

As the war entered its fourth year in 1918, Kertész was off filming exteriors in the Tatra Mountains between Slovakia and Poland. Because of the collapse of Imperial Russia and the overthrow of the czar by the Bolsheviks, what had been the Eastern Front was no longer a war zone. Kertész immediately began shooting footage for four films while doing preproduction work on an entire slate of movies that equated to making one feature per month in 1918.

Phönix released seven pictures directed by Kertész over the following months. *Az árendás zsidó* (The Jewish Tenant) allowed him to probe the presence of anti-Semitism. An Orthodox Jewish couple living under serflike conditions is evicted from their home by an unfeeling landowner. On the road to an unknown future, they discover the corpse of the landowner's wife, who has committed suicide, leaving an infant daughter. The couple adopts the child, becomes wealthy, and returns to the landowner's estate to reunite the grown daughter with her ruined father.

With *A 99-es számú bérkocsi* (The Rental Car Number 99), based on a novel by R. F. Foster, Kertész delved into the world of crime mystery. He cast his fellow National Theater alumnus Bela Lugosi, whom he had already used in *Lulu* and *The Colonel,* as an undercover detective probing a robbery-homicide. Despite Kertész's and Lugosi's being friendly since performing onstage in *Anna Karenina* in 1911, there was friction. After the Phönix lab overexposed a reel of film during final production, the thirty-six-year-old Lugosi proved more than a match in proud stubbornness with his director. In a typical on-the-set display of imperial brusqueness, Kertész ordered Lugosi to do retakes to replace the ruined scenes. The actor, put off by Kertész's manner, refused and was excoriated in front of the entire company. Lugosi stalked off the set and did not return until Kertész agreed to apologize to him in front of the crew. This was one of the early occasions in which the director had to eat crow in order to finish a film. Anger was a transitory emotion with him. The picture always came first.

Kertész finished four more Phönix productions, concluding in September with *Júdás* (The Judas), his final completed feature for Phönix. In October 1918 Austria-Hungary sued for peace, and the Habsburg monarchy was dissolved on October 31. Germany surrendered in November. But the conclusion of World War I brought little celebration in Hungary.

The Allies strove to ensure that the defeated Austro-Hungarian Empire would never rise again. The result was punitive geographic dismemberment. A new Hungarian Democratic Republic would be cobbled out of what was a third of the former Kingdom of Hungary. Slovenia became part of the new state of Czechoslovakia. Transylvania and Bukovina were partitioned by Romania; Galicia was absorbed by Poland with Bosnia; and Croatia, Dalmatia, and Slovenia joined with Serbia into what would eventually become Yugoslavia. One-third of Hungarians suddenly found themselves living outside their own country.

The Treaty of Trianon, signed under protest by Hungary in 1920, neutralized the Hungarian army down to a token militia. The navy was entirely eliminated, since the country was now landlocked. The remaining population faced shortages of essential goods, an uncertain government, and a deterioration of law and order. The Spanish flu pandemic raised the misery index. The disease swept across Europe in summer 1918, killing thousands of young men in the trenches and countryside before moving into the cities. It also had an effect on the Hungarian film industry. Most of the cinemas were temporarily shuttered and the always-open coffeehouses in Budapest closed early every day.

Surrounded by pandemonium, Kertész continued making films. In October 1918 he abruptly left Phönix and joined Semper Film Company. He took with him a large contingent of talent, including Victor Varconi. He also left a trio of films undone, including *A napraforgós hölgy* (The Sunflower Lady), which he had begun in June.

The exact reason for his departure remains unknown; it may have been studio infighting, lack of money, or the belief that there was a better opportunity at Semper to produce his own scripts. But Kertész would never again possess control over all phases of film production, as he had during his tenure at Phönix.

He helmed three films for Semper: *Varázskeringő* (The Magic Waltz), *Lu, a Kokott* (Lu, the Cocotte), and *A Víg özvegy* (The Merry Widow).

He completed the last of these in December 1918 before he was stricken with influenza, which required prolonged bed rest.

Political change in Hungary was moving along at a faster clip than a Phönix film production. Many in the film industry were agitating to be nationalized by the government to protect their jobs and to guard against the encroachment of films imported from the United States and other countries. The tumult in Hungarian cinema was a microcosm of the upheaval occurring throughout the entire country owing to inflation, unemployment, and shortages of coal and food. The bejowled Hungarian entertainer S. Z. Sakall recalled postwar Budapest as "a huge stirred-up anthill. . . . There was misery everywhere." The Hungarian film community coalesced into several organizations that pitted intellectuals and union workers supporting the nationalization of the industry against much of the established order of actors, directors, and executives.

After the dissolution of the monarchy, the Social Democrats under Count Mihály Károlyi established a coalition government that couldn't quell social unrest. It also lacked the means to contest the absorption of Transylvania by Romania and sought someone more forceful to fight for Hungary's territorial independence. Béla Kun, leader of the Hungarian Communists, believed he was such a force and moved quickly to fill the power vacuum. Kun was a willful roughneck who had learned to spout leftist polemics after becoming a prisoner of war in Russia, converting to Communism, and fighting with the Bolsheviks during the Russian Civil War. After an effective campaign of speeches and labor strikes, he orchestrated a merger of the two parties that elevated him as the dominant figure in a new government. Amid much optimism, the Hungarian Soviet Republic was established on March 21, 1919.

The new regime immediately turned postwar depression into chaotic disaster. Courts and the rule of law were abolished in favor of revolutionary tribunals. Magazines and newspapers were banned or shut down. Private property was nationalized, taxes were canceled, and millions of acres of privately held Hungarian farmland were merged into huge collective farms to be run by the state. Fortunately, Kun's wild plans lacked the support of his uneasy Social Democratic partners, many Communists in his own party, and, most critically, Vladimir Lenin and the Bolsheviks, who were preoccupied with establishing their hegemony in the new Soviet Union.

Kertész remained apolitical; he simply wanted the maximum amount of freedom and money to make bigger and better films.

Shortly after the new republic was established, a National Committee of Cinema was formed, and a cadre of his colleagues were assigned to responsible positions: Ladislaus Vajda and Béla Balogh were appointed artistic commissioners, Iván Siklósi was on the Exhibition Committee, and Alexander Korda was placed in charge of all film production. Kertész was notable for his absence from a high-profile position. It is possible that his often-autocratic deportment came back to haunt him. The producer István Radó knew Kertész during this period and later wrote that Phönix's former production chief held court at the Café New York like "a noble visitor." According to Radó, Kertész was "stuck-up" and condescended to his colleagues. The director eventually found himself appointed to something called an Actors Examiner Jury.

Kertész soon found it impossible to embrace the Communist regime as many of his colleagues had. Conformance to a political system so rigid that books, magazines, and films were run through an ideological meat grinder was contrary to the cinematic freedom he yearned for. He began to consider other options outside his homeland. In the interim, he kept his head down and played for time. The rapidly changing political landscape in Budapest validated his calculation to straddle the fence.

An internal coup attempt against Béla Kun on June 24, 1919, caused secret police and regime thugs to begin rounding up and executing undesirables labeled as counterrevolutionaries. Anyone of prominence associated with the previous regime was categorized as disloyal. So were former military officers. Since Kertész fit both categories, he felt doubly at risk.

His dilemma gave birth to a colorful yarn related by his stepson, John Meredyth Lucas, years afterward: "Mike went home and remained quiet until, one night, came the dreaded pounding on the door. Red Army Guards were there for him. He said a quick good-bye to his mother and family, expecting it to be his last." According to Kertész, he was taken to a palace for interrogation and pushed into a large room. "In the far corner of the enormous room, a man sat working at a desk, his back to the door. Mike waited uncertainly, not knowing whether to speak or simply wait. After what seemed an eternity, the man turned toward the light and jumped up, throwing his arms wide. 'Mishka!' After a stunned silence, Mike drew his first easy breath. It was Korda." Alexander Korda immediately offered him money and a film assignment, telling him, "We've got it made. . . . You begin directing your first picture tomorrow, *Red Banner.*" A stunned Kertész made a lame inquiry about the script, and Korda shrugged and told him to make do. The anecdote concludes with

Kertész filming *Red Banner* for several weeks in the mountains with "a detachment of Alpine troops" while Kun was being overthrown in Budapest. Later, after Korda was jailed by the new regime and eventually made his way to Vienna, Kertész returned the favor by offering his now-threadbare colleague a job at Sascha-Film as his assistant.

This serendipitous tale of Korda rescuing his childhood friend by sending him into the mountains to make a film and Kertész reciprocating later on in Vienna by bailing out a destitute Korda was an entertaining fiction worthy of an Eric Ambler novel. There is no record of Kertész's arrest or detention during 1919.

Kertész was assigned by Korda during this period to direct *Jön az öcsém* (My Brother Is Coming), an eleven-minute propaganda film that was a thinly disguised biographical treatment of Béla Kun. Iván Siklósi composed the titles, and Kertész cast his wife, Ilonka, as the worker's spouse who welcomes her revolutionary brother-in-law back to the fold.[1] *My Brother Is Coming* was filmed in several days and released on April 3, a mere two weeks after Kun was elevated to power and before the arrests and executions began in June. After that, Kertész went on to film the May Day parade celebrations in Budapest and was in the process of doing other work for the regime as he quietly planned his departure from Hungary.

Béla Kun conscripted the Hungarian Red Army to fight the Romanians, whose annexation of Transylvania remained unacceptable to a majority of Hungarians. Kun's army was routed and his 133-day-old government dissolved on August 2, 1919. Kun fled to the Soviet Union, where he was executed during Stalin's 1938 Red Terror purge. After sacking Budapest and its environs under the guise of war reparations, the Romanians withdrew and anointed Admiral Miklós Horthy, a right-wing Christian and former monarchist, as ruler. Horthy consolidated his power by unleashing a retaliatory reign of terror worse than Kun's. Former government functionaries, leftists, scientists, writers, artists, intellectuals, and particularly Jews were targeted. The anti-Semitism that had simmered beneath the surface under the Habsburgs was quickly brought to a boil.

The Hungarian film industry suffered terribly, as the new regime considered cinema to be decadent propaganda run by Jews for the deposed Communists. Horthy unleashed an onslaught that resulted in the near-obliteration of Hungary's early cinema. (Destruction of much of the remaining Hungarian film archives occurred during a one-hundred-day siege and sack of Budapest by the Soviet Red Army near the end of World War II.)

The historian István Nemeskürty observed: "The soldiers of Miklós Horthy singled out the art of film to be honored by their special attention. . . . Cinemas were given as rewards to soldiers wearing crane-feathered caps—symbol of the counter-revolutionary army; war widows, leftist citizens and Jews were driven out of their cinemas."

Actors, directors and many others associated with Hungarian cinema fled the country, since no one wanted to share the fate of Sándor Pallós, a film director who was tortured to death by Horthy's men.

Alexander Korda was arrested in October 1919 and held at the Hotel Gellert, the headquarters of Horthy's secret police. Either through a case of mistaken identity or (more likely) because Korda's volatile wife, Maria, was threatening to turn his arrest into an embarrassing international incident, Korda was released and left Budapest in early November. He rode in comfort with his wife on the train to Vienna and checked into a suite at the Imperial Hotel.

Korda arrived in Vienna just in time to attend the November 21, 1919, premiere of Kertész's first feature for Sascha-Film. Kertész had slipped out of Budapest in June with his wife and daughter and was then living and working in Vienna. He had departed in such a hurry that his final Hungarian production, an adaptation of Ferenc Molnár's *Liliom,* was left unfinished. Kertész decided that, like Bela Lugosi and others who had also fled, he was not going to stick around to be measured for a noose.

The cultural freedom of early twentieth-century Hungary that shaped the lives of Kertész, Korda, and many of their contemporaries had disappeared. Although Kertész would return to Budapest to visit his mother and siblings after the political upheaval settled down, he turned the page on his homeland and began a new life. For a generation of talented Hungarians, many of whom ended up in Hollywood, memories of Budapest became the topic of wistful dinner table recollections.

6

City of Film

During the uncertain period after World War I, the former capital of Austria-Hungary expanded its rich artistic heritage into the new domain of motion pictures. Vienna, the so-called City of Dreams, would become Michael Kertész's City of Film. And it was now Michael instead of Mihály, as the director thought it was better to Germanize his first name to ease his assimilation into what was a similar but different culture. Kertész and his family relocated to Vienna at the behest of his newest benefactor: Count Alexander "Sascha" Joseph von Kolowrat-Krakowsky.

For a movie mogul, Kolowrat had an appropriately melodramatic lineage. The wealthy son of an Austrian count and a Russian cigarette manufacturer's daughter, Kolowrat was born in Glen Ridge, New Jersey, in 1896 because his father was temporarily exiled in the United States after shooting a man during a duel. After attending university in Belgium, Kolowrat plunged into a variety of action-packed avocations, including car racing, aviating, motorcycling, ballooning, and cinematography.

The young aristocrat was an intellectual and a technological visionary. He spoke numerous European languages and possessed far-sighted ideas about the potential of motion picture production—ideas he conceived after visiting the Pathé studios in Paris and filming a car race in the Alps in 1910. After inheriting his father's Bohemian estates and fortune, Kolowrat began his film career by producing a series of shorts featuring Austria's first comedy team, Cocl and Seff. He achieved commercial success with his feature *The Millionaire Uncle* and founded Sascha-Film in 1914. He cleverly contrived to be appointed head of the Austro-Hungarian Imperial Press Office film department during World War I. In that role he exercised sole control over the creation of wartime newsreel documentaries, which he routinely altered for propaganda purposes. He built his own studio in the Sievering district of Vienna in 1916. Kolowrat not only survived after being on the losing side of the war, but also prospered.

The location of his vast estates amid post–World War I borderlines automatically made the count a citizen of Czechoslovakia. The man in charge of producing propaganda newsreels for the vanquished Central Powers reinvented himself as a bystander businessman from a neutral country. Kolowrat built a series of shell distribution companies throughout central and eastern Europe that were controlled by Sascha-Film. He also created an American branch of Sascha and became the Austrian distributor for Paramount Pictures. In addition to his wide range of professional interests, the affable, oversized count was a womanizer of legendary repute. Victor Varconi, who would join the cinematic exodus to Vienna, recalled that Kolowrat always carried a heavy topcoat over his arm, even on the hottest days: "This was because he had discovered most girls prefer [the coat] to the grass. He was always prepared and, incidentally, most successful."

The count had attempted to lure Kertész away from Budapest several times during the war. As the Hungarian political situation deteriorated, they'd made an agreement: Kertész would make films under the congenial oversight of the count, who would provide the director and his family an elegant lifestyle in one of the most beautiful cities in Europe. Adapting quickly to his new surroundings, Kertész was joined by a large number of émigrés from Budapest. Viennese cafés replicated the atmosphere of his former haunts; the director was frequently seen holding forth with the Kordas and Ladislaus Vajda, among other colleagues. Kertész respected the count's willingness to plow his considerable resources into film production and enjoyed their shared passion for the nuts and bolts of filmmaking. But the count's other interest left him nonplussed: "It was never clear if I was in the study of a motion picture magnate or the studio of a motor racing industrialist. The office was covered with technical objects, small models of racing cars, and enormous maps of Austria dotted with small flags that marked the distance of car races that he had competed in."

Kertész's debut for Sascha was his opening gambit to turn his wife into a movie star. *Die Dame mit dem schwarzen Handschuh* (The Lady of the Black Glove) is a dark melodrama that Kertész originally developed at Phönix Film. Lucy Doraine plays an early version of the femme fatale: a convict scarred on one hand, which she conceals with a glove. Kertész also began a professional association with a young cinematographer named Gustav Ucicky, the son of the famed Viennese painter and secessionist

Gustav Klimt. Ucicky became Kertész's cinematographic Boswell, lensing virtually every significant movie that Kertész made for Sascha-Film.

Kertész's next feature, *Boccaccios Liebesnächte* (Boccaccio's Love Nights), starred the popular Ica von Lenkeffy and Pál Lukács. (The latter, as Paul Lukas, would edge out *Casablanca*'s Humphrey Bogart for the Best Actor Oscar in 1943 for *Watch on the Rhine*.)

Kertész reached an agreement with Kolowrat for a slate of films that he would direct and Doraine would star in. Kertész's treatment of his wife as an idealized cinematic female proved highly influential. His depiction of women onscreen would reflect the European cinematic culture of the 1920s: women were often portrayed as predatory, duplicitous, and sexual, yet also vulnerable, with a capacity for moral redemption.

As he had done at Phönix to maximize budget and scheduling, Kertész cut costs by shooting multiple films simultaneously on location. He traveled to Bosnia and Croatia, and then filmed the interiors back at Sascha studios. *Die Stern von Damaskus* (The Star of Damascus) and *Die Gottesgeißel* (The Whip of God) comprise a continuous story that was released as two separate films. But slanting his movies toward making his wife a glamorous star was a challenge. In addition to her demanding temperament, Doraine presented a visual test even for a director as skilled as Kertész. She did not possess a figure born for the camera. A pleasing face highlighted by a pair of luminous eyes competed with a flat-chested torso that abruptly broadened to wide hips. Kertész strove to film his wife draped in a cloaking wardrobe and emphasized her facial appeal.

Doraine's reputation as a versatile actress who could play comedic material as well as melodrama gained traction with the lighthearted *Mrs. Tutti Frutti,* which Kertész concluded with a startling visual gimmick: a sheet of paper filling the screen is torn asunder by the startling appearance of a baby, the happy protagonists (Doraine and the Viennese actor Alphons Fryland), and their matchmaker doctor (Josef König). The characters form the shape of a heart before the final dissolve.

Sascha-Film had emerged in the top rank of cinematic production in Europe. To complement his production facilities at Sievering, Count Kolowrat commissioned the construction of a huge outdoor set in the Prater, a vast public park in Vienna's Second District. Kertész made use of this set for *Herzogin Satanella* (Duchess Satanella). The Prater set and location filming in Vienna, the French Riviera, the Italian Lake Garda, and Venice make *Duchess Satanella* visually lush. Doraine vamps her way through a veritable catalogue of femmes fatales, alternately portraying a

Japanese geisha who fatally ensnares a naval officer, a French baroness who seduces a priest of the First Estate, and an Indian beauty whose marriage to a sultan results in their mutual downfall.

Although Kertész was on his way to becoming an internationally known filmmaker, his new career in Austria was becoming ominously reminiscent of his stewardship of Phönix-Film. Instead of the apocalyptic troika of war, epidemic, and revolution, this time it was the looming specter of postwar hyperinflation. Austria and a prostrate Germany spent what they had on unemployment and food relief, and then printed more money and spent even more. The value of Austrian kronen dropped like a stone in the Danube. In January 1919 one U.S. dollar was worth 17.09 Austrian kronen. By August 1922, a single dollar bought 77,300 kronen as the inflation rate approached 10,000 percent. But Count Kolowrat continued pumping his money into productions and Kertész kept directing. As before, people attended the cinema in droves to forget their troubles.

Kertész was having his own troubles as well: his marriage to Lucy Doraine was crumbling. According to his future stepson, John Meredyth Lucas, "Mike had a European attitude about marriage. It formed a stable home, provided comfort, but was not expected to confine one's pleasures." The director possessed a romantic soul that was complemented by a turbo-charged libido. Irving Rapper, who would learn his craft at Kertész's elbow two decades later at Warner Bros., described his directorial mentor as "a sex maniac."

Kertész exuded charm and power in an industry where beautiful women were readily available; it is surprising, then, that he became involved with a young lady who worked in a bank. But Mathilde Foerster aspired to be much more than a clerk in a teller's cage. She arrived in Vienna from her native Galicia in 1905 and lived in the Ottakring district with her family. Known as Thilde by friends and family, she was well educated and aspired to become a writer. According to her granddaughter, Thilde might have met Kertész while trying to sell a script she had written: "She loved to ice skate and was a real romantic. . . . She had a soft spot for books with romantic melodramatic plots." Foerster and Kertész became involved during the winter of 1919, and their son, Michael, was born the following year. The director's subsequent behavior was far from chivalrous. After he agreed to provide financial support, Kertész's interest in supporting his son quickly waned. For the director, it was the onset of a pattern of behavior that was not just indiscreet, but disreputable.

While working for Sascha-Film, Kertész would father two more children by different women. His daughter Sonja was born in 1923 and another son—also named Michael—arrived in 1925. Their mothers were both bit players or extras in his films. Kertész's affairs bore a striking resemblance to his pattern of making films: he would immerse himself totally in a project until it was completed, then move on to the next with hardly a backward glance.

His habit of constant progression and seeming inability to sustain intimate relationships did not necessarily mean that he didn't care about his children. In 2000 his granddaughter Ilona Ryder told a German newspaper: "He led quite a dissolute life but maintained contact with all of his children. He loved his children. . . . I see him both lovingly and critically, but at any rate honestly." On the basis of the director's subsequent behavior toward Foerster and his firstborn son, and the disavowal of his children that came to light after his death, Ryder's assessment seems more sentimental than accurate. In the end, Kertész remained true to himself. He permitted nothing—not family, money, sex, or fatherhood—to interfere with his passion for filmmaking.

At the end of 1921, Kertész traveled back to Budapest to visit his mother and siblings. As he had done when he was riding high at Phönix-Film, he used his filmmaking earnings to take care of them. Although the Hungarian political situation remained tense, it was apparent that Horthy's ardor for repressing the Jewish intelligentsia had cooled. Kertész and other exiles were apparently allowed to enter the country to visit their families and leave unmolested, as his presence in Budapest was reported in *Theater Life* magazine on December 4, 1921.

Kertész finished two more 1921 productions starring Lucy Doraine. *Frau Dorothys Bekenntnis* (Madame Dorothy's Confession) told the story of Dorothy Robey (Doraine) almost entirely in flashback. He followed with *Wege des Schreckens* (The Terror Road), also known as *Labyrinth des Grauens* (Labyrinth of Horror). This was another tragedy-laden drama in which Doraine portrayed a woman of humble origins who is persecuted into prostitution by a reprehensible criminal of a brother.

Kertész's films did brisk business throughout the European market, but Count Kolowrat was not content with the status quo. The aristocrat-mogul was convinced the time was ripe for Sascha-Film to penetrate the vast market of the United States with a blockbuster epic. Michael Kertész was eager to turn his vision into reality.

7

Monumental-Filme

Cinematic epics were not an American invention. Italy's Enrico Guazzoni began the genre in 1912 with his lavish production of *Quo Vadis?* The picture featured five thousand extras amid ornate sets, and it became an international hit. Subsequent productions included *The Last Days of Pompeii* (1913), directed by Mario Caserini and Eleuterio Rodolfi, and Giovanni Pastrone's *Cabiria* (1914), a stupendous two-hundred-minute epic that featured the eruption of Mount Etna set against the historical backdrop of the Second Punic War.

These motion pictures profoundly influenced D. W. Griffith. For his mammoth production *Intolerance* (1916), Griffith refined Pastrone's pioneering moving-camera technique. His filming of the colossal Babylon sets continues to inspire awe a century later. Count Kolowrat viewed *Intolerance* during a research visit to the United States in 1920 and was transfixed by its epic scale and innovative use of four parallel stories from different historical epochs, cleverly intercut to relate a single moral lesson.

The ever-ambitious mogul gave Kertész the go-ahead to begin pre-production on *Sodom and Gomorrah*. The director immediately began developing the complex story line with his favorite scenarist, Ladislaus Vajda. Vajda worked on *Sodom and Gomorrah* with Kertész while concurrently writing Alexander Korda's *Samson and Delilah* (1922). Korda had left Sascha-Film and was making his own biblical opus showcasing his mercurial wife, Maria, under the production auspices of Vita-Film; it premiered in Vienna in December 1922, three months after *Sodom*. The two countrymen, who shared much professionally and culturally and were both married to young ingénues they had made into stars, now produced thematically similar epics. The professional association remained cordial but distant—Kertész is credited for costume design on *Samson and Delilah* because he let his colleague use the thousands of costumes and wigs made for *Sodom*.

The final scenario for *Sodom,* laden with melodramatic sexuality, would encompass eleven acts divided into two autonomous stories— "The Sinner" and "The Punishment"—corresponding to the film's title of *Sodom and Gomorrah: The Legend of Sin and Punishment*. Not surprisingly, Kertész positioned the ubiquitous femme fatale (Doraine) as the centerpiece of the film in the tripartite roles of Mary Conway, a Syrian princess, and Lot's wife.

Griffith's and the Italian epics might have inspired him, but *Sodom and Gomorrah* was Kertész's singular creation: a unique construction of drawing-room melodrama and lurid sexuality, an elephantine biblical epic of such gigantic proportions that it eclipsed in scale all the similar films that had preceded it. "Monumental-filme" was what the Germans called it. *Sodom and Gomorrah* was all that, and more.

Period publicity releases included claims of "eighty thousand extras, seven thousand animals, two hundred thousand costumes, thirteen thousand wigs, thirty-eight thousand pairs of shoes, and seven hundred rugs." The production would take nearly two years; Kolowrat and Kertész ran what amounted to a virtual employment agency for the state of Austria, given the seemingly endless legions of actors, extras, technicians, artisans, designers, costumers, and craftspeople, augmented by contingents from the Austrian army and police force. Walter Slezak, who would become one of Hollywood's most respected character players, remarked in a 1970 interview: "Have you any idea what 14,000 extras requires? It means approximately 1,200 . . . makeup artists, then circa 2,000 costumers: the people had to all be fitted for wigs, that was an unbelievable expense."

The overwhelming volume of wardrobe commissioned for *Sodom and Gomorrah* included eleven costumes for Lucy Doraine, personally designed by the costumer of the Austrian National Theater. The critic Béla Balázs believed Kertész had succumbed to "prop madness."

In addition to studio sets, Kertész used the imperial gardens at a Laxenburg castle and Schönbrunn Palace for exteriors. He required a huge tract of land to construct and stage the sets that he had in mind for the Syrian and Sodom sequences. A large, open area called the Laaer Berg, which was partially occupied by a trash dump outside the center of Vienna, proved ideal. After persuading Kolowrat to lease the land, Kertész had laborers construct a series of interconnected offices and barracks to house the production designers, artisans, and carpenters who would fabricate the sets, as well as create staging areas for the cast, crew, and extras.

The prominent architects Julius von Borsody, Hans Rouc, and Stefan Wessely designed the massive sets constructed for the Sodom sequence. The Temple of Astarte rose to 230 feet in a series of levels reminiscent of the Tower of Babel. It included a huge staircase up the center, which was bisected by side staircases that extended to the top of the structure, adorned in Assyrian-Babylonian style. There was also a large platform built for the interior set of the temple, containing a thirty-two-foot-high statue of the goddess Astarte. The assembled sets became a source of wonder; no one in Austria had seen anything like them before. The quoted budget for the film was 500 million Austrian kronen, roughly $10 million in today's dollars. *Sodom and Gomorrah* became the most expensive motion picture to that date.

Kertész wanted a new, young actor to play alongside his wife and Victor Varconi. According to Varconi, Leo Slezak, the famed tenor of the Viennese Opera, visited Kertész on the set one day. The elder Slezak delivered Walter, his twenty-year-old son, to the director, imploring, "Do something with this boy, if you can. He's my son, my own flesh and blood. Yet he can't sing. He can't act. What can I do with him?" Walter's more colorful recollection of his screen debut involved a chance encounter in a Viennese bar:

> A few tables away were seated two men and a woman. The woman pointed at me—the two men turned around and looked me over carefully. I recognized her—she was Lucy Doraine, then a famous motion-picture star. . . . Then one of the two men got up and walked over to my table, sat down and said: "With your kind permission, I have imagined you." That sentence was delivered with a straight face and the thickest possible Hungarian accent. I must have looked very stupid, because he continued: "You do not understand—you are my vision." For a moment, I thought an escaped lunatic was talking to me and I was ready to humor him. "Of course, I understand." "No, you do not," he said, sadly. "But I will explain. My name is Michael Kertesz. I am preparing *Sodom and Gomorrah,* the legend of sin, and we need beautiful young man—and you are beautiful young man."

The director learned that this beautiful young man was a banker, not an actor. "That's not good," said Kertész. "We want an actor—but who

Walter Slezak, Curtiz's "beautiful young man," made his screen debut in *Sodom und Gomorrha* in 1922 (author's collection).

knows, maybe you have talent." After testing the newcomer, Kertész concluded that the neophyte possessed ample acumen to go with his good looks. With the legal consent of his famous father, Leo (who was also was given a small part in the picture), the career of Walter Slezak was launched.

After months of preproduction and with the huge Laaer Berg sets still under construction, Kertész began shooting on August 10, 1921. The director was in his element: his system employed interconnected megaphones, a bevy of assistant directors with light signals to initiate the mass movement of extras, and a telephone system to coordinate the complex logistics.

S. Z. Sakall encountered Kertész on a *Sodom and Gomorrah* location, a field marshal directing his troops: "The sight before us was certainly impressive. My childhood friend, Michael Curtiz, stood on top of a two-story-high director's rostrum and gave his orders through a megaphone. A crowd of many hundreds hung on every word. And he was talking German."

The director was riding high, remarking for public consumption: "At the moment, I am working on the biggest film of my life . . . which is as big as one only once gets to make in his lifetime." Kertész also bragged that the success of Austrian cinema was due in no small part to the profusion of imported Hungarian talent, including Vajda, Doraine, Varconi, and, of course, himself. Events would soon dilute some of his bravado.

Disaster struck in the form of a windstorm that swept through Vienna at the end of October. Walter Slezak recalled arriving at the Laaer Berg with Kertész and Doraine and initially thinking the chauffeur had driven them to the wrong location. The standing sets, including the temple, had been completely destroyed. "We were too stunned to talk; even Mike was speechless. We got out of the car and surveyed the wreck: lumber, stucco and lots of painted cloth were all that was left of the Temple of Astarte."

The decision was made to complete all the interior scenes and then rebuild the temple sets and wait for spring. According to Slezak, the principal cast remained on salary for thirty weeks waiting for the final exterior shooting to resume in May 1922. Kolowrat borrowed upward of 60 million kronen, and the Sascha money spigot continued to gush.

Given the scope and complexity of the shoot, many mishaps were to be expected. As a general rule, safety on early movie sets was a secondary consideration at best. Adding to the risk on *Sodom and Gomorrah* was Kertész's cavalier attitude toward the well-being of his performers, particularly when it came to his insistence on staging a sequence in the precise manner he envisioned it. While rehearsing a battle scene on a temple staircase in April 1922, Kertész demonstrated how an extra should react by shoving him against a railing. The railing gave way and the man was severely injured. In an era before workman's compensation insurance, the performer filed a formal criminal complaint and the director was charged with negligence. Sascha was obliged to pay the man off, as Kertész escaped liability.

For some of the final scenes, Kertész had upward of twenty ambulances standing by; they would be needed. He and his assistant director, Arthur Gottlein, engaged a pyrotechnician named Otto Wannemacher to coordinate the destruction of Sodom. According to Slezak, Wannemacher was "a wonderful little man; on his right hand he had only two fingers, three on his left hand—the rest he had exploded away. And a piece of his nose was missing. But, undaunted by these little detonated misfortunes, he kept handling explosives with great casualness, always with a lighted cigar in his mouth."

During his first day on location, Wannemacher's creation of a landslide using explosives proved so effective that he partially buried a camera crew. He also inadvertently substituted a can of dynamite for black powder underneath a float on a lake carrying Lucy Doraine away from the destruction of Sodom and Gomorrah. The intent was to create a bow wave that would overturn the raft, and Slezak would come to the rescue. Doraine, wise to the ways of both moviemaking and her husband, insisted on a demonstration of the stunt before the first take. A large explosion belched a geyser of water into the air and reduced the float to kindling as Doraine unleashed a whirlwind of Hungarian invective on her husband. It was another outburst in a marriage that had become as doomed as the Temple of Astarte.

The couple would separate before the end of the picture. Vajda had to rewrite several scenes, and the existing footage of Doraine would be creatively redistributed as she abruptly left for Germany. Kertész didn't miss a beat, on or off the set. He was openly having affairs with other women.

The final destruction of the temple was high drama that turned to farce. With thousands of extras in place along with film industry executives and government brass hats standing by, Kertész signaled Wannemacher, who depressed the detonator boxes. The explosions lifted the temple set several feet, and then it sat right back down without collapsing. Kertész and the production staff howled as Wannemacher ran for his life. The demolition scene was eventually finished and production wrapped on July 14, 1922.

There are unsubstantiated reports that some of the special effects resulted in injury and death for a number of extras, leading to criminal charges being lodged against Kertész. The director again avoided any significant penalty. Wannemacher was jailed for a period and a 500,000-kronen fine was paid by Sascha-Film. In addition to his erratic pyrotechnician, Kertész enjoyed the assistance of the Austrian Army High Command in the form of landmines, smoke bombs, and various pyrotechnics. According to one report, "They fired more ammo and dynamite than some of the bloodiest battles of the war. During filming, fire brigades and ambulance car teams were constantly deployed, standing by, and the latter had to aid crew members quite often."

Kertész shot miles of film. Part 1, 7,000 feet, premiered in Vienna on October 13, 1922. Part 2, coming in at 12,953 feet, for a total running time of 296 minutes, premiered a week later. The final cut included a twenty-one-minute prologue that disappeared after the original two-part release was combined (and censored) into a shortened version that could be viewed in a single sitting in 1923. Apparently the Austrians believed a single version would be more marketable (they were right), while the German censors were uncomfortable with the overt sexuality and possible political ramifications. Although the sex could be partially rationalized as "biblical," the allegorical connection of Sodom and Gomorrah to contemporary Weimar decadence made Berlin's postwar government bristle. Both these edited versions deleted the entire Syrian sequence.

For years *Sodom and Gomorrah* was thought to be lost, until a partial reconstruction was done by Filmarchiv Austria in 1987. More material was subsequently located throughout Europe, which resulted in a final restoration negative in 2002. As the film's production reports, script, and editing and censorship records are lost, and nearly five thousand feet of original footage remains missing, it is impossible to precisely replicate the film's intended continuity. What remains for the modern viewer is an unwieldy spectacle with flashes of brilliance. The camera is mostly stationary, some of the acting does not hold up well, and the restored film lacks a coherent structure. It is possible that the production of *Sodom and Gomorrah* grew so large and so complex as to be unmanageable even for Michael Kertész.

In 1922–23 *Sodom and Gomorrah* played successfully around the world, and Sascha-Film actually reported a profit by October 1923, an outcome that had appeared unthinkable the previous summer. The American release was extremely successful despite the fact that it was cut to ninety-two minutes and retitled *The Queen of Sin*. *Variety* praised the film's biblical sequences while making unkind comments about the physical appearance of some of the actors: "The film fans of the continent must have a lot of beef as far as the leading women are concerned, and Lucy Doraine fills that requirement fully. . . . Their leading men are all heavy, pouchy individuals of over 50 while their juvenile leads, it seems, must have been recruited from the cradle, so immature do they appear, both in stature and in histrionic ability."

Kertész couldn't have cared less. He was residing in a sumptuous villa in Vienna's garden district that Count Kolowrat had purchased for him along with a new automobile in gratitude for his work. He was now the internationally known director of an acclaimed film. And two weeks after completing *Sodom and Gomorrah,* he began work on his next picture.

At the urging of Count Kolowrat, Kertész decided to adapt the epic play *Young Medardus,* written by the Viennese dramatist Arthur Schnitzler in 1910. The title character is Medardus Klähr, a young student who resists Napoleon's occupation of Vienna after his father is slain at the Battle of Austerlitz in 1805, only to fall in love with an exile from a French royal family. Kertész's production would be laden with huge battle sequences and the overarching presence of Napoleon, balanced by the tragic romance of the ultimately doomed couple.

Vajda and the reclusive sixty-one-year-old Schnitzler created a workable scenario that reduced the complex five-hour stage drama to approximately one hundred minutes of film. There were sensitive political issues to consider. Schnitzler, the son of a prominent doctor and a close friend of Sigmund Freud, ditched medicine in midlife to take up writing and had become a controversial figure. His 1893 play *Anatol,* concerning the sexual affairs of a despondent playboy, was the center of a storm of public criticism.

And that reaction was muted in comparison to what was provoked by *Reigen,* a ten-act play written by Schnitzler in 1897 but not performed until 1920. Schnitzler's scene-by-scene depiction of sexual intercourse within different societal classes incited pandemonium, including a riot in Vienna. The hullabaloo was capped by a 1921 obscenity hearing in Berlin. It resulted in Schnitzler's acquittal despite the trial's blatant anti-Semitic overtones.[1]

Young Medardus skirted social criticism with a story that was thematically romantic rather than sexually controversial. The play had wide patriotic appeal to Austrians and was Schnitzler's most popular work. Despite their differences in nationality, temperament, and background, Kertész and Schnitzler had several things in common. Both were indifferently observant Jews who were obsessively preoccupied with sex, and they shared a secular artistic perspective that emphasized the interrelationship of love and tragedy with life and death.

Repeating the formula of *Sodom and Gomorrah,* Julius von Borsody and Artur Berger recreated Old Vienna by designing ornate sets at the Laaer Berg. Once again, Count Kolowrat spent lavishly on the production and exercised his political influence to convince the Viennese National Guard to act as extras during the prodigious scene in which Napoleon's army marches into Schönbrunn Palace. Kolowrat was gambling on hitting it big with another epic in a short-circuiting economy. When principal photography on *Young Medardus* began in January 1923, French and Belgian troops occupied the industrial Ruhr Valley in Germany to ensure that war reparations were paid in goods, rather than worthless paper money. A disastrous period of hyperinflation had begun in Germany that would soon spread to Austria.

Although considerably older than the fictional Medardus Klähr, the omnipresent Victor Varconi performed ably in the title role. For Varconi's romantic counterpart, Kertész decided on Ágnes Esterházy, a striking-looking Hungarian actress from Kolozvár.

Kertész and Doraine's messy divorce was chronicled in the Viennese newspapers during the latter part of 1922. Doraine claimed that her husband was jealous, quarreled with her, and even hit her on at least one occasion. According to her lawyer, "In spite of his jealousy, he hadn't been faithful and cheated on her several times." Kertész's attorney maintained that Doraine was "lewd, even alcoholic."

Their daughter, Kitty, ended up in the custody of her mother after the divorce was finalized in August 1922. She was sent to a convent school in lower Austria while her parents made cameo appearances in her life. The contrast between the austere convent and the opulence of luxurious villas and hotel suites on holidays became part of Kitty's confused childhood.

Young Medardus was acclaimed for its immense battle sequences with thousands of extras and gunfire, smoke, and explosions. It also benefited from the painterly mise-en-scène that Kertész was becoming known for; the critic Béla Balász called it "the largest and most beautiful war tapestry cinematography." Kertész displays his visual sophistication in the use of lighting with silhouettes—one splendid sequence frames a huge shadow of Napoleon—along with his spatial compositions of interior shots. *Young Medardus* emphasized characterization and emotional angst, the Napoleonic era serving as a historical backdrop. The film suffered from staginess and its proximity to Abel Gance's *Napoléon* (1927), a movie so epochal that no other picture can be fairly compared to it.

These problematic comparisons were also partially caused by the severely edited version of *Young Medardus* that was created by Sascha-Film for export to France. Kolowrat was not going to deny himself the French cinema market out of nationalistic loyalty. Retitled *Gloire* as a paean to Napoleonic grandeur, the repurposed epic emphasized Michael Xantho's supporting role as the Little Corporal in posters and publicity materials.

It was noted in the Hungarian theatrical press that Kertész deviated from his normal approach with *Young Medardus* to create a "stylized art film." What had actually occurred was that he had evolved into a director who was supple with any type of material. At the premiere of *Young Medardus* on October 5, 1923, the director—with an eye on his public image—contrasted the identity and viability of European cinema with the more technically advanced product coming out of Hollywood: "Many European cinema productions offer a simple imitation of the American films as a weapon in the fight with the competition. I believe that we are not going to win anything with this approach. On the contrary, we are going to lose our individuality; this is the basis of our artistic being. As sources for our topics and themes, cinema must serve our art, our national sentiments, our culture, our individualism. . . . Only in this way will we be capable of saving our cinematic production from disappearing."

Although Kertész clearly understood that economic conditions were adversely affecting the future of cinema in Europe and his own film career, he believed that bigger and better movies would win out.

8

Exodus in Red Heels

It was a star-crossed period for Michael Kertész in 1923. Even though the director had helmed a pair of impressive box-office hits, his future was fraught with uncertainty.

The hyperinflation spreading from Germany sounded the death knell in Austria for what had been one of the world's leading film industries. From a robust twenty-five independent production companies that produced seventy-five feature films the previous year, film studios withered to a mere three firms in a matter of months. Three thousand Austrian film industry employees lost their jobs. Imports from Hollywood inundated the cinemas. Kertész could see the writing on the wall; despite having the most sophisticated studio facilities in Europe (Vita-Film at Rosenhügel Studios and Sascha-Film at Sievering), film production in Austria was dying.

Kertész's private life was in disarray as well. His acrimonious divorce cost him dearly in attorney's fees and child support. He was paying these bills while Doraine was dividing her time between Munich, starring in a film for her new production company, and Venice, where she vacationed: "I stay here a week, then I go to Monaco for the car races." In January 1923 a determined Mathilde Foerster took him to court to make him legally acknowledge the paternity of their son, Michael. Kertész was ordered to provide financial support for his son. The director was infuriated over what he considered a deliberate public humiliation. The experience seemingly hardened his heart. By refusing to support his child and holding a grudge, Kertész exacerbated what would become a continued source of embarrassment and heartbreak.

On August 11, 1923, Kertész welcomed the arrival of his latest child, Sonja, by the actress Teresa Dalla Bona. At the same time he was grieving for his father, who had recently died in Budapest at the age of seventy-

Curtiz with the cast and crew of *The Avalanche* (1923). Mary Kid and Victor Varconi are to Curtiz's immediate left (courtesy of the Lucas family).

eight.[1] He continued to support his mother, whom he worshiped. Thanks to the apparently bottomless pockets of Count Kolowrat, Kertész maintained his supremacy as the chief director-supervisor of Sascha-Film and held a senior position in the Austrian cinematographers union while helping his younger brother David get a leg up as an assistant director.

Kertész journeyed to Innsbruck in the Tyrol to film *The Avalanche* (1923), a dramatic study of a man conflicted by his relationship with a pair of women. The film costarred Varconi and Kertész's newest discovery, the German actress Mary Kid. Kertész next helmed *Nameless*, a remake of *The Charlatan*, which he had directed in Hungary in 1917. One reviewer observed, "If we look at this film, we have the impression that we're watching an American movie." Early the following year, Kertész lost his favorite leading man. Victor Varconi signed a contract with Cecil B. DeMille and left Vienna for Hollywood.

Even though Kertész and Vajda had their contracts renewed for five years in December 1923, rumors surfaced in the newspapers about the imminent demise of Sascha-Film. Both Kolowrat and Kertész believed that the only avenue to Sascha's survival would be the production of another epic with international box-office appeal.

Kertész found what was necessary in H. Rider Haggard's 1918 novel *Moon of Israel*. The international craze for all things Egyptian (sparked by the discovery of Tutankhamen's tomb) was still viable. The project was designed as a challenge to the Hollywood competition generally and Cecil B. DeMille's *The Ten Commandments* specifically.

To obtain production funds, Kolowrat sold the British Commonwealth distribution rights to the theater magnate Sir Oswald Stoll, owner of Stoll Pictures Productions Ltd., which produced films at London's Cricklewood Studios. Stoll's investment allowed Kertész to send a second-unit crew to Egypt for six weeks of exterior filming for the pyramid and desert scenes that used a large number of extras. The count was also maneuvering to stall his uneasy creditors at the von Rothschild-founded Creditanstalt Bank.

Moon of Israel is an ancient love tale colored by religion; Moses and the Exodus furnish the background of the story. Vajda and Kertész's adaptation retains the first-person narration of the novel while emphasizing the love story between the Israelite slave girl Merapi (the Moon of Israel) and Prince Seti, son of the Pharaoh Menapta. Because the film required international box-office appeal, Kertész abandoned his practice of frontloading the cast with Hungarian players—except for the title role. For Merapi, he chose Maria Corda, the Transylvanian wife of his friend and colleague Alex Korda. Like Lucy Doraine, Maria had become a star in her husband's films. Although she was on her way to becoming an insufferable prima donna better known for the abusive tantrums directed at her famous husband, Kertész coaxed a superior performance from her.[2]

More striking than beautiful, Corda had luminous eyes—appearing dilated, as if she were drugged—that heightened her portrayal of Merapi as more than a downtrodden slave girl drawn into a love affair with the son of an oppressive pharaoh. Merapi is possessed of supernatural powers; she is a biblical Circe who causes statues to disintegrate while conjuring up a plague of darkness to destroy Thebes. The Chilean actor Adelqui Migliar acquitted himself equally well as Prince Seti. Rounding out the cast was twenty-two-year-old Arlette Marchal as Userti, the betrothed of Prince Seti. She was a captivating French actress who would end up at Paramount three years later, appearing in *Hula* and *Wings*.

For the last time, the Laaer Berg would be the location for an epic film. Artur Berger, who had worked on *Young Medardus,* and Emil Stepanek, one of the *Sodom and Gomorrah* production designers, created the massive sets of Tanis, the capital of ancient Egypt circa 1230

Maria Corda in a swimsuit, with her husband, Alexander Korda (pointing), during a Laguna Beach visit with Curtiz and Bess Meredyth during the late 1920s (courtesy of the Lucas family).

B.C. With an estimated five thousand extras, *The Moon of Israel* rivaled *Sodom and Gomorrah* in terms of production values. But Kertész and the producer Arnold Pressburger avoided some of the mistakes of the previous epic. Accidents were reduced, and instead of creating countless elaborate costumes and props, the extras, particularly the Israelites, were clothed in simple garb; the ornate costumes were reserved for the actors playing the relevant Egyptian characters.

The Moon of Israel is Kertész's outstanding silent epic. His use of the camera guides the audience through the blended saga of romance and biblical story to the tragic denouement wherein Seti clutches his dead Merapi. Both lovers had been beyond despondent over the death of their son, who was struck down by the plague wrought against first-born Egyptians.

Kertész brought his mother from Budapest to visit the set. In a later interview, the recently widowed matriarch expressed pride about her eldest son and his latest epic: "Poor boy, he is working a lot. He's up on his feet from dawn until late evening. . . . I found myself in a large constructed 'film city' . . . they have been building for two months. They were shooting with 5,000 extras, eight cameramen, ten assistant directors, and horse-riding messengers were helping my son."

The climactic parting of the Red Sea remains a bravura sequence of silent cinema. *The Ten Commandments* had been released to great fanfare in Hollywood on December 4, 1923, and the sense of nationalistic competitiveness on the part of Kolowrat, Kertész, and their crew to develop an equally impressive Red Sea sequence cannot be overstated. The technology developed for the biblical cataclysm was as simple as it was clever: a large wooden structure, made to release one hundred cubic meters of water simultaneously from both sides, remained out of the camera frame. After the actors were filmed in the ostensible area of the receded Red Sea, the wall of water shown on both sides was actually a plaster prop that blended perfectly with the black-and-white film using a double exposure of the negative. The sea subsequently crashing down on the Egyptian army was the water from the wooden structure cascading into a closed trough that was twenty-six feet long and three feet deep. The receding of the sea was the original shot of the crashing water run in reverse.

The Moon of Israel was screened for a select audience in Berlin during the first week of October and officially premiered on October 24 at the Eos Cinema in Vienna. Kolowrat expensively decorated the Eos in an Egyptian motif that aped Sid Grauman's new Hollywood Boulevard movie palace. The reviews were positive and the box-office returns throughout Europe were handsome.

The European success was gratifying, but *Moon of Israel* needed to be a hit internationally, particularly in America. No one had reckoned on the machinations of a wily Hungarian, Adolph Zukor, president of Famous Players-Lasky (reorganized as Paramount Pictures in 1927), who produced *The Ten Commandments.*

Oswald Stoll determined to lease the London Pavilion as the site of the U.K. premiere of *The Moon of Israel.* Famous Players-Lasky was then the leaseholder on the theater. Although Zukor decided to approve a sublease permitting Stoll to screen *Moon of Israel* for an entire month at the Pavilion to avoid embarrassing a powerful mogul in his own country, he had no intention of allowing Kertész's epic to compete with *The Ten Commandments* in the United States.[3]

The print of *The Moon of Israel* that was shown at the premiere in London and intended for distribution to the United States was an edited version that was missing some of the violence—arrows sticking out of soldiers—and passionate kisses, while including English subtitles written by H. Rider Haggard. This cut would never be seen in an American movie theater. Famous Players-Lasky bought the American distribution rights and refused to exhibit it. Although Kolowrat and Stoll received their up-front fee, anticipated U.S. box-office receipts evaporated. Zukor kept *The Moon of Israel* in archival purgatory until the summer of 1927, when he sold a stripped-down, sixty-five-minute version to Joseph P. Kennedy's FBO studio. By that time, the principals involved in both *The Moon of Israel* and *The Ten Commandments* had long since moved on.

Despite being outwitted by Zukor, Count Kolowrat made a respectable profit. But a successful film could not correct economic conditions in Austria. A new currency, introduced on December 20, 1924, replaced the Austro-Hungarian krone at a rate of one schilling to 10,000 kronen. The free fall slowed, but it was too little, too late. American movies continued to flood the market and talent was exiting.

In an ironic twist, Kolowrat had indirectly invented one of the entities that was then competing against him. The count's wartime newsreels for the former Austro-Hungarian government proved so effective that they spurred the Germans to establish Universum Film, or UFA, in 1917 to create wartime propaganda films. For a time UFA had a seat on the Sascha-Film board of directors. UFA eventually merged with other firms and, with the backing of the Weimar Republic government, became a fierce competitor to Austrian film companies. The era of the Austrian monumental film was over. Kolowrat and Kertész quickly pivoted to a project that was in keeping with the changing times. It was specifically designed to be emblematic of the mid-1920s Jazz Age, characterized by its new morality and sexual frankness.

Das Spielzeug von Paris (The Toy of Paris) (1925), based on Margery Lawrence's novel *Red Heels,* was unlike any of Kertész's previous Sascha-Film productions. Instead of spectacle or melodrama, Kertész's adaptation revolved around an irresistible cabaret star named Célimène, who is pursued by two radically different men along with assorted characters who wander in and out of her dizzying orbit as she soaks up the high life of nocturnal Paris.

Kertész was happy to leave Vienna to scout talent and film exteriors for *The Toy of Paris* in France. His personal life remained turbulent: his third child, Michael, was born on April 28, 1925. The mother was eighteen-year-old Franzeska "Franzi" Vondrak, a Sascha-Film extra with whom the director had been keeping company since *The Moon of Israel.*

Kertész needed a new face for *The Toy of Paris.* After watching Lili Damita onstage and meeting her in Paris, the director was transfixed. He had discovered the authentic Célimène, a petite vixen who could cast a carnal spell on every man she desired.

Born Liliane Marie-Madeleine Carré in Blaye, France, in 1904 (some sources list 1901), Damita appeared in the revue at the Casino de Paris at the age of sixteen and was a supporting actress in a half dozen French films before being spotted by Kertész. Damita loved to flaunt her sexuality, once responding to an admirer's comment about a form-fitting blue dress, "If monkeys can have blue asses, I can have blue tits!" (After marrying her in 1935, Errol Flynn ruefully admitted to a friend that though Damita had intellectual limitations as a spouse, "she was the greatest lay in the world.") Kertész was smitten. He began an affair with Damita as production began on *The Toy of Paris.* The shared passion of director and star added more fire to an already overheated story.

An eclectic international cast complements Kertész's vivid imagery of a hedonistic Parisian nightlife as a nocturnal universe peopled by elderly lechers, beautiful women, assorted crooks, gays, and drunks amid the magnificent set designs of Artur Berger. After fifteen films with Kertész, the cinematography of Gustav Ucicky was a virtual storyboard of the director's visual conceptions. The dance numbers staged against the hazy

Curtiz and Lili Damita during filming of *Das Spielzeug von Paris* (The Toy of Paris; 1925) (courtesy of Photofest).

background of the smoky Parisian nightclub have a completely different, adult sensibility from those of the conventional Hollywood musicals Kertész would direct years later.

Kertész's affair with Damita sharpened his portrayal of runaway lust onscreen. Célimène is shown kissing her female friend on the mouth and orgasmically emoting, and there are many scenes with overt sexual symbolism.

Because of his financial concerns, Kolowrat compelled Kertész to shoot two different endings to *The Toy of Paris*. The director was unhappy about altering what he considered to be a stellar finale but he had no choice. The blatant sexual content would make distribution difficult in certain countries, and the count needed every dollar. The version distributed in England, Austria, and Germany featured the alternative ending that concluded on a note of melodramatic emancipation: Célimène searches out her husband, Miles Seward, during a driving rainstorm, seeking the redemptive love of marriage to curtail her continual self-indulgence. She ends up dying of pneumonia after completing her moral testament, thereby satisfying certain audiences and censors.

Kertész's preferred finale, which was shown in France and Spain, finds Célimène recovering from her bout with pneumonia and returning to a life of lighthearted profligacy at the nightclub. Both versions include a racy sequence showing a scantily clothed Damita stuck in the mud on a road as a car prepares to run her down. The director convinced his star-lover to stage this scene without using a double.

Kertész's happiness about working in Paris was palpable: "You can't believe what a joy it is to film in Paris, where they greet those who want to work in movies with courtesy and welcome that's unheard of. There's a genuine international company of people there. . . . Almost everybody travels to Paris to make films. It is my pleasure to tell the readers that my movie *The Toy of Paris* turned out well, and in it you will be introduced to a splendid young actress, Lili Damita."

For Kolowrat, obtaining financing was becoming problematic. After his relationship with Oswald Stoll played out, he looked to Germany, whose recovering economy and burgeoning film industry offered opportunities for collaboration. Kolowrat worked out a financial deal with Phoebus-Film AG, a component arm of UFA. The agreement also allowed Sascha-Film to gain a toehold in the German market and avail itself of lower production costs by moving film operations to Berlin.

In November 1925 Kertész began production on *Fiaker Nr. 13* (The Horse Cart Number 13), adapted from an 1880 novel. Damita played the

Curtiz directing *Fiaker 13* (The Horse Cart No. 13; 1926) in Paris; Gustav Ucicky is behind the camera (courtesy of the Lucas family).

lost child of a millionaire raised by an elderly Parisian cab driver and his wife. This charming picture benefits from Kertész's insertion of a melodramatic lost love theme and the participation of the talented Paul Leni as production designer.

While he was shooting *Fiaker Nr. 13*, the director's concentration was disrupted by the presence of several strangers. He became irritated and asked the interlopers to leave. As Kertész recalled in a 1947 interview, "One of the two men whisper something to my assistant and my assistant tells me that Mr. Warner, of America, is watching me and will give me a job."

9

A Family Business

Harry Warner was searching for talent to support his growing film production company in the United States. After interviewing Kertész, Warner departed for New York on the S.S. *Berengaria* on February 24, 1926. Before leaving, he cabled his younger brother Jack, who was in charge of production at the Warner Bros. movie studio at Sunset Boulevard and Bronson Avenue in Hollywood. He reported that he was impressed by Kertész and wanted to see *Moon of Israel,* the film that Adolph Zukor had contrived to bury. Harry was characteristically suspicious about why the epic hadn't played in America. Jack unearthed a *Moon of Israel* print and both brothers were "laid in the aisles" by Kertész's work. According to Jack, his older brother exclaimed, "We've got to get this man to Hollywood!"

The offer of a Warner Bros. contract took Kertész by surprise. He hadn't expected anything tangible so soon after his brief meeting with Harry. Uncertain about his future with Sascha-Film, Kertész had initiated a handshake agreement with the independent German producer Jakob Karol before his meeting with Warner. After the director fessed up to Harry about his agreement with Karol, Warner offered to pay Karol off to the tune of $15,000 to free up Kertész to join Warner Bros. Kertész considered Karol an opportunist who was trying to pry money out of Warner, but he was flattered that the American wanted him badly enough to pay off the German. It was an archetypal decision by the eldest Warner brother, who carefully measured risk against reward, but wasn't afraid to take chances. In the spring of 1926, Harry and his brothers—Albert, Sam, and Jack—were poised to surge away from the Hollywood pack of independent film entrepreneurs.

Their father, Benjamin Wonskolaser (the surname was changed to Warner soon after he arrived in the United States), was a Polish Jew who had immigrated to Baltimore and discovered that the streets were not paved with gold. He tried selling goods to railroad workers in Virginia and was swindled by a brother-in-law. He next traveled to Canada to deal in fur pelts and was fleeced again. Returning to Baltimore, he switched to running a grocery store, working sixteen hours a day and yet never making enough money to support his large family.

He passed his strong devotion to Judaism on to his first son, Harry, who was born in 1881. Although the family eventually settled down in the hardscrabble town of Youngstown, Ohio, where the elder Warner made ends meet as a grocer and butcher, it was a life of unrewarding toil. Never forgetting their father's humiliations and feeling ostracized for being Jewish and poor, the brothers closed ranks and worked together against the world.

In the beginning, it was a balanced team. Harry and Albert were temperate in personality, opportunistic in business, and reflected the rectitude of their father. Harry was perfectly cast as the abstemious elder who put his family, his religion, and his country first. Albert Warner possessed the effervescence of an undertaker; he deferred to his older brother in nearly all matters.

Sam and Jack were more assimilated, impulsive, and, in Sam's case, talented. Sam was a charming risk taker whose high-roller personality and intuitive technical acumen were complemented by a ferocious work ethic. While the brothers respected Sam on his own terms, Jack, the youngest, Canadian-born in 1892, felt compelled to attract attention and acted the clown. The chasm between Harry the sober patriarch and Jack the perpetual kid brother often seemed unbridgeable. But Sam could do everything, including keeping the peace between Harry and Jack.

In 1904 Sam prevailed on his brothers to invest one thousand dollars in a movie projector. It was said that they hocked their father's gold watch or sold his delivery horse to close the deal. They achieved an immediate return on their investment by screening *The Great Train Robbery* in a tent pitched in their Youngstown front yard. They then exhibited the film at carnivals in Ohio and Pennsylvania. Harry sold a bicycle shop he owned and joined forces with his brothers to open a pair of movie theaters in New Castle, Pennsylvania. The brothers quickly realized that there was a great deal of money to be made in the embryonic movie business. After building up a film exhibition exchange called the Duquesne Amusement Company in Pittsburgh, they were forced to abandon it by the Edison Trust monopoly, which charged usurious fees to exhibitors until broken up by the courts in 1915. The brothers went back into distribution and eventually established a film exchange business with offices in New York, San Francisco, and Los Angeles. Even after teaming with Carl Laemmle to distribute his Universal films, the business proved to be a financial roller coaster between struggling to establish territorial rights to distribute a particular film and absorbing grievous losses for a box-office turkey. Soon the brothers were aspiring to produce movies rather than distribute them.

After making an educational film on venereal disease for the Army Signal Corps during World War I, the brothers struck gold by securing the movie rights to the book *My Four Years in Germany* by James W. Gerard, the U.S. ambassador to Germany before America entered the war. Their docudrama propaganda film reviling German militarism earned them a profit of $130,000, which paved the way for the establishment of Warner Bros. Pictures Inc. While Harry and Albert ran the business end from New York, Sam and Jack set up shop in a tiny downtown Los Angeles studio, cranking out cheap serials. Sam and Jack also established a relationship with Motley Flint (W. C. Fields would have adored that name), president of Los Angeles's Security Pacific Federal Bank. Flint believed in the future of the film industry generally and Warner Bros. specifically. It was his bank that provided the funding to upgrade the new ten-acre Warner studio site in Hollywood in 1923.[1]

Always mistrustful of outsiders, Harry was convinced that the brothers were getting cheated by distributors and wanted to control both the distribution system *and* the theaters that allocated and exhibited Warner films. He needed access to financial resources at reasonable interest rates to finance his expansion plans. It was a tough sell. Many banks were wary of the movie industry. Harry's successful 1924 courtship of the financier Waddill Catchings assured the future of Warner Bros. After signing onto the Warner Board of Directors, Catchings lined up multiple banks that had never previously lent a nickel to a movie studio to provide a multimillion credit line for the Warners. Harry immediately bought up Vitagraph Studios and its distribution exchanges, and he then commenced purchasing movie theaters. A vertically integrated company began to take shape.

It was Jack who signed their first major star, Rin Tin Tin. After the dog's first movie, *Where the North Begins* (1923), was a smash hit, the thirty-year-old mogul hired a twenty-one-year-old gap-toothed Nebraskan named Darryl F. Zanuck as a screenwriter. Zanuck was a whirling dervish who could dash off a Rinty script lightning-quick while working frenetically on other projects. He was responsible for so many Warner screenplays during his first two years at the studio that he adopted several "noms de screen" to confound distributors who complained that all the Warner films seemed to be written by the same person. The Rin Tin Tin pictures sustained the studio through lean financial times (Jack dubbed the dog "the mortgage lifter") as Zanuck's meteoric rise began.

The brothers also moved into radio with Sam Warner's establishment of the third commercial radio station in greater Los Angeles. More important, Sam got wind of a new process for synchronizing sound to film from the station's audio technician. After traveling to New York and witnessing the process at Western Electric's Bell Laboratories, he became positively evangelical about the sound-on-disk process as the wave of the future in the movie business. Harry eventually gave his assent in 1925 for a licensing deal with Western Electric for the new process that he believed would combine recorded classical music with silent pictures. By the time Warner Bros. extended their offer to Kertész, movie sound was well on the way to becoming a reality.

How much of this background was Kertész aware of as he pondered the Warner contract offer? Surely he would have known about the much-ballyhooed engagement of John Barrymore and the subsequent success of *Beau Brummel* in 1924. He was also aware that Warner Bros. had signed the German director Ernst Lubitsch two years earlier and that the relationship had soured. Lubitsch was given carte blanche to create his own films but achieved middling box-office results. He soon departed for the greener pastures of Metro-Goldwyn-Mayer.

What was clear to Kertész was that Warner Bros. was on the rise and needed a skilled and experienced film director. In the end, perhaps the deciding factor was that the apex of the movie business was in Hollywood. He would be on the outside looking in as long as he remained in Europe.

The contract he was offered was remunerative but not what Warner was paying its top-line talent. He would receive a salary of $15,600 per year (approximately $215,000 in 2017 dollars), at a rate of $300 per week. The contract escalated over four years to a maximum of $36,000 per annum. Although Warner Bros. agreed to advance him $2,000, which he would have to pay back to the studio at the rate of $200 per month, they also arranged for Jakob Karol to pay Kertész $200 a month: that $2,400 was applied to the $15,000 purchase price of Kertész's contract from Karol.

Kertész's Warner contract ceded every conceivable benefit to the employer. The rights to any creative work by the director, including scripts, magazine articles, theater and radio appearances, and phonograph records, along with any plots or ideas that he might conceive while under contract, were deemed the property of the studio. Furthermore, his pay would be suspended if he were unable to perform his duties or was absent for a period of more than two weeks for any reason, "illness, death in the family, and Divine Act included." Kertész was required to assist with editing, continuity, title construction, and anything else associated with an assigned film. This contractual full nelson was routinely applied to hired talent during the early days of the Hollywood studio system but not nearly so punitively in Europe, where the director was considered more of an artist.

Kertész was unfazed by any contractual mumbo-jumbo. His confidence was unbounded. It was more than self-assurance; it was arrogance, an egotistical belief in his proven abilities as a filmmaker that had been honed during his fourteen years behind the camera in Europe. He had directed upward of seventy films, many of them commercial successes, while also becoming a technical virtuoso. Kertész knew acting and actors and had an impressive track record of finding and nurturing talent, developing scripts, working with writers, and producing, editing, and orchestrating complex epics with casts of thousands. In short, he believed that it was Michael Kertész who was best equipped to show Warner Bros. and Hollywood how to make better and more successful movies, rather than the other way around.

Before leaving the continent, Kertész wrapped up his final film for Count Kolowrat. His cinematic trifecta with Lili Damita concluded with *The Golden Butterfly,* produced under the new Phoebus-Film–Sascha banner. The vivacious Damita portrayed an adopted restaurant cashier, Lilian, with a passion for dancing who ends up emotionally torn between her stepbrother and a dashing impresario who wants to make her a big star. She pursues her professional dancing career with lamentable consequences: after an onstage accident, Lilian becomes permanently disabled as her two suitors continue to vie for her love. Kertész filmed the picture in Berlin; exteriors were shot in London and Oxford.

The affair between Kertész and Damita concluded with their last film. Despite a number of modern sources averring they were married for a year or so before Kertész left for Hollywood, there is no evidence that such a union occurred. The passage of time dimmed their initial passion and, as both director and star were resolutely focused on themselves, it was an amicable parting. In light of Damita's subsequent misadventures after being lured to Hollywood by Samuel Goldwyn in 1928, Kertész was doubtlessly thankful that he never wedded the tempestuous temptress. (There would be a future connection between the pair nine years later at Warner Bros.)

As he signed the Warner contract on May 10, 1926, in Berlin, the director realized that he was severing close ties with his immediate family in Hungary. Hollywood was effectively a million miles away. For Kertész, this was emotionally wrenching. He made a final trip to Budapest to see his mother and siblings before boarding the train to Cherbourg, France, and sailing on an ocean liner to New York. His divorce arrangement with Lucy Doraine did not allow his daughter Kitty, then eleven, to live with him until she attained the age of twelve. Under her mother's sponsorship, Kitty had become a child actress with Emelka Films (later Bavaria Films AG) in 1923 and appeared in her first German feature, which was shot in Munich. She recalled her childhood in Europe during an interview with *Theater Life* in the early 1930s: "Already at age eight, I became acquainted with filmmaking when I appeared in the Emelka drama *Dying Love,* in which I had such great success that the whole German press celebrated me. From then on, my time was divided between the convent and traveling. At the age of ten, I traveled the whole continent with my mother, who is my best friend."

Although Doraine and Kitty would soon follow Kertész to Hollywood, their lives would become increasingly cordoned off from his—a continuation of how their relationships evolved in Europe.

For Kertész, cutting his European ties also included another change of surname. Judging from Warner Bros. studio correspondence, the switch from Kertész to Curtiz occurred almost simultaneously with his hiring. The name alteration apparently went hand in hand with being signed as a new commodity at the studio. It is also probable that the Warners believed that the director's Hungarian surname had a "foreign" connotation that would be negatively construed.

Faced with the loss of his ace director, the indefatigable Count Kolowrat promoted Curtiz's cinematographer, Gustav Ucicky, to be his principal director, and a new slate of films planned for the following year. But the producer didn't have much time left for movies, as he was diagnosed with pancreatic cancer in the summer of 1927. Count Alexander Kolowrat died on December 4, 1927, at the age of forty-one. An overlooked figure in cinematic history, he remains the godfather of Austrian film and the person most responsible for guiding Michael Curtiz's pre-Hollywood career.

Curtiz with his daughter Kitty in the early 1920s (courtesy of the Lucas family).

As Curtiz watched the coastline of France disappear from the stern of the ocean liner, he shook off any uncertainty over his decision to leave Europe and concentrated on the new biblical epic that he was discussing with Harry Warner. The film he envisioned could be made only in Hollywood.

10

Hungarian in the Promised Land

One of the most fanciful myths perpetuated about Curtiz concerns the circumstances of his arrival in the United States. According to numerous sources, including Jack Warner, Hal Wallis, and Curtiz himself in later studio press releases, Curtiz's ocean liner, the *Leviathan,* arrived in New York harbor amid great fanfare. Jack, who seldom permitted truth to interfere with an anecdote, related his version of the story in his memoir:

> Harry promised Curtiz press conferences and a gala reception.
> . . . As the steamer slid up the Hudson River to the dock there
> were fireboats hurling spears of water high about the ship, there
> was a band playing martial music on shore, and the sky was on
> fire with Roman candles and bursting rockets. Mike was so over-
> come that he wept. . . . I never had the heart to disillusion him
> about the noisy and vunderful welcome for the great Michael
> Curtiz on the waterfront. He just happened to arrive in New York
> on the Fourth of July.

This amusing story embellishes the Curtiz legend, but it is entirely fictional. Curtiz had arrived in New York on June 6, 1926. There were no bands, fireworks, or press conferences. His stay in America was authorized for only six months under the Immigration Act of 1924; he had arrived without any type of work visa. Whether Curtiz left Europe in such a hurry that he simply forgot about obtaining a visa or Warner Bros. was remiss in their responsibilities as his employer, this situation became a recurring headache for the director and his studio.

Harry Warner, in Chicago on a business trip, wasn't there to meet him. Albert Warner delayed the start of the next leg of Curtiz's journey to Los Angeles in order to wait for the return of the elder Warner brother "so

Under way to the Land of Plenty: Curtiz on board the *Leviathan* en route to New York City in June 1926 (courtesy of Photofest).

that they [Curtiz and Harry] might go over some stories and other matters before he left New York for Hollywood." When Harry arrived, he and Curtiz had an extended conversation about the biblical movie that the director had broached when the pair first met in Europe. Harry assured his new director that production would commence on his epic shortly after he arrived in Hollywood and met with Jack at the studio. Curtiz was thrilled and continued working on his outline, titled *Noah's Ark,* while on the train to the West Coast. The trip took just under four days. Reality set in immediately upon his arrival in Los Angeles.

Standing at the old Central Station, Curtiz felt like a stranger in a strange land. No one from the studio met him. He managed to locate and ride the streetcar from downtown, arriving at the Warner Bros. studio at 5800 Sunset Boulevard in Hollywood, on Monday morning, June 21, 1926. His initial meeting with Jack L. Warner could not have been more deflating. Ushered in to see the production chief, who was having the kinks worked out on a massage table, Curtiz brandished his *Noah's Ark* treatment and eagerly inquired when he could start production. According to Curtiz, Jack replied, "We have decided not to do that. Leave your script on the massage table. You will make *The Third Degree.*"

It eventually dawned on Curtiz that he had been caught up in the sibling infighting between Harry and Jack. Jack had no intention of surrendering his prerogatives as vice president in charge of production to anyone, particularly his bossy older brother, who regularly sniped at him from New York. Jack would not tolerate Harry's issuing edicts regarding when *Noah's Ark* or any other film would be made. It was a lesson the director never forgot. Curtiz assiduously avoided getting into the middle of future Warner family squabbles. The youngest Warner also believed— quite correctly—that before Curtiz could be entrusted to helm an expensive epic whose failure might break the studio, he had to demonstrate success with more modestly budgeted films. The disappointed director began preproduction on *The Third Degree,* a crime story based on a 1908 stage drama by Charles Klein.

There were major challenges for Curtiz to overcome in order to successfully complete his first American feature: (1) he could not read English; and (2) he knew absolutely nothing about the American criminal justice system. As he recalled two decades later, "I didn't know what to do, but I know my entire career depends on it." After privately commissioning a translation of the play into Hungarian and reading it over, he was momentarily downcast. He dictated a memo that was translated into

English and sent to Jack Warner stating that *The Third Degree* was "a rather poor and naive story" and suggested how to enhance it to make it suitable for the screen. He then summarized his feelings about his initial film assignment: "If you think this film will be a moneymaker and with a clever writer, also your ideas added, then I will be willing to do this picture, but this picture *The Third Degree* does not give me a fair opportunity to introduce my best abilities and capacity."

Jack Warner was adamant that his new director should prove himself by directing a medium-budget production of this literary property (which Warner Bros. inherited when they bought Vitagraph Studios in 1924). The scenarist Bess Meredyth was brought in to write the story treatment; the screenwriter Raymond Schrock and the former newspaper scribe C. Graham Baker were assigned to construct a shooting script with Curtiz, who dictated a three-page memo on recommendations to punch up the story. The thrust of Klein's play concerned the dangers of unchecked police interrogation (i.e., "the third degree"), which could cause an innocent man to confess to a crime he hadn't committed. *The Third Degree* had been filmed twice before, in 1913 and 1919, and would be revived on radio in 1936.

Curtiz got himself up to speed on American criminology and police procedures by contacting Eugene Biscailuz, the Los Angeles County undersheriff. Biscailuz was sympathetic to the earnest Hungarian who begged for his advice. Curtiz spent the next ten days literally living at the Los Angeles County Jail, learning the ropes and absorbing everything: "I am up every morning at four o'clock studying fingerprint, eating with detectives, going to morning line-up. When I finish, I know more about jail system and American criminals than the technical director they pay big dough to tell me about such things."

As specified by Curtiz, *The Third Degree* script expanded on the social-injustice premise of a falsely accused man who marries a circus performer. The screenwriters also added a detailed prologue that enabled the director to add circus action sequences that were not part of the original story. One spectacular scene was a motorcycle accident during a stunt aptly titled "The Whirl of Death." The other was a forty-foot dive by a daredevil into a small pool of water. When Hal Wallis asked him why he added these scenes, Curtiz responded, "I felt something extra was needed."

The circus sequences were the first instances of the director's pattern of behavior during his formative years at Warner Bros. He would

the first phot of 'Third degree' 20ᵗʰ Sept. 1927
on the Vitagraph lot for Warner Brothers.

Curtiz's Warner Bros. debut, *The Third Degree* (1926). Curtiz's name is misspelled on the sign, and the photo is annotated with the incorrect year (courtesy of the Lucas family).

be assigned and agree to a certain script or story and then add or delete sequences and dialogue during filming as he saw fit. This latitude might have been okay for Curtiz and his colleagues in Europe, but not at Warner Bros., where Jack Warner relentlessly monitored budgets and shooting schedules. Darryl Zanuck, followed by Wallis, would add more road-blocks, as both producers considered an approved script a consecrated parchment not to be trifled with. For years Curtiz would intermittently engage in battles over the content of films that he always believed were his but were actually theirs.

Jack Warner supported his new director on *The Third Degree* by assigning Heinz (Henry) Blanke as assistant director. Blanke began as a cutter at UFA before becoming a production assistant for Ernst Lubitsch. He accompanied Lubitsch to Warner Bros. and remained after the German director moved to MGM in 1926. After heading the Warner production office in Germany for two years, Blanke returned to Hollywood for an unprecedented twenty-eight-year career at Warners as production supervisor and line producer. He would play a pivotal role in Curtiz's career as the associate producer for some of the director's best films. The cinematographer was Hal Mohr, who enjoyed a six-decade career in Hollywood. Mohr admired the new director's creativity and ability to work alongside the camera: "He [Curtiz] had great artistic instinct. . . . I was really surprised by the beauty of some of the shots we got."

Keenly aware of what was riding on his debut, Curtiz pulled out all the stops on *The Third Degree*. With a cast headed by the studio's top female star, Dolores Costello, and a skilled ensemble of character players (Louise Dresser, Rockliffe Fellowes, Tom Santschi, and Jason Robards Sr.), the director employed nearly every camera trick he had learned and created some new ones.

For the high-dive sequence, Curtiz had Mohr position the camera under the transparent bottom of the pool. His use of expressionistic visual devices included contrasting diagonals in a montage of multiple staircases to convey the weariness of Robards's character's fruitless job-hunting, a near-constant use of sloping camera angles, a long traveling shot trolling down a garbage-strewn street, extreme close-ups of Robards's face sweating and fingering his dry lips during the police interrogation, and a series of split-screen circus sequences that the *New York Times* reviewer described as "an orgy of dissolves, but in quite a number of cases these are emphatically effective." In an era before optical printing, Mohr recalled running the film through the camera more than eighty times to achieve the multiexposure overlays that Curtiz wanted. The director even had Mohr shoot through a drop of glycerin on the camera lens during a scene in which Dolores Costello becomes dizzy, to better convey her disorientation. The final fade-out, in which the circus ringmaster places his hat over the lens, was an acknowledgment of the camera's primary role in Curtiz's first Hollywood film.

Some of this visual alchemy was over the top for U.S. reviewers, who thought the film was good but that Warner Bros.' newest director was trying too hard. *Variety* favorably compared *The Third Degree* to E. A. Dupont's 1925 circus-based drama *Variety*, but the reviewer added that the Hungarian director's camerawork was "too much of a good thing." Curtiz's use of the camera was an attempt to entice audiences to become more involved in the story. He wasn't into self-aggrandizement; he was trying to make a distinctive movie.

The critics might not have been the only ones who misinterpreted his work as technical grandstanding. According to Curtiz, he was fired three times during production of *The Third Degree* after Jack Warner previewed his rushes. Warner said afterward that Curtiz made two movies—a crime story and a circus picture. He was never in actual danger of being let go, but his angst about the success or failure of his first American picture was genuine. The Warners were actually quite satisfied and enjoyed Curtiz's camerawork; it was the principal reason they'd hired him. Most critically, their new director brought the film in on time and on budget. From a cost of $208,000, *The Third Degree* grossed $413,000, a respectable profit.

After the December 1926 release of *The Third Degree,* Jack Warner notified Curtiz that *Noah's Ark* had been postponed indefinitely. The Warners were counting pennies more closely than usual. The studio had lost a million dollars in 1926. Their fight to bring sound to the screen had sent Warner Bros. stock soaring during the summer, but it had all come crashing down by the end of the year.

Warner Bros. borrowed $4 million to establish the Vitaphone Company to franchise their new sound system—masterminded by Sam Warner—which debuted in New York on August 6, 1926, with talking shorts and the sound music score for the John Barrymore vehicle *Don Juan.* But neither theater owners nor studios were buying. Western Electric quadrupled the price to install Vitaphone sound systems in movie theaters, and the other four major studios that owned theaters—Paramount, MGM, Fox, and RKO—colluded not to license the Vitaphone system until all of them possessed a universally shared sound system of their own making. The bank loan ran out, and Harry Warner had to sell his stock to keep the studio afloat. At one point, Jack Warner had Henry Blanke store the studio cameras at his home in the evenings to avoid the possibility of having them seized by the banks.

More troubling to Curtiz was his immigration status. As a business visitor, he could legally stay in the United States only until December 1926. An extension had to be requested by his employer. Although another six-month extension was eventually requested by Warner Bros. and approved by the U.S. Department of Labor at Ellis Island, Curtiz found himself in the uncomfortable position of being beholden to Harry and Jack Warner in order to remain in Hollywood. He had fallen in love with his new home. In the United States there were few class distinctions and an absence of monolithic government; this was intoxicating to someone who came of age under an emperor's rule and survived the chaos of war. During a 1946 interview, the director evinced his feelings about America: "Everybody is human beings. I learn democracy here. Where I came from wasn't freedom. When I am a little kid I am on street, a policeman pass and say, 'Long live king and beat the Jew.' When I come here, the buildings are marvelous; but most important, always the underdog is the hero. I observe and I never forget."

Curtiz's initial rapture would ripen into a fierce patriotism that strongly influenced his future work. Now he had to figure out how to stay put and direct meaningful pictures.

His immigration situation exacerbated his lack of leverage to argue with Jack Warner about assignments, budgets, and the like. It is a reasonable supposition that Jack used Curtiz's immigration status to elicit the director's cooperation in matters large and small. For the studio boss, it was a handy way of keeping the leash taut on a valued employee. Curtiz received a continuing $200-per-week bonus in April 1927 that would be augmented by another $300 per week the following year after the first two options on his original three-year contract were picked up. Despite the pay increases, Curtiz had to accept whatever film he was assigned and do the best he could. It is not a coincidence that he became much more insistent about demanding better assignments at Warner Bros. after he became a U.S. citizen in 1936.

Curtiz's second Warner Bros. picture, *A Million Bid,* again starred the angelic-looking Dolores Costello. It was another recycled melodrama based on a stage play that Vitagraph initially filmed in 1914. The story is a mélange of torturous circumstances involving a forced marriage, attempted rape, rescue at sea, and amnesia; it featured Warner Oland (the Swedish actor who became the first cinematic Charlie Chan) and a young William Demarest. An exciting sea storm in which Costello, Oland, and Betty Blythe are tossed around by cascades of water on a sinking ship was

Curtiz's dress rehearsal for *Noah's Ark* the following year. One scene revealed a darker side of the director to Hal Mohr: "We had a darling little baby in . . . *A Million Bid,* and the baby was supposed to cry. So Mike would go up to say something to the woman who was holding the baby, and he'd fuss around, adjusting the diaper or something. The baby would start to cry, and he'd turn on the camera. I took about four or five takes before I caught on to what the sonofabitch was doing: he was pinching the baby to make it cry."

Mohr might have been the first person at Warner Bros. to become outraged by Curtiz's willingness to resort to any means necessary to get a scene in the can. He wouldn't be the last.

Curtiz began his long association with Darryl F. Zanuck when he directed *The Desired Woman* in 1927. Although the director had the dependable Anthony Coldeway to punch up Zanuck's Sahara Desert story concerning a comely British royal (Irene Rich) involved in a love triangle with a pair of Royal Army officers, the premise was strictly clichéd. Curtiz persuaded Zanuck to let him shoot near Yuma, Arizona, to give some sense of visual reality to a weak story.

The director was also saddled with Prince Michael Romanoff as a technical adviser. Romanoff, an endearing professional imposter who convinced the gullible of his lineage to the deposed Russian imperial family, persuaded Zanuck that he possessed expertise as a former British army major in the Sudan and would be invaluable to the production. Prince Michael, better known to the police as Harry Gerguson, spent most of his time pursuing Warner ingénues and living the high life until his imposter status was exposed on the front page of the *Los Angeles Examiner.* Leaving town quickly, he would eventually return to open the legendary Romanoff's in Beverly Hills, holding court for decades as a restaurateur, bit actor, and friend to the stars.

Curtiz's next assignment was more of the same: *Good Time Charley* was another period melodrama. The stolid Warner Oland costarred with Helene Costello, younger sister of Dolores, whose tragic life would be truncated by alcoholism, tuberculosis, and barbiturate addiction.

With his immigration extension expiring again, Curtiz composed an earnest letter to Harry Warner. He treated all the Warners respectfully, but he always showed the highest degree of deference to Harry. He worked for Jack, but Harry was responsible for bringing him to America and he never forgot it. Curtiz appealed to the Warner patriarch: "I am very anxious not only to remain in America, but to become an American citizen. Since I have arrived, I have realized that this is the country that promises to fulfill my highest artistic ambition. Even though I could get another extension for six months or a year, this continuing matter of extensions causes a permanent concern. . . . Would you try to be so kind to get me a number in the quota . . . and in due time become a citizen."

Warner Bros. had previously sent a letter to Will Hays at the Motion Picture Producers and Distributors of America (MPPDA) requesting assistance on Curtiz's first immigration extension in 1926. Hays offered no help and unkindly pointed out that a large number of Germans working in the motion picture industry routinely overstayed their temporary business authorizations. The studio had little option but to request another extension for Curtiz, which was granted under a five-hundred-dollar bond posted by the studio with the Department of Labor at Ellis Island.

Curtiz had planted his flag at Warner Bros. and had another year to continue to prove his worth. He also had another reason for desperately wanting to remain in America: he had fallen in love with the "clever writer" of *The Third Degree* and wanted to get married as soon as possible.

11

A Loving Collaboration

Shortly after arriving at Warner Bros., Michael Curtiz was introduced to Bess Meredyth on the set of *Don Juan*. One of Hollywood's top writers, Meredyth had worked on the scenario for the John Barrymore swashbuckler and had also written the outline for *The Third Degree*. The details of their working relationship during Curtiz's film debut remain unknown, but a personal connection between the pair was definitely established.

The upshot of their first meeting was an invitation from Meredyth for Curtiz to join her and some friends at a beach party. Curtiz rented a car to drive to the ocean and experienced one of his many difficulties with automobiles. A Curtiz anecdote retold for decades has him driving a car for weeks in second gear and consequently burning up the engine because he wasn't aware the transmission needed to be shifted into a higher gear. He drove the car onto the beach, where it became stuck in the sand, and the partygoers spent most of the afternoon assisting him in getting it out. By the time the excavation concluded, the director and writer had charmed each other thoroughly, and they began keeping steady company. In addition to their mutual immersion in filmmaking, they shared an irreverent sense of humor, a total lack of pretentiousness and, at the time, a mutual physical attraction. As Bess recalled, Curtiz's wardrobe wasn't exactly Southern California chic: "Ah, you couldn't forget him, darling. He had a long coat down to his ankles and a black hat, and for two years we tried to ditch that coat every time we went out! He always insisted on having the thing, and finally at the end of two years he got wise to the fact that it wasn't the thing to wear."

Curtiz's most enduring relationship would be with a woman who became much more than a lover. Meredyth would become his most trusted collaborator—someone he could bounce ideas off and work closely with on story and script development. She would also acclimate her new beau

Curtiz posing with a longtime nemesis: an automobile. His Hungarian handwriting on the photo reads: "I think I've sent you one about this—on the automobile at the studio's yard" (courtesy of the Lucas family).

to the insular Hollywood social scene. Her circle of friends included the influential Hearst columnist Louella Parsons, screenwriter Frances Marion, writer Gene Fowler, Darryl and Virginia Zanuck and, since she was a founding member of the Academy of Motion Picture Arts and Sciences, just about everyone else who mattered in Hollywood. Meredyth's legion of colleagues quickly embraced the man who would become her husband.

Meredyth might not have been cinema royalty, but by the time she met Curtiz, she had servants, held lavish dinner parties, and owned a tan Lincoln driven by a chauffeur. She had achieved her success through equal amounts of talent and toil. Born Helen Elizabeth MacGlashan in 1890, she displayed a knack for writing in a fiction column in the local newspaper in her hometown of Buffalo, New York. After her impulsive teenage marriage to a football player was quickly annulled, she toured in vaudeville and stock productions before entering the budding motion picture business in 1911, working for D. W. Griffith at Biograph Studios.

Moving to Universal, Meredyth became the scenarist and star in the

Bess the Detective movies, which she produced and costarred in with her husband (since 1917) Wilfred Lucas. Incredibly prolific, she composed more than one hundred movie scenarios for both shorts and features in less than ten years and became an expert in the nuances of filmmaking. Bess was in the vanguard of the golden age of female screenwriters; women wrote half of all the films produced under copyright between 1911 and 1925. When it first emerged, the movie industry welcomed the participation of women just as enthusiastically as it would later exclude them.

After changing her name to Bess Meredyth (to better fit on a marquee) and giving birth in 1919 to her son, the future director John Meredyth Lucas, she and her husband traveled to Australia to make three films, including *The Man from Kangaroo* (1920). By the time they returned to Hollywood, the film capital had outgrown its freelance roots—Wall Street investment money was creating a more corporate studio structure—and Wilfred Lucas had become a forgotten actor who had difficulty finding work. His wife's career as a writer proceeded to soar; her projects included *The Red Lily* (1924) and a high-profile rewrite of *Ben-Hur* (1925) shot on location in Rome. Their marriage foundered, and their 1925 divorce came after several years of living apart.

After Curtiz finished *The Third Degree* and moved on to other features, Meredyth remained on the Warner Bros. lot, writing *The Sea Beast* and fending off the advances of John Barrymore before the Great Profile found solace in the arms of his costar and future wife, Dolores Costello. After her marriage ended, Meredyth moved out of her Crescent Heights Boulevard house and engaged a suite of rooms at the Hotel Roosevelt, where Curtiz became a constant visitor. As their relationship became closer, so did their partnership.

Curtiz struggled to master English. Meredyth reviewed scripts with him, explained the meanings of words and phrases, and shared her considerable expertise as a scenarist and story editor. The director gradually acquired a rudimentary degree of competency in reading and writing in the language of his adopted country. Meredyth's attempts to improve his conversational skills met with significantly less success. Hungarian is a Uralic language rooted in postpositional and compound words. Native Hungarians can find it particularly challenging to pick up prepositional phrases and inflections that are common in English. As a citizen of the Habsburg Empire, Curtiz had been compelled in elementary school to learn German by rote memorization. He applied himself zealously to the task of learning English in the same manner. Located in a stack of Curtiz ephemera retained by his grandson Michael Lucas were several composition notebooks with many pages of vowels, consonants, and diagrammed sentences annotated in pencil by Curtiz.

Curtiz frequently used erratic phrasings and applied words out of sequence. And his Hungarian accent was thicker than the densest goulash. Usually everyone understood what he meant even if it sounded funny, but he could become incoherent, particularly when excited or lost in thought. Those who assumed he was a buffoon because of how he spoke ended up chagrined by their presumption. His difficulty in discerning the nuances of screenplays written in English would cause him the most problems during his career in Hollywood.

The director eventually turned his linguistic deficit to his advantage. The PR benefits of "Curtiz spoken here"—a sign that his property master Herbert "Limey" Plews posted outside his sets—cloaked the legitimacy of his intermittent struggle with the language of his adopted country. He also pretended not to understand English whenever the situation suited him. Curtiz's Hungarian colleague Steven Sekely arrived in Hollywood in 1939. He remarked on Curtiz's linguistic reputation within the Hungarian émigré community: "I was speaking English better than Mihály Kertész, who lived there for years and never spoke it well. There has been much said and written about Kertész's English, that he knew English better than he cared to show it—because this way (owing to his poor English), they always wrote and talked about him."

For his growing circle of friends and colleagues, his manner of speech was part of his charm. Certainly it was for Meredyth, who adored Curtiz exactly the way he was. The smitten couple was seeing so much of one another that they were taking turns spending the night at Curtiz's Hollywood apartment and Meredyth's suite at the Roosevelt. John Meredyth Lucas remembers his mother's account of Curtiz's marriage proposal:

Mother said, "It would probably be simpler if we were married."

"Bessky," he said, nodding sadly, "I like very much we should be marry but—" He looked away. . . . His voice was very low. "I am Jew," he told her.

"I know," Mother said. "I have no idea what I am."

Mike looked incredulous, "Is not matter?"

Michael Curtiz and Bess Meredyth were married in a civil ceremony on December 7, 1929.[1] The seven witnesses included Louella Parsons. In

Bess and Curtiz at Laguna Beach, circa late 1920s (courtesy of the Lucas family).

addition to being the father of four children, the director was now a stepfather to nine-year-old John, known as Jack.[2]

John Meredyth Lucas remarked on the early years with his stepfather, "Mike made an effort to establish a family relationship." When the director was in preproduction and maintaining somewhat normal working hours, there were dinners at Musso & Frank on Hollywood Boulevard, followed by movies at the Egyptian Theatre. Curtiz also favored the Friday night prizefights at the American Legion Stadium and was a habitué of the Filmart Theatre on Vine Street, where he could keep up with the world of European cinema. It was the beginning of an enriching relationship that lasted for the balance of Curtiz's life. Hardly a traditional father figure, but more than a friend, Curtiz and "Jick," as he called his stepson, would spend decades living and working together.

Curtiz and Meredyth eventually settled at 1017 Roxbury Drive in Beverly Hills. Their house was a luxurious setting during a halcyon era in Hollywood. There was no smog or traffic and little crime. People left their doors unlocked and awoke to the singing of birds rather than the hum of freeways. Highly compensated movie people, particularly the stars, existed in a protective bubble in which any transgressions were swept under the carpet by a watchful studio publicity apparatus and an accommodating press corps. At the time, a meal in an upscale restaurant cost no more than a dollar, and the salary of a comfortable middle-class American was around $6,000 per year. By comparison, the Hollywood upper crust made astronomical sums. Greta Garbo earned $5,000 per week in 1928, during an era of negligible income taxes. Curtiz, whose own salary would be bumped to $1,200 per week by 1929, was on his way to becoming well off. But he and Meredyth were spending the money as fast as it came in. It didn't matter. Life was good, and it seemed there would always be another film to make. And, for a very long time, there was.

Hollywood was a small town where status was typically stratified by power. Curtiz and Meredyth brought together an eclectic mix of people, not necessarily reflective of the industry social hierarchy. They entertained frequently, young Jack being safely ensconced at his uncle's. Evening gatherings usually included a film screening, dinner, and copious drinking, although never by Curtiz. The director ate and drank sparingly, although he and Meredyth did hire a Hungarian cook to feed the legions of European friends and artists who flocked to their house. Meredyth became a kind of den mother for Curtiz's colleagues arriving from Europe. *Theater Life* noted: "Miss Bess Meredyth is not only a superb scenarist but in her spare time a guardian angel of the Hungarians in Hollywood." Nearly every newly arrived Hungarian artist or show business person had a party thrown in his or her honor by Curtiz and Meredyth.

The director never lost his preference for his native cuisine. He regularly ordered cases of Tokay, a white wine made with Furmint grapes grown in the Tokaji region of his homeland, from a well-known Hungarian gourmet store in New York. Most of the transplanted Hungarians in Hollywood—Bela Lugosi, Irén Biller, Ernest Vajda, and Paul Lukas, among others—did likewise. None could be without their "Toke," as they dubbed the sweet wine of their homeland.

The Roxbury Drive residence was the only place in town where a Saturday night party might feature W. C. Fields juggling plates, Louella Parsons trolling for gossip tidbits to use on her new weekly radio program, Darryl Zanuck gesticulating with his ever-present cigar, and new arrivals such as Ernest Vajda, Paul Lukas, Lajos Bíró, and Alexander Korda enjoying an exquisitely prepared Hungarian dinner.

At the time, much of the buzz at Hollywood parties concerned the new talking pictures. Sound in films had a number of different creative pioneers, including Lee de Forest and William Fox, whose Movietone newsreels rivaled the Vitaphone shorts that Warner Bros. had been producing

Curtiz and Alexander Korda at Laguna Beach, circa late 1920s (courtesy of the Lucas family).

in increasing numbers since 1926. The October 6, 1927, debut of *The Jazz Singer* at the Warner New York theater in Times Square, with its synchronized dialogue and Al Jolson song sequences, was a sensation. The picture ended up grossing more than $2.6 million against a cost of $422,000, putting Warner Bros. back in the black and liberating Harry Warner to renew his expansionist business policies.

The *Jazz Singer* debut played out against a family tragedy. Sam Warner, the person most responsible for popularizing sound to film, died the day before the premiere owing to complications from a sinus infection that spread to his brain; it was just a year before the discovery of penicillin. The emotional bond that unified the brothers began to fray. Harry and Jack's increasingly contentious relationship became one of Hollywood's longest-running family dramas.

Warner Bros. announced a slate of twelve Vitaphone features for 1928, in addition to a full complement of silent films. Curtiz would direct *Tenderloin,* a crime drama starring Dolores Costello and Conrad Nagel, who was borrowed from MGM. *Tenderloin* was misleadingly advertised as "the first feature-length voice film released," ignoring the dialogue sequences in *The Jazz Singer* and the first all-talking feature, *Lights of New York,* released in July 1928. *Tenderloin* included four Vitaphone talking sequences (approximately fifteen minutes each) primarily featuring Costello. Both *Variety* and the *New York Times* reported opening-night audiences laughing out loud at them. *Variety*'s review elliptically described the situation as "being virtually the first try at character-talking from the screen and owing to the hard-boiled first-night audience seeing it too cold-bloodedly . . ." Indeed, the scenes had been inserted in a somewhat ad hoc manner and were delivered by actors inexperienced in the new, rudimentary medium.

Insult was added to injury by a princely two-dollar ticket charge levied to defray the costs of outfitting theaters for sound. Opening-night audiences felt rooked by what appeared to be a blatant gimmick. Despite Curtiz's visual flourishes along with some daring dance-hall sequences, *Tenderloin* was categorized as an experiment and mostly forgotten after sound gained a firmer footing. Jack Warner could not have cared less about negative reviews. Michael Curtiz's first sound picture, made at a cost of $188,000, grossed $886,000 domestically.

Curtiz publicly embraced the new Vitaphone sound-on-disk process as a second cinematic renaissance, but in reality he, like many other filmmakers, initially loathed it. The most frustrating aspect was ceding the personal authority of his set to what he perceived as lesser entities beyond his control. Sound mixers—"sound bums," as Curtiz derisively called them—often spoke in incomprehensible techno-babble accompanied by the arrogance that came with their sudden power. Also, the need to cluster actors around microphones concealed in props drove him crazy. The cameras had to be contained in small, soundproof booths to squelch the noise of running gears, which nearly asphyxiated the cameraman.

Early talkies reflect a rudimentary method of editing to account for the narrative maintained by dialogue. The lighting also had to be changed from noisy arc lights to quiet, but horrifically hotter, incandescent lights, which roasted actors and crews. In a matter of months, soundstages came into existence as studios began to commit huge resources to the new technology. It was an enormous change that caused short-term chaos in the industry, as no one really knew how the sound revolution was going to turn out. Actors began taking elocution lessons, and even quitting pictures if they flunked a sound test. Performers from the Broadway stage who were surmised to have vocal talent were rushed to Hollywood. Directors could no longer verbally coach their actors throughout the filming of a scene. The musicians who had played mood music on the set or were employed by movie theaters to accompany films lost their jobs. The international language of silent film that Curtiz and other pioneers had mastered as an art form was coming to an abrupt end.

Much of Curtiz's frustration over sound would emerge later in the year. He was finally able to begin the biblical spectacle that he had journeyed from Europe to make. After the death of Sam Warner, Darryl Zanuck was appointed head of film production under Jack Warner. Now that the studio was flush again, Zanuck and Curtiz got the green light to begin production on *Noah's Ark*. Both their futures as well as that of Warner Bros. would be invested in a colossal motion picture that would be Hollywood's last great silent epic. Neither producer nor director realized the full gravity of the risks he was taking.

12

Hollywood's Great Deluge

During the sweltering summer of 1927, Michael Curtiz wrote to Jack Warner imploring him to authorize the start of production on the special effects in *Noah's Ark* before work began with the actors. Curtiz was trying to appear helpful to the production chief by pointing out that the studio would save money by avoiding having the principal actors drawing salaries while he was occupied with planning the special effects.

In fact, Curtiz was beyond impatient about the delays on *Noah's Ark* and was prodding Warner to get things moving. He knew that once the money spigot was opened, it would be difficult to shut it off. Warner apparently ignored Curtiz; no director needed to tell him when to take actors on or off salary, particularly before the first take had been printed. Moreover, it would be the Effects Department, not the film's director, who would be handling the trick shots. The unanswered memo was another reminder to Curtiz of who was really in charge. Although the anxious director had another eight months before shooting the first scene on his cherished project, much had already been accomplished. The story and script preparation that began when he arrived at the studio were completed. But *Noah's Ark* would end up being a different film from the one Curtiz had originally envisioned.

The principal creative challenge was to design a modern-day parallel story to the flood that would unify the movie and resonate with audiences. Curtiz's treatment deployed the familiar melodramatic love triangle he'd employed in several of his European movies, followed by a spectacular version of the biblical flood. His female protagonist is fated to become a vestal sacrifice before she is rescued and taken to the ark as the rest of the world is swept away.

Warner and Zanuck deemed Curtiz's version unsuitable. The modern story's linkage to the biblical sequence was too vague. Curtiz's undated treatment is annotated with "A Michael Curtiz Production" across the top of the title page of the original outline, which Curtiz began in France, discussed with Harry Warner, and worked on during his initial journey to Hollywood. The front cover is annotated "Mr. J. L. Warner"; comments in pencil appear to be in Warner's handwriting:

Send to Darryl. Biblical part ok.
1/3 modern, 2/3 Biblical Cost $750,000 or more.
Build on Vita lot. Lease ground somewhere for this picture (DeMille)

Jack Warner's ruminations turned out to be partially correct. The *Noah's Ark* sets were built on the Vitagraph lot without having to lease another studio's facilities, but the story ended up being more evenly divided between modern and biblical. The cost of the picture would rise to $1 million, an enormous investment that Warner Bros. would not exceed until eight years later with *The Charge of the Light Brigade*.

Enter Bess Meredyth, whose story used World War I as a modern plot parallel to the biblical saga. As would be true of so many of Curtiz's future films, the specific collaborative details between Meredyth and her soon-to-be husband on the *Noah's Ark* treatment remains unknown. But in light of their already close relationship, it can be presumed that they jointly worked on it.

Warner Bros. house scribe Anthony Coldeway finessed the Meredyth-Curtiz scenario into a *Noah's Ark* continuity during March 1927. There is also an unsigned first-draft story dated June 22, 1926, that was apparently written by Darryl Zanuck. The producer personally oversaw the details of the final script and decided that the film would open with a post-deluge matte shot of the ark on dry ground as Noah and his family offer prayers for their salvation. A montage of biblical settings and scenes of modern Wall Street avarice follows before the present-day story begins. Travers (George O'Brien), Al (Guinn "Big Boy" Williams), Nickoloff, a disreputable Russian secret service agent (Noah Beery), and Marie, a German showgirl (Dolores Costello) survive a crash of the Orient Express and take shelter at a nearby inn. Nickoloff attempts to rape Marie and is knocked silly for his trouble by Travers. When soldiers arrive and inform all that war has been declared, Nickoloff asserts that Marie is a spy. She flees to Paris and marries Travis. The couple becomes separated when Travis joins Al in the U.S. Army. He accidentally kills his pal while fighting at the front. Nickoloff—now an Allied officer—discovers Marie performing with a Paris dance troupe. When she refuses his advances, he has her sentenced to death by firing squad as a German spy. Travis returns to save her as an exploding shell buries the group underneath the remains of a church. As they await their doom by suffocation, the bearded minister from the Orient Express (Paul McAllister) orates the parallel story of Noah's Ark.

Miriam (Dolores Costello) is the betrothed of Japheth. She is kidnapped by the minions of King Nephilim (Noah Beery) as a virgin sacrifice to the pagan god Jaghuth. Noah's son Japheth (O'Brien) attempts to rescue Miriam, but he is blinded by a hot iron and shackled with other slaves to a huge millstone. God summons Noah (McAllister) and communicates his intentions to destroy humanity with a colossal flood. Noah is directed to build an ark to save his family and all the animals in creation. Howling wind and rain destroy the temple as the Great Flood rises to engulf humanity. A Jehovian lightning bolt frees Japheth, who locates Miriam in the aqueous pandemonium, and they make their way to the ark. As Japheth carries Miriam into the ark, a ray of heavenly light restores his sight as King Nephilim and his subjects drown in the surging floodwaters. The action returns to the present as rescue workers save the trapped contingent—less the deceased Nickoloff. Travis and Miriam embrace and walk off with Allied soldiers as the Armistice is declared and a new era dawns for a hopeful world that has been cleansed of war.

The story was officially credited to Zanuck, whose name was emblazoned above that of the director on the opening titles. The young producer boasted to the *Los Angeles Times*: "We had just a name to begin with. Just a name, *Noah's Ark*." He noted Curtiz's involvement with a brief aside: "Yes, of course there was a director. Michael Curtiz directed all the dramatic work." Curtiz understood the twenty-six-year-old's craving for prestige—Zanuck was making a quantum career leap over his standard identification as the writer of Rin Tin Tin movies. Credit grabbing by the principals of a major film was a standard Hollywood operating procedure that dated back to Cecil B. DeMille's barn.

Curtiz concentrated on directing the actors and staging spectacular sequences featuring large masses of people in the midst of apocalyptic destruction. The results would be unforgettable, especially for the participants.

Most of the principal actors in *Noah's Ark* were freelance performers or borrowed from other studios. George O'Brien was touring Europe with the director F. W. Murnau when he was hastily summoned home by

A Warner Bros. contingent greets Darryl and Virginia Zanuck at the Pasadena railroad station on February 19, 1928. Bess is on Zanuck's right. Curtiz is next to Wallis in the middle row (courtesy of the Lucas family).

Fox to be lent out at $1,500 per week. Noah Beery, whose métier as Hollywood's most odious villain reached its peak when he was signed for an exorbitant $3,000 per week, was matched by the slapstick comedienne Louise Fazenda—recently wed to Hal Wallis—who received fourth billing for her brief appearance as an innkeeper. The former Broadway actor Paul McAllister and future Warner Bros. contract player Guinn "Big Boy" Williams rounded out the primary cast. Williams, a brawny, hard-drinking Texan, would spend a long career on horseback in studio back lots and Hollywood polo fields while appearing in four Curtiz-helmed Westerns.

Production got under way in March 1928. Although Curtiz would shoot some exterior scenes at Big Basin Redwoods State Park at Santa Cruz and the Iverson Ranch in Chatsworth, the major scenes of *Noah's Ark* were filmed at the old Vitagraph Studio, a former Los Feliz sheep ranch. The studio gates at the corner of Prospect and Talmadge streets became jammed with hordes of people when it came time to film the huge

Curtiz sits on the steps of the Temple of Jaghuth set built for *Noah's Ark* (1928). His handwriting reads: "During construction—[working] on the changes of [construction] plans" (courtesy of the Lucas family).

processional scene into the Great Festival of Jaghuth. By one account, it was a tableau straight out of Nathanael West's *The Day of the Locust*: "The police officer raises his hand and hundreds of cars stop, waiting for the sign that permits them to progress again. The cars are heading to

Talmadge Street. The roads are clogged around the six gates of Warners with heavy-duty trucks, Buicks, Chryslers waiting to get in. Cavalries of extras, technicians, carpenters, Negros, Japanese, Chinese are marching in. Inside the gates, tall buildings are towering towards the skies. Syrian temples, Babylonian streets are next to reconstructed forests—and on top of a hill, there it is: the Ark."

More than five thousand extras were costumed and made up in a vast array of tents reminiscent of an army camp. Many were sprayed with dark body makeup to appear more Middle Eastern. Reflectors and special lighting equipment were everywhere. Wranglers brought in elephants, oxen, lions, and numerous other animals for the ark embarkation sequences. Anton Grot's production design rivaled Curtiz's Viennese spectacles: a tremendous palace set stretching 385 feet long and 85 feet high. The sculptor and makeup artist Charles Gemora designed and constructed the ornate idols. Fred Jackman's special effects department outdid itself with detailed glass paintings for matte effects, the construction of realistic miniatures for the wreck of the Orient Express, and the long shots of the Great Deluge. For the orgiastic festival highlighted by the sacrifice of Miriam, Curtiz designed a blueprint that detailed the position of every player down to the last extra—and used a siren to start eleven cameras rolling simultaneously. He boasted extravagantly to a visiting reporter from Budapest: "*Noah's Ark* is a long-held dream of mine. I carried it with myself from Europe because only the American technology and American money can make it come true. The American newspapers doubted that one could make a film about Noah, this hazy biblical figure that would be entertaining and exciting. Well, I solved this impossible problem. I divided the movie into two parts, the first one takes place in biblical times, the second takes place in the present. I set it during the First World War."

Curtiz concluded the interview with a dubious disclaimer about how well he was getting along with the entire company. His true colors surfaced immediately afterward, when he grabbed the loudspeaker and yelled at a group of extras milling about, "Go on!" The director's brusque manner alienated more than a few members of the cast and crew who thought his obsession with realism bordered on lunacy.

The phlegmatic George O'Brien wasn't one of the naysayers. Strikingly handsome and riding high after his performance in Fox's *Sunrise,* he respected Curtiz's passion for cinematic verisimilitude as embodied by his superhuman work ethic: "I talk of my own little inconveniences, but they were nothing compared to his. For three months, day and night, Mike drove forward ceaselessly."

Decades later, O'Brien recalled Curtiz's direction before the sequence in which Japheth's eyes were put out: "When I was to be blinded with a hot poker, he said, 'George, I want you to come very close, my boy. I want the audience to scream.' And I'll tell you. I could feel the heat of that thing [an actual red-hot iron]. I screamed bloody murder and I went through the rest of the picture [acting] blind. That was an experience!"

O'Brien's dedication would be further tested when the Danish actor Anders Randolf, playing the leader of King Nephilim's soldiers, hurled a collapsible spear at him that failed to collapse:

> The spear was supposed to disappear. . . . It didn't disappear except into me. I was supposed to fall. . . . I fell back and the blood started to roll out and I saw Curtiz watching me. They wouldn't stop the camera in those days. Dolores Costello broke away and fell over me. She screamed, "He's stabbed! He's stabbed!" Finally they said, "Cut!" and Curtiz said, "Don't touch him! Are you all right, George?" "Yes, I'm all right." "I want to get the close-up!" So they ground away a few feet away from me really bleeding, and then I was picked up and the doctor came and he washed it out and so forth. I had a pretty good tan, but under the lights, the wound showed, and they to keep touching it up with body makeup.

Curtiz couldn't resist the opportunity to film the actual impalement of one of his actors, and likewise, the Warner Bros. publicity department seized the occasion to tout the realism of their biblical epic. A photograph of a smiling O'Brien in costume, displaying his bandaged wound while posing next to a studio nurse, graced the *Noah's Ark* press guide.

For some on the set, it must have seemed like divine retribution when Curtiz experienced a mishap of his own. Twelve-year-old Jack Warner Jr., who skipped school to watch the exciting climactic scenes, witnessed it. A stuntman had just performed a fall down the temple steps, and it was not to the director's liking:

> Curtiz fixed the poor recumbent wretch with a middle European stare and went on, "This, Mister Stunt-faller, is how I vant." He then raced all the way up the stairs to the temple gates, collapsed

dramatically and pirouetted down the steep flight, arms and legs flailing, the perfect picture of a heroic death. Curtiz lay at the foot of the stairs, breathing heavily, then shrieked loudly in Hungarian. . . . Fortunately, only his left leg had been broken. He was rushed off to the hospital while the company called lunch. They waited an hour until he returned in a wheelchair and in a leg cast to resume his place beside the camera. He cleared his throat and yelled at the stuntman, "Now you dummy—get your ass up those stairs and fall down the vay I showed you."

The Warner Bros. publicity department sent out a release stating Curtiz broke his leg after falling off an elevated camera platform. This episode paled in comparison with his staging of the Great Deluge. For years, people in the film industry who never saw *Noah's Ark* or knew little about Michael Curtiz remembered the anecdote of the crazed movie director who drowned several extras while making a biblical epic.

The cinematographer Hal Mohr believed that the majority of the flooding sequences could be achieved through the use of process effects intercut with close-ups involving a select group of stunt people and breakaway temple sets constructed of balsa wood: "I knew . . . that Jackman could take a miniature of a tremendous amount of water, and tremendous columns collapsing, and blue-backing them over this action, make it look as if it was a one-piece film."

But other than long shots of temple miniatures being flooded, Curtiz had no intention of using special effects for the majority of his shots of the Great Flood. A crew of 139 technicians constructed a system of three tanks holding four million gallons of water (or one million gallons under pressure, or possibly 800,000 gallons from a main reservoir, according to differing accounts from Jack Warner and Darryl Zanuck) that would pour down myriad spillways (140, according to Zanuck) and topple the columns. The large number of extras directed to take their places had no idea what was going to occur. Outraged when he discovered the plan, Hal Mohr confronted Curtiz and Zanuck: "I said, 'Jesus, what are you going to do about the extra people?' He [Curtiz] said, 'Oh, they're going to have to take their chances.' I said, 'Not as far as I am concerned. I'll never have anything to do with a thing like that.' . . . They insisted they were going to do it the way they wanted to do it, so I told them to shove the picture and walked off the set."

Barney McGill took over for Mohr. Fourteen cameras ground away simultaneously as nearly every incandescent light in Hollywood illuminated the set. At a signal from Curtiz, the water from the tanks sped down the spillways.

The scenes of the Great Deluge that were printed are spectacular; the footage remains awe-inspiring. The damage inflicted was considerable. Dolores Costello recalled the ordeal as "brutal." Interviewed by David Gill for Kevin Brownlow's epic *Hollywood* documentary series, she called the movie "mud, blood, and flood," and, after a pause, added, "There was much blood." With a decided edge to her voice, she went on: "Mr. Curtiz had been told which were the breakaway and which were the permanent parts of the set. And they had longhorn steer in there and human beings and some dummies. But he put the human beings where the real set was and the dummies where the breakaway was because he wanted 'realism,' as he called it."

Curtiz and Zanuck didn't realize or gave no consideration to the force of the water. Walls of water came crashing down from multiple directions. The impact toppled and broke apart the sets, sweeping away everything in the water's path. Propelled by the water, wood and other debris became deadly missiles. Extras were knocked down by wreckage while others swam for their lives with the panicked cattle. Dolores Costello fainted from the force of the water hitting her in the stomach and reportedly caught pneumonia. George O'Brien, who was rendered sightless by spirit gum makeup and was tied up when the water was released, had boards tear off both of his big toenails.

And what of Curtiz? According to a cameraman, Byron Haskin, he was "screaming at the extras from the sidelines and hurling two-by-fours at them" when they attempted to stand up instead of being swept away. Although Haskin, who variously described Curtiz as "a freak," "a loser," "a masochist," and "a weirdo," might not have been the most objective observer, it was clearly a debacle. Costello remembered that many people were injured: "I found a man leaning against my dressing room door. He was heavily bandaged, and I said, 'What's wrong?' He said, 'Thirty-eight ambulances have left. I am in better condition than most of them and they're coming back for me. I think somebody's been killed."

Was anyone actually killed? Hal Mohr claimed that one man lost a leg and "a couple of people were injured to the point that they never did recover." Numerous contemporary accounts mention the deaths of three people but don't provide any supporting documentation. The film historian Anthony Slide wrote, "It is generally believed that there was at least one fatality." The Warner Bros. legal files and *Noah's Ark* materials contain no details about any deaths. The files are also missing the daily production reports and any evidence concerning injuries, lawsuits, or the hospitalization of extras. There was nary a mention in a local newspaper of any difficulties or injuries occurring during the making of *Noah's Ark*. It was as if the incident never happened. One brief article lauded Curtiz, the vigorous new Warner Bros. director, for his inspirational leadership in directing the sequence: "A miracle of concentrated energy is Michael Curtiz, who in making the flood scenes of *Noah's Ark* shamed timorous extras by himself plunging into the swirling deluge. It was wintry weather and as a result, he was taken severely ill. But the experience seems not to have daunted his enthusiasm."

Inspiring the fainthearted to attempt feats of cinematic bravado was a touchstone of Curtiz's directorial style, but this account strains credulity. Though it is possible that the eyewitness accounts might have been unintentionally embellished over the years, there is little doubt that a number of people were severely injured in what was clearly a case of gross negligence. The responsibility also rested on the shoulders of Zanuck, who backed Curtiz to the hilt. There are no recorded expressions of regret from Curtiz, Zanuck, or Jack Warner about the toll of the *Noah's Ark* flooding sequence. In an Orwellian touch, the *Noah's Ark* press guide gaily stated that there was "little need for the services of the hospital staff" at the studio during the filming.

Viewed retrospectively, the lack of documentation about the consequences of the flood sequence isn't surprising. The files for Warner films produced during 1920s, now housed at the Warner Bros. Archive at the University of Southern California, are mostly lacking the detailed production reports and related correspondence that are routinely part of the records of films beginning in the mid-1930s. Either the material was lost or discarded, or the studio removed it before the donation of the records to USC. It is also not certain if Warner Bros. documented the daily routine of filmmaking with the administrative zeal that was applied during the following decades.

It is also probable that the news blackout was stage-managed by the studio. Still fresh in the public's mind was the St. Francis Dam tragedy that killed hundreds of people north of Los Angeles in March 1928. Hollywood studios at that time didn't hesitate to protect their interests by any means necessary. The writer Budd Schulberg once recalled the power wielded by the moguls: "Hollywood was like Liechtenstein or Luxembourg. The district attorney was on the studio payroll; you could and did commit murder, and it wouldn't be in the paper." The studios kept the district attorney's office greased with cash in the form of campaign contributions while studio security chiefs colluded with the local police to quash scandalous incidents involving contracted talent.

During the Roaring Twenties and into the next decade, Los Angeles was the prototypical wide-open town. The Los Angeles Police Department resembled a crime family. A criminal defense attorney of the period observed: "You know, in Chicago the gangsters paid off the police but the gangsters did the job. In Los Angeles, the police were the gangsters." In 1938 L.A. Mayor Frank Shaw achieved the distinction of being the first U.S. mayor to be successfully recalled after a police captain was convicted of planting a bomb in the house of a Shaw opponent. District Attorney Buron Fitts, who was acquitted of perjury and bribery charges in 1934 and survived an assassination attempt in 1937, was believed to have accepted a bribe to drop the investigation into the 1932 death of Paul Bern, an MGM executive who was the husband of Metro's star Jean Harlow. Jack Warner was impressed enough to hire Fitts's head investigator, a man named Blayney Matthews, as his studio security chief. A former Warner Bros. employee described the taciturn Matthews as "the silent custodian of more studio secrets than even the Brothers."

The Hollywood newspapers were similarly acquiescent to the wishes of the movie moguls. No reporter was going to bite the feeding hand by launching an investigation into why so many people were injured during the making of a movie. For the Warners, it was a simple matter to pay off anyone severely injured, or their families, while steering the episode away from the jurisdiction of law enforcement and keeping it out of the newspapers.

During an era before workplace safety laws and labor unions, movie studios were under virtually no obligation to protect employees on set or on location. Safety was usually a determination made by the individual; the studio's attitude could be summed up by the adage "Do you want the job or not?" For instance, when the stuntman Joe Bonomo was assigned by Cecil B. DeMille to play a Christian slave who is thrown into a pit filled with live alligators in *The Sign of the Cross* (1932), the director reminded him just before rolling the cameras, "If any alligator gets you, the studio won't be responsible."

Working in films with action sequences was dangerous. From 1925 to 1930, 10,794 people were reported injured in movie productions filmed in the state of California. Of these, 55, primarily stuntmen, were killed. During the production of Clarence Brown's *The Trail of '98* in 1927, three men, including the stuntman Red Thompson, drowned in the Cooper River. Stunt people knew what they were getting into and were paid to take risks. What made the *Noah's Ark* debacle so scandalous was Curtiz's and Zanuck's apparent indifference to the safety of the untrained extras whom they put in harm's way.

Extras got a day's pay and that was about it. There was little training beyond being made up and told where to stand and when to move. Curtiz specifically chose many of the extras based on their athletic heft. Local high school athletes and college football players who were selected, including John Wayne and Andy Devine, were grateful for the cash.

For "the goddamn murderous bastards," as Hal Mohr labeled Zanuck and Curtiz, the most serious consequences of *Noah's Ark* would be bad reviews. After the Hollywood premiere of *Noah's Ark,* the notices were favorable, as *Variety* singled out Curtiz's direction for particular praise. But critics outside Hollywood were not nearly as kind. The *New Yorker* thought the film was "an idiotic super-spectacle." A major British paper termed it "a film of triumph and failure" and believed the dialogue during the Vitaphone sequences was "ridiculous." The *New York Times* praised some of the imposing sequences but labeled the film "wearisome" and remarked that the Vitaphone lines exchanged by Costello and O'Brien were "inept" and "frequently border[ed] on the ridiculous."

Even though Zanuck made judicious cuts to the Vitaphone sequences and other footage to reduce the running time from 135 to 105 minutes, it was evident that Curtiz conceived *Noah's Ark* as a silent movie. The talking scenes were mawkish. "It's wonderful how a train wreck brought us together, isn't it, Marie?" Travis murmurs into Marie's ear as drunken soldiers sing in the background.

Some of the unintentionally funny dialogue was made worse by the intermittent malfunctioning of the Vitaphone system. During the premiere of *Noah's Ark* in Chicago on April 9, 1929, a glitch resulted in Al instead of Marie cooing to Travis, "He said kiss me again for France." The audience howled with laughter.

While the acting, particularly by Costello and O'Brien, was effective and the biblical scenes spectacular, the parallel modern story was laden with absurd coincidences. The opening footage—visually impressive scenes of the Tower of Babel under construction and a slave being crushed by a stone block (a blatant theft from *The Ten Commandments*)—and an orgiastic feast with a huge statue of a Golden Calf that was borrowed from Exodus rather than Genesis amounted to a biblical highlight reel. Accentuating the inherent weakness of the film were the platitudinous titles, some of which appeared to have been sourced from a poorly written comic book. Several cards that didn't default to biblical quotes relied on trite phrases ending with exclamation marks. Zanuck privately described his first big production as a mess; the writer Arthur Caesar later castigated him for "taking a book that's been a hit for nineteen hundred years and making a flop out of it." But *Noah's Ark* wasn't a failure; it simply wasn't a box-office hit on the order of *The Ten Commandments* and *The King of Kings*. With a cost of just over $1 million, it grossed more than $2.3 million, half of that amount accruing in foreign markets.[1]

The film premiered at Grauman's Chinese Theatre on November 1, 1928. Hosted by the actor Conrad Nagel, the gala affair included a chorus of singers drawing a curtain back to reveal a mock-up of the ark, complete with live animals. After the film concluded, the leading players came onstage, taking bows to thunderous applause. The Hollywood glitterati then repaired to an opulent party at Bess Meredyth's house. Meredyth and Curtiz were identified in the press as being engaged; the fact that they were unmarried and living together went unmentioned. In addition to a large Warner Bros. contingent, including Dolores Costello, George O'Brien, Jack Warner, and Darryl Zanuck, nearly every Hollywood A-list star and studio executive showed up to pay homage. Curtiz basked in his success with some of his former European colleagues. Victor and Anna Varconi, Alexander and Maria Korda, Mr. and Mrs. Paul Leni, and the recently arrived Lili Damita, "surrounded as usual by a trail of men," were all present to congratulate him for his triumphant magnum opus.

Curtiz's low-key demeanor at his victory party was a mixture of delight and relief. Although he had successfully completed the picture that he had journeyed to America to make, he also realized that the flooding debacle might have cost him his career. By protecting themselves from scandal, Harry and Jack Warner shielded Curtiz from any potential backlash and strengthened the mutual bonds of loyalty. As the champagne flowed and the actor Fritz Feld entertained on the living-room piano, the director could not be faulted for believing that he was on a rapid ascent, with more important pictures on the horizon. But this scenario would be another story requiring significant revisions.

13

General Foreman

Following the release of *Noah's Ark,* Michael Curtiz's professional fortunes were aligned with those of the country's fastest-rising movie studio. Warner Bros. assumed a majority interest in First National—one of the major Hollywood movie studios—complete with a sixty-two-acre site in Burbank that became the Warner production and corporate hub, along with a surplus of First National contracted talent and infrastructure. The acting talent absorbed by Warner Bros. included Richard Barthelmess, Douglas Fairbanks Jr., and Loretta Young. Inherited personnel working behind the camera were the director Mervyn LeRoy and cinematographers Lee Garmes, Ernest Haller, and Sol Polito.

In November 1929 Harry Warner bought out the remaining one-third of First National stock from a cash-strapped William Fox. The bold acquisition stunned the other Hollywood studio heads, particularly Adolph Zukor at Paramount, who had alternately wooed and fought with First National. One competitor admitted, "It would have made more sense if First National had bought Warner Brothers."

Appalled by what he perceived as featherbedding, Jack Warner fired one hundred First National employees during his first week of ownership, including the cowboy star Ken Maynard and the entire Western film unit. He appointed his publicity director, Hal Wallis, to acclimate the new vassals to the realities of life under the Warner Bros. shield. The tightfisted Wallis could make beads of sweat appear on the forehead of a Lincoln-head penny. He was on his way to becoming a shrewd executive capable of managing every detail to make good movies fast and cheap. First National production costs of $300,000 per picture were reduced to an average of $100,000. It was the beginning of an assembly-line process that doubled output to eighty-six feature films in 1929. For legal and tax purposes, both companies maintained their names separately for some years. The government approved the First National acquisition contingent on the periodic release of films that carried the names of both studios until 1938, but the product of both entities was one and the same: Warner Bros.

Curtiz played a key role in the newly merged studio. During a five-year period ending in fall 1934, he directed an incredible total of thirty feature films—an average of six per year. He drove himself savagely, moving from one picture to another without a break. Although his pictures were well crafted and most of them were profitable, Curtiz struggled to distinguish his work from that of others. His films were mostly conventional endeavors; thanks to the Depression, there would be no epic productions on the order of *Noah's Ark* for a long time.

Curtiz did his best on each project at hand. He insinuated himself into preproduction script development, adding and deleting scenes, changing dialogue, trying to improve the material. Despite his dictatorial reputation, Zanuck was amenable to input and often incorporated the director's suggestions. Curtiz learned just how far to nudge Zanuck without alienating him or causing him to lose his formidable temper.

Their collegial working relationship ripened into friendship, especially after the producer left Warner Bros. to cofound Twentieth Century Pictures, which would later merge with the bankrupt Fox studio into Twentieth Century-Fox. Their wives became thick as thieves. Curtiz's granddaughter Liz MacGillicuddy Lucas recalled numerous parties and events with "Uncle Darryl and Aunt Virginia" during her childhood at the director's Encino ranch. Congeniality endured because of Curtiz's flattering deference to Zanuck, who treated all his relationships as competitive exercises of power.

Once production was under way, Curtiz was left alone to do whatever he wanted so long as the budget and schedule weren't exceeded and the script wasn't blatantly rewritten. He typically visualized how to improve a certain scene on set. He would watch the initial run-through and shake his head, saying something like "Is too much hammy," and then rework it into something more authentic. He also redoubled his efforts to master the nuances of sound direction.

Curtiz's films released in 1929 are currently unavailable. Judging by contemporary reviews and available production documentation, none of them seems to have been exceptional, even though they added considerably to the Warner Bros. bottom line. *The Glad Rag Doll* and *Madonna of Avenue A* reunited Curtiz with Dolores Costello. Dubbed "The Belle of the Screen" the star remained an automatic box-office draw. *Madonna*

One of Darryl Zanuck's costume parties; Curtiz is dressed as George
Washington at the far right of the second row. How many stars can you spot?
(Courtesy of the Lucas family).

of Avenue A included Vitaphone talking sequences for slightly more than
half the seventy-one-minute running time, whereas *The Glad Rag Doll*
was released as a talking feature in its entirety. (A silent version was also
released for theaters not yet converted to sound.)

The Glad Rag Doll centers on a hit song of the same name, alternately
played and sung on the Vitaphone soundtrack. With Costello portraying
a conniving showgirl being pursued by a Philadelphia society swell, the
movie was a tremendous hit, grossing more than $1 million against a cost
of $143,000.

Years after the release of *Madonna of Avenue A*, Curtiz claimed to
have written the movie's story while in the throes of resolving contractual issues with Warner Bros. His assertion of authorship might well be
authentic. The film criticizes the American preoccupation with the ac-
cumulation of personal wealth—a premise that would recur in several of
Curtiz's later films.

The Gamblers was an adaptation of a play by Charles Klein, writer
of *The Third Degree*. The plot involves a corporate swindle by a father-
son executive team (George Fawcett and Jason Robards Sr.) that is com-

plicated by a love triangle involving H. B. Warner and Lois Wilson. Jack Warner increased the modest budget allocated to Curtiz, hoping to catch lightning in a bottle a second time. Mordaunt Hall of the *New York Times* assessed the picture as "expertly directed," remarking that the dialogue scenes, problematic in previous Curtiz films, were well-recorded and competently acted.

These successes earned Curtiz his most lavish budget since *Noah's Ark* when he was assigned *Hearts in Exile*. The drama is based on John Oxenham's novel, which was first filmed in 1915. "Far-fetched" is a polite term to describe its story of the delicately beautiful Vera, a Czarist-era Moscow fishmonger who is in love with a self-indulgent student but marries a well-to-do man who is banished to Siberia. There were also musical numbers and a different ending to the European release. The *Washington Post* stated that Curtiz "made egregious blunders" and that the director "leaves much to be desired as a director of camera drama for American consumption."

All the studios were groping for a winning formula to replace the artistry of silent movies. In searching for a contemporary identity for their movies, Warner Bros. needed new stars. The studio had the world's top male performer under contract, but the great Al Jolson was beginning to lose a bit of his cinematic luster.

A phenomenon onstage and in his first couple of films, Jolson was the highest-paid entertainer of his era—the first Jewish superstar. He was also an insecure egomaniac whose handling required a large amount of patience. "Jolie" loved to be loved and was on constantly. He was the only star in the history of the studio who could barge into Jack Warner's office unannounced to share corny jokes. But even a showbiz deity couldn't guarantee indefinite success. Jolson's third film, *Say It with Songs* (1929) did less than half the business of 1928's *The Singing Fool*.

It was hoped that matters would improve when Curtiz directed him in *Mammy*, released in March 1930. Curtiz added considerable visual attributes to his adaptation of the original Irving Berlin play *Mr. Bones*. Jolson plays an iterant minstrel singer who is caught in a love triangle and framed for an attempted murder. The director added several parade scenes, including a handsome opening with Jolson and the minstrel company marching into town and singing in a rainstorm, along with two-strip Technicolor sequences of the production numbers. Curtiz and Jolson got along fine. The director observed, "Because he's so big a personality, he's not difficult to direct. He is tireless, he is enthusiastic."

Mammy amounts to a series of melodramatic episodes strung around Jolson's renditions of Berlin's songs, in many of which the star and the company perform in blackface. Although the picture was one of the more entertaining of Jolson's movies, *Mammy* grossed less than $200,000 over its considerable cost. Jolson starred in six films for Warner Bros., but he never succeeded in making the transition from dynamic stage performer to movie actor.

Curtiz directed five films in 1930 that allowed him to become more facile at handling dialogue sequences and the evolving process of Technicolor. *Under a Texas Moon* is the earliest surviving Warner Bros. film shot entirely in Technicolor. The technique had evolved from hand-painting color directly onto the film during the era of the Lumière brothers to Herbert Kalmus's patented Technicolor dual-color method called "two strip."

Despite the penurious nature of Warner Bros., the studio wasn't going to be left behind on a major technical innovation. After watching *The Viking* and *The Desert Song* in 1928, Jack Warner signed contracts with Technicolor for upward of twenty films. By 1931 color had been significantly improved by a dyeing process that increased visual clarity. The cost and inordinate amount of lighting required was regarded as a trade-off for the spectacular result of color on the screen.

The rub was that Technicolor's camera team and engineers had to work alongside the studio's cameramen during filming to properly execute and safeguard their process. Natalie Kalmus, the founder's wife, was the "color supervisor" for every Technicolor film production in Hollywood. She became a terrible nuisance as an ad hoc art director, insisting, for instance, on the use of neutral colors in background compositions and interposing herself into the creative process rather than acting as a technical adviser.

Thus, just as he had started becoming accustomed to working with sound, here was another new technology that irritated Curtiz. The director was already cranky, as he was having difficulties with Frank Fay, the star of *Under a Texas Moon*, who had recently been signed by Jack Warner. Fay was part of the entourage of theatrical talent summoned to Hollywood after the advent of talkies. He originated a vaudeville act that made him a top headliner. A master of ceremonies who commanded the stage with pithy jokes, insults, and ad-libbed remarks, Fay invented the style that became widely imitated by Jack Benny, Milton Berle, and other funnymen. In show business terms, Frank Fay was bigger than big; he was huge. He was also married to twenty-three-year-old Barbara Stanwyck, whose film career was beginning its own spectacular ascent.

Curtiz would direct Fay's four features at Warners. The working relationship instantly became problematic when the director ordered Fay's red hair to be dyed black so that the Irish American performer would resemble a Mexican in *Under a Texas Moon*. Fay didn't care for anyone telling him what to do, particularly a Hungarian Jew in jodhpurs who spoke in broken English. Fay, a notorious anti-Semite, made little effort to hide his feelings.

His unbridled arrogance was fed by an ego so gigantic that it made Al Jolson seem a paragon of humility. When asked during a court proceeding to list his occupation, Fay responded that he was the world's greatest comedian. Curtiz could barely tolerate him and gritted his teeth through their films together. Offscreen, Fay's life gradually evolved into a melodrama. His erratic disposition was worsened by an increasingly serious drinking problem. According to Myrna Loy, who played an ingénue in *Under a Texas Moon*, Curtiz and Fay weren't on speaking terms during production.

Aptly advertised by Warner Bros. as "The Biggest Surprise of the Year," the startling premise of Frank Fay as a singing Mexican cowboy thwarting cattle rustlers and eventually riding off into the sunset with Myrna Loy after she attempted to poison him was complemented by Curtiz's location photography. Technology had advanced sufficiently to permit the director to film Technicolor sound sequences in Red Rock Canyon National Park, in the high desert near Victorville. There was a daring scene of a woman with partially exposed breasts frolicking under the Tahquitz Canyon waterfall in Palm Springs that drew the ire of the Massachusetts Board of Censors. The director also staged a specialty dance number and a funny sequence with Fay unknowingly serenading the occupants of a brothel and being humiliated when an overweight actor laughs at him, exclaiming, "It is not necessary to serenade *these* señoritas!"

Despite its seeming absurdity, the picture was highly successful, and the studio raked in even more cash after buying the music firm that published the title song sung by Fay. Nothing encourages professional reconciliation more than success. Fay and Curtiz reached an accommodation that allowed them to work together: each man respected the other's expertise while suppressing his personal dislike of the other.

Curtiz's *The Matrimonial Bed* and *Bright Lights* (both 1930) incorporated some of Fay's stage performance acumen that would bore movie audiences. The former is a French-based bedroom farce in which Fay played an amnesiac who marries Sylvaine (Lilyan Tashman) after a train crash and then encounters his previous wife (Florence Eldridge), who has since married Gustave (James Gleason). The picture is amusing in spots, but it has the static appearance of a stage play.

Bright Lights is a musical filmed in two-color Technicolor. It would end up being pulled by Zanuck and released in a black-and-white version. The film opens on the eve of the final performance of a great musical star, played by the underrated former Ziegfeld star Dorothy Mackaill, who is marrying a society dandy (James Murray). As the accolades pour in, a flashback reveals her seedy beginnings in a crowded South African dive. Musical numbers titled "Cannibal Love" and "Song of the Congo" are sandwiched around Fay and the always-repugnant Noah Beery vying for her affections.

Aside from Fay's flaccid presence, the musical scenes in *Bright Lights* have some genuine pizzazz, although nobody would confuse Curtiz with Busby Berkeley. A genuine movie star was necessary to carry the material in these pictures. Fay transfixed live audiences, but his flair simply didn't come across on camera. It was also evident that Curtiz was having limited success in convincing him to accept direction.

Curtiz and Fay tried once more in early 1931 with *God's Gift to Women*, starring Fay as a Parisian bon vivant Casanova-type trying to reform and win the hand of Diane (Laura La Plante). A tarted-up Joan Blondell and an underused Louise Brooks provide additional visual distraction in a film laden with sexual innuendo. It is the most enjoyable of the four Curtiz-Fay pictures, which is damning with faint praise. It includes some nightclub sequences that demonstrate the fluid camera movement Curtiz would become known for. The film was shot in nineteen days and included several musical numbers that were cut before release. Zanuck believed musicals had become unpopular and wanted to minimize the studio's risk. *God's Gift to Women* still lost more than $100,000, and Fay was finished at Warner Bros. He degenerated into acute alcoholism. As Barbara Stanwyck's star rose and her husband's receded, the inevitable joke emerged: Which Hollywood actor has the biggest prick? The punch line: "Barbara Stanwyck." After their marriage spiraled into physical abuse, Stanwyck divorced him in 1935. Fay had a return to glory on Broadway in *Harvey* during the 1940s, before descending into a permanent stupor.[1]

Fay's remaining contract was bought out, as were the contracts of other artists who were not clicking at the box office. In 1929 Jack Warner retired Rin Tin Tin—the dog's popularity had run its course—and brought in the respected actor George Arliss for the title role in *Disraeli*. The veteran British thespian immediately enhanced the profile of the studio by winning an Academy Award.

Warners was beginning to shift toward more contemporary material, but Curtiz was handed yet another trifling assignment with *A Soldier's Plaything* (1930). Zanuck somehow convinced himself that the silent comedian Harry Langdon and clean-cut Ben Lyon could replicate Fox's winning World War I Flagg and Quirt duo (played by Victor McLaglen and Edmund Lowe). The movie opens with a cleverly staged fight scene between Lyon and Fred Kohler, but it quickly gets bogged down in a hodgepodge of drama and comedy interspersed with musical numbers.

Once again, Zanuck couldn't resist playing around with the footage and removed the musical sequences. His cuts reduced the running time to under an hour, which meant that the picture wouldn't play effectively in theaters; double bills were not yet popular. The editing ruined a marginal film and guaranteed its commercial failure. *A Soldier's Plaything* would be one of Curtiz's least successful films by posting a loss of $137,000.

James Oliver Curwood's rugged adventure novels and short stories about the Canadian and Alaskan far north have been adapted into literally hundreds of movies and television programs, from *Looking Forward* (1910) to *The Bear* (1988). *River's End: A New Story of God's Country*, published in 1919, was adapted for the screen three times.

In Curtiz's 1930 version, a Royal Canadian Mounted Policeman named Conniston and his guide, O'Toole, track Keith, an escaped murderer into the far reaches of the Canadian north. Upon capturing Keith, Conniston discovers that the murderer is a dead ringer for him. Keith gets the drop on both men and leaves them to die, then experiences a change of heart and returns to help them. Conniston subsequently dies of a frozen lung, and O'Toole, convinced of Keith's innocence, allows him to assume Conniston's identity. When Keith returns to Conniston's headquarters, he discovers that he has been cleared of the murder charges, but he cannot reveal his identity because it would appear that he murdered Conniston.

Curtiz convinced Zanuck that the dual role of Keith and Conniston needed a rugged new face. Zanuck agreed and arranged to borrow Charles Bickford from MGM. The craggy, red-haired actor had been signed by MGM after a sensational 1925 turn on Broadway in Jim Tully's *Outside*

Looking In. He quickly earned a reputation as "difficult" by constantly quarreling over scripts and film assignments. He was let go by Metro after telling Louis B. Mayer "fuck you" when the mogul insisted that the actor finish his role in *The Sea Bat* (1930). In addition to being stubborn, Bickford was an intimidating presence. As a kid he shot a trolley conductor in the forehead for running over his dog and was later rumored to have killed a man he caught in flagrante with his wife.

Bickford was sold on *River's End,* however, and gave an excellent performance. Although pleased with the picture, Bickford loathed Curtiz, who he believed was "burdened by a terrible inferiority which he manifested by screaming gratuitous insults at little people who were in no position to fight back." The actor also claimed that he needed fourteen stitches because of an on-set accident in which sled dogs attacked him, and that his misfortune amused Curtiz, whom he disparagingly described as a "sadistic weightlifter."

Bickford's youthful costar Junior Coghlan viewed Curtiz much differently, believing he was "as tender as any director I ever worked for." In a key scene with Bickford, the fourteen-year-old had to break into tears. It wasn't easy, and Curtiz patiently worked with him. Coghlan remembered that it came together perfectly. Curtiz immediately printed the scene and remarked, "God, that kid is good. He can cry quarts on demand." Curtiz's deftness in crafting the sequences with the dual Bickford characters onscreen together, through the skillful application of double exposures and astute blocking, was a masterful bit of technical acumen for its time. *River's End* was a critical success that turned a moderate profit.

Curtiz began receiving assignments that others couldn't handle; for example, Jack Warner attempted to replicate the studio's success of 1926's *The Sea Beast* by producing a sound version of *Moby Dick* with John Barrymore reprising his role as Captain Ahab. They doubled down by filming a German-language version loosely based on Melville's classic using the same sets during off-hours with a different cast and crew. Producing duplicate versions of films for foreign distribution was not unusual at that time. Universal Studios, for instance, was filming *Dracula,* starring Curtiz's friend Bela Lugosi, during the day and a Spanish language version of Bram Stoker's vampire story with different actors at night.

Lloyd Bacon was assigned to direct the all-German cast of *Dämon des Meeres* (Demon of the Sea), which included William Dieterle and Lissy Arna, but he found that he couldn't communicate effectively with many of his actors. So the two directors were switched around. *Demon of the Sea* premiered on March 2, 1931, in Berlin. Dieterle remembered the film as "great fun," despite the long hours that the cast and crew worked.

Curtiz made a lasting impression on Dieterle, who became his directorial colleague at Warners. Zanuck expected all his directors to be accomplished enough to progress on a film even if the script wasn't ready or was being revised. Dieterle ruefully recalled: "If a director wasn't fast enough or gave them too much trouble, they replaced him, usually with Mike [Curtiz]. Mike did everything. He could finish a picture at 11 and at 1 P.M. start a new picture. He was extraordinarily talented. He didn't always know what he was doing, but he had such an instinct for film, he could do it. I couldn't. If I didn't have my script, I was helpless."

Jack Warner apparently concurred with Dieterle's assessment. He presented Curtiz with a new contract on April 4, 1929, that raised his pay to $1,200 per week (and gave him another bump in 1931 to $1,500).

Although he was viewed as highly skilled and versatile, always doing his utmost while adhering to increasingly austere budgets and tight schedules, Curtiz was the equivalent of a general foreman at the Warner Bros. film factory. He was competing against Alan Crosland, William Seiter, Roy Del Ruth, Lloyd Bacon, Archie Mayo, Frank Lloyd, Mervyn LeRoy, William Beaudine, Alfred Green, and some sixteen others. Although most of Curtiz's films were profitable, the studio's heavy box-office hitters were Crosland (*On with the Show!*), Bacon (*The Singing Fool, Say It with Songs*), Del Ruth (*Gold Diggers of Broadway, The Terror, The Desert Song*), and Mayo (*My Man, On Trial, Sonny Boy*).

Curtiz was privately frustrated with his assignments but put his feelings aside when he got behind the camera. He was more anxious over his immigration status, as his final passport extension was set to expire on March 31, 1930. After an urgent consultation with an attorney, facilitated by Harry Warner, Curtiz was advised that because his initial entry status was as a visiting businessman with multiple extensions, he had to physically leave and reenter the country to start the clock running toward becoming a naturalized U.S. citizen. Another key element in resolving his immigration status was his marriage to Bess Meredyth.

Curtiz and Bess departed on a vacation to Europe in August 1931. They arrived back in the United States on the S.S. *Europa* from Cherbourg, docking in New York on August 24, 1931. The ship's manifest listed "Michael Kertesz" as a "film manager." Curtiz's Declaration of Intent to become a U.S. citizen, filed in the Southern District Court in Los Angeles on October 19, 1931, reports his initial entry into the United

States as August 24 of the same year. Curtiz noted on his nationalization form and all subsequent citizenship application folderol that his initial entry into the country was in 1931 instead of 1926. In any case, he was now a legal resident alien who could petition to become a naturalized citizen in five years' time.

As the Depression deepened, the economic future of the country and particularly the film industry appeared increasingly uncertain. Curtiz was unfazed; he had seen much harder times in Europe. He remained confident that he would prove himself as a great American director so long as he could continue making movies at Warner Bros.

14

Pre-Code in Synthetic Flesh

Curtiz's exceptionally busy period at Warner Bros. in the early 1930s coincided with what would be termed the pre-Code era of Hollywood films.

In 1922 the studio moguls appointed former Republican postmaster general Will H. Hays the czar of the Motion Picture Producers and Distributors of America (MPPDA) to improve Hollywood's public image after a series of scandals (most prominently the rape and manslaughter trials of the slapstick star Fatty Arbuckle and the unsolved murder of the director William Desmond Taylor). Because of continued protests by religious groups and local censors over the perceived licentious content of movies, Hays and the studio heads signed off on a new code of standards in March 1930 that would govern film content while ostensibly seeking to promote American moral values. Taboo subjects included premarital sex, out-of-wedlock childbirth, drug addiction, adultery, and prostitution.

Despite the acceptance of the Hays Code, actual implementation rested with the studio heads. As the Depression deepened, the moguls became desperate for sure-fire box-office hits. Banned subject matter increased after establishment of the Code, which remained an unenforced public relations fig leaf until mid-1934. And more than any other studio, Warner Bros. would push the envelope on salacious material.

Darryl Zanuck paved the way for a new style of contemporary cinema with *The Doorway to Hell,* released in October 1930. Two newly signed Warner contract players, Edward G. Robinson and James Cagney rocketed to stardom as unrepentant gangsters in *Little Caesar* and *The Public Enemy.* The Warner gangster movies filled a cultural niche by melding social commentary with dramatically vivid depictions of urban violence. American law enforcement, the judiciary, capitalism, and other sacred cows would be raked over the coals by screenwriters—many of them former newspaper scribes—including Ben Hecht, John Bright, W. R. Burnett, Earl Baldwin, Lucien Hubbard, and Oliver Garrett. Decades before the term "ripped from the headlines" entered the entertainment lexicon, it was standard operating procedure for Zanuck. The early 1930s allowed only the shrewdest of tough survivors to claw their way to the top of the heap. It was the era of Warner Bros.

Once a Warner screenplay was approved, it was rarely changed. As the writer-producer Casey Robinson explained, "Warners was the greatest studio for writers because Jack Warner wouldn't pay for rewrites, he wouldn't pay for reshooting." Occupied by contracts, publicity, and budgets, Jack seldom read a script and was often contemptuous of writers. He referred to his screenwriting stable as "schmucks with Underwoods." His philosophy proved to be an artistic double-edged sword. The movies helmed by Curtiz and other contract directors kept Warner theaters constantly supplied with new product. But the frenetic pace of production and refusal to spend money to improve an obviously troubled feature guaranteed that a certain number of bad movies would be released. Warner and Zanuck didn't care so long as several moneymakers followed a stinker. The primary objective was hewing to a production schedule that ground out the movies like sausage.

Assigned a new film roughly every two months, Curtiz directed *The Mad Genius*, starring the illustrious John Barrymore. The Great Profile's box-office cachet might have been fading, along with his periods of sobriety, but he remained a formidable talent. Barrymore had recently starred in the title role of Archie Mayo's *Svengali,* which garnered enthusiastic notices after general release in April 1931.

Zanuck didn't wait for *Svengali* to be released before rushing Barrymore into *The Mad Genius.* Curtiz began filming on March 9, just sixteen days after *Svengali* wrapped. Although *Svengali* was a critical triumph, it was not a financial success that justified a follow-on film of the same ilk. All the same, the studio wanted to squeeze one last feature out of Barrymore before the expiration of his expensive contract.

Jack Warner had purchased the rights to Martin Brown's drama *The Idol* for $15,000 the previous year. The play was a flop, but the leading role was tailor-made for Barrymore. He dominates *The Mad Genius* with his baroque send-up of a Svengali-like character, the embittered puppeteer Tsarakov, who rescues a young Fedor (Frankie Darro) from an abusive father (Boris Karloff). The club-footed Tsarakov lives vicariously through Fedor—played as an adult by Donald Cook—whom he develops into the most accomplished ballet dancer in the world. Tsarakov is a sociopathic Sol Hurok; he controls his dance company by keeping his ballet master, Serge Bankieff (Luis Alberni), hooked on dope while sustaining Fedor's loyalty with an entourage of compliant ballerinas. His insipid assistant Karimsky (Charles Butterworth) inspires ruthless scorn. Karimsky mentions that he's taking pills to help his head and Tsarakov replies, "Maybe you're not putting them in the right place."

Jack Warner pushed Curtiz to finish the picture quickly to minimize production costs inflated by Barrymore's $175,000 salary. During the casting phase, Darryl Zanuck recycled a number of the principals from *Svengali* to maintain thematic continuity in *The Mad Genius*. Marian Marsh, the teenage ingénue who was reportedly selected for the role of Trilby in *Svengali* because of her resemblance to Dolores Costello, was cast as Nana. The most notable repeat performer other than Barrymore was the art director Anton Grot, who became an integral contributor to many of Curtiz's best pictures. His sets in *The Mad Genius* distort the traditional spatial design of staircases, doors, and windows. Grot also incorporated low-set ceilings that Curtiz shot in claustrophobic style, a decade before the cinematographer Gregg Toland popularized the process in *Citizen Kane* (1941).

Taking his cue from Jack Warner, Curtiz drove the entire company beyond the point of exhaustion. The first day of shooting lasted until 8:10 p.m. at the Warner Studio on Sunset. On the second day, Curtiz worked with Barrymore and Charles Butterworth all day, then filmed a rainy scene with circus wagons in Burbank until 1:30 the following morning. It continued that way for the duration, including Saturdays and Sundays.

A fed-up Barrymore, in constant pain because he was limping around on his clubfoot prosthetic while working three consecutive weeks with only one day off, compared laboring under Curtiz's direction to being a finalist in a marathon dance competition. The seventeen-year-old Marian Marsh was more positively caught up in the moment. Although she accused Curtiz of being temperamental, she also believed that the director "was charming, too—a marvelous flair, and I loved his enthusiastic manner. He made things *go*."

Vitagraph's huge theater set was used extensively for the production numbers. During one sequence the hot lights set off the sprinkler system, drenching the company, yet Curtiz still kept going. He wrapped production at 2:40 a.m. on April 1, with a fade-out of Barrymore's clubfoot, nine days ahead of schedule. Almost as an afterthought, the eighty-one-minute picture was released in early November 1931, six months after the realization that *Svengali* did not have the box-office coattails that Warner and Zanuck had predicted.

Despite Barrymore's performance and Curtiz's skillful mise-en-scène, *The Mad Genius* was a commercial failure, which was due in part to the star's huge salary. Thornton Delehanty in the *New York Post* called it "an opulent orgy, careening on the fringe of lunacy," whereas the *New York Times* tabbed Curtiz's staging of the production "brilliant."

Barrymore's sagging box-office numbers reflected his increasingly cosmopolitan appeal. The dashing heroic figures of Don Juan and François Villon had transitioned to the thoroughly despicable Svengali and Tsarakov characters that were unattractive to less sophisticated audiences that resided where the Warners owned a lot of their theaters. The picture lost $41,000 and Barrymore left the studio to sign at MGM.

The gloomy year 1931 concluded with an $8 million loss that caused the studio to retrench. Everyone except the brothers had his or her pay cut, and production time for features was reduced to less than twenty days unless Jack Warner personally waived that limit.

In December 1931 Curtiz had his weekly pay reduced to $1,400 per week after he signed a contract extension in April. During the summer, Mathilde Foerster had brought him to heel for nonpayment of child support for their son, Michael, who was residing in Germany. After his arrival in Hollywood, the director's compliance with the 1923 Viennese support settlement became intermittent. An agreement was negotiated requiring Curtiz to pay $3,500 in a lump sum and $200 per month in continuing support until his son reached his majority. A seething Curtiz refused to meet with Foerster and empowered his attorney to sign the agreement for him on July 15, 1931.

The director was also dissatisfied with the results of *The Woman from Monte Carlo*. The picture was made as a vehicle to introduce the German actress Lil Dagover to American audiences in what would be an ill-fated Warner attempt to clone Greta Garbo and Marlene Dietrich. Five years earlier, Dagover had been brought over by Paramount, along with the director Erich Pommer, did nothing, and returned to Germany. Possessed of a dark, alluring appearance and a deep voice, she had an impressive acting résumé that included a featured role in *The Cabinet of Dr. Caligari* (1920) along with Fritz Lang's *Destiny* (1921) and F. W. Murnau's *Tartuffe* (1925). After signing her, Jack Warner orchestrated a publicity buildup culminating in the January 1931 production of *The Woman from Monte Carlo,* which was released during the same week as MGM's debut of *Mata Hari,* starring Garbo.

Dagover plays a Viennese femme fatale married to a French navy commandant. She becomes a stowaway on her husband's ship while seemingly having an affair with one of her husband's officers. The script has Dagover vamping away in both English and German. Despite the presence of Walter Huston and Warren William, the movie conveys the impression of being exactly what it is: a slapped-together project that was rushed through for publicity purposes.

The positive aspects included a climactic naval battle using miniatures that the director drew from his *Atlantis* experience to stage. Curtiz and Dagover reportedly didn't get along. Immediately after the fiasco of her Hollywood debut, the actress retreated to Berlin, where her career continued for more than half a century.

Curtiz's next picture was more rewarding. *Alias the Doctor* was a personal project—a remake of *The Charlatan,* which he had directed in Hungary in 1917 and again in 1923 for Sascha-Film. He'd lobbied Jack Warner and Zanuck for more than a year to buy the rights to Imre Földes's play. Warner eventually forked over $10,000: $4,000 to Földes and $6,000 to Universal, which had optioned the property back in 1927.

Curtiz cast First National holdover Richard Barthelmess as Karl Brenner, a German farm orphan who takes the rap after Stephan, his foster brother, performs an illegal operation while the pair are attending medical school. On the day of his release after serving a two-year stretch in prison, Karl discovers the erratic Stephan dead of consumption. Subsequently saving the life of a child by performing a revolutionary operation, Karl assumes Stephan's identity and goes on to become a famed surgeon before his past inevitably catches up to him. The adaptation of Földes's play, compressed into a truncated sixty-one-minute running time, becomes such a breakneck series of contrived coincidences that one begins to wonder why poor Karl ever left the family farm.

Niven Busch, attending his first Hollywood story conference as a young writer on *Alias the Doctor,* recalled that Barthelmess "had a face-lift, which reduced his facial expressions to one: a lowering look of bewildered menace. His face was frozen, which is very impressive under the right circumstances—which do not arrive in every scene." Barthelmess became an emblematic example of a major silent film star whose career withered away in sound pictures.

Yet there are also genuinely dramatic moments. *Alias the Doctor* is visually compelling owing to the skillful artistry of Curtiz. Anton Grot's Germanic set designs recall *The Cabinet of Dr. Caligari* and F. W. Murnau's *The Last Laugh* (1924). Curtiz's deft mixture of dolly shots, innovative camera angles, silhouettes, and well-timed close-ups relates the drama in such stark visual terms that the movie transcends its dated story.

Alias the Doctor was a profitable picture even in light of Curtiz's successful filibustering for additional scenes and retakes, which raised the cost of the production.

Curtiz finally got a crack at more contemporary material with *The Strange Love of Molly Louvain* (1932). Based on the play *Tinsel Girl*, Curtiz lucked out with the dual casting of the pre-Code siren Ann Dvorak in the title role alongside the ultimate hard-boiled reporter, Lee Tracy. The picture opens with Molly getting kicked to the curb by the socially prominent Ralph Rogers (Don Dillaway), who can't bear to bring his impregnated lower-class girlfriend home to mother. As *Molly Louvain* is a quintessential pre-Code parable about women making bad choices, Molly opts for sharpie Nicky Grant (Leslie Fenton), and, after a quick montage of license plates, she drops off her baby girl with a caregiver to continue living with her erratic lover, who has graduated to stickups in order to make ends meet. After she becomes entangled in a botched robbery, a wounded Nicky falsely tabs Molly as a crime queen. She dyes her hair blond and goes into hiding as the dragnet goes out. The avian-voiced Cornell (Lee Tracy) contrives with the police to use Molly's child to coerce her surrender, not realizing she is the dame living across the hall to whom he is pitching bare-knuckled woo. Curtiz keeps the pace frenetic as Molly surrenders to a coldhearted police lieutenant, who forces her to sign a phony confession in order to see her daughter. Dvorak's bravura performance struck a resonant chord with Depression-era audiences who were also struggling to make the best out of the bad hand that life had dealt them.

Curtiz took care in several scenes to make the police appear as callous as possible and included an insider slant that has the police reporter Cornell receiving a telegram with an offer to become a Hollywood screenwriter. The rotund Guy Kibbee as a dim-witted police sergeant assigned to water plants in the squad room shakes his head and offers a line worthy of Ben Hecht: "Everyone is in Hollywood writing books and scripts. There are no reporters left."

Curtiz brought out the best in Ann Dvorak; it is unfortunate that they were never teamed up again. Life would imitate art, as Dvorak eloped to

Europe with her *Louvain* costar Leslie Fenton in July 1932. The actress's vanishing act opened a lengthy period of discord between her and Jack Warner. The squabble evolved into a disagreement about pay and disputed allegations about the actress's health that culminated in Dvorak's unsuccessful lawsuit that sealed her eventual dismissal from the studio.

It was the first of several legal fights between Warner Bros. and their artists over pay and movie assignments that continued for more than a decade. The independent-minded James Cagney was suspended in 1932 after Jack Warner refused to renegotiate his contract, which amounted to a pittance in view of the huge popularity of his films. Warner's capricious treatment of top-drawer talent often made Curtiz's job as a filmmaker more challenging than it already was.

As Depression-era losses mounted, Zanuck cast about for story ideas that would lure people into theaters, while Jack Warner was saddled with his languishing Technicolor deal. Horror became a Hollywood staple in 1931, beginning with *Dracula,* followed by *Frankenstein* and *Dr. Jekyll and Mr. Hyde,* both released at the end of the year. Although the process of using red-orange and blue-green two-strip color had recently been enhanced, the studio's moratorium on musicals had halted making new films in color. Because the cost of each Technicolor print was more than double the outlay for a black-and-white one, nothing would be produced in color during early 1932 unless it was a surefire gambit.

With the acquisition of a play titled *The Terror* by Howard W. Comstock and Allen C. Miller in January 1932, Zanuck decided to create a different kind of Technicolor film for Curtiz to direct. On January 18, 1932, the *Los Angeles Times* reported that Bela Lugosi and Loretta Young would costar in *Doctor X,* but Zanuck eventually signed Fay Wray and the Broadway leading man Lionel Atwill instead. The Canadian-born and Hollywood-bred Wray was in preproduction with the producer Merian C. Cooper on *King Kong,* and Atwill, a British stage actor of skilled elocution, would begin to leave his indelible mark as one of Hollywood's maddest scientists. *Doctor X* captured Wray's initial cinematic scream and permitted Atwill his earliest opportunity to skulk about a fantastically configured laboratory set. The script was by Earl Baldwin and Robert Tasker, the latter having originally taken up screenwriting while serving time in San Quentin for armed robbery. Zanuck and Curtiz would subsequently change *Doctor X* into something much different from what was originally intended.

Zanuck believed a frightening Technicolor movie would make money, but Jack Warner didn't want to publicize *Doctor X* as a horror film because he was leery of offending exhibitors. *Doctor X* ended up becoming a strange hybrid: Warner Bros. publicized it as a comedy-mystery with a surprise ending despite the gruesome story about a serial killer (the "Moon Killer") involved with cannibalism and dismemberment. The casting of Lee Tracy as yet another nosy, fast-talking reporter underscored Zanuck's reluctance to stray from the populist success of previous films. Curtiz began production on March 19, 1932, with a twenty-four-day schedule; Jack Warner's twenty-days-or-less mandate had proven untenable. Although Curtiz took time to design an additional scene that added suspense to Atwill's red-herring character, Zanuck eventually had to drop five scenes from the script to ensure that his director stayed on schedule. By the second week, Curtiz ramped up to shooting fifteen hours per day. The final week of eighteen-hour days climaxed with a twenty-hour marathon that had the director completing twenty-seven camera setups into the wee hours of the next morning. *Doctor X* wrapped four days behind schedule.

Adding to the ordeal was the Technicolor two-color film that required four times the lighting of a black-and-white feature. In an era before air-conditioning, the *Doctor X* soundstages were akin to an illuminated sauna. During an extended scene with four wax likenesses of the Moon Killer's previous victims onstage, the prop figures melted under the hellish arc lights. Curtiz ordered in extras from Central Casting to pose as statues and shot a different scene until they arrived. After each take, all the actors retreated as far away as possible from the suffocating heat of the lights.

Two different cameramen were grinding away. Ray Rennahan, the contracted Technicolor cinematographer, filmed the movie in color, while Jack Warner ordered the filming of a sequential black-and-white negative that was shot by Richard Towers. The black-and-white print allowed for international distribution of *Doctor X* to locales where color movies were not viable. The manufacture and striking of a black-and-white print for a Technicolor production violated the spirit of Jack Warner's agreement with Herbert Kalmus. The different film modes also meant that the actors had to do additional takes whenever film ran out or when glitches occurred with the Technicolor camera. As a result, some of the dialogue varies between the two versions.

In addition to the ungodly hours and unpleasant working conditions, the director's demeanor didn't enhance the company's morale. Fay Wray

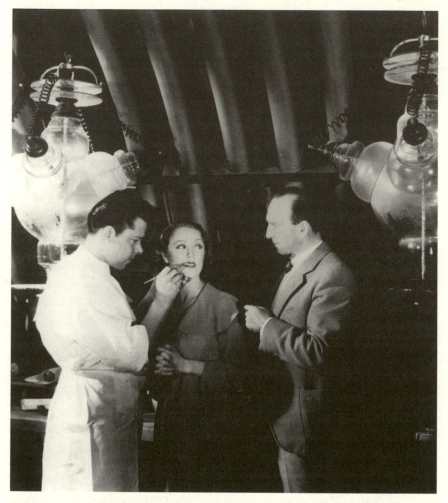

Curtiz scrutinizes Perc Westmore applying lip gloss to Fay Wray during filming of *Dr. X* (1932) (courtesy of Photofest).

was accustomed to authoritarian realism after being directed by Erich von Stroheim in *The Wedding March* (1928). But even that experience didn't prepare her for Curtiz working a short schedule: Michael Curtiz "was a machine of a person—efficient, detached, impersonal to the point of appearing cynical. He stood tall, militarily erect; his calculating, functional style made his set run smoothly, without humor. He had a steely intelligence and moviemaking know-how that made you feel there was a camera lens inside his cool blue eyes."

The actress also witnessed an instance of Curtiz's dismissive behavior that bordered on outright cruelty: "Looking through the finder one day at a group of extras, he called out to one, 'Move to your right . . . more . . . more . . . more. . . . *Now* you are out of the scene. *Go home!*' So wicked, it was almost funny."

And then there was the director's frustration over breaking for lunch. When the company went down to Laguna Beach for a day to film a scene, the actress observed Curtiz pacing in the sand talking to himself while the cast and crew were eating their boxed lunches: "Why should they eat? I don't eat! Why should we be wasting this time?"

Curtiz again received a lot of help from Anton Grot, whose morgue and laboratory sets were exquisite. He explained his philosophy in the film's press book: "We design a set that imitates as closely as possible a bird of prey about to swoop down upon its victim, trying to incorporate in the whole thing a sense of impending calamity, of overwhelming danger."

Curtiz's framing of different shots, beginning with the opening of the film on a pier outside the New York morgue, appears painterly in their composition. Scenes inside the lab added to the creepy mood: Preston Foster intently peering at a living heart in a beaker, John Wray's visual discomfort after the police notice his possession of a racy magazine,[1] and Harry Beresford wearing a lab jacket spotted with blood. The director designed the movement of his camera so that the audience would follow the action of the participants with a heightened atmosphere of suspense. In the *Doctor X* press book, Curtiz dubbed this technique "the curious camera."

In the sequence in which the one-armed Preston Foster is revealed as the Moon Killer, he attaches a synthetic-flesh appendage and smears himself with Max Factor makeup. This was a genuinely frightening apparition in 1932. The gradual application of the makeup was made even more eerie by a hydraulic lift in which Curtiz seated the actor. Slowly raising Foster's height from a sitting position accentuated the visual sense of a man being transformed into a taller, more primeval creature. Foster was doubled by a larger stuntman during the climactic fight with Lee Tracy, which ends with the Moon Killer becoming a screaming funeral pyre, falling through an upstairs window into Long Island Sound.

The suspenseful tempo created by Curtiz overcame several lapses in the credibility of the script. The addition of slapstick comedy touches, which included Tracy stumbling into skeletons and reacting to falling objects, attempted to lessen the grim mood of the picture. Curtiz also snuck in an initial scene in which Tracy makes a telephone call from what is obviously a brothel.

Mordaunt Hall of the *New York Times* praised Curtiz's direction of a film that made "'Frankenstein' seem tame and friendly." *Doctor X* nearly tripled the studio's investment, and a follow-up film with the working title *The Wax Museum* was planned to begin production in September 1932.

During the interim, Curtiz directed *The Cabin in the Cotton* between May 9 and June 13, 1932; it was released in late October. The film was Warner social commentary transferred from the usual urban environment to below the Mason-Dixon Line. Richard Barthelmess played the son of a sharecropper caught in the middle of a dispute between the self-entitled owner of a plantation (Berton Churchill) and the financially desperate sharecroppers. Complicating matters is Barthelmess's simultaneous romantic involvement with a sharecropper's daughter (Dorothy Jordan) and the plantation owner's trampy spawn, played by twenty-four-year-old Bette Davis.

Perhaps the compromised ending of the film placated the Warners— the depicted strife between the plantation owner and sharecroppers bore an uncomfortable resemblance to the actual working relationship between the brothers and their employees. The second-unit footage that included long shots of sharecroppers working in fields of cotton was authentic. The location manager, Bill Guthrie, traveled with a camera crew to Stovall, Mississippi, to film on a large plantation. Although the purpose of the filming was supposed to be a secret, the Warner crew barely escaped a tar-and-feather brigade from the nearby town. The locals apparently didn't appreciate a bunch of Hollywood Yankees showing up to make a movie based on a novel by Harry Harrison Kroll that depicted white plantation owners as dishonest while expressing a modicum of sympathy for sharecroppers, whose bleak existence had essentially remained the same since Reconstruction.

At the time, there wasn't an inordinate amount of difference between the segregated South and a Hollywood soundstage. Included in Jack Warner's résumé of unpleasant character traits was racial bigotry. He steadfastly resisted for decades to produce a picture with black actors playing anything other than background characters exuding subservient clichés. In 1951 Warner forced the screenwriter Ivan Goff to change James Cagney's African American roommate in *Come Fill the Cup* to a character played by the veteran Irish American actor James Gleason. "You think Cagney's gonna be under the same roof as a nigger?" demanded Warner.

He also turned down the opportunity to produce *Porgy and Bess*. The only African American employees at Warners and the other studios during this period were gofers and shoe shiners. The black drop cloths used to prevent inadvertent illumination on soundstages were routinely referred to as niggers. "Put a nigger on that arc," a gaffer would call out within earshot of a black employee. It was taken for granted that the African American characters in *The Cabin in the Cotton* and other Hollywood movies would be obedient, musically inclined stereotypes.

Although Curtiz usually offended people on an individual, rather than a collective, basis, his language difficulty inadvertently created a racial faux pas overheard by the company of *The Cabin in the Cotton*. Giving a speech from a camera boom through a bullhorn to a large group of black extras hired to play cotton pickers, Curtiz exhorted them to "behave 'like Southern peasants' . . . from the terrible time when the South was fighting the East." His geographical perspective on the Civil War elicited quizzical looks. The director then added an additional flourish when Barthelmess was settling the dispute between the planters and sharecroppers. John Meredyth Lucas recalled the scene:

> Mike instructed them over the bullhorn, "When the hero come out from the courthouse, all the niggers should throw up the hand and shout happy from—" He broke off, startled as the assistant director apologetically snatched the bullhorn from his hands.
>
> "Jesus, Mike, you can't say that!"
>
> "What I say wrong?"
>
> "You can't call them that," the assistant explained. "They're colored. You have to say colored."
>
> "Oh," Mike took the bullhorn again. "I am terribly sorry what I say," he apologized to the extras. "I speak so lousy my English." Then, more firmly he began again. "When the hero come out, all the *colored* niggers should throw up the hand and—"
>
> The assistant had already collapsed.

The actor George Murphy would repeat this episode almost word for word in his memoir after allegedly observing Curtiz directing a group of African American soldiers during the filming of a musical number for *This Is the Army* (1943). The anecdote would be trotted out yet again by the actor Paul Picerni, who claimed it happened during the filming of *The Will Rogers Story*. In fact, Curtiz bore no ill will toward any ethnic group.

In many respects, he was enlightened about race in America. His youthful poverty imbued him with a lifelong empathy with those who had to struggle against insurmountable odds. In a 1945 interview, Curtiz was asked how the European mind functions when it considers the American Negro in films. His answer was unhesitatingly clear-cut: "To me, the Negro is like anyone else. When I came to America, I was told a difference was made. However, in this business you cannot attach any importance to the color of a man's skin. The thing that counts is whether or not he is a good actor." Actual deeds backed up Curtiz's response. In 1950 Curtiz cast the respected Afro-Cuban actor Juano Hernandez in *Young Man with a Horn* and *The Breaking Point* as a major supporting player. He also integrated African American actors into a number of crowd scenes and production numbers in *Roughly Speaking* and *Night and Day*.

The Cabin in the Cotton was Curtiz's first film with Bette Davis. He damaged their working relationship almost before it began. The director wanted a sexy ingénue for the part of the plantation owner's daughter but was ordered by Zanuck to use Davis. A frustrated Curtiz vented behind the camera during a close-up between Barthelmess and Davis, fuming loudly enough for the actress to overhear him calling her a "God-damned-nothing-no-good-sexless-son-of-a-bitch." As a third-billed contract player, Davis swallowed the insult but never forgot it. She relished her role, which included her favorite line of movie dialogue—"Ah'd like t' kiss ya, but ah just washed mah ha-ir"—but it was an unpleasant experience. She recalled: "My director made my life hell every day. Mr. Curtiz ignored my needs completely."

Although Curtiz and Davis would make seven films together, she believed he devoted an inordinate amount of time to the camera rather than the actors, especially her. Although she remained at the studio until 1949, Curtiz directed his final picture with her in 1939. Davis developed into such a powerhouse that she became a handful for any director to manage. Vincent Sherman and William Wyler coped by sleeping with her.

Davis also appeared in *20,000 Years in Sing Sing*, which Curtiz directed in August and September 1932. Although she received second billing to Spencer Tracy, the nominal star of the picture was the book on which it was based, written by the Sing Sing prison warden Lewis E. Lawes.

James Cagney was originally scheduled to play the lead and William Wellman to direct, but that notion went down the drain after Cagney temporarily left the studio in a breach-of-contract dispute. Lawes's deal gave him script approval, and he favored Spencer Tracy, whose record of playing men behind bars was second to none at that time. Tracy came to the attention of Hollywood while starring in the Broadway prison drama *The Last Mile* (and then took time off from the play in 1930 to make his feature debut alongside Humphrey Bogart in *Up the River* at Fox). Jack Warner had little choice but to fork over $10,400 to Fox to borrow Tracy.

Curtiz and the cinematographer Barney McGill used still photos taken at Sing Sing prison in Ossining, New York, to match the close and medium shots intercut into footage that the director Ray Enright and a second-unit crew shot at the prison. Anton Grot's sets included detailed reconstructions of the mess hall, the barbershop, various industrial shops, and death row—and an exact replica of Lawes's office at Sing Sing, even down to the volumes in his bookcase. The cellblock sequences that constitute the majority of the dramatic scenes were filmed at the Metro lot in Culver City, where the set for *The Big House* (1930) remained intact.

Curtiz was stuck with another twenty-four-day schedule and felt compelled to push the company past the point of endurance with a series of eighteen-hour days. A Warner contract actor, Lyle Talbot, who was in the cast said, "Mike must have hated his wife, because he never wanted to go home." The sole hiccup was the actor Warren Hymer, who had recently been let go from Fox because of a bad drinking problem. On August 15, two days after Curtiz had begun filming, he showed up late and was drunk. Hymer wouldn't get into his wardrobe and was sent home. He arrived hungover the next day and promptly got into an argument with Curtiz, who called him out in front of the company for his behavior. Spencer Tracy took charge and told Hymer that if he didn't straighten out, "I'll walk out and refuse to finish the picture while you're in the cast." Hymer finished the picture more or less sober, although he was late several more times. After pulling the same stunt later at Columbia and getting thrown off the lot, the tough-guy actor earned the respect of nearly everyone in Hollywood by reportedly urinating on Columbia mogul Harry Cohn's desk. He eventually drank himself out of the movies and died at age forty-two.

Curtiz composed a masterly opening with prisoners moving in regimented lines in the cellblock, superimposed graphic numbers denoting the length of their sentences. The numbers and the prisoners increase as they march in place in front of their cells, transitioning to an overhead shot of an assemblage of convicts in the prison yard with a huge "20,000" graphic unveiling the title of the movie as the musical score crescendos. A

Curtiz and the cameraman Barney McGill line up a shot of Spencer Tracy and Lyle Talbot in *20,000 Years in Sing Sing* (1932) (courtesy of the Lucas family).

moving aerial shot of the prison interspersed with the opening credits follows; framed shots introduce the principal players until the camera zooms into the interior of a fast-moving train taking Tommy Connors (Tracy) up the river.

20,000 Years in Sing Sing was social commentary blended into a

Warner Bros. gangster melodrama. Along with Curtiz's direction, what makes the picture memorable is the screenplay that eschewed overt preaching. Tracy is excellent as a flawed but admirable gangster adhering to his personal code. Arthur Byron is similarly convincing as the tough, cigar-chomping warden, revealed to be a compassionate man. As Connor's girlfriend, Davis exudes authentic love and loyalty. The quality of the acting adds dramatic viability to a story that might have foundered with a lesser cast. Curtiz's staging and compositions are unrelentingly grim. The shaded lighting—prison-bar shadows are pervasive—and the versatility of the camera shots invigorate every scene. The sound is much improved as well. Warner Bros. had transitioned out of the cumbersome Vitaphone disk recordings and was employing Photophone sound-on-film technology.

Rehabilitation of convicted criminals was a relatively new concept in 1932, when many American prisons resembled medieval hellholes designed solely to inflict punishment. Warner Bros. exposed the stark inhumanity of prison life in *I Am a Fugitive from a Chain Gang*. The picture caused a sensation when it was released the week before Thanksgiving 1932 and grossed more than $1 million. Opening six weeks later, *20,000 Years in Sing Sing* offered a social remedy to the conditions exposed in *I Am a Fugitive* by presenting Lawes's book as a public plea for the humane treatment of convicts. Curtiz's picture also doesn't default to a moralistic conclusion that characterizes later Warner dramas such as *Angels with Dirty Faces* (1938) and *Each Dawn I Die* (1939), which had to conform to the rejuvenated Production Code.

Economic hard times continued to grow worse for the vast majority of Americans. Though a new president was offering a beleaguered nation hope that happy days were here again, the brothers Warner were not so sure.

15

Regime Change

The Warners abandoned their traditional allegiance to Republicanism to actively support Franklin D. Roosevelt for president in 1932. Jack Warner observed: "The country is in chaos. There is revolution in the air. We need a change." The mogul rounded up campaign contributions and organized a star-laden FDR campaign rally at the Los Angeles Coliseum. After Roosevelt's inaugural, the youngest Warner would go fishing with the new president and slept a night in the White House.

The period of 1932–33 was a financial nightmare for Hollywood. The desultory effects of the Depression and the outlays for sound conversion became a double whammy for the studios. Thirty percent of the movie theaters controlled by the studios—five thousand venues—were closed down; people were enticed to watch movies at the remaining theaters by dish nights and other exhibitor giveaways. RKO lost $10 million and Paramount $21 million, and both filed for bankruptcy protection. Warner Bros. reported $14 million in red ink and owed more than $100 million to the banks. Despite the gloomy news, Harry Warner was determined that the family business would never fall under the control of Wall Street bankers.

The movie industry's response to the temporary crisis of closed banks in March 1933 was one of panicked avarice. Under a plan quickly approved by all the major studios under the auspices of the Academy of Motion Picture Arts and Sciences Emergency Committee, all studio employees making more than $50 per week had their salaries temporarily reduced by 50 percent for eight weeks, ostensibly for cash-flow purposes. After two months, Price Waterhouse would examine the studios' financial records and advise the Academy whether employee pay could be restored to previous levels.

Darryl Zanuck became upset about the entire situation. He didn't believe the salary cuts were necessary, and the Warners hadn't consulted him before notifying the entire studio about the plan. But he voluntarily reduced his own salary for the eight-week duration. At that time, Price Waterhouse duly advised the Academy that salaries should be reinstated at previous levels. All the studio chiefs agreed, except for Harry Warner. It didn't escape notice that Harry and Jack had never reduced their own salaries; the notion of shared sacrifice was anathema to all the moguls. The money from the salary reductions was never returned to Warner employees. By reducing his own salary after arguing against the reductions, Zanuck crossed an executive Rubicon in siding with the rank and file over his own bosses. However indispensable he might have seemed, Zanuck's name was not on the studio water tower.

Long wary of the eldest Warner, Zanuck considered Harry a hypocritical Ebenezer Scrooge whom he couldn't stomach any longer. After a heated argument between the pair at the Brown Derby restaurant, the producer tendered his resignation on April 14, 1933. Zanuck, who invented the successful style of Warner Bros. pictures, immediately partnered with Joseph Schenck at Twentieth Century (which would merge with Fox Film two years later to become Twentieth Century-Fox). He finally had his own movie studio.

His departure created a path of ascension for Hal B. Wallis, who was named the studio's production chief. Wallis had been Zanuck's assistant for four years. It has been surmised that Wallis produced the First National films and Zanuck the Warner Bros. productions, but the surviving studio records from before 1935 are incomplete on this score. Wallis knew from personal experience what he was getting into. He was eating lunch with Zanuck at the Brown Derby when Harry Warner summoned Wallis's soon-to-be-former boss from the table for their final confrontation.

Although the two men shared a Jewish heritage and a ferocious frugality, Jack Warner and Hal Wallis had little else in common. Nothing about Wallis resembled the insecure vindictiveness and yen for cornball shtick that characterized the youngest Warner. Harold Brent Wallis was a sober, self-contained man who'd had to grow up fast after being born Aaron Blum Wolowicz in turn-of-the-century Chicago. His father, Jacob, was a tailor from Belarus who became a degenerate gambler. After bankrupting his family, the elder Wallis abandoned them. His son went to work when he was fourteen to support his mother and three sisters. After becoming successful as a salesman for the Edison General Electric Company, Wallis moved to Los Angeles with his tubercular mother and the rest of the family.

The oldest sister, Minna, was also a hard charger who landed a job drawing up contracts for a Los Angeles law firm. She recommended to one of her bosses' clients that her younger brother would be the ideal candidate to manage the Warner Bros. Garrick Theatre on Eighth Street and Broadway in downtown Los Angeles. She later introduced Hal to Sam Warner, who hired him on the spot. Her brother's career was the first of many launched by Minna Wallis, who became a powerful Hollywood agent credited with discovering Clark Gable, among other stars.

Hal Wallis became an acknowledged expert in every phase of the movie business. He spent hours in the editing room with the younger Zanuck, learning cutting and continuity; he mastered exactly how the varied parts of a film should be fitted together. He knew exhibition and publicity inside out. He lived budgets, scripts, and casting. A lover of the theater, Wallis possessed exceptionally tasteful judgment about material for movies. Over the years, he would develop a reputation as a "starmaker" by spotting and signing new talent. Wallis also became a virtuoso at hiring skilled people for key staff positions while paying them as little as possible and rarely extending gratitude or credit publicly to anyone who ever worked for him.

A major attribute that Wallis did not possess early in his career was a sensibility about filmmaking beyond what was economically viable. Although he was a quick study, his unawareness resulted in sporadic eruptions of frustration. Wallis usually conducted himself as a gentleman in person and rarely raised his voice, but his executive deportment was immediately apparent to everyone on the lot.

Like a generalissimo, Wallis expected unquestioning obedience from subordinates and brooked neither delay nor criticism. "There were two Hal Wallises," recalled the screenwriter Julius Epstein. "Hal Wallis at the office was efficient, impersonal, cold. If you were walking across the lot and you met him, he would always say, 'When are you going to finish that script? Are you making a life career out of that script?'" One had to earn Wallis's respect in order to survive. Robert Lord, who made a successful transition from writer to associate producer, recalled him as a straightforward boss: "If Hal respects you, there's no problem. If he doesn't, he'll cut you to pieces." The other Wallis, away from the grind, was shy and amiable—a person few people at the studio knew existed. He rarely acknowledged the existence of underlings. Those lowest on the Warner corporate totem pole, including the studio messengers, loathed him.

Wallis's interoffice memos were often akin to Zeus flinging lightning

A filmmaking triumvirate: Jack Warner, Michael Curtiz, and Hal Wallis
(courtesy of the Lucas family).

bolts from Mount Olympus onto the scurrying mortals below. It was
a technique in keeping with the Warner culture, which stressed the requirement to compose every request into a written communiqué. The line
"Verbal messages cause misunderstandings and delays (please put them
in writing)" adorned the bottom margin of Warner Bros. memoranda in
bold text. Wallis forgot nothing and was brilliant in his ability to manage
hundreds of details on multiple films simultaneously. His endless missives
chided nearly everyone at the studio about something: "I am still waiting
for your response," "I don't understand why I need to ask you again," or
most severely, "I am damn sick and tired of your crossing me." Wallis regarded any type of nonresponsiveness as a personal betrayal. The already
feverish activity on the lot attained an even higher level of intensity.

Wallis is credited with supervising several of Curtiz's films, including
The Strange Love of Molly Louvain and *Mystery of the Wax Museum*.
The latter picture proved to be an artistic tour de force by Curtiz.

Jack Warner and Herbert Kalmus settled their wrangle over Technicolor caused by *Doctor X;* there would be no duplicate black-and-white
version made of the next Technicolor film. The new picture would be the

third and final First National color feature under their existing agreement. Warner's attempt to substitute shorts for the third Technicolor feature apparently fell on deaf ears, as Kalmus felt double-crossed by the mogul's previous chicanery.

Charles Belden's story "The Waxworks" was sold to Warner Bros. for a piddling $1,000. It was adapted into a more structured screenplay by Don Mullaly and Carl Erickson. Lionel Atwill was brought back for a meatier role as the sculptor Ivan Igor, a maniac horribly scarred as a result of his business partner's burning down his London waxworks. The spectacular fire sequence, masterfully staged by Curtiz, encompassed four soundstages and took nineteen hours to film. Then the action shifts to New York, where it is gradually revealed that the insane Igor purloins both corpses and living people, coating them in wax, to keep his museum stocked with replicas of famous personages. Fay Wray, who bears an unfortunate resemblance to Marie Antoinette, appears in a role that gives her little to do other than demonstrate her famous scream.

Aside from Atwill, the key player is Glenda Farrell as a sassy, wisecracking newspaper reporter in prototypical Warner pre-Code style. The spunky Farrell gives much better than she gets from her obnoxious editor, played by Frank McHugh, who peppers her with sarcastic ripostes. After *Five Star Final* (1931), it was seemingly impossible for Warners to conceive of any movie that didn't include a wiseacre reporter and an editor clipping off snappy dialogue.

Double entendres that tested the censor's office are sprinkled throughout the script of the seventy-seven-minute feature. In a flouting of the Production Code, the character of Professor Darcy, Igor's assistant, is portrayed by the actor Arthur Edmund Carewe as a drug addict. Many elements of *Doctor X* are greatly improved on. Natalie Kalmus's selection of background colors for standing sets, makeup, and costume colors, Ray Rennahan's photography, Grot's spectacular design of Atwill's subterranean laboratory (which includes an exotic wax tank), and Perc Westmore's horrific makeup jobs were all uniformly superb. *Mystery of the Wax Museum* remains the most striking surviving example of the two-strip Technicolor process during the early sound period.

What *Doctor X* and *The Mystery of the Wax Museum* also shared were the actors' misery in laboring under the blinding Technicolor lighting—an ordeal worsened by Curtiz's punishing agenda, which commenced on September 26, 1932. Interviewed by the future film archivist Scott MacQueen, Glenda Farrell remembered: "Michael Curtiz was very—exacting. I liked him, we got along fine, but he worked people to death. We all collapsed one night on *Wax Museum*. He worked us for twenty-three hours. We all had hysterics and collapsed. They had to let us have the next day off to stay in bed."

The unreasonable hours were a result of Curtiz's quest for perfection. Because he understood editing, he filmed scenes from a variety of angles rather than "cutting in the camera." He also developed a habit of visualizing certain camera setups and then changing his mind when he suddenly came up with a better idea. The director never arranged a setup or moved his camera without a definite purpose that he believed would improve the film. Curtiz explained the rationale of his visual modus operandi in the film's press book:

> Odd, unusual camera angles should never be used for their own sake though the temptation to do so is often great, especially to the man who has an aptitude for thinking in them. The only reason for using an angle, in presenting a scene that would not seem the usual one to the onlooker, is to obtain a definite effect upon the spectator, which can be gained in no other way. You wish to arouse at that point a feeling of surprise, of terror, of repulsion, of admiration—and to emphasize it, the person or thing you are photographing must be presented from a special angle. Otherwise the natural, straightforward method of recording a scene in pictures is the one that holds the spectator's interest, keeps the story moving and preserves the flow and tempo of the action. It is very easy, in a story like *Mystery of the Wax Museum*, for instance, to overdo the bizarre, startling angles. That is why I used them throughout the picture sparingly, and always with a definite purpose in mind. Unless one is chary of the employment of them, their effect is very quickly blunted, and thereafter they become a nuisance instead of a help. Much more effective is the specialized type of lighting that we used to establish and build up a mood that we wished to communicate with the spectator. This was particularly true in the sequences laid in the two waxworks—the London one and the New York museum. In each, without being too obvious in our lighting, we tried to arouse in the spectators' minds a vague, intangible feeling of uneasiness, mystery, a sinister something lurking in the shadows, never shown but only suggested.

Curtiz ponders his next setup while the morgue monster waits during the frenetic production of *Mystery of the Wax Museum* (1933) (courtesy of Scott MacQueen).

Because of his artistic approach, Curtiz wasn't moving fast enough. On Saturday, October 15, he attempted to play catch-up by working the cast and crew until five o'clock the following morning. The result was eleven scenes and a superhuman forty setups. The picture was now so far behind schedule that its supervisor, Henry Blanke, had Curtiz work nearly around the clock, finally wrapping the morning after Halloween.

Curtiz's ruthless work ethic earned him admiration but not affection. Fay Wray ended up preferring the tender mercies of King Kong to those of Michael Curtiz: "He was like part of the camera. . . . He was very efficient, I'm sure. I guess I could respect that. But I didn't like him and I didn't think he was a good or very nice person."

During the initial take of the climactic scene, in which Wray breaks through Atwill's wax mask to reveal the horrific burned face underneath, she didn't know what to expect. Curtiz prevented her from seeing Westmore's makeup so as to elicit a spontaneous reaction for the camera. The makeup was so revolting that she froze after one piece fell away, and Curtiz quickly cut the scene. "You should have kept hitting and hitting until it was all broken away," he exclaimed. A reserve wax mask was quickly applied, and the scene—inspired by Lon Chaney's *The Phantom of the Opera* as repurposed by Don Mullaly—was reshot to Curtiz's satisfaction.

Mystery of the Wax Museum was not critically well received upon its release on February 18, 1933. Though Curtiz's skillful direction garnered positive notices, the picture was unloved. The *Los Angeles Times* claimed that Glenda Farrell "will pass as the reporter, although I've seen her do better portrayals." *Variety* complained that the picture was mistimed and predicted that it wasn't going to be a big moneymaker. The *New York Times* called it "too ghastly for comfort."

Audiences disagreed. *Mystery of the Wax Museum* became a major success that ended up grossing more than $1.1 million. Curtiz was now in a much better position as a director. Most of his pictures reflected an increasing acumen, and their success helped guarantee the continued survival of Warner Bros. during the depths of the Depression.

Curtiz's own social drama with Mathilde Foerster continued to play out as he ceased paying the required child support for their son, Michael, that had been stipulated in the legal agreement of 1931. In early 1933 Foerster traveled from Europe to Hollywood in an attempt to get Curtiz to pay up. She penned an emotional letter to Jack L. Warner:

> As Mr. Michael Curtiz is employed in your studio I feel obliged to inform you about my case pending against him.
>
> From the enclosed documents you will see that Mr. Curtiz admitted paternity in court in 1923 and was held responsible for the support and education of his son in accordance with his means. In 1931, we entered the enclosed agreement, which he fulfilled until November 1932.
>
> When Mr. Curtiz stopped paying, I had to come to America to proceed against him. I left my son in a very good school in Germany, where we resided. They would have kept him on credit, until this case should be decided. But Hitlerism broke out, the child had to flee over the border to avoid anti-Semitic mistreatment.
>
> He is now in the care of Jewish charity organizations, in bad health, without any money.
>
> The trip and the legal expenditures have taken all my resources. I am a visitor in this country and therefore am not allowed to work. I earn nothing and can send nothing to my son.
>
> Mr. Curtiz is drawing a salary, in proportion to which it must be immaterial whether he pays $7 or $50 weekly for the support of his child. Nevertheless he refuses to send him any money at all, although he has not paid one dime since November.
>
> Furthermore he threatens to drag out this case as long as possible through unnecessary and malicious complications. By this action our son would be harmed mentally and physically for the remainder of his life.

Mr. Curtiz is perfectly aware of these facts but his only reaction is to calculate that I should be forced through necessity to accept the miserable amount of $30 monthly and thereby lose the right to ask for any more.

I cannot do this. But I also cannot let my child bear the consequences of this shameless cruelty and meanness, this legally disguised maltreatment.

Should Mr. Curtiz continue to leave his son in public charge in order to profit financially by this situation, it is not at all improbable that he might encounter the open protest of large Jewish organizations throughout the country. These organizations, which still believe in humanity, are in a position to judge his character by his actions.

I don't expect you to believe my statements without proof. My lawyer, Mr. Seymour S. Silverton, whose integrity is beyond any doubt, will certainly give you any wanted information.

I know, Mr. Warner, that you have children too. So I hope that you understand my attitude in this matter. I am acting in defense, not of myself, but of the helpless child in Europe who is Mr. Curtiz's son as well as mine.

It was a futile effort. Jack Warner was immune to familial sentiment. In 1958 the mogul would bar Jack Warner Jr., his only son, from the Burbank lot and cut him completely out of his life. It is unknown if there was a discussion between Warner and Curtiz concerning Foerster's letter, although the inclusion of the letter in the studio's legal files makes it appear likely.

In February 1933 Foerster's lawsuit made a brief splash in the newspapers but accomplished little else. Despite her assertion about the inability to find work, she managed to land a job as a reader and scenario writer at RKO. She sent for young Michael, who came to live with her in a Santa Monica bungalow while she continued her legal battle on behalf of her son. On October 9, 1934, Curtiz filed a cross-complaint in Los Angeles Superior Court denying paternity and requesting that Foerster's lawsuit be dismissed. He claimed that the original order of the Austrian court to pay 2,000,000 kronen amounted to only $45 or $55 a month by 1931. The director also stated that Foerster used fraudulent representations to elicit the $200-per-month support.

The judge disagreed with Curtiz's complaint and ordered a trial date

Mathilde Foerster poses for a wire service photo as she goes to court with her child support case against Curtiz in 1933 (author's collection).

set for December 1934. On December 9, 1934, shortly before the trial, Curtiz ended eleven years of contentiousness by agreeing to a settlement requiring him to pay $150 a month in child support for his fourteen-year-old son. The legal ordeal, particularly the denial of paternity, resulted in the two becoming permanently estranged. Michael Foerster recalled his arrival in America and the famous father who chose to ignore him:

> About 30 days after leaving Le Havre and the Europe that was about to be swallowed up by Hitler, I arrived in another world, in San Pedro, California. . . . My mother had rented a bungalow for 28 dollars a month which was a typical rent for a small house or apartment in the thirties, and we set up housekeeping. . . . My father paid us $150 a month child support, which at that time was a very nice middle class salary. Though, to put it in perspective, my father, as one of the top directors in Hollywood, earned perhaps $5000 per week. [Curtiz was making $2,000 per week in 1934.]

Although Michael and his mother managed to scrape along reasonably well, there were some painful moments, as Michael later remembered:

> One day in a Thrifty's drug store, my mother saw some movie people that she had known in former days. She ducked out, hoping they had not seen her. She was shabbily dressed. She began to cry because they were all successful and elegant and she looked so poor and down at the heel. They were *"shöne, elegante Frauen,"* she said, and that's what she wanted to be. She rarely showed emotion, so I remember the incident vividly. I too felt shabby and impoverished but I accepted it as my more or less normal state.

Michael's daughter Michelanne Forster offered her viewpoint concerning Curtiz's treatment of his oldest son:

> I think you can say that my Grandfather eventually met his financial obligations towards his eldest illegitimate son, but he never showed any generosity or warmth towards him while he was growing up. It was only when my Dad got out of the army, where he served as an interpreter in the latter part of the war, that [Curtiz] made a friendly overture, offering to get my Dad some kind of job at Warner Brothers. But by then the damage was done. No doubt the dynamic between my Grandmother and [Curtiz] had something to do with this breach between father and son.

Although further details concerning the relationship between Curtiz and Foerster that caused more than a decade of legal acrimony remain unknown, the director's treatment of his firstborn son appears heartless. Curtiz's record of providing financial support to his other "outside" children is unclear. According to Ilona Ryder, he sent money to his children's mothers when he could or remembered to do so. But when it came to his daughter Kitty, it was a different story.

The director sent for Kitty in April 1930, after she had completed her education in the convent and was living with Lucy Doraine in Berlin. The fourteen-year-old made the long journey from Bremen, Germany, on board the ocean liner *Europa* to New York and then by the cross-county train to Los Angeles. After settling her in Hollywood, Curtiz paid for private tutors, including language and singing lessons, while attempting to impose a degree of parental discipline that turned out to be a lost cause.

Kitty was a worldly-wise teenager who had grown up fast under the erratic parenting of her movie-star mother. She was indifferent to the dictates of an absentee father who'd had little to do with her upbringing and spent nearly every waking moment directing or preparing to direct films. Kitty enjoyed becoming acquainted with her new stepmother—it was impossible not to warm up to Bess Meredyth—but she was a fish out of water in Hollywood. In a press interview after she returned to Europe in an attempt to reignite her career as an actress, Kitty said she'd initially been excited about beginning a new life in America under the auspices of her father, but that her enthusiasm had quickly faded: "That happiness all but dissipated as soon as I learned my way around Hollywood. . . . It was not the life I desired: on one hand, the strenuous, fast-paced work, on the other hand, the excessive partying, and in that gap between the two, there is barely a break, a pause. I'd love to live a life that is more profound, more humane."

Kitty's mother also experienced difficulties adjusting. After she was touted as the next Pola Negri and signed a contract to make *Adoration* at First National in 1928, Lucy Doraine's movie career experienced a permanent dissolve. There were a couple of featured supporting roles, a bit part in *Hell's Angels* (1930), and her final screen appearance, in a German-language version of *The Trial of Mary Dugan,* filmed at Metro in 1931. Doraine's Hungarian accent contributed to her downfall in talking pictures by the age of thirty-three. Her personal life became erratic, including a series of divorces and a scandal involving her and her third husband being accused of attempting to extort six thousand dollars from Douglas Fairbanks Jr. After marrying a wealthy avocado grower in 1935, she dropped from public view.

Curtiz's life remained anchored at Warner Bros., where he spent the balance of 1933 directing several of the new stars who had been hired away from Paramount in 1931. There had been a gentlemen's agreement between the major studios not to raid one another's talent. As the Warners were not gentlemen and needed to increase the profits of their pictures with greater star power, it was a straightforward matter to sign William Powell, Kay Francis, and Ruth Chatterton to contracts that effectively doubled their salaries. Although the *New York Times* ran a story in large type entitled "War on Paramount by Warners Reported; Ruth Chatterton and William Powell Signed by Latter Firm, It Says," Paramount continued to do business as usual with Warner Bros. by lending out Gordon Westcott and Jack La Rue for Curtiz's next several features.

William Powell acquired his movie acting chops while playing mostly villains in silent films. His melodious voice and effortless screen presence proved to be perfect for sound productions. Powell's transition from scene-stealing heavy to sophisticated leading man was cemented after playing S. S. Van Dine's bon vivant detective Philo Vance in three Paramount films during 1929–30. Warner Bros. promptly put their newly minted urbane star in *The Road to Singapore* (1931) a dud, followed by *High Pressure* (1932), a sophisticated comedy directed by Mervyn LeRoy, and then the delightful *Jewel Robbery* (1932), in which Powell was perfectly cast as a fast-talking con man opposite Kay Francis.

Curtiz directed Powell in *Private Detective 62* (1933) and *The Kennel Murder Case* (1933). The former is a deft adaptation of a *Black Mask* magazine story. Powell plays a down-on-his-luck diplomat who is compelled to take a job as a partner in a disreputable investigative firm owned by a corrupt Arthur Hohl. After being financed by a gambler to frame a society dame (Margaret Lindsay), Hohl assigns Powell to do the dirty work; the outcome is, predictably, ethical rebellion, romance, and a denouement involving a murder frame-up that was a dress rehearsal for the *Thin Man* series. In *Private Detective 62,* Curtiz cleverly repurposed the unemployment montage sequence that he had used in *The Third Degree* (1926). The director had Powell negotiating endless stairs interspersed with inserts of fluttering overdue-rent notices and job rejection slips.

The Kennel Murder Case is one of Curtiz's more enjoyable films from the early 1930s. Powell plays Philo Vance for the fourth and final time in what is clearly the best outing of the popular sleuth series that totaled fourteen movies made between 1929 and 1947. By the summer of 1933, Powell was a major movie star and Warner Bros. wanted to remind everyone who had him under contract. *The Kennel Murder Case* opens with a moving searchlight on venetian blinds, which open and rise to display a Chinese vase with the bold credits descending: "WILLIAM POWELL RETURNS AS PHILO VANCE."

Powell's turn is a lower-octane version of Nick Charles. His elegant charm is a distinct improvement over the literary Vance, an arrogant, intellectual fop who wore a monocle.

A brisk tempo was an essential attribute for a murder mystery with a wordy screenplay. Curtiz retained much of the dialogue—the script was faithful to the book—without slowing the pace and was brilliant in employing barn-door wipes, split screens, dolly shots, and angled perspectives to accelerate the action through a rapid seventy-three minutes.

An emblematic example of the director's visual style is a sequence showing five suspects being fingerprinted. Curtiz depicts the first person bending over the squad room inkpad, then a quick wipe to the next person, then the next, until all five suspects are covered. Transitions are seamless: "Send a wire to the police and say . . ." then a quick cut to a cop reading the telegram out loud to a colleague. Another innovative aspect is the superbly crafted miniature of adjoining houses that illustrate a significant plot point. Although the solution to the locked-room mystery is revealed as a piece of mundane movie trickery more appropriate to a Charlie Chan picture, Curtiz presents it in such a manner as to make it appear as forensic reality instead of cinematic sleight of hand.

The Keyhole (1933) stars Kay Francis and George Brent in the first of their six feature films together. The movie, which begins and ends with the camera peering through a huge keyhole, has the familiarity of a well-worn high-heeled shoe. Brent and Francis fall in love with all of the attendant complications that Curtiz could cram into sixty-nine minutes. Most notable is the presence of Kay Francis. She projected an image onscreen that filmgoers found enrapturing. Tall (at five feet nine), Francis possessed the beauty of a Madonna. She became a major female movie star during the Depression years and was the queen of the Warner Bros. lot during the mid-1930s. She showcased the work of Orry George Kelly, Warner Bros.' chief costume designer. Although Orry-Kelly, as he fashioned himself, would dress many of the great stars of Hollywood in a career that thrived until his death in 1964, none of them was more extravagantly costumed than Kay Francis. In *The Keyhole* she donned twenty-three different costumes.

William Dieterle began filming *Female* on July 17, 1933, became ill after nine days, and was replaced by William Wellman. Wellman directed for the next ten days, until Jack Warner halted production. Warner screened Wellman's footage and reportedly disliked the performance of George Blackwood. Blackwood was cast as one of the numerous male employees whom Alison Drake (Ruth Chatterton)—the high-powered and vibrantly sexual CEO of an automobile company—invites to her house to first seduce and then exile to the firm's distant Montreal office.

For whatever reason, Warner uncharacteristically ordered scenes reshot using Johnny Mack Brown in place of Blackwood, along with some additional sequences to bolster what he considered a weak film. By September, Wellman was directing *College Coach*. Curtiz was tasked with the retakes beginning on September 3 and wrapped the picture ten days later. As a reward for reshooting in record time, Curtiz ended up with the sole screen credit, even though he directed little more than a third of the picture.

Although Chatterton's character conducts her business and love affairs in the imperial style of a dynastic Manchu empress, the screenplay transitions to her head-over-heels pursuit of Jim Thorne (George Brent), a proletarian engineer with traditional family values. The finale, in which Alison is resigned to marry Thorne and remain at home to have his babies doubtlessly enraged feminists. *Female* remains an interesting pre-Code film for its suggestion that a woman could be as professionally ruthless and sexually carnivorous as any male executive.

Although dwarfed by the rebound in musicals (Darryl Zanuck's final contribution to his former employer was the gargantuan proceeds garnered by *42nd Street* and *Gold Diggers of 1933,* which collectively grossed more than $5.5 million), Curtiz's pictures continued to reap significant profits. He still acted as the studio's directorial supernumerary, shooting ten hours of retakes on William Wellman's *The Mayor of Hell.*

From Headquarters was slated for Curtiz, but he managed to sidestep what he perceived a routine mystery programmer.[1] In a June 24, 1933, memo to Hal Wallis, he claimed the assignment would hurt his career: "My sole objection is that it is a mystery story following directly the "Kennel Murder Case." If I had the opportunity to do this late, I'd be glad to do it, but with two mystery stories right in a row, I am afraid I wouldn't do justice to the second one. Moreover, you would be labeling me as the "Dracula" director of Hollywood. . . . I'd appreciate it very much if I could be given a comedy or comedy drama to do in between these other two."

Curtiz wanted to counter any perception that he couldn't successfully direct lighter material. Wallis was amenable. He removed Robert Florey from *Goodbye Again* and assigned Curtiz to direct what was an early screwball comedy. It is a minor delight. Warren William sheds his reputation as a cad and stars as a celebrity romance novelist, Kenneth Bixby, dubbed "The Man Who Understands Women," who is on a book tour in Cleveland with his secretary-lover, Anne Rogers (Joan Blondell). Women are eagerly snapping up his books during a scene in a bookstore featuring titles including *The Boudoir Cloister, Ecstasy,* and *The Woman Who Gave.*

Julie Wilson (Genevieve Tobin) arrives at Bixby's hotel suite believing she is the romantic inspiration for the heroine in his latest novel after a long-ago fling. She throws herself at a bewildered Bixby, who isn't sure that he even remembers her. Julie's doltish husband, Harvey (Hugh Herbert), along with her younger sister, Elizabeth (Helen Chandler), and Chandler's snooty lawyer-fiancé (an amusing Wallace Ford wearing horn-rimmed glasses), all run around attempting to pry Julie away from Bixby for their own individual reasons.

Blondell was never better than in this film. She serves up smart-aleck palaver to William, who volleys it right back. Naturally, they end up together at the conclusion of sixty-six rapid-fire minutes. *Variety* got it exactly right: "Perfect for audiences of quick wit, but too slick for others." Fortunately, there were enough clever theatergoers who appreciated this amusing picture.

Despite his successes, Curtiz was becoming impatient. The director desperately wanted to make a truly significant film and resolved to do so. He aptly summarized his professional dilemma: "If I don't follow my head, I'm a shoeshiner."

Like the cowboy who feels fenced in, Michael Curtiz also decided he was tired of living in Beverly Hills and that he needed land—lots of land.

16

Home on the Range

It was originally Bess Meredyth's notion to sell the Roxbury Drive house and move out to the San Fernando Valley. A valley ranch had become Hollywood chic during the 1930s. Bob Hope, Bing Crosby, Clark Gable, Carole Lombard, and W. C. Fields were some of the notables who had already migrated to the rural environs on the other side of the Cahuenga Pass.

The valley at that time was a 222-square-mile mélange of bridle trails, citrus groves, farms, and ranches amid large tracts of undeveloped land. Encino resembled a stagecoach rest stop: its group of small buildings was clustered on Ventura Boulevard, and the main drag, Sepulveda Boulevard in Van Nuys, remained unpaved. Many residents got around on horseback. Automotive travel to the Hollywood studios was extremely hazardous. Sixty-four people were killed in traffic accidents on the mostly dirt roads of the valley in 1934.

Bess traveled to the western area of the valley to inspect a hilltop Tudor-style house on Oakdale Avenue, north of Ventura Boulevard in what was then Canoga Park (now Woodland Hills). The house reminded her of a Highland manor she had recently visited in Scotland while writing *The Iron Duke* for Gaumont-British Pictures. It was a brownstone manor that had been lavishly appointed by a Depression-era financier who was then residing behind bars; he had invested $250,000 in developing the twenty-five-acre ranch; 10 percent of the total was used for extensive landscaping and flowers. She took her husband to look the place over. Curtiz became rapturous over what would soon be called the Canoga Ranch. Curtiz and Bess forked over more than $100,000 to purchase the property.

As an impoverished Jew growing up in Budapest, Curtiz could have only dreamed of owning such a domain. The director found himself the master of an estate that would have been the envy of Count Kolowrat.

Curtiz could afford to live like a baronial squire. His Warner Bros. contract had been increased to $2,000 per week in March 1934. Considering that the average annual household income during the same period had fallen to $1,524, the director was a Southern California Croesus.

The Canoga Ranch became a secondary obsession. Curtiz and Bess oversaw numerous upgrades, including a polo field, stables for a dozen horses, a skeet range, and a photographic studio. (While these improvements were under way and the Roxbury house was already sold, Curtiz, Bess, and John lived at the Colonial House, a swank apartment building off Sunset in Hollywood.) He engaged Anton Grot to design a small guesthouse as an office for Bess. He also enlarged the kitchen to include a bar and added a garden between the back of the house and the large swimming pool, which featured showers and changing rooms. The house itself had a giant living room with a twenty-five-foot ceiling and a bay window at either end. According to John Meredyth Lucas, Curtiz usually sat at a desk in front of one of the windows to work on his scripts: "In my memory he is always there, making notes in his nearly indecipherable handwriting and unique spelling." The ranch eventually grew to include outlying barns with livestock plus a staff to help run it. Curtiz and Bess usually entertained on weekends. Instead of the large parties that characterized their tenure in Beverly Hills, there were more intimate gatherings around the pool complemented by skeet shooting or Sunday matches on the polo field.

Curtiz had become addicted to polo several years before he moved out to the Valley. After settling at the ranch, he hired an experienced hand to maintain his polo ponies and trailer. There were twenty-five outdoor polo fields in the Los Angeles area during the mid-1930s. Curtiz traveled on weekends to fields in the Valley and the Riviera Polo Field (currently the location of Los Angeles' Paul Revere High School) to play polo with Zanuck, Will Rogers, the writer Niven Busch, Walter Wanger, Paul Kelly, Leslie Howard, Johnny Mack Brown, Spencer Tracy, and Walt Disney, among others. The sport became so popular with the movie colony that several of the studios formed teams that competed against one another. The Warner team that included Zanuck, Curtiz, Busch, and others was called "Los Amigos." The hypercompetitive Zanuck became known for pacing around his office during story conferences while swinging a sawed-off polo mallet, working to improve his wrist action. After Zanuck left Warners to run Fox, he organized another team at his new studio and hired ringers to play for him.

Other than movies and sex, there was nothing Curtiz enjoyed more than polo (courtesy of the Lucas family).

Sunday polo matches at the Riviera drew a large number of paying spectators who, as Niven Busch recalled, loved to "watch us make asses out of ourselves." Curtiz had acquired an odd way of sitting forward on a horse in his Hungarian Army days and played polo from that position. "Now of course, he couldn't get back to hit, but he'd dribble, and he was a very good dribbler," remembered Busch. "But he was always riding up on his horse's neck and so everyone called him a pommel fucker."

Curtiz and Hal Wallis saddle up at the Canoga Ranch (courtesy of the Lucas family).

Polo was dangerous. Disney crushed several vertebrae after falling off his horse and sold his polo ponies in 1938. Zanuck's nose was squashed when his mallet ricocheted back into his face. Niven Busch recalled four fellow players being killed in a span of three years. The outbreak of World War II curtailed the huge popularity of the sport in Hollywood. After Zanuck returned from the war, he became a croquet fiend.

Despite his ungainly appearance in the saddle, Curtiz was a skilled rider and loved inspecting his land on horseback. Though he maintained his frenetic work schedule, Canoga Ranch allowed him some introspective moments away from the relentless studio grind.

The director wrapped *Mandalay* toward the end of 1933. After watching the prerelease cut in December, Jack Warner raved to Hal Wallis, "It is a hell of a good women's picture, in fact, it's great!" Warner went on to tell Wallis to make some specific changes concerning dialogue and plot along with "the usual speeding-up."

In referring to *Mandalay* as a "women's picture," Warner pigeonholed a movie that by the standards of the time was perversely explicit. The original leading actors had opted out: Ruth Chatterton refused the starring role of a prostitute and was replaced by Kay Francis. George Brent claimed he didn't want to travel to Stockton for ten days of location filming in November. Wallis decided to go with the reliable Ricardo Cortez. Also in the cast was Lyle Talbot, who reported that the *Mandalay* cast was chilled to the bone in their light tropical costumes during riverboat scenes shot on the nearly frozen San Joaquin River, which was doubling for tropical Burma. The frigid weather didn't prevent Kay Francis from modeling another stunning array of Orry-Kelly costumes, many of which appeared to be made out of surgical gauze.

Francis starred as Tanya, a White Russian refugee who is living on a luxurious yacht in Rangoon, Burma, with a gunrunner, Tony Evans (Cortez), as her lover. Shortly after professing his undying love to Tanya, Evans sells her to an underworld chieftain, Nick (Warner Oland), to settle a debt. After initially declining to join Oland's legion of nightclub hookers—who are highlighted by Curtiz in an eye-catching sequence—Tanya becomes a celebrated prostitute nicknamed Spot-White (a wag at the bar remarks that her name should be "Spot-Cash") who blackmails the British colonial provost for passage out of Rangoon aboard a river steamer to Mandalay. On board the boat, she falls in love with a ruined doctor (Talbot)—"We're two wrecked people who need each other"—triggering a climactic confrontation with Nick. The film proved to be a delightful distraction, particularly for Kay Francis fans, who savored her histrionics as a fallen woman who redeems herself.

Although *Mandalay* was beautifully filmed, Wallis chided Curtiz for shooting too much coverage and angles that he claimed were a waste of time. The director was simply ensuring that there was enough footage for the editor, but Wallis, always watching the budget, disagreed. Curtiz continued making the picture in his way. He ignored Wallis's cutting notes and didn't consult with him about any of the changes he made. The director must have thought he was back in France with Lili Damita when he added a racy sequence with Francis and Cortez. Wallis lost patience and sent Curtiz a lengthy memo:

> Your stuff is beautiful and I don't want to start limiting you and restricting you to shooting the actual script as you are doing such a good job on the whole. However when you show Kay Francis in the bathtub with Cortez in the shot and a close up of Kay Francis

in the tub and show her stepping out of the tub and going into Cortez's arms, then you get me to the point where I am going to have to tell you to stick to the script and not do anything else. For god's sake, Mike, you have been in pictures long enough to know it is impossible to show a man and a woman who are not married in a scene of this kind. The situation in itself is censorable enough with Cortez and Francis living together. . . . It is impossible to put it in a picture so why the hell do you shoot it and make it necessary to go back and make retakes or cut the scene so the charm is gone out of it. . . . I am going to have to cut the scene now with Cortez sticking his head in the hatchway in a close-up and Kay Francis coming into the two-shot with the audience ever seeing her, on the other side of the room and this is only because you do such god damn silly things.

Curtiz devised a solution that retained his risqué concept while mollifying Wallis and the censor. Cortez leans in through an open hatchway and ogles an unseen Francis, who is out of sight in the bathtub, and they exchange dialogue. The camera moves across the room to Francis, who has hopped out of the bath, obviously nude but with a towel wrapped around her, running to the hatchway. Covered with the towel, she stands on a platform and leans forward through the open hatchway to kiss and embrace Cortez. Cut to a side view of Francis's lower thigh down to her feet as the towel drops to the floor and the scene dissolves.

Francis's turn as a prostitute-poisoner nearly drove Joseph I. Breen at the newly created Production Code Authority (PCA) censor office round the bend. He loathed almost all the Warner pre-Code movies, calling them the "lowest bunch we have." An ardent Roman Catholic, Breen viewed the Code as consecrated doctrine. Administratively skilled and bigoted, he assumed a position of unrivaled power over film content as Hollywood's chief censor for two decades. With the ascendancy of a Democratic administration in Washington, D.C., eager to regulate the movie industry, the Legion of Decency's protests—including a circulated pledge for all Catholics to remain away from "debauching movies"—and an entity called the Motion Picture Research Council insisting that movies corrupted the minds of children, Hollywood studios had little choice but to acquiesce to a legitimate, self-regulating solution or have control of their product wrested from them.

In July 1934 the PCA replaced the good-old-boy Producers Appeal

Board, which had routinely overridden censor decisions. From then on, every film would be issued a PCA approval certificate; fines for noncompliance would be levied against producers and theaters. Pictures would be rigorously scrubbed of objectionable material during preproduction, and many pre-Code movies would disappear from theaters. Warners would be denied a reissue certificate for *Mandalay* in 1936, as Breen wrote to Jack Warner: "This picture also has the basic Code violation of presenting the heroine as an immoral woman." He also forbade the re-release of *Female:* "A cheap low-tone picture with a lot of double meaning, wise-cracks, and no little filth which they think is funny."

The major studios adjusted rapidly. Hal Wallis started to move the studio's emphasis away from Zanuck's front-page fare while continuing to grind out the programmers that kept Warner theaters supplied with new films.

Curtiz completed another pair of movies before the shift in censorship enforcement irretrievably altered film content. *Jimmy the Gent* (1934) was his first feature with James Cagney (his ten hours of retakes on *The Mayor of Hell* did not include any scenes with Cagney). Their extended collaboration would be hugely beneficial for both of them. On the part of Cagney, it was a relationship of decidedly mixed emotions: "Mike was a pompous bastard who didn't know how to treat actors, but he sure as hell knew how to treat a camera. He was one of those few directors who could, at need, place a camera where it would do the most good. So I give Mike respect there, and when you got through a picture with him, you could be confident that it was well done. But, as I said, he just didn't know how to treat actors. He left me alone because he knew I'd knock him on his ass if he didn't."

Among the New York stage actors who came to Hollywood during the early sound era, none of them had a more grounded sense of their own worth than James Cagney. His insistence on being paid in proportion to what his pictures earned, not to mention becoming one of the leaders of the Screen Actors Guild and fighting for saner working hours and standardized compensation resulted in continual conflict with the studio. Cagney's intense loathing of Jack Warner—he referred to the mogul privately as "the shvontz" ("prick" in Yiddish)—was mutual.[1]

Cagney's sense of fair play and social justice, developed on the mean streets of New York City, imbued him with a low tolerance for those he considered superfluous hacks. Most Warner Bros. directors apparently fit into that category, since, in Cagney's view, the majority of guidance he received was self-aggrandizing bullshit. Cagney thought Mervyn LeRoy was a phony self-promoter who married Harry Warner's daughter, and he dismissed the overbearing Anatole Litvak as a "natural-born asshole." The actor extended his respect only to those he believed actually earned it, primarily the actors, screenwriters, cinematographers, and crew. Curtiz was an exception. Cagney admired his abilities even as he disapproved of him personally.

In *Jimmy the Gent* Cagney plays a roughneck sharpie who is running a racket chasing down heirs of wealthy men who die intestate and is not above creating a fictitious relative in order to be paid a percentage of the inheritance as a finder's fee. In a visual statement at odds with his type-casting as a gangster, Cagney sports a bizarre haircut with the sides and back of his head shaved to bare skin, reminiscent of a Prussian field marshal. The actor also employed a Paleolithic-era New York accent littered with broken grammar.

Cagney rebelled further against his tough-mug persona by adding touches of humor and other bits of business that leavened his character while eliciting the consternation of Hal Wallis. Wallis complained to Curtiz that Cagney was "trying too hard to characterize" and not acting "in the typical Cagney manner," requesting that the director get the top star back on the desired track of playing a hoodlum. Apparently he'd forgotten that the movie was supposed to be a lighthearted farce. Curtiz, who approved of the way Cagney was playing the role, simply ignored the memo. Cagney carries the film with one of his most enjoyable turns. Produced for the typical Warner bare-bones budget of $151,000, *Jimmy the Gent* was highly successful.

The Key (1934) reunited Curtiz with William Powell. Under his Warner contract, Powell had the right to select one of three offered scripts from the studio. He chose an unusual romantic story set against the Irish rebellion in 1920. It was based on a London play of the same title that Warner Bros. purchased for the princely sum of $20,000 in October 1933. The working title, *Isle of Fury,* was changed back to *The Key* after Wallis became uneasy that the former might offend Irish moviegoers. The completed film avoided favoring either the British or the Irish by simply using the conflict as a background for melodrama. This technique of adapting controversial subject matter while not taking sides became a key element of Wallis's production strategy.

Powell portrays a British army captain, Bill Tennant, sent to Dublin to enforce martial law. He discovers his old army pal, Andy Kerr (an infernally taut Colin Clive), married to his former sweetheart, Norah (Edna Best). Powell and Best renew their passionate romance as she prepares to leave Andy—until the Irish kidnap him. Tennant arranges Andy's eventual release on his own authority. Although he is arrested and charged with treason, Tennant is content to have reunited Norah with her husband.

Curtiz had established a signature method of creating the opening shot in his films by fluidly moving his camera through a window, keyhole, banister, or similar obstruction to a close-up of a character or an object that established the theme of the picture. *The Key* opens with a Dublin clock tower tolling midnight and transitions as the camera glides through a rubbernecking crowd observing what is shown to be the order of martial law posted on a wall in extreme close-up. Curtiz then frames a two-shot of a Dubliner and his wife reading the notice:

Wife: It's a sorry midnight that clock is striking for Ireland.
Husband: It's not striking for Ireland: It's tolling for England!

Curtiz's fog-shrouded vision of Dublin is paired with the tried-and-true romantic triangle that is brought off effectively by the three principals. Although the *New York Times* praised Curtiz's direction, Wallis was less than impressed when he discovered that Curtiz, Robert Presnell Sr. (associate producer) and Frank McDonald (dialogue director) had rewritten portions of the script without telling him. Wallis put the hammer down: "I want you to stop this. It is god damn silly and I won't stand for it. This is final."

Wallis continued to elevate the studio's level of material when he assigned Curtiz to direct *British Agent,* based on R. H. Bruce Lockhart's 1932 book *Memoirs of a British Agent,* a best-selling sensation in England and the United States. The author was the British vice consul whose tenure in Moscow from 1912 to 1918 spanned the final years of the czarist regime and the chaotic establishment of the Soviet state under Lenin and Trotsky. His insider memoir, rife with criticism of his government's diplomatic missteps, his eventual misgivings about the Communist regime, and his love affair with a Ukrainian aristocrat and a probable double agent, was ripe for adaptation to the screen.

The preproduction of *British Agent* included a couple of novel ideas that went nowhere. Wallis toyed with the notion of engaging the great directorial romanticist Frank Borzage to helm the film before deciding to give it to Curtiz. Jack Warner attempted to negotiate with the Soviet government to be the first Hollywood studio to have a film crew shoot second-unit footage in the Soviet Union. In 1934 Joseph Stalin was beginning to shift his murderous focus to his Communist Party cohorts after concluding the state-sponsored collectivization famine of 1932–33 that killed millions of Russian peasants. Concealing the true nature of his regime was an imperative for Stalin, and Warner's request was denied.

Despite being confined to the studio lot, Curtiz wasn't handicapped, as he was given what was then a hefty budget of $475,000. He made the most of it by using forty-one different sets and a large cast, including a superabundance of extras—a Warner press release ballyhooed 1,500 people—for scenes depicting the fall of the Russian Provisional Government to Lenin's Bolsheviks. Emulating the visual military bravado in *Young Medardus,* Curtiz ordered more than three thousand rounds of blank ammunition discharged during street combat sequences, which filled the early summer air in Burbank with gun smoke.

He created some beautiful scenes, including an ornate diplomatic ball through which his camera beautifully glides before the setting is disrupted by machine-gun fire that destroys a series of mirrors. With his memories of the 1919 Hungarian upheaval still vivid, Curtiz strove to depict the Soviet revolutionaries of 1917 in an appropriate light. There is a sequence with a diplomat seeking out a Red Army officer for assistance. "I am glad I found you, colonel," the relieved diplomat remarks as the group strolls away into a misty fade-out. In the next scene the man is stood up against a wall with other inconvenient unfortunates and shot.

The British leading man Leslie Howard played diplomat Stephen Locke, a character modeled on Lockhart. The lissome clotheshorse Kay Francis as an aristocratic Russian-turned-committed Red, Elena Moura, who falls in love with Locke, initially appeared to be miscast. But Francis responded with one of her most appealing performances.

It was challenging even for Curtiz to condense the sprawling saga of the overthrow of the provisional government by the Bolshevists, Locke's fruitless attempts to keep the Reds fighting the Germans, and the attempted assassination of Lenin amid a romance-stained tale of betrayal and redemption. Although all this is shoehorned into an eighty-minute running time, *British Agent* manages to hold together nicely until the end, when, in the wake of Lenin's attempted assassination, Elena and Locke are about to be executed. After a trumpeting announcement of Lenin's miraculous recovery, a blanket amnesty is issued for all political prisoners. This denouement is capped by a sappy fade-out at a Moscow train station, where Locke and Elena exchange banal dialogue about chewing gum. The ridiculous finale mars what is otherwise an effective film.

Curtiz hit the ground running after *British Agent* in order to take an extended vacation. He and Bess had planned a tour of Europe that included a rendezvous with Darryl and Virginia Zanuck. According to John Meredyth Lucas, Curtiz's frantic departure to catch an ocean liner in New York was a scenario straight out of a screwball comedy: "As soon as Mike called the final 'Cut,' a studio driver rushed him to Burbank airport. The plane, slow as they were in those days, would cut two days off of the trip and get him to New York in plenty of time to meet Mother at the boat. Unfortunately, however, Mike got himself on the wrong plane. It was going to New York but with innumerable stops along the way and would arrive after the ship had sailed."

After realizing what had happened, Warner Bros. personnel sent telegrams to Bess and made telephone calls to the airlines and the office of Fiorello H. LaGuardia, the recently elected mayor of New York. The plane took a more direct route and a Warner employee, accompanied by a New York police escort, whisked the director from the airport to the ocean liner, which had departed with Bess on board after waiting a half-hour past sailing time. Curtiz was conveyed to the liner via a harbor patrol boat, jumped aboard the gangway, and stood with Bess at the rail watching a couple of seamen wrestle his luggage aboard. "Is not bad trip," offered Curtiz, "but I think so I like better the train."

After a stopover in Paris, Curtiz was received as a conquering hero when he and Bess arrived in Budapest. There were myriad banquets and public tributes as the couple was literally besieged by dignitaries, admirers, job seekers, and an endless array of relatives, including Curtiz's mother and siblings. After exhausting themselves in Budapest, Curtiz and Bess traveled to his secondary hometown of Vienna. He gave his wife a detailed tour of the city, and then the couple went on an extended antiquing spree to furnish the Canoga Ranch. Curtiz purchased a Meissen clock, an ornate candelabra, and Biedermeier furniture.

After Curtiz arranged to have his purchases shipped home, it was onto the train for Germany. He received another rousing reception, but Berlin was no longer the freewheeling city of UFA films and anything-goes cabarets. There were visible signs of Nazi-sponsored anti-Semitism, but the Nuremberg Laws abolishing German citizenship and basic human rights for Jews were not instituted until September 1935. Curtiz was a

Curtiz and Bess pose outside the Hungarian Parliament building in Budapest in 1934 (courtesy of the Lucas family).

celebrity foreigner who was allowed to travel unmolested. After several days in Berlin, he and Bess departed for the French Riviera.

At Cap d'Antibes they relaxed with the Zanucks. Twentieth Century-

Fox's chairman, Joseph Schenck, who had the gorgeous Merle Oberon in tow, joined them. Curtiz's boyhood friend Alexander Korda was also present. Korda had found the American studio system unsuitable for his artistic temperament. After four indifferent years in Hollywood, he divorced the volatile Maria Corda and returned to Europe in 1930. He founded London Films, produced *The Private Life of Henry VIII,* and reinvented himself as Britain's first film mogul. He eyed Oberon's apparent designs on Schenck—his former colleague at United Artists—askance: "She has him by the grip of death," Korda confided to Curtiz and Bess. "He buys her very expensive jewelry. I worry that he plans to marry her. She merely works for what she can get from him." Oberon was under contract to Korda, but the mogul secretly craved more than a professional relationship.

Curtiz was enjoying himself so much that on August 3, 1934, he cabled Hal Wallis for a short extension of his vacation, which was immediately approved. The holiday was capped by a gala banquet in Monte Carlo that Curtiz and Bess attended along with the Zanucks, Schenck and Oberon, Douglas Fairbanks and his fiancée, Lady Ashley, and other assorted glitterati. Korda continued his sotto voce diatribe about Oberon-as-gold digger to anybody who would listen. The evening climaxed with Schenck's announcement of his engagement to Oberon, followed by multiple toasts and best wishes from all present.

Curtiz and Bess departed Villefranche on the S.S. *Rex,* which docked in New York on August 8, 1934. By the time they arrived back in Los Angeles on the Golden State Limited, Schenck had dissolved his engagement with Oberon. Korda's Machiavellian strategy had worked. He was already keeping company with Oberon and married her in 1939. After Korda was knighted in 1942, Oberon became Lady Korda. When Bess remarked on the seemingly inexplicable shift in Korda's attitude toward Oberon, Curtiz shook his head, exclaiming, "Hungarians!"

The director returned to the studio before the end of the month, refreshed and ready to begin work on a new picture. Warner Bros. decided to address the volatile topic of industrial strife by synthesizing a play titled *Bohunk* by Harry Irving and the short story "Jan Volkanik" by Judge Michael A. Musmanno into a screenplay titled *Black Hell* that was earmarked to star Paul Muni.

Judge Musmanno was a former labor lawyer and ardent supporter of workers' rights. The son of a coal miner, he had been appalled by the 1929 murder of a Pennsylvania miner, John Barcoski, who was beaten to death by the Coal and Iron Police, a group of anti-union sluggers employed by the mining companies. As a state legislator, he worked with the governor to have the murderers prosecuted and all company-hired goons banned from the coalfields. The Barcoski murder and its aftermath inspired him to write "Jan Volkanik," for which Warner Bros. paid him $6,666.67 to adapt for the screen.

Wallis was leery about the potential reaction of the coal industry, whose trade association had already written to Will Hays complaining about the movie before it was even produced. Wallis subsequently told associate producer Robert Lord to tone the story down: "We could not deliberately set out to attack the coal industry and I feel that we should make all changes indicated by Breen, and if necessary, bend over backwards to eliminate anything unfavorable to the coal mining industry."

Wallis convinced Jack Warner to change the title from *Black Hell* to the less provocative *Black Fury* after the film began production. The miner Joe Radek is portrayed by Muni as a tragic figure whose fiancée, Anna (Karen Morley), runs off with another miner. Instead of the mining firm's unenlightened labor practices, it is Muni's morose guilt and fury that trigger his initial opposition to the company.

Contrary to the reality of the Barcoski case and the stark nature of Musmanno's story, the police goons led by the brutal McGee (Barton MacLane) are portrayed as a rogue force controlled by a group of racketeers. After McGee murders the head of the miners' union and wounds Radek, Anna reappears and helps her former lover out of the hospital. Radek bests McGee in a vicious fight and threatens to blow up the mine until the company comes to an agreement with the union that retains previously negotiated wages and benefits.

Black Fury was further cleansed of any possible controversy before it was previewed. The depraved conditions of the mineworkers are accurately depicted, but the mining executives are portrayed as honest-john businessmen upholding free-market capitalism. Byron Haskin, the film's cinematographer, sarcastically observed: "So an unnamed agency gets all the blame. The unions, the workers, and the management all come off like real nice guys." The final cut strengthened the burgeoning reputation of Warner Bros. as a producer of socially significant pictures while allowing the studio to avoid publicly aligning itself with either management or labor. Although the political straddling act didn't fool anyone in the know, it was noteworthy that *Black Fury* was made at all. However hypocritically, Warner Bros. addressed a subject that no other Hollywood studio would have touched in 1934.

Muni's cachet had skyrocketed with the smash success of *I Am a Fugitive from a Chain Gang* (1932). Jack Warner locked him up in June 1933 with a lavish contract of $50,000 per picture and no more than two pictures per year. Muni was allowed to continue working onstage and was also given script approval. He was touted as the studio's most esteemed actor—he would win the Best Actor Academy Award for *The Story of Louis Pasteur* (1936)—as Hal Wallis continued the evolution into more prestigious pictures.

A veteran of the Yiddish theater and the Broadway stage, Muni immersed himself in each role by studying every nuance of his character. During the filming of *Black Fury,* he read Louis Untermeyer's poem "Caliban in the Coal Mines" aloud every morning before departing for the set. Muni's wife, Bella, served as his drama coach.

Curtiz and Muni had an initial confrontation after the director advised Muni several times that he was overacting. When his counsel was ignored, Curtiz accused his star of behaving like a ham. Muni responded defensively that he knew what he was doing, "After all, I know a little something about acting. I've been on the stage for thirty years." Curtiz's calm riposte: "That is the trouble, Mr. Muni." Muni realized he should not be playing to the balcony, but to the camera and toned it down accordingly. He ended up appreciating Curtiz, believing that the director could be "light as whipped cream and deep as a mine shaft." Muni's performance as the tragically bewildered miner is one of the finest of his career.

In September 1934 Curtiz journeyed to Pennsylvania with a film crew to shoot second-unit footage for *Black Fury.* After meeting up with Judge Musmanno in Pittsburgh, they went to the nearby coalfields and directed the filming of the background sequences of the mining operation and its environs that open the picture. Curtiz terrified the cinematographer Byron Haskin after scrambling up a narrow ladder on a 150-foot-high coal tipple to indulge his yen for variant camera perspectives:

> He yelled, "Bunnie!" I looked up, and this bum is halfway up holding a finder. "A great shot from up here. Come on up and take a look." I said, "I can tell what it looks like from down here. It's O.K. with me." "No, you must come up and see." God, I climbed up on this damn thing, assailed by vertigo in the worst way. I almost fell off, getting up to where he was. I said, "O.K."— I didn't even look at the shot. He was satisfied and rushed down leaving me up there! By myself!

Curtiz and the crew inspected the mines and also visited the shack-like residences where the miners lived in wrenching poverty. Each house possessed a single lightbulb, and Haskin remembered seeing two children lying in a bed covered with flies. The coalfield housing reminded Curtiz of his childhood days in Budapest.

Curtiz wrapped *Black Fury* six days behind schedule. It was a technically challenging picture. Hal Wallis got upset about the lack of lighting in several scenes inside the mine set, which was a tunnel constructed on the Warner back lot. Haskin replicated the miner's hat lights by staging small spotlights around the set and having them manipulated by electricians following the movements of the actors rather than lighting the set in a conventional manner. It was an innovative approach that he convinced Curtiz would work, but the profiles of the actors were too dim against the pitch-black set. Curtiz had Haskin go back and use conventional lighting so he could reshoot several scenes. He was being pressured by Jack Warner to work faster than he possibly could. The conscientious Robert Lord interceded on his behalf:

> I know you are not satisfied with the progress Curtiz is making on *Black Hell*. But also, I don't think you quite realize what a difficult picture it is to shoot—I mean *physically* difficult. At least a half of the picture consists of fights, mob scenes, coal mining scenes, etc. Today, the company started in the mine set on the back lot. And, Jack, ten minutes on that set would convince anyone that working there must inevitably be tough and rather slow. It is small, cramped, dark, crowded with timbers, piles of coal, etc. Even the placing of camera and sound equipment presents a real physical problem. Don't take my word for it. Go on the set and see for yourself. I am convinced that we will have a great picture, despite all difficulties, if only you will be a little lenient and not hammer Mike until you completely discourage him. Please Jack.

The *Black Fury* company experienced an authentic disaster shortly before production wrapped. On December 4, 1934, a fire began in a machine shop adjacent to the mine set where Curtiz was filming (now the corner of Warner Boulevard and Avon Street). It quickly spread, and Curtiz led the cast and crew in an attempt to extinguish the flames. The studio fire department, aided by the Burbank, Los Angeles, and Hollywood bri-

Curtiz contemplates Barton MacLane leading a bunch of union-busting goons in *Black Fury* (1935) (courtesy of the Lucas family).

gades, battled the blaze; Dick Powell, Warren William, Helen Morgan, and Kay Francis manned the fire line until it was extinguished.

The damage was extensive. In addition to losing a majority of the back lot, sets, shops, and soundstages, a film storage vault that included many of Curtiz's pictures from the 1920s was incinerated. Jack Warner calmed employees and investors by quickly issuing a statement that the studio would use the Vitagraph and Sunset studios along with the undamaged soundstages to maintain film production while the Burbank facilities were being rebuilt.

A successful picture also helped offset the calamity. Jack Warner was ecstatic over the final cut of *Black Fury,* which had undergone an extensive editing and preview process for six months before it was released. The mogul praised it to Hal Wallis: "I saw *Black Fury* tonight and I want to go on record right now—in fact, I am sure—that this is as good a picture as *Fugitive.* It's really great."

The major newspapers largely echoed that impression. The *San Fran-*

cisco News raved about Muni: "It is a far more subtle performance he gives as the bewildered miner than he gave as the chain gang fugitive or *Scarface*"; it also praised Curtiz's direction. The *New York Times* was equally complimentary, calling *Black Fury* "the most notable American experiment in social drama since 'Our Daily Bread.'"

Black Fury and Muni's performance were inexplicably omitted on the 1935 Academy Awards ballot. Despite the snub, Muni finished second to the eventual Best Actor winner, Victor McLaglen, as a write-in candidate. It was the last year the Academy permitted write-in votes.

Black Fury was a defining film for Curtiz. He was handed his largest budget since *Under a Texas Moon* and entrusted with a politically sensitive subject starring the studio's most prestigious actor. His direction of the location footage in Pennsylvania created a realistic background. In addition to Muni's stellar turn, Curtiz elicited superb performances from a strong supporting cast, including MacLane, Morley, J. Carrol Naish, John Qualen, Tully Marshall, Akim Tamiroff, and Ward Bond.

The sole disappointment was that *Black Fury* did not become a box-office smash to match *I Am a Fugitive from a Chain Gang*. Even so, it grossed an extremely respectable $802,000. By that time, Curtiz was poised to direct a picture that would permanently elevate his professional status.

17

The Dream Team

While Curtiz was attempting to grab the directorial brass ring at Warner Bros., he was also coping with his daughter Kitty, who had returned to Europe, ostensibly to pursue her dream of becoming an actress. In the summer of 1933, Curtiz saw her off to Berlin with a large amount of cash and a letter of recommendation to study with Max Reinhardt. But instead of enrolling in Reinhardt's acting school, she reportedly joined a dance group as a chanteuse.

As soon as Curtiz discovered Kitty's change of plans, he desperately fired off telegrams to friends in Berlin and asked them to intercede to prevent her from signing a contract with the dance troupe. Kitty sent word back that she would do whatever she pleased and relocated to Budapest in January 1934 to work in a nightclub while avoiding her uncles and other relatives who lived there.

In an interview Kitty gave to Andor Váró (published in *Theater Life* on January 14, 1934), she represented herself as the manager of the Parisian Grill. Váró diplomatically questioned the veracity of her management credentials—he casually mentioned that she was being advertised merely as a jazz singer at the club—and she defensively maintained that her current singing gig was part of an orchestrated plan with her parents, who were helping her jump-start her stalled show business career:

> My mother, just like my father, the world-famous director, Mihály Kertész, adores me, and it's their desire to break away from my thus-far-decadent lifestyle and become a serious actress and find a prestigious job that fulfills my edgy nerves—and I admit my ambition. . . . My father gave Lucy $25,000 as an advance on my dowry. . . . My father came up with the idea that my mother and I should rent the Városi Theater. I don't want to list the fi-

nancial details now and our artistic plans, but I have to stress that our plans are serious.

Lucy Doraine wrote to her daughter: "Dear Kitty, I am glad to hear that you're willing to do some real work and that you would like to perform until our plans with the Városi Theater become true. I don't mind, do what you please. As for the matter of Graf K., I can only make this remark: I would be very happy if your marriage plans would be realized."

It is improbable that Curtiz would have had anything to do with leasing a theater in Budapest for his ex-wife and daughter to perform in, particularly after attempting to prevent Kitty from signing a contract in Berlin with a dance troupe. Kitty was interviewed again after moving her act to the Élysée Bar in Budapest. This time she vented frustration as the offspring of celebrity parents: "I got tired of being called 'Lucy Doraine's child' or 'Michael Curtiz's daughter.' I wanted to be somebody on my own! Hollywood was impossible. My parents were too famous. When I tried to get a screen job, directors would look at me and think: 'So you're trying to break in on your father's reputation!' Yet, I had ambitions and I think talents of my own."

Kitty also complained about social complications caused by her striking physical resemblance to her mother:

And the minute a boy showed interest, it was the worst of all. The next thing I knew, he would be saying, "How like your beautiful mother you are!" And if I introduced him to my mother—bang! The whole thing was off and he would be in love with her. . . . I was happy to have a youthful and lovely mother . . . but to have men admire me because I resembled her—how awful! No, I was doomed to be just a daughter so long as I stayed in Hollywood. So I went away and came here. Even then, they offered to help me—and a letter from my father would have eased things—but I didn't want that. So I started off on my own and was accepted at the Élysée and they're billing me as "Lucy Doraine's daughter"!

She left Budapest in February 1934 without notifying anyone of her whereabouts. A newspaper report said that one of her family members begged Kitty on behalf of her father to return to Hollywood. She refused and stated that she didn't care about either of her parents, and that if they continued to pursue her, she would renounce the use of either of their surnames. Curtiz hired a New York detective agency to track Kitty down. In May 1934 she was located working as a singer in a cheap cabaret in Athens, Greece. When she didn't appear for work one night, she was found unconscious in her hotel room from some type of "sleeping drug" and rushed to a hospital. Kitty's suicide attempt created an international wire service headline—"One 'Hollywood Daughter's' Tragic Fight to Save Her Soul"—while she continued to resist her father's entreaties to return to Hollywood. The article concluded: "Kitty, the pathetic career-seeker, dropped out of public view again after the Athens affair—and, no doubt, is pursuing the will-of-the-wisp of an independent career in a city, if she can find one where her parents aren't known."

Traveling to Europe to be with his daughter was apparently out of the question. Kitty's rejections convinced Curtiz that a forced reunion would be counterproductive. She eventually settled in London and enrolled in college, studying art. For her father, there were the films that had to be directed. The unrelenting schedule at the studio helped him shrug off any despondency over his daughter. Curtiz's facility to blot out personal relationships in order to maintain focus on filmmaking had been perfected long before.

He was briefly reunited with a star he hadn't worked with in more than five years. Al Jolson was cast for a final time at Warners in *Go into Your Dance*. Jolson's star power was fading, as was his marriage to Ruby Keeler. The insecure superstar overrode Archie Mayo by providing ad hoc direction to Keeler and quarreled over how many close-ups he was getting compared to his wife. Curtiz was brought in to direct six different scenes during the third week of January 1935 and returned on March 13 for a brief retake of Jolson and Joseph Crehan at the Vitagraph Studio.

Hal Wallis next assigned Curtiz to direct the Perry Mason mystery *The Case of the Curious Bride* in January, over the objections of the production supervisor, Harry Joe Brown. (All the associate producers who reported to Wallis were referred to as "supervisors" in studio correspondence and were not given screen credit by Jack Warner until 1938.) Brown wanted Alfred Green as director because he believed that "Curtiz goes in for more spectacular shots than practical ones, and *Curious Bride* needs a jovial sort of fellow on the set to keep the company happy and human." He went on to recommend that Curtiz direct *The Florentine Dagger,* a programmer mystery about the Borgia family, saying that the mundane project "really needs what Mr. Michael Curtiz could give it." Wallis refused Brown's request to change directors.

The Perry Mason series and other crime mysteries were a fresh initiative at Warner Bros.; the studio publicity department dubbed these films "Clue Club Pictures." Wallis wanted these features to be of high quality despite the usual lean budgets.

Warren William had debuted as Perry Mason in *The Case of the Howling Dog,* which was directed by Alan Crosland and released in September 1934. Suave without dash, with an angular screen presence at more than six feet in height, William was in the process of being repurposed from the leading pre-Code cinematic cad in prestige films to a debonair sleuth and leading man in programmers. A skilled actor with a resonant voice, William was the sole contractual alternative to play Mason after the departure of William Powell to MGM. He was a quiet, introspective man who loved designing and building things on his Encino ranch and held several patents for his inventions.

Wallis wanted *Curious Bride* to imitate the humorous chic of *The Thin Man* and *Forsaking All Others* (both 1934), another MGM film scripted by Joseph Mankiewicz. Curtiz took his producer's guidance and ran with it. *Curious Bride* is the most entertaining of Warner's six Perry Mason films. William's turn as a gastronomically inclined legal virtuoso who prepares gourmet dinners in his favorite Fisherman's Wharf eatery with his wiseacre coroner pal Wilbur Strong (Olin Howland) and his factotum, Spudsy (Allen Jenkins), is a delightful change of pace. Under Curtiz's direction, Perry Mason proves to be a clever protagonist who isn't above employing sneaky tricks to tie up the DA's office and the San Francisco Police Department in knots.

After his morgue gags in *Doctor X* and *Mystery of the Wax Museum,* Curtiz couldn't resist a reprise, including a close-up of shoes crossing a welcome mat at the entrance to the city morgue. *Curious Bride* unreels with verve, wrong turns, and a surprising denouement that eschews a courtroom scene (much to the displeasure of the series' author, Erle Stanley Gardner, who included a courtroom finale in almost every Perry Mason story). Gardner had ample reason to become dissatisfied with Warner Bros.' handling of the Mason franchise. Three different actresses were shuttled in and out of the Della Street role—Bette Davis took a suspension rather than appear in *The Case of the Howling Dog*— and the studio replaced Warren William with Ricardo Cortez, who was followed by Donald Woods. The studio used five different directors for the six Mason pictures, and each feature was less successful than its predecessor.

Curtiz used an unusual device to conclude sequences by having the camera go out of focus just before the cut. An annoyed Hal Wallis told Harry Joe Brown to have Curtiz stop it, as he believed this type of wipe-off was the province of Fred Jackman's special effects department, not the director: "Will you tell him that I brought this up again and this is the last time that I am going to ask him to cut it out. I am writing to you as apparently he can't read English, so will you explain to him in person."

At this juncture, Curtiz could read English passably and had an assistant to keep track of the stream of memos from the production team. He was simply ignoring Wallis, and that always got the executive producer excited in the wrong way. Wallis also nagged him about the number of times Curtiz was having Allen Jenkins "swing that blackjack around" because of his worry that the film wouldn't pass the review of the PCA and state censor boards. He also urged Curtiz to have Jenkins's character, Spudsy, played broader, for more obvious laughs. Jenkins continued to play the part as originally conceived, including twirling his blackjack during the opening credits. In the face of Wallis's relentless attention to detail, which spilled over into needless micromanagement, Curtiz selectively disregarded his dictates. Despite the success of *Curious Bride,* the working relationship between producer and director would become further strained by the importance of the pictures that Curtiz was directing. Wallis adored Curtiz's talented drive but was increasingly frustrated that he couldn't bend the director to his will.

In 1934 Warner Bros. purchased Teddington Studios, in southwestern London, and used the facility to produce lean-budgeted British programmers nicknamed "quota quickies." These pictures increased the number of Warner Hollywood imports that could be exhibited in the United Kingdom under a regulatory law. Irving Asher ran Teddington for Warner Bros. One day he spotted an Australian actor named Errol Flynn in a flop play and offered him a screen test. Flynn's test impressed Asher, who cabled Jack Warner about the young actor in October 1934: "Signed today seven years' optional contract best picture bet we have ever seen. His twenty-five Irish looks cross between Charles Farrell and George Brent same type and build excellent actor champion boxer swimmer guarantee he real find."

Jack Warner arranged to have Flynn make the journey from London to Hollywood. The publicity department initially touted Flynn as a native-born Irishman rather than an Aussie from Tasmania. Delmer Daves, then a Warner screenwriter, remembered the young Flynn appearing in the now-lost Teddington programmer *Murder at Monte Carlo* (1934) as a wonderfully good-looking man with seemingly little else going for him: "He seemed self-conscious. But he *was* the handsome man who was to conquer a few million female hearts, and he was signed based more on that attribute than any evident acting ability."

In his notoriously inaccurate autobiography, *My First Hundred Years in Hollywood*, Jack Warner claimed he not only saw Flynn's test, but also met him at Teddington Studios and "hired him on impulse," a claim not supported by any other account or documentation. It is notable that in Jack Warner's ghostwritten memoir, the name of Hal Wallis goes completely unmentioned. Wallis asserted in his memoir that it was he who told Asher to send Flynn to Warner Bros. Errol Flynn always gave credit to Jack Warner for his big break. Over time, the mogul and star developed an unusually close relationship. Although Flynn would periodically raise Warner's blood pressure with his salary demands and unprofessional behavior, the two got on. Warner couldn't help admiring the charming rake he nicknamed "The Baron." For his part, Flynn dubbed Warner "Sporting Blood."

Wallis wasn't initially excited about Flynn and appeared disinclined to cast him in any type of production—a curious reaction for someone who later claimed to have discovered the star. Flynn arrived on the Burbank lot in December 1934 and settled into a bungalow at the Garden of Allah in Hollywood that adjoined the dwelling of Lili Damita. He had become involved with Damita when the pair found themselves together on the ocean liner *Paris* steaming from England to New York in November 1934.[1] Their shipboard fling became a permanent relationship, and they married in June 1935. Busying himself with tennis by day and Lili by night, Flynn waited for the studio to cast him in a movie. After reportedly considering him for a small part in *A Midsummer Night's Dream*, Wallis did nothing. Jack Warner became fed up and eventually ordered that Flynn be cast in *The Case of the Curious Bride*. The mogul was not interested in a discussion as he made his feelings clear to Wallis:

> I overheard a typical Mike Curtiz–Harry Joe Brown squawk about not wanting to use Errol Flynn in *Case of the Curious Bride*. I hope they did not change you because I want him used in this picture, first because I think it is a shame to let people like Curtiz and Harry Brown to even think of opposing an order coming from you or myself and, secondly, when we bring a man

all the way from England he is at least entitled to a chance and somehow or other we haven't given him one. I want to make sure he is in the picture.

Wallis couldn't ignore such a categorical directive from Warner. Flynn was cast as the murder victim who is shown in flashback for about a minute near the end of the movie. He tussles with Donald Woods and is impaled on a broken mirror shard without uttering a line of dialogue. Several weeks later, Flynn got five minutes of screen time in the comedic programmer *Don't Bet on Blondes* (1935).

A convergence of circumstances, timing, and luck rapidly elevated Errol Flynn to the top tier of the movie star firmament. The Warner cinematic identity—founded on rapidly paced contemporary stories produced on the cheap—was transitioning. The studio would retain several of the key stars who helped shape the working-class personality of its films—James Cagney, Edward G. Robinson, Bette Davis, and Pat O'Brien—while casting them in pictures with different themes. With Wallis squeezing what was left out of performers such as Dick Powell, Joan Blondell, and Kay Francis, Jack Warner continued to sign new talent, including Flynn, Olivia de Havilland, Humphrey Bogart, and Ann Sheridan.

Warner Bros. would produce an increasing number of literary-themed, historical, and biographical pictures that were in keeping with the contemporary vogue and bore Hal Wallis's personal imprint. Wallis was a fervent Anglophile and history buff—his Sherman Oaks estate home was constructed and decorated in the Tudor style. Because these newer films were more complex and expensive, the Warner studio organization had to expand infrastructure and, above all else, control costs more closely.

As a result of the December 1934 fire that destroyed a significant portion of the lot, Jack Warner had a number of replacement soundstages built with increased capabilities, including Stage 16, which remains the tallest on the Warner lot. He reorganized the studio to centralize his control over operations. T. C. "Tenny" Wright was promoted to the key position of studio production manager. An ex-boxer, stuntman, and assistant director, Wright had been at the studio since 1929. Profane and shrewd, he was approachable and generally well liked by the grips, gaffers, painters, electricians, sound mixers, script clerks, assistant directors, and unit managers who reported to him. He became an integral part of the moviemaking process at Warner Bros. The associate producer David Lewis understood Wright's importance to the studio: "Tenny Wright was a very reasonable man. He respected quality and, if you showed him something, and he understood it, he would be of great assistance. Over many years his wisdom was invaluable to Warners and the quality of their productions."

Wright always had one of his assistants on the set or locale of every major ongoing production. This allowed him to react quickly to any production or script changes that required different scenery, props, or sets. Bill Schaefer, who was Jack Warner's secretary for forty-five years, believed Wright operated like an old-style New York ward heeler: "Tenny was a good Irishman with good sources, and that's how Tammany Hall worked. And I think Wallis resented it." Jack Warner also brought back the producer Bryan "Brynie" Foy and assigned him to ramrod the studio's output of B films. The dual-feature program was fast becoming the norm in American movie houses: 85 percent of all theaters were running double bills by 1936.

What this organizational revamp meant for Curtiz was that Wallis had more real-time eyeballs to scrutinize his every move. David Lewis, who learned his craft under Irving Thalberg at MGM and joined Warner Bros. as an associate producer in 1937, believed that "the studio was marvelously organized for quality and efficiency, where MGM had not been. The whole atmosphere, in spite of all the gripes, was conducive to the best possible creative activity."

The fresh talent, improved facilities, and revamped organization coalesced with the production of *Captain Blood*. The studio acquired the rights to Rafael Sabatini's novel in 1925, when Harry Warner bought Vitagraph Studio, which had produced a silent production of *Captain Blood* in 1924. In the era when *Treasure Island, The Count of Monte Cristo, The Scarlet Pimpernel* (released in 1934), *The Three Musketeers,* and *Mutiny on the Bounty* (released in 1935) were being produced at RKO and MGM, Wallis and Jack Warner believed that *Captain Blood* was a potential winner. Preproduction began in December 1934, and Harry Joe Brown was assigned to supervise the film under Wallis. Curtiz was overjoyed at being assigned the director in March 1935. Ever since the *Noah's Ark* debacle, he had been yearning for a major production loaded with people, action, effects—and the budget to support it all. Much as Curtiz wanted to be exclusively involved in every detail of *Captain Blood,* the director had to helm two other films while remaining engaged in preparations for *Captain Blood.*

Bette Davis would sue Jack Warner in 1936 because of her frustration over the lousy movies he kept putting her in even after she prevailed on the mogul to lend her out to RKO for *Of Human Bondage* (1934), which made her a major star. But *Front Page Woman* (1935) wasn't one of the pictures that specifically raised her professional ire. It is a rapid-tempo yarn about rival reporters (Davis and George Brent) who are in love, though Davis refuses to marry Brent until he admits that she is as good a reporter as any man. The picture was a typical Curtiz feature highlighted by energetic performances and superb camerawork.

Irving Asher struck gold again when he watched a five-year-old female prodigy doing a benefit show at the London Palladium. Sybil Jason was a native South African who could sing, dance, and do celebrity impressions. She appeared in a British movie, *Barnacle Bill,* and was preparing to return to Cape Town when Asher sent the film to Warner and Wallis. The duo believed they'd found their box office riposte to Twentieth Century-Fox's Shirley Temple phenomenon. A contract offer was immediately tendered to Jason's family.

Jason's Warner Bros. debut was *Little Big Shot* (1935) based on a story by Harrison Jacobs. It was almost identical to Paramount's *Little Miss Marker,* which was a month ahead in the preproduction process. Jack Warner considered suing, but his contracts attorney, Roy Obringer, pointed out that since neither studio had produced a viable film, Jacobs was probably the only person who could sue anyone; the result would be counterproductive.[2]

Instead of Sorrowful Jones accepting a little girl as an IOU for a $20 bet (the premise of *Little Miss Marker*), *Little Big Shot* confidence men Steve and Mortimer (Robert Armstrong and Edward Everett Horton) have lunch with a colleague who is ducking a gang of crooks and is accompanied by his little girl, Gloria (Jason). After gangsters kill Gloria's father, the two con artists attempt to place her in an orphanage before resolving to take care of her themselves while enlisting a heart-of-gold hatcheck girl, Jean (Glenda Farrell), to help them. Gloria's singing and spot-on impressions of Greta Garbo and Mae West buttress Steve and Mortimer's livelihood of conning suckers.

Importing a child actress from a foreign land might have been a delicate situation for the studio to manage. It wasn't. A trouper wise beyond her years, Jason was one of the few child actors of that era who actually enjoyed her work and wasn't intimidated by Curtiz's volatility: "Michael Curtiz was probably one of my favorite directors, but as brilliant as he was, he was a mass of contradictions. Quick to temper one moment, and yet very gentle and understanding in the next. I could see, young as I was, how very difficult it was for the adult actors to handle. But handle it they did, for they realized that the results of his direction produced excellent acting performances."

Curtiz's insistence on realism was again on display in *Little Big Shot*. A scene at an orphanage playground was scheduled for the studio back lot until Curtiz convinced Wallis to move the company to the grounds of the Los Angeles Orphans Home (later known as the Hollygrove Home for Children), located next to Paramount. A slightly older girl amid an assembled group of children from the orphanage kept bobbing around and spoiling the shot. After talking to the girl twice and imploring her not to move, Curtiz lost it after three blown takes. Jason remembered the director's rage: "The veins in his forehead and temples stuck out, his eyes got a wild look and his voice got loud and hysterical. All of this happened when that poor child moved ever so slightly once again. This time, she was so scared that she raced away from the scene and ran to the swings and slide area situated on the other side of the playground."

In her memoir, Jason fast-forwarded to 1972. After studying a Warner still of that group scene, a friend of the fidgety girl recognized her as none other than Norma Jean Baker, the orphanage's most famous alumna. This meant that Michael Curtiz was technically Marilyn Monroe's first film director, although he was probably never aware of it.

Beyond losing his temper at a future superstar, Curtiz resorted to a bit of physical abuse in order to wrap the picture. During the finale, Jason had to scream on cue and couldn't do it, despite multiple attempts. She remembered, "So much so did he believe in realism, that, earlier, when the assistant director suggested that the scream could always be dubbed in, Mike adamantly said no. Michael Curtiz got the realism that he wanted because he had borrowed a long hat pin from wardrobe and used my little buns like a pin cushion." Decades later, she viewed the director's technique philosophically: "Instead of being hurt, either physically or mentally, I was glowing with pride that I had actually let out a good, loud scream!"

Although the use of a hatpin on a child's backside enhances Curtiz's reputation as a directorial sadist, it is germane to consider the behavior of some of his contemporaries. Norman Taurog related the fake death of Jackie Cooper's pet dog in order to have the child star—who was Taurog's own nephew—sob real tears during the filming of *Skippy* (1931). A furious Cecil B. DeMille was prevented from striking Dickie Moore with a riding crop by a social worker during the remake of *The Squaw Man* (1931), and William Wyler reduced Marcia Mae Jones to hysterics with a ferocious rant on the set of *These Three* (1936). During Hollywood's golden era, directors and parents regularly resorted to callous tricks to get an emotional reaction out of a child performer. Although moral relativism is not an excuse for bad behavior, Curtiz was probably no worse than some of his peers when it came to directing children.

Little Big Shot was successful, but nobody confused Jason with Shirley Temple, who had no less a fan than President Roosevelt. Although Jason's talent was undeniable, her distinctive South African accent nonplussed critics and audiences. After making several features and shorts at Warner Bros., she left the studio and was out of the movies by 1940.

While Curtiz was selecting a hatpin to motivate Sybil Jason, Warner and Wallis were attempting to cast the lead roles in *Captain Blood*. For the part of Arabella Bishop, Warner wrote to William Randolph Hearst inquiring if Marion Davies would be interested in the part. Although Hearst had moved his longtime lover to Warner Bros. from MGM the previous year—along with her twenty-room studio bungalow that the magnate had built on the Culver City lot—the thirty-eight-year-old Davies was totally unsuited for *Captain Blood* and declined.

Warner's offer might initially have appeared to be an ill-advised entreaty that made Wallis reach for a bottle of bicarbonate, but it was actually a clever move. Warner arranged with Hearst to use his Cosmopolitan production company, which the press lord had established for Davies, as the flagship production entity for *Captain Blood*. This allowed Warner to garner additional publicity from Hearst's empire of newspapers and periodicals while offsetting Warner's financial outlay for the production.

Finding the lead actor for *Captain Blood* proved difficult. Although the trade papers announced in June 1934 that Warren William would play the title role, he was never under serious consideration. Borrowing Clark Gable or Ronald Colman from Louis B. Mayer was out of the question. Fredric March and Leslie Howard refused the part. Warner and Wallis eventually set their sights on Robert Donat, who had recently scored in *The Count of Monte Cristo*. Thanks to the ubiquitous Irving Asher, Donat signed a Warner contract for *Captain Blood* in December 1934. Jack Warner congratulated Asher with his typical hyperbole: "First, I want to thank you for the splendid part you played in getting Robert Donat signed up. I consider this the biggest thing done in pictures in the past several years."

The biggest thing in pictures quickly became a litigious mess when Donat attempted to back out for health reasons. Jack Warner took him to court. To Warner, a contract was a contract, even if the star of *Captain Blood* had to be wheeled into the Burbank soundstage on a gurney. After Donat's doctor attested that the actor's severe asthma would not allow him to perform, the contract was voided. There might have been other factors involved. Although Donat's medical condition was legitimate, Warner believed that the actor and Alexander Korda had double-crossed him in order to remain in England and star in Alfred Hitchcock's *The 39 Steps*

Preproduction had now lasted for six months and Warner Bros. still didn't have a star for *Captain Blood*. Or did they? The film's screenwriter, Casey Robinson, claimed that the inspiration for casting Errol Flynn came from Harry Joe Brown during the filming of *The Case of the Curious Bride* back in January. According to Robinson, Brown and Curtiz had a confidential chat with Lili Damita, Errol Flynn's soon-to-be wife, who was also a friend of Ann Alvarado, who would marry the mogul in 1936: "Annie says, 'Leave it to me.' Sure enough a week later, Harry Joe was called into Jack Warner; and we go in and Warner looked across that desk—I'll never forget the look he gave us across that desk. He said, 'Boys are you blind?' Do you know we've got the greatest Captain Blood right here under contract?' 'Who, Jack?' He says, 'His name is Errol Flynn.' And Harry Joe says, 'Only you would have thought of it.'"

Jack Warner might have been in charge of production at his studio, but the future Mrs. Warner was definitely in charge of him. The youngest of the brothers roused the ire of the entire Warner clan when he left his first wife, Irma, for Ann, a gorgeous raven-haired shiksa who had been previously married to the actor Don Alvarado (born José Paige). Although Jack Warner didn't marry Ann until January 1936—after Irma had charged him with desertion and filed for divorce—the couple had been living together since the end of 1933. Much to the horror of strait-laced Harry Warner, his younger brother was squiring Ann around to Hollywood premieres and parties; everyone knew who the de facto Mrs. Jack Warner was. If Ann mentioned something to Jack about casting Errol Flynn as *Captain Blood*, the mogul would have listened.

What doesn't add up is that if Warner selected Flynn in January or February 1935 during the filming of *Curious Bride*, why would the studio still be conducting screen tests of Flynn and other actors for the lead role five months later? By June, Wallis was having Mervyn LeRoy direct tests of George Brent and Flynn for *Captain Blood*. Brent's tests were poor, but Flynn showed promise. Wallis wasn't convinced and ordered Harry Joe Brown to shoot another set of tests with the recently arrived Ian Hunter on June 27. There was a final set of scenes with Flynn opposite a contract player, Jean Muir, directed by Curtiz, in which the actor performed scenes selected by Wallis, who emphasized the importance of getting it right: "Please let's not have any slip-ups on these series of tests, as the result of them will determine whether Flynn is to do the part."

The decision was made to proceed with a virtual unknown in the title role of Warner's most expensive film produced since *Noah's Ark*. In a letter to Irving Asher on July 8, Jack Warner summarized the casting of Flynn with the acumen of a prophet: "However we have placed Errol Flynn in the big role of *Captain Blood* and am sure Flynn will come through with flying colors. His tests are marvelous. If he has anything at all on the ball he will surely come out in this picture and go to great heights. If he hasn't it will be one of those things, but we will do all in our power to put Flynn over in grand style."

After a screen test with Flynn, it was decided to have Olivia de Havilland, a nineteen-year-old contract player, play Arabella Bishop. De Havilland had recently parlayed an understudy role in the Max Reinhardt stage production of *A Midsummer Night's Dream* that played at the Hollywood Bowl into a seven-year contract at Warner Bros.[3]

Her transition from Max Reinhardt providing nuanced guidance about Shakespeare to the fast-paced direction of Mack Sennett's former editor Ray Enright on *Alibi Ike* (1935) was the thespian equivalent of being drenched with a bucket of cold water. After reprising her stage turn in the filmed version of *A Midsummer Night's Dream* (1935)—a commercial letdown that took nearly a decade to earn back its $981,000 cost—de Havilland yearned for professional recognition in meaningful pictures. Warner Bros. would never be the place for her to realize her ambitions. For the time being, she contented herself with financial security and long hours while mastering her craft.

Production began on *Captain Blood* on August 7, 1935. The stakes were high for everyone concerned, but especially for Hal Wallis. It would be his most significant production since taking over for Zanuck, and he was determined to make good. Despite any initial misgivings he had about Errol Flynn, Wallis was fully committed to the actor's success. Adding pressure was Jack Warner's order that the picture be brought in at under $1 million. Wallis would manage *Captain Blood* down to the last detail. Both his ego and his ambition demanded that the picture bear his personal stamp. Wallis informed Harry Joe Brown and Curtiz that there would be zero tolerance of anything less than verbatim adherence to the approved script and his orders. Curtiz dismissed the directive as typical front-office huffing and puffing. He believed that he would wring a credible performance out of Flynn while directing the film in his own way.

Although shooting in sequence was anathema to Wallis, *Captain Blood* proceeded in approximate lockstep with Casey Robinson's script. The early scenes with Flynn as Dr. Peter Blood being sentenced to death for treating a wounded Lord Gilroy and, after commutation, being shipped as a slave to Port Royal, Jamaica, were inconsistent. Flynn's acting was erratic. When he tensed up, the neophyte performer was sweating and nervous, his jaw clenched and the action stilted. When he relaxed and let himself go, he commanded the scene with star magnetism. One week into production, Wallis complimented Curtiz but nudged him to pay more attention to Flynn and advised him to decrease what he considered excessive camera movement:

> Your last two days dailies have been excellent. The action and the photography and composition are all fine. . . . I would cut down on the use of dollies unless they are necessary for the action. . . . I think Flynn is doing very well, except that in the courtroom I thought you played him down a little too much. . . . It seems to me you could have gotten a little more fire in him. . . . He plays a little too much in a monotone . . . so, in your direction, give him a little more of this action and let him have a little more fire.

The problems were not due to a lack of effort on Flynn's part. Although Curtiz was saddled with a novice actor who wasn't inclined to exert himself at anything that wasn't adventurous fun, Flynn was eager to cash in on his golden opportunity. "I worked as hard as I knew how," he wrote in his memoir. At one point, when the actor was weakened by a recurrence of malaria picked up during his roustabout days in New Guinea, he gulped down a large amount of brandy and kept going. Other than this episode, Flynn remained sober and deadly serious.

At one point, Curtiz exhorted Flynn, "You are thrilled, excited! Let me see the tinkle in your eye." According to de Havilland, the director's approach to eliciting a performance wasn't exactly an exercise in confidence building: "He [Flynn] wanted to be a success so badly and when we

Hal Mohr, Errol Flynn, and Curtiz on the set of *Captain Blood* (1935) (author's collection).

sat in that screening room to look at the first dailies, Mike ridiculed the footage unmercifully. And Errol did nothing, there was nothing he could do, not then when he was starting, but I could feel the hurt for him on the other side of the room."

Curtiz's brutal critique of a raw Errol Flynn, in order to shape his performance—a philosophy in keeping with his view of actors as directors' marionettes—would end up paying immediate dividends. But it would also eliminate any possibility of a collaborative relationship between the director and his soon-to-be star. Flynn quickly tired of Curtiz's autocratic demeanor and channeled his frustration into mastering his performance. As the second month of shooting began, his line readings exuded more authority, although Wallis continued to fret about his looking scared to death at the beginning of several scenes. He also believed that de Havilland lacked spark and had Curtiz reshoot her initial meeting with Flynn at the Port Royal slave market. Wallis had Curtiz move the two stars away from the large group of actors and extras assembled on the slave block and get more close-ups of both of them. The retake was considerably better.

Flynn improved so quickly that before the end of the production schedule, Curtiz was authorized to reshoot a number of the actor's earliest scenes in order to improve the picture. One key retake of the enslaved Flynn stealing a kiss from de Havilland on location in Palm Springs was rewritten by Casey Robinson and shot two weeks after the company had finished production at the end of October. As Flynn and de Havilland got their feet under themselves in *Captain Blood,* there was an undeniable sexual chemistry. Wallis caught on to it late in the production and pushed Curtiz to capture it on film.

Aside from insisting on spontaneity from Flynn and the other actors, Wallis grew furious about Curtiz's predilection for altering wardrobe and props, adding or changing dialogue, and dropping or creating new scenes. There was a profound disagreement between producer and director over the visual concept of the picture. Wallis wanted to cut back and forth with a greater amount of close-ups of the actors as they were speaking or reacting to dialogue in order to advance the narrative. He was not unjustified in believing that Curtiz was emphasizing visual composition and camera movement at the expense of the story.

Wallis peppered the director with angry memos—too many bowls of fruit and candlesticks in the foreground of shots, not enough people in the hold of the slave ship, the dizzying movement of the camera to simulate the rocking of the ship, the changing of dialogue in the script, not enough close-ups of Flynn—until finally exploding:

> I have talked to you about four thousand times, until I am blue in the face, about the wardrobe in this picture. I also sat up here with you one night, and with everybody else connected with the company, and we discussed each costume in detail, and also discussed the fact that when the men get to be pirates that we would not have "BLOOD" dressed up. Yet tonight, in the dailies, in the division of the spoils sequence here is CAPTAIN BLOOD with a nice velvet coat, with lace cuffs out of the bottom, with a nice lace stock collar and just dressed exactly opposite to what I asked you to do. . . . What in the hell is the matter with you and why do you insist on crossing me on everything I ask you not to do? What do I have to do to get you to do things my way? I want the man to look like a pirate, not a molly-coddle. You have him standing up

here dealing with a lot of hard-boiled characters, and you've got him dressed up like a God-damned faggot. . . . You get one good day's dailies and then you go all to hell again and do everything ass backwards. . . . I suppose that when he goes into the battle with the pirates (the French) at the finish, you'll probably be having him wear a high silk hat and spats. . . . Don't have him dressed up like a pansy!

Wallis concluded that he would personally approve all further Flynn costumes and ordered Curtiz to leave the set and see him immediately so the producer could discover "why it is that you insist on doing things that I tell you not to do."

There is no record of the subsequent conversation, just as there was no noticeable change in Flynn's costumes. The film opened with Peter Blood as a gentleman doctor in a fancy robe, and that image was maintained after his transition from slave to pirate was completed. Flynn continued to be garbed in a long coat with cuffs in several other scenes, to no appreciable detriment.

Curtiz continued to ignore Wallis. In a September 5 interoffice communiqué akin to a papal bull, Wallis ordered Curtiz to immediately cease changing dialogue in the script without his approval. He specifically directed Curtiz to reshoot a scene in which the character of Don Diego (Pedro de Cordoba) recited a line of dialogue concerning the Spanish conquest of Port Royal. In his memo, Wallis annotated what was in the script and what Curtiz shot that was slightly different, and he added a sentence for clarification. Wallis's directive to reshoot was disregarded, and the scene remained in the final cut as Curtiz filmed it.

The vitriolic memoranda were less about what was best for *Captain Blood* and more an expression of impotent frustration by Wallis, who discovered that he could not control every nuance of the production from his office. Curtiz eventually reacted to being continually lambasted, but in a manner contrary to what Wallis wanted. Although he had often and would later be accused of overshooting and wasting film, the director uncharacteristically shot several scenes with less coverage than normal. By resorting to cutting in the camera, he left little opportunity for the editor to construct the scenes differently. Curtiz was also responding to the ceaseless urging from Jack Warner, who wanted him to move along faster, as the picture was behind schedule. There is no indication that the constant barrage of criticism from Wallis disheartened the director; it simply made him more determined.

Curtiz imbued *Captain Blood* with as much realism as he could muster, particularly in the Port Royal slavery scenes. There is a detailed sequence of a man being branded with a hot iron, the flogging of Jeremy Pitt (Ross Alexander), and overseers whipping slaves who are chained to a large milling wheel, the mayhem being overseen by a vile Colonel Bishop (Lionel Atwill). Wallis was leery about the violence, but most of it made it through the Breen office. After Robert Lord watched a preliminary cut of the film, he wrote Wallis a withering note: "Why do you have so much flogging, torturing and physical cruelty in *Captain Blood*? Do you like it? Does Mike like it or do you think audiences like it? Women and children will be warned to stay away from the picture—and justly so."

Wallis seemed more concerned about why Curtiz was filming the shirtless older pirates with hairy potbellies. The final battle sequence of Blood's crew vanquishing a squadron of French vessels off Port Royal was magnificently staged despite Wallis's fretting about too much gun smoke from the shipboard cannons obscuring the background. With cutlass in hand, Blood clips off rousing dialogue in close-ups that would have sounded like clichés if uttered by almost any other actor. Jack Warner's instincts were spot-on: a star had been born in a single film. *Captain Blood* consecrated Errol Flynn as the greatest movie swashbuckler since Douglas Fairbanks. The picture also gave an immediate lift to the career of Olivia de Havilland. Hal Wallis might have referred to her as "the girl" in his memoranda but her onscreen synergy with Flynn made them a bankable team. Even though the picture does not hold up as well when compared to Curtiz's subsequent swashbucklers with Flynn—the budget limitations are obvious at times—its energy still shines.

What cinched the *Captain Blood* magic was the musical score, composed by Erich Wolfgang Korngold. Jack Warner may have scrimped in certain arenas, but the music department, headed by former Vitaphone orchestra conductor Leo Forbstein, wasn't one of them. The addition of Korngold initiated the transformation of what was essentially a nightclub band into an accomplished orchestra staffed by world-class musicians. By the time the composer Max Steiner and orchestrator Hugo Friedhofer (the future recipient of the Oscar for *The Best Years of Our Lives* score in 1946) joined Warner Bros. in 1937, the studio had created a music department that became the gold standard. Korngold wasn't nearly as prolific as Steiner, but his lavishly orchestrated scores added an exquisite veneer of

Curtiz rides the camera dolly while filming the *Captain Blood* slavery sequences as Guy Kibbee, Errol Flynn, and Robert Barrat look on (author's collection).

emotion that perfectly complemented several of Curtiz's most prestigious films. The two composers shared a similar quick wit that transcended their amiable professional rivalry.[4]

To the relief of Jack Warner, Curtiz brought in *Captain Blood* in at a cost of $995,000. A smash hit, it grossed more than $2.7 million. The picture was nominated for five Academy Awards: Best Picture, Best Director, Best Screenplay, Best Sound Recording, and Best Musical Score. Although it didn't win, it was evident that Warner Bros. had assembled a dream team of producer, director, and star. Wallis's frustration over Curtiz's stubbornness quickly receded as they both basked in the glow of success. Now, if only the executive producer, the director, and their newest star could all get along on their *next* picture.

18

The Reason Why

After *Captain Blood,* Curtiz was assigned a programmer that became an effective film. *The Walking Dead* initially appeared to be another half-hearted effort to cash in on the horror genre. Wallis expected Curtiz to bring it in on an eighteen-day schedule that was unrealistic because of the number of setups required. There was also the attention to detail lavished by Curtiz, most notably the nearly eight hours he took to perfect the lighting for a brief close-up of Boris Karloff's face as he returns to life on an operating table. The production closed five days behind schedule, on December 21, 1935; three days of added scenes and retakes were shot on January 6 through 8.

In the five years since he had played a bit part in *The Mad Genius,* Karloff had become a star in *Frankenstein,* followed by a series of successful Universal horror films. He was signed for the lead role in *The Walking Dead* at $3,750 a week with a four-week guarantee. Karloff later remembered that Curtiz appeared to hesitate after their initial interview back in 1931, yet hired him anyway. On *The Walking Dead* set, Curtiz explained his earlier behavior to the very British actor: "The reason I called you in [for *The Mad Genius*] was because I thought you actually were a Russian. Your name is Karloff—it certainly sounds Russian. When you came in, you seemed so anxious to get the job that I decided to let you have it."

The Walking Dead proved an auspicious reunion of actor and director. It is a well-designed parable about the meaning of death, in which Boris Karloff projected the eerie pathos that transfixed audiences of his Universal horror films. Frank S. Nugent, never a fervent admirer of the genre, wrote in the *New York Times,* "Horror pictures are a staple commodity, and this one was taken from one of the better shelves."

Warner Bros. hired Irving Rapper as a dialogue director, and he thus began a long-term relationship with Curtiz beginning with *The Walking*

Curtiz directs Boris Karloff in *The Walking Dead* (1936); Hal Mohr is perched on the dolly wheel (courtesy of the Lucas family).

Dead.[1] Some studios combined the tasks of the dialogue director and the script supervisor into a single job function. Warners didn't. The studio assigned specialty clerks on each set to annotate the script for continuity and editing. It was useful for Curtiz to have a skilled dialogue director on hand, particularly when the actors became befuddled by his Hungarian-laced syntax.

Articulate, British-born, and gay, Rapper arrived from the New York stage after a brief stop at MGM. He hit it off immediately with the rough-hewn Hungarian director, who loudly abused English and considered a lunch-hour tryst with an ingénue a part of a typical workday:

He came into the office, very Hungarian, spoke with a heavy accent, adjusted his tie like George Raft and that hat. "Irving, I hear you are genius for Broadway and Forty-second Street." I knew immediately there was a sympathetic chord there. "If you answer me one question right, you have the job." So I guess there was a good job sold on me and I said, "What's the question?" "Have you ever worked with a Hungarian before?" I said, "I worked with the greatest Hungarian in the world." "What the hell you mean? Who is this?" I said, "Ferenc Molnár; we did all his plays." And he smiled like this and said, "Here's the script, tell me what stinks in it and you're my boy."

Rapper worked with Curtiz on nine films. Although he humorously complained at one point, "I have developed cauliflower of the Eustachian tubes listing to the demoniac Magyar explanations," he revered Curtiz as "a great, great director." Rapper, who became a gifted director in his own right with *Now, Voyager* (1942) and *Deception* (1946), extolled the man he would call his mentor:

Michael Curtiz was the most sympathetic man I ever worked with, and I owe a great deal to him . . . in spite of the fact that he murdered the English language and [was] full of malaprops all the time, which made the people hysterical, so they never got angry at him. He was rather rough and severe. But by the time they deciphered what he meant, they lost their anger. Mike had a sharp ear for what sounded [good]. . . . He could tell what sounded right immediately. And of course his expertise with the camera was terrific.

Curtiz's ability to take charge of any film with virtually no advance preparation had become a notable strength. He continued to be rushed into the breach whenever something had to be done in a pinch.

Wallis produced another hit with *Anthony Adverse,* the studio's biggest-budgeted film to that date. The picture was based on an elephantine best seller about an eighteenth-century English foundling who rises to business prominence amid global adventures and familial melodramatics. When the film's director, Mervyn LeRoy, asked Jack Warner if he had read the novel, the mogul wisecracked, "Read it? I can't even lift it!" With seventy-eight speaking parts, period costumes, and costly sets, *Anthony Adverse* would prove to be a long and complex shoot: seventy-two days and a final cut that ran for 141 minutes. The box-office payoff was big, and the picture won four Oscars.

Curtiz was assigned to direct *Anthony Adverse*'s opening shot on the final day of the original sixty-day production calendar. Jack Warner, close to a panic attack because of the ballooning budget, ordered Wallis to use whoever was available to finish the picture immediately. On February 3, 1936, Curtiz dutifully traveled up to the Santa Susana Pass with four doubles, eleven extras, and five horses, and had the scene in the can by the end of the day. He pitched in with even greater alacrity than usual, as he was attempting to convince Wallis to let him direct *The King's Guard*. Based on a poem by Alfred, Lord Tennyson, and eventually titled *The Charge of the Light Brigade,* the picture was designed as a follow-on vehicle for Errol Flynn and Olivia de Havilland and to emulate the success of *Captain Blood* and Paramount's *The Lives of a Bengal Lancer* (1935).

The script for *Light Brigade* by Rowland Leigh and Michel Jacoby was historically ludicrous even by Hollywood standards. The famous charge at the climax of the Crimean War was linked to the British 27th Lancers regiment stationed in India, which was seeking revenge against Amir Surat Khan of Suristan in northwest India, who allied himself with Imperial Russia and slaughtered the British garrison at Chukoti, including the regiment's dependents. A revenge-obsessed Geoffrey Vickers (Flynn) discovers that the amir has fled India and is at the Russian lines at Sebastopol opposite Vickers and the 27th. He forges a written order from the British commander that allows him to lead the brigade's impossible charge against the well-fortified Russian positions. Vickers and the amir die on the battlefield as Tennyson's poem is emblazoned on the screen. The charge is portrayed as turning the tide of the Crimean War.

It was absolute applesauce. The amir, Suristan, the 27th Lancers, and Chukoti were fictional entities. The charge occurred in 1854 against the Russians during the Battle of Balaclava. Sebastopol was under siege until the following year and had nothing whatsoever to do with the charge. The actual charge was an ignominious blunder that accomplished nothing other than the useless killing of several hundred British soldiers. The script's contrivance of an evil Indian amir who initiated a treacherous massacre and ended up allied with Russians during the Crimean War was a fantasia that established the British Raj theme of the film, with which Wallis sought to replicate the success of *The Lives of a Bengal Lancer.*

The anglophile in Wallis fretted about the grotesque historical inaccuracies: "If we are to save ourselves from a lot of grief and criticism in England, we must make our picture [as] historically accurate as possible." But it was too late to worry about truthfulness and the possibility of hurt feelings across the Atlantic Ocean. The cast was assembled, the sets were being built, and the script was written. Wallis settled for opening the film with a detailed disclaimer that declared that the story and historical events were fictionalized.

Eager to direct an epic with spectacular battle sequences in multiple locations, Curtiz begged for the assignment. Wallis let him sweat it out a while. The executive producer used Frank Borzage as a stalking horse to extract a promise from Curtiz to stick to the script and follow orders. Curtiz pledged total obedience, then reneged as soon as the cameras rolled.

He shot himself in the foot with Jack Warner by reinforcing the perception that he wasn't overly concerned about the script. Warner recounted to Wallis a luncheon conversation he had with Curtiz about the forthcoming epic:

> All he [Curtiz] talked about were the sets and that he wants to build a fort somewhere else, and all a lot of hooey. I didn't hear him say anything about the story. In other words, he's still the same old Curtiz—as he always will be! Bischoff was there at the time, and I told him that we don't want to go any place for the fort or any other locations other than the ones you have already picked out, so for Lord's sake, get ahold of Mike and set him on his prat and let him make the story and not worry about the sets. Let the Art Director worry about this; he's getting paid for it.

It was as if Curtiz believed he was still at Phönix-Film in Budapest or lunching with Count Kolowrat. Warner was running the most efficient movie factory in the world. He wanted Curtiz to direct *Light Brigade* and wasn't interested in any of his ideas about production design and sets, particularly if they would cost additional money.

Wallis, Curtiz, and the rest of the production team mapped out the script with specific scenes scheduled for Lone Pine, Lake Sherwood in Ventura County, Lasky Mesa, and Chatsworth, out in the San Fernando Valley. Before he headed up to Lone Pine, Curtiz added to the list of pre-approved sequences. He wanted to reinstate a horse stampede and a guerrilla attack that Wallis had previously removed. Tenny Wright cautioned that these additions would cost more money, but Curtiz got his way and the guerrilla attack was reinstated. The horse stampede was "restored" by inserting stock footage of running horses obtained from Futter Studios in a film-swap deal.

After reading the script, Curtiz was dismayed by the dull wrap-up.

He laid out his concerns to Wallis: "I know in my heart, you must feel as I do, that after a terrific climax, it would be dangerous to allow the story to end in a conversation between two old characters. I beg you to consider seriously my suggestions, knowing that we must find a more effective ending." Curtiz and Irving Rapper wrote a thoughtful finale with a lap dissolve from the dead Errol Flynn on the battlefield to a debate in the House of Commons decrying the military disaster, which culminates in Benjamin Disraeli's saving the day with a stirring speech, stating that "our bitter rancor, gentlemen, will not resurrect our dead." The scene shifts to a parade scene of the 27th Brigade in which Lord Raglan presents a posthumous Victoria Cross to Flynn for the final fade-out.

Wallis responded courteously to Curtiz but refused to use the proposed ending. Ego may have played a part, but in the end, it was about money. The executive producer was not about to build another set or hire more actors for a newly conceived ending with production already under way. Wallis even attempted to obtain footage from *The Lives of a Bengal Lancer* to save money on *Light Brigade*, but Paramount turned him down.

Although the *Light Brigade* would be a beautifully shot picture, it certainly didn't appear that way to Wallis shortly after the start of production. He was determined to curtail Curtiz's peccadilloes before the picture progressed too far to stop him. Curtiz immediately indulged his habit of changing approved wardrobe after adding a clutch of white egret feathers to Surat Khan's (C. Henry Gordon's) turban. Wallis had the scene filmed over again and threatened to fire Curtiz off the picture: "I'm not going to suffer through this picture with him like I did on *Captain Blood* and I am not going to fight him all the way through."

After discussing in detail with Curtiz what was needed before the director went to Lasky Mesa to film the Chukoti fort sequences, Wallis previewed the initial dailies from the location with disgust. Besides the fact that Curtiz had filmed Flynn through a rotating waterwheel, Wallis was distraught over footage that Curtiz shot inside the fort that was muddled with people who were not principal actors. There were women with pots on their heads and children running around, along with assorted goats and horses. Curtiz envisioned the fort as it was in the script: a small frontier outpost crowded with soldiers and sepoys along with their families, who were to be slaughtered by the amir's barbarous host. Wallis wanted long lines of British troops in formation, clean shots of a tidy headquarters, and, above all else, close-ups of the actors whenever they uttered a word of dialogue.

Once again, it was the cinematic cultural divide between the executive producer who grew up in Chicago watching plays and nickelodeons and the director from Budapest with an artistic sensibility—and a reverence for realism—bred into his bones from the time he directed his first film (when Wallis was fourteen years old). Despite their growing friendship, Wallis was fed up. In a detailed three-page memorandum, he laid out instance-by-instance where he thought Curtiz was going wrong with the filming, sending copies to the associate producer Sam Bischoff and Tenny Wright. Wallis concluded in purposeful language: "I have to go through this with you on every picture and I am beginning to wonder why. . . . This is the last note that I am going to write you on this picture. . . . From now on, I will expect you to shoot the script and the story, and I want you to stop shooting through foreground pieces. I want the camera in the clear, and I want you to forget about all of this crap about composition because if the story is no good you can take the composition and stick it!"

Four days later, Wallis upbraided Curtiz for not shooting close-ups from different angles, that is, cutting in the camera. He wrote another note to the director and the tone was ominous: "I remember about four months ago when you came to my office and pleaded to be allowed to make this picture and promised me that if you got it you would absolutely behave and do everything you were told to do and I would not have any trouble with you on the picture, but I have had one headache after another."

It had finally become personal for Wallis, and Curtiz realized he was licked. The director had to compromise or he would be removed from the film. Quitting was not an option. If he walked off the picture, his career would be jeopardized. He had seen firsthand what happened to people who crossed Jack and Harry Warner, and his application for U.S. citizenship was still pending. Curtiz began letting the close-ups and two shots run full, and he reduced the number of foreground compositions in favor of the style Wallis preferred.

Both Flynn and de Havilland were unhappy about laboring under a director they considered a tyrant as well as with a script that seemed to be a juvenile adventure story. Flynn looked smashing in his British uniform along with his new mustache (championed by Jack Warner), which the actor would maintain for nearly his entire career. There were no more of the sweaty palms and clenched teeth of *Captain Blood*. His comfort in front of the camera allowed him more time to reflect on the vagaries of movie stardom. No one was more let down than Flynn when it was announced that Curtiz, and not Borzage, would direct *The Charge of the Light Brigade*. Working outdoors in the freezing mountains of Lone Pine with spartan accommodations and bad food, Flynn found his distaste for his director evolving into a hatred that raised his frigid body temperature. Even though the company was in Lone Pine for only a week, Flynn felt like a member of the Donner party trapped in the Sierra Nevada during the winter of 1846: "The wind was like a knife; it cut through everything, and it raced through our thin costumes. . . . Meantime the hard-boiled Curtiz was bundled in about three topcoats, giving orders. . . . I didn't know enough to tell him to give me one of his coats, or to drop dead. He didn't care who hated him or for what. He'd keep us waiting hour after hour sitting on the horses, freezing to death."

Being immersed for long periods in the fetid water of Lake Sherwood or buffeted by the heat and dust of the San Fernando Valley didn't improve Olivia de Havilland's disposition, and neither did her role in the film. Inserted into its historical contortions is a trite love triangle between Vickers, Elsa (de Havilland), and Flynn's brother, Perry, a fellow soldier played by Patric Knowles. Elsa is betrothed to Geoffrey Vickers, who returns to India to find her in love with his younger brother. It was the same dusted-off plot from dozens of other potboilers. She ended up disliking Curtiz nearly as much as Flynn: "Curtiz was a Hungarian Otto Preminger, and that's that. He was a tyrant, he was abusive, he was cruel." After viewing the completed film, de Havilland thought her performance was awful.

David Niven, who was borrowed from Sam Goldwyn and cast as Flynn's heroic aide, claimed that Curtiz's language malapropisms were a "source of joy to all of us." The future author recalled Curtiz's staging of horses during one scene. "'Okay,' he yelled into a megaphone, 'Bring on the empty horses!' Flynn and I doubled up with laughter. 'You lousy bums,' Curtiz shouted. 'You and your stinking language . . . you think I know fuck nothing. . . . Well let me tell you—I know FUCK ALL!'"

In his memoir Niven also wrote about Curtiz's personal involvement in a cruel practice that allegedly resulted in the mass crippling and destruction of horses: "Curtiz ordered the use of the "Running W," a tripping wire attached to a foreleg. This the stunt riders would pull when they arrived at full gallop at the spot he had indicated, and a ghastly fall would ensue. . . . Flynn led a campaign to have this cruelty stopped, but the studio circumvented his efforts and completed the carnage by sending a second unit down to Mexico, where the laws against mistreating animals were minimal, to say the least."

"Bring on the empty horses!" Curtiz and Errol Flynn during production of *The Charge of the Light Brigade* (1936) (courtesy of the Academy of Motion Picture Arts and Sciences).

Niven's account was partially accurate. Flynn apparently did report the maltreatment of horses to the Humane Society at some point. He despised any type of cruelty toward animals and blamed Curtiz for the abuse. Flynn's widow, Patrice Wymore, told me, "I know Errol was terribly incensed at his [Curtiz's] treatment of animals." But contrary to Niven's assertion and other published reports, no portion of *The Charge of the Light Brigade* was filmed in Mexico. His claim concerning Curtiz's responsibility regarding the mass inhumane treatment of horses appears to have been grossly exaggerated.

Nearly every man in Hollywood who could skillfully ride a horse—including the author's great uncle—appeared in the film. Curtiz himself did not necessarily order the Running W to be used. Use of a trip wire held by the rider and attached to a foreleg was standard practice in the industry at that time. Yakima Canutt, the legendary second-unit director and godfather of movie stuntmen, lost just two animals to freak accidents in more than half a century of continually handling horses in action movies. In his memoir Canutt provided clarity concerning the use of the Running W: "It was something that caused a lot of controversy for stuntmen and Western producers. I remember reading an article written by an officer of the Humane Society that stated we were tying wires on the horses' legs and crippling them so badly that they had to be killed after the stunt. The Running W, used right, will not cripple a horse. I have done some three hundred Running Ws and never crippled a horse."

After Canutt demonstrated the proper use of the Running W for a group of Los Angeles Humane Society officials at Vasquez Rocks, they approved the practice for use in *Virginia City,* a 1940 Curtiz film starring Errol Flynn. Canutt remembered: "It was generally understood in Hollywood that Flynn had reported to the Humane Society about horses being mistreated, but it wasn't on *Virginia City.* I did a couple of Running W's for him in that picture, and he always watched me doing it and all he ever said was, 'Now why don't all the fellows do them that way?'"

Unfortunately, Canutt wasn't assigned to *Light Brigade.* The second-unit director hired to direct most of the key action sequences was B. Reeves "Breezy" Eason. According to the director Andrew Marton, Eason was "a crazy, drunk Irish-American, happy-go-lucky, who had the uneducated man's flair for doing the right thing at the right time." He was generally regarded as the best second-unit action director in Hollywood. Eason earned his nickname by reportedly always printing the initial take of an action shot, but the moniker could also be ascribed to his attitude toward safety. Eason took extreme risks in directing action sequences and was indifferent about the treatment of animals so long as he captured the necessary footage. Although his work was usually confined to Westerns, Eason made his reputation by directing the chariot race in the 1925 version of *Ben-Hur,* a production marred by perhaps the worst episode of prolonged animal abuse in motion picture history.[2] Canutt diplomatically remarked about Eason, "I sincerely admired him for his ability as an action director, but I always felt that he took too many risks."

The bulk of the action sequences were filmed at Lasky Mesa during the first week of June; Curtiz and Eason directed the charge scenes using separate units. The scenes required 280 extras and 340 horses and were filmed with multiple cameras along a thousand-foot bulldozed road that paralleled the horse riders. The scenes included explosions from rigged detonations on an open plain, as men on horseback at full gallop took falls. At least two stuntmen were hospitalized with severe leg injuries. The final stunt and action sequences were filmed in Sonora, California, near the foot of the Sierra Nevada Mountains. The company had already been lucky after a spooked elephant ran amok during an earlier leopard-hunt action sequence in the film that Eason had shot at Lake Sherwood. The agitated pachyderm was caught before any injuries occurred. Warner Bros. would experience nothing but misfortune during the week of June 14 in Sonora.

The Sonora location was logistically favorable—a wide plain in a valley surrounded by mountains on three sides—but the ground was a thin layer of soil over solid rock. Eason approved the site and had a six-hundred-foot-long trench excavated along one edge of the plain to install a car with multiple cameras that could film the riders at a low angle, along with other trenches for camera placement. The use of dynamite created dagger-like protrusions in ditches that resembled craters. After a day for setups, Eason began filming stunts and horse falls with more than sixty riders, upward of eighty-one horses (approximately thirty of these were locally purchased), sixteen cameramen, numerous assistants, a fire engine, and an ambulance. By the last day of filming, *two* ambulances were needed.

Powder technicians rigged dozens of explosives that were triggered as the riders galloped through the mayhem toward the end of the valley. One technician was treated for sunstroke and a stuntman reportedly broke his neck. Other riders were injured when they were thrown or fell on the rocky terrain. The horses fared worse. After Eason concluded filming the stunts, including six Running Ws and six pitfalls, two injured horses had to be put down and another subsequently collapsed and died. The local chapter of the ASPCA discovered what was going on and dispatched a representative to investigate before the company could leave or cover up what had happened.

On June 29, 1936, three Warner employees, including Eason's first assistant, Jack Sullivan, pled guilty in court to animal cruelty and were sentenced to pay a fine of fifteen dollars and received a suspended ten-day jail sentence for using the trip wires that caused the death of the horses. Frank Mattison, who fretted about the second unit expending overhead funds by sitting around in Sonora, viewed the situation as a nuisance. Mattison facilitated the court pleas without first conferring with the Warner legal department. The guilty pleas to animal cruelty by Warner Bros. employees were reported in San Francisco newspapers and picked up by the Associated Press. More than one thousand letters of protest poured into the studio. Animal welfare organizations in America and England began to line up against the film.

Jack Warner wasn't about to let his expensive epic suffer from bad publicity that he considered manifestly unjust. He immediately orchestrated a legal counterattack. The studio's attorney Roy Obringer accused the ASPCA investigator of exaggerating the events, which opened the floodgates for Humane Society articles relating the deaths of "three or four hundred horses." The studio maintained that none of the destroyed horses had been injured because of the use of the Running W or trip wires. Obringer and A. J. Guthrie traveled to San Francisco and showed the local head of the Humane Society photos of the dead horses, which had no trip wires attached to their forelegs. The ASPCA was unconvinced and stood behind its investigator. Archival Warner legal files revealed that the ASPCA investigator who originally showed up in Sonora, a man named Girolo, hit up Frank Mattison for a hundred-dollar "loan" and later tried to extort additional money from Warner Bros. personnel. The studio theorized that Girolo notified the San Francisco newspapers about the guilty pleas when his second shakedown attempt was rebuffed.

The attending veterinarian, Warner Bros. employees, and other principals on the scene provided signed statements and sworn affidavits that attested to the nature of the injuries of the two horses that were put down, along with the third horse that subsequently died of heart failure. There was a fourth horse that was killed as a result of falling and striking a sharp rock during a scene filmed in Chatsworth. Unable to reverse the guilty pleas of its employees, Warner Bros. concentrated on correcting reports about the deaths of numerous horses. The studio successfully sued the Women's Guild of Empire in Great Britain for libelous statements about the film, as well as a recommended boycott.

As a result of the legal and publicity ramifications caused by their alleged mistreatment of horses, Warner Bros. instituted an internal policy requiring a Humane Society representative to be present at every film production involving horse stunts. Running W and pit falls were permanently banned in December 1940.

Although it is possible that more horses could have been killed, there is not a scintilla of evidence that other animals died or that Warner Bros. orchestrated a cover-up. The mythical mass murder of horses during the production of *Light Brigade* ended up historically tarring a single individual: Michael Curtiz was identified as being responsible for the "carnage," to use David Niven's term. That the director wasn't even present at the location where most of the animals were injured and put down and was a skilled rider who loved horses didn't matter. Although the treatment of horses on this film didn't come close to the horrors of *Ben-Hur* during the previous decade, Curtiz's reputation as a directorial martinet made it easier for Flynn, Niven, and others to ascribe the blame to him. It also didn't help that Breezy Eason removed his name from the credits in deference to Curtiz. Conversely, it is debatable whether Curtiz would have done anything differently even if he had been present in Sonora. The very nature of the production lent itself to severe injuries to horses and their riders.[3]

Curtiz was in his element. He loved working outdoors, staging the battle scenes, coaching the actors, and manipulating the cameras to best advantage. At Lake Sherwood he jumped up on a large boom and acted out the scene to several hundred extras by brandishing his microphone like a rifle. The columnist Sheilah Graham skirted Tenny Wright's ban on visitors and observed Curtiz in action at Calabasas: "'More smoke up here,' shouts director Michael Curtiz. 'British and Russian lancers, get on your horses!' yells his assistant Jack Sullivan. In the general confusion an electrician at the switchboard pushes a button and a large explosion results. A horse throws its rider. 'No matter what happens, no matter who gets hurt, no one is to run into the shot,' warns Sullivan. 'If anyone gets wounded, he gets extra pay,' reminds Curtiz."

Light Brigade charged to the top of the box-office charts, bringing in grosses that were nearly identical to *Anthony Adverse*'s. The bravura sweep of the film, the heart-stopping battle scenes, and Max Steiner's thrilling score—his first of over 150 for Warner Bros.—overcame any concerns about cruelty to horses, a weak script, and the rewriting of military history.

This latest success was in stark contrast to Curtiz's personal life, which was undergoing another tumultuous episode. At the end of the summer, Bess Meredyth left Canoga Ranch and moved into a rented house in Bel Air. In her September 5, 1936, divorce petition, she claimed that Curtiz's behavior made it "unsafe to live with him as his wife." She also stated in the overheated rhetoric of divorce filings that Curtiz told her and mutual friends that "he did not love her, hated her, and wished she was dead." She believed that she was "in danger of a nervous breakdown."

The marriage had been damaged by Curtiz's serial philandering. Meredyth initially fought back whenever she discovered one of her husband's extramarital dalliances. She owned a cottage at Laguna Beach that the couple used for holidays and short vacations. She sold it after discovering her husband had used it for a tryst while he was supposed to be directing an evening shoot on *Captain Blood*. Her remonstrations occasionally became physical. Irving Rapper remembered Curtiz showing up one morning with a black eye that was attributed to a quarrel with his wife. For Meredyth, it was a continual series of skirmishes in a war she came to realize there was no hope of winning.

Curtiz viewed his intimate relations with women as akin to eating or breathing: sex ran a close second to filmmaking. It was the classic male double standard: Meredyth was required to be the faithful wife, social companion, and collaborator while her husband did whatever he wanted. She loved him and believed in a monogamous marriage. His continual unfaithfulness hurt her terribly.

John Meredyth Lucas theorized that it was his mother's inability to control Curtiz's philandering that caused her to disengage from her screenwriting career and take to her bed. She read mysteries and worked on jigsaw puzzles while being attended to by nurses and servants. "Whatever her drive had been, it was gone by this time or, perhaps, transmuted into self-destruction. She had always made the rules—she divorced Burton [her first husband], she got rid of my father. Now that she had someone she couldn't control, it made her 'sick.' Today her illness would probably be diagnosed as depression." Divorce lawyers shuttled in and out of the leased Bel Air home while Curtiz brooded at the Tudor manor in Canoga Park.

The peril that forced Curtiz to bend his knee to Hal Wallis during *The Charge of the Light Brigade* was the terrifying possibility of his directorial career being curtailed. As his anger cooled, he realized that his reputation would suffer grievously if Meredyth divorced him. She was more than a wife. She collaborated with him on scripts and counseled him about studio politics. Professionally and socially, she remained an important person in Hollywood. Curtiz's whirl of screening nights and parties with Darryl and Virginia Zanuck, Hal and Louise Wallis, and the like had been predicated on his marriage. He was now a social third wheel and hated it. He was also worried about the effect of a financial settlement as the result of a divorce. Meredyth went through money as fast as it came in. Curtiz was not financially astute, either. That he was concerned about money while making more than two thousand dollars per week— not including his wife's screenwriting income—indicated that their spending had spiraled out of control.

The culture of Hollywood high society revolved around a cadre of powerful men—Zanuck, Warner, Mayer, Wallis—accompanied by highly competent spouses who adhered to a silent compact. The wives supported their husbands and were charming hostesses while turning a blind eye to philandering so long as it didn't become scandalous. While Curtiz didn't fully understand why Meredyth wouldn't adhere to this unspoken understanding, he also realized that his affairs had been indiscreet. He loved his wife and, perhaps more important, he respected her talent. He returned, apologized, and wooed her all over again. The seventeen-year-old John Meredyth Lucas recalled the reconciliation in basic terms: "Soon the divorce lawyers ceased to come to the Bel Air house with their documents and one evening Mike appeared at the dinner table. We moved back to the ranch."

Curtiz also moved on with his career. He directed the final courtroom scene and several sequences for *Black Legion* (1937). This picture was one of the most declarative Warner Bros. social commentary films of the 1930s. It was viewed as such a risk from a career perspective that Hal Wallis asked the principal director, Archie Mayo, if he wanted his name removed from the credits. Although the societal abuse of African Americans went unmentioned in the script, which focused on the mistreatment of "foreigners" by hooded Klansman types, *Black Legion* reflected the studio's most admirable instincts by taking a stand against a rising tide of intolerance both at home and abroad.

Harry Warner was deeply concerned about the ascension of Hitler in Europe and the links between Nazism and American anti-Semitic organizations such as the Klan, the German American Bund, and Father Coughlin's Union Party. Warner Bros. abandoned the German film market in 1933 after Nazi brownshirt thugs beat up Philip Kaufman, their Berlin manager, looting his house and stealing his car. Harking back to the beginning of his career in *My Four Years in Germany* (1918), Harry Warner expressed the desire to produce a Nazi exposé feature titled *Concentration Camp*. He backed down only after fierce resistance from Joseph Breen at the MPPDA, who was fearful of offending a foreign country under the Production Code. The other moguls simply could not countenance writing off the German market and supported Breen. *I Am a Fugitive from a Chain Gang* would be the last big Warner hit to play in Germany until after World War II.

Harry and Jack Warner would continue to sound the alarm about the mushrooming threat of Hitler by slanting the content of selected features and initiating a series of hyperpatriotic shorts produced by Bryan Foy. Harry expunged anything remotely pro-Nazi from Warner movie theaters, including newsreel footage of the German heavyweight Max Schmeling's twelfth-round knockout of Joe Louis in June 1936 at Yankee Stadium.

Curtiz's next film, *Stolen Holiday* (1937), is loosely based on a 1930s French bond scandal involving a Russian émigré named Serge Alexandre

Stavisky who either was murdered or committed suicide after his chicanery was exposed. Claude Rains plays the con man, Stevan Orloff, to the hilt, and Kay Francis, perfectly cast as a fashion designer set up in business by Orloff, displays her usual assortment of dazzling Orry-Kelly gowns while reciting dialogue that was scrubbed of the letter "r" to help cloak her speech impediment.

Jack Warner loved Rains after watching his initial screen test, telling Wallis, "He can certainly do everything, and do it right, that Warren William used to do wrong. We want to keep him in mind." *Stolen Holiday* was the first time Rains was directed by Curtiz. They became unabashed admirers of one another during their eleven films together.

During preproduction, Curtiz offhandedly remarked to Kay Francis that the script for *Mistress of Fashion*—the working title of *Stolen Holiday*—was lousy. Apparently he was referring to a first draft and hadn't read the revised script. Wallis responded with frustration: "If you don't like a script, why don't you come up and tell me and maybe I would take you off it and give you something to which you are more sympathetic. After giving you assignments like *Captain Blood* and *The Charge of the Light Brigade*, it seems to me you would be a little more careful. . . . It now makes it twice as hard for to get Francis into the picture in a pleasant frame of mind. . . . Perhaps you would be happier if I let you do a couple of Foy pictures." Wallis was still pulling his hair out over his talented but exasperating director: "It just seems useless for me to write you or talk to you about these things. You go right out and do them over again. I don't know what to make of you. Are you just naturally antagonistic, or do you think we're all nuts, or what is it?"

Stolen Holiday was completed nine days over schedule; the production department blamed Curtiz for the delays because he shot too much film. It was another Kay Francis vehicle that turned a respectable profit and was quickly forgotten.

Francis became an object lesson for Curtiz and everyone else on the lot of what could happen to you if you got on the wrong side of the Warners. After signing a three-year contract at $5,250 per week with the understanding that she would star in *Tovarich* (1937), Francis decided that Jack Warner had lied to her—not a particularly unusual occurrence—when the plum role went instead to Claudette Colbert. In her anger, she decided to sue to obtain a release from her contract. She refused to settle, went to court, and then inexplicably backed down at the last moment and returned to the studio. Rumors circulated that Warner blackmailed her by threatening to expose an alleged lesbian relationship. Francis chronicled numerous sexual affairs with men in her diaries, but never mentioned a female liaison or the lawsuit. Harry and Jack next launched a scurrilous campaign to browbeat her into violating her expensive contract by putting her into programmers, taking her dressing room away, and so on, eventually ending her tenure at the studio and permanently damaging her career.

In December 1936 Curtiz became an American citizen. It hadn't been a foregone conclusion. There is a tantalizing entry in his immigration case file of an anonymous letter dated August 11, 1933, with the notation "relating to fraudulent nature of Michael Kertesz," and signed by "a Hungarian spectator." Mathilde Foerster, the long-aggrieved mother of Curtiz's first son, Michael, apparently wrote the anonymous letter. She (accurately) reported that Curtiz perjured himself by stating on his 1931 nationalization petition that he had no children other than Kitty. She further advised the U.S. government that Curtiz had fathered three illegitimate children by different European women.

Curtiz was summoned by the Los Angeles office of the newly constituted U.S. Immigration and Naturalization Service and interviewed about the letter on September 9, 1933. Under oath, he denied paternity of his son and claimed that the letter was part of a continuing effort by Foerster to get more money out of him after he had settled out of court to avoid further scandal while denying paternity. The anonymous nature of the letter, the nebulous possibility of non-American children residing in Europe outside U.S. jurisdiction, along with Curtiz's prominence as a film director apparently convinced the INS official to dismiss the entire matter. Curtiz's citizenship application moved forward without any further delay and was finalized on December 4, 1936. Bess Meredyth remembered the trying period before her husband obtaining his cherished citizenship: "Ah, that was an awful time, really. He had a tutor that followed him around, he was on the set, he was everywhere with him. He learned two thousand questions, absolutely two thousand. He used to have us cue him, we didn't know, we couldn't answer the things to save our lives, we didn't know American history, but he knew it all. Then he finally went out, of course, to be sworn in as an American citizen and almost died . . . they only asked him three little questions."

It turned out that the INS examiner was a film buff who pumped the director for movie gossip. Curtiz complained to Bess afterward, "Goddamn, why hell, all this time I break my head to be American and he ask me only goddamn actors?"

19

Falling Fruit

Basking in the dual triumphs of *The Charge of the Light Brigade* and his new American citizenship, Curtiz stepped up to finish the production of *Marked Woman,* starring Bette Davis. He completed ten scenes and four and a half pages of script on December 29–30, 1936, after the assigned director, Lloyd Bacon, departed on his honeymoon. Curtiz's efforts garnered the gratitude of Hal Wallis: "Dear Mike, I saw the stuff you did on *Marked Woman* and it was very well done. I appreciate your jumping into this picture on such short notice and helping out, and your dailies are really swell."

Wallis was doubly grateful after Curtiz's handling of a dicey assignment in the fall of 1936. *Mountain Justice* was based on the Edith Maxwell murder case that had transfixed the nation. Maxwell, a twenty-one-year-old schoolteacher, arrived home late on a July evening in 1935 in rural Wise County, Virginia, and was confronted by her dictatorial father, who began to beat her. The elder Maxwell ended up dead on the kitchen floor, bludgeoned by either a blunt instrument or (as alleged) Edith Maxwell's high-heeled shoe. Maxwell was arrested and convicted of murder by an all-male jury on circumstantial evidence. Whether she actually killed her father—she possibly took the rap for her mother, who was initially charged—or if the elder Maxwell expired from a heart attack has never been conclusively proved. Reporters turned Maxwell into a cause célèbre, putting the face of "The Lonesome Pine Girl" above the page-one fold on newspapers across the country. They dramatized the story with fanciful yarns replete with Appalachian familial feuds, moonshine, and corrupt law enforcement.

In December 1935 Harry Joe Brown recommended to Hal Wallis that the Maxwell story be adapted for Bette Davis. Davis would be eliminated from consideration as Luci Ward's draft script, titled *Hill Billy Justice,* went through several iterations. Wallis was being cautious about a topical but grim story. He had the studio research department study all aspects of the Maxwell case in an attempt to remove any trip wires that could result in litigation. The screenwriter Norman Reilly Raine adapted the story and expunged the most blatant similarities to the actual Maxwell case.

Warner Bros. negotiated a payment of one thousand dollars to Maxwell, which was paid to her brother Earl. Earl Maxwell endorsed *Mountain Justice* after attending a preview at Burbank. He purportedly wrote a letter, resembling a legal form, which complimented the studio on the realism of the picture while carefully noting that the completed film possessed distinct differences from the actual events and characters. The Maxwell family desperately needed the money. Edith Maxwell was running short of funds after appealing her twenty-five-year sentence. She languished in prison until 1941, when Eleanor Roosevelt wrote a letter on her behalf that resulted in a full pardon from the governor of Virginia.

Edith Maxwell became Ruth Harkins (Josephine Hutchinson), an altruistic medical assistant who attempts to bring health care to a rural region populated by insular mountain folk. Her father, Jeff (Robert Barrat), is a cruel ignoramus who forbids her to have any kind of life other than the one he permits. At a local carnival, Ruth falls in love with Paul Cameron (George Brent), an out-of-town lawyer who is seeking to try her father for killing a surveyor who inadvertently trespassed on his property. Ruth ends up testifying against her father, who is convicted. A sympathetic judge and jury give him a light sentence. When the father returns from prison, he attacks Ruth, dies for his trouble, and his daughter is tried for his murder.

Curtiz began filming on September 10, 1936. As always, he took care to imbue the project with period realism. At his initiative, the courtroom set for the trial of Jeff Harkins was designed from a realistic sketch obtained from a Wise County court clerk. A Kentucky schoolteacher was hired as a technical adviser to ensure "authenticity in speech, customs, and costumes of America's forgotten people." The studio obtained six Kentucky coonhounds that Curtiz staged around the courtroom set, along with thirty corncob pipes, forty-three plugs of chewing tobacco, fifteen gourds, twenty-seven jars of preserves, fourteen hundred yards of calico, and two dozen watermelons imported from Hope, Arkansas. Curtiz staged the Ruth Harkins trial on the Warner city street set, re-creating the county-fair atmosphere of the Virginia hill country with an overflowing crowd outside the local courthouse.

The picture quickly fell behind schedule. Josephine Hutchinson, ill with a variety of ailments, was absent from the set. Other delays were caused by the location shooting in the unseasonably cold mountains near Big Bear Lake. Hutchinson and George Brent were reciting affectionate dialogue through chattering teeth and the result did not please the director. Hutchinson remembered: "We got the giggles again, and Mike Curtiz was furious. The studio finally sent up warm clothing and liquor to keep us comfortable during the rugged stay."

Hal Wallis rejected the footage of this particular sequence, aptly terming the acting "cold," and was incredulous that Curtiz would film a love scene with Brent wearing a hat. The scene was reshot, along with a new sequence of Brent and Hutchinson's initial meeting at the carnival, which Curtiz wrote with Irving Rapper. More retakes were required. The picture went nearly three weeks over schedule.

Most appealing to Curtiz was staging the bedroom fight scene between Ruth and her father. The director at one point framed Barrat in silhouette, beating Hutchinson with a whip against the backdrop of an "Honor Thy Father and Mother" wall hanging. He turned the final confrontation between father and daughter into a pier-six brawl. Frank Mattison, the unit manager, related the progress of the fight scene to Tenny Wright and Wallis: "Mike is making this into another struggle such as they had in *The Spoilers*. I believe that you will agree with me that what he is getting on the screen is worth the time he has lost here."

The imposing Barrat, whom James Cagney described as having "a solid forearm the size of an average man's thigh," obscenely overpowers the demure Hutchinson, who vividly recalled the sequence: "Barrat had been a boxer, he was a sweet man, but he didn't know his own strength. Once he hit me so hard I went out like a light. When it was all over, I looked like a bad avocado." Mattison obliquely reported Barrat's kayo of the film's female star: "Miss Hutchinson passed out yesterday afternoon and had to let her go home early. This fight scene has been very strenuous, but Mr. Curtiz hopes to finish it today by using a double all the way through and putting close-ups of Miss Hutchinson."

Mountain Justice is one of Curtiz's forgotten pictures. Deftly photographed by Ernest Haller, it is an entertaining but flawed film. Hutchinson lacked star power, and George Brent is miscast. Exemplary character performances by Barrat, Guy Kibbee, Margaret Hamilton, Fuzzy Knight, and Russell Simpson bolster a grab bag of topical plot points.

The scattershot script addresses the urgency of rural medical care,

Curtiz stages a memorably unequal fight scene with Josephine Hutchinson and Robert Barrat in *Mountain Justice* (1937) (courtesy of the Lucas family).

abusive treatment of women, child marriage, women's legal rights, and mob violence. The climactic notion of redneck goons avenging the accidental death of the despicable Barrat character by attempting to lynch his daughter, who was already unjustly sentenced to twenty-five years in prison, takes dramatic license to absurd extremes. The *New York Times* critic Frank S. Nugent wrote off *Mountain Justice* as "closer to the taste of the Beverly hill-billies than Tennessee's."

Released at the end of April 1937, the film returned a modest profit. The Warner legal department concluded it would be better off not to exhibit *Mountain Justice* in Virginia. The decision eliminated any ticket revenue from the state's ninety-odd Warner-affiliated theaters.

If there is a single film emblematic of the Warner Bros. style that emerged from the Depression, *Kid Galahad* may well be it. Based on Francis Wallace's serialized *Saturday Evening Post* story, it concerned a young bellhop who gets hooked up with a boxing manager and his girlfriend and becomes the titular pugilist. The manager becomes furious when he discovers that his fighter is keeping company with his cloistered kid sister. He maneuvers the inexperienced Galahad into a match with the champion, who is controlled by a gangster. After conniving with the gangster to arrange an ostensible fix, the manager experiences a last-minute change of heart and exhorts his young pugilist to win the bout.

In addition to Curtiz's rapidly paced direction, *Kid Galahad* is rousing entertainment owing to the cast, headed by a trio of legendary Warner stars. Edward G. Robinson had recently signed a lucrative contract extension. One of the studio's biggest stars, he was perfect as the irascible, fast-talking boxing manager, Nick Donati. He recalled that Jack Warner's wooing of him for the new contract included an insight into the mogul's feelings about actors:

> When he came to my house (can you imagine!) to discuss a new film with me (a script of *Kid Galahad* under his arm), he was all smiles and darlingness. . . . We discussed (boringly) the difficulties he was having with Jimmy, Bette, and Livvy. . . . I told him he treated actors badly. At this point he nearly sobbed, and by God, he was sincere about it. Who were these people? Nobodies that he'd transformed into stars, arranged for them to have money, deference, houses, international fame. And how was he being paid back? They were nailing him to the cross.

Bette Davis had also returned to the fold. Unable to reach a new agreement with Warner over creative control, she signed a contract with an Italian producer to star in movies made in England and left the country in June 1936. As she was still under contract, Jack Warner had her followed to London, obtained an injunction to prevent her from working abroad, sued her for breach of contract in King's Bench Divisional Court, and won. When Davis returned to Burbank, she discovered that her gutsy stand had garnered her newfound respect. Jack Warner went out of his way to accommodate her wishes and raised her salary to two thousand dollars per week. After she had starred in *Marked Woman,* it appeared that she had finally reached a turning point after years of striving for better parts. Davis later believed that the role as Robinson's girlfriend, "Fluff," in *Kid Galahad* continued her career upswing by "consolidating my position with the public." The rise of "the Fourth Warner Brother" had begun.

As for Humphrey Bogart, he was paying his dues playing heavies after making his Warner debut as a gangster in *Three on a Match* back in

1932. He signed a seven-year contract with Warner Bros. after replicating his stage role as "Duke" Mantee in *The Petrified Forest* (1936). With a few exceptions, Bogie would continue to play characters named "Bugs," "Red," "Baby Face," "Rocks" and "Whip" during the next five years. The principal variation in his roles was the precise timing of his gut-shot death during the final reel. Bogart's philosophy was to keep showing up and continue working, and eventually good things would happen. He would ultimately be proven correct beyond his wildest dreams. In the meantime, he would play "Turkey" Morgan, the crooked boxing promoter in *Kid Galahad*.

Although the film was tightly directed, it was the fight scenes that Curtiz focused on. Boxing movies were a relatively new phenomenon, and he sought to put ring realism on the screen. The director used one of newcomer Wayne Morris's (Curtiz spotted him at the Pasadena Playhouse and had Wallis sign him to play Galahad) uncredited ring opponents, the former light welterweight champ Mushy Callahan, to assist him in staging the boxing sequences. Callahan appropriately concluded his career in pictures as a bit actor and boxing expert, begun under Curtiz, by playing the referee and serving as the technical advisor in the 1962 remake of *Kid Galahad* starring Elvis Presley.

The boxing sequences were state-of-the-art at the time. One take took Curtiz by surprise. Bette Davis recalled Wayne Morris's authentic physicality in the ring, which caused the director's startled reaction: "'Fake fight! Retake! Fake fight—awful!' Curtiz screamed, but it was difficult to redo because Wayne's opponent was unconscious. He had knocked him out cold."

Film Daily tabbed *Kid Galahad* "the best fight picture ever screened." The *San Francisco Examiner* weighed in: "Michael Curtiz has directed it with a masculine vitality which gives a robust tempo and virility to the picture." Reviewers also raved about twenty-three-year-old, six-feet-two Wayne Morris. The *New York Times* labeled the young newcomer "the Warners' latest astronomical discovery" in a picture that is "lively, suspenseful and positively echoing with the bone-bruising thud of right hooks to the jaw." The normally collected Howard Barnes of the *New York Herald Tribune* called Wayne Morris "the best find that the films have made since Tyrone Power took over leading roles." Morris's screen career would turn out to be solid but relatively unspectacular, and it was truncated by his war service. He would achieve enduring fame as a decorated U.S. Navy fighter pilot ace, earning four distinguished Flying Crosses and other honors during World War II.

And by 1937 Errol Flynn possessed star power in spades. After completing *The Charge of the Light Brigade,* he starred in *Green Light* and the sumptuous *The Prince and the Pauper.* Both pictures, particularly the latter, were major successes, so now any Warner-Flynn film was surmised to be a guaranteed moneymaker. His new project was Curtiz's *The Perfect Specimen,* a comedy that Jack Warner originally conceived for Robert Montgomery and Marion Davies. Flynn costarred with Joan Blondell. Olivia de Havilland and Blondell were appearing in other films on the lot and it became a race to see which actress would be available first for *The Perfect Specimen.* This process of elimination occurred after Hal Wallis dithered over obtaining Carole Lombard, Miriam Hopkins, or Rosalind Russell to star opposite Flynn.

The story of a wealthy heir brought up in seclusion in order to become the perfect man, only to discover the foibles of life and love from the gardener's sister was a clever premise for a comedy. But the film was credible only to those whose imaginations could embrace the improbable notion of May Robson raising Errol Flynn and keeping him incommunicado on a posh estate during his formative years. The script also had a piecemeal quality after nine different writers had labored on it. Elements of slapstick and sophisticated humor simply did not hang together well. Most critically, the hoped-for chemistry between Flynn and Blondell was noticeably diluted.

Much of the onscreen uncertainty was attributable to Flynn. Screwball comedy was not the actor's forte, although he desperately wanted it to be. Jack Warner was willing to indulge his star occasionally with this type of picture, though he knew that his bottom line was always better off when Flynn held a gun or a sword in his hand.

The picture received mixed reviews, but audiences liked it. Warner spent $14,000 to run a full-page ad in the Scripps-Howard newspapers with a chart calculating Flynn's height, weight, and box-office value, deeming them all perfect. Although *The Perfect Specimen* was far from it, the film made a boatload of money, and Curtiz was handed a more substantive assignment.

Wallis believed *Gold Is Where You Find It* (1938) would mine major box-office receipts. It was a three-color "new" Technicolor production that adapted Clements Ripley's serialized novel about a hydraulic gold-mining syndicate versus wheat farmers in 1870s California. Curtiz rushed from *The Perfect Specimen* to begin *Gold* location filming on August 21. The truncated interval between films gave the director precious little time to plan what would be a complex production staged at an old mining site near Weaverville, California.

In addition to directing a large cast, Curtiz would be required to stage scenes with numerous extras and special effects, including a rousing finale of a dam giving way. Large outdoor sets were constructed with massive fire nozzles blasting water at the mountainside and wooden sluice runs carrying the muddy slurry down the mountain, where the gold ore was harvested from settling vats. The movie depicted the resultant runoff flooding the wheat fields in the Sacramento Valley. The environmental debacle leads to a confrontation. The landowner, Colonel Ferris (Claude Rains), rallies the farmers against the nefarious San Francisco mining syndicate as the heroic mining engineer Jared Whitney (George Brent) falls in love with Ferris's daughter, Serena (Olivia de Havilland).

When Tenny Wright banned all visitors, particularly relatives, from the Weaverville location, Curtiz arranged for his stepson, John Meredyth Lucas, to join the company as an apprentice script clerk. As Lucas recalled, the location had the trappings of a military camp: "A huge tent city was built in the wilderness, housing the crew, actors and hundreds of extras. . . . It was a gigantic project and the construction workers fiddled constantly with the sets, even in the long shots. Their unnecessary delays caused Mike, always impatient with anything that held up filming, to shout over the bullhorn, 'Hey carpenter, don't do a genius job out from it. Mr. Warner won't see it.'"

Curtiz had considerable justification for anxiety. In addition to directing the multifaceted production on location, he was also coping with a barrage of acerbic correspondence from Wallis. The producer claimed that Curtiz ruined a scene between de Havilland and Margaret Lindsay by adding "atrocious dialogue," and that a brief shot of Rains during the final flooding scene was "the most amateurish thing I have seen in years."

Then there were the unwieldy Technicolor cameras used for the three-color filming: large blue boxes that had to be carefully lugged up to the mountain locations. Curtiz lambasted the Technicolor crew: "Hey, Technicolor bums, when you write your memoirs for the next generation, tell them how goddamn slow you work on your things." As John Meredyth Lucas witnessed, Curtiz defied one of the epistles from the first lady of Technicolor when filming a love scene against the backdrop of a beautiful mountain sunset: "Mike was told the Technicolor cameras could not possibly shoot into backlight. Mike said, 'On my responsibility, you goddamn do it.' 'But Mr. Curtiz,' the Associate sputtered, 'Mrs. Kalmus gave us specific instructions that—' 'Mrs. Kalmus,' Mike told him, 'don't shoot my goddamn picture.'" When the Technicolor associate wanted to drive to the nearest phone, Curtiz declared, "'The sun don't wait for Mrs. Kalmus. . . . We make the shot, and then you call.' It turned out to be a sensational scene and changed Technicolor's thinking about that particular rule."

Gold Is Where You Find It opened to mixed notices. Howard Barnes thought the movie was "ornamental rather than engrossing," with the exception of the sequence of the dam collapse: "Michael Curtiz had directed this minor cataclysm with all of the vigor and melodramatic excitement that are wanting in other sequences." An overwritten script replete with preaching and clichéd characterizations offset the gorgeous Technicolor photography and well-staged scenes (a sequence inside a crowded Barbary Coast café is beautifully shot).

The ending, with a concluding judicial speech, unctuously delivered by Henry O'Neill, is better suited to a civics class. The leaden finale is only slightly more stilted than the pedantic opening monologue about California, which resembles a *Voice of the Globe* travelogue. It was unusual for a Curtiz film have such lethargic stretches. The director knew he was working from behind with a weak script. One day during production, he shook his head and remarked to Irving Rapper, "The tempo is okay, but the pause stinks."

The tandem of de Havilland and Brent is also less than inspired. Wallis justifiably criticized Curtiz's direction of the final fadeout, as the pair stand like statues staring into the sunset reciting dialogue "like school children at their graduation exercises." But he did not elect to have the scene rewritten or compel Curtiz to go back and reshoot the ending.

Much of the message-driven pomposity in the film was attributable to Robert Buckner (this was his first credited screenplay). He would become infinitely better at writing for movies and lasted fifteen mostly distinguished years at the studio. The native Virginian would write or produce (or both) seven of Curtiz's films, holding writing credits for *Yankee Doodle Dandy* and *Life with Father*. He believed Curtiz was a "cinematic genius" whose talent behind the camera was intuitive: "Mike could make a picture when he didn't know what it was about."

There had been several films portraying the legendary English brigand Robin Hood, starting in 1908 with *Robin Hood and His Merry Men,* directed by Percy Stow. Douglas Fairbanks was the most recent incarnation in the aptly titled *Douglas Fairbanks in Robin Hood* in 1922. Although the athletic star-producer-writer excelled in the portrayal of the English folk hero, there was little more than pageantry and acrobatics to flesh out the Robin Hood legend onscreen. In the summer of 1935 the costume designer Dwight Franklin suggested to Jack Warner that James Cagney would make a "swell Robin Hood." Preproduction plans for Cagney to star in a Robin Hood epic, announced in the fall, were shelved after Cagney's relationship with the studio deteriorated to the point that he was suspended in November 1935.

Warner's new top star, Errol Flynn, was immediately cast as Robin Hood, and Hal Wallis urged Jack Warner to "publicize this now and let Cagney know he is losing these properties by his attitude." Suffice it to say that *Robin Hood* would have been an entirely different movie with Cagney clad in green tights, swinging from vines in Sherwood Forest.

Before production could begin, Warner Bros. had to finalize a deal in September 1936 to purchase the rights and materials owned by MGM. These materials included a pair of Robin Hood treatments written by Bernard McConville, an outline by Philip Dunne, and a continuity from Reliance Pictures. Warner acquired all of the research, treatment, and script materials for $23,910.88 but would be limited to making a picture titled *The Adventures of Robin Hood* that specifically could not be an operetta or employ any music or lyrics that MGM ostensibly planned to use in a future Robin Hood musical production. As part of the agreement, Warner granted Metro the rights to the operetta version of Robin Hood, but MGM was restrained from making a Robin Hood operetta for two and a half years after the release of the Warner Bros. movie. A sweetener was added after Louis B. Mayer complained that the scope of Warner's Technicolor production would result in "milking" the value of the retained Robin Hood property. Jack Warner released the rights inherited from First National to the picture *Quo Vadis* to MGM for $2,500. Metro did eventually produce the blockbuster epic *Quo Vadis* in 1951, but the announced Robin Hood musical was never made.

Rowland Leigh completed a first-draft Robin Hood script that Hal Wallis panned for its ponderous character development and flowery dialogue. The screenwriters Norman Reilly Raine and Seton Miller used more modern phraseology that would resonate with audiences without compromising the period nature of the picture. The writers leveraged some of the purchased materials from MGM to create an original story that expanded on the Robin Hood legend of stealing from the rich and giving to the poor. Warners continued to insert twentieth-century themes of social justice in their films—as European war clouds continued to gather—even if the setting was medieval mythology in merrie olde England. At one point Robin Hood exclaims, "Saxon, Norman, what does that matter? We're all Englishmen! It's injustice I hate, not the Normans!" Wallis, sensitive as always to British history, had a studio researcher, Herman Lissauer, review the script word by word to ensure the use of accurate terminology. Certain phrases ended up being omitted, including a reference to Friar Tuck's consuming a hogshead of ale when it was discovered that a hogshead was the equivalent of forty-eight gallons.

Wallis assigned Henry Blanke to produce and William Keighley to direct. Keighley was a former stage actor and director who had found a home as a contract director at the studio beginning in 1932. Although born in Philadelphia, he affected a British accent acquired during his days as an actor in an English theatrical company. The urbane Keighley incongruously experienced his greatest success with several of the studio's most hard-boiled gangster pictures: the monster hit 'G' Men, starring James Cagney, and *Bullets or Ballots,* with Edward G. Robinson. He had recently helmed *The Prince and the Pauper* and got on famously with Errol Flynn. The clincher came when Flynn implored Wallis and Jack Warner to assign Keighley to the picture instead of Curtiz. They eventually acceded, leaving Curtiz dejected. He rightfully believed that he was perfect for *Robin Hood*.

Keighley began rehearsals and Technicolor tests with Flynn on August 12, 1937. The sixty-day production schedule began on September 27 at Bidwell Park in Chico, California. A good 350 miles from Burbank, the 2,400-acre park offered a natural canopy of trees. Carl Jules Weyl, the art director, spruced up the scenery with prop tree trunks and even spray-painted some of the foliage green for Technicolor purposes. Big Chico Creek would be the site of the first scene Keighley filmed, in which Robin Hood is knocked into the water by the quarterstaff of Alan Hale's Little John.

Hale had portrayed this same character in the 1922 edition of *Robin Hood* and would do so a final time in *Rogues of Sherwood Forest,* released six months after his death, in January 1950. Hale became the most identifiable face in the Warner Bros. stock company. Through thirteen films opposite Flynn and eleven pictures directed by Curtiz, his onscreen blarney became a touchstone for audiences who became comfortably accustomed to his comedic mugging.

The rest of the supporting cast was faultless. Claude Rains portrayed

Alan Hale, Curtiz, and Peter Lorre kibitz outside the Warner commissary (courtesy of the Lucas family).

evil Prince John as an effeminate backstabber and was a perfect contrast to Flynn's virility. Basil Rathbone, a freelancer, was hired as Sir Guy of Gisbourne. His character's arrogant knavishness was augmented by the actor's superior fencing ability. Guy Kibbee's contract at Warner Bros. had not been renewed, so Wallis brought in the rotund Eugene Pallette as Friar Tuck. In addition to being under contract, Patric Knowles was one of Flynn's off-set acolytes. Knowles got the role of Will Scarlett because Flynn's pal David Niven was vacationing in England. The rest of the principal cast included Ian Hunter as the late-appearing King Richard, Melville Cooper as the bumbling sheriff of Nottingham, and the officious Montagu Love as the purple-robed Bishop of the Black Canons. Una O'Connor as Maid Marian's servant and Herbert Mundin as one of the Merry Men were written in for additional comic relief.

Jack Warner originally wanted Anita Louise cast as Marian because she was not assigned to a picture at that time. Warner hated for any contracted actor to draw a salary while idle. He quickly came to his senses and switched to Olivia de Havilland.

By the time de Havilland arrived at the Chico location on October 22, Norman Raine was revising the script on location and had gotten into an argument with Keighley over the inclusion of a jousting tournament with which the director wanted to open the film. Wallis was forced to arbitrate, and the tournament scene eventually was tossed out. The producer had taken a major risk with the production schedule, given Northern California's typical weather during the late summer and early fall. Tenny Wright warned him in a September 7, 1937, memorandum rain was already having an effect on Curtiz, who was in Weaverville, 120 miles north of Chico, frantically attempting to finish *Gold Is Where You Find It*: "*Robin Hood* will not start until the later part of this month, September, and the rains generally set in around the first of October." Wright concluded: "I mean by this—is it worth gambling on the weather?"

As Wright knew, Wallis was committed to filming in Chico and couldn't change the entire schedule less than three weeks before the start of production without delaying the picture. Wright neatly covered himself with Jack Warner by ensuring that the executive producer, not the production manager, owned this particular decision. Overcast skies and rain disrupted filming in September and October. An additional complication was a flulike virus that intermittently laid out Alan Hale, Patric Knowles, and other members of the cast. By the time Breezy Eason arrived in Chico on October 26 with thirty-four horses and five buses filled with stuntmen and support staff to shoot some of the location action sequences, the film was already a week behind.

New scenes had been added to the picture, and the costs were mounting. Wallis had been supporting a "Warner City" location of four hundred people in Chico for more than a month, and the project was growing so large that he split the company into two units under Keighley and Eason. The Eason contingent included a Humane Society representative to observe all the stunts with horses.

And of course Errol Flynn was enjoying being Errol Flynn. He and Patric Knowles occupied their spare time by renting a private plane at Chico Municipal Airport; Knowles was a licensed pilot and began teaching Flynn to fly in between trips to the hotel bar. Wallis became apoplectic. He fired off a telegram to the unit manager, Al Alleborn, demanding that the aerial hijinks cease immediately. Flynn ignored orders to stop flying during the production even after Wallis issued a veiled threat to Knowles to knock it off or consider a career as a freelance actor. A Civil Aeronautics Authority official eventually confiscated Knowles's pilot license pending resolution of the studio's specious complaint to the Screen Actors Guild that the actor was illegally performing as a stunt person by flying an airplane with Flynn.

Shortly after Flynn was grounded, his wife, Lili Damita, arrived in Chico for a visit. She enveloped Flynn in a boa constrictor–like embrace and posed for photographers while looking askance at Olivia de Havilland, whom she considered a threat. Damita need not have bothered. After several weeks on location, de Havilland was fed up with having to play another romantic partner to Flynn, who had lately resorted to juvenile tricks to annoy his sensitive costar and throw off her performance.[1]

Flynn was dissatisfied at what he was being paid under his contract. He attempted to enlist a makeup man, Ward Hamilton, in a scheme to delay the picture by complaining about his beard, wig, and makeup in order to gain more compensation "by hook or by crook." In response to Flynn's request about his hairpiece, Wallis tasked Perc Westmore with designing a more suitable wig; meanwhile, Roy Obringer deposed Hamilton and filed the affidavit away for future reference.

After returning to the Warner soundstages at Burbank, Flynn shuttled so many ingénues on and off his dressing room divan that the crew started placing bets on how many women would be required to sate Robin Hood in a single day. Jack Warner and Hal Wallis were more than willing to put up with Flynn's shenanigans. What they were viewing in the dailies was nothing short of spectacular. Errol had *become* Robin Hood. His humorous dash and heroism literally leapt off the screen.

But Wallis was deeply concerned about the picture itself. Although many of the scenes that Keighley filmed in Chico had a light, humorous touch that played well, the overall tone as a robust adventure was sorely lacking. A week before the company left Chico, Wallis wrote to Henry Blanke and expressed dissatisfaction with Keighley's judgment regarding the camera setups. He specifically identified a scene of a single line of men moving through the forest that ran on endlessly for 1,600 feet of uncut film. The camera had been placed too far away, and the men in the frame looked like miniatures. There were also long shots in Technicolor that were out of focus. "Keighley does not know how to shoot action sequences," declared Wallis.

Robin Hood was nine days behind schedule by the time the company departed Chico for Burbank on November 8. With weather no longer a factor, Wallis and Blanke expected the pace to accelerate. But after filming a portion of the archery contest scene at Busch Gardens in Pasadena, Keighley continued to fall farther behind. He had to be coached by Al Alleborn to work out his setups in advance with Breezy Eason so the two units could collaborate on the sequences involving both acting and action. On November 10 Wallis reviewed the state of affairs with Henry Blanke: "I imagine that we are two weeks behind schedule on *Robin Hood* so far. After yesterday's talk, you know what that means in terms of dollars and cents. I wish you would go through the script again and have a talk with Keighley and see if there aren't additional scenes that we can cut out of the picture at this time. Perhaps by now, Keighley has a different perspective on the stuff and what is not needed, and he may have some ideas for cuts."

Approximately two weeks later, Wallis made a command decision. The majority of the action sequences were yet to be filmed, and neither Blanke nor Wallis had confidence that Keighley could direct them with the required grandeur and sweep. With the latest budget projections exceeding $2 million and the studio's newest star on display, it simply had to be a success. Wallis knew how to bring the picture home: Curtiz would take over as director. The executive producer discussed the situation with Jack Warner, who concurred. Curtiz was euphoric at being asked to come to the rescue.

Precisely how Wallis explained the switch to Keighley is not recorded. Although newspapers reported that Keighley withdrew from the picture "following a disagreement over production methods," he remained a significant director at Warner Bros. In his memoir Wallis confirmed why Keighley was assigned to direct the film to begin with: "Unfortunately, the action sequences were not effective, and I had to replace the director in mid-production, an unheard-of event at that time. I felt that only Mike Curtiz could give the picture the color and scope it needed. The reason we hadn't used him in the first place was because Errol had begged us not to."

The handover of the directorial reins occurred on November 30, when Al Alleborn brought Curtiz and his assistant director, Jack Sullivan, up to speed so they could start filming the banquet scene the next day. Curtiz convinced Wallis to replace Tony Gaudio with Sol Polito as cinematographer. The director also brought in Irving Rapper as dialogue director and Limey Plews, his good luck charm, as prop man. Plews had to scramble to get ready: "I found that I had ninety-seven props to make in one night."

As Alleborn recorded, Curtiz immediately set an energetic pace on his first day: "Curtiz looked over the Castle set and lined up every shot which we are doing today. Looked at rehearsal of the men who are dueling; also looked at the cast for their fight which takes place at the end sequence." Two days later, on December 3, Alleborn raved about the energy exuded by Curtiz and his team: "I think this company with a new crew is moving along 100% better than the other crew. . . . The balance of the work that is left to do in the Castle has been walked through and explained to everyone concerned, including Mr. Wallis and Blanke, who have approved of the way Mike is to play it and the set-ups necessary for the action."

Knowing Curtiz so well, Wallis was a bit less sanguine when he cautioned Henry Blanke: "There is one thing that we will have to watch with Mike. In his enthusiasm to make great shots and composition and utilize the great production values in this picture, he is, of course, more likely to go overboard than anyone else as he just naturally loves to work with mobs and props of this kind."

Although Curtiz did overshoot Flynn's escape from the palace banquet with an excess of angles and stunts, Wallis's hard-nosed editing pared the sequence down to the essential action. Things were simpatico between Wallis and Curtiz for the balance of the production, except on one occasion when the director could not resist the urge to rewrite a scene between Flynn and de Havilland. Wallis sent Curtiz a chastising memo and quickly moved on. Even though Curtiz had made up a day on the schedule by December 7, there was no conceivable way he could make up more than two weeks. And ultimately, Wallis did not ask him to try. He knew Curtiz would finish as quickly as possible. The filming of establishing shots without principal actors continued into the evening, as the director spent upward of eighteen hours a day on the set. And after handing Curtiz the megaphone, Wallis dedicated more resources to make *Robin Hood* a blockbuster.

Retakes of scenes directed by Keighley were ordered. The sequence depicting the ambush of the treasure caravan shot in Chico was augmented by Curtiz at Sherwood Forest in eastern San Fernando Valley, a namesake location from the 1922 Douglas Fairbanks version that was also filmed there. Curtiz had the Merry Men scooting up the trees toward the swinging vines and branches and then, as he put it, "the boys should fall from the trees like fruit" onto the Norman horsemen. Curtiz also completely reshot the initial entrance of Robin Hood and Will Scarlett with much greater panache. He directed additional archery contest footage at the Midwick Country Club in Alhambra.

For the scene in which Robin Hood greets Maid Marian before leaping into her room from the vines on the castle wall, Curtiz ordered two glass shots that added a river and bridge in the background. The follow-on love scene enabled de Havilland to wreak a little revenge on Flynn for his upstaging antics in Chico. Their kissing grew authentically passionate during multiple takes; Flynn was urged on by Curtiz, who was directing from his seat on a camera boom: "That kiss—she would not melt butter. Don't hold her like she was a hot potato. Crush her!" Flynn required minimal encouragement. De Havilland humorously recalled more than half a century later that she gave her costar an erection that strained against his green tights. Their *Robin Hood* love scenes are among the best in their nine Warner features together.

It was in the interior sequences in Nottingham Castle that Curtiz particularly excelled at staging. The banquet and fight followed by Robin's escape from the castle, the coronation of Prince John, and the final battle with the climactic sword duel were all filmed on the studio's Stage 1 during December. Curtiz was determined to better *Captain Blood*'s swordfight sequence using the same pair of actors. His creativity unshackled, he turned the final confrontation into superlative artistic imagery. Their duel is a masterful composition of swordplay that traverses a winding castle stairway with choreographed falls, then tumbles over a candelabra; their blades lock across a table, which gets kicked over after a rapier-like amputation of a lighted candle. The dueling is interspersed and accentuated with an exchange of lighthearted billingsgate between the two actors. Curtiz had Sol Polito position his lights so the swordsmen cast their shadows against the massive castle pillar as his camera glided through the sequence. The only problem was a shot inside the castle that was later revealed to have an extra in period dress on the fringe of a crowd of soldiers eating an ice cream cone that had to be cut.

Flynn inaccurately stated in his memoir that he performed all of his own *Robin Hood* stunt work, but he and Rathbone did enact the majority of the dueling sequence, less several of the falls. The Belgian fencing master Fred Cavens coached them on how to seem authentic onscreen

Errol Flynn's expression says it all about being directed by Curtiz in *The Adventures of Robin Hood* (1938), as Olivia de Havilland waits at the castle window (courtesy of Photofest).

while dueling with prop swords. The film appropriately ignored the fact that sword fencing was a warrior technique not taken up until centuries after the medieval period of Robin Hood. While Cavens acknowledged that Flynn was an athletic quick study, he was much more impressed by Rathbone, who took fencing lessons and worked extremely hard: "He [Rathbone] has excellent form and is the most colorful of all the people I have taught. I doubt that he would do well in competition, but for picture purposes, he is better than the best fencer in the world."

The only mishap with the scene occurred when Rathbone's stuntman Fred Graham broke his ankle doing the actor's final fall. Stuntman Buster Wiles (Flynn's pal) doubles Flynn in the scene where Robin escapes from the gallows after a well-timed arrow fells the hangman and he leaps on a horse with his hands bound behind him to make his escape.

For another Douglas Fairbanks–like gag, Curtiz called Wiles over and, using his nickname for the stuntman, who often sang on the set, told him, "Singing Marie, you pretend to cut rope, hold on, go up." As the cameras rolled on the Warner back lot, Wiles took a hack at the portcullis rope and was neatly pulled up to the top of the castle battlement as the portcullis gate rose.

Howard Hill, a famed archer and bow hunter, shot the majority of the arrows in *Robin Hood*. In addition to launching countless arrows into padded stuntmen who were getting $150 per arrow shot into them from Warner Bros., Hill orchestrated the most famous archery trick shot in history: in the archery tournament scene, he shot at the target with an arrow already in the bull's-eye and split the existing arrow.[2] The adventurous Hill became a close friend of Flynn, who launched him on a new career of Warner Bros. shorts about archery and hunting, along with bit parts and doubling for Flynn in movies.

Flynn's work was thoroughly professional after the company returned to Burbank. Despite his occasional hijinks and professed loathing of Curtiz, he buckled down—he was late to the set only once—and after finishing the picture, he departed for a scheduled vacation on his yacht in January. The production finally closed on January 14, 1938, thirty-seven days behind schedule. Production reports indicate that of the 416 individual scenes in the film, 302 were added *after* production had begun in August 1937.

Although the film was yet to be edited and scored, Jack Warner knew that he had something special and acknowledged the man who was responsible. He authorized a $2,500 bonus to Curtiz and, in a letter to Roy Obringer, instructed the studio attorney to increase Curtiz's pay: "When we exercise the next option of Mike Curtiz's contract, he goes to $2600 per week commencing May 1938. We are now giving him a $200 weekly bonus. On this date, May 26, I want you to increase this bonus to $400, making it a flat sum of $3000 weekly."

Wallis closely supervised the editing of the film with the goal of accelerating the action by dropping extraneous bits. He and Curtiz both believed in hindsight that *Captain Blood* had run too long at 119 minutes; the 1951 reissue would be reduced to 95 minutes. *The Adventures of Robin Hood* was finalized at 102 thrill-packed minutes.

Besides the editing and the laborious transfer of the Technicolor three-color dye prints, the most important postproduction task was the music score. Erich Wolfgang Korngold left the studio in May 1937 to work on an opera in Vienna. Korngold was still smarting over his Academy Award for *Anthony Adverse* being presented at the dinner ceremony to Leo Forbstein, the head of the Warner music department, rather than to him. Korngold's name wasn't even mentioned during the presentation. Although Forbstein sent Korngold an apologetic note and ran an ad in *The Hollywood Reporter* that recognized Korngold as the actual composer of the Oscar-winning score, Korngold refused to accept the statuette until after Forbstein's death, in 1949.

On January 22, 1938, Korngold was at his Vienna home working on his opera *Die Kathrin* when a telegram arrived from Wallis asking him if he could be in Hollywood in ten days to write the score. Korngold cabled his acceptance and noted that he would arrive at the studio on February 7. After attending a screening of a rough cut at the studio on February 8, Korngold was despondent. He wrote Wallis a regretful letter: "*Robin Hood* is no picture for me. I have no relation for it and therefore, cannot produce music for it. . . . Let me say 'no' definitely and let me say it today when no time has been lost for you as yet, since the work print will not be ready until tomorrow."

Korngold returned to his Toluca Lake residence. Three days later, on February 12, the composer learned of the Anschluss, or union between Germany and Austria. The annexation of Austria was the overture of Hitler's dominance of Europe: the Nazi dictator and his troops would march into Vienna a month later, ending Austria's existence as an independent country. Korngold heard this news as Leo Forbstein rang his doorbell.[3] At the behest of Warner, Wallis, and Blanke, Forbstein begged the composer to reconsider. Given the seismic events in Europe that he had learned of just a moment before, he relented and agreed to compose the *Robin Hood* score.

After his family made it safely out of Austria on the last open train to Switzerland in mid-March, the composer went to work. Jack Warner extended the general release date of the film to May 14, 1938, allotting Korngold seven weeks to compose his score. Korngold's son George later recalled: "My father was on the verge of stopping several times. I shall never forget his anguished protestations of 'I just can't do it!' which I over-heard in the middle of the night through my bedroom wall. He was suffer-ing, and at the same time producing one of his finest scores."

Korngold's *Robin Hood* music became an extraordinary triumph. The composer relied on his father's recommendation to use as the foun-dation the overture *Sursum Corda,* opus 13—Latin for *Lift Up Your Hearts*—that Korngold had composed in 1919. It was influenced by Rich-ard Strauss's tone poems. The score would be written like an operetta: each major scene and character was linked to an appropriate theme. It is not an exaggeration to state that no other Hollywood movie was ever more brilliantly enhanced by a music score. Warner Bros. recognized the uniqueness of Korngold's achievement by using his score to promote the film. A special radio broadcast of the composer conducting the studio or-chestra playing major excerpts and Basil Rathbone narrating the story oc-curred on May 11, 1938, three days before the film's general release.

According to Jack Warner, *Robin Hood*'s Pomona sneak preview was greeted by the most enthusiastic reception in the studio's history. The response to additional previews was just as ecstatic. Wallis cabled New York after an April 24 preview screening at Warner Bros.' Hollywood Theatre to say that the reception was "absolutely sensational. Spontane-ous applause throughout the picture. Terrific hand at finish. Review sen-sational. Important people throughout business phoning congratulations this morning. . . . Its success without question."

The Adventures of Robin Hood cost $2,033,000 to produce and would gross almost twice that during its initial release. It was nominated for four Academy Awards, including Best Picture. It won three: Best Art Direction, Best Editing, and Best Music, Original Score, by Korngold. The composer reveled in his redemptive triumph by personally accept-ing his Oscar.[4] In the three-quarters of a century since its release, the film remains a masterpiece. The gorgeous Technicolor photography and exquisite production design accentuated by Korngold's music produced a synergistic work of art that has proven immune to age. The script, com-posed with straightforward elements of legend, romance, humor, and dash, has not become dated, either. All the performances remain spot-on, particularly those of the two leading stars.

Errol Flynn was at the peak of his powers in 1938. He would later profess hatred of being typed as the humorous swashbuckling outlaw, but, with due respect to Douglas Fairbanks, no other actor has been better suited to play such a challenging role with more panache.

Hal Wallis, Errol Flynn, and Olivia de Havilland chat during *The Adventures of Robin Hood* while Curtiz studies his ever-present script (courtesy of the Lucas family).

Not wanting to repeat the experience in which she recoiled observing herself onscreen in *The Charge of the Light Brigade,* Olivia de Havilland claimed long afterward that she did not see the film when it was first released. She eventually watched it with her young son in Paris during the 1950s and was transfixed: "I had no idea it was so good. It was enchanting, and I thought, good gracious, it's a classic, it really is a classic! When we made those films, we had no idea what we were making, that we making the best of their kind. We were, and that was marvelous."

In giving Curtiz full marks for *The Adventures of Robin Hood,* it would be unjust to overlook the contributions of William Keighley. Filmmaking is a collaborative art, and the film would have been different without his work in Chino. Ditto for Henry Blanke, who skillfully protected Curtiz by preventing Wallis from micromanaging every aspect of the production. Blanke's presence allowed Curtiz to direct the picture in magnificent style with minimal interference. Much credit is due to Hal Wallis, who uncharacteristically gambled by committing additional resources at a moment when the picture's ultimate success appeared extremely iffy. He also corrected his original mistake of assigning Keighley to the picture by having Curtiz take over at a critical juncture. In shaping the entire production, Wallis made *Robin Hood* his picture as much as Curtiz's.

Robin Hood was also a transition point in Curtiz's relationship with Wallis. Although the latter would continue to be periodically frustrated with what he considered the director's excesses, Wallis from this point forward muted the demeaning tone of his criticisms. Never again would he seriously consider removing Curtiz from a picture. Wallis was evolving into a world-class producer and he concurrently became a more fervent advocate of Curtiz. Curtiz's success enhanced the executive producer's own professional reputation. Wallis never forgot what Curtiz did for him on *Robin Hood*. They became closer friends.

Curtiz directed approximately one-half to two-thirds of the film that ended up in the final cut. But much more important than the amount of footage was the uplifting vigor of the director's personality imbued in the picture. De Havilland, who retains few pleasant memories of working with Curtiz, offered an honest, if reluctant, testimonial to the success of *Robin Hood:* "Oh, he [Curtiz] was a villain, but I guess he was pretty good. We didn't believe it then, but he clearly was. He knew what he was doing. He knew how to tell a story very clearly and he knew how to keep things going; you had to transmit vitality. I was astounded by *Robin Hood*'s vitality, its effervescence. That was a revelation, and I thought, well, he had something to do with it, and he did; I have to admit that."

20

Cash Cow

Curtiz was now poised to embark on the most successful portion of his career. After twelve years, he had merged his cinematic style with the rapidly paced Warner Bros. house technique pressed on him by Zanuck and Wallis. Curtiz's understanding of exactly what he wanted in front of the camera accentuated his ability to direct his actors.

His technical acumen was complemented by an acute awareness of the background details of the stories he was putting on film. He continued his quest to learn everything possible about his adopted country. By performing his own research, he acquired a unique insight beyond jingoistic gratitude. Whether it involved a metropolitan newsroom, a small town, or an urban slum, his desire to absorb U.S. history and culture would be reflected in the sensibility as well as the reality of his work. Despite his battles with the English language, Curtiz had become a quintessentially American film director.

His major liability, as perceived by some of the writers who worked with him, was a lack of understanding of how a story needed to maintain thematic continuity. Curtiz could spitball dialogue to correct or enhance individual scenes, but he didn't always recognize broader flaws. He certainly strove in every instance to bring a realistic tale to the screen. In working with writers, he attempted to extract a reason for everything. Like Hitchcock, he designed his films with the audience's reaction in mind. "Curtiz wants no question in the mind of the audience as to why anything happened," claimed Robert Buckner. Like most directors who cut their teeth in silents, he was more of a visual storyteller who eschewed dialogue whenever possible. The screenwriter Casey Robinson observed: "With Curtiz, I must say that the quality of the picture depended on the script. He would get the best he could out of the script, but sometimes if he . . . had a lousy script, it would be a lousy picture. If he had a good script, it would be a beautiful picture."

John Meredyth Lucas viewed his stepfather's dilemma as the inevitable catch-22 of being a director at a studio where writers wrote and directors directed: "Mike's problem is that he was too good at his trade. He would direct any script the studio forced on him. . . . A great director can make a bad story better but never make it great."

As the screenwriter of *Four's a Crowd,* Casey Robinson had firsthand experience with the creation of an indifferent script. In an interview he dismissed the film as "a program comedy." Starring Errol Flynn, Olivia de Havilland, Rosalind Russell, and Patric Knowles, *Four's a Crowd* was scarcely a programmer. And its failure was due to more than poor writing. From its inception, Warner Bros. had struggled with the production of successful comedy features. Humor was an institutional deficit exemplified by the personalities of the men who ran the studio. Harry Warner was a mirthless man who took taciturnity to tight-lipped extremes. Jack Warner's sense of humor made the Three Stooges resemble light-comedy sophisticates. The actor Richard Erdman recalled that all the Warner contracted talent were compelled to appear at annual banquets for the studio distributors held on one of the soundstages, where they pretended to laugh at Warner's hideous jokes delivered from the center dais: "It was terrible. And if nobody laughed, Warner figured no one heard him, so he repeated himself at greater volume."

Hal Wallis and Curtiz rarely indulged in laughter on the job and never at their own expense. The funniest lines from the screenwriter contingent emanated from the youthful Epstein brothers, who enjoyed poking fun at Jack Warner and his studio. The Epsteins' sardonic humor would soon have a significant influence on several of Curtiz's important films.

Wallis understood that a successful Ernst Lubitsch–style comedy—without Lubitsch—was difficult, if not beyond him: "Light comedy requires that special light touch, and the results are seldom as rewarding commercially." The best that he could muster in early 1938 was an attempt to copy a success produced by another studio, using some of its actors. For *Four's a Crowd,* he borrowed Rosalind Russell from Metro and Walter Connolly from Columbia. The story about a newspaper editor (Flynn), his reporter (Russell), the paper's young owner (Knowles), and a tycoon's daughter (de Havilland) wooing each other through comedic complications and ending up with different mates was adapted from Wallace Sullivan's story "All Rights Reserved." It was a nearly direct lift from MGM's *Libeled Lady* (1936), which was also penned by Sullivan.

Curtiz was given the assignment because William Dieterle was directing *Blockade* for the producer Walter Wanger, and Edmund Goulding, who had worked on the script, turned the assignment down. Curtiz spent several days at the *Los Angeles Herald Examiner* observing in order to faithfully re-create the bustle of a working newsroom. The film was visually permeated with the director's verve, but it proved more nettling than funny. Casey Robinson's insider dialogue, which seemed sophisticated on the page, simply didn't play well. Curtiz vainly attempted to improve the screenplay as Casey Robinson reported in a memo to Wallis: "What Mike regarded as a serious weakness in the middle of the picture (What he asked for and could not find an answer for was some reason why the newspaper must find the identity of H. Louis Brown). . . . This is not meant as a criticism of Mike—whose ideas are very helpful and who is only trying to improve the picture. Naturally I cannot make all the improvements Mike wants in the script."

The production of *Four's a Crowd* was also less than amusing. The schedule coincided with the disastrous flood of 1938 wrought by tropical storms that swept through Southern California, killing more than 120 people and postponing the Academy Awards for a week. All four stars became ill with the flu. De Havilland was frustrated to be playing yet another consort to Errol Flynn. She was further dismayed about being directed again by Curtiz. According to production correspondence, she was late, didn't know her lines, and brought production to a halt one evening when she "walked off the set and refused to work any longer."

In an attempt to overcome the script's deficiencies, Curtiz added dashes of visual comedy that impressed Wallis: "All of those pieces of business of putting the dog under the waste basket, and getting de Havilland out of the room, and the rouge on the teacups, the added business with the skeleton . . . were excellent."

By combining various action scenes, Curtiz brought the picture in $12,000 under budget, even though he finished eleven days behind schedule. *Four's a Crowd* grossed under $1 million, reinforcing the front office's conviction that Errol Flynn should remain a swashbuckling action star.

Wallis's story editor, Irene Lee (later Irene Lee Diamond), was proficient at guiding viable properties to her boss for acquisition and recommending appropriate writers. After drawing Wallis's attention to "Sister Act," a Fannie Hurst short story that was published in Hearst's *International Cosmopolitan* in March 1937, Lee nudged Wallis to assign it to Lenore Coffee. Coffee fashioned an elegantly structured screenplay out of Hurst's story about the musical Lemp family.

Lee also reminded Wallis that the best writer to finish the job also had a twin brother who was just as talented. Julius and Philip Epstein were the sons of a livery stable owner from New York's Lower East Side. After being educated at Penn State, Julius went to Hollywood in 1933 as a ghostwriter for Jerry Wald. The Wald-Epstein association was said to have inspired Budd Schulberg's 1941 acid Hollywood novel *What Makes Sammy Run?* Wald was the fast-talking Hollywood operator Sammy Glick, and Epstein the long-suffering writer Julian Blumberg.

"Julie" Epstein wised up quickly to the mores of Hollywood credit grabbing after Wald sold one of Epstein's original screenplays to Warner Bros. as a jointly written project in 1935. Julie was soon working as a Warner Bros. contract writer. His brother, Phil, also passed through a brief initiation as Wald's ghostwriter and eventually joined Julie at the studio. "The boys" would become a peerless screenwriting team, functioning more or less as a single entity. They excelled equally at composing entire scripts and punching up existing screenplays with witty, effervescent dialogue. Lenore Coffee's final draft of *Sister Act* (the working title of *Four Daughters*) was given to Julie Epstein to polish the lines before Curtiz began filming in April. Wallis, a stickler for having a completed script in hand before start of production, blew his stack to Henry Blanke about Epstein's slow progress: "What in the world is Epstein doing all this time on *Sister Act*? I thought we had a pretty good script and it was just a matter of his going through the last half of the story, or the last third, and doing a little touching up of the dialogue. The whole job shouldn't have taken more than a week, and he has already been on it about three. What the hell is the matter with him anyway? Does he want to work or doesn't he?"

The Epstein brothers would become famous (or, rather, infamous, in the view of Jack Warner) for writing no more than two hours a day. Wallis calmed down after he read Epstein's completed pages, full of superb dialogue that brought the characters to life. And the casting of *Four Daughters* matched the quality of the screenplay. Claude Rains played a music professor, Adam Lemp, and his four musically inclined daughters were the singing Lane Sisters—Priscilla, Lola, and Rosemary—plus a contract actress, Gale Page.

Errol Flynn turned down the leading role of Felix Deitz, the charming if frivolous composer who moves into the Lemp household and falls in love with Priscilla Lane. After reading the script, he realized that the starring role was a second banana to the ostensible supporting character of Mickey Borden. The newcomer Jeffrey Lynn was given the Deitz role as his big opportunity.

A street-toughened product of the Bronx, Julius Garfield (he had changed his surname from Garfinkle in 1932) had left the Group Theatre when he didn't get to play the lead role in the Clifford Odets 1937 Broadway play *Golden Boy*. Odets had written the part of the young violinist-boxer for Garfield, but the play's director, Harold Clurman, decided to cast Luther Adler, his brother-in-law. After a screen test at Warner's New York office resulted in a $750 per week contract for two pictures, Garfield took the Super Chief to Los Angeles and presented himself to Jack Warner. Warner, who viewed overtly Jewish actors as a possible business risk, attempted to convince him to change his first name: "People are gonna find out you're a Jew sooner or later," he told the young actor, "but better later."

Garfield resisted being renamed "James" after the deceased President—"Remember, they shot him"—and settled for John. The Epstein brothers befriended him and arranged with Curtiz to shoot a screen test for *Four Daughters* with Garfield as Mickey Borden. Another version has Curtiz viewing a Metro screen test of Garfield. By whichever circumstance, Curtiz immediately told Wallis that they had their Mickey and a whole lot more: Garfield's appeal was palpable. Jeffrey Lynn saw it after watching his own screen test: "I also got to see Garfield's test. Now, I'd never heard of this guy John Garfield, but after I saw the test I said, 'Whoever does get in this picture with him [Garfield] better step aside, because he's got the film.'"

Curtiz and Garfield got on extremely well. Although it took him a while to decrypt the director's bollixed syntax, Garfield realized that Curtiz knew exactly what he was doing. Conversely, the director observed that the young New Yorker who possessed the intangible movie star charisma was dedicated to his craft. He warmed up to Garfield personally, too: They'd both been youthfully impoverished urban Jews graced with a unique artistic sensibility wedded to fierce ambition. Curtiz was the perfect director for Garfield; he taught the Group Theatre alumnus that in front of the camera, less is more. The actor remained grateful to Curtiz, whom he credited with his breakthrough: "Mike discovered me. He had wanted Burgess Meredith for the part of Mickey Borden, but Meredith was going to Europe. Mike saw a test I made for Metro which refused to sign me and said, 'That's my boy.'"

Four Daughters is charming schmaltz for the first thirty minutes—until Garfield makes his entrance. Unshaven, tie askew, hat tilted back, he cynically assesses the interior of the Lemp household (a veritable template for *Better Homes and Gardens*): "Rug on the floor, smell of cooking in the kitchen, piano, flowers. It's homes like these that are the backbone of America. Where's the spinning wheel?"

Four Daughters became John Garfield's picture but it was also Curtiz's. Insulated again by Henry Blanke, the director exerted himself to instill every bit of painstaking craftsmanship in the film. The opening sequence is pure Curtiz. As the credits dissolve, the camera glides through a flowering dogwood tree outside the Lemp residence to the sound of the professor rehearsing a Schubert composition with his daughters. The camera travels through the window into the house, pausing on Lemp's doctorate of music certificate on the wall. It then unobtrusively gives us individual close-ups of the family playing their instruments. Curtiz seamlessly establishes the setting of the film before the first word of dialogue.

Garfield's suicide as Mickey Borden is similarly striking. We see him driving a car with the perspective alternating between his face and his view of the snowy road through the windshield as the wiper sweeps off the snowflakes. Lighting a cigarette with wide-eyed resolve, he switches off the windshield wipers. There is a quick close-up of his foot pushing the accelerator to the floor, then his anguished expression, and the windshield turns opaque with snow as the scene dissolves. Billy Wilder remarked that this sequence "was one of the very best suicides ever in a picture. . . . It's a wonderful, wonderful pictorial invention."

Wallis praised Curtiz's dailies but urged Henry Blanke to hurry him along:

> We must pick up time on this thing, as it would be bad enough with Flynn in the picture to be four days behind schedule, but he must realize that without a big name cast, the more we can save on this picture, the more chance we will have of having a successful picture. You must keep after Mike and see that he doesn't take too much time. . . . Naturally, these long, involved set-ups in the kitchen, moving around from one to another and all that on the dolly eat up plenty of hours. . . . Will you please talk to Mike about this and see that he starts doing simpler shots, because after all . . . we move right into close-ups anyway.

Wallis's anxiety over the schedule lacked any consideration of the time required for the director to work with the actors. Jeffrey Lynn might have been eclipsed by Garfield's turn, but he made a favorable impression that was never equaled in his future films. The experienced Claude Rains claimed that Curtiz taught him the difference between stage and movie acting by showing him "what not to do in front of the camera."

Lynn remembered Curtiz's direction as inspirational:

> Remember that scene at the piano with Garfield and May Robson when she offers him tea? Well one day Curtiz called the whole cast together, and he told us the story as he saw it. And what that scene meant to all of us. He must have talked for almost an hour, and as he finished tears were streaming down his face. We couldn't speak! We were so entranced by this tough Hungarian weightlifter telling us about this slice of American life, and if I had any doubts about the film, I forgot them there and then. I figured if he was going to be that serious about the film, then I knew I had to be.

Despite the fretting about the schedule, Curtiz finished just two days behind. The *New York Times* gave the picture an unqualified rave: "A charming, at times heartbreakingly human, little comedy about life in a musical family of attractive daughters which occasionally is ruffled by the drama of a masculine world outside, Four Daughters . . . tempts one to agree with Jack Warner's recent assertion in the advertisements that it is the climax of his career." The *Chicago Herald Examiner* extolled its director: "Michael Curtiz's direction approaches perfection." Jack Warner sent an unusually warm note of praise to Curtiz, shown in the accompanying illustration.

Four Daughters holds up well, even though its representation of small-town Americana seems a bit faded after the passage of three-quarters of a century. It had wit, charm, and wholesome storytelling, and the dark aspect of Garfield's character infused it with an appropriate melodramatic flavor. It was nominated for five Academy Awards. In addition to Curtiz for direction and Coffee and Epstein for writing, there was Garfield's performance for Best Supporting Actor and the coveted nomination for Best Picture. Although the film won no Oscars, it was a hit that would spawn three additional films: *Daughters Courageous* (1939), *Four Wives* (1939), and *Four Mothers* (1941). Curtiz would direct the first two follow-ups as he reveled in the formation of one of the most valued entities sought by a studio: a franchise.

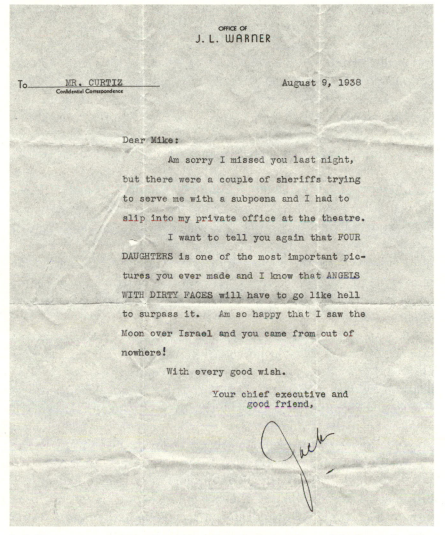

Jack Warner memo to Curtiz re: *Four Daughters* (courtesy of the Lucas family).

James Cagney's hiatus ended in January 1938. After he was released from his original Warner contract in Los Angeles Superior Court on March 16, 1936, Cagney starred in a pair of films, *Great Guy* (1936) and *Something to Sing About* (1937), for Grand National Pictures. Few people watched these films, as the other major studios had closed ranks with Warner Bros. and refused to book them. Despite the show of solidarity, Jack Warner realized his two-year-old lawsuit against Cagney had boomeranged. He caused his top star to be released from his contract and had received nothing in return other than legal bills and bad publicity. When William Cagney began preparing a lawsuit against Warner Bros. for professionally ostracizing his brother, Jack caved and ceded a then-unprecedented amount of money and authority to a contracted actor.

Cagney's new five-year contract with Warner Bros. was groundbreaking: he agreed to make eleven pictures at the rate of two or three a year, plus one to close out his previous contract. He was guaranteed $150,000 per picture plus 10 percent of the gross over $1,500,000. He'd have twelve consecutive weeks of vacation on his Martha's Vineyard estate, and William Cagney would be the associate producer on all his films. Cagney also had script approval and an option to submit his own story ideas. The most extraordinary aspect of the deal was termed a "happiness clause." He could cancel his contract at the conclusion of any film or given year if his relationship with the studio was determined to be "obnoxious or unsatisfactory to him." Since "obnoxious" was a polite term for how Cagney and Jack Warner felt about each other, the new contract was a marriage of tenuous necessity.

Boy Meets Girl was an inauspicious return by Cagney. Directed by his pal Lloyd Bacon, what had been a hit Broadway farce became another misfired Warner Bros. attempt at comedy. Bacon acquiesced to Wallis's demands by moving matters along at a racehorse pace. The result was Cagney and his costar Pat O'Brien unintelligibly barking their lines at one another. Cagney waited until the picture was finished, then clipped out a negative review about his staccato delivery and mailed it to Wallis. It was clear that something better was needed.

Angels with Dirty Faces was an original story written by Rowland Brown about the friendship of two city boys who grow up to become a gangster and a priest. Brown, who was reputed to have ties to Detroit's Purple Gang, was cash-strapped at the time. When he discovered that Warner Bros. was interested, he took his story to Ben Hecht and Charles MacArthur, who were glad to polish up the yarn for their friend. Hal Wallis eventually purchased it from Brown for $12,500 and assigned Curtiz to direct. Wallis believed that Curtiz was strong enough to help him control the Cagney brothers. Curtiz had never helmed a true gangster picture, but his assignment proved an astute decision—although not for all the reasons Wallis originally intended.

John Wexley and Warren Duff were tapped to do the difficult job of adapting Brown's story to the screen. The studio received a great deal of negative correspondence from the Production Code Authority; a film based on the relationship between a hoodlum and a Catholic priest received Joe Breen's undivided attention. The Cagney brothers were upset that the final shooting script diluted some of the dramatic aspects that had originally attracted them to the property.

Rather than locking horns with Jack Warner, the brothers decided on subterfuge. James Cagney would "suggest" changes on the set to shape the story in the desired manner. The Cagneys discovered a staunch ally in Curtiz. Both the star and the director made changes and additions that raised *Angels with Dirty Faces* to the level of something memorable.

The creative atmosphere on the set inspired others in the cast—Pat O'Brien, Humphrey Bogart, and George Bancroft—to suggest dialogue improvements. This leniency did not extend to the Dead End Kids. Leo Gorcey overstepped the boundaries one day when he ad-libbed a cue line to James Cagney, who reacted in character: "I gave Gorcey a stiff arm right above the nose. Bang! His head went back, hitting the kid behind him, stunning them both momentarily." Cagney told the kids to "cut out this goddamned nonsense" and had no further trouble with them.

The original Dead End Kids—Billy Halop, Bobby Jordan, Huntz Hall, Leo Gorcey, Bernard Punsley, and Gabriel Dell—came to Warners after Wallis convinced Jack Warner to purchase their contract from Sam Goldwyn.[1] It was a brilliant move to incorporate them into *Angels with Dirty Faces,* as it made it possible for the story to be about more than the star-crossed destinies of the gangster Rocky Sullivan (Cagney) and Father Jerry Connolly (O'Brien). It also provided the punchy finale about Rocky "dying yellow" to save the slum kids who idolize him.

Less perceptive was Wallis's haranguing of Curtiz about Cagney's acting, recalling what occurred during *Jimmy the Gent.* Wallis apparently believed that every Cagney performance should be a repeat of the actor's Tom Powers character in 1931's *The Public Enemy.* Cagney was creating a unique persona as Rocky Sullivan while Wallis remained fixated on an ominous stereotype. Curtiz ignored the producer's entreaties. He well knew that, in terms of characterization, Cagney directed Cagney. In a major part of his transition to Hollywood filmmaking, Curtiz listened to actors who were interested in the betterment of the picture while only pretending to pay attention to stars solely concerned with the betterment of their careers.

Wallis harped on Curtiz about overshooting, as did Jack Warner, who visited the set on July 15 and was observed "urging Mike along." There was also the usual difference of opinion between Curtiz's compositions and Wallis's insistence on close-ups. Wallis, however, was perceptive regarding how to film the Dead End Kids in reactive shots that captured their unique personalities. He also recognized that Ann Sheridan's line readings needed to be more emotive, referring to the actress in correspondence as "the girl," the identical term he used for Olivia de Havilland during *Captain Blood*. With the exception of his criticism of Cagney, Wallis's observations on how to accentuate the other performances were spot-on.

Even though Wallis habitually scolded Curtiz for changing dialogue, he was not inclined to do much about it this time out. He could hardly castigate his director for deviating from the script while allowing the film's star to do the same thing. The clincher was that Wallis realized that the alterations by Cagney, Curtiz, and the others were improving the picture. In one instance, when Wallis discovered that Curtiz had prepared an additional scene with Pat O'Brien launching an anti-gangster crusade from a radio station, he lodged no objection even though an unbudgeted set had to be built. And there was flexibility on both sides. Although Cag-

Curtiz observes a shot of James Cagney and Ann Sheridan in *Angels with Dirty Faces* (1938) (courtesy of the Lucas family).

ney considered Hal Wallis a front-office shill for Jack Warner, he realized that he couldn't totally ignore the executive producer. Cagney initiated a discussion with Wallis that resulted in the expansion of a key sequence that included details that the screenwriters had omitted from Rowland Brown's story.

After killing Frazier (Bogart) and Keefer (Bancroft), Rocky engages in a running gun battle with the police and is trapped in a warehouse. Father Connolly arrives to reason with him over a police loudspeaker, and Rocky briefly takes him hostage before being apprehended. After listening to Cagney, Wallis sent a memo to associate producer Sam Bischoff inviting him and Curtiz to a meeting in order to incorporate Cagney's "gutty" ideas into the film.

An emboldened Curtiz added shots to this sequence. The production manager, Frank Mattison, scrambled to give the director what he needed and reported back to Tenny Wright: "While the shots he has added are no doubt building up the sequence, there is no mind-reader on the lot that can keep ahead of Mike when you turn him loose with machine guns, revolvers, bullets and gas bombs. I think he would rather play cops and robbers than eat."

Curtiz attempted one visual flourish in the gun battle that might have ended James Cagney's comeback permanently. The director blocked out a scene with the star standing at an open warehouse window firing blanks at the police below, then ducking back against the wall as actual machine gun bullets shatter the window. The same marksman who had barely missed Cagney during the filming of *The Public Enemy* was standing by while Curtiz reassured the star that the stunt was perfectly safe. Cagney refused to play the scene with live ammo. He told Curtiz to make it a process shot that could be edited in later. The director reluctantly acquiesced. And indeed, when the machine gunner fired for the camera, one bullet hit the steel window frame and ricocheted into the wall exactly where Cagney's head would have been.

Pat O'Brien recalled another instance when Curtiz's reckless exuberance created a nerve-wracking moment. The director insisted that a scene establishing the divergent childhood paths of the protagonists be filmed at the downtown railway yard. Two juvenile actors playing the Cagney and O'Brien characters are seen stealing pens from a boxcar and are pursued by the police. In the film, Jerry Connolly escapes and becomes a priest, whereas Rocky is caught and begins his journey through reform school and prison. Curtiz had the boys cross the tracks in front of a moving train that was traveling too fast. One of them had a (choreographed) fall and was helped up as the pair scrambled away just in time to escape the on-rushing train. O'Brien remembered: "The train barely missed hitting the two boys, who leaped aside like salmon. The shaking engineer clambered down out of his cab; he looked like death at bargain prices. Mike, a true Hungarian, just smiled at him. '*Very* good. This was part of the action of our story. I purposely did not tell the two boys before you go so fast.'" The film crew had to restrain the train engineer from attacking Curtiz, who shook his head afterward and asked, "How do you get realism if not take chances?"

Curtiz imbued authenticity of a less hazardous nature in the early scenes depicting life in the ghetto. He had fifty-six pushcarts imported from New York City along with four hurdy-gurdies to dress up the set of a slum neighborhood. To open the film, the director transitioned from a man on the street reading a newspaper headline about Warren Harding's presidential election to a moving-crane shot of a tenement street set encompassing four city blocks. The period vegetable pushcarts, the laundry hanging on fire escapes, and a variety of horse-driven carriages are accentuated during a visual transition from the 1920 neighborhood of Rocky Sullivan and Jerry Connolly to the same locale eighteen years later, after Rocky emerges from prison.

To depict the passage of time, Curtiz employed an identical shot using a late 1930s headline about an airplane circling the globe and once again perused the neighborhood by crane. Although it is recognizably the same slum, including the "Dock Street" sign, the storefronts are changed, there is less laundry hanging about, and the streets are now jammed with automobiles. The camera follows a radio van festooned with loudspeakers blaring music that passes by Connolly's neighborhood parish, where he is directing the boys' choir as the adult Rocky enters the church. Curtiz's staging of action during the film is brilliant; Sol Polito's shaded photography and Max Steiner's score instill an ominous mood.

Cagney put his heart into playing Rocky Sullivan. Drawing on a boyhood memory of a Yorkville street pimp by appropriating his "what d'ya hear, what d'ya say" greeting while lifting his arms and rolling his shoulders, the actor turned in a classic performance that provided fodder for generations of Cagney impressionists. The denouement (Father Jerry begs Rocky to die as a coward to avoid becoming a posthumous hero to the slum kids who idolize him) is wonderfully composed. Curtiz decided to film Cagney and O'Brien's final conversation in the death cell in a single, continuous take that lasted a full twelve minutes before editing. Both actors nailed it on the first try.

Curtiz talked the production department into providing iron doors and bars for the set where Cagney walks the last mile and rode the camera dolly that filmed the grim scene. The death cell set and corridor to the electric chair were built to the exact specifications of the Sing Sing prison death house. The finale of a struggling Rocky Sullivan in silhouette being strapped into the electric chair while screaming for his life remains chilling. Cagney later claimed it took three days to film the execution sequence, during which he lost four pounds. It was worth it.

Angels with Dirty Faces wrapped on August 10, 1938. Its November release was sensational. Cagney won the National Board of Review and New York Critic's Circle Award, but he lost the Best Actor Oscar to his pal Spencer Tracy for *Boys Town*. Curtiz and Rowland Brown were also Oscar-nominated.

It was an incredible year for Curtiz, even though neither *Four Daughters* nor *Angels with Dirty Faces* earned him a Best Director Academy Award. Darryl Zanuck sent him a telegram after the Oscars the following February, commiserating that his friend had lost the award on a "technicality," since Curtiz garnered the most aggregate votes. His work was universally recognized as outstanding, and his pictures grossed more than $8 million. *Angels with Dirty Faces* was one of the top moneymakers of the year, raking in more than $2.3 million against an investment of $633,000. Curtiz had become the directorial cash cow for Warner Bros.

The director capped off his most successful year in Hollywood yet by helming an epic Western. Although Twentieth Century-Fox's *Jesse James* (1939), followed closely by John Ford's *Stagecoach* and Cecil B. DeMille's *Union Pacific,* are rightly credited for rescuing Westerns from the doldrums of Poverty Row, a major Western production had been germinating at Warner Bros. for some time. In February 1938 Jack Warner responded to Hal Wallis's proposal about a movie biography about the legendary lawman Wyatt Earp: "We would really have a box office attraction in this all over the world, as these Western epics go great in America, and it would be sensational in Europe. . . . With the western streets we have at the ranch and at the studio, we could get a good fast director like Lloyd Bacon to shoot it and I don't know if Muni would do this or not, but it would be swell of him to play Wyatt Earp."

Although the notion of Paul Muni as Wyatt Earp seems ridiculous, Warner was convinced that the esteemed actor could play any imaginable historical figure except Beethoven because, as he memorably told Henry Blanke, "Nobody wants to see a movie about a blind composer." But Muni would be cast in the title role of *Juarez* instead, and Wallis had to come up with a viable star.

The Wyatt Earp notion was abandoned as Robert Buckner fashioned a screenplay about the fictional Wade Hatton, a Texas cattleman who arrives in Dodge City and cleans up the West's version of Sodom and Gomorrah. Although Buckner inserted some social editorializing about railroad capitalism and women's rights, the yarn was pure entertainment. There would be shoot-outs, saloon brawls, cattle stampedes, and speeding locomotives, all in Technicolor. *Dodge City* would be a sprawling, six-gun tableau specifically written for Curtiz to direct.

Casting the picture became an acute problem by July, as it was scheduled to be finished before the end of the year. Even though Curtiz was assigned, the studio still didn't have the picture cast or the script completed. The associate producer Robert Lord pressed Wallis for Gary Cooper—under contract to Paramount—and then suggested James Cagney. Cooper was unattainable and Cagney had already agreed to star in *The Oklahoma Kid*, directed by Lloyd Bacon; his contract precluded any arbitrary recasting, and Wallis didn't even bother considering him. Warner Bros. had Errol Flynn under contract. Why look any further?

Although it resembled the *Captain Blood* casting debacle all over again, the circumstances were different. Flynn was an established star who was completing a prestigious role in *The Dawn Patrol*. He craved the carefree life on his yacht far more than life on horseback at a remote location with his least favorite director. He also believed he was ill equipped to star in such a uniquely American genre. After he read the script, his agent, Noll Gurney, sent a memo to Jack Warner outlining his client's concerns: "He seems a little dubious about his ability to play a part that is so essentially American—or accentuated, as he puts it—but Bob Lord is so enthusiastic about Errol for this part, and I know you are too, that I feel if we have a talk together it will give Errol some confidence."

Lord, Wallis, and Warner led the cheerleading; Robert Buckner provided Alan Hale with some expositional whimsy in the script about Hatton's (Flynn's) being a British soldier of fortune who "was with the English Army over in India, then a hoo-rah revolution in Cuba before he started punching cattle in Texas." The star came around. In truth, it wasn't nearly as difficult as haggling with Cagney or Muni. Flynn was an insecure free spirit who wanted to get paid what he felt he was worth. *Dodge City* continued to provide the means of a rollicking life of drinking, wenching, and sailing on the *Sirocco*.[2]

Production began on a sour note when Flynn arrived unable to work. Wallis fumed about it to Tenny Wright:

Last night I found out that Flynn arrived the morning of the 9th, was met by Berry and then for some reason or other Berry left him and picked him up again that night, and in the meantime Flynn did some damned fool thing or other and showed up on location with a sprained ankle. Consequently, the whole first day Mike was handicapped by having to shoot close-ups because Flynn couldn't get his boots on, and the entire second day Mike had to shoot around him, making odd shots and long shots, while Flynn stayed in bed and had his ankle treated. . . . Don't you think that I knew what I was talking about when I asked you to have a man meet Flynn at the boat and take him right to the location, or do you think that I just sit up here and think these things up for my health or because I like to?

Flynn was again cast with Olivia de Havilland, who was at the end of her professional tether. She begged Jack Warner to lend her out to David O. Selznick to play Melanie in *Gone with the Wind*. He refused, telling her Selznick's big picture would end up being a gigantic flop (after he tried to option it) and ordered Wallis to assign her to *Dodge City*. A bundle of raw nerves after making three movies in six months, de Havilland reported to location in Northern California, near Modesto, where Curtiz began production on November 10, 1938. Long afterward, she described *Dodge City* as "an awful experience." She remembered, "I was in such a depressed state, that I could hardly remember the lines." Errol Flynn didn't help her dreary demeanor. The actor-continued to resort to childish scene-stealing tricks, twirling horse reins and fiddling with grass during their two-shots when his costar was speaking her lines.

Her frustration over how she had been continually cast as Flynn's romantic sidekick fueled her determination to land the role in *Gone with the Wind*. She also had more than artistic concerns to be upset about. As a costar, she was getting paid little more than the character actor Frank McHugh received for a secondary supporting role. Jack Warner's serial mishandling of Olivia de Havilland would end up triggering a chain of events that shook the studio system to its very foundations.

Curtiz with Olivia de Havilland during filming of *Dodge City* (1939). One reason for her unhappiness during the production is grasping her right arm (courtesy of the Academy of Motion Picture Arts and Sciences).

At the Modesto and Little River locations, Curtiz directed the cattle drive and covered wagon sequences flawlessly before making his first major deviation from the script. Abbie Irving's (De Havilland's) loutish, drunken brother, Lee (William Lundigan), was supposed to be gunned down in self-defense by Hatton after nearly causing a cattle herd to stampede the wagon train. Curtiz decided to have Hatton wound Lee in the leg after he tries to shoot Rusty Hart (Alan Hale). Hatton subsequently rescues Abbie from the spooked livestock that trample Lee to death. Curtiz sold Bob Lord on the script change, but no one bothered to tell Hal Wallis, who asked Lord about it: "Was it your idea or was it Mike's on location to have the boy killed by the steers running over him rather than by Flynn shooting him. I am just curious to know if Mike is starting to reconstruct the story on location."

But Curtiz's decision to use cattle as the final executioners made Hatton a more unvarnished hero. A major theme of *Dodge City* is how Abbie comes to realize that Hatton is an honorable man who resorts to violence only when he is given no choice. Would she be more sympathetic to audiences by falling in love with the man who shot her brother through the heart? Curtiz's modification of this sequence was visually stimulating while strengthening the story line. Wallis left it alone and three days later wired Curtiz: "Very happy over progress you are making. Hope you can finish in time to be home for Thanksgiving. If you do it will be Thanksgiving for all of us. Regards. PS took Freckles out yesterday Hal." The light-hearted reference to Freckles, Wallis's horse, which the producer boarded on Curtiz's ranch, underscored the fact that the director was on solid ground.

After wrapping up the location work, the company returned to the studio and divided the remaining shooting time between the Warner Ranch in Calabasas and the studio lot. Curtiz encapsulated the crowded, lawless atmosphere of Dodge City as a Babylonian boomtown of the old West. Every scene was staged with masterly background composition, particularly when Hatton and Rusty kibitz their way down a main street that is packed with people walking, talking, loading wagons, and saddling horses.

The director then pulled out all the stops in filming the mother of all Western saloon brawls on a huge set spread over two soundstages. According to production records, Curtiz deployed 176 extras and stuntmen in a prolonged sequence of barroom carnage that served as the inspiration for the finale of Mel Brooks's 1974 comedy *Blazing Saddles*. To trigger the donnybrook, the director used a device that he would repeat in a future film: Ann Sheridan warbles "Marching through Georgia" from the stage as a large contingent of Union veterans joins her in song. Guinn Williams initiates a competitive chorus of "Dixie" with a group of fellow Southerners at the bar and mayhem breaks out. Four years later, "La Marseillaise" would drown out "Deutschland über Alles" in *Casablanca*.

Although Wallis was inclined to let Curtiz have his head, he eventually ordered Robert Lord to move on after the director worked on the roughly four-minute sequence for more than a week. "I hope that Mike is through shooting the fight. . . . We have enough film already for two or three fights, and if he isn't through with everything by now, I want it stopped today." The spectacular scene was estimated to have cost $112,000, the most expensive brawl yet filmed. The experienced Lord stumbled several times in supervising the production, apologizing to Wallis at one point, "I am sorry to trouble you with these details, but having once become caught in the trap of Curtiz's enthusiasm, I do not intend to become a victim again so soon."

Curtiz stayed on schedule until near the end of the year, when matters began to go awry. De Havilland became ill, took to her bed for a time, and looked so colorless in the dailies that Curtiz called for additional makeup. The company had been split into two units, Curtiz handling both of them. The director came down with a severe sore throat right after the New Year. Illness didn't stop him from chewing out Errol Flynn and his roistering pal Bruce Cabot on the morning of January 5, when they both showed up hung over and not knowing their lines, which added another day to the production.

Curtiz dropped a lot of Buckner's dialogue, as he was directing what was inherently an action picture. Wallis eventually sent an SOS to Curtiz about the finale: "Please level with me on the ending of the picture which you are going to shoot. . . . I don't want to end the picture on that phony laugh of Olivia de Havilland's." Curtiz tied it off with a Buckner rewrite that had Flynn and de Havilland riding off into the sunset in a wagon.

Curtiz took to his ranch to recover for a spell. On the rare occasions when he was not working, he enjoyed his rural domain, despite a couple of disconcerting episodes. He'd doubled the amount of land originally purchased in Canoga Park, then added another house to the property at Bess's urging, only to have all of the plumbing fixtures—bathtub, sink, toilet—stolen by enterprising thieves during construction in February 1937.

A disaster was averted thanks to Curtiz's employment at Warner Bros. One day a catastrophic brush fire threatened to destroy his ranch when the flames jumped across Ventura Boulevard and began to move up the hillside. Bess phoned Curtiz at the studio and advised him that although family, staff, and horses were being safely evacuated, it appeared that they were going to lose the house and outlying structures. The director notified Jack Warner from the set that he would have to attempt to rescue his home from the inferno. After a momentary pause, Warner told him to continue filming and dispatched the studio fire department to Curtiz's residence, more than fifteen miles distant. The department had been expanded to a fully equipped brigade after the disastrous 1934 blaze that destroyed a large portion of the back lot.

John Meredyth Lucas remembered the rescue effort: "Within half an hour, we had the Warner fire hose trucks and equipment rolling down toward the polo field and the oncoming flames. Although ranches near us suffered damage, we lost not a single building."

The director's social life was minimal during the workweek, but he had to respond to an occasional summons from the boss. Warner invited Curtiz to join his party for a late evening at the Cotton Club in Culver City, a Prohibition-era den of iniquity modeled on the famous Harlem venue. Warner coerced Curtiz to accompany him, even though the director politely told the mogul that he simply wanted to have a sandwich and go to bed. Curtiz rose at five o'clock each morning so he could be the first person on the soundstage. He never ate lunch and was in the middle of directing a picture. Warner wouldn't hear of it. He gave Curtiz a stack of chips and led him to the roulette wheel, where the director quickly lost it all. Warner, tucked in at the blackjack table, plied Curtiz with additional chips; the director eventually snuck out the back door in search of food. All the restaurants and drive-ins along his lengthy drive home were closed, so he took to his bed tired and hungry. The next day, he received a letter from Warner on the set that he showed Bess and John later that evening:

Dear Mike,
    Congratulations again on a wonderful picture. You certainly have the magic touch.
Jack
P.S. Please send your check for three thousand for the chips.

After patching up their marriage, Curtiz and Bess Meredyth had settled into a comfortable routine. In addition to the whirl of premieres, parties, and polo matches, the couple continued to collaborate. Bess reviewed Curtiz's scripts, adding or deleting dialogue and making structural recommendations. It would be a fascinating but impossible task to discern how many of the Curtiz script changes that so exasperated Hal Wallis originated with her. Her close friend Frances Marion was adamant that Bess's contributions to her husband's films were considerable: "While she had retired from an active job at the studio, all the producers with whom Curtiz worked knew that sparks flew from her anvil into every picture that her husband made, although Bess refused to take any credit."

Curtiz revered her talent, along with that of his stepson, "Jick," who would soon turn twenty and ascend from script clerk to dialogue director with the Warner "B" unit. Curtiz also assisted his wife's ex-husband, Wilfred Lucas, who had fallen on hard times, by giving him bit parts in his and other Warner films.

But despite the apparent harmony, there were distinct fault lines. In an era when a three-bedroom house cost less than $4,000, rent averaged $27 per month, and gasoline cost 10¢ per gallon, Curtiz was living paycheck to paycheck while making $3,000 per week—which would be bumped to $3,600 in 1939.

How much of his weekly salary went to support his three out-of-wedlock children in addition to Kitty is unknown. His main profligacy was the stable of polo ponies. His wife was a different story. Her ceaseless spending on lavish parties, an entourage of servants and attendants, antiques, expanding the ranch, and the like exceeded the normal Hollywood extravagance. As Curtiz pursued his sexual infidelities, albeit with greater discretion, it is likely that his wife's apparent obliviousness to the value of money may have constituted a retributive marital tithe. The director viewed his finances with increasing concern, but he simply couldn't say no to Bess when it came to money.

There were other degrees of separation as well. Curtiz's spartan lifestyle, reflecting moderation in food and drink, plenty of exercise, and early bedtime around constant work, had chiseled him into a vigorous fifty-two-year-old. Although he possessed the then-universal vice of cigarette smoking—he went through several packs of English Ovals daily—he appeared so fit that young actors such as Jeffrey Lynn could refer to him as a weight-lifter. Meredyth was increasingly taking to her bed to be waited on, ate whatever struck her fancy, and was putting on weight. Their joint horseback rides around the property became less frequent, and they occupied separate bedrooms. Although she was three years Curtiz's junior, Meredyth increasingly resembled an older woman with a younger husband.

Curtiz was also supporting Kitty, who was completing her art studies at City College of New York. The amount of financial support that he provided for his other three children during this period is unknown. He never spoke to anyone in Hollywood about his two namesake sons or daughter Sonja in Europe.

By the end of 1938, Hitler's acquisitive intentions in Europe were evident to all but the most obtuse. Yet appeasement abroad and isolationism at home remained the order the day. Curtiz's mother and his siblings remained in Hungary while the director monitored events with increasing apprehension. For Harry and Jack Warner, it was time to initiate bolder action in rallying the country to what they perceived as a clear and present danger to everything they had accomplished. Curtiz would direct more movies and cope with a personal crisis before joining the vanguard of what would become a cinematic crusade.

21

Reaching Their Majority

Curtiz came to the rescue again after John Garfield was cast in Brynie Foy's production of *Blackwell's Island*. After his Oscar nomination for *Four Daughters,* Garfield had his screen career stereotyped much like Cagney's and Flynn's had been after they initially hit it big with Warners. He would be cast in a series of roles similar to the Mickey Borden character. In *They Made Me a Criminal* (1939), Garfield portrayed a chip-on-his-shoulder prizefighter on the run from a bum rap.

After Garfield's second film racked up a big profit, Jack Warner screened the incomplete *Blackwell's Island,* which had been shelved owing to legal and production issues. The picture foundered under the uncertain direction of William C. McGann, who was removed after filming three different endings—all deemed unsatisfactory. Warner did not want his newest star appearing in a bad programmer, but was unwilling to lose money by canceling a nearly completed film. He ordered Curtiz to fix the picture.

In *Blackwell's Island* Garfield plays a sharpie reporter uncovering a bribery racket in New York's island prison. The picture was factually based on the imprisoned mobster Joey Rao's corruption of the warden and prison staff on Welfare Island, which turned the institution into a country club for Italian gangsters. The resultant scandal caused the jail to be closed in 1934. The risk-averse Warner Bros. legal department pushed for a disclaimer on the released film that (absurdly) disavowed any relationship to actual events.

Curtiz directed a week of retakes in September 1938. He also added scenes, shaping the film into something acceptable. His work included the staging of a climactic speedboat sequence. The result was a lively seventy-one-minute diversion that did no harm to either Garfield's career or the studio's reputation.[1] What was initially viewed as a potential embarrassment grossed a quarter of million dollars over its modest cost.

246

Curtiz spent the last week of January 1939 directing *Sons of Liberty,* a two-reel short subject. A pet project of Harry and Jack Warner, the story of the Revolutionary War financier Haym Salomon was a culmination of their series of short subjects celebrating America's heritage. These shorts were aimed at contrasting U.S. democracy with the totalitarian metastasis under way in Europe and the Far East. The fact that Salomon was a Jewish patriot was a major point of emphasis. Unlike the other Warner short subjects that trumpeted American history and values, *Sons of Liberty* was produced like a full-blown feature film.

Hal Wallis personally oversaw the production. Curtiz understood that this was a special assignment and responded with enthusiasm. He vigorously believed in the film's laudatory theme concerning the founding of American democracy, even as he continued to worry about his family in Hungary.

Sons of Liberty was shot in Technicolor with Claude Rains as Salomon; he was supported by an impressive cast of character actors, including Gale Sondergaard, Donald Crisp, Montagu Love, Henry O'Neill, and James Stephenson. The film would win an Oscar in the narrow category of Best Short Subject (Two-Reel).[2] *Sons of Liberty* is a handsome film, but it does not hold up well. Crane Wilbur's narrative is dated, as is Montagu Love's unctuous impersonation of George Washington, complete with a fake nose. It served, however, as a timely reminder about American exceptionalism, and critics and the public raved about it. Jack Warner was delighted and awarded Curtiz a three-thousand-dollar bonus.

Dodge City had its world premiere in Dodge City, Kansas, on April 1, 1939. The former frontier Babylon was now a quiet midwestern city of ten thousand souls. Warner Bros. chartered a special train dubbed the Dodge City Special out of the new Union Station in downtown Los Angeles and loaded it with two hundred actors, reporters, studio brass, and an ample amount of booze. The entourage included the studio police chief Blayney Matthews, a security detail, and four prostitutes, who served the dual purpose of entertaining the randy actors and reporters and allowing the actresses on board to be relatively free from drunken advances. The picture was another Curtiz-orchestrated stampede to theater box offices. Most of the reviewers tabbed it as it was: a handsomely made, sprawling Western that was as frivolous as it was enjoyable. *Dodge City* would be the sixth-highest grossing Hollywood movie released during the banner year of 1939.

Two of the principals were conspicuously absent from the gala premiere. Olivia de Havilland had disembarked from the train at Pasadena in order to continue playing Melanie in *Gone with the Wind*. Her resolve to pursue the part included a secret screen test orchestrated by David O. Selznick and the director George Cukor after she returned from Modesto in December 1938. The test was a technical violation of her Warner Bros. contract, but she was past the point of worrying. She arranged a luncheon with Ann Warner and convinced the mogul's wife to persuade her husband to lend her out for Melanie.

Curtiz was also missing from the Dodge City express. He was already at work directing another picture, *Daughters Courageous*. He also had no desire to be stuck on a train with a bunch of hard-drinking Warner actors.

Daughters Courageous was not precisely a sequel to *Four Daughters*. "Dissimilar but alike as much as possible" is a more accurate description. The movie was based on the play *Fly Away Home,* which had had a six-month Broadway run in 1935. Despite the differences of story and character, the casts were nearly identical: John Garfield, Jeffrey Lynn, Claude Rains, the Lane sisters, Gale Page, Frank McHugh, May Robson, and Dick Foran. To ensure that the two pictures were linked in the public's mind, Jack Warner launched a publicity campaign to replicate the success of the earlier picture and changed the title at least four times until it dawned on him that "daughters" was the best tie-in. The parallel between the casts was played up in press releases and advertising.

Rains played the role that Thomas Mitchell essayed onstage as Jim Masters, a restless wanderer who returns to his Carmel, California, beachfront home after two decades of globetrotting. A stranger to his family, he attempts to reconnect with his quartet of daughters even as his long-suffering ex, Nan (Fay Bainter), plans to marry a community pillar, Sam Sloane (Donald Crisp). John Garfield portrays Gabriel Lopez, the nonconformist son of a Monterey fisherman. Allergic to work, he attempts to con the gullible by selling an ostensible fragment of Moby Dick's tooth while wooing Buff (Priscilla Lane). Masters and Lopez eventually realize that they are cut from the same cloth. They depart to travel the world together so that Nan can marry Sloane, and Buff avoids the identical marital trap that waylaid her mother.

The whimsical wholesomeness of *Daughters Courageous*—and that of *Four Wives,* a continuation of the Lemp family saga that Curtiz directed during August and September 1939—could have been successful only before the advent of World War II. The country was emerging from the doldrums of the Depression and maintained its insular enthusiasm for the most saccharine of family values even as events around the globe were foreboding. Commercially, the lighthearted improbabilities of *Daughters Courageous* and *Four Wives* were a response on the part of Warner Bros. to MGM's spectacularly successful *Andy Hardy* pictures, albeit with lesser results. The final entry, *Four Mothers,* directed by William Keighley, was released in January 1941; the Hardy series continued well into the 1940s.[3]

Movie patrons were content to overlook the irrationality of *Daughters Courageous* and *Four Wives*. Jim Masters's homecoming is presented as a temporary inconvenience for his ex-wife and daughters instead of the unwelcome reappearance of a selfish cad. In *Four Wives,* Ann Lemp Borden (Priscilla Lane) muses about her deceased husband's unfinished musical composition (the husband is John Garfield as Mickey Borden in flashback) and renews her romance with Felix Dietz (Jeffrey Lynn) only weeks after hubby's suicide. (The vowels in his surname had inexplicably been transposed between the two films.) She is also pregnant with Mickey's child. Dietz ends up saving the premature baby with an emergency blood transfusion as Ann listens to him conduct Mickey's completed symphonic composition on the radio from her hospital bed.

A great deal of adroitness was required to put across this type of fantasia. There was the remarkable work of the Chinese-born James Wong Howe, one of Hollywood's leading cinematographers. A pioneer of low-key, expressionistic lighting and lithe camera movement, Howe signed a seven-year contract in 1938 after Jack Warner witnessed his exquisite work in *Algiers*. Howe's technical background and dedication made him a perfect candidate to work with Curtiz. The director finally had a collaborator who attempted to beat him out as the first person to arrive on set each morning. Howe would shoot four movies for Curtiz. "I thought he was wonderful," said Howe. "The crews hated him. He was tyrannical and rotten to them. But he was great. I learned a lot from him." Howe himself would develop a similar reputation for dyspeptic impatience with many of his colleagues.

But it is inaccurate to say that everyone on Curtiz's set loathed him. Over time, he surrounded himself with highly skilled people who understood his unique vernacular and respected his perfectionist drive. Along with Limey Plews and Irving Rapper, there were the assistant director Jack Sullivan, cinematographer Sol Polito, property master Scotty More, and rugged stuntmen such as Buster Wiles and Sailor Vincent, among other regulars. A Curtiz set bubbled with excitement. The producer Rob-

Curtiz and James Wong Howe prepare to shoot a scene in *Daughters Courageous* (1939) with Priscilla Lane (behind the couch), Gale Page, Fay Bainter, Lola Lane, and Rosemary Lane (courtesy of the Lucas family).

ert Lord observed, "Curtiz had more energy, more drive, than anybody, he never sat down."

Although Howe's visual style could be adapted to any director or studio, it was believed that he would mesh well with the high-contrast, shadowed photography as practiced by Warner Bros.' house lensers Sol Polito, Ernie Haller, and Tony Gaudio. What Howe did not anticipate was the tight control that Warner Bros. exercised over every aspect of their filmmaking. Any technical suggestion that might alter the house style or cost more money was usually rejected. Success was increasingly based on repetition of what had worked previously instead of the daring innovations that had characterized Warner Bros. during the advent of sound and Technicolor. When Howe wanted to film James Cagney's boxing sequences in *City for Conquest* (1940) with a handheld camera, Jack Warner dismissed the request, telling him to use a regular studio camera in lieu of some "hand-held toy." Howe would have to wait until the boxing scenes in *Body and Soul* (1947), which he shot holding a camera while gliding around the boxing ring on roller skates. It was always about speed at Warner Bros., and the meticulous Howe was never known as a fast worker. At first, Curtiz was impatient with Howe on *Daughters Courageous*. He mentored him on how to plan the camera setups in advance in order to move more quickly. Howe's pace improved, and his photography remained superb.

When Howe came down with a severe sore throat during *Daughters Courageous*, Ernie Haller replaced him, much to the dissatisfaction of Curtiz. Henry Blanke dashed off a memo to Hal Wallis imploring him to return Howe to the picture as soon as possible: "I must agree with Mike that the photography of Haller is adequate but in no way reaches the beauty that we got when Howe was photographing. . . . Mike asked me to please see that he is put back on the picture immediately, and I must join Mike in his plea."

Howe completed *Daughters Courageous* and split duties with Sol Polito on *Four Wives*. Jack Warner continually harried Curtiz to move faster. The production staff recognized that this ceaseless pressure was counterproductive. After Curtiz finished a Herculean day of work in a frantic effort to close the schedule gap, Frank Mattison wrote to Tenny Wright: "I wish you would send the above information to Mr. J. L. Warner which will show how much Mike can be speeded up under stress, but I doubt if it is a good policy and we will get as good a picture when he makes 24 set-ups in a day." Both pictures ended up with cost-to-gross ratios that made Warner gleeful. *Daughters Courageous* grossed $1,225,000 on an investment of $580,000, and *Four Wives* did $1,477,000 after an outlay of $614,000.

Sandwiched between this pair of successes, Curtiz experienced his first significant disappointment in nearly a decade.

Elizabeth the Queen was conceived as a starring vehicle for Bette Davis, who was enjoying a banner year after *Dark Victory* and *The Old Maid*. Her portrayal of Carlota in *Juarez* was one of the few high points in a gargantuan, meticulously produced epic that cleverly used the Emperor Maximilian as a metaphor for Hitler but possessed the entertainment value of a history textbook. Hal Wallis was insistent about casting Davis in an Anglophile spectacle filmed in Technicolor. Although he screen-tested Geraldine Fitzgerald, he informed Jack Warner, "I think when you see the test of Geraldine Fitzgerald . . . you will agree that the only one to play this part is Bette Davis." As Queen Elizabeth, Davis would play a character analogous to her own mercurial temperament.

The picture was an adaptation of Maxwell Anderson's 1930 play depicting the power-laden, romantically doomed relationship between Elizabeth and the Earl of Essex. The play debuted in England and was done on Broadway by the Lunts. Wallis purchased the rights in February 1939 for $30,000 and had it adapted by Norman Reilly Raine and Aeneas MacKenzie. Although the screenplay eliminated much of Anderson's English blank verse, Bette Davis beseeched Jack Warner to cast Laurence Olivier as Essex.

Olivier had starred in the British-made *Fire over England* (1937)—a remarkably similar picture in which Flora Robson played Queen Elizabeth—and the soon-to-be released American-made *Wuthering Heights*, but he was not a big-name Hollywood star. For Jack Warner, who was spending more than a million bucks on a period costume drama, the only actor who merited consideration was Errol Flynn. Davis acquiesced but remained dissatisfied with Flynn, whom she considered an acting lightweight.

The jousting between the two stars replicated the story between the queen and earl. After a chat between "Sporting Blood" (Warner) and "The Baron" (Flynn), the title was altered from the sedate *Elizabeth the Queen* to the more swashbuckling *The Knight and the Lady*. In a letter to Jack Warner tinged with the tone of a sovereign, Davis insisted that the film's title be changed to reflect her starring supremacy and included a bald threat: "You force me to refuse to make the picture unless the billing is mine." Warner countered by proposing *The Lady and the Knight* while reminding Flynn that he was being paid more than Davis and isn't that what really mattered? Then Warner realized that "you cannot call a Queen a lady" and had to change the title yet again. The final designation of *The Private Lives of Elizabeth and Essex* eventually mollified the two stars but damaged the picture's commercial viability.

Flynn's relationship with Davis became more strained after the cameras began rolling. During the rehearsal of a scene in which Elizabeth had to slap Essex, Davis smacked Flynn with "that little dainty hand, laden with about a pound of costume jewelry, right across the ear. I felt as if I were deaf." Flynn claimed that he took his revenge in a later rehearsal when he turned a playful pat into a fearsome swat to Davis's derriere that lifted her two feet off the ground. He noted in his memoir, "It wasn't a very pleasant picture to make, for me, that is."

Curtiz hadn't directed Davis since *Kid Galahad*. There was a snippet in the *Hollywood Reporter* that William Keighley was originally scheduled to direct *Elizabeth and Essex* but left on vacation, which resulted in Curtiz landing the assignment. Irving Rapper claimed that he convinced Davis to request that Curtiz helm the picture: "She said, 'Whom would you suggest?' I said, 'As far as the studio is concerned, I would put somebody who will counterbalance the great poetry of Maxwell Anderson with the clang of armor in action. Take Michael Curtiz.' She did."

In all likelihood, Rapper's recommendation and Keighley's vacation schedule had little to do with Curtiz's selection. There was no way that Jack Warner would entrust a picture of this magnitude to any other director than Curtiz. In terms of value measurement, Curtiz would be paid a greater sum ($45,500) than either Flynn or Davis.

Curtiz knew that Davis would get her own way as Queen Elizabeth, but he let the actress know that his modus operandi hadn't changed. "When you work with me, you don't need lunch, just take an aspirin," he advised on the first day of shooting.[4] Davis rolled her eyes and did what she pleased. The director and star immediately clashed over her wardrobe; Davis preferred the historically accurate, bulkier costumes designed by Orry-Kelly that she donned for the costume tests. Curtiz didn't like them and convinced Wallis to have a lighter wardrobe prepared for filming. When production began, Davis simply wore the original costumes.

What the star and director shared was a burning desire to make the best picture possible. They coexisted on that basis alone. Davis could be peremptory in a manner that mirrored Curtiz's own impatience. When she felt Curtiz's instructions were overlong, she would chirp, "Shut up, Mike, and let's get on with it."

Curtiz had much more difficulty directing Flynn. During preproduction, Hal Wallis vainly attempted to keep Flynn available by discouraging him from disappearing for "jaunts on his boat," as he was on salary and needed for still photography, makeup, and wardrobe tests. During a long shoot that lasted from May 11 to July 6, Flynn was habitually late to the set and frequently unable to remember lines. According to one Frank Mattison report, "We lost considerable time because of Mr. Flynn's continual blowing up in his lines. We made 20 takes all on account of Flynn. Mr. Curtiz dismissed him at 5:00 pm as it was absolutely impossible to accomplish any more than he had already done." Another Mattison memorandum noted: "It seems as though Mr. Curtiz can make fast time until he gets with Errol Flynn and then we slow down to a walk."

Though Humphrey Bogart could get away with memorizing his dialogue while nursing a hangover before an early morning call, Flynn could

Curtiz attempts to direct Bette Davis in *The Private Lives of Elizabeth and Essex* (1939) (author's collection).

not. Even sober, Flynn frequently forgot his lines. He always had time for mischief, though. Curtiz was reportedly carrying on a dalliance with Davis's stand-in. Flynn informed the director that he had slept with the same ingénue and caught the "most incredible" social disease. Curtiz quickly left the set to be examined by his doctor.

There was another display of angst on the set courtesy of Olivia de Havilland, who was finishing *Gone with the Wind* in Culver City. Warner ordered Hal Wallis to arrange her return to Burbank to play a secondary part as Lady Penelope Gray. Her name was below the title; her role consisting primarily of reacting to Davis and Flynn. De Havilland's casting in *Elizabeth and Essex* amounted to blatant score settling by Jack Warner. The mogul was determined to punish her for the *GWTW* screen test subterfuge and manipulation of his wife. De Havilland lost her composure with Curtiz in front of the entire company. Frank Mattison chronicled the meltdown:

> I had another display of temperament last Saturday afternoon from Miss de Havilland; to wit at 5:15 pm when we started to rehearse a scene between her and Miss Fabares [Nanette Fabray], she informed Mr. Curtiz that she positively was going to stop at 6:00 pm, but Mr. Curtiz told her unless she stayed and finished the sequence, he positively would cut it out of the picture. Miss de Havilland expressed herself before the company and Mr. Curtiz came right back, with the result that she made a display of hysterics before the company and it became necessary for me to dismiss the company at 6:15 without shooting the sequence. In as much as this sequence of 2 pages was inserted at Miss de Havilland's request, I believe that we definitely should not shoot it and uphold Mr. Curtiz in this matter.

The disagreement was eventually ironed out, and the scene was shot and included. Although de Havilland's life at Warner Bros. had become miserable, she also knew that outbursts made her appear unprofessional. She penned an apologetic letter to Jack Warner, essentially blaming the episode on Curtiz for attempting to shoot the scene so late in the evening and becoming tactless when she objected. Her distaste for the director was so visceral that she identified him in her note as "a certain person," then as "a certain man who means well." Long afterward, she summarized the episode forthrightly: "I lost my cool, which was not like me, and which is unforgivable."

Curtiz refused to allow any distractions to slow him down. *Elizabeth and Essex* was one of his most efficiently directed pictures. A large part of the effectiveness was due to his use of outside talent, including Vincent Price, Henry Stephenson, and Henry Daniell, who would become a

Curtiz favorite. Virtually all the outside actors finished their scenes on schedule and did not need to be held over and continued on salary. More money was saved after Tenny Wright implemented a system whereby no sets could be built or modified without a requisition bearing his signature. Thus, the addition of unbudgeted sets, a habitual temptation for Curtiz, was removed from his bag of tricks. Always seeking to discover another method of squeezing a nickel hard enough to asphyxiate the buffalo, Wallis ordered Wright to design and construct the standing sets for *Elizabeth and Essex* so they could be reused for the forthcoming *The Sea Hawk*. There were also very few retakes or added scenes. Curtiz ended up bringing the film in one day ahead of schedule and under the projected budget.

Even so, he took the time to do it his way. De Havilland was nonplussed by Curtiz's direction in one scene when he told her, "I should want you to sit a little more feminine." She sat as demurely as possible while Curtiz rehearsed this scene repeatedly and then shot multiple takes. No one on the set understood what Curtiz wanted even after he finally got it. He communicated more effectively during a key scene between Davis and Flynn that was not intimate enough. "Please, please, make me a love nest from out of it," he begged. He also brought de Havilland up short when she began to affect a rather phony British accent—"You speak too much from afternoon tea"—telling her to knock it off.

Wallis was concerned more about how the Elizabethan wardrobe and Anton Grot's sets would appear in expensive Technicolor than in critiquing Curtiz's composition of individual scenes. With the capable Robert Lord as associate producer, Curtiz directed with minimal interference and, as usual, strove for realism. The nineteen-year-old Nanette Fabares (Fabray) made her film debut as Elizabeth's young lady-in-waiting. She remembered Curtiz telling her during wardrobe tests that she had to have her braces removed forthwith: "Vot are those wires on your teeth? They must go!" Fabray duly visited her dentist, and the braces disappeared for two months.

Elizabeth and Essex is an exquisitely crafted picture, well written and acted, particularly by Bette Davis in a powerhouse performance. The gorgeous Technicolor photography accentuates the magnificent costume and set design. According to de Havilland, Davis experienced a change of heart decades later and praised Errol Flynn's performance after a screening of the film at the singer Mel Tormé's house in the mid-1970s. "Damn, he's good. I was wrong about him all the time," she declared. There is no known expression of similar sentiment from Davis concerning the film's director.

Expectations for the picture to become a huge financial hit would not be met. Gradwell Sears, general manager for sales, had warned Jack Warner back in August: "The reaction to the title *The Private Lives of Elizabeth and Essex* is extremely bad. I am getting letters of protest from every part of the country and my own people tell me that wherever they go, exhibitors are objecting. . . . They say it smacks of Alexander Korda and that in the south, midwest, and small towns particularly, it will be confused with an English picture, which as you know do very little business."

Sears begged Warner to change the title to something that directly implied romantic adventure. Warner refused, possibly because the picture was a British historical drama rather than a Flynn swashbuckler or a Davis melodramatic weeper. The studio chief believed that if he vigorously promoted Davis and Flynn, the picture would be a hit. He was wrong. *Elizabeth and Essex* grossed approximately $500,000 over its cost of more than a million dollars: hardly a disaster, but nothing close to the anticipated success of such a touted, expensive project. It was nominated for four Academy Awards and won none.

For Curtiz, the disappointment was momentarily deflating. The director realized that the oldest of Hollywood clichés, "You are only as good as your last picture," was also the most accurate. During his time in Hollywood, he watched as the careers of several European contemporaries ended abruptly with professional failure, often accompanied by personal tragedy. The great F. W. Murnau ended up broke and dead on Pacific Coast Highway after an auto accident in a car driven by his Tahitian boyfriend. Benjamin Christensen returned to Denmark in disgrace after failing at MGM. The Romanian director Marcel De Sano retreated to France and committed suicide in 1936.

Working as a script clerk on Warner Bros.' *Confession* (1937), John Meredyth Lucas witnessed the professional demise of the director Joe May. The English language and the moviemaking assembly line flummoxed a bewildered May. The temperamental E. A. Dupont slapped one of the Dead End Kids for mocking his accent while directing *Hell's Kitchen* (1939) and was replaced by Lewis Seiler. Dupont didn't direct another picture for more than a decade before resurfacing to helm bottom-of-the-barrel fare like *The Neanderthal Man* (1953). Curtiz, who couldn't conceive of a life without directing movies, vowed that he would not allow his career to slip by making flops.

He was also coping with a family calamity that occurred shortly after he wrapped *Elizabeth and Essex*. Kitty had returned to Hollywood from New York without informing either of her parents and was found in a hotel room at 5849 Sunset Boulevard, her wrists slashed. At the Georgia Street Receiving Hospital, where she was treated for a severed artery, she told medical personnel that she had failed to pass her final examinations at CCNY and was afraid to tell her father. She sobbed, "I was so lonely and I didn't know who to turn to." She told the police: "I tried to kill myself. . . . My parents have been divorced and I've been going to school most of my life." One observer described the twenty-three-year-old as being "highly nervous and highly strung." Kitty's psyche had been battered by a lifetime of being farmed out to nannies, convents, boarding schools, and colleges, and her suicide attempt represented an unsurprising cry for help. According to one report, she said: "Tell my father I am so sorry. I was rash and I am a coward."

The saga of the attempted suicide, including photos of a distraught Kitty in her hospital bed, appeared in newspapers coast to coast. Curtiz rushed to the hospital and told reporters that his daughter had been attending school abroad and in New York and that he had last seen her during her Easter vacation. He said that after Kitty was released, she would recuperate at the Canoga Ranch, and that he and Bess would be retaining a private physician and a therapist.

Despite her personal turmoil, Curtiz's daughter possessed a unique perspective about her obsessive father:

> Once a journalist told my Father that he was the "General of the Cinema" and this name stuck to him because no one moves and molds the masses like him—and this is a fact recognized even by Eisenstein during a trip to Hollywood. He has that solid calm, that rapid determination he needs to direct the masses and the suggestive strength of his personality with which he bends people to his will. My Father believes that there are capacities or innate faculties that predestine an actor for a part, that not even the most ample talent replaces this natural predisposition. My Father has a lot of contact with his actors. He examines them without any objection and always gets to know their personalities and characteristics down to the smallest detail. He has a lot of good friends who have never acted in his pictures because my Father abhors the protectionism of cliques and entourages. To his actors, he demands absolute naturalness. He hates the theatrical.

Curtiz posing with his mother, Aranka, and Julia MacGlashan, Bess Meredyth's mother (courtesy of the Lucas family).

> In the middle of the wasteful luxury that reigns in Hollywood, he lives with a spartan simplicity and demands the same of those around him. His coworkers and actors love him very much. They behave with him privately as if they were part of his family. . . . But when the hour of working comes, to all he will yield an iron-clad discipline.

The maintenance of his ranch and his wife's spendthrift habits were precipitating a different type of crisis. He was so short of cash that he obtained a personal loan of $7,100 from Jack Warner on July 20 and made arrangements for $400 per week from his salary to go into a Bank of America account that he kept secret from Bess. He needed every penny to get his family out of Hungary and support them after they arrived in the United States. Curtiz managed to relocate his seventy-seven-year-old mother to America. Aranka Kaminer arrived in New York on the *Queen Mary* on April 20, 1939, and traveled by train to Los Angeles with her eldest son, who met her when the boat docked. Curtiz leased a house for her at 4035 Dixie Canyon Avenue, in what is now Sherman Oaks. The house included a housekeeper named Mrs. Alpert, who cooked kosher for the strictly observant Kaminer. John Meredyth Lucas described Curtiz's mother as "a frail, stooped woman with a will of iron." Curtiz's reason for not bringing his mother to the Canoga Ranch was obvious: Bess Meredyth and Mrs. Kaminer had not gotten on when they met in Budapest.

His two brothers David and Gabriel had to reside in Tijuana, Mexico, while awaiting legal disposition of their request to enter the United States. They would remain there for two long years. Of his siblings, Curtiz was closest to David. He believed that David possessed a singular talent similar to his own and had always looked out for him, dating back to when he arranged to have him cast in *Death of Dracula* in 1921. Curtiz would support both his brothers and help them start their own Hollywood careers.

His other brother, Lajos, remained in Budapest, along with their sisters, Regina, Margit, and Kornelia. His sisters were married, and their husbands chose to remain in Hungary with their families. It was a tragic decision. The Nazis deported Margit and her family in 1944. Her husband and two children died in Auschwitz. Although Margit and a daughter survived the Holocaust and eventually immigrated to the United States, there was more to the story, according to the Hungarian film critic György Báron, whose uncle married a Kertész relative. Báron related some of Margit's story to the film historian László Kriston:

> It was after the war that her brother brought her to America. The three Kertész boys have long been living there; they were extremely successful and well-off, and their conscience had bothered them for not having brought out Margit in time, when they could still have done that. When they came to their senses, it was too late. Kertész reportedly sent a military aircraft—probably from a European base of the U.S. Air Force—which was stationed in Europe—to Pozsony [now Bratislava, Slovakia] to pick up Margit. Curiously, Margit's son, Uncle Lorand, was already in America. He studied at the Sorbonne in Paris, and left Europe with the last ocean liner in 1941. Mihály helped him when he came to America. He went into the American military and fought in the war in the Far East.

How Curtiz could arrange for a U.S. Army Air Corps aircraft to scoop up his sister in Hungary after the war is unexplained, although it is possible that Jack and Harry Warner could have pulled some strings for him.

Jack and Ann Warner visit with Curtiz's mother at the Canoga Ranch (courtesy of the Lucas family).

With Germany's invasion of Poland on September 1, 1939, America's mood began to shift from indifferent isolationism to worried concern. But most of the country had miles to travel before catching up with the vigorous anti-Nazi campaign of the Warners. During a meeting of the Hollywood Anti-Nazi League at the home of Edward G. Robinson, Groucho Marx offered a toast to Warner Bros. as "the only studio with any guts."

The studio's abandonment of the German film market was followed by its subsidizing of the Hollywood Anti-Nazi League, including Warner radio broadcasts in Los Angeles that mocked Hitler as well as the studio's production of the patriotic shorts and social-consciousness features. Once again, it was the brothers standing together against outsiders, but this crusade was about survival rather than dollars.

Confessions of a Nazi Spy premiered on April 27, 1939, at the Warner Beverly Theatre. The German American Bund sued the studio (the case was thrown out of court), German consular offices railed, and Jack Warner received death threats. *Confessions* opened the door to more provocative anti-Nazi films. The Warners, who pioneered so many advances in the industry, were achieving another first: the commitment of major resources by a Hollywood studio to an unabashed propaganda campaign to shape American public opinion on *the* major issue of the day.

Yet they remained focused on making movies that delivered pure entertainment. Curtiz was assigned to a Western intended to replicate the blockbuster success of *Dodge City*. Robert Buckner composed an original screenplay titled *Gold Train,* a Civil War saga about a sultry dance hall girl who contrives with a Confederate prison warden to smuggle $5 million in gold out of Virginia City in order to rescue the dying Confederacy in 1864. The supposedly fact-based narrative was made even more implausible by the casting of thirty-nine-year-old Miriam Hopkins as a southern ingénue opposite Errol Flynn. Flynn, who had become resigned to Westerns, reportedly didn't want Olivia de Havilland in the picture and insisted on a different costar. The newcomer Brenda Marshall and Ann Sheridan, a Flynn favorite, were considered and rejected. The studio eventually decided on Hopkins because she was already on salary. Flynn again lobbied to have Curtiz replaced as director; Warner refused.

Curtiz approached what would be titled *Virginia City* with his usual vigor, but there were delays and disruption. Wallis's schedule had *The Sea Hawk* ready to begin in January 1940, which compelled him to start production in November on *Virginia City* without a finished shooting script. In addition to being incomplete, Buckner's script, as revised by Norman

Reilly Raine and Howard Koch, possessed inherent weaknesses that necessitated even more rewriting. Adding to the challenge was the decision to have Curtiz shoot the majority of the exterior scenes in northern Arizona. He toured the area with Joseph Barry, the location manager, and fell in love with the stunning Schnebly Hill vistas in Sedona.

In an October 11, 1939, memo to Wallis, Curtiz submitted a detailed list of twenty changes to the 105-page partial screenplay that addressed the opening and ending of the picture, but no middle. In addition to deleting eight scenes, the majority of Curtiz's changes incorporated the addition of quick cuts, the removal of a long opening montage, and strengthening the story by enhancing the character development between Flynn, Hopkins, and Randolph Scott. Most of these recommendations were reflected in the final shooting script.

The company arrived at Flagstaff via chartered train on November 3, 1939, and overflowed the town's three hotels and several motor courts. Many of the actors and crew, including Hopkins, Bogart, and Scott, were lodged in a hotel fifty-four miles away. A team of construction workers had already arrived to assemble sets and build floats to move covered wagons on water during a river sequence. Forty-eight horses were sent out from the studio by train, and another 250 were leased out of Flagstaff.

According to a newspaper interview with Flynn, the location production of *Virginia City* offered beautiful scenery, but was hard work: "We are routed out of bed at 5 am, bolt down breakfasts at 5:30 am, shiver in the cold, dark morn, and roll away in the buses at 6 am. . . . One day we are at Schnebly Hill, looking deep down into the depths of glorious Oak Creek Canyon, resembling Colorado. The next we are ninety miles away at Round Hills, starving in a wagon train as it staggers through a Nevada sand storm (produced in Arizona by Hollywood wind machines)."

With twelve limousines, six passenger buses, seventeen eight-ton trucks, two sound units, two station wagons, a couple of camera cars, a huge generator truck, and nearly two hundred people, the location shoot was conducted like a military campaign as Curtiz led the troops.

According to Yakima Canutt, Curtiz conceived one of the best horseback stunts in *Virginia City:* "Yucca, I have a good gag, can you do it?" he asked. After Canutt promised a quick yes or no, Curtiz explained what he wanted: "Well, you are doubling for Flynn, you are riding his horse leading another horse. You are riding like hell to get away—they are shooting at you and your horse gets hit. He does what you call a Running W. When he falls, you catch the saddle horn on the other horse and do a pony express. You know, when your feet hit the ground, you bounce up on the horse and keep going. It must be done in a fast run."

Canutt stared at Curtiz in wonderment. "I was amazed at him," declared the stuntman. "This was a good gag and I wondered why I hadn't thought of it myself." Canutt agreed to do the stunt for $250 and nailed it in the first take.

Curtiz was up each morning before light. Despite the amount of time it took to get crew, equipment, and actors to the different locations, he would carefully choose his camera setups and always rehearse the actors before the first take. The stars were professional and got along fine— with the exception of the leading lady. Difficult under the best of circumstances, Hopkins loathed being forced to appear opposite Errol Flynn in a Western. She hated the script and let everyone know it. According to Orry-Kelly's unpublished memoir, she schemed to make his costumes appear to fit her poorly in order to delay the picture while attempting to have the script revised to enhance her role.

The studio tried to keep the actors busy on the weekends with publicity visits by Flynn to an annual carnival in Flagstaff, and a screening of *Elizabeth and Essex* at the Orpheum Theatre. A highlight of the location shoot for Flynn and his costar Randolph Scott was discovering seven female swimmers in a disabled car on Highway 89. The girls were headed to the coast to appear as nymphs in Billy Rose's Aquacade show. They changed both the flat tire and the itinerary of the ingénues. Flynn remarked over a week later, "They're still here, to see how movies are made."

Although previous accounts of *Virginia City* attributed production delays to several weeks of torrential rain in northern Arizona that reputedly sickened Errol Flynn, an examination of weather reports disproves this fiction. It was the incomplete script that chafed Flynn and the rest of the company. Flynn cabled Hal Wallis on November 11: "It is quite impossible to proceed with this picture without the middle of the script (stop) do you think I belong to the Gestapo, I won't tell anyone what is in it I am on your side —Errol."

The pages eventually showed up but had to be reviewed by Curtiz and his comments routed back to Wallis and the associate producer Robert Fellows. Wallis told Fellows to show the completed script only to Curtiz and especially not to Miriam Hopkins. He and Curtiz had added a scene for the actress to mute her constant complaints, but they didn't want to deal with her until they were ready.

Curtiz held Byron Haskin over to complete second-unit work on location. The director told Mattison he needed only eight shots. After Wallis approved the extension, Curtiz slipped Haskin a list of twenty different shots. When Mattison put Curtiz on the spot over the discrepancy, the director shrugged and said the added shots would help the picture. Tenny Wright fumed to Wallis about Curtiz's duplicity: "If this isn't double-talking, I don't know what the devil it is."

When Curtiz began the interiors back in Burbank, Wallis became alarmed at the escalating costs and schedule delays. The revised schedule indicated five more weeks of filming, which would take production into the next year. Wallis had all but ceased berating Curtiz about these issues. Still, with the deadline of January staring at him, Wallis urged him to move faster: "When we started out to do this picture, we had a long talk about it, and largely through your persuasion, we decided to do *Virginia City* as it promised to be a simple picture, and one which you in your own words said that you could knock off in no time, as it was difficult and you would finish the early part of December, and then you would have three to four weeks in between so we could start *The Sea Hawk* on January 2nd. Now the picture is two weeks over schedule and we are still slowing down." As an example, Wallis cited a sequence that he believed should have taken much less time: "It is a simple scene, and instead of trying to get ninety odd angles of three men sitting behind a table talking to Errol Flynn, it is a very simple matter to do it in three or four setups, so why make a big production out of a relatively unimportant sequence?"

Wallis also appealed to the director not to change any more dialogue on set. After thirteen years of dealing with Curtiz, the executive producer might have been better advised to attempt to square a circle. Using Robert Fellows as an intermediary, Curtiz stood his ground: "In general, Mike doesn't feel that the dialogue comes up to what he feels is required from the situation and individual scenes and he feels he can improve the scenes with an occasional dialogue change."

It wasn't only Wallis who objected to Curtiz's incessant alteration of dialogue. Robert Buckner took umbrage over a comedic scene that Curtiz added. He wrote to Fellows: "This is the little number which Curtiz, Flynn and Big Boy Williams cooked up among themselves. . . . We have worked for months to keep just such corny crap out of *Virginia City* and as the writer I don't wish to be thought responsible for such amateurish bilgewater." Buckner's complaint fell on deaf ears. The "amateurish bilge-

Cooking up some script changes with Errol Flynn, Alan Hale, and Guinn "Big Boy" Williams during production of *Virginia City* (1940) (author's collection).

water," a brief reunion scene among Flynn, Williams, and Alan Hale, remained in the final cut.

Curtiz did move along faster while continuing to infuse more quality into the production. Fellows advised Wallis that Curtiz wanted to punch up the river-crossing scene (filmed in Victorville in mid-December) with more action that could be edited into the picture. The director wanted to shoot it in Chatsworth instead of Red Rock Canyon in Calabasas. Wallis scrawled on the memo, "How much will it cost?" This was different from the usual financial angst from Wallis. He was completely burned out from the constant strain of managing every major Warner production over the previous five years. He uncharacteristically disappeared for a week in mid-December, during the most critical time of the production. Fellows advised Curtiz on December 13 that Wallis was ill: "Hal is quite sick. From what I can find out, he is close to a nervous breakdown and doesn't intend to come in until some time next week."

Curtiz continued to shoot the picture in his inimitable fashion. He had young Dickie Jones run around the interior of Sound Stage 2 six times

The Warner Bros. "A" team: Sol Polito and Curtiz (courtesy of the Lucas family).

before dashing into a scene with Errol Flynn. When Jones expressed confusion about why he should do this, Curtiz replied, "Because you must be out from breathing!" When a number of people on set guffawed at the director's grammatical misfire, Curtiz narrowed his eyes and fired back, "Anybody who should talk when I am shooting this scene should be kicked to death by a jackass and I'd like to be the one to do it!"

Curtiz wrapped *Virginia City* on January 3, 1940. It ran seventeen days over schedule and well over the original $890,000 budget, coming in at $1,179,000. Frank Mattison defended the final results by pointing out they basically made it up as they went along: "If you look at the script, you will find we had more blue pages than white pages, and I know of no scene in the picture in which changes were not made on the set during shooting.[5] Yet with all, I believe this picture is going to be a very good picture and will justify the trouble and expense we had in making it." He was correct: *Virginia City* grossed $1 million over its cost. Audiences overlooked the weaknesses (Humphrey Bogart plays a Mexican bandit) throughout the unwieldy saga and concentrated on Flynn and the action. It is a beautifully photographed film. Sol Polito had become Curtiz's visual doppelganger; *Virginia City* was the ninth of sixteen films that they collaborated on. So attuned were they to each other, they often communicated with nods, grunts, or glances. The Italian-born photographer addressed the director as "Miska," his childhood nickname reserved for an intimate few.

Jack Warner replicated the *Dodge City* premiere formula by leasing another train, filling it with stars, reporters, and booze, and sending it to Virginia City and Reno for the premiere. Still sulking, Miriam Hopkins refused to attend or promote the picture. Once again, Curtiz excused himself from attending the gala opening. He was preparing for another big swashbuckler starring Errol Flynn.

22

The Swash and the Buckler

Curtiz began directing *The Sea Hawk* at the end of January 1940. A screen adaptation of Rafael Sabatini's best seller was a given after the success of *Captain Blood*. It was planned as an elaborate picture, but there were specific limitations designed into the production.

The discouraging results of *Elizabeth and Essex* caused Jack Warner to shy away from employing Technicolor on the studio's big-budget epics for nearly two years. The mogul believed that the return on investment for color wasn't worth the risk. In addition to having Tenny Wright repurpose the *Elizabeth and Essex* sets, Curtiz, Henry Blanke, and a rejuvenated Hal Wallis decided that the studio would use footage from *Captain Blood* to supplement *The Sea Hawk*'s main battle sequence. Neither Warner nor Wallis cared to chance shooting the picture on board a ship at sea, where weather, accidents, and other unforeseen circumstances might cause costly delays.

Warner Bros. was planning for more than one picture when they invested $150,000 in the construction of Stage 21 on the Burbank lot. The installation of water mains, drain piping, and sewer grates made it possible to fill the entire soundstage with up to five feet of water. An English man-of-war and a Spanish galleon were constructed side by side; between them was a deeper rectangular pool that allowed stuntmen to fall off rigging or go over the side of either one to land in the simulated "ocean."

The production of *The Sea Hawk* reflected the apex of studio infrastructure at that time. The two ships inside Stage 21 were mounted on wheels with hydraulic rams that could tilt either or both vessels to give a rocking or sinking effect. In addition to the creation of a vast muslin cyclorama that served as the background horizon, Anton Grot and his assistant, Leo Kuter, developed a water ripple and wave illusion machine. The special effects coordinator Byron Haskin supplemented the ship sets with state-of-the-art eighteen-foot miniature vessels. With the exception of a scene in which Flynn and his men arrive on a beach (shot at Point Mugu) and another sequence shot at the Warner Ranch in Calabasas, *The Sea Hawk* was filmed in its entirety on the soundstages and back lot. But staying close to home didn't make Errol Flynn any happier.

Flynn's attitude about making pictures and, more specifically, making them with Curtiz had become extremely negative. Even though he had achieved his ambition of becoming a movie star, there was an element of self-loathing in the hedonistic actor. He believed that Warner Bros. had turned him into a caricature, and the focal point of his frustration was Curtiz. In addition to being fed up with the director's behavior toward both actors and horses, Flynn believed Curtiz was responsible for typecasting him as a comic-book hero of Westerns and swashbucklers.

While unable to avoid being directed by Curtiz, Flynn used his star power in attempting to force the studio to allow him to choose his leading ladies. Hal Wallis resented having his prerogatives usurped. In July 1939 Wallis wrote to Curtiz to make "a complete, thorough test of Dennis Morgan in the character of the leading role for *The Sea Hawk*." It was a gesture born of frustration. There was nobody but Flynn for the role of the English buccaneer Geoffrey Thorpe. Although originally announced as the costar, Olivia de Havilland became unavailable. Flynn and de Havilland's roller-coaster relationship, characterized by spurts of mutual attraction, ambition, and jealousy, was at that point on the downswing, and Flynn reportedly didn't want her in the picture.

After testing Jane Bryan, Ida Lupino, and Geraldine Fitzgerald, among others, the studio settled on Ardis Ankerson, whom Warner Bros. had renamed Brenda Marshall. The gorgeous brunette had been groomed in a couple of Foy productions and *Espionage Agent* (1939). Another in the long line of unknown and famous actresses who were tested as Scarlett O'Hara by David O. Selznick, Marshall was deemed ready for her big opportunity as Doña Maria in *The Sea Hawk*. She turned out to be no Olivia de Havilland. Marshall had an aura of steely reserve, and there was minimal chemistry in her scenes with Flynn.

The supporting players were first-rate: Claude Rains, Donald Crisp, Flora Robson as Queen Elizabeth, the perpetual Alan Hale, James Stephenson, Gilbert Roland, and the oily Henry Daniell as Lord Wolfingham, the chief villain. At this point, Curtiz cast all the supporting players in his pictures. For *The Sea Hawk* he engaged Victor Varconi, his first star from the early days in Transylvania, for a small role as a Spanish general.

Still unsettled over the *Virginia City* debacle, Wallis ensured that he had a solid shooting script in hand for *The Sea Hawk*. Seton I. Miller's outline, entitled "Beggars of the Sea," was partially inspired by a 1936 Delmer Daves treatment that portrayed Geoffrey Thorpe as a fictional version of Sir Francis Drake. Miller's script was revised several times and then lay fallow as Warner Bros. proceeded with *The Adventures of Robin Hood*. Curtiz and Henry Blanke were enthusiastic about Miller's work and pressed Wallis to move forward. After the studio scheduled *The Sea Hawk* for early 1940, Howard Koch revised the script and made the historical situations reflect present-day realities. Although Flynn's character is a piratical rogue, Koch shaped the narrative into a modern treatise against totalitarian tyranny. *The Sea Hawk* thus became another Warner Bros. broadside against Nazism. The final shooting script had absolutely nothing to do with Sabatini's novel, save the title.

Wallis was determined that the script not be tinkered with. He attempted to restrain Curtiz from making changes during the first week of production. After commenting negatively about a scene Curtiz shot with Flynn and a monkey, which included dialogue that was not in the script, one can hear the sigh in his memo to Curtiz: "What are you going to do about this? Are you going to keep harassing me all through this picture or are you going to shoot the script?" Curtiz continued to insert dialogue and bits of business. He surreptitiously kept Koch on the set for a time to assist him with dialogue changes. After Koch became too intrusive, he was banished by Curtiz, who posted a guard at the soundstage door to keep him out. At one point, Flynn referred to Queen Elizabeth several times as "madam" rather than "Your Majesty" or "Your Highness." Although Curtiz's correction of the wording was technically accurate, Wallis fumed, "It sounds instead like somebody having a conversation with the owner of a hook shop." There was also a sequence that Curtiz devised in which Brenda Marshall distracts a curious guard while Flynn hides in a coach. It fit nicely into the story and remained in the final cut.

During the second week of shooting, Wallis praised Curtiz's dailies as "beautiful." After mildly remonstrating over the usual business of shooting too many angles, the producer concluded that "everything is going along nicely," and "I have been able to eat all of my meals regularly."

Wallis' digestive idyll didn't last long. He had a fit after enumerating several scenes Curtiz filmed that were either inadequate or changed without authorization. He demanded that Blanke provide a daily list of shots, cut for cut, that Curtiz would be directing inside the set of the ship, and that nothing would be filmed "unless I okay it." Blanke protected Curtiz by patiently explaining to Wallis that all the footage that the director shot was necessary, while dutifully providing the shot list and sticking with Curtiz on the set until the sequence was completed.

Because of Flora Robson's contractual prearrangement to appear on Broadway in *Ladies in Retirement*, Curtiz filmed all her scenes first. Robson's closing speech as Queen Elizabeth was a clear call of support for a beleaguered England, which stood alone against Germany in the summer of 1940: "But when the ruthless ambitions of a man threaten to engulf the world, it becomes the solemn obligation of free men, wherever they may be, to affirm that the earth belongs not to any man, but to all men." Her stirring words, which transitioned into a final dissolve with a shot of the British fleet, were included in the British version of *The Sea Hawk* but were missing from the American release, which had a more pedestrian ending.

When Flynn experienced his habitual problem with remembering lines, Robson gently chided him about holding up the picture. Flynn thereupon applied himself so diligently that the actress remembered Curtiz being startled and remarking, "What's the matter with you? You know all your words?"

Curtiz and Sol Polito quickly moved on to the culminating swordfight between Flynn and Henry Daniell. It was conceived to be visually more compelling than the stellar Robin Hood duel. Curtiz was obsessive about having Polito ensure that the two combatants cast their shadows all over the huge Anton Grot set. The Belgian fencing master Fred Cavens and Curtiz staged the duel with great care, but the sequence required extensive editing because of the athletic ineptitude of Henry Daniell. Curtiz admired Daniell's acting, but he should have known better than to use him in this particular role, according to Frank Mattison: "Mr. Daniell is absolutely helpless and his close-up in the duel will be mostly from the elbows up. Mr. Curtiz was greatly discouraged . . . but there is nothing we can do as it will be impossible to go back and change to someone else in this part. The casting office and everyone connected with this picture were duly warned of Mr. Daniell's inability to fence long before the picture started and we knew of him being taken out of a part in *Romeo & Juliet* because he could not handle a sword."

Curtiz became ill with the flu while directing the duel. The bug swept through the company, laying out Jack Sullivan, Alan Hale, and others. There was no filming on February 19. The following day Curtiz remained

Curtiz poses with Ralph Faulkner, a fencing double, on the set during filming of *The Sea Hawk* (1940) (courtesy of Photofest).

bedridden at the Canoga Ranch and Flynn left the set with a hundred-degree-plus temperature. By the end of February, the picture was a week behind. A diminished Curtiz directed a weakened Flynn, who could wield a sword no more than several hours a day against Daniell (who was doubled extensively by two stuntmen, Ned Davenport and Ralph Faulkner). The swordfight sequence was finished by March 2.

After recovering from his flu bout, Flynn appeared to lose interest. He had been relatively well behaved and was turning in a superior performance. The director encouraged him to play Geoffrey Thorpe as a patriotic Englishman of action rather than a mischievous brigand. It would be different from the wronged Peter Blood, the impudent Robin Hood, and the arrogant Earl of Essex, and the star took to it with gusto. Then Flynn began to miss calls, show up late, leave early, and forget his lines. Despite working ungodly hours, Curtiz was falling farther behind.

Tenny Wright and Mattison implored Flynn to behave himself. The star eventually acknowledged that he could do better, but he believed that Curtiz unfairly blamed him for putting the picture behind schedule after everyone had come down with the flu and the sword duel had dragged on for two weeks. The columnist Sidney Skolsky was on hand when Curtiz compelled Flynn to perform a scene repeatedly, to the point that the writer expected the star to "pull a gun" on the director. After Flynn finally played the scene to Curtiz's satisfaction, the director praised his star with a fresh Curtizism: "Errol, you worked hard. But it's all right. You can't get anything for nothing unless you pay for it."

There would be additional concern about the amount of coverage Curtiz gave to the whipping of the galley slaves. According to the film historian Rudy Behlmer, Flynn became upset at Curtiz over the excessiveness of these sequences. Wallis was worried about the reaction of Breen and the PCA and told the director to tone it down. There was another delay after Brenda Marshall fell off a horse in Griffith Park on a Sunday afternoon when she was riding with her future husband, William Holden. She experienced internal bleeding and had to be hospitalized for a week while Curtiz shot around her.

Curtiz filmed some of the Panamanian sequences in an area adjacent to the back lot called 30 Acres. Anton Grot and his staffers turned the 500,000-square-foot parcel of land into a Central American swamp. A specific performer sought by Curtiz was not made available, as Mattison confirmed to Tenny Wright: "Mr. Curtiz is very anxious to have an alligator or crocodile in the swamp, but in accordance with your instructions, I am telling him we cannot get it for him."

Despite having hunkered down with Blanke to identify the *Captain Blood* battle footage that would be repurposed for *The Sea Hawk,* and agreeing with Wallis in July 1939 that no other battle scenes would be needed, Curtiz decided he needed new sequences of cannons firing, sections of the ship being broken out by cannonballs, and stunt people falling into the water and swinging between the two boats. Apparently he chose not to mention these additional shots to Henry Blanke or Hal Wallis; he simply had the action staged and filmed it. Wallis fulminated to Blanke: "It seemed to me that I issued instructions to everyone, you, Mike and Tenny Wright, that we were not to shoot any of this sort of thing, yet the stuff seems to be scheduled every day, the stuff is shot, we keep squawking, the cost keeps mounting and nobody does anything about it. I am personally am getting damned sick and tired of the whole goddamned mess."

Blanke explained to Wallis that in addition to the *Captain Blood* stock shots, new action footage was needed.[1] Curtiz's battle scenes were superbly choreographed, like miniature narratives. Wallis's notion that the nautical battle action could be depicted solely through the use of stock footage was emblematic of the difference between the executive producer, who viewed movies as the product of an assembly line, and the director, who considered every film a personal artistic statement. By the time Wallis put his foot down, Curtiz's battle scenes were ready to be edited into the picture, and he shifted his concentration to filming the principals during the final battle.

The Sea Hawk gave rise to a memorable Curtiz anecdote related by James Cagney to Peter Bogdanovich many years later. According to Cagney, the director was shuttling back and forth topside on Stage 21's man-of-war, peering through his viewfinder. As he strode around the confined space, the actors scurried out of harm's way, with the exception of an older man who had a bit part as a minister. After repeatedly dodging the pacing Curtiz, the flustered thespian stepped backward off the side of the ship and landed with a sickening thud on the stage floor. Curtiz glanced downward, viewed the prostrate figure being administered to and clipped off in his distinctive accent: "Get me another minister!"

Like so many Curtiz yarns, it didn't matter if the episode actually happened so long as it sounded as though it might have. Raymond Massey claimed that during the filming of *Santa Fe Trail* (1940), Curtiz was framing a shot with his hands and crowded up against an elderly actor who was going to play a parson. Curtiz stepped backward into the parson, who promptly disappeared down an empty water tank on the process stage: "Before he hit bottom, Mike muttered, 'Get another parson!' A pile of folded tarpaulins broke the parson's fall and he wasn't badly hurt." In Ronald Reagan's account from the same picture, an elderly actor on a scaffold dodged Curtiz until stepping backward, falling, and breaking his leg. According to Reagan, "Mike walked across, looked down where he lay on the ground, turned to his assistant and said, 'Get me another minister.'"

These anecdotes illustrate what Massey termed "a mean streak," reflecting Curtiz's indifference to the welfare of actors. Many performers who worked with him would not disagree with this assessment.

There was an actual accident involving an older actor falling and injuring himself during production of *Santa Fe Trail*. Legal correspondence in the studio archives noted the spinal injury of a sixty-five-year-old character actor named Horace Carpenter that occurred during the production. An employee who didn't set up mattresses correctly for a planned fall was blamed for Carpenter's mishap. Any involvement by Curtiz is unmentioned.

The Sea Hawk wrapped on Saturday, April 20. The picture finished in sixty-eight days—twenty days past the original schedule. Curtiz included thirty-four additional scenes. Although the final cut had an unusually long running time (slightly more than two hours), no one complained. Erich Wolfgang Korngold's brilliant musical score and the well-written script accentuated Curtiz's visual pageantry, but the box-office draw was Errol Flynn at the peak of his powers. Although *The Sea Hawk*'s final budget swelled to $1.7 million, the film grossed a million dollars over the cost. It made Jack Warner even more cash during a 1947 re-release, when it was edited down and paired with *The Sea Wolf*.[2]

Despite the success of his latest film, Errol Flynn undoubtedly gritted his teeth when he read *Time* magazine's review: "For Hungarian director Michael Curtiz, who took Flynn from bit-player ranks to make *Captain Blood* and has made nine pictures with him since, it should prove a high point in their profitable relationship." He now had to cope with the perception that Curtiz was responsible for his success, and he loathed the fact that "Errol Flynn" had become synonymous with "swashbuckler." The word, with origins dating back to sixteenth-century combat, aptly depicted the tumultuous relationship between Flynn and Curtiz. "Swash" was to strike something violently, while a "buckler" was a small, round shield hefted by a handle at the back or worn on the forearm.

Before beginning *Santa Fe Trail*, Curtiz traveled to New York for a week in May. It wasn't a true vacation because he didn't know how to relax. Having briefly passed through New York several times while going to and from Europe, he was eager to explore the city. He was also pulling scout duty by attending a pair of plays to which the studio owned the film rights: *The Man Who Came to Dinner* and *The Male Animal*. His whirlwind immersion began upon arrival, with dinner followed by the acclaimed *There Shall Be No Night* at the Alvin Theatre. After the final curtain, Curtiz visited at least five nightclubs and cruised through Manhattan with the columnist Walter Winchell, whose car was equipped with a radio that monitored police calls. The next morning, he strolled by the fruit and vegetable pushcarts lining Bleecker Street, scrutinized medieval art at the Cloisters, and crossed the Triborough Bridge to look over Long Island. He returned to grab a quick lunch, visit the New York Stock Exchange, and then watch a matinee at Radio City Music Hall. After dinner the same evening, he attended *The Male Animal* before embarking on another round of nightclubbing.

"That list is only for the first two days," Curtiz told Theodore Strauss of the *New York Times* on his last day in town. "I have also have been to the World's Fair twice. I have seen several movies to watch the audience reaction. I have gone to the broadcast studios. I went to . . . a taxi dance hall and talked with the hostesses." Asked about the challenge of pleasing New York film audiences, Curtiz broke it down: "The 20 percent, including the comparatively sophisticated folk, which is 'most difficult to please, nothing is ever right,' and the 80 percent, the average man in the street, 'easy to laugh, easy to cry.'" Curtiz related how he coped with the dilemma that amounted to a summary of his career at Warner Bros.: "I compromise. I take a simple story and try to handle it artistically."

Casting about for another Flynn vehicle, Jack Warner asked Robert Buckner if he had any ideas about an action tale concerning the building of the railroad through Kansas in 1857. Buckner replied that the big event in Kansas during that time concerned the abolitionist John Brown and the Free State movement being pitted against the proslavery forces in a guerilla conflict that transformed the region into "Bleeding Kansas." Buckner elaborated on John Brown's involvement with the Pottawatomie Massacre, where he had five defenseless men hacked to death, and the Harpers Ferry raid, which pushed the nation toward the Civil War. Warner liked what Buckner told him. "Fine, go ahead," said the mogul. "We'll make the son of the bitch the heavy."

Buckner's screenplay and Raymond Massey's acting turned John Brown into a psychopathic prince of darkness. Massey's florid performance could have been the centerpiece of a relevant biography about a transformational American figure. This was an Errol Flynn picture produced by Warner Bros., however. *Santa Fe Trail* became another exercise in preposterous historical bowdlerizing.

Flynn played J. E. B. "Jeb" Stuart alongside a grinning Ronald Reagan as George Armstrong Custer. An ensemble of young actors including Frank Wilcox, David Bruce, William Marshall, and George Haywood rounded out the ensemble of neophyte cadet classmates who would become the iconic Civil War generals James Longstreet, Phil Sheridan, George Pickett, and John Hood. In the script, all these members of the Long Gray Line graduate from West Point in 1854 and are sent to Kansas to guard the frontier. That these men actually graduated in different years with entirely variant careers (George Custer being last in his class, in 1863) was irrelevant. The studio's researcher Herman Lissauer consulted the public relations officer at West Point and provided him with a copy of Buckner's script. The West Point officer was appalled, but he tried to be helpful: "I realize that you have a problem. . . . If it is not too late to change the script, I think we could obtain information for you on names that are significantly less known, who are nearer the 1854 period."

Several last-minute changes had to be made. The character of General George McClellan was removed from the final scene of John Brown's hanging when it was noted that he wasn't in the army at that time. Roy Obringer cautioned that the implication that the social reformer Henry Ward Beecher financed Brown's raid on Harpers Ferry might result in a libel suit from Beecher's family. The Beecher scene was excised.

When not on the set pursuing Brown and his brigands, Flynn's and Reagan's characters vied for the affection of Olivia de Havilland. She concluded that since she wasn't going to get the roles she wanted at Warner Bros., she might as well keep her name above the title in a picture that would probably be another hit.

Van Heflin's character, Carl Rader, provides the story's connection between John Brown and his revolutionary chaos and the military law and order represented by Stuart and Custer. Rader is a firebrand abolitionist who fights with Stuart at West Point, gets cashiered, and becomes a hired gun for Brown and his forces. With his flashbulb eyes and dismissive sneer, the versatile Heflin was doing a warm-up for his most twisted role, a decade later, in Joseph Losey's *The Prowler* (1951). The actor Gene Reynolds remembered a rehearsal in which Heflin exchanged lines with Flynn. Heflin was playing it broadly until Flynn exclaimed, "For God's sake, wipe that smirk off your face!"

There was byplay throughout the picture between Tex Bell (Alan Hale) and Windy Brody (Guinn "Big Boy" Williams). Although both actors etched credible careers as comedic relief valves, they were never more annoyingly infantile than in *Santa Fe Trail*. Their scenes were added to leaven the seriousness of the grim John Brown sequences. Transitions from a sepulchral Brown vowing to cleanse slavery from the land with blood to Bell and Brody joking over a packhorse or playing a banjo come across as awkwardly inappropriate.

A railroad being built across Kansas established in the first reel inexplicably disappears until the end of the picture, and the film's connection with the Santa Fe Trail remained obscure. Curtiz boned up by reading the antiquarian tome *The Story of the Santa Fe* by Glenn Danford Bradley and then lost the rare book, greatly embarrassing Lissauer, who had borrowed it from a senior official at the Santa Fe Railroad.

Production began in mid-July. Aside from the railroad sequence shot in Modesto, the bulk of the picture was filmed at the studio, the Warner Ranch, and other San Fernando Valley locations. Because he knew that the story was flawed, Curtiz was more impatient than usual. A rehearsal with the actor Alan Baxter as one of John Brown's sons spiriting a family of slaves out of Kansas via train didn't proceed well. Curtiz exclaimed: "What's the matter? Do you think I am going to spend all day on this? We've got to get to those scenes with the Dead End Kids!" By "Dead End Kids" he meant Flynn, Reagan, Heflin, William Lundigan, and others.

Gene Reynolds was borrowed from Metro to play John Brown's youngest son, who wants nothing to do with his fanatical father. Being directed by Curtiz was an abrupt change of pace for the seventeen-year-old actor, who had been guided deferentially by Frank Borzage and Clarence Brown:

> I was in a wagon doing a tracking shot . . . and Curtiz is hanging on the camera, on the camera dolly on the truck that is driving the camera. . . . And he's yelling across me, he says, "The big guy up there from MGM," you know, he was trying to get me to do more with that scene and we went around and around three times and he was finally satisfied. It [*Santa Fe Trail*] was positive because I felt the work came out well. But [with Curtiz] it was also kind of traumatic. . . . His way of getting something out of you was saying "Oh for God's sake, what are you doing? Come on let's have something."

The difficulties with Errol Flynn continued. At one point Wallis and Jack Warner became so frustrated with the star's behavior that there were discussions of reporting his conduct to the Screen Actors Guild or even terminating his contract. During the first four days of shooting, Flynn didn't receive a call because Curtiz was filming scenes with Raymond Massey. He rushed into the studio, confronted Wallis, and claimed that the Stuart part wasn't important enough for a star of his magnitude. After cooling off, Flynn reviewed the script and discovered how significantly his role figured in the story. Ronald Reagan recalled how Flynn's anxieties affected his behavior: "Errol was a strange person, terribly unsure of himself and needlessly so. He was a beautiful piece of machinery, likable, with great charm, and yet convinced he lacked ability as an actor. As a result, he was conscious every minute of scenes favoring other actors and their position on the screen in relation to himself. He was apparently unaware of his own striking personality."

Reagan also became aware of his costar's scene-stealing tricks. During a rehearsal, Flynn had a quick word with Curtiz and rearranged a scene of actors grouped around a campfire so that Reagan would be standing away from him and behind the shoulders of the other actors when it was his turn to recite dialogue. After surreptitiously scraping together a pile of dirt, Reagan ascended his homemade plinth and appeared in the frame of the shot as the future president of the United States delivered his lines.

The associate producer Robert Fellows advised Tenny Wright that Flynn's attitude was one of continual complaint: "He precedes every state-ment with the fact that he is trying to do his best and then launches into a tirade against this picture and all of the outdoor pictures he has ever been in. He has refused, as you know, to accept a late afternoon call and work into the night."

Curtiz attempted to get along with Flynn, particularly when there were visitors on the set. After wrapping up the scene at the Warner Ranch in which Brown surrenders to Stuart, Curtiz walked out of the round-house with a grin, saying, "How'd you like those bums in that scene?" to a visiting reporter. When the reporter expressed the wish that it hadn't gone so smoothly so she could watch Curtiz lose his famous temper, the director laughed and replied: "Heet's all propaganda. . . . Reely, I am very lovable person. Eesn't that so Errol honey?" Flynn walked by, trailed by his schnauzer, and responded tersely, "You're a lovable bum, Mike honey."

Curtiz's obsession with realism remained unabated. During a fight scene between Rader and Stuart, a prop chair thrown at a window simply broke apart. Curtiz substituted a real chair without consulting the prop-erty master, Limey Plews, or the actors. During the second take, the chair flew through the window, taking out the glass and part of the wall.

Santa Fe Trail's portrayal of African Americans was particularly of-fensive. According to Wallis, Curtiz compounded matters by adding a sequence of a group of slaves breaking into a spiritual when John Brown informs them that they have been freed. Wallis's written comments to Curtiz exhibited the stereotypical attitude of a 1940s-era Hollywood stu-dio executive toward people of color: "They get up and start singing, and it sounds just like the Hall Johnson Choir with beautiful voices in har-mony . . . instead of a lot of poor old niggers who are freed slaves. It is so theatrical and so phony that it ruins the scene."

The movie presents slavery as a social irritant. Everything would be worked out if not for John Brown, Rader, and other miscreants stirring up trouble. Three-quarters of a century after Appomattox, the Civil War remained vivid in the minds of many Americans. Many descendants of those on the losing side also happened to live where Warner Bros. owned a lot of movie theaters. Jeb Stuart becomes a hero of two minds. In one scene he condemns slavery and then modifies his view that the violence in Kansas "will be stopped when we hang John Brown. Then the South can settle her own problems without a loss of pride of being forced into it by a bunch of fanatics." This unusual ambivalence of a Flynn character is a result of another of Wallis's sociopolitical equivocations hatched to make the movie a salable product.

In mid-September, while the film was being edited, a restless Wallis toyed with the idea of excising its most dramatic scene: John Brown's hanging. Buckner and Curtiz reacted with frustration: "What *is Santa Fe Trail* in any honest analysis but the story of John Brown? That's the very thing that makes it important from the ordinary Western. *We must see the end of John Brown.*" They prevailed, and the execution sequence, beautifully staged by Curtiz, stayed in, although the silly final dissolve has Stuart and Kit Carson Holliday (de Havilland) exchanging marriage vows on the miraculously reappearing train.

The December 13, 1940, world premiere of *Santa Fe Trail* in Santa Fe, New Mexico, was accompanied by the usual hoopla. Unmentioned in the publicity campaign was the disparagement from critics that included retired army personnel and a federal judge. The critiques noted the erroneous use of modern repeating rifles in 1859, Curtiz's re-creation of the Harpers Ferry attack as a set piece Civil War battle, and Buckner's comingling of a hodgepodge of military notables. Bosley Crowther, beginning his inexplicably long tenure as a *New York Times* film critic, referred to the fictional grouping of future generals as Warner Bros. "graduating them en masse to Kansas, like a troop of adventure-loving Rover Boys."

Nobody at the studio cared about the critical carping. *Santa Fe Trail* grossed nearly $1.5 million over its cost.

Curtiz's next film was based on a superior literary work and was one of his more distinctive pictures. Jack London's *The Sea Wolf* had been adapted to the screen an astonishing six times since its publication in 1904. The original notion was for Mervyn LeRoy to direct Paul Muni, who would star as the dictatorial captain Wolf Larsen. Muni advised his agent that he wouldn't consider the project unless Rafael Sabatini, Sidney

Howard, or Eugene O'Neill agreed to write the screenplay. By 1940 Muni and LeRoy were both gone from Warner Bros. After initially considering the director Anatole Litvak, Wallis decided it was a perfect Curtiz project: another rousing adventure picture. Curtiz parroted the studio party line in a publicity release: "I have always said that I love action in pictures and finally I found my ideal picture: one that is all action." But he would direct *The Sea Wolf* in an entirely different style from that of a Flynn swashbuckler.

Edward G. Robinson enthusiastically accepted the role of Wolf Larsen. "No actor could ask for more—no actor nearing fifty, that is," he declared. Jack London created Larsen as a literary refutation of Nietzsche's superman. Robinson viewed the character through the modern political prism as a Nazi "in everything but name."

Ida Lupino, John Garfield, and Alexander Knox rounded out the starring cast. Lupino played the part of Ruth Brewster with sloe-eyed sincerity. She respected Curtiz as a gifted director, even though he mostly ignored her Davis-like recommendations on how to direct her scenes. She loved working with Garfield and intensely disliked Robinson. She remarked about the star: "When we worked together, it was easy for us to hate each other and we continued that way!"

Wallis courted George Raft for the part of George Leach, the fugitive seaman who signs on aboard the *Ghost* and runs afoul of the sadistic Larsen.[3] Raft turned the part down by inaccurately telling Wallis that the George Leach role amounted to "little better than a bit." Raft correctly surmised that Robinson as Wolf Larsen would own the picture, and he was not willing to play second fiddle to any other Warner star.

Garfield was delighted to be in *The Sea Wolf*. Even though Leach was a supporting part, it was an opportunity to celebrate the work of the legendary Jack London, whose novels had been devoured by nearly every American boy during the first four decades of the twentieth century. He would also be reunited with Curtiz, with whom he remained close after *Four Daughters*.

Alexander Knox, a Canadian actor with British stage and film experience, played the idealistic novelist Humphrey Van Weyden, who is trapped on the nightmarish ship after a ferry collision casts him and Ruth Brewster adrift. The thirty-four-year-old Knox projected a mature empathy that was a perfect contrast to Wolf Larsen's sadism. Knox was taken aback upon encountering Curtiz his first morning on the picture. He was looking over the set of the sea cabin when Curtiz burst in, pacing and agitated. The director began ordering him to rearrange the props, assuming he was from the prop department, as it was too early for any actors to be called. After Knox made it clear who he was, Curtiz apologized, and Knox concentrated on comprehending the unique directorial syntax.

The screenplay by Robert Rossen was an expansion from an outline by Abem Finkel and Norman Reilly Raine. The son of a rabbi from the Lower East Side, Rossen was an ideal fit for Warner Bros. After arriving at the studio in 1936, he wrote or cowrote *Marked Woman* (1937), *They Won't Forget* (1937), *Racket Busters* (1938), *Dust Be My Destiny* (1939), and *The Roaring Twenties* (1939). Hal Wallis continued using him later on at Paramount for *The Strange Love of Martha Ivers* (1946), *Desert Fury* (1947), and *The Accused* (1949). Rossen's breakout picture would be the award-winning *All the King's Men*, which he wrote, produced, and directed at Columbia in 1949.[4]

Rossen played up London's story, with its theme of social Darwinism, as a comment on fascist totalitarianism and altered the main characters. Humphrey Van Weyden was no longer the romantic partner of Ruth Brewster, and the Leach character played by Garfield was built up and paired with Brewster. The PCA prevented Brewster from being portrayed as a prostitute, as she was in the novel, so Rossen turned her into a tough-as-nails escapee from a women's prison. Larsen philosophizes that he is the living exponent of Milton's blank verse by reigning over his nautical hell. His inward fear grows as he begins losing his eyesight, contemplating the loss of control over his brutish seamen.

Curtiz cast every supporting part with care. Barry Fitzgerald excels as the repellent ship's cook, who threatens Van Weyden with a knife, informs on crewmembers, is thrown over the side, and loses his leg to a shark. Gene Lockhart is similarly credible as the alcoholic Dr. Prescott, who saves Brewster's life with an emergency blood transfusion from Leach. He is rewarded with a torrent of abuse from Larsen and ends up committing suicide.

Instead of a rousing adventure film, Curtiz staged *The Sea Wolf* as an exercise in anxiety-laden dread. The opening credits are reminiscent of *Bride of Frankenstein*'s: the title lunges out at the audience as Erich Wolfgang Korngold's score creates an atmosphere of trepidation.

The balance of the picture emphasizes the dreary claustrophobic conditions on board the *Ghost*. The scenes are shaded in a foggy haze that sunlight barely penetrates. The shots of the ship in motion are silently sepulchral. Byron Haskin's superb miniatures—he was nominated for a spe-

Curtiz and Sol Polito line up a crane shot during production of *The Sea Wolf* (1941) on Warner's massive Stage 21 (courtesy of the Lucas family).

cial effects Oscar—are complemented by the 130-foot-long, 32-foot-wide set of the *Ghost* assembled by a team of seventy-five carpenters on Stage 21. In staging the ferry collision, Curtiz drew on his 1913 Nordisk experience in *Atlantis*. He used less than two minutes of film, with several quick cuts, to chronicle the maritime disaster that is accompanied by a chorus of female screams.

Because *The Sea Wolf* was an exercise in cinematic minimalism, Curtiz didn't receive the usual written critiques from Wallis about the expansiveness of his direction. The depictions of violent action are short and sharp. And his direction of the actors was similarly on point. The sequences between Lupino and Garfield demonstrate that the director could elicit the essence of a scene despite his struggle to communicate. Lupino recalled how Curtiz threw himself into describing what he wanted: "Curtiz would come over when we were doing *The Sea Wolf* and say, 'Lupe, Lupe, Lupe, listen to me, you do a little . . .' and then he'd explain it forever. Afterwards Julie [Garfield] would say, 'I don't understand a goddamn thing he was saying, but I think he was right.'"

Curtiz deleted a number of scenes from Rossen's script that tended to make the Larsen character sympathetic. It was a rare instance of Wallis approving of the director's tinkering; he urged Curtiz and Henry Blanke to have Robinson play Larsen as a noxious brute: "Whenever Robinson gets into these philosophical discussions, particularly with Van Weyden, the tempo seems to lag and Robinson seems to change his character. In the other scenes on deck, he was swell, he was tough and hard. . . . Let's at all times keep Eddie in character. Keep him hard, tough, and don't let him become too much of an intellectual."

Curtiz achieved the proper balance by trimming some of Rossen's dialogue-laden exchanges while maintaining the theoretical depth of the Larsen character as more than a thuggish heavy.

With regard to Robinson, there was another agenda in play. During *A Dispatch from Reuters* (1940), Jack Warner observed that Robinson had begun to appear older onscreen and worried about his continued box-office appeal. Warner consulted Roy Obringer before production began on *The Sea Wolf* about the possibility of canceling Robinson's contract, which guaranteed the actor starring roles for nearly two more years. Warner eventually opted for greater subtlety. The mogul began to offer parts that he knew the actor would turn down. Robinson left the studio in 1942.

Curtiz brought *The Sea Wolf* in on schedule and at just over a million dollars. After presenting Wallis's son Brent with a model of the *Ghost*, Curtiz and the crew celebrated at the wrap party that, according to Lupino, was highlighted by the director's being ceremoniously pitched into the Stage 21 water tank by cast and crew.

Henry Blanke and Hal Wallis had to launch a frantic postproduction effort to prevent Jack Warner from changing the title of *The Sea Wolf* to

The Law of the Sea. Warner worried that audiences would confuse *The Sea Wolf* with *The Sea Beast* or *The Sea Hawk*. Blanke wrote an impassioned memo about the continued popularity of London's novel, which swayed the studio chief.

Instead of chartering a train, Warner Bros. engaged the S.S. *America* out of Los Angeles harbor to premiere *The Sea Wolf* on March 21, 1941, during the liner's at-sea transit to San Francisco. The picture was a solid success, grossing more than $800,000 over its cost. Nearly all the major reviews were positive. *The Sea Wolf* remains a superior film despite the continued search for the long-missing ten minutes of footage that was excised for the double bill re-release with *The Sea Hawk* in 1947. Current versions of the film clock in at eighty-seven or ninety minutes instead of the originally released version of one hundred minutes.

With America's involvement in the war becoming more of a certainty, Jack Warner and Hal Wallis decided on a fail-safe approach: casting their stars in military-themed pictures. *Dive Bomber* was originally conceived for James Cagney, but instead became an Errol Flynn paean to the U.S. Navy Air Corps. The Buckner screenplay was adapted from a story by a U.S. Navy aviation pioneer, Commander Frank "Spig" Wead, who also contributed to the script.

Flynn plays a crusading flight surgeon attempting to devise a medical solution for altitude blackout among aviators. Curtiz wanted to showcase the lissome Hollywood High School grad Alexis Smith, who had been signed the previous year and was given a prosaic part as Flynn's girlfriend. (The Canadian-born actress would remain at the studio for a decade as a cooperative if underappreciated contract player content to accept roles that other actresses turned down.) Warner borrowed Fred MacMurray from Paramount in exchange for lending out Olivia de Havilland for *Hold Back the Dawn*.

Jack Warner decided that a return to Technicolor was warranted after the studio obtained a pledge of extensive cooperation from the U.S. Navy. Secretary of the Navy Frank Knox gave the studio veritable carte blanche on the use of base facilities, ships, planes, runways, hangars, and trucks. The realization that Hollywood could assist with the coming war effort had begun to dawn on Washington politicos.

Second-unit background was filmed at Eglin Air Force Base in Florida and Hickam Field in Honolulu, while Curtiz took the principal company to North Island Naval Air Station in San Diego for two weeks of location filming beginning on March 20, 1941. The navy allowed Curtiz and the

While making *Dive Bomber* (1941) at North Island Naval Air Station in San Diego, Curtiz is joined by Commander Frank "Spig" Wead, a visiting John Ford, and Errol Flynn (courtesy of the Lucas family).

company to embark on the aircraft carrier U.S.S. *Enterprise* to film carrier flight operations. These sequences gave rise to a time-honored Curtiz anecdote originally related by Ralph Bellamy: "We got all the long shots and medium shots called for in the script during our week at sea, but Mike saved the close-ups to shoot against the superstructure of the *Enterprise* while we were returning to its San Diego base. This was good planning." Time was of the essence, as the director was hurriedly shooting close-ups to match the previous shots while giving directions to the crew and actors over the ship's public address system. As the carrier approached land and the engines backed down, a huge billow of smoke descended between the camera and the actors. "In his own special dialect, Mike went to pieces," continued Bellamy. "He lost all control of himself. He exploded over the public address system to the assistant director [Jack Sullivan], 'Tell de captain to blow the smoke de udder vay!'"

A fallacious account claimed that Curtiz ranted at navy brass and liaison officers like tardy dress extras. In reality, he went out of his way to be polite to everyone wearing a uniform. He was required to shoot many critical aviation sequences in single takes and was dependent on the navy's cooperation. Bellamy confirmed:

> Curtiz had to be on his best behavior. . . . Even though he couldn't give any direct orders, he was always grabbing officers by their sleeves as they walked by and saying things like, "My good man, do you think you could go over there and do this for me?" . . . No, he didn't call anyone a bum. Jack Warner would have yanked him out of there by the seat of his pants if he had done so. . . . I'd worked with Mike Curtiz before, but this is the first time I've seen him humbled. He was used to being a dictator, but not on this trip.

Wallis was pleased with the location dailies even though he believed Curtiz had captured enough footage of airplanes flying overhead during a scene of a graduation ceremony to "make a two-reel short." According to the associate producer, Robert Lord, Curtiz "never misses a day without wanting something rewritten," even though most of his changes were relatively minor. Lord noted that Curtiz's collaborative nature created the kind of delays that a director like John Ford never would have tolerated: "The dialogue director, the assistant directors, the property men, the principal actors, etc. etc. . . . Today these people continually suggest changes in the script. They do this in all sincerity—with the best intentions in the world—thinking that they are improving the picture."

According to Lord, Errol Flynn's chronic insecurity was a major irritant: "Flynn . . . does not like his part; he has already been after me to take things away from Joe [MacMurray] and give them to him. Most of his changes cannot be made without wrecking the story completely. . . . I am going to have trouble with him for weeks." John Meredyth Lucas turned twenty-two years old on the set: "Errol sulked quite a bit of the time after he found that MacMurray, who had been borrowed from another studio, was getting a much larger salary that he was."

As usual, the principal concern became Curtiz's inability to stick to the production schedule—which was devised by people who hadn't ever directed a film. Because of the location shooting and the continual script changes, the director returned to the studio more than a week behind. Jack Warner wrote Curtiz an imploring note:

> I know you could not judge schedules when you were in San Diego, but when you are here at the studio you should stay on

schedule, in fact better your time. The picture is now practically nine days behind on a forty-eight day schedule.

Every one of your pictures, Mike, goes over by a whole lot of money. In the past, I wasn't so worried, but with conditions in Europe today and the future looking very dark, I am frightened to spend on any picture over a certain amount. Therefore, I am appealing to you to see if you cannot speed up your work. Maybe you are trying for too many angles that we don't need and will never see in the picture. If the picture is finished and we need anything, you know we always go back and get it, therefore, if you should accidentally miss something, believe me, I will be the first to see you pick it up after the picture is out.

I am depending on you as my long-standing friend and one of the most important directors in the business at least not to lose any more time and try to make up some of it. I know you will get more work done each day, for you, myself and everyone else in these trying times must dig in and do twice as much or even more than we used to do in normal times.

Warner sent a copy of the note to Wallis with the comment: "If the attached note to Mike Curtiz does not do the trick, I don't know what will." Curtiz well knew that after production concluded on any of his pictures, his ability to add or change anything on his own initiative would be non-existent. This was precisely why he labored so hard to put everything possible into his films before the front office got hold of it.

In response to Warner's missive, Curtiz pushed the cast and crew harder while still refusing to move on until he got exactly what he wanted. At one point, he became dissatisfied with his perceived inadequacy of MacMurray and Regis Toomey reacting to altitude sickness and cut the scene, yelling, "Please, everybody sweat now!"

After twelve features with Curtiz, Errol Flynn finally snapped. Near the end of the film, he reportedly grabbed the director around the throat and began choking him. In his memoir, Flynn claimed the incident occurred during filming of *Santa Fe Trail,* writing that he'd received a cut on the cheek from a galloping stunt rider. Flynn maintained that Curtiz had had the tip guards removed from the prop swords without telling the actors. But Flynn's story doesn't square with the fact that Curtiz directed him in *Dive Bomber* after *Santa Fe Trail.*

Flynn also wrote about a stuntman named Bill Meade who died after falling off his horse and becoming impaled on a sword during the filming of *They Died with Their Boots On;* he laid the blame on Curtiz for needlessly ordering a third take of a cavalry charge sequence. But this also never happened. Curtiz did not direct a frame of *They Died with Their Boots On.*[5] Flynn probably confused the Meade story with an actual occurrence during the same movie. The rider who died was a polo player–turned–stuntman named Jack Budlong, the son of a wealthy automobile executive; he volunteered to perform in the film on a lark. He insisted on using a real sword rather than a prop during a charge scene and ended up being thrown off his horse and impaled. He was rushed from the Warner Ranch to Cedars of Lebanon hospital, where the twenty-eight-year-old died several days later from peritonitis. Budlong's family sued the hospital for negligent treatment, but the coroner ruled the death was accidental.

Flynn's attack on Curtiz during *Dive Bomber* reportedly necessitated two men to pry him off. The episode circulated through the studio but managed to stay out of the newspapers. Olivia de Havilland was given to understand that the confrontation was "a lethal, lethal scene." As Flynn put it, "I deemed it wiser not to work with this highly artistic gentleman who aroused my worst instincts." Curtiz tried to patch up matters by buying Flynn an expensive cigarette lighter but was left feeling humiliated. The two men never worked together again. It was an unfortunate finale to one of the most successful collaborations between a director and a star.

A more pleasant recollection of Curtiz from the set came from the character actress Ann Doran, who had a small part as Fred MacMurray's date:

> Oh Mike. Lovely, lovely Mike! I was under contract to Paramount and they called me to . . . go over and meet the director, Mike Curtiz. Well, I had heard about Mike Curtiz, and I had heard some pretty wild stories about him. You know, a volatile man. He'd tell you everything in Hungarian and you didn't know what he was talking about. He turned around with his arms in the air, looked at me and came over. He said, "Oh my darling, you have such charming . . ." He was always charming to me. Absolutely charming. He would get so angry once in a while and would storm about the set; always in his Hungarian. I didn't know what he was talking about, what was upsetting him, and I always figured it wasn't me. . . . But this was Mike. He was fun. I really enjoyed working with him.

Archduke Otto von Habsburg of the defunct Austro-Hungarian Empire visited Curtiz's *Dive Bomber* set. After publicity pictures were taken with Curtiz greeting his could-have-been sovereign, Bess Meredyth asked her husband if he had spoken to the archduke in German or Hungarian. He replied, "Why hell I talk foreign? I speak English. I am American."

Dive Bomber wasn't a great film, but with Flynn and MacMurray on the marquee along with the Technicolor aviation footage and the patriotic narrative, it became one of the most profitable Warner movies of 1941. Even so, it was dwarfed by the year's most popular movie, also produced by Warner Bros. The studio had brought in Howard Hawks to direct Gary Cooper in *Sergeant York,* which grossed an incredible $7 million.

If Curtiz suffered from professional jealousy, he didn't show it. Much as he had as the head of Phönix-Film during World War I, Curtiz would achieve several of his greatest professional accomplishments while the world was at war.

23

The "Pinochle" of His Career

Curtiz was on the telephone from Halifax, Canada, reporting back to Hollywood every evening. His latest picture, *Captains of the Clouds,* appeared to have a lot going for it. James Cagney was accompanied by beautiful Technicolor photography in the first American feature filmed entirely in Canada.

America wouldn't enter the war until the end of 1941, but Canada had been fighting Germany since September 1939. At the urging of the heads of the Canadian Air Service and film boards, Warner and Wallis conjured up this tribute to Canadian bush pilots to support the overall war effort. Cagney realized the script was mediocre, but there were fringe benefits to working with Curtiz on location in Canada: "The plot was the same old crap: I'm a no-good who winds up doing good. On the positive side, after our doing *Angels with Dirty Faces*, Mike Curtiz was not only used to my adding dialogue or changing it, but actually encouraged it, and it was fun doing that." Cagney did at one point become fed up with the director's routine mistreatment of nonstar actors and gave it back to him in spades: "He gave one of the actors a hard time for no discoverable reason. I took Mike on the side and started to lace into him but good. He said, 'Jeemy, I am a sheet-heel, no?' I said, 'You are a sheet-heel, yes!' I really came down on him for his meanness, which in this instance was ample and quite deliberate. I saw he was hurt by what I had said to him, but it had to be said. This was the only moment I ever had with him when I realized that he *could* be sensitive and sorry."

Cagney also received a mild concussion after refusing to use a stunt double for a scene in which he was knocked into a lake by a plane propeller. Aside from those two episodes, the actor enjoyed the hospitality of the Canadians and palling around off-camera with cast members Dennis Morgan, George Tobias, and Alan Hale.

The location shoot wasn't nearly as much fun for Curtiz, who was routinely lambasted for his script changes by Wallis, and Jack Warner kept asking him why he was behind schedule. The special effects coordinator Byron Haskin witnessed Curtiz being tag-teamed over the phone by both executives: "They'd bounce him around like a pingpong ball for twenty minutes, absolutely tear him to pieces. . . . Finally he'd hang up and shake his head: 'Bunnie, I jump out of the window. These guys drive me crazy.'"

The logistics were daunting. A majority of the crew was housed in a remote army barracks, and autograph seekers deluged a second-rate Ottawa hotel where Cagney and the other stars were staying. The Italian-born Sol Polito experienced difficulty with the immigration authorities when he attempted to enter the country—Canada was at war with Italy—and then suffered a mild heart attack. Curtiz refused to shoot the film without his paisan behind the camera. Fortunately, Polito quickly recovered.

The gorgeous color photography of Canadian lakes and forests by an Oscar-nominated Polito was supplemented by breathtaking aerial sequences filmed by Winton C. Hoch, Charles Marshall, and Elmer Dyer. There was also a stirring excerpt from Churchill's famous Dunkirk speech voiced by the actor Miles Mander and an actual Canadian Royal Air Force graduation ceremony featuring Air Marshal William A. "Billy" Bishop, the great World War I Canadian aerial ace. Warner Bros. premiered the film simultaneously throughout the British Commonwealth in London, Ottawa, Cairo, Melbourne, Toronto, Winnipeg, and Vancouver, in addition to New York. Jack Warner had the prints delivered to all the premiere locales by Royal Canadian Air Force planes.

But neither the visual grandeur nor publicity efforts could overcome the pedestrian screenplay by five different writers that could have been culled from any of a number of Zanuck-era quickies. *Time* magazine characterized Cagney's role as "thankless," and Bosley Crowther observed that Warner Bros. would have been wiser to leave the first hour of the 113-minute picture on the cutting room floor. The critics weren't buying tickets, though. *Captains of the Clouds* garnered profits of more than $1.3 million.

By the time the picture was released on February 12, 1942, the country was embroiled in World War II and Curtiz was directing one of his finest movies. The notion for a biographical film about legendary show business powerhouse George M. Cohan had been kicking around Hollywood since the late 1930s. All but forgotten today, it is germane to recall how iconic a figure Cohan was during the first decades of the twentieth century. The father of American musical comedy, who claimed to be born on July 4, 1878, began treading the boards at age eight in the family vaudeville act. During his career, he wrote more than 150 original songs, including the standards "You're a Grand Old Flag" and the country's most popular song during World War I, "Over There." With Sam Harris, Cohan produced more than fifty musicals and plays on Broadway; at one point five of their shows ran simultaneously. Cohan did it all: he was a playwright, composer, lyricist, actor, singer, dancer, and producer. Although the majority of his work has become badly dated, Cohan *was* the American musical theater from 1904 to 1925.

By 1941 he was ill and realized that his days were numbered. His ego was piqued by the notion of a film biography to enshrine his legacy (he had already published his autobiography at the age of forty-seven), but he had serious misgivings about films. He had appeared in several silent movies that failed to capture his feisty style. After his popularity had begun to fade, Cohan starred in two early talkies. The second, *The Phantom President* (1932), was a fiasco. Cohan compared the experience to a stretch at Leavenworth Penitentiary and vowed never to return to the West Coast.

But impending mortality mellowed his outlook. He negotiated with Samuel Goldwyn—who initially committed to a Cohan film starring Fred Astaire before the actor-dancer dropped out—and consulted with his close friend, the actor Edward McNamara. A former Irish cop who made more money pretending to be one onstage and in films, McNamara was also a pal of James Cagney. McNamara urged Cohan to consider Cagney to play him while simultaneously pitching the project to the star. Around the same time, *Variety*'s publisher, Abel Green, advised Jack Warner about Cohan's interest in a bio-musical film. Warner and Hal Wallis were intrigued. Wallis contacted William Cagney about having his brother portray George M. Cohan and was surprised when James turned it down.

Cagney was reticent because of his feelings about the entertainer. Cohan had an infamous falling-out with Actors Equity in 1919 after he opposed a strike by actors from the perspective of an owner-producer. His refusal to join Equity damaged his reputation throughout the profession. As a charter member of the Screen Actors Guild (he would be elected SAG president in September 1942), Cagney was diametrically opposed to Cohan's position. Cagney's trade-unionist liberalism, nurtured by his impoverished background and accentuated by a poisonous relationship with Jack Warner, led to an instinctive mistrust of bosses, particularly producers. Although he respected Cohan as a great performer, he couldn't countenance portraying a man he regarded as an antiunion reactionary.

But changing political winds convinced Cagney to reverse his decision and to reexamine some of his own positions. In August 1940 an ostensible Communist Party member named John Leech testified during Los Angeles grand jury proceedings that Cagney, along with other famous Hollywood personages, including Humphrey Bogart, Fredric March, and Franchot Tone, were Communists, members of Communist "study groups," or contributor-sympathizers. With regard to Cagney and many of the others, the charges were demonstrably false, but the newspapers had a field day. The city's corrupt district attorney, Buron Fitts, made movie-star patriotism a centerpiece of his ultimately unsuccessful reelection campaign. Another publicity-seeking DA in Sacramento had previously accused Cagney of having Communist ties back in 1934 (that charge was eventually quashed).

Bill Cagney, summoned to a meeting with Jack Warner, had to rehabilitate his brother's reputation, and fast: "[Warner] told me in no uncertain terms that if my brother didn't clean his skirts of this charge, he was going to destroy him." James had already been moving politically right at the behest of his wife by shedding some of his extreme left-wing friends, such as the screenwriter John Bright, and maintaining a more conservative social circle that included Robert Montgomery and his Irish Mafia pals Pat O'Brien, Lynne Overman, and Frank McHugh.

William Cagney contacted Martin Dies, chair of the House Un-American Activities Committee (HUAC), and arranged for James to testify in front of HUAC. Dies, whose committee accused ten-year old Shirley Temple of being a Communist dupe in 1934, eventually issued a public statement clearing Cagney. The actor's opposition to *Yankee Doodle Dandy*, as the Cohan picture was eventually called, evaporated. As William related to the writer Patrick McGilligan, he told his brother: "We're going to have to make the goddamndest patriotic picture that's ever been made. I think it's the Cohan story."

Yet animus persisted between Wallis and the Cagneys. James regarded Wallis with disdain, viewing him as a front-office suit responsible for reinforcing the actor's image as a screen gangster. The chill was mutual. "He [Cagney] and I never became friends," admitted Wallis. "He was cold to me and I wasn't particularly fond of him." Wallis continued to brood over being forced to accept William Cagney as an associate producer. The younger Cagney was no shrinking violet, either. He was an activist who never hesitated to put his elder brother's interests ahead of the studio's. Fully aware of the battle lines, Curtiz would walk a tightrope to maintain relationships with both sides while directing *Yankee Doodle Dandy*.

Wallis assigned Robert Buckner to write the script. Buckner's specialty was drama and Westerns—he had no experience with musicals or lighter material—but he did a thorough job that took more than half a year. He moved to New York to work with Cohan and ended up befriending him. Cohan's contract gave him script and title approval in addition to his $125,000 fee and 10 percent of the gross receipts over $1,500,000. He also had final say on characters and all references to his family. Cohan approved Cagney to portray him but had his own ideas about the screenplay.

Cohan attempted to sanitize his life on screen. He especially wanted to expunge any romantic or personal aspects from the screenplay and stubbornly resisted any effort to portray his life as other than a series of professional triumphs. Even so, "The Man Who Owned Broadway" was also a realist. During a period of back-and-forth frustration over the script, he wrote to Buckner and Wallis: "Four-fifths of the people who remember me are dead. This younger generation doesn't know me. If you can't lick the storyline, I'd rather call the deal off and return the contract than see a picture made that wasn't right—personally to me or commercially to Warners."

After Cohan submitted 170 pages of script changes, Buckner, along with Wallis and William Cagney, carefully crafted a letter that begged Cohan to allow them to take a limited amount of dramatic license in order to produce an entertaining musical biography. Using the recently successful *Knute Rockne All American* (1940) as an example, the trio beseeched Cohan: "This is our main plea, Mr. Cohan. Without your faith in our sincerity that this is not merely another commercial product, pure and simple, or in our ability to handle the subject with above-board frankness and good taste, we are completely helpless to proceed."

The letter swayed Cohan, who eventually compromised to a limited extent. The script was revised to introduce a fictional Mrs. Cohan named Mary, who would be played by sixteen-year-old Joan Leslie. There would be no mention of his first wife, who left him in 1907 (and would unsuccessfully sue Cohan and Warner Bros. over the film), or his second (successful) marriage. Cagney, who was uncomfortable displaying any type of sexual intimacy onscreen, would further downplay the romantic angle. Cohan's relationships with other characters, including his family and particularly his partner, Sam Harris, were idealized. It became the story of a triumphant show-business personality living a storybook life.

Though Cohan consented to the script, there was still James Cagney to contend with. When the star read through Buckner's final draft (with contributions by the screenwriter Edmund Joseph) on his Martha's Vineyard farm, he was appalled: "I read it with incredulity. There wasn't a single laugh in it, not the suggestion of a snicker. And this was a script purporting to be about a great American light entertainer, a man who wrote forty-four Broadway shows, only two of which were not comedies."

Cagney refused to do the movie unless the script was gone over thoroughly by Julius and Philip Epstein, who had impressed him with their work on *The Strawberry Blonde* (1941). The Epsteins later downplayed their role, viewing the project as flag-waving corn that they'd agreed to work on only because William Cagney repeatedly asked them to. But they made numerous contributions, including transforming the stilted relationship between the Cohan and Mary characters into a charming romance. Comic scenes between the music publisher characters Goff and Dietz were added, and they also built up the character of the couple's daughter, Josie Cohan, played by Jeanne Cagney. Most significantly, they added the "Over There" coda, which concluded the film on an upbeat note. *Yankee Doodle Dandy* wouldn't have been a success without the Epstein brothers. Cagney's biographer Patrick McGilligan described the final product as a Horatio Alger version of Cohan's life. After watching the film, Cohan's daughter, Georgette, remarked, "That's the kind of life Daddy would have liked to live."

During the production, Robert Buckner continually complained about the changes to his screenplay. He challenged the studio's intention to grant the Epstein brothers equal screenwriting credit, informing Wallis that he was ready to take the issue to the Writers Guild: "I spent seven months on that job, all the research, all the selling of Cohan, all his changes, weeks working with Curtiz and his ideas. I appreciate many of the laughs which the Epsteins have inserted, but I do not feel (nor do they) that their contribution, time or physical efforts justify an equal share of the screen credit. . . . This script is one (I think the only one) I've ever felt so strongly about that I am ready to go to bat for."

The Epsteins considered Buckner a respected colleague and were glad to defer credit over an issue that they felt had become embarrassing. The other pair of brothers reacted differently. The Cagneys viewed Buckner as a Wallis loyalist who delivered a lousy script, attempted to undermine them, and was now trying to ace out the writers most responsible for the film's success. Despite the friction, production would begin on schedule, even as it became shaped by bigger events.

Sunday, December 7, 1941, was Curtiz and Bess's twelfth anniversary. Characteristically, they celebrated the occasion together, but separately. Bess remained in bed at the ranch while Curtiz was out on the skeet range with Henry Blanke and Robert Stack, then a youthful national skeet champion–turned–actor. John Meredyth Lucas recalled the day:

> I was reading when I heard a shout from Mother. I ran into her bedroom. . . . Over the radio we heard the ominous tones of H. V. Kaltenborn announcing the Japanese raid on Pearl Harbor. I grabbed the station wagon, raced down to the skeet field and relayed the news. The skeet match broke up quickly. I went back to the house because Ann Sheridan and George Brent had come to lunch. I brought a portable radio out to the pool and the three of us listened, drank and ate. The extent of the damage to the fleet as not yet released but clearly the damage was terrible. It was a very quiet lunch.

The Japanese attack, followed by Hitler's declaration of war against the United States on December 11, capsized the isolationist movement in the U.S. Congress, which had continued to target Warner Bros. for their openly anti-Nazi films. After Pearl Harbor, the Washington isolationists performed a pirouette in considering how Warner Bros. and the other Hollywood studios could best help America win the war.

The morning after Pearl Harbor was the first day of production on *Yankee Doodle Dandy*. Rosemary DeCamp, cast as Cagney's mother, recalled the real-life drama that occurred before the cameras rolled:

> The crew was standing still with grave faces. Jeanne Cagney, Walter Huston and I, made up and elaborately costumed, were staring at a little radio emitting the sound of President Roosevelt's voice along with a lot of static. Mike Curtiz the director and Jimmy Cagney came in through the freight dock and walked across the big soundstage toward us. Mike started to speak, but Walter held up his hand. The president finished with the grave news that we were now at war with Japan and Germany. Then, the national anthem blared forth. Some of us got to our feet and

sang the lyrics hesitantly. At the end, Jimmy said, clearing his throat, "I think a prayer goes in here . . . turn that damn thing off." Someone did. We stood in silence for a full minute. Jeanne and I dabbed our made-up eyes carefully. Mike bowed and with his inimitable accent said, "Now boys and girls, we haff work to do . . . we haff bad news . . . but we haff a wonderful story to tell the world. So let us put away sad things and begin."

From that momentous first morning, everyone on the set understood that *Yankee Doodle Dandy* would be a special picture. DeCamp believed that the crew and the actors "worked in a kind of patriotic frenzy, as though we feared we might be sending a last message from a free world because the news was very bad indeed during those months in the winter of '41 and '42."

The outbreak of the war was certainly a motivating factor, but it was the seamless collaboration between Cagney and Curtiz that inspired the rest of the company. After their previous experiences on *Angels with Dirty Faces* and *Captains of the Clouds,* star and director had developed a bond of trust. Curtiz knew he did not have to explain to Cagney how a scene should be played, nor did Cagney need to tell the director how to shoot the picture. Curtiz was also on his best behavior with the rest of the cast and crew, realizing that anything less would not be tolerated by the Cagneys. Curtiz understood that *Yankee Doodle Dandy* belonged to James Cagney. He put the star front and center in nearly every scene.

Joan Leslie, who would celebrate her seventeenth birthday during the production, remembered that the collaborative synergy on the set was unique for a Warner Bros. film: "Mike was so happy because he had everything he wanted: a wonderful script, a terrific cast, and don't ever sell Bill Cagney short as the associate producer! He was on set every day and deeply involved in every aspect of the production. But it was Jimmy who inspired everyone, especially Mike. Jimmy suggested and added so many things and Mike would say, "Okay, Jimmy, that sounds great." It was a beautiful thing to see."

Curtiz was delighted just to *be* the director of *Yankee Doodle Dandy.* The flag-waving jingoism and the overt sentimentality that future critics would characterize as maudlin were, to him, the picture's most appealing aspects. Curtiz wore his American patriotism like a badge of honor— even more so with war recently having been declared. During the production, the columnist Ezra Goodman quoted Curtiz expressing ardor for his adopted country: "If a man is born in a country where there is liberty, he takes it for granted. But for European men—like myself—who lived through the First World War and much suffering, there is in my heart a deep love and appreciation for liberty and freedom here. To me the American spirit is more important than to most others." Shortly before the cameras rolled, Hal Wallis wrote Curtiz a private note: "Dear Mike, As always my best wishes on the picture, particularly this one, because I know how enthusiastic you are about the subject matter."

Yankee Doodle Dandy was also special in other respects. Asked how he liked working on it, Curtiz replied, "Vunderful. This time I work without horses, guns, cowboys, airplanes, Indians, sabers and Errol Flynn." Yet Curtiz remained Curtiz. "He was a ruthless authoritarian with an eagle eye," remembered Rosemary DeCamp. "He could walk on a crowded set with extras and instantly spot the one with a missing earring, or twisted tights or running mascara." Joan Leslie recalled how Curtiz continued to rely on Bess Meredyth when a seemingly intractable script problem arose. "He would take it home and his wife, you know, is a very fine writer . . . and the next morning, he would come back, he'd say, 'I know what we're going to do.' And we'd just bang into it and it was as smooth as silk."

In addition to DeCamp, Leslie, and Cagney's sister, Jeanne, the key supporting cast included Walter Huston as Cohan's father, Jerry, Richard Whorf as Sam Harris, George Tobias (a Cagney favorite), the former vaudevillian Walter Catlett, and Curtiz's Hungarian contemporary S. Z. "Cuddles" Sakall, who would become a jowl-shaking fixture of the Warner stock company. Irene Manning as the Broadway star Fay Templeton and Frances Langford provided musical interludes between the song-and-dance numbers featuring Cagney.

Cagney screened *The Phantom President* (1932) in part to mimic Cohan's nasal New England accent. His turn incorporated many of Cohan's movements—including the stiff-legged dancing style—and delivery during the musical numbers, but the performance was 100 percent Cagney. As he put it, "I didn't have to pretend to be a song-and-dance man. I *was* one." This self-assessment was spot-on despite Cagney's inability to carry a tune. He didn't need to be a singer, according to Joan Leslie: "Jim doesn't sing, because he couldn't sing worth a darn. He'd talk it, and every now and again, he'd hit a note . . . but he had so much energy and such a presence that it didn't seem like he couldn't sing." Cagney rehearsed musical numbers until he was convinced they were perfect—then he practiced

James Cagney and Joan Leslie perform the "Harrigan" number in *Yankee Doodle Dandy* (1942) as Curtiz watches from far left, cigarette in hand (courtesy of the Lucas family).

them again. DeCamp spoke for the entire cast when she said of Cagney, "We all tried to live up to him."

For Curtiz, working with Cagney was the equivalent of having a codirector. For the charming "Harrigan" number, Cagney walked it through with Joan Leslie. After glancing at Curtiz, who nodded, Cagney did a run-through followed by the first take that was printed by Curtiz.

James Wong Howe was the director of photography. Years later, Howe reputedly disparaged both Curtiz and *Yankee Doodle Dandy* to the writer Charles Higham. Howe's remarks—"He knew almost nothing about lighting; he couldn't even tell the cameraman how he wanted the lights to look"—do not square with either Curtiz's expertise or Howe's statements to other interviewers. The notion of Curtiz not knowing how he wanted a set lighted is absurd. The prop man Limey Plews recalled Curtiz's expertise for an interviewer in 1946: "Suppose he makes a scene today. Two weeks later, when he is making a connecting scene, he'll remember the exact lighting he used fourteen days before, what lens he used and what exposure, where the actors were and where the camera was." Asked if she believed Curtiz was more a technician or an actor's director, Joan Leslie responded: "He was absolutely both. He knew exactly what he wanted. I think he was completely in sync with Jimmy Wong Howe, and I heard that Jimmy was slow, but he was wonderful."

Jack Warner stuck to his usual practice of pressuring Curtiz after the first ten days of shooting: "I am not at all satisfied with the amount of dailies you are getting every day. . . . We want to finish up the picture on time and with the holiday season here it is going to be tough to get work done. Will appreciate you stepping on it and I know that you will." It apparently didn't occur to Warner that because of war blackout requirements, the studio suspended night operations as of December 15. Movies could now be made only during daylight hours.

Seymour Felix, who won an Oscar for his dance direction in *The Great Ziegfeld* (1936), was brought in to direct the musical numbers and choreograph the dancing. He immediately clashed with Cagney and Curtiz. The bickering escalated, and Felix was fired after a showdown with Wallis. LeRoy Prinz was then brought in to choreograph. It would be the first of eleven films that Prinz would work on with Curtiz; the director would refer to him forever after as "Prince LeRoy." Their relationship began poorly, as Frank Mattison noted to Tenny Wright: "Mike Curtiz came on the set Saturday afternoon and bellyached about what he had seen in the dailies of this finale number. He was telling Prinz he was very much disappointed. Naturally, you and I know that anything Mike does not shoot himself, personally, is never any good. I really think this little fellow Prinz might take a punch at Mike's nose if he adds insult to injury like he did after both numbers that Prinz has shot so far."

In addition to the bravura turn by Cagney and the contributions of the screenwriters, there were the faultless arrangements of Cohan's music by Ray Heindorf and the wonderful montages of Broadway by Don Siegel. Curtiz conceived the remarkable staging of the "It's a Grand Old Flag" number, writing to Wallis: "This seems to me to be the most important number in the show, particularly now in view of the declaration of war. It must be sold, not only musically, but also with a dramatic setting that brings out its theme and spirit. I have discussed this idea with Bill Cagney and he approves of it. Carl Weyl has built a miniature and drawn sketches to illustrate my plan, and I can best show these to you on the stage."

Curtiz sold it after rehearsing the rousing number in front of an audience that included Wallis and Jack and Harry Warner. The principal actors march on moving conveyor belts in front of dancers in formation holding flags as Cagney performs a stiff-legged jaunt up and down the ranks before joining his costars in the first line of dancers. The scene opens up to a memorable tableau. Curtiz drew back the camera boom to capture the materialization of a backdrop of the Capitol dome, and the entire stage is awash in flags and dancers; the scene concludes with a huge projection of Old Glory. It remains the most memorable number in the film.

Curtiz also repurposed the "Over There" number so there would be an audience of soldiers singing with Cagney and Frances Langford. He worked out Jerry Cohan's deathbed scene after entreating the Epstein brothers to "give me the tear in the eye" sentiment. The brothers eventually complied, writing what Julius believed was pure hokum: "So we wrote the death scene with the Cohan trademark—'My mother thanks you, my father thanks you,' and so on. We thought it was hilarious. We thought they'd never use it. But they did and it was one of the best scenes in the film." Joan Leslie remembered how Cagney's emotional power affected the entire crew, particularly Curtiz:

> I stood at the door, not wanting to intrude on . . . this very special scene with a father and son. And Jimmy cried over that first scene, he cried and cried. Now he cried on every take; the closeups on the two shots, on the turn-around, even on Walter's closeups, he cried enormous tears that spanked down on the covers of the blankets and you know the guys up on the walkers about the set and behind the scene, they were watching and crying too! Mike ruined a take he was crying so hard. But, I mean, we were all so touched by it that we felt we were losing our father. It was just Jimmy at his best.

Curtiz paid Cagney the ultimate directorial compliment while sobbing: "Cheeses Chrisdt, Jimmy, beautiful, beautiful."

Curtiz convinced William Cagney and Wallis to scrap a scene written by the Epstein brothers that detailed the flop of Cohan's play *Popularity* in favor of the original Buckner script, which he revised with new dialogue. All told, he submitted seven different scenes to William Cagney that he wanted to include in the picture and changed or added additional bits of business.

The younger Cagney drew the line at Curtiz's proposed opening rewrite before Cohan initially meets with President Roosevelt. The director's concept of transitioning from Cagney as Cohan backstage in FDR makeup in *I'd Rather Be Right* to President Roosevelt's White House study was thoughtfully constructed, but William Cagney was not interested in changing the beginning of the movie on the fly. Curtiz persisted, and the associate producer eventually appealed to Hal Wallis: "I would be most grateful if you would knock this idea out of Mike's brain once and for all."

Curtiz unsuccessfully campaigned to have Sidney Blackmer play Franklin Roosevelt after testing several other actors, including Taylor Holmes and Regis Toomey. Portraying any sitting president, much less Roosevelt, in a movie was a sensitive matter in 1942. It was eventually decided to use a Canadian actor named Jack Young, who was billed as "Captain Jack Young." Young was filmed exclusively from the rear; the radio announcer Art Gilmore provided the FDR voice track.

There was a brief dustup over S. Z. Sakall, who was playing Schwab, a potential backer of a Cohan musical. Cohan is pitching the play to Sam Harris while Schwab sits at a table, supposedly listening with rapt enthusiasm. Instead, the former Budapest stage comedian trolled for laughs by mugging and offering ad libs. An annoyed Cagney pulled Curtiz aside: "Mike, this scene with Sakall is, for chrissake, a *plot* scene. We have to hear what the hell I am saying, and now this old bastard keeps muttering and repeating everything I say. I know he's doing it for comic effect. For *his* comic effect. I've got plot to get over and I want him to stop it." Curtiz initially refused to tell Sakall to knock it off because his countryman was such a big star back in Hungary. But Cagney persisted, and Curtiz's directorial instinct overcame his reluctance to insult an esteemed colleague from his past life. Most of the actor's comic reactions during the sequence were cut.

Despite the commitment of the studio to the success of *Yankee Doo-*

dle Dandy, Wallis cracked the whip on the budget. Early on, he scaled back Curtiz's requisition for a parade sequence: "All that we need here is Walter Huston running out, getting caught up in a section of the parade for a couple of quick lines of dialogue and then exit, and yet for this you have ordered 16 firemen, 20 policemen, a 12 piece band, 20 G.A.R. veterans, 20 soldiers, 70 women, 70 men, 15 children, a hand pumper, 4 carriages, 4 cannon. If we are going to make this picture for less than two or two and a half million dollars, you are going to have to cooperate with me."

After fourteen years at Warner Bros., Curtiz had acquired the hide of an armadillo. He either ignored the dictates of the front office or lived with them and moved on. The Cagneys were considerably less tolerant. Wallis's typical nitpicking over minutiae such as the use of a horse in the "Little Johnny Jones" musical number struck them as deliberately adversarial. From the sidelines, Robert Buckner continued slinging barbed memos to Wallis, wringing his hands over the changes to the script that were being hidden from Cohan. At one point he wrote to Wallis: "For your information, Curtiz must learn some day to stay within the regulations of a contract. We have a specific contract and agreement for this picture with Geo. M. Cohan and we have violated it in many places."

The behind-the-scenes acrimony was unseen by most of the cast and crew, but both Cagneys became fed up with the incessant infighting. After Wallis quarreled with Bill Cagney about setting up a third unit to film the prologue, James Cagney notified Warner Bros. that he was exercising the "happiness clause" in his contract and would be leaving the studio at the end of the picture. Jack Warner and Wallis quickly backed off and tried everything they could to persuade him to change his mind.

An immediate benefit of Cagney's resignation was that his brother was permitted to function as an actual producer for the balance of the picture rather than as a Hal Wallis sock puppet. Jack Warner's ritualistic hounding of Curtiz on the schedule and Wallis's micromanaging receded. The production proceeded in comparative harmony, and the sense of collaborative joyousness is evident in the picture. It was one of Curtiz's happiest experiences at Warner Bros. As promised, the Cagney brothers left the studio to set up their own production company and did not return to Burbank until financial necessity compelled a reunion, which resulted in the production of *White Heat* in 1949.

Yankee Doodle Dandy wrapped on April 27, 1942. Although the forty-eight-day production schedule was more than doubled, it was brought in at a relatively economical $1,532,000. Jack Warner launched the biggest publicity campaign in studio history. The gala May 29 premiere in New York at their Hollywood Theater doubled as a war bond drive: general admission tickets cost $25, and choicer seats came at escalating prices in the 1,600-seat movie palace. In a single evening, $4,750,000 in bonds were sold. It was the first day of what would be an incredible nineteen-week run at the New York Hollywood, which totaled more than $323,000 in ticket sales. *Yankee Doodle Dandy* would gross more than $6 million on its initial release as Hollywood's second-most profitable film of the year.

The picture garnered unqualified critical raves. Even the *New York Times* curmudgeon Bosley Crowther was wowed: "There is so much in this picture and so many persons that deserve their meed of praise that every one connected with it can stick a feather in his hat and take our word—it's dandy!" The *Los Angeles Daily News* noted: "If *Yankee Doodle Dandy* is the best in a long line of Cagney successes, it is also the high spot in Michael Curtiz's directorial career." Curtiz agreed, categorizing the film in his typically mangled syntax as "the pinochle of my career." It is a beautifully composed movie of superb economy. Throughout all the dramatic scenes and superlatively staged musical numbers, there is not a wasted minute of film. Curtiz would remember the debut of *Yankee Doodle Dandy* in Hollywood as one of the high points of his life.

Opening night at the Warner Hollywood, tailored to coincide with a $5 million "Build Ships" drive, was another triumph; the film received standing ovations during the "Grand Old Flag" number and the closing credits. In a cable to Cohan, Jack Warner called it "the most inspirational opening since the beginning of motion pictures. You were with me every minute of the running of the picture. The world is deeply indebted to you for permitting me to make the picture of your great American life. You have done another great service."

Warner's decision to withhold the script changes from Cohan until after the film was finished was a gamble that paid off. In April he had a print delivered to the ailing entertainer at his Monroe, New York, vacation home. After watching the picture in a hall over the town firehouse, Cohan sent James Cagney a cable: "Dear Jim, How's my double? Thanks for a wonderful job, Sincerely, George M. Cohan." Cohan succumbed to cancer on November 5, 1942.

The charming vivacity of *Yankee Doodle Dandy* continues to resonate with modern audiences. The film is also a reflection of Curtiz's appreciation for a departed era of traveling players and vaudeville acts that

Curtiz directs *Yankee Doodle Dandy*, flanked by James Cagney and James Wong Howe (author's collection).

paralleled his own formative years in Hungarian music halls and provincial stage productions. Despite his hardboiled demeanor, Curtiz could be extremely sentimental. *Yankee Doodle Dandy* brought out this nostalgic sense from the fifty-five-year-old director, figuratively glancing over his shoulder at bygone days.

The film was nominated for eight Academy Awards, including Best Picture. Curtiz lost the Best Director award to William Wyler for *Mrs. Miniver,* the only 1942 film more financially successful than *Dandy.* Cagney won for Best Actor and made a typically modest acceptance speech. He placed the Oscar statuette on William Cagney's desk the following morning. It was a gesture of gratitude to a beloved brother for broadening his public persona from tough guy to accomplished song-and-dance man.

After *Yankee Doodle Dandy*'s smashing premiere, he and his brother ran a large ad in the *Hollywood Reporter* that thanked Julie and Phil Epstein for their contributions while pointedly omitting Buckner and Edmund Joseph.

Cagney maintained an evenhanded opinion about Curtiz, even though they never worked together again. In a memorable acceptance speech after receiving the American Film Institute's Life Achievement Award in 1974, Cagney paused during his recitation of thanks to friends and colleagues from his early days at Warner Bros. Raising whitened eyebrows and stifling a smile, the seventy-four-year-old cinema legend said, "And the unforgettable Michael Curtiz." There was a loud guffaw, doubtlessly from an old Warner Bros. hand in the huge ballroom.

Curtiz had moved into the most rewarding period of his career. His next film proved so consequential that it would eventually obscure his own legacy.

24

Fundamental Things

Success has many fathers and none more so than *Casablanca,* the most enduringly popular movie in cinema history. From Jack Warner and Hal Wallis tussling over the 1944 Best Picture Oscar, to both men claiming exclusive credit for creation of the film in their memoirs, to the different screenwriters and other participants weighing in with their varying recollections, and the numerous books and essays detailing and debunking every possible aspect of the film, one thing remains certain: decades later, everybody involved with the making of *Casablanca* still wanted to come to Rick's.

Despite the voluminous historiography, *Casablanca* remains worthy of reexamination. The film was the product of some of the best Hollywood talent of 1942, working at peak pitch on what was thought to be just another picture. Shortly before producing his final film, *Rooster Cogburn,* in 1975, Hal Wallis remarked about *Casablanca:* "We started out to make a good picture. We never dreamed it would become a classic."

The morning of December 8, 1941, when America declared war and Curtiz began production on *Yankee Doodle Dandy,* Stephen Karnot, a Warner Bros. story analyst, read the play *Everybody Comes to Rick's* and sent a summary and a detailed twenty-two-page synopsis to Wallis three days later. Karnot was prescient about the cinematic possibilities: "Excellent melodrama. Colorful, timely background, tense mood, suspense, psychological and physical conflict, tight plotting, sophisticated hokum. A box office natural—for Bogart, or Cagney, or Raft in out-of-usual-roles, and perhaps Mary Astor."

Irene Lee, Wallis's story editor, had discovered the unproduced play on a trip to New York and recommended that Wallis buy it. This is borne out by archival records and the recollections of the screenwriter Julius Epstein. After Wallis approved the $20,000 purchase—a hefty sum for an unproduced play—Lee is said to have given the initial screenplay assignment to the Epstein brothers. The notion that she did this on her own authority is specious. Wallis zealously reserved the right to select the writers to create screenplays for his films. Lee certainly could have recommended the Epsteins to Wallis.

Irene Lee (later Irene Lee Diamond) would survive all the *Casablanca* principals and maintained her claim to be the person who initially saw the play's potential as a movie. According to Lee, Wallis remained in character after *Casablanca* became a huge hit; in addition to claiming credit for discovering *Everybody Comes to Rick's,* he responded to her request for a modest bonus with a dismissive "That's what you're here for." Though Lee admired Wallis's considerable abilities as a producer (their relationship also reportedly included a brief affair), she had little choice but to accept her status as a highly competent female employee working in a male-dominated industry. It was an inequitable situation exacerbated by Wallis's reluctance to share credit with anyone.

There is also an assertion by the screenwriter Casey Robinson that he read *Everybody Comes to Rick's* during a train trip to New York with Wallis and urged him to buy the play. Robinson's substantiated contributions to *Casablanca* were significant, but this is one of several claims that remain unverifiable.

Murray Burnett and Joan Alison wrote the play *Everybody Comes to Rick's.* Burnett's inspiration came during a trip to Europe in 1938. The virulent anti-Semitism in Vienna significantly altered Burnett's outlook about the coming war. He also visited a French nightclub with a black piano player and was inspired to create Rick's Café and the Sam character.

Thirty years after the film was released, Burnett took legal umbrage against *Casablanca* screenwriter Howard Koch. Koch had dismissed the play as having little or nothing to do with the film and assumed credit for the motivations of nearly all of the film's principal characters. He also dismissed the play as having had little or nothing to do with the film. He made these claims in the April 1973 edition of *New York* magazine and in the foreword to his book *Casablanca: Script and Legend,* published the same year. Burnett sued everybody involved. Koch later apologized and admitted that Burnett's complaint was justified. Even so, Burnett lost his defamation lawsuits.

The challenge of attributing specific creative contributions to *Casablanca* is primarily due to the fact that at least seven different writers worked on it separately, with the exception of the Epstein brothers, who always worked together. Despite Koch's assertion that he worked with the Epsteins for ten days on the script, there is no formal or informal record of the various *Casablanca* writers ever collaborating directly with each other.[1]

The progression of the script was analogous to the manufacture of a bicycle wheel. Wallis was at the hub, adding the different writers as spokes. The balance of the writing mostly involved shaping the motivations and behaviors of the key characters rather than broad plot restructuring: Burnett and Alison's play remained the spine of the film.

By the time the Epsteins began to write the *Casablanca* screenplay in mid-February 1942, Hal Wallis's role at the studio had changed, as he had signed a new contract with Jack Warner on January 12. His new contract specified that "A Hal Wallis Production" or "Produced by Hal Wallis" should appear after the film's main title in a size that left no doubt whose picture it was. The contract gave him carte blanche with respect to actors, scripts, directors, and technical and production staff to produce four Warner films per year. The four films would later be renegotiated to six. In addition to a lavish weekly salary, he was entitled to 10 percent of the gross profits after each picture realized 125 percent of its cost.

Wallis initially believed that he'd finally reaped his due benefits after decades of successful toil. But he had encroached on Jack Warner's narrow boundary of tolerance concerning the perception of who ran the studio. The once-close relationship between the pair became a ticking time bomb.

As the Epstein twins began work on the script, Wallis sent an outline to William Wyler in Sun Valley, where he was vacationing and playing gin rummy with Darryl Zanuck. After not receiving any interest from either Wyler or Sam Goldwyn for a loan of the director, Wallis sent the play to Curtiz, William Keighley and Vincent Sherman. Sherman responded that he would love to direct *Casablanca,* but the producer opted for Curtiz.[2] Curtiz was captivated by the dual concepts of the war and the relationship between Rick Blaine and Ilsa Lund. He immersed himself in preproduction planning with Wallis.

Press reports concerning the possibilities of different actors appearing in *Casablanca* were primarily the result of the Warner publicity mill's placing phony plants in the trade papers and gossip columns. Ronald Reagan was never a serious consideration to play Rick. *Casablanca* was designed specifically for Humphrey Bogart, as confirmed by Wallis's memo to Steve Trilling, head of the casting department.

With nine years and thirty films under his belt at Warner Bros., Bogart had finally established himself as a leading man. He starred in *Across the Pacific* (1942), a war-themed reunion of the principal cast of *The Maltese Falcon*, which he was finishing when he was assigned to *Casablanca*. But he still needed a role as a romantic leading man to get him truly on top. Wallis decided that *Casablanca* would be the picture.

A pair of memos exchanged by Wallis and Jack Warner disproves the oft-repeated myth of George Raft's being offered and turning down the role of Rick Blaine. Warner wrote to Wallis on April 2: "[Raft] knows we're going to make it and is starting a campaign for it." Wallis's response: "I have thought over very carefully the matter of George Raft in *Casablanca* and I have discussed this with Mike and we both feel that he should not be in the picture. Bogart is ideal for it, and it is being written for him, and I think we should forget Raft for this property. Incidentally, he hasn't done a picture here since I was a little boy, and I don't think he should be able to put his fingers on just what he wants to do when he wants to do it."

Curtiz had avoided directing Raft, whom he considered a no-talent star. He respected Bogart as a highly professional performer, although he thought the actor never exhibited any inclination toward preparation. After *Casablanca,* Curtiz observed: "Humphrey Bogart never study, but he is always great."

In his defense, Bogart hadn't required a lot of preparation during the long years of collapsing on Warner soundstages after being shot with blanks. Curtiz would direct Bogart differently from when the actor played heavies for him in *Kid Galahad* (1937) and *Virginia City* (1940). He allowed Bogart to find himself as Rick Blaine. Their professional relationship would evolve despite becoming strained by the end of the picture. Bogart loathed the director's verbal malice toward those who couldn't fight back. Yet he had genuine appreciation for Curtiz's abilities. When Bogart signed a landmark contract with Jack Warner in 1946, the document included directorial approval. He provided a list of five acceptable candidates: John Huston, Howard Hawks, John Cromwell, Delmer Daves, and Michael Curtiz.

Casting Ilsa Lund was a different matter. Wallis initially opted for Ann Sheridan, but that was when the character was still the trampy American named Lois Meredith from Burnett's play. Someone advised Wallis to change Lois Meredith to Ilsa Lund. It was apparently Casey Robinson who did the convincing. Robinson, Warner Bros.'s highest-paid screenwriter, was extremely close to Wallis. He claimed in a 1974 interview that he "got the idea to use not two Americans, but a European girl and an American, and to tie the story . . . into World War II and the refugees."

Robinson said that the notion of using a European woman occurred to him because he was falling in love with a Russian ballerina named Tamara Toumanova. Toumanova did receive an Ilsa Lund screen test for *Casablanca* and married Casey Robinson in 1944. Robinson also stated that Wallis originally offered him *Casablanca* to write and was piqued that the producer then assigned the Epsteins to "my picture."

Robinson's recommendation of a foreigner to replace the Lois Meredith character was relayed to the Epstein brothers, who responded from Washington, D.C., with their typical panache: "While we handle the foreign situation here, you try to get a foreign girl for the part. An American girl with big tits will do. Love and Kisses, Julie and Phil."

After a request to borrow Hedy Lamarr was rebuffed by Louis B. Mayer, the French actress Michèle Morgan was tested but was found wanting. Wallis began a dialogue with David O. Selznick for the services of Ingrid Bergman. As the script was very much a work in progress, Wallis sent the Epstein brothers to relate the story to Selznick's assistant Dan O'Shea. The Epsteins ended up in front of Selznick, who was ensconced behind his desk during lunchtime, slurping down a bowl of soup. Julius Epstein realized that after droning on for nearly twenty minutes, he hadn't even mentioned Bergman. "So I said, 'Oh, it's going to be a lot of shit like *Algiers*.' And Selznick looked up and nodded to me that we had Bergman."

After producing *Rebecca* in 1940, Selznick had become Hollywood's most prominent loan shark for contracted talent. He rented out his stable of actors, which included Bergman, Vivien Leigh, Joan Fontaine, and the director Alfred Hitchcock, at top-drawer prices above their salaries and pocketed the overage. These deals allowed Selznick to maintain his lavish lifestyle while staying ahead of his gambling losses. In addition to being paid $3,125 per week for an eight-week loan of Ingrid Bergman, David O. Selznick Productions received the services of Olivia de Havilland from Warner Bros. for the identical number of weeks and dollars. (Selznick promptly lent out de Havilland to RKO for *Government Girl* so he could get paid again without having to produce a movie.)

Selznick maintained the right to take an acute interest in how Bergman would be photographed and dressed in *Casablanca*, and he sent several of his infamously long memoranda to Wallis on the subject. It was all part of an orchestrated plan to build up Bergman, whose films since *Intermezzo* (1939) had been successful but unspectacular. Selznick hoped that *Casablanca* would be a major hit, as he planned to lend Bergman to Paramount for an even bigger payday to costar with Gary Cooper in *For Whom the Bell Tolls.*

Bergman didn't have a clue what *Casablanca* was about, but she was immediately put at ease by Curtiz, who charmed her thoroughly. She later wrote, "I greatly enjoyed Mike Curtiz, who really taught me quite a bit." Curtiz likewise admired Bergman's concentration. She was also refreshingly absent the movie-star sense of entitlement.

Curtiz called everyone "baby," but he addressed Bergman as "Christmas baby," meaning that she was extra-special. There was no doubt that he was attracted to her. But his days of sleeping with his leading ladies were long gone. He satisfied himself with an alluringly platonic relationship during the production. In a candid moment, he reflected on his dealings with actors generally and Bergman in particular: "I am very critical of actors, but if I find a real actor, I am first to appreciate it. I am very contemptuous to unreal things. I try to express myself real. It is very difficult to get down-to-earth result with actors who don't act at all. I am not too much popularity, but I think Miss Bergman is my friend."

Curtiz's mentorship of Bergman included his recommendation that she cease playing roles such as the governess in *Adam Had Four Sons* and the barmaid in *Dr. Jekyll and Mr. Hyde* (both 1941). He advised that attempting to professionally stretch herself in the Hollywood of the 1940s would end up limiting her career; in addition to being true to the audience, she had to also be true to herself, and the Ilsa Lund character was completely genuine. One of Curtiz's chief contributions to *Casablanca* was his enabling Humphrey Bogart to become a star while reminding Ingrid Bergman how to remain one.

Curtiz wanted the Dutch actor Philip Dorn to play Victor Laszlo, but Dorn was already cast in *Random Harvest,* in production at Metro. He was adamant about having an appropriate European actor to match Bergman. Wallis warned him that he might have to settle for somebody different:

> I have been going over with Trilling the possibilities for the part of "Laszlo" and aside from Philip Dorn, whom we cannot get, and Paul Henreid, who I am sure will not play the part when he reads it, there is no one else that I can think of. I think you should

Curtiz presents mistletoe to his "Christmas Baby," Ingrid Bergman (courtesy of the Lucas family).

satisfy yourself on this point; that is, that there is no one available, and then begin to adjust yourself to the thought that we might have to use someone of the type of Dean Jagger, Ian Hunter or Herbert Marshall or someone of this type without an accent. I am as anxious as you are to have a type like Philip Dorn in the part, but if there is no one available there is just nothing that we can do about it.

Paul Henreid initially believed that the Laszlo part was a loser and turned it down. But after being impressed while watching the rushes of *Now, Voyager* (1942), Wallis upped the ante to costar billing with Bogart and Bergman and assumed the balance of Henreid's existing contract with RKO. Henreid accepted the part but had misgivings after the picture was finished. He'd ended up getting the girl . . . but also not. Henreid brought a precise chord of noble integrity to the part of Victor Laszlo that proved integral in making *Casablanca* work.

The rest of the cast fell into place. As the Sam character, Wallis briefly considered casting the jazz pianist and singer Hazel Scott, who he thought would be "marvelous for the part," or Lena Horne, instead of an African American male actor. The notion was discarded because of the controversy that would ensue over a desirable woman of color being perceived as possibly having a romantic relationship with Rick Blaine. Casting a woman in the role would also detract from the love affair between Rick and Ilsa. Upon further review, it was deemed more acceptable for Bogart to have a black male companion.

After initially ordering Steve Trilling to sign Clarence Muse to portray Sam, Wallis acceded to Curtiz by casting the drummer-singer Arthur "Dooley" Wilson instead. Wallis tepidly termed Wilson's screen test "pretty good," but Curtiz believed he was markedly superior to Muse, whose acting struck the director as stereotypical. The pianist Elliot Carpenter, the only other African American on set, played the piano just off camera while Wilson fingered the keys. In addition to "As Time Goes By," Wilson's voice was used for "It Had to Be You," "Shine," and "Knock on Wood." The critical accolades Wilson received for his portrayal of Sam validated Curtiz's faith in him.

Curtiz and Wallis both surmised that Claude Rains would be perfect as Captain Renault. The Epstein brothers revered Rains and ended up writing their most delightfully sarcastic dialogue for him. Julius Epstein later admitted that he and his brother initially couldn't understand why Wallis and Curtiz didn't use a French actor instead of Rains, but that *Casablanca* would never have become what it is without him.

Conrad Veidt, a major silent film star who played the somnambulist in *The Cabinet of Dr. Caligari* (1920), proved similarly ideal as Major Strasser. Veidt was a passionate anti-Nazi with a Jewish wife who fled Hitler's Germany and became reconciled to playing Hollywood Nazis in order to make a living. Otto Preminger was tested for the Strasser role but would have to wait another decade to portray a memorable Nazi in Billy

Wilder's *Stalag 17* (1953). According to Julius Epstein, Curtiz urged Veidt to finesse the Strasser character into an aristocratic villain rather than a stereotypical Nazi thug.

Peter Lorre and Sydney Greenstreet were added as Ugarte and Ferrari. Greenstreet was already under contract, and Wallis borrowed Lorre from Universal. Both Greenstreet's and Lorre's roles are small, but their kinetic ability to captivate audiences made them prominent. The Ferrari role was built up, along with Greenstreet's salary, to make the corpulent actor congenial toward the smallish part. The corrupt aura of his sinister bulk, adorned in a fez and wielding a flyswatter (a Curtiz touch) added considerable (and literal) heft to the picture.

Peter Lorre was the knuckleball of Hollywood character actors. Curtiz was never fully certain what he might utter when the cameras rolled—except that it was bound to be excellent. With protruding eyes and a murmuring voice like a sinister kewpie doll, he famously played the child murderer in Fritz Lang's *M* (1931), the Japanese detective Mr. Moto, and the effete Joel Cairo in *The Maltese Falcon*. Lorre's subtle brilliance concealed a disastrous morphine addiction that eventually destroyed him. An inveterate practical joker, he provided comic relief on the set by surreptitiously extinguishing Curtiz's cigarettes with water from an eyedropper. According to Paul Henreid, Lorre hooked up a microphone that picked up the live action of a Curtiz lunchtime tryst behind the soundstage flats, to the immense enjoyment of several members of the cast. This story is probably apocryphal, as production records indicate that Henreid and Lorre were never on the set of *Casablanca* at the same time.

Memorable lines that became embedded in popular culture—including "Round up the usual suspects," "I am shocked, shocked to learn that gambling is going on in here," and "The Germans wore gray, you wore blue"—were the creations of the Epstein brothers, who would be paid for twelve weeks as the principal screenwriters. "Here's looking at you, kid" was either an Epstein inspiration or a Bogart ad lib that was incorporated into the script. And the most famous of all, "Play it again, Sam" was never in the script or uttered by Bogart in the film.

The screenwriters didn't have an easy time working with Curtiz, whose story conception often relied on his mind's eye as the camera, building the picture scene by scene. During the studio-system era, story continuity was the writer's principal consideration, and Warner Bros. screenwriters rarely were allowed to visit a set. That John Huston was allowed to write and direct *The Maltese Falcon* was a rare exception. Jack Warner ran his studio with a specific individual assigned to every function of the moviemaking process. His blood pressure rose precipitously whenever someone had the temerity to attempt to change the role that he, as the head of the studio, had designated for him or her.

Julius Epstein recalled the process of working with Curtiz on *Casablanca:* "Curtiz was marvelous on the visual side of directing. He knew just when the cigarette smoke should curl backwards; when to move; when not to move. . . . We all knew, of course, that the night before the story conferences Mike would get his directions (regarding the script development) from his wife, Bess Meredyth, who was one of the great silent screenwriters, and then come in and tell us what Bess had said. But sometimes Mike would forget what to say! I wish I had a tape recording of those story conferences!"

John Meredyth Lucas had a similar memory of Curtiz telling Epstein that he was displeased with a certain scene in *Casablanca.* When asked for specifics, the director scowled and said, "Goddamn, I don't remember what hell Bess tell me."

Casey Robinson elaborated about Curtiz and screenwriters: "I think Mike was one of the great directors of scenes. He was one of the great directors of people, especially young people. He knew nothing whatever about story. . . . He didn't get along with writers because you couldn't talk to him, you know? He didn't know what hell you were talking about. He saw it in pictures, and you supplied the stories."

To be fair, the notion of Curtiz's alleged inability to comprehend story continuity doesn't take into consideration that the *Casablanca* screenplay was continually being rewritten during the entire production. Curtiz acted several times to restore equilibrium to what he perceived to be an unbalanced script. Although Curtiz and Wallis thought that the initial Epstein script was superbly written, they both believed it was incomplete. Who was Rick Blaine? What was his background? How did he end up owning a Casablanca saloon? To address this, Howard Koch was assigned to write an entirely new screenplay after meeting with Curtiz and Wallis on April 6.[3]

Koch incorporated his political views into the script. Liberalism combined with antifascism was a mainstream sentiment in the Hollywood of 1942. Rick was molded into a closet idealist, a "sentimentalist," as Captain Renault termed it. In one scene penned by Koch, Renault remarks that Rick "ran guns to Ethiopia" and "supported the Loyalist side in Spain," implying that Blaine was a member of the Abraham Lincoln

Brigade that fought Franco during the Spanish Civil War. After Blaine parries that he was well paid for his work, Renault provides the touché: "The winning side would have paid you more."

Other polemics by Koch made Rick much more than a cynical saloonkeeper nursing a broken heart. Blaine jokingly warns Major Strasser that the Third Reich would be well advised to stay out of "certain areas of New York." Koch even provided Sydney Greenstreet's Ferrari with a line about the futility of isolationism. He also added the vignette of Rick arranging to have the young Bulgarian girl and her husband (played by Jack Warner's stepdaughter Joy Page and Helmut Dantine) win at roulette in order to purchase an exit visa so that she won't have to sleep with Captain Renault. Koch claimed in his memoir that the memory of his wife being allowed to win at a Palm Springs casino by a compassionate croupier inspired this scene. In a rebuttal to Koch's often-fabulist recollections, Casey Robinson averred that Curtiz was the creator of the roulette–exit visa scenario.

Curtiz expressed concern that the love story between Rick and Ilsa was getting lost amid the Epstein brothers' wisenheimer humor and Koch's speechifying. Wallis agreed and had the screenwriters Lenore Coffee and Casey Robinson review the script. Coffee wrote an alternative (and ultimately unused) storyline in less than a week, before Wallis took her off salary. Robinson generated a detailed seven-page memorandum on May 20—five days before Curtiz started shooting—that significantly shaped a final element of the story: "My impression about *Casablanca* is that the melodrama is well done, the humor excellent, but the love story deficient. Therefore, my comments are almost all concerned with the latter."

Robinson suggested a number of changes to the script that would be incorporated in the final version. One key addition was a solitary entrance of Ilsa into Rick's Café, and her insistence that Sam play "As Time Goes By," to emphasize the symbolism of the song to the Rick-Ilsa affair. His other recommendations included the meeting between Ilsa and a drunken, bitter Rick in the darkened café and the sequence in which Ilsa explains why she left Rick and how she venerates her husband. He also clarified the somewhat ambiguous relationship between Ilsa and Victor Laszlo. Robinson concluded by laying out the dynamics that would end the picture on an emotional high note: "Now you're really set up for a swell twist when Rick sends her away on the plane with Victor. For now in doing so, he is not just solving a love triangle. He is forcing the girl to live up to the idealism of her nature, forcing her to carry on with the work that in these days is far more important than the love of two little people. It is something they will both be glad for when the pain is over."

Curtiz began filming *Casablanca* on Monday morning, May 25, 1942, on Stage 12A, sporting a bandaged right hand from a Sunday-afternoon polo injury. He had received his usual portentous message from Jack Warner the previous Friday: "These are turbulent days and I know you will finish *Casablanca* in top seven weeks. I am depending on you to be the old Curtiz I know you to be, and I am positive you are going to make one great picture."

On his first day of shooting, Curtiz had a heated confrontation with the sound mixer Francis Scheid. They despised one another but often had to work together. Despite his résumé of hits, Curtiz was not permitted to select the technicians for his assignments. The Warner Bros. production technical staff reported to Tenny Wright. Wright usually tried to please, but he was not going to foul up other pictures or compromise his assignment schedule solely on the basis of Curtiz's whims. Apparently not even Hal Wallis, armed with his new contract, could overrule Wright. Wallis had ordered Wright to assign James Wong Howe as the cinematographer for *Casablanca,* but he and Curtiz ended up with Arthur Edeson because Howe was already committed to *The Hard Way* and Wright refused to move him.

Curtiz had loathed sound mixers since the days of his early Vitaphone pictures, when he was required to kowtow to know-it-all Western Electric technicians. Over the years, he vented pressure on set by using the soundman as his verbal piñata. Scheid described Curtiz to Aljean Harmetz as "a miserable bastard" who treated him with disdain during their half-dozen pictures together. According to Scheid, Curtiz shot the first scene of *Casablanca*—a portion of the flashback love scene in a Paris café—in a low-ceiling set where he couldn't place a microphone: "I told him there was no way to put a mike in. He said, 'Oh shut up, you dumb sound man.'" After several line readings from a two-page scene, Scheid stopped the recording and told Curtiz that it sounded lousy. "He got red in the face, completely red in the face. . . . He said, 'The hell with you, the hell with you, to hell with you.' I said, 'To hell with you.' You could have heard a pin drop" as Scheid stalked off the set.

Expecting to be fired, Scheid reported to work the next day. He discovered that Wallis had sent a memo that morning to George Groves, head of the sound department, complaining that the hum of a sun arc lamp ruined the scene, and the delay in replacing the lamp prevented the scene from being shot. Wallis explained the incident to Groves on the basis of what he had been told by Curtiz: "My question to you is, why didn't the mixer hear the hum of the sun arc during the twelve rehearsals? Why didn't he speak up at that time, which would have given the company plenty of opportunity to replace the lamp while other rehearsals were taking place? As I understand it, the mixer's argument was that there were too many other noises for him to have heard the sun arc during the rehearsals, but this was not the case as the scene was a very tender, delicate one and Mike called for absolute quiet on the set."

According to Scheid, Curtiz lied to Wallis about the episode with the microphone, making up the story of the defective sun arc lamp to cover himself for not having the scene completed. When Scheid walked onto the stage the next morning, Curtiz greeted him, "I'm sorry you got mad at me." Scheid, who would become a combat photographer during the war, never wavered in his version of the first day's events or his view of Curtiz as a cowardly bully.

While Curtiz was butting heads with the sound recorder, Wallis was making life challenging for the veteran cinematographer Arthur Edeson. A former portrait photographer, Edeson began his film career in 1911 as a camera operator at the Éclair Studios in Fort Lee, New Jersey. His credits included *The Thief of Bagdad* (1924), *All Quiet on the Western Front* (1929), *Frankenstein* (1931), and *Mutiny on the Bounty* (1935). More recently he was behind the camera for *The Maltese Falcon* and *Sergeant York* (both 1941). A diminutive pipe smoker nicknamed "Little Napoleon," Edeson was nearing retirement but remained a formidable talent. He was one of the cinematographers who, before filming a scene, personally marked the actors' positions with a piece of chalk, adjusted the lights with the stand-ins in place, then darkened the chalk lines so the actors knew exactly where their marks were.

Curtiz and Edeson got along fine, although there was the usual heartburn over work rapidity, as the production manager Al Alleborn noted: "Edeson and Mike are having their little argument now and then, but nothing serious. You know how Mike is. Edeson is doing his damnedest, but he is not as fast as we would like him to be." Wallis initially took Edeson to task for taking an hour and a half to light the café set for the contentious initial scene that Curtiz never shot. He reminded the cinematographer, "You were present at all the meetings we had about all the war emergencies and the necessity of conserving money and material and I must ask you to sacrifice a little on quality, if necessary, in order not to take these long periods of times for setups."

A written reminder from Wallis to minimize the amount of time required for camera setups was nothing new. But there was a fresh sense of urgency owing to the war. Since Pearl Harbor, the studio's culture of frugality had become a relentless campaign of penny-pinching. Jack Warner was particularly eager to use the war as an excuse for new economies. The studio newspaper, the *Warner Club News,* carried an editorial exhorting all employees to save nails: "Without them, we cannot build sets, without sets, it would be almost impossible to make pictures."

Harry Warner gave a speech to employees with the theme "Waste Is More Deadly Than Sabotage." The waste highlighted by the elder Warner specifically referred to the overuse of film stock. The translation: if Curtiz and the other Warner directors shot too many takes, it was no longer simply a case of being wasteful; they were sabotaging the war effort. Jack Warner delivered a lecture to all the directors on the lot about the conservation of film stock. A memo from Jack to Curtiz near the end of the production nagged about minimizing the use of film: "Dear Mike: I can't understand why a 54-second take must be started seven times. You must cut down on the amount of positive and negative film."

The government's War Production Board had established price limits on building almost everything, including studio sets. Materials such as rubber and nylon were scarce. Rationing of gasoline and other commodities began in earnest by May 1942. More skilled tradesmen left Warner Bros. because of the draft or better job opportunities in war-related industries than any other studio.

Yet the zealous practice of constantly scouring their business operations to save or recoup the most minuscule amounts of money would hold Warner Bros. in good stead during the war years. Nothing was overlooked. Curtiz received an officious letter from Roy Obringer on January 22, 1942, insisting that the studio's highest-paid film director, at $3,600 per week, immediately remit $26.95 to settle an overdue bill for personal phone calls.

Beyond the routine parsimony, innovative cost reductions were realized on *Casablanca*. Wallis sent Curtiz a memo ten days before the cameras rolled concerning set use: "We are building a portion of a Railroad Station for *Now Voyager*. . . . I have an idea that it can be easily adapted for your railroad station in the retrospect of the addition of a sign and a piece of railing, as suggested in the sketch you showed me the other day. Will you please look over the model or the plan . . . as we can take advantage of a good set without cost."

Casablanca was not an expensive film. Nearly the entire picture was shot on studio soundstages and the Warner lot's French Street. The sole location scene was Major Strasser's deplaning arrival, which was filmed at the metropolitan airport in nearby Van Nuys. Curtiz finished at the airport in a single day and had a glass technician capture the matte background of Casablanca behind the plane on the tarmac. The original budget of $878,000 ended up increasing to slightly more than $1 million because of the salaries of the cast and the writers who worked throughout the production.

Bogart received $36,667. Henreid and Bergman were paid $25,000 each. Rains got $4,000 per week with a five-week guarantee, Veidt $5,000 per week for five weeks, and Greenstreet $3,750 for two weeks. Much to Wallis's frustration, Greenstreet overran his two-week guarantee and cost an additional salaried week. Curtiz received $73,400, considerably more than anyone else on the picture, including Wallis, although the producer's base salary didn't include the profit percentages that were a part of his new deal with Jack Warner.

Wallis had his own ideas not only about what he wanted to see onscreen but how it should be accomplished. Another memo to Arthur Edeson was specific about what he desired: "I want to again ask that you get as much contrast as possible in lighting the picture, especially in the scenes in Rick's Café. I am anxious to get real blacks and whites, with the walls and the backgrounds in shadow and dim, sketchy lighting." The sensitive Edeson was wounded by the criticism and didn't react the way Wallis requested. After viewing the dailies, Wallis followed up with Curtiz two days later: "Again I want to say that I don't think the Café is dark enough. I think there is too much general lighting and somehow or other the place doesn't seem to have the character to me that it should have. Either we should have something on the walls, some matting or decorations of some kind, or we should have less general illumination. Everything is too generally lighted."

The lighting memorandum illustrates Wallis's maturity as a creative producer. He knew exactly how Rick's Café should appear onscreen: with shaded lighting through a haze of cigarette smoke and an absolute minimum of reflected light. A review of Wallis's communications throughout the production of *Casablanca* finds them to be civil, reasoned, and insightful. *Casablanca* would reflect a great deal of Wallis's personal vision, including the live parrot he had placed outside the Blue Parrot Café.

But the producer never outstripped Curtiz's own visualizations. The flourishes of Bergman knocking over the glass in the Paris café, the Vichy water bottle hurled in the trash by Rains at the finale, and Bogart's curling cigarette smoke that precedes the flashback sequence underscore Curtiz's brilliance. One of Casablanca's most striking attributes is its exquisite imagery. Perhaps the most emblematic example is the initial interior sequence in Rick's Café. It is a visual panorama of waiters with trays, patrons, and soldiers, all moving about or seated in the crowded nightclub in a faultless choreography of bustle. The sequence transitions from a close-up of Dooley Wilson singing into a dolly shot that reveals the darkly lit interior before dissolving into a quick series of shots of shady black marketers surreptitiously touting all manner of escape to a mixture of bewildered Europeans.

One can't help wondering if Curtiz's formative years in Budapest cafés influenced his vision of Rick's. And it is more than his fluid camera movement and skilled composition that create the authenticity. The actors appear to be European refugees because, for the most part, they were. Many of the bit actors in *Casablanca* were expatriates who had fled the Nazis. Curtiz personally cast each of them.

Many were Jewish refugees. One notable duo was Ilka Grüning, who played Mrs. Leuchtag, and Ludwig Stössel (a distant relative of the author), who portrayed her husband. Grüning was a sixty-six-year-old Viennese actress—the oldest performer in the film—who appeared with Conrad Veidt in a 1919 German silent of *Peer Gynt,* made a trio of movies for F. W. Murnau, and worked with Max Reinhardt. She left Germany after the Nazis came to power and didn't work for nearly nine years until appearing in Vincent Sherman's *Underground* (1941). Stössel was an Austrian stage actor who transitioned into German films, including Fritz Lang's *The Testament of Dr. Mabuse* (1932). He fled to the United States after the Anschluss and forged a long career in Hollywood that included the short-lived *Casablanca* television series and a string of TV commercials wearing lederhosen as that "Little Old Winemaker" for Italian Swiss Colony wine.

Among the credited players was young Helmut Dantine, the son of a prominent Austrian railroad executive. Dantine became a leading anti-Nazi agitator in Austria and organized youth riots before being interned in a concentration camp and eventually making his way to the United States. He became an actor who played Nazis in *Random Harvest* and *Desperate Journey.* There was also a refugee husband-and-wife team. Marcel Dalio, a French movie star who played the croupier who hands over the gambling winnings to Captain Renault, was married to Madeleine Lebeau, who as Rick's jilted girlfriend starts a fight between a German officer and a French soldier in the café.[4] All told, thirty-four nationalities appeared in the film.

Although he eschewed the fisticuffs, Curtiz gleaned inspiration for the famous "La Marseillaise" scene from his *Dodge City* (1939) saloon fight, reusing the competing-song concept, this time with the French national anthem drowning out "Deutschland über alles," sung by Major Strasser and his cabal. The gargantuan character actor Dan Seymour, who played the doorman at the gambling den in Rick's, watched the crowd of actors on the café set during the number and noticed that many were actually crying. He recalled, "I suddenly realized that they were all real refugees."

Curtiz attempted to keep some of the bit actors on salary during the balance of the picture, but the ever-vigilant Wallis stymied him: "I am going over the bit list with the Casting Office and I find that you had planned to carry several characters . . . and others through the picture. . . . We have a terrifically expensive cast as it is, and I am not going to put anybody on for longer than they are needed."

Hiring additional extras and giving low-level jobs to friends and relatives had long been a habit for Curtiz. For somebody perceived to be hardhearted, Curtiz often went out of his way to help others. Rex Schroeder, a longtime teamster for Warner Bros., was given his first job by Curtiz in the early 1930s because his family knew the director. Schroeder recalled that Curtiz habitually hired additional extras during productions in November and December so that people would have money for the holidays.

Wallis also expressed his disapproval of Curtiz's selection of Leo Mostovoy to play the bartender at Rick's. The director quickly replaced him with Leonid Kinskey. The Russian-born actor was a drinking pal of Bogart's and is memorable as "Sascha." Kinskey claimed that Bogart spoke with Curtiz and got him the part.

Perhaps the most important casting selection made solely on Curtiz's initiative was that of his old Hungarian friend S. Z. Sakall as Carl, the headwaiter of Rick's Café. He craved Sakall's humor, which he believed would balance the film, but he had to perform some skillful negotiating to make it happen. Sakall demanded $1,750 per week and a four-week guarantee. The engagement duration was beyond the limit of Wallis's financial tolerance. He wrote to Curtiz, "If Sakall will do the part on a two-week guarantee, I will pay him the $1750. It is up to you to work on him."

Curtiz convinced both parties to compromise. Sakall was signed to play Carl at his price with a three-week guarantee. His comic timing and empathetic reactions resulted in his part's being built up to where he had more scenes than all the other supporting players except for Claude Rains and Conrad Veidt.

Curtiz claimed that he spoke with many of the refugee actors and incorporated into the film some of their actual experiences, including the trading of jewelry for exit visas and encounters with pickpockets. When the *Casablanca* cast held a party for him on July 8 to celebrate his fifteenth anniversary at Warner Bros., Curtiz responded to Hedda Hopper's query about his predilection for directing films laden with Americana: "Maybe it's because I've been through so much hell over there, and seen so many people without liberties that I love to do the American story."

Although the publicity department typecast Curtiz as a benevolent patriot, he reverted to the mercurial autocrat on the set. When matters went awry and the soundman wasn't available, he would explode at actors who had relatively unimportant parts. Paul Henreid recalled that he, Bogart, and Rains once threatened to walk off the picture after Curtiz's mistreatment of a German bit actor:

> We could both hear Curtiz screaming at the German actor. "You stupid son of a bitch! Can't you understand English? Can't you do what I tell you? Don't try to think, you idiot—just listen to me and don't be such an asshole." . . . I asked, "Does Curtiz do this all the time, talk like that?" "He can be a real son of a bitch to the bit players," Bogie said, "but watch the way he treats us." He was right. When Curtiz saw us his face and manner changed and he smiled. "Gentlemen, what can I do for you?"

Rains informed Curtiz that his verbal abuse must cease immediately or three of his stars would be taking their leave from the set: "We don't want to hear an ugly word from you to anyone on this stage." The chastened director struggled to hold his temper in check until the end of the picture.

As filming progressed into July, the screenplay rewrites continued; new pages were being brought to the set each morning. On July 6 Wallis informed Curtiz:

> I see tomorrow that you are shooting in the Café with Laszlo and Ilsa arriving and with Renault putting Lazlo under arrest. All of this is in the new rewrite on which we are working with

Koch with the exception of scene 245 where Ilsa asks Rick if he has arranged everything. I am attaching the new dialogue to take the place of this scene. . . . I am also attaching the new ending as Koch and I have finally worked it out. I think you will find that it incorporates all of the changes you wanted made and I think we have successfully licked the big scene between Ilsa and Rick at the airport by bringing Laszlo in at the finish of it.

Wallis ended the memo with a question that encapsulated the challenge of the revisions: "One more thing: do you feel that we have enough dialogue from Ilsa on Page 1 attached? This is the scene where she says "We were married three weeks when Victor got word they needed him in Prague." You will remember that in the different versions from the Epsteins, Casey and Koch, we used to have Ilsa tell quite a long story and this has now been boiled down to just a couple of speeches. Do you think that this is enough?"

Wallis continued to have speeches revised during the month of July. The constant rewriting meant Curtiz had to scramble, and it became a race to finish the picture on schedule. Curtiz uncharacteristically apologized to the actors at one point because of the short time they had to memorize the new dialogue and rehearse. At the same time, he continued to fight for what he believed was good for the picture.

Curtiz had argued vehemently with Koch for inclusion of the flash-back scene between Rick and Ilsa in Paris, featuring a montage of a car ride and champagne toasts that established the basis for their romance. Koch didn't think the sequence was relevant, and Curtiz overrode him. Koch later acknowledged that the sequence made the film better.

After filming the flashback, Curtiz had to contend with Wallis because he had decided to drop some of the dialogue from the latest revision of the script. Wallis insisted that all the dialogue be used for the part of the flashback that depicted Rick and Ilsa's drive through Paris and into the countryside. Curtiz believed the sequence played better without words and ignored him. Wallis's memo of May 28 demanded that the scene be reshot with the dialogue. The scene in which Bogart says to Bergman, "I'm sorry for asking. We said no questions," was reshot, but the flash-back process shot of the pair in the car remained without dialogue, as Curtiz originally filmed it.

Curtiz also replaced the musical number "Tabu" with "Tango of the Roses," a performance by the soprano Corinna Mura and her guitar, during Bergman's initial entry into the café. The substitution allowed the insertion of a brief piano interlude in order to easily cut to Dooley Wilson when Bergman mentioned him. Wallis brought in Casey Robinson for three weeks of rewriting some of the love sequences. According to Julius Epstein, he and his brother rewrote (again) much of the flashback sequence that Robinson had previously rewritten from their own draft. Epstein claimed: "Only one line [by Robinson] remained, we couldn't get it out. 'A franc for your thoughts.' And we fought it. But we couldn't get it out."

As *Round Up the Usual Suspects* author Aljean Harmetz observed, it is impossible to apportion precise recognition for the various elements of the *Casablanca* screenplay: "One cannot give all the credit for the love story to Robinson just as one cannot give all the credit for the politics to Koch or credit every funny line to the Epsteins. Each of the writers won and lost, was rewritten and rewrote."

Curtiz concentrated on controlling what he could. His perfectionism occasionally exceeded the forbearance of even those who genuinely liked him. At one point, he shot iterative takes of Claude Rains doing nothing more than walking into the café set. Not understanding what was wanted, Rains became exasperated and made his next entry on a bicycle, much to the delight of Bogart and the crew.

Wallis, Curtiz, and the writers weren't the only people exerting themselves to make *Casablanca* better. Bogart had gotten inside the skin of his character. The cynicism that Rick Blaine used to cloak his sensitive soul fit him like a glove. Although Bogart was uncomfortable in some of his love scenes with Bergman—he had to wear three-inch wooden lifts on his shoes when standing next to his five-foot-nine costar—his metamorphosis into a romantic leading man was complete. Bogart cared deeply about his craft as an actor. He understood that *Casablanca* would be only as good as he made Rick Blaine. He had meetings with Koch and Wallis over the script while becoming increasingly at odds with Curtiz.

When displeased, or when on call but not in front of the camera, Bogart would return to his chessboard. During *Casablanca,* the actor played an extended by-mail game with Irving Kovner, the brother of a Warner Bros. employee, and in person with Henreid. Bogart spent so much time at chess that Koch said this was why he composed the initial appearance of Rick Blaine in *Casablanca* sitting behind the chessboard in the rear of the café. Bogart was more assertive than usual on the set. In addition to threatening to walk off with Rains and Henreid, he once told Curtiz to "shut up" when the director was badgering Leonid Kinskey. According to Henreid, when Curtiz blew his top at Rains for flubbing his lines near the end of the production, the trio kept their pledge and disappeared for several hours. The impromptu exit made Curtiz frantic, then effusively apologetic when they eventually returned and filming resumed.

Matters came to a head when Curtiz, Bogart, Bergman, Henreid, and everyone else did not know precisely how the picture was going to end. Casey Robinson's preproduction memo (along with the original play) punctures the myth of the totally unknown ending. There was little doubt about the route that the finale would follow, given that the Production Code would not permit a married woman to desert a noble husband to remain with her saloonkeeper lover. And killing off Laszlo in order to allow Ilsa and Rick to be reunited would ruin the picture. There was also the problem of what to do with Rick after Ilsa and Laszlo left on the plane to Lisbon.

Koch later recalled numerous meetings among Wallis, Curtiz, Bogart, and the rest over the ending. Curtiz became more nervous. Bogart got crabby. Bergman was uncomfortable; her eight-week option was nearing its end, and she was looking forward to finishing, particularly after she found out that the director Sam Wood was going to borrow her from Selznick to star in *For Whom the Bell Tolls*. Bergman said afterward that she was unsure which actor to express love to during her close-ups as she still didn't know whether she was going to end up with Blaine or Laszlo. She claimed Curtiz and the writers couldn't tell her because they didn't know, a recollection that is not borne out by Casey Robinson's May 20 memo referring to Ilsa and Victor leaving at the end of the film. She also spoke about an ending that was never filmed that had her remaining with Rick. But there is no record of this alternative finale, and it appears unlikely that such a denouement would have progressed beyond the discussion phrase. Bergman distinctly remembered that "every lunchtime, Curtiz argued with Wallis" over the script. The director tried to calm the anxiety of the actors, one scene at a time. Bergman recalled: "Every morning we said, 'Well who are we, what are we doing here?' And Curtiz would say, 'We're not quite sure, but let's get through this scene today and we'll let you know tomorrow.'"

Howard Koch's ending—Rick and Captain Renault ruminate over a chessboard, the noise of the departing airplane in the background—was tossed. Julius Epstein asserted that he and Philip were driving to the studio one day near the end of production when they turned to each other and said, in unison, "Round up the usual suspects." Although the identical twins frequently finished each other's sentences, this recollection seems

The *Casablanca* shoot was an anxious time for both of the two stars and the director (courtesy of the Lucas family).

apocryphal. They had written of Rick's killing Strasser and then Renault's shielding Rick in their draft script back in May. This solved half the problem; the challenge remained: how to handle Rick and Ilsa's parting.

Koch kept rewriting and changing the words. The need for personal sacrifice in wartime became the key that unlocked the puzzle. It was finally shot on July 17, but not until evening. Bogart and Curtiz had a major disagreement about the final scene that would be filmed on Stage 1 against the backdrop of a prop mockup of an airplane. Al Alleborn's report to Tenny Wright chronicled the situation: "During the day the company had several delays caused by arguments with Curtiz the director, and Bogart the actor. I had to go get Wallis and bring him over to the set to straighten out the situation. At one time they sat around for a long time and argued, finally deciding on how to do the scene. There were also numerous delays due to the cast not knowing the dialogue, which was a rewritten scene that came out the night before."

Precisely what Bogart and Curtiz quarreled about has been forgotten. The fact that Alleborn needed to summon Wallis indicates that the dispute was heated, as Wallis visited the sets of his films only occasionally. He had three other pictures in production concurrently with *Casablanca*. It is possible that Bogart initiated a quarrel with Curtiz because he didn't know his lines that morning and needed to stall until he memorized them.[5] The new dialogue included the "You're getting on that plane" and "We'll always have Paris" colloquy. Jill Gerrard, Curtiz's last surviving intimate, said that the director told her the argument was over how the ending was to be played. Perhaps some of the *Casablanca* magic was created by the alchemy of acrimony that so often characterized a Curtiz set.

The refinement of dialogue continued until the very end of the picture. Bogart clipped off an ad lib as he shot Major Strasser at the airport— "All right, Major, you asked for it"—that Wallis removed for censorship reasons. Even the self-defense killing of a Nazi during wartime was perceived as subject to the compensating moral values dictates of the Production Code. The Bogart ad lib remains in the original *Casablanca* preview trailer, even though the scripted dialogue ("I was willing to shoot Captain Renault and I am willing to shoot you") was restored to the feature. Curtiz or the actors devised the bit of business about Captain Renault's suggesting to Rick that he might arrange passage to the Free French garrison in Brazzaville and accompany him; this dialogue doesn't appear anywhere else, until it was penciled in after the fact on the editor's cutting script. Principal production on *Casablanca* was completed on July 22.

It was fitting that Hal Wallis had the last word. Dissatisfied with the film's final line of dialogue, delivered by Rick to Renault, Wallis eventually came up with, "Louis, I think this is the beginning of a beautiful friendship." He sent it to Curtiz via memo. Bogart would return from his yacht to record this sentence at the end of August. It was dubbed into the soundtrack as the pair disappeared into the oil-laden fog vapor on Stage 1.

Curtiz directed his final scene of *Casablanca* on August 22. It was a brief sequence of a French soldier reading a teletype report into a telephone about the murder of the German couriers and the theft of the letters of transit. The last major attribute of *Casablanca*—the music—would be a principal aspect of postproduction.

The composer Max Steiner didn't just dislike "As Time Goes By"; he hated it. Steiner's wife remembered her husband coming home from the studio after receiving the *Casablanca* assignment and bitterly complaining, "They have the lousiest tune, they already have it recorded, and they want me to use it." Steiner's prodigious talent made it not unreasonable for him to object to being forced into such heavy use of someone else's composition. Although a kindly man, he was a perfectionist who was probably more deserving than Curtiz of the sobriquet "workhorse." His music would eventually grace more than 350 feature films. He was assigned *Casablanca* as he finished the score of *Now, Voyager,* for which he would win an Academy Award, one of three Oscars he received for twenty-four nominated film scores during his career. Steiner also composed the Warner Bros. fanfare that had opened their movies since 1937.

Few composers other than Steiner turned out more distinguished work while laboring under the draconian time constraints imposed by Warner Bros. and the other studios. "The work is hard and exacting, and when dreaded 'release date' is upon us, sleep is an unknown thing," he wrote in his unpublished memoir. Steiner once worked fifty-six consecutive hours to finish a film score and relied on Benzedrine tablets to complete *Gone with the Wind* in time for the premiere.

"As Time Goes By," a 1931 song by Herman Hupfeld, so entranced Murray Burnett that he wrote it into *Everybody Comes to Rick's.* Elliot Carpenter's piano rendition and the dialogue in which Ilsa asks Sam to play it and then hums the tune were already recorded on the film's soundtrack. Steiner reportedly refused to use the song when it was initially assigned. Although it seems unlikely, Wallis supposedly considered reshooting the specific scenes that included the song. When he discovered that Bergman had already cut her hair to appear in *For Whom the Bell Tolls,* Steiner, "a fast-talking, hypersensitive gnome," composed the score using "As Time Goes By."

It would prove to be one of the most enduring music film scores using a predetermined theme song. "As Time Goes By" ended up on the top ten of *Your Hit Parade,* the NBC radio program, for twenty-one weeks. The once-forgotten pop tune reigned for the month of April–May 1943 as the number-one song in the country. Because of a musician's strike, the original 1931 record of the song by Rudy Vallee was re-released and saw a big spike in new sales. Steiner had his earlier title music from *The Lost Patrol* (1934) reorchestrated by Hugo Friedhofer to open the film.

Steiner's score and *Casablanca* became inseparable. The composer's ability to convey emotion and delineate characterization by seamlessly linking creative music cues within the movie was brilliant. Curtiz knew it and sent Steiner a telegram after the preview of the answer print: "Dear Max: We previewed *Casablanca* last night. My congratulations to you for marvelous music. Perfectly catching all moods and drama, this is your best and most brilliantly conceived work. Thanks."

Gone with the Wind and *King Kong* aside, Curtiz's praise of Steiner was accurate. But the composer didn't believe it, then or ever. He kept practically nothing about the picture in his papers and rarely spoke of it. He maintained his sense of humor, though. On the final page of his *Casablanca* music score that he passed to Friedhofer for orchestration, Steiner wrote in pencil, "Dear Hugo: Thanks for everything. I am very pleased with you! Yours, Herman Hupfeld."

In addition to Curtiz's praise for Steiner, there were other early indications that *Casablanca* was a special movie. Art Silver, who made the trailers and viewed most of the studio's film product with disdain, thought *Casablanca* was a terrific film. Then there was Joseph Breen. In his capacity as Hollywood's censor, Breen and his staff had to watch every movie made by all the studios in town. Breen normally had little or nothing to say about any film other than its conformity or lack thereof to the Production Code. In a surprising phone call to Hal Wallis, Breen raved about *Casablanca*. Wallis wrote a memo to the studio's publicity maven, Charles Einfeld, about the censor's passionate endorsement: "He [Breen] told me it was not only one of the most outstanding pictures to come off the lot in some time, but one of the best he had seen in some years. . . . I thought perhaps this enthusiasm might inspire you to plan a campaign for *Casablanca* as a really big picture."

The film was initially previewed on September 22 in Pasadena. Einfeld and other studio representatives were ecstatic; the Epstein brothers were not. Julius Epstein wrote a note to Hal Wallis telling him that he thought the picture "was a big flop." Like the proverbial elephant, Wallis never forgot and made sure that Epstein brothers didn't either. Julius ruefully recalled: "Thereafter, he kept that memo in his desk. Whenever we had an argument with him about anything, he would open his desk, take out that memo, and give it to us."

After another enthusiastically received preview, several of the audience cards indicated that the film should have shown Blaine and Renault's escape from Casablanca. Wallis immediately considered adding a new scene to change the ending of the picture. He was probably also reacting to Benny Kalmenson, Albert Warner, and the studio's other New York executives who wanted to change the ending after the Allied invasion of North Africa on November 8. Wallis reacted so rapidly that he erroneously described this added scene as a retake:

There will be a retake on *Casablanca* involving Claude Rains and Humphrey Bogart, and about 50 or 60 extras. Free French uniforms will be required for all of these. We will need the deck of the freighter on Stage 7. The scene is to be a night scene with fog. . . . Rains is in Pennsylvania, and I am asking Levee (his manager) to get him out here as quickly as possible as I want to make these scenes this week if possible. Curtiz will shoot. . . . I think it will probably take two nights to complete.

David O. Selznick was at the preview and wired Wallis the next morning:

Dear Hal: Saw *Casablanca* last night. Think it is a swell movie and an all-around fine job of picture making. Told Jack as forcibly as I could that I thought it would be a terrible mistake to change the ending, and also that I thought that the picture ought to be rushed out. . . . Mike Curtiz's direction was, as always, splendid. He is clearly one of the most competent men in the business. I am most grateful to you and to Mike Curtiz for the superb handling of Ingrid. Thanks to you two, and of course to Ingrid, the part seems much better than it actually is; and I think it will be of benefit to her, and therefore of course to me.

Jack Warner, swayed by Selznick's entreaty and the overall preview reaction, forbade Wallis to change the ending of *Casablanca*. In a November 12 memo to the corporate cabal in New York, Warner decreed hands off: "Will definitely not touch picture as previewed it again last night and audience reaction beyond belief. From main title to the end, there was applause and anxiety. Hundreds said do not touch the picture. My personal opinion is if picture is touched now it will become a patched job."

For a mogul who was not regarded as being particularly intelligent, Jack Warner had an intuitive sense of what would and wouldn't work. A year earlier, he had prevented Wallis from changing the title of *The Maltese Falcon* to *The Gent from Frisco*. In addition to nixing the idea of a new ending, he also allowed the war to assist him in marketing the film. He moved up the release date from a projected June 1943 to Thanksgiving Day 1942 at the Hollywood Theatre in New York to leverage the publicity from the Allied landing at Casablanca several weeks earlier. This initial ten-week New York opening was followed by the film's general release on January 23, 1943, timed to coincide with the meeting between Roosevelt and Churchill in Casablanca.

The *Casablanca* release, synchronized with momentous events in North Africa, boosted the picture's success. War news had become all-consuming. World War II was waged on a magnitude of ferocity unimaginable to present-day Americans. By the time of *Casablanca*'s November premiere, there had been nearly 40,000 American combat casualties. During the meeting between Roosevelt and Churchill the following January (Stalin did not attend), the determination of unconditional surrender by the Axis was announced. Victor Laszlo's closing declaration to Rick Blaine, "Welcome back to the fight. This time, I know our side will win," was more than a throwaway line of wartime propaganda. It was a genuine affirmation of a shared commitment.

However much the initial surge of patriotism may have boosted it, *Casablanca* succeeded on its own merits. Critics and audiences adored it. Bosley Crowther wrote an unequivocal rave in the *New York Times*: "Yes, indeed, the Warners here have a picture which makes the spine tingle and the heart take a leap. . . . We will tell you that Michael Curtiz has directed for slow suspense and that his camera is always conveying grim tension and uncertainty. . . . In short, we will say that *Casablanca* is one of the year's most exciting and trenchant films."

It was the sixth-ranked box-office success of 1943, grossing $4,496,000. In addition to winning Academy Awards for Best Picture, Director, and Writing, it would garner five other nominations for Best Actor (Bogart), Supporting Actor (Rains), Cinematography (Edeson), Editing (Owen Marks), and Music (Steiner). David O. Selznick's gratitude to Wallis and Curtiz rang true. Bergman's performance in *Casablanca* helped boost *For Whom the Bell Tolls* into the top position as 1943's highest-grossing film.

Casablanca became America's symbol of what it meant to be on the right side in a world starkly divided between good and evil. What no one anticipated was the future ascent of the film into a rarified firmament of popular culture that few movies occupy.

There was a 1955 re-release coinciding with an ill-considered Warner Bros. TV series starring Charles McGraw as Rick that added another $6,859,000 to the studio coffers. Humphrey Bogart did not live to see *Casablanca* become beloved by the sons and daughters of the Greatest Generation, who originally watched the film in movie theaters. The *Casablanca*-Bogart cult began in 1957 with screenings of Bogart movies at the Brattle Theatre in Cambridge, near Harvard University, and quickly took root around the country. Jack Warner sold his movie catalogue to televi-

Curtiz delivers his acceptance speech with the Academy Award finally in hand (courtesy of the Lucas family).

sion in 1956, and *Casablanca* became one of the most-watched movies on TV over the next two decades.

Dooley Wilson sang about how "the fundamental things apply as time goes by," but he could have been extolling those attributes that sustained Warner Bros. at its zenith: superb acting by charismatic stars and supporting actors, efficient production, a timeless screenplay constructed by a stable of skilled writers, excellent photography, and inspired direction. It was a picture that the key participants strove to improve until the last possible moment.

The film gave birth to a cottage industry. There was an attempted play by Epstein; a spoof film, *Play It Again, Sam* (1972), by Woody Allen; another aborted television series; myriad plays, books, essays, and articles; and countless references and assorted tie-ins. It is always near the top of "best film" compilations; the British Film Institute named it the greatest film of all time in 1983. Sam's old piano from Rick's Café sold at a New York auction in 2014 for $3.4 million, more than three times what it cost to make the movie. As for the mythical letters of transit that Bogart slipped into the same piano, they were purchased for $118,750.

The film critic Andrew Sarris characterized *Casablanca* as "a happy accident" that was a notable exception for those true believers of the auteur theory. To the contrary, *Casablanca* and Michael Curtiz's career at Warner Bros. contradict the shopworn theorem of giving sole credit to a director. *Casablanca* is better described as cinematic magic that occurred accidentally on purpose.

Even though Curtiz consistently credited Hal Wallis for his most enduring success, *Casablanca* never would have been what it became without his brilliance. Jack Warner clearly agreed, as he extended Curtiz's contract and anointed Julius and Philip Epstein producers.

A sequel with the working title of *Brazzaville* was contemplated in spring 1943. Curtiz was assigned to direct, and a synopsis was written with a prospective cast that included Geraldine Fitzgerald and Sydney Greenstreet. The project quietly died. There was also the notion of a companion picture starring Bogart and Ann Sheridan. Instead, audiences got *The Conspirators* (1944), a wartime potboiler directed by Jean Negulesco and starring Hedy Lamarr—accompanied by the usual suspects, Henreid, Lorre, and Greenstreet.

Curtiz began directing another picture three days before *Casablanca*'s November 27 New York premiere. His next pair of films would remain in thematic step with the war. One would become his most controversial and the other his biggest box-office success at Warner Bros.

25

"Those fine patriotic citizens, the Warner Brothers"

June 22, 1941, would become one of the most significant dates of the twentieth century. Hitler's invasion of the Soviet Union ultimately sealed his fate. This strategic blunder was compounded by another fatal miscalculation six months later: Germany's declaration of war against the United States. The Soviet dictator Joseph Stalin, Hitler's theretofore loyal ally, was forced into an unbeatable alliance with the United States and Great Britain against the Axis powers. Although it wasn't apparent at the time, the stage was also set for decades of future Cold War divisiveness that included convulsions for the American motion picture industry.

The grim necessity of America and the Soviet Union being joined at the hip as allies to defeat Nazism caused a sigh of relief in many quarters. President Roosevelt viewed the U.S.S.R. as the linchpin that would allow America to win the war in Europe. Antifascist liberals in America who had become estranged from domestic Communists because of the 1939 Hitler-Stalin nonaggression pact (more accurately described as a mutual aggression pact against Poland and Finland) became reunited with the true believers who had rationalized the Soviet collaboration with the Nazis. In addition to sharing a hatred of fascism, there were those on the left who, reduced to despair by the Great Depression, perceived Communism and the Soviet Union as an alternative socialist Utopia. As Lillian Hellman declared to the writer Allen Rivkin after Germany's attack on the Soviet Union: "The Motherland has been attacked!" In truth, there were few Americans with any genuine insight into what had and was actually transpiring inside Stalin's Russia.

Accurate reporting about the Soviet Union had presented a daunting challenge since the 1918 revolution. The number of foreigners allowed access to the country was kept to an absolute minimum; internal movement had become restricted in 1932. Strict Soviet censorship prevented information leaving the country through normal channels. There was also Stalin's ability to pose as an accommodating pragmatist rather than the ruthless despot he had become. This act hoodwinked visiting VIPs, including H. G. Wells and George Bernard Shaw. Several prominent journalists, most notably Walter Duranty, the chief Moscow correspondent for the *New York Times,* who were aware of the horrific human toll realized by Stalin's policies, deliberately falsified their reporting.[1] The terror famine of 1932–33 that killed ten million people in Ukraine and the Northern Caucasus region was scarcely reported in the West.

It was this mélange of wartime necessity, idealistic delusion, and obstructive propaganda that resulted in Curtiz's most controversial directorial assignment at Warner Bros.

Joseph E. Davies had been a high-powered trial lawyer defending corporate clients before entering Democratic politics. He was married to the cereal heiress Marjorie Merriweather Post, reputedly the richest woman in the United States, and also served as the first chairman of the Federal Trade Commission. Davies was the American ambassador to the Soviet Union from 1936 to 1938. A close confidant of President Roosevelt since they had served together in the Woodrow Wilson administration, Davies obtained F.D.R.'s approval and, after Hitler attacked the Soviet Union, began compiling a book that was based on his personal diaries and confidential State Department documents, which were declassified for his use. John Franklin Carter, who authored the syndicated column *We, the People,* assembled the material for the book, and Spencer Williams and Stanley Richardson, who were journalists assigned to Moscow when Davies served as ambassador, did the ghost-writing. *Mission to Moscow* was rushed into publication less than a month after the attack on Pearl Harbor.

Davies's narrative that the U.S.S.R. was a misunderstood, fair-minded, socialist-style government simpatico to American values gained considerable traction. In particular, his depiction of Stalin as a pragmatic leader was a boon to the perception of the Soviet dictator in the West. *Mission to Moscow* sold 700,000 copies and was translated into thirteen languages. It was presented as a documentary record of the U.S. government's viewpoint of the Soviet Union and published with the blessing of the State Department and President Roosevelt. How *Mission to Moscow* became a major film production was a question that would be pursued by the House Un-American Activities Committee (HUAC) after the war.

HUAC specifically queried Jack Warner in 1947 about the making of

Mission to Moscow. The committee was ferreting around for purported Communist infiltration of the motion picture industry. Warner testified under oath that Davies originally contacted Warner Bros. to make the film. This account matched Davies's own story about how his book was adapted for the screen. Warner later changed his testimony and stated that his brother Harry read *Mission to Moscow* and contacted Davies about filming it.

Mission to Moscow was raw meat for the postwar political class of Red hunters because of its endorsement of the Soviet Union generally and of Stalin specifically. When compared with other pro-Soviet movies, including RKO's *Days of Glory* (produced by Casey Robinson and starring his wife, Tamara Toumanova), Goldwyn's *The North Star,* and MGM's *Song of Russia, Mission to Moscow* stood as the most striking example of pro-Soviet propaganda produced by Hollywood. The British historian Colin Shindler sarcastically observed that the film was "riddled with such political bias as to make *Triumph of the Will* look like an objective current affairs program."

The question that remained unclear after the HUAC hearings was exactly why Warner Bros. strove produce a pro-war movie out of a boring, overlong political tome.

Jack Warner wrote a fabulist account in his 1964 memoir in which Roosevelt was behaving like a Hollywood agent, pitching *Mission to Moscow* to him over dinner at the White House: "'Joe [Davies] is anxious to make it into a picture,' Mr. Roosevelt said. 'He wants Warner Brothers to do it. What do you think, Jack?' 'It would make a powerful film,' I said. "But I'd also like to know what *you* think.' The President was thoughtful for a moment, and he tipped his long cigarette holder in my direction. 'Jack,' he said, 'this picture must be made, and I am asking you to do it.' 'I'll do it,' I said, 'you have my word.'"

Warner said that he considered the president's request "an order." He also claimed that Roosevelt confided to him that he was worried that Stalin would form a second alliance with Hitler if the Nazis prevailed in the battle for Stalingrad, and "we simply couldn't lose Russia at this stage."

Warner's memoir omitted any mention of his HUAC testimony, which included an affirmation under oath that the U.S. government "never cooperated" with the making of *Mission to Moscow*. Warner added the startling observation during his testimony in executive session that the Columbia University philosopher John Dewey, who had panned the film after it was released in 1943, was a "Trotskyite."

Howard Koch recalled in his memoir being summoned to a meeting with Harry and Jack Warner. After informing Koch that he could not refuse this particular screenplay assignment, Jack discussed his attendance at a recent White House dinner with Ambassador Davies and President Roosevelt. Roosevelt supposedly handed Jack a copy of *Mission to Moscow,* saying, "Our people know almost nothing about the Soviet Union and the Russian people. What they do know is largely prejudiced and inaccurate. If we're going to fight the war together, we need a more sympathetic understanding."

Robert Buckner, the producer of *Mission to Moscow,* harbored no doubt who originated and approved the idea of making the film:[2] "I knew that F.D.R. had brainwashed him [Davies] and the Warners as well, into making the film; as F.D.R. said in a meeting at the White House: 'to show the American mothers and fathers that if their sons are killed in fighting alongside Russians in our common cause, that it was a good cause, and that the Russians are worthy allies.' This statement was relayed to me by Harry Warner, head of the studio, who was present when F.D.R. spoke in front of Davies, [Soviet Foreign Minister] Litvinov, Harry Hopkins and others."

By whichever account, it is evident that *Mission to Moscow* was adapted into a feature film because President Roosevelt believed that the movie would aid the U.S. war effort. Despite Harry's intense loathing of Communism, the brothers believed it was their patriotic obligation to support the president and help win the war by any means necessary. Under these auspices, *Mission to Moscow* was shepherded into production.

The Warners didn't realize what they were getting into. What they believed would be a pro-American war film highlighting the Soviet Union as a U.S. ally ended up bearing no resemblance to any picture ever produced in Hollywood. Joseph Davies was determined that the movie would reflect his personal viewpoint of Stalin and the Soviet Union. It was a false narrative that dated back to the beginning of his ambassadorial service.

When Davies arrived at Moscow to assume his post in 1936, Stalin was administering what became known as "the Great Terror." He achieved absolute autocracy by eliminating anyone who could rival his power or raise an independent voice. It was a wholesale purge of the Communist Party, the Red Army, the secret police, and all other state, local, and international organs including intelligentsia, foreigners, and anyone else he deemed inconvenient or disloyal.[3] Stalin's preferred method of disposing of senior members of the party was the show trial. High-ranking officials were arrested and tortured until they signed prepared confessions of plotting coups or being spies; they were then subjected to a public tribunal for "wrecking" (the Soviet equivalent of sabotage). These trials served an additional purpose by blaming the catastrophic results of the agricultural collectivization and mass famine earlier in the decade on invented foreign plots and alleged "wreckers."

The defendants were faced with manufactured evidence, lying witnesses, and scripted confessions before the court arrived at the predetermined conclusion of a death sentence. Many of these doomed men confessed with the understanding that they and their families would be spared. Stalin had the condemned executed, along with most of their families. Those who were spared disappeared into the vast network of Soviet forced-labor camps.

It was against this backdrop of barbarity that Davies extolled Stalin in *Mission to Moscow* as "a great leader" who "insisted on the liberalism of the constitution" while "projecting actual secret and universal suffrage." The ambassador reported the show trials to the State Department as genuine. Concerning the twelve defendants in the Trotsky-Radek treason trial in 1937 who confessed, pled guilty, and were executed, Davies wrote: "To assume that this proceeding was invented and staged . . . would be to presuppose the creative genius of a Shakespeare and the genius of a Belasco in stage production." Davies also posited that that Stalin "had cleansed the country and rid it of treason." His unabashed endorsement of Stalin and his regime cannot be ascribed solely to naïveté. During his tenure as ambassador, Davies and his wife were allowed to purchase valuable Russian artifacts at negligible cost, including a pair of the jewel-encrusted "Imperial" Easter eggs made for the czar by Karl Fabergé and a diamond-studded crown used at Imperial Russian weddings. These objects of art remain on display at Marjorie Post's Hillwood residence in Washington, D.C., which was turned into a museum after her death in 1973.

The deal that Davies received from Warner Bros. for *Mission to Moscow* was a $25,000 payment along with script approval. The former ambassador assumed supervisory authority over the development of the screenplay and didn't hesitate to claim that "every change was at the personal request of the president." There was little that Warner Bros. could do to rein him in. The Office of War Information (OWI) had veto authority over any movie, and the government could declare Warner picture production as nonessential to the war effort and cut off supplies of their film stock.

Under the circumstances, Jack Warner had to be extremely careful. Robert Buckner was assigned to produce. The studio chief believed that after Buckner's ability to bond with the contentious George M. Cohan during the pre-production of *Yankee Doodle Dandy,* he was the most qualified person to manage what would clearly be a challenging relationship with Joseph Davies.

According to a magazine profile of Curtiz published in December 1958, he was ushered into Harry Warner's office as the studio patriarch unlocked his desk and handed the startled director a copy of *Mission to Moscow.* Curtiz blanched, telling Warner, "But you know I am anti-Communist." "I know," said Warner, "so am I. But the Russians are now our allies and President Roosevelt would like us to make the picture." Both of the Warners wanted Curtiz to direct because he was best suited to handle a large cast and would be able to finish the picture as quickly as possible. Jack Warner also counted on Curtiz's ability to perform under pressure. On November 9, 1942, Warner wrote to him: "Today you start the most important picture of your wonderful career. I know you will come through with flying colors which has always been the Curtiz credo." It would be an assignment that the director would recall without pleasure.

After unsuccessfully attempting to convince Robert Sherwood to write the screenplay, Davies insisted the studio hire his friend the novelist Erskine Caldwell. Caldwell had no previous experience as a screenwriter. His draft combined the purge trials into a single event and opened the film with Haile Selassie's famous appeal to the League of Nations after Italy invaded his country in 1936. These aspects were retained in the final screenplay, which was written by Howard Koch.[4]

Koch admittedly knew nothing about Russia and insisted that he be able to bring on a technical adviser of his own choosing. Warner agreed. Koch hired Jay Leyda, a man he described as "a valuable ally" who was "sympathetic to the Soviet system." Originally a photographer, the Detroit-born Leyda had attended the Moscow State Film School, studying under the Soviet film pioneer Sergei Eisenstein and serving as an assistant director on Eisenstein's film *Bezhin Meadow.* Leyda left the Soviet Union in 1936 after Eisenstein recommended that he accept a job offer (assistant film curator at the Museum of Modern Art) and avoid being swept up in the purges. Leyda brought a complete print of Eisenstein's classic *Battle-*

ship Potemkin with him to MoMA and would become a respected film historian specializing in Russian and Chinese cinema.

Although Leyda's influence on the content of *Mission to Moscow* is believed to have been minimal, his papers archived at New York University included his written notes to Koch titled "Changes to *Mission to Moscow*." Leyda's recommendations insinuated that the Nazis were working with elements of the Soviet regime to overthrow Stalin and that the trial depicted in the film needed to indicate that the condemned men were guilty of treason. Leyda's political point of view (he was reportedly a member of the Communist Party of America [CPUSA]) was simpatico with Koch's, and both men were sympathetic to Davies's perspective. Leyda believed that the film's "positive accomplishments . . . fortify me." Koch was untroubled by the predisposition of his script to deify the Soviet regime. As he remarked about the opening scene at the League of Nations, in which Litvinov supports Haile Selassie: "Let the Soviet-haters scream."

The script's message, repetitively delivered in ham-handed fashion, was that the Russians were a happy, hard-working lot thriving under the benevolent rule of Stalin. Davies took the unprecedented step of inviting Foreign Minister Litvinov to his New York country estate on Lake St. Regis in the Adirondack Mountains to review the script with him to ensure that its characterizations of Litvinov, Stalin, and the Soviet Union were accurate. Koch and Buckner also spent time at St. Regis going over the script with Davies. Buckner was uncomfortable with Davies's increasing interference, but his hands were tied.

Davies apparently raised an objection to Curtiz as the director, but he changed his mind after flubbing on Erskine Caldwell and being reassured by Buckner and Warner. Koch was also initially unhappy with Curtiz. He wrote in his memoir that he believed the director was "miscast for a film in which most of the action would be verbal exchanges." Of greater concern, the screenwriter believed, was that in Curtiz's younger days he "had been involved in revolutionary politics in his native Hungary, but . . . he had left them there . . . in America he was strictly apolitical." In addition to the implication that Curtiz needed to pass a political litmus test to direct *Mission to Moscow,* Koch had already forgotten about *Casablanca* and wasn't aware of *British Agent*. He possessed no knowledge about Curtiz's background in Hungary, including the circumstances of his direction of *Jön az öcsém* (*My Brother Is Coming*). If Koch was worried that Curtiz's political neutrality might somehow dilute his written paean to the Soviet Union, it was a case of misplaced anxiety.

Curtiz did not contrive to alter the script. Although relentlessly pro-American, he *was* apolitical. After being exposed to some of the early excesses of Soviet-style Communism, Curtiz harbored no delusions about Stalin. Although he "reluctantly accepted" the *Mission to Moscow* assignment, he was more well informed than Koch and others at the studio realized. He skimmed through *Soviet Power* by Hewlett Johnson, the so-called Red Dean of Canterbury, which he borrowed from the studio research department. This book was a compilation of Soviet propaganda tracts that included such insights as Stalin "leading his people down new and unfamiliar avenues of democracy." Curtiz also read the first comprehensive biography of Stalin (written by the disaffected Communist Boris Souvarine), which was critical of the Soviet dictator.

Curtiz was foursquare with the Warners in support of President Roosevelt and the war effort. As a Jew who had recently scrambled to get his mother and brothers to America, he knew that Hitler and the Nazis had to be eradicated. He considered *Mission to Moscow* a job of work and, as always, did the best he could. The Koch screenplay became just another script rather than a geopolitical treatise tainted by pro-Soviet propaganda. Buckner recalled that "even after the script was finally written and approved, Curtiz had to be reminded almost daily of the events he was directing." Despite his usual tunnel vision, it was obvious that this particular picture was being controlled by powers far beyond the Warner executive suite. This was neither the time nor the picture for making a personal directorial statement. In a marked departure from his usual form, there are no recorded instances of Curtiz changing or adding dialogue in *Mission to Moscow*.

On September 23 Davies submitted twenty-four pages of script changes and recommendations to Buckner and Curtiz. Since Davies had previously approved everything that Koch had written and there was barely more than two weeks before start of production, both producer and director became upset. Buckner attempted to finesse these issues, particularly the sequence featuring a brief meeting between Davies and the president, by inviting the ambassador to Hollywood to discuss his concerns. It would continue to be rough going; Davies submitted additional changes to the script that elaborated on the worst excesses in his book. The most egregious examples concerned the 1939 Soviet invasion of Finland and the characterization of the Stalinist purge trial that was the heart of the film. Davies insisted on adding dialogue indicating that Russia did not invade Finland. The final cut included Walter Huston as Davies reciting this whopper after being asked about the Soviet invasion of Finland in 1939: "Russia knew she was going to be attacked by Hitler so the Soviet leaders asked Finland's permission to occupy strategic positions to defend herself against German aggression. She offered to give Finland twice as much territory in exchange, but Hitler's friend Mannheim refused and the Red Army moved in."[5]

When Buckner challenged Davies on the veracity of this startling revisionism, the former ambassador stated that he possessed "privileged knowledge." Buckner said that Davies was "often prone to pulling this 'mysterious knowledge' to silence us." Portions of Davies's book (including his confidential cables to the State Department describing the existence of the Terror and the havoc wreaked on the Soviet economy by Stalin's policies) were absent from the final script. According to Buckner, Davies also insisted on changing the key purge trial sequence to clearly indicate the guilt of the defendants even though the script left this point ambiguous. Buckner believed that this falsehood crossed a line. Sensing that history would harshly judge both him and Warner Bros., Buckner forced a showdown with Davies. As he related it to the author David Culbert:

> Davies insisted upon the guilt. I went to the brothers Warner and told them that I thought a great historic mistake was being made. They called a meeting with Davies and myself to settle the point, and Davies made one of the most beautiful poker-play bluffs I have ever witnessed. Instead of answering our questions he asked how much the film had cost to that point. I had the figure at hand, just under one million dollars. Davies said, "All right, let's say one million as a round figure. I will give you the million here and now and will take over the negative of the film from you." He took out a checkbook and pen and prepared to write the check. I don't think he ever would have done so but the Warners and I knew that with Mrs. Davies' money behind him he could have paid such a sum. The Warners were tempted to call his bluff but they didn't at last, and Davies won his point that the Purge Trials would "make clear" that the victims were guilty as traitors and Trotskyites. At this decision I offered to resign as the producer, but Warner would not let me.

Davies also waded into the casting process. He contacted Fredric March, urging him to play the leading role. March declined. Walter Huston was eventually tapped to play Davies, and Ann Harding played his wife. Harding, who had recently returned to the screen after a five-year hiatus, was paired with a young Eleanor Parker as Davies's daughter. Parker was at the beginning of a career that would blossom into postwar stardom. She found Curtiz's directorial temperament to be less fearsome than she'd heard rumored: "Mike Curtiz had a reputation for being difficult with actors, but he was completely professional and polite with me. Also, he knew exactly what he was doing as a director. I had no problems."

After production began, Davies and his wife relocated to the Beverly Hills Hotel for two months to observe the filming. He was given a star dressing room and treated like an executive producer. He kept Roosevelt in the loop about the progress on the picture, meeting with him in October and November 1942. He also cleared the simulation of the president's voice in the movie. Davies was regularly quoted in the trade papers about *Mission to Moscow,* declaring at a January press conference, "There is no man in the world I would trust more fully than Joe Stalin or Maxim Litvinov, Vyacheslov Molotov or Marshall Clementi Voroshilov." He apparently did not share the same degree of confidence about the film's director.

The former ambassador asked Curtiz why Walter Huston wasn't made up to resemble him as the other actors portraying contemporary figures, such as Churchill, Stalin, and Molotov were. "That, Mr. Davies," responded Curtiz with his usual tact, "is because you are not famous." Davies got the last word. He forced the studio to shoot a six-and-a-half-minute prologue in which he introduces the film: "My people were pioneers. They came to New Orleans in a sailing ship. I was born in Wisconsin, educated in the public schools, graduated from the University of Wisconsin, and went to Washington as one of Woodrow Wilson's young men." He lauded the Warner brothers as "those fine, patriotic citizens" and gave a ringing affirmation of the "integrity, honesty of the Soviet Union" According to Howard Koch, Jack Warner chalked up the introduction to Davies's future presidential ambitions and let it go.

It was left primarily to Curtiz to cast the rest of the film. The supporting cast of nearly 180 included almost every character player in Hollywood who could muster a foreign accent. In addition to the Viennese Oscar Homolka as Litvinov and the Belgian Victor Francen essaying a watered-down version of the feared prosecutor Vyshinsky, there was Curtiz's favorite British character player Henry Daniell as Hitler's foreign minister, Von Ribbentrop, the Italian-born Frank Puglia portraying the trial judge, and Americans Gene Lockhart as Soviet Foreign Minister Molotov and Leigh Whipper as Haile Selassie.[6] Konstantin Shayne, a native Russian actor, added ethnic credibility as the doomed Nikolai Bukharin, and a Broadway actor named Manart Kippen briefly portrayed a pipe-smoking, avuncular Joseph Stalin. Captain Jack Young and the voiceover specialist Art Gilmore reprised the over-the-shoulder depiction of President Roosevelt that they had created in *Yankee Doodle Dandy*. Despite the pedantic nature of the film, it simply could not be a Warner Bros. picture without an ancillary character whose sole purpose was comic relief. George Tobias filled this niche as the family servant.

The beginning of production was less than auspicious. Curtiz managed to have his stepson elevated out of the "B" unit to be the film's dialogue director. After two days on the job, Lucas got into a public argument with an actor, and news of the quarrel reached Robert Buckner. Curtiz couldn't save him, and the young man was bounced back to programmers. Years afterward, Lucas ruefully remembered, "I consider my stupidity at losing that job prime among the many dumb things I have done." Less than two weeks later, the lack of an authentic technical assistant became evident. Jay Leyda might have been familiar with Russian cinema and was helpful in obtaining Soviet newsreel footage, but he knew nothing about how Soviet cadres dressed, marched, or communicated. Al Alleborn explained the dilemma to Tenny Wright:

> Mike is raising hell with me—regarding not having a Technical Man who knows the maneuvers and execution and drill, salute, etc, as well as the wardrobe and costuming of the people. . . . I explained to Mike that . . . it is impossible as there is no one in Hollywood. Mike did have a man who he thought was good, but I know and you know that he is nothing but an extra and has been here in Hollywood for years—a Russian extra. So Tenny, we are going ahead just as we have in the past and make the best of it.

Curtiz soldiered on, intermittently bored with a picture that stifled his normal creativity. He had some of the usual difficulties with the cinematographer Bert Glennon while coping with the continually changing script. Koch was delivering new scenes for the actors to memorize and rehearse that were being shot later in the day, exactly as had happened on the *Casablanca* set. Despite these revisions and Davies's continued interference, the film remained on schedule. Curtiz enjoyed staging the opening scene with Haile Selassie addressing the League of Nations. Curtiz directed the scene (four hundred delegates reacting to Leigh Whipper as Selassie) like "a conductor leading a symphony." He bellowed to the entire company: "When the Negus [Selassie] speak, I want the crowd to react. I want the crowd to go like an ocean." What helped make *Mission to Moscow* visually distinctive was the excellent work of the montage specialist Don Siegel, who seamlessly integrated the extensive newsreel and stock footage into the film. According to Koch, Curtiz was worried that the continual sequences of talking heads during the 124-minute running time would make the picture flat. Although his concern was justified, the final cut of *Mission to Moscow* was a skillful blend of direction and editing. Koch wrote a lyrical ending to the film using a biblical quotation that overlaid a scene of happy Russians plowing furrows on the steppe that Buckner jettisoned for a more prosaic finale.

Curtiz got no "Get Out of Jail Free" card when it came to his excessive use of film stock. Early on he had to shoot ten takes of a scene because of a minor actor playing a German official. Alleborn noted in the production report: "Henry Victor could not remember his lines, we put them on a blackboard and everything else trying to get this scene, but it was impossible for this man till the tenth take. This scene could not be broken up and did not concern a lot of dialogue."

Jack Warner wrote to Curtiz: "You cannot shoot 10 takes. You know there is a war on, Mike, and you must conserve film, so why don't you do this." A week later, he fired off another memo: "Please Mr. Curtiz, there's a war on! We can't start 12 times on a short scene. We *must* stop doing this! How are we going to win the war?" Curtiz had finally had enough:

Dear Jack—Believe me, it is not a pleasure to reshoot a take ten and twelve times. It disturbs me as much as it does you. There are always reasons for it what with actors breaking down on their lines or faulty mechanism slowing it up. You refer in particular to the short scene. Walter Huston broke down 11 times, therefore necessitating these repeats. I wasn't able to overlap because it was one shot. These things occur and are really beyond my control.

Jack, of our 130,000,000 Americans, I am foremost in the desire to win the war.

Production concluded during the first week of March 1943. The OWI claimed that *Mission to Moscow* "will make a great contribution" to the Allied cause. The audience feedback from an initial sneak preview in Hol-

Hal Wallis, Curtiz, and Colonel Jack L. Warner (courtesy of the Lucas family).

lywood was positive, and Jack Warner reportedly allocated $500,000 to promote the film. Two weeks before the premiere, Joseph Davies made a final demand. His wife wanted a scene of her character in a cosmetics shop with Molotov's wife. Buckner gritted his teeth and convinced Ann Harding to return with Curtiz to film this sequence on April 15.

After Davies screened the film at the White House for President Roosevelt on April 21, Warner Bros. held a star-spangled preview in Washington, D.C., for four thousand people. The cascade of criticism began immediately after the general release of the picture on April 30. The brickbats didn't come only from those on the Right. Two noted liberals, John Dewey of Columbia University and Suzanne La Follette, niece of the famed progressive senator, castigated the film in the *New York Times*. Dewey had led an independent commission with La Follette that had investigated Stalin's purges. He categorized *Mission to Moscow* as "the first instance in our country of totalitarian propaganda for mass consumption—a propaganda which falsifies history through distortion, omission or pure invention of facts." Dewey and La Follette enumerated most of the film's more damning attributes, including deletion of any mention of the 1939 Hitler-Stalin pact, the whitewashing of the purge trials, the overtly negative portrayal of prewar Britain and France, and the unfavorable portrayal of the U.S. Congress, contrasted with the film's presentation of "the Soviet dictatorship as an advanced democracy."[7] There was the additional fiction of the Red Army Marshal Mikhail Tukhachevsky being portrayed as one of the defendants in the trial sequence. There had been no public trial for Tukhachevsky; Stalin had him tortured and executed in June 1937. Manny Farber wrote in *The New Republic* that he was ready to vote to give *Mission to Moscow* "the booby prize," as the film "made up its own facts" to praise the Soviet Union.

Other reviews were favorable. Bosley Crowther believed that the picture attempted "to convey a realistic impression of fact" and that the purge trial sequence was "briefly, but effectively played." In the *Nation*, James Agee wrote that *Mission to Moscow* would "hasten and intensify our cooperation with the Soviet Union" while aptly describing the film as "the first Soviet production to come from a major Hollywood studio."

Not surprisingly, the Warners stood their ground and fought back. Harry Warner sarcastically remarked, "We would hate to be known as the company that made the most successful musical film of this great war for freedom." Jack Warner was particularly aggrieved by William Randolph Hearst's reprinting of the Dewey–La Follette broadside in his newspapers. After all, hadn't Jack hired Marion Davies in 1935, going so far as having her dressing room towed from MGM to the Warner Bros. lot while he partnered with Hearst's Cosmopolitan Pictures? Warner urged Hearst to publish Dr. Arthur Upham Pope's defense of *Mission to Moscow* in "the interest of fairness."[8] The venerable yellow press lord was having none of it. In a cordial response, Hearst wrote: "Your film, Mr. Warner, gives 'the other side of the case'—the communist side—quite completely. . . . I am sorry that we disagree on the proper function of the press—and of the moving picture. But I am sure that you will realize that our attitude toward your screen product (an attitude so frequently favorable, but in this case frankly critical) is guided by no personal unfriendliness, but merely by a sense of public duty."

Warner countered with a rejoinder that he would repeat during his later HUAC testimony: *Mission to Moscow* was no different from the rest of his studio's pro-war films, including *Sergeant York, Air Force,* and *Action in the North Atlantic.* He might have actually believed this. Although much later Warner defaulted to the essential truism that his studio complied with what President Roosevelt requested of it, the only other alternative would have been to admit that the content of the film got away from them primarily because of the influence of Joseph Davies. That untenable option was never considered. Public admission of error was not a trait embraced by any of the studio moguls, particularly the brothers Warner.

The net outcome of *Mission to Moscow* on the hearts and minds of Americans regarding the Soviet Union proved negligible. The focus on immediate war news blotted out everything else. *Mission to Moscow* grossed little more than $100,000 over its cost of $1.5 million, but the huge outlay on publicity and distribution made it a financial loser. According to Buckner, it was "not a disaster" but "never broke even." It was shown overseas to American troops and in the Soviet Union; Joseph Davies traveled back to Moscow to personally screen the picture for Stalin. Buckner ran into the English-born Madame Litvinov on New York's Fifth Avenue after the picture had been released and asked her how *Mission to Moscow* was received by the Soviet leadership. According to Buckner, she said: "It was hilarious. My husband was there. Everybody saw himself portrayed on the screen and they got a great kick out of that. But there were so many things in the picture that never occurred. My husband said later that in the entire history of the Kremlin there had probably never been as much laughter."

What was more profound was how *Mission to Moscow* affected the movie industry. The Cold War took root in Hollywood years before Winston Churchill would speak of an "iron curtain" descending in Europe. Sam Wood, the director of *Goodbye, Mr. Chips, Kings Row,* and *For Whom the Bell Tolls,* was a right-wing zealot who viewed domestic Communism as a clear and present danger. *Mission to Moscow* motivated Wood to join with the screenwriters James Kevin McGuiness (described by no less than Ronald Reagan as a Red-baiter), Casey Robinson, and Morris Ryskind, along with the director-producers Victor Fleming, King Vidor, Walt Disney, Clarence Brown, and others to form the Motion Picture Alliance for Preservation of American Ideals in February 1944. The organization's stated goal was to counteract what its founders believed was Communist influence in the motion picture industry. The politics in Hollywood became toxic after the war. During his 1947 HUAC testimony, Jack Warner got even with Howard Koch for causing him so much trouble when he threw him and other screenwriters under the bus by naming them as Communists or fellow travelers. Koch was blacklisted primarily because of the *Mission to Moscow* debacle.

All this came later. In May 1943 the critical barbs aimed at *Mission to Moscow* wounded Curtiz. He felt that his loyalty to America and the war effort was being questioned. Buckner wrote to Jack Warner: "Mike Curtiz is very upset by all the criticisms and is taking it personally. I have been holding his hand and reassuring him that life will go on as usual." Life was indeed proceeding, as Curtiz began helming what would be a deliriously popular wartime extravaganza that would expunge anybody's doubts about his patriotism.

The legendary composer and lyricist Irving Berlin decided to create a Broadway show as a fund-raiser for the military in the spring of 1942. Berlin's creativity was rejuvenated by the war. "'Songs make history and history makes songs,' he declared. It needed a French Revolution to make a 'Marseillaise' and the bombardment of Fort McHenry to give voice to 'The Star-Spangled Banner.'" Berlin obtained the permission of Army Chief of Staff General George Marshall to create the show as a tribute to the army, staffed it with soldiers as well as actors, and opened it on July 4 at the Shubert Theatre in New York. *This Is the Army* became a sensation, and Berlin took it on a national tour. By the time the tour ended in San Francisco on February 13, 1943, the revue had raised $2 million for the Army Emergency Relief Fund. Berlin sold the film rights to Jack Warner for $250,000 and donated all the proceeds to the relief fund. The deal for the picture reflected Warners' willingness to support the war effort. Jack Warner's original proposal was for the studio to completely finance the picture and donate 50 percent of the profits to army relief after the outlay to produce, promote, and distribute the film was paid for. The ink on the agreement was barely dry when Harry Warner decided that the Army Emergency Relief Fund should receive all of the profits from *This Is the Army*.

Hal Wallis produced the film under the auspices of Jack Warner. Warner had elbowed Wallis aside on *Mission to Moscow,* an act that the producer was ultimately grateful for. Their relationship had begun to deteriorate. Warner's desire for control was apparent in a memorandum to Wallis: "I personally want to do all the communicating with the War Department on *This Is the Army,* that all requests for people pertaining to whatever we may desire. . . . Please acknowledge receipt of this note and if you have corresponded with anyone send me the file so I can follow up and inform them that from here on all correspondence will be handled by me."

And it was now "Colonel Warner," as the studio boss had wrangled himself a U.S. Army commission. His military title is appended to much of Warner's studio correspondence during the war, and the studio employees were told to refer to him by his army rank.

Curtiz's assignment to *This Is The Army* was a foregone conclusion. Berlin admired Curtiz's work with his material in *Mammy* and wrote to Jack Warner: "I understand Mike Curtiz is going to do another picture before *This Is the Army.* I realize he couldn't stay idle all this time, but I do hope he will be able to come on with Wallis and Robinson because he has a very sympathetic approach to this story and will be very helpful in the conference."

Warner reassured Berlin: "It is true that Mike Curtiz is going to do *Mission to Moscow* first, but he will be through a month or eight weeks before *This Is the Army* starts, and with the entire enterprise being in the capable hands it is, you need not have one minute of fear."

The director began shooting *This Is the Army* on February 25, 1943, less than three weeks after *Mission to Moscow* wrapped. *This Is the Army* was a complex undertaking; the studio worked closely with the War Department, which eventually assigned a lieutenant colonel as a full-time liaison with the studio. The 350 soldiers assigned to the show were housed in a ten-acre outpost built by Tenny Wright's prop department and named Camp TITA. Located on a vacant lot behind the studio, the post was built to military specifications; it consisted of thirteen wooden-floored, furnished tents, a shower house, latrines, an admin building, a PX, and a telephone exchange.

While not involved in filming, the troops had to rise at reveille, appear on parade, and perform military drill while being marched in and out of the studio every day in formation. In order to distinguish between the actual soldiers and the 4-F actors in uniform, the studio issued the actors armbands. The future playwright Max Wilk served in the First Motion Picture Unit and was assigned to *This Is the Army*. Wilk recalled that "if you saw a colonel with a 'W-B' on his arm, you were free to ignore him. . . . It was a heady sensation."

The G.I.s found that bivouacking near Hollywood had its benefits. The studio employees mobbed them as if their arrival from the Burbank train depot signified that the war was over. In the evenings, they were able to mingle with the movie stars at the Hollywood Canteen. More than a few soldiers managed to land rooms out in town. One lucky private contrived to commute to work every day with Ingrid Bergman, who was starring in Warner's *Saratoga Trunk*.

Lieutenant Ronald Reagan, assigned to the First Motion Picture Unit, received permission from the army to appear in the film with a cast including Joan Leslie, George Tobias, Alan Hale, Stanley Ridges, and Dolores Costello. It was the only occasion Costello worked with Curtiz after the *Noah's Ark* debacle, and it would be her final screen appearance. Casey Robinson and Claude Binyon wrote the script, and the Epstein twins polished the dialogue. *This Is the Army* was essentially a hodgepodge of musical numbers and songs. Minimal elaboration was necessary for a Technicolor musical starring the borrowed-from-MGM George Murphy as Johnny Jones's (Reagan's) father, Jerry. Irving Berlin's World War I revue *Yip Yip Yaphank*, written during the lyricist's 1918 military service at Camp Upton, New York, provided the biographical theme. The film featured Kate Smith singing "God Bless America" and the heavyweight champion Joe Louis among other guest stars who were featured in musical numbers written by Berlin.

The composer also reprised his "Oh How I Hate to Get Up in the Morning" number from *Yip Yip Yaphank*. The workaholic Berlin excelled at writing lyrics rather than singing them. In front of the camera, he resembled exactly who he was: a fifty-four-year-old man in a doughboy uniform intoning in a reedy twang. As Berlin's voice weakened near the end of the number, a grip on the set remarked, "If the fellow who wrote this song could hear this guy sing it, he'd roll over in his grave." Curtiz captured the number in a single take. Ronald Reagan said later that he was introduced to Berlin five times during the production. During their final encounter, the composer told Reagan, "It's very possible that you could have a career in show business." Despite his absent-minded deportment, Irving Berlin was the ultimate patriotic mensch. The composer donated every dollar he made from the film, including royalties from "God Bless America."

Wallis, Irving Berlin, Curtiz, and Casey Robinson assess matters during filming of *This Is the Army* (1943) (courtesy of the Lucas family).

Even with the cooperation of everyone involved, there were problems. The head of advertising informed Jack Warner that the musical numbers in which men dressed as chorus girls would cause *This Is the Army* to be denied an export license in Latin America because "female impersonators do not exist in Latin America: men in women's clothing are highly insulting and revolting to Latin sensibilities and censors." Although the comedic musical numbers were no more offensive than Milton Berle in drag on television several years later, these scenes were diluted. More ominous was a Berlin musical chorus written to conclude the movie. "Dressed Up to Kill" had accurate but appalling lyrics, as a group of soldiers sang in a chorus that was choreographed with lunging bayonets:

Dressed up to kill,
Dressed up to kill,
Dressed up for victory.
Oh we don't like killing,
But we won't stop killing
Till the world is free.

No one would confuse this particular number with "God Bless America." Ezra Stone, the voice of radio's Henry Aldrich and Berlin's stage director, was assigned to the picture in his uniformed rank as a master sergeant. He and Berlin had a permanent falling-out over the song. Stone believed that the lyrics were immoral and began initiating a public relations campaign against the song after the composer refused to pull it. When Jack Warner began receiving protest letters from church groups, and the OWI condemned the lyrics, he wired Wallis and Irving Berlin: "We will be very wise if we immediately change this chorus, therefore you should wire me new lyrics at once. Suggest new words, Dressed up to Win, etc. This movement may result in very serious damage to entire production and to us personally because when mass church organizations start after you, you haven't got a leg to stand on."

The chorus was changed in favor of a montage of scenes that built to a crescendo orchestrated by Curtiz. Max Wilk remembered, "We had acquired a new commanding officer—Mike Curtiz." According to Wilk, Curtiz "would turn out to be a more demanding and critical boss than any drill sergeant, but from *him,* we'd accept it without a murmur. Curtiz had a hell of a lot more talent than any officer we'd had to deal with."

Warner Bros. carpenters swarmed over Stage 22 and built a huge set—"a veritable Mount Everest"—of ramps and moving stairs along with a forty-foot statue of Uncle Sam and a huge American bald eagle. It was the patriotic equivalent of the towering Astarte set in *Sodom und Gommorrha* or the Temple of Jaghuth from *Noah's Ark,* except there would be no intervention of a biblical cataclysm. The army contingent from Camp TITA resembled a bull's-eye seated on the massive set. Curtiz exclaimed, "Ve got to fill up de goddamn Uncle Sam!" The studio had the War Department truck in hundreds more soldiers in uniform, some of whom were bearing flags of all the Allied countries. After days of rehearsals, Curtiz shot the scene from an elevated crane dolly that took him almost to the roof of Stage 22. Hundreds of arc lights illuminated more than six hundred soldiers, who lip-synched the playback lyrics of Berlin's "This Time Is the Last Time." The word *kill* was changed to *win,* and the bayonets remained in their scabbards. It took two exhausting days before Curtiz was satisfied.

Because of the war, Curtiz's salary became an issue. The Wage Stabilization Act enacted in October 1942 froze prices, wages, and salaries at current levels in an attempt to combat inflation during wartime. This requirement was piled on to the complicated process of using contracted actors who could draw military pay only during the picture. *This Is the Army* actors and technicians who were not in the military were paid at greatly reduced rates. Reagan was paid his lieutenant's stipend of $250 per month; MGM received $28,333 for George Murphy, as the actor voluntarily worked for free. The practical effect of wartime regulations and patriotic volunteerism significantly lowered the outlay for a picture whose profits were already pledged. Curtiz voluntarily contributed his directing services, but his constant need for cash put him in a bind. Studio attorneys wrote a letter to the government about the director's predicament: "Mr. Curtiz has agreed, as a patriotic gesture, to render his services as the director of *This Is the Army* without compensation. Unfortunately, Mr. Curtiz finds himself in a position where he is in need of funds; he has frankly explained the situation to our client and has requested a loan of the sum of $40,000 to be advanced to him over a period of twelve weeks. The sum is to be deducted from the salary of Mr. Curtiz after he completes his work on *This Is the Army* and he is again assigned to a regular commercial production." After the government approved the arrangement, Warner's legal department head, Roy Obringer, relayed the following instructions:

> Please charge Mike Curtiz's salary from Feb 17 until he completes directing *This Is the Army* into an undisclosed account so that no salary paid to Curtiz will be charged to *This Is the Army*. We are entitled to have Curtiz direct a picture for us without cost either during 1943 or 1944 or, in the alternative, if the Wage Stabilization Act is repealed, to modify his contract so that the compensation payable to him during the period of 2 years after the repeal will be reduced in the aggregate by the amount he is paid while directing *This Is the Army*.

Curtiz went along with the conditions of the loan but couldn't help noticing that Hal Wallis and the Warners didn't offer to waive a penny of their salaries. One can't help wondering what, if any, role Jack Warner played in Curtiz's "patriotic gesture" to forgo his salary for the picture. The renewal of the director's contract on April 10, 1943, boosted his pay to four thousand dollars per week for fifty-two weeks and included an eight-week layoff period.

In addition to the pay hassle, Curtiz was aggravated by the fragmented nature of the production. Hal Wallis lamented "the peculiar manner in which we are forced to shoot the 'Army' picture, with principals tied up in the numbers, waiting for orchestrations, waiting for certain personalities to sing the songs, etc." Also onerous was the chore of providing direction to active-duty soldiers through their noncommissioned officers, who hadn't yet mastered the rudiments of "Curtiz spoken here." Joan Leslie recalled his direction of a scene shot down the coast in Oceanside:

> It was a simple little scene, a short scene. But we ran into all kinds of trouble. There we were in the middle of a gravel pit at Camp Pendleton with soldiers and everybody standing around. This was a "no privacy" movie set. Curtiz was up on a crane trying to get the camera angle for a demanding shot. . . . Many things went wrong and that's when he got all out of sorts and he was out of temper and I don't blame him. It was really difficult. He had to make up a love story that started with George Murphy and Rosemary DeCamp. It came up to Ronald Reagan and me, and this story had to be woven into a plot. And still he had to show all of those vaudeville acts and make it seem entertaining. As you know, this didn't always work.

Curtiz made it all work. *This Is the Army* would be his biggest Warner Bros. success as measured by first-run box-office numbers. The film on its initial release realized an incredible $9,309,000 against a cost of $1,870,000. It was Hollywood's highest-grossing film of the year. Harry Warner had Senator Happy Chandler of Kentucky enter his letter into the *Congressional Record* on December 18, 1944, noting that Warner Bros.' donations to the Army Emergency Relief Fund were projected to reach $7 million. A memorandum in the archival files recorded that $7,550,000 would be eventually forwarded to the relief fund. A 1955 re-release of the film grossed millions more; this time the money flowed directly into the studio coffers. Curtiz's reputation was buoyed by the smashing success. But being recognized as one of Hollywood's most successful directors would be followed by a dose of humility.

On August 8 he began direction of the long-anticipated *Casablanca* sequel that wasn't a sequel. *Passage to Marseille* was based on the Charles Nordhoff and James Norman Hall novel *Men without Country*. The story involved five French escapees from Devil's Island, picked up by a French freighter manned by a divisive mixture of Free French adherents and a pro-Vichy contingent. The studio spent six months in preproduction, including half of that time building a French freighter mock-up inside Stage 21. A quartet of *Casablanca* principles was reunited; Bogart, Rains, Lorre, and Greenstreet; Michèle Morgan was added as Bogart's loyal wife. Curtiz finally got to cast Philip Dorn along with the stock company ensemble of Victor Francen, George Tobias, and Helmut Dantine. James Wong Howe was cinematographer, Max Steiner scored, and the Casey Robinson–Jack Moffitt script seemed solid. It appeared that Curtiz possessed all the ingredients for a hit wartime melodrama, but it wasn't meant to be.

He experienced misgivings during preproduction. Already reading the tea leaves concerning Hal Wallis's future at the studio, Curtiz bypassed the producer and sent Jack Warner a wire expressing his concern about the studio's $2 million investment in *Passage to Marseille,* as the war might be concluded before the picture was released. He was wrong about the timing of the war's end, but he was rightly concerned about the commercial viability of an expensive war-themed picture.

The film's 110-minute running time seemed even longer because of the complex, three-flashback-deep narrative initiated by Claude Rains as a French aviation captain, Freycinet, speaking to a war correspondent, Manning (John Loder) at a Free French air squadron in England. The confusing story becomes further weighted down by excessive dialogue. Bogart stars as a gutsy French editor, Jean Matrac, whose liberal crusading gets him railroaded into Devil's Island. He leads Lorre, Dorn, Tobias, and Dantine in a daring escape through the jungle to be picked up by the aforementioned freighter. Matrac circumvents a mutiny engineered by a swinish Major Duval (Greenstreet) and shoots down a German dive-bomber before dying heroically as a pilot for the Free French. The most contentious sequence has Matrac machine-gunning the German survivors clinging to the debris of the downed plane. After finishing the crew off, Matrac gestures at the French sailors killed by the airplane strewn about the decks and clips off to Captain Malo (Victor Francen), "Look about you and tell *me* who are the assassins." This slice of wartime realism kicked up a brisk squall of protest from various religious groups and earned the picture a B rating from the Legion of Decency. Warner Bros. didn't entirely roll over this time. The original scene was left intact for domestic releases, although the OWI ordered it excised from foreign distribution prints.

Bogart may have envisioned Jack Warner thrashing about in the water as he took aim on the German aircrew. In addition to coping with his unraveling marriage to the alcoholic Mayo Methot, the actor had been forced by Warner to star in *Conflict*, a noirish mystery that he had refused to do unless the script was rewritten. The actor reneged when he thought the revised script was worse than the original. Warner was livid. He told Wallis, "If you can get [Jean] Gabin for *Marseille*, by all means do so." Bogart eventually gave in to Warner's arm-twisting and appeared in *Conflict*, which wrapped two weeks after *Passage to Marseille* began production.

No one was happy during the making of *Marseille*. Philip Dorn had a bad knee, Lorre didn't know his lines, and the unhappy Bogart remained surly throughout the nearly four-month production. He remarked afterward that anyone could have played his role. Curtiz zeroed in on Michèle Morgan and sought to break her down in order to mold her performance. Morgan despised him:

> Within hours, he proves to be the most unpleasant director I've ever known. He looks like a Tartar, and this Hungarian is a terror. Somehow I have become his mark, his pet peeve, his scapegoat. He is a sadist, watching for (no, expecting) each of my failings. Of course, the more he does this the more I make mistakes. Before and after each take, there is an insulting comment, a wounding word, anything to break me and hurt my already low morale. Each night I have trouble to sleep, dreading the next day, knowing I'll have to go back to my torturer.

According to Morgan, her costar wasn't exactly supportive either. Bogart showed "nothing but morose neutrality. He had his own problems, mostly marital. He hadn't yet met Lauren Bacall. On the first days of shooting, Bogart distanced himself from Curtiz by telling him off, with a few choice words."

Curtiz was at odds with nearly everyone as the picture slipped behind schedule. He confronted Bogart one morning after the star arrived on set, disheveled from the previous evening, as noted by the production assistant Eric Stacey: "The rest of delays during the day were due to Humphrey Bogart (this information from Mr. Curtiz) suffering from a very bad hangover and being very unruly and hard to manage; Mike said he lost an hour and a half through the day due to Bogart's condition and he did not complete the work he planned for the day."

Curtiz also quarreled with Howe over his glacial pace and a perceived

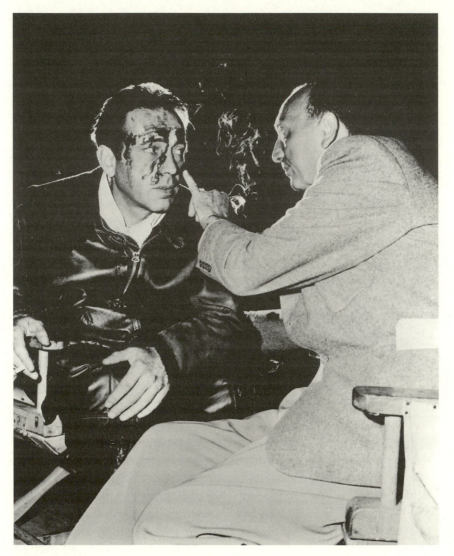

Curtiz applies faux blood to Bogie's face in *Passage to Marseille* (1944) (courtesy of the Academy of Motion Picture Arts and Sciences).

lack of initiative. Howe eventually walked off the picture on October 2. Stacey submitted a detailed report:

> Considerable trouble caused today through Jimmy Howe deciding to walk off the picture. This was straightened out and Jimmy

returned to work right after lunch. . . . The reason for the late start was a very complicated boom shot through fog. Jimmy Howe wanting to quit is connected with the various electrical problems on this stage. The root trouble with all this lies in Mr. Curtiz himself and not in Jimmy Howe. It is an old story that all of us know so well and if Mike would only be patient and not try to run the Camera Dept., the Effects Dept., the Electrical Dept. and all the other departments and give orders all day long everyone would be able to function more efficiently. By Jimmy threatening to quit and walk off the show, he was endeavoring to protect the Electrical Dept. who were having trouble keeping the arc from flickering. . . . He was trying to stand up for his gaffer who was getting the brunt of the squawks from Mike.

Curtiz also created a confrontation with the effects supervisor, Sid Loranger, who rigged the explosives to the prop ship and was assigned to trigger them during the battle sequence with the airplane. Curtiz kept moving George Tobias toward the explosions until he was too close. Loranger intervened and advised Curtiz, "The actor is going to get hurt; I will not activate these effects." Curtiz told Loranger he was fired. When Loranger began disconnecting the wiring to the charges, Curtiz demanded to know what he was doing. The effects man responded: "Nobody is going to trigger these devices that I installed." Curtiz flew into a rage and summoned Tenny Wright to the set. After assessing the situation, Wright chewed out Curtiz, telling him that Loranger would remain as the effects supervisor. Filming resumed with Tobias positioned a safe distance away from the explosive charges.

Adding to the overall discord was the deteriorating relationship between Wallis and Jack Warner. At the end of November, Warner sent Wallis an apoplectic telegram accusing the producer of hogging credit for his productions by deliberately omitting Warner's name from a newspaper story. After receiving Wallis's response, which blamed the reporter for excising Warner's name, the studio chief all but accused his executive producer of being a liar: "Stop giving me double talk on your publicity. . . . I will take legal action if my name has been eliminated from any article or story in any form shape or manner as being in charge production while you were executive producer and in charge production since your new contract commenced."

In a telegram to Charles Einfeld, Warner complained about Wallis:

"Sick and tired of taking all credit and I become small boy and doing most of work."

Jack had inadvertently pinpointed his own behavior. Like the kid who doesn't get picked for the playground team, his jealousy resembled that of a petulant child.

By the beginning of 1944, the team of Warner, Wallis, and Curtiz, which had spawned so many successful movies, entered cinematic hospice as Wallis contemplated life after Warner Bros.

With the help of Don Siegel and a second unit, Curtiz finished *Passage to Marseille* twelve days behind schedule. The picture was a dud, losing $417,000, although the foreign release eventually put it in the black.

Needing a rebound, Curtiz was assigned the lighthearted *Janie*. Thematically similar to the director's *Four Daughters* and its follow-ups, *Janie* was adapted from a hit Broadway play. The encroachment of an army base upsets the routine in the idyllic town of Hortonville and especially the love life of Janie Conway (Joyce Reynolds) and her boyfriend, "Scooper" Nolan (the newcomer Richard Erdman).

For the eighteen-year-old Erdman, *Janie* was the stuff that dreams are made of. A chum from Hollywood High, the future director Albert Band, landed a job at Warner Bros. and read the script for *Janie*. Believing that his pal was perfect for the Scooper role, Band notified the casting office about Erdman, who worked two newspaper routes each morning to support himself and his mother, a waitress at the Ivar House restaurant in Hollywood. Before he realized what was happening, the young thespian, whose experience hadn't progressed much further than a high school play opposite his classmate Gloria Grahame, was being ushered into Curtiz's inner sanctum. Seven decades later, Erdman was still a working actor, and his memory of his initial encounter with Curtiz remained indelible:

> If there was a god on the Warner Bros. lot at that time, it was Mike Curtiz. He was fifty-seven years old when I met him. He emerged from his inner office wearing jodhpurs, a plaid sport jacket, and a cravat. And riding boots. His head was smallish, bald, tan, and atop his burly upper torso, it gave him the appearance of a very alert turtle. He glanced at me, blinked and then said, in a very thick Hungarian accent: "Do-ink for me dee scene vid dee Janie, on dee beach." "Yessir!" "In ten minutes." "Yessir." "After phone call." "I'll be ready." He nodded, turned to his secretary, Esther: "Get writer-bums on phone. Now!" I studied

the script. *Dee scene vid dee Janie, on dee beach* was short. I read it and read it and read it. "Writer-bums!" growled Curtiz as he stormed out of his office. Then he turned to me as his expression changed abruptly.

A benign, considerate smile creased his face.

"Esusink," he said. Gently. "Do-ink for me now dee scene."

But I didn't read. I had the short scene memorized. I turned to Esther-Janie and performed the scene with all the energy I could summon up. She cued me as well as any secretary could and when we finished I just stopped. I couldn't bring myself to look at Curtiz. "Do-ink again," he said politely. "Exactly dee same. Only better. Do-ink now."

"Yessir!" I said. And we did it again, better, I felt.

Curtiz nodded, watching me. Then he turned to Esther.

"Talk do dee Alex Gottlieb. And dee Friedman. Making contract." Then he turned to me. "You are Scoopy," he said. Two days later I was signed to play Scooper Nolan with a seven-year contract. With Warner Bros. and Michael Curtiz as my champion. "It's the Lord's will," said Mother. I agreed with her, although His Name was Michael Curtiz as far as I was concerned.

Janie did more than launch Erdman's career. Audiences weary of war and war movies turned out in droves. Al Jolson sent his old pal Jack Warner a telegram after a preview: "Saw *Janie* last night. Warner Bros. stock should be selling at 100 a share. Not only should you feel proud but also Mike Curtiz, Gottlieb and everyone connected with it. I never heard an audience scream and yell so much in my life."

The movie's schmaltzy charm of fictional teenage life in small-town America went over big in the summer of 1944. The picture grossed more than $1.7 million over its cost.

By the time *Janie* was released, the Allies had landed in France and the tide of the war had turned. Hal Wallis had left the studio, and Curtiz, with his *Casablanca* Oscar resting on the mantel at the Canoga Ranch, remained on top.

26

Victory Garden

The war years sped by for Curtiz. Long days at the studio were interspersed with leisure time on Saturday nights and Sundays at the Canoga Ranch. Though his dedication to polo began to taper off, Curtiz's passion for shooting skeet remained constant. He wore a jacket around the ranch adorned with a sleeve patch that bore a "50" insignia, indicating that he'd successfully hit fifty consecutive targets without a miss.

World War II motivated everyone to support the Allied cause. John Meredyth Lucas remembered "the war had gotten Mother out of bed." Bess became involved with the British War Relief Society during the early years of the war. She joined Virginia Zanuck and many other friends in supporting "Bundles for Britain." Started in a New York City storefront, the wartime charity ultimately delivered $1,500,000 in clothing to a belt-tightened United Kingdom along with another million in cash.

Then there were the ubiquitous victory gardens championed by the government to support the war effort. Bess seeded a large plot adjacent to the main house to raise vegetables for the family table. Although she diligently tended the garden, it wasn't productive; the local rabbit population became nighttime saboteurs. After an unsuccessful attempt to fence off the garden from the pests, Curtiz initiated an evening stakeout with his shotgun. After spotting a rabbit, Curtiz shot it in the leg, then experienced an epiphany as the injured creature piteously attempted to drag itself to safety. According to John Meredyth Lucas, the episode brought forth a compassionate side from Curtiz that was rarely witnessed on a film set:

> Mike watched, horror-stricken. Then, calling for help, he carefully captured the wounded rabbit. We had a veterinarian we used for all our dogs. Mike had Mother get the vet out of bed and took the rabbit to the animal hospital. The rabbit made a

slow but satisfactory recovery and was ultimately turned loose on the ranch again. "Why hell we need garden?" Mike asked Mother. "We doesn't eat much vegetable." Henceforth we bought our greens at the market. Mike had always loved rabbit cooked the French provincial way, but as far as I know, he never again ordered this dish.

On April 4, 1944, Jack Warner voided Wallis's contract after accusing him of negotiating with other studios just as the two men were in the midst of arranging a financial settlement. After reviewing multiple offers from nearly every studio in town, along with one from J. Arthur Rank in Great Britain, Wallis decided to set up shop at Paramount Pictures in July 1944. He initiated a partnership with Joseph Hazen, a disaffected Warner Bros. financial vice president. Their company's agreement with Paramount's president, Barney Balaban, was refreshingly simple. Wallis produced whatever movies he wanted with no interference. He delivered the completed negatives to Paramount and divided up the money with the studio.

Wallis began building up his own stable of contracted talent. He wooed Curtiz to join him as his principal director. Curtiz wavered briefly—Wallis was a trusted friend—but decided to stay where he was. The studio in Burbank had been his home for nearly two decades, and Wallis—the new Wallis, out from under the aegis of Warner Bros. and its considerable resources—was not yet a proven commodity. Curtiz also wanted to make more money, and Wallis had a justified reputation as one of the stingiest men in Hollywood. Unable to land Curtiz, Wallis opted for William Dieterle, the former Warner effects supervisor Byron Haskin, and the director Lewis Allen. The trio would helm a number of popular postwar film noirs for Wallis's company.

With Wallis gone, Curtiz experienced a sense of liberation. He also sensed that Jack Warner would never again share power as he had done with Zanuck and Wallis, and he thus reasoned that he would now have greater access to the studio chief concerning creative decisions. He began to formulate definitive plans to produce his own pictures. Curtiz was a hot commodity, as a letter from Darryl F. Zanuck to Jack Warner in November 1944 demonstrates:

My dear Jack: I wondered why you avoided me before you left for the East. . . . I am now certain, after receiving your letter, that it had to do with none other than our old Hungarian friend, Mike Curtiz. . . . I have not directly or indirectly made Mike Curtiz an offer to come to Twentieth Century-Fox, nor has anyone else associated with this company made him an offer. I have heard, however, that David Selznick, Hal Wallis, and Bill Goetz have made Mike offers. I do not want to make a definite accusation, but nevertheless my information on this subject comes from reliable sources. . . . None of this, however, justifies me in stealing anyone from anyone else or in any unfair practice. On the other hand, if Mike Curtiz ends up with Wallis or Goetz or Selznick, what have you gained? You should have an understanding with Mike and if you are going to sign him you should sign him now. If you fail to sign him, then he is on the open market, and I will do my utmost to convince him to come with us.

While Warner pondered how to keep his top director content, future events would show that Curtiz was prescient about the nature of Wallis's successor. There wasn't one. Instead, Warner elevated Steve Trilling from casting director to chief assistant, the line producers reporting to Warner via Trilling. Although Trilling was administratively competent and affable, his principal attribute was abject fealty to Warner. According to the production assistant Martin Jurow: "Steve Trilling was Jack Warner's executive assistant. Poor man! J. L. treated him shamefully, working him without mercy and without a single word of praise or gratitude. Everyone brought their complaints to Steve, with gripes ranging from the location of their dressing rooms to their desire for more publicity. When Steve relayed them to J. L., the bombastic studio chief was always ready to shoot the messenger."

Curtiz was already communicating directly with Warner about assignments. In February he turned down *God Is My Co-Pilot,* writing to the studio chief: "I have continued to read and re-read *God Is My Co-Pilot* in the hope I could work out a satisfactory solution to the many problems the present script presents. Unfortunately, I have not been successful. . . . As it stands now, there is so much included that is cliché and routine and so little that is honest and interesting and new. All in all, the story seems much less worth the effort and hardship and financial outlay that will be required."

God Is My Co-Pilot was reassigned to Robert Florey and became a syrupy war programmer that was released a month before V-E Day. Instead, Curtiz's next assignment became *Roughly Speaking.* Warner Bros. purchased the best-selling autobiography of the novelist Louise Randall Pierson for $35,000. Her saga of youthful poverty after the death of her spendthrift father is the beginning of a lengthy story of college, marriage, four children, and a divorce, all followed by nursing her kids through the trauma of polio. Pierson's second marriage, which added another child, was accompanied by financial success that evaporated during the Depression and was subsequently renewed as her sons enlisted to fight in World War II. Pierson's four-decade odyssey as a liberated woman was a challenging project; the chronicle was difficult even for Curtiz to compress into a coherently paced comedy-drama. Lengthy running times were anathema to Jack Warner. An initial 150-minute cut was edited down to 125 minutes, then trimmed to 117 minutes before general release in February 1945.

Pierson was anointed as the film's technical adviser; the screenwriter Catherine Turney condensed the author's memoir into a viable shooting script. When Curtiz suggested to Pierson that he wanted Rosalind Russell to portray her, the writer was doubtful: "But we don't look anything alike!" Curtiz knew that none of the Warner female stars could portray Pierson's Yale-buffed veneer embedded with self-determined grit. He explained to Pierson that movie acting was not about physical similarity, but who could best convey the story while entertaining the audience: "How much better if the people do not look like the real people. Then you are not confined by what the real person was like, what the real person's reaction was. You create a new character who happens to be in the same situation."

Ann Doran, who was in the film, remembered visiting with Pierson at the Hollywood premiere of *Roughly Speaking:* "She [Pierson] was ecstatic. She said, 'There were facets of it [her life] I didn't realize even as I was going through it at the time.' But this was Mike's idea. . . . He looked at everything as the impact on the audience, what it was going to mean to them. And he gave them more of an impact than the real. . . . Even though truth is stranger than fiction, sometimes it is not as moving as fiction. And he gave that story so much more because he did play against type. But this was Mike."

Jack Warner had dispersed all of Wallis's ongoing projects to his stable of producers. First among equals were the veteran Henry Blanke and the fast-rising Jerry Wald. Blanke and Curtiz had been extremely close for years, although their volatility could make the working relationship ap-

Curtiz with his friend and mentor Henry Blanke (courtesy of the Lucas family).

pear adversarial. Ann Doran recalled being startled by their deportment, noting that "Blanke would come on the set and the two of them would scream and holler at each other and then I'd find out afterwards that they were just discussing where they were going to have dinner that night."

In addition to Rosalind Russell, *Roughly Speaking* also showcased the multitalented Jack Carson as Pierson's second husband, Harold. Carson could sing, dance, and play both comedic and dramatic parts. "I don't know if anyone really appreciated how talented Jack Carson was," said Joan Leslie, who costarred with him in *The Hard Way*. "He could do everything." Curtiz, who would use him in six pictures, had the utmost respect for Carson. Usually cast as the fast talker or stumblebum sidekick who never gets the girl, Carson was gratified that he got to clinch with

Russell just before the final fade-out. "But don't think I am giving up laughs for sighs," said the self-deprecating actor to a reporter. "It's just that some kind-hearted person has got the idea that I wouldn't frighten all the girls, that perhaps a few might tolerate me in a romantic scene."

The large number of Randall-Pierson children in the cast created opportunities for several neophyte actors. After receiving a medical discharge from the navy in 1944, Robert Arthur borrowed money and traveled to Hollywood from his hometown of Aberdeen, Washington. He had virtually no experience other than a few high school plays and winning a radio announcer's contest when he was fourteen. His ex-vaudevillian landlady lined him up with an agent, and he began haunting the studio casting offices. Curtiz agreed to hear him read for *Roughly Speaking*: "For Mr. Curtiz, I worked up a scene between a boy and girl and played both parts. Everybody laughed, except Mr. Curtiz. 'Vot is dot scene?' Curtiz asked. 'It's a comedy scene,' I replied. 'But your character, Frankie, Mrs. Pierson's youngest son, is going avay to vor.' So, to get in the right mood, I thought about the time my dog died, doing the scene over again in a serious manner. 'Hire dot boy,' instructed Curtiz. 'He'll break dair hearts.'"

After being signed for a week and extended for two more, Arthur leveraged an opportunity during a scene filmed around a dining room table:

I have to toast my mother on her birthday and say, "Ma, I think you're swell and I love you." Mr. Curtiz called out, "Keep the cameras on Bobby. Let's see vot he can do vit dis scene." So, I ad-libbed a lot of banter with Jack Carson about the wine we were all drinking, saying things like, "Ma, this is the first wine, I've ever had—officially." And made something of the scene. Miss Russell was off-camera giving me wonderful support. On the strength of this scene, Warners gave me a seven-year contract.

The first day Arthur walked on the set, Louise Randall Pierson spotted him and declared, "My God, it's Frankie!" Arthur ended up living with Pierson, her husband. and their son Frank for two years.[1] The movie was an intoxicating experience for Curtiz as well. There were no more notes from Wallis scolding him about changing the script or exhorting him to minimize camera angles. *Roughly Speaking* is one of Curtiz's most overlooked films. Highlighted by Russell's stellar turn, it is a heartwarming picture: well written, nicely performed, and beautifully shot. The finale in a crowded soundstage that doubles for New York's Grand Central Station is a singular example of Curtiz's ability to imbue sentimental intimacy into a scene frantic with people.

Although reviews were uniformly positive, there was muted criticism that the film didn't possess the depth of Pierson's best-selling memoir because of the protracted story line, which was too complex for the screen. *Roughly Speaking* was not a financial success. Although the picture took more than a decade to earn back its investment of $2,156,000, it was a different kind of movie for Curtiz, as it concerned the life of a divorced single mother. He would double down on that theme with his next picture, which was in the forefront of a new style of postwar American movies.

James M. Cain was originally offered $25,000 from MGM in 1935 for the screen rights to *Double Indemnity*. He was not amused when the studio reneged on the offer because of pressure from the PCA. Eight years later he accepted $15,000 from Paramount for the rights—Joe Breen's ardent enforcement of the Production Code effectively cost him ten grand. Cain was a newspaper writer who went to Hollywood to scribe for the movies, but he never acquired the knack of effective screenwriting.[2] His novels were a different matter. The world according to Cain was a blunt instrument lashed together by untidy people, dark corners, and bad endings. His unique style of first-person narration, characterized by the absence of formal dialogue identification, constituted a new form of popular literature. Cain's work was perfectly timed to be in the vanguard of the post–World War II film noir movement.

The script of *Double Indemnity,* eventually penned by Billy Wilder and Raymond Chandler, was approved by the PCA in 1943, and the picture was released by Paramount the next year. It was followed by a host of other films laden with themes of avarice, adultery, murder, and sexual obsession that reflected a hybrid style that would later be termed film noir. The war, hard-boiled crime fiction, and émigré directors ushered in a new mode of cinema that plumbed the darker aspects of contemporary society. To an extent, the studio system was growing up with the country.

Cain published *Mildred Pierce* in 1941. It deviated from the testosterone-tinged tenor of his previous novels. His protagonist was a woman who emerges from the shambles of a Depression-era divorce to build a successful restaurant chain. Mildred's will to control everyone in her orbit becomes sidetracked by her bottomless craving for the withheld love of her daughter, Veda. Veda is an operatic singer whose manipulation eventually destroys her mother's success. In her fruitless pursuit of Veda's affection, Mildred loses everything, including her second husband, Monte, a craven weakling who has an affair with Veda. In the finale Mildred is back in her bungalow, preparing to break open a bottle to get smashed with Bert, her first husband. Getting this sordid saga onscreen would take some doing.

Mildred Pierce became the brainchild of the producer Jerry Wald. The title role would go to Joan Crawford, who was scooped up by Warners after being jettisoned by MGM in 1944 as box-office poison. If not for the tenacious efforts of Wald, the studio would have missed out on a huge hit film and a legendary comeback by a great star.

Of the numerous type-A personalities who swelled the ranks of the movie business, Jerry Wald was the whirlingest dervish of them all. He began as a kid writer with a nose for selling radio stars, and himself, when he landed at Warner Bros. as a neophyte screenwriter in 1934. The young comer possessed an innate talent for ingratiating himself with those who were more experienced—the Epsteins, Richard Macaulay, Mark Hellinger—in order to learn the ropes while they did most of the heavy lifting. Wald was an idea guy: he gushed forth scenarios, treatments, script ideas, film titles, and casting choices like a bubbling spring. The director Curtis Bernhardt remembered: "Jerry Wald's enthusiasm was something to behold. In story conferences, he would jump up and pace up and down, telling us a big scene that he thought up. Then, one of us would say, 'But Jerry, that's shit.' He'd respond, 'Okay, I've got another idea.' He was a completely intelligent guy, always had a new idea, never got discouraged."

Maintaining a file of more than two thousand stories that had piqued his interest, Wald conceived endless scenarios while understanding what was necessary to turn his visions into reality as well. He also tended to relationships better than any other producer on the lot. In stark contrast to Hal Wallis, Wald was a tireless cheerleader. He spewed out countless memos that encouraged, complimented, and stroked. With *The Hard Way* (1943), *Destination Tokyo* (1943), *The Very Thought of You* (1944), and *Objective, Burma!* (1945), Jerry Wald was on the ascent at Warner Bros.

Joan Crawford was on an opposite trajectory. Always looking for a bargain, Jack Warner signed her for one-third less than her former MGM salary. He didn't even greet her when she arrived at Burbank. "That has-been!" he grumbled to his assistant, Martin Jurow. "Why waste my time? We're only using her because Stanwyck's too busy. I've got better things to do than to say hello to that dame." Warner's view of Crawford as a default selection for *Mildred Pierce* may not have been entirely accurate. Barbara Stanwyck was quoted late in life as being ardent in her desire to portray Mildred: "I desperately wanted the part. I went after it. I knew what a role for a woman it was, and I knew I could handle every facet of Mildred. I laid my cards on the table with Jerry Wald. After all, I'd done a dozen pictures at Warner's, including *So Big* and *Meet John Doe*. I'd paid my dues. I felt Mildred was me."

This story suggests that Wald was wooing Crawford for the role from the very beginning; Curtiz strongly favored Stanwyck until Crawford humbled herself by doing a screen test that won him over.[3] She didn't have a lot of competition. Bette Davis turned the part down, declaring afterward, "I didn't want to do a rags-to-riches melodrama and I couldn't stand to work for Curtiz again." Ditto for Ann Sheridan. "I didn't like the story," admitted the so-called Oomph Girl. "Mildred was too tough and the kid was a horror." Joan Crawford hadn't starred in a feature film in nearly two years. Since arriving at Warners in 1944, she'd made a solitary cameo appearance in *Hollywood Canteen* (1944) and inflamed Jack Warner by turning down a series of formulaic scripts. At one point, Crawford reputedly asked Warner to take her off salary since she wasn't working. The stunned studio chief didn't know what to make of his new star. How the hell did they run things over at MGM, anyway?

At Wald's urging, she reread *Mildred Pierce*. Cain's novel both intrigued and frightened her. Viewed in the context of future allegations, Crawford offered this irony-tinged platitude for the *Saturday Evening Post*: "As I have two adopted children, I felt I could understand Mildred and do the role justice." This opinion was issued for public consumption after she had received her Oscar for *Mildred Pierce*. Her initial assessment was considerably less sanguine. Although she was pushing forty, Crawford had little inclination to portray the mother of a teenage daughter who seduces her second husband. The former Lucille LeSueur, who had overcome a rotten childhood to become one of Metro's biggest stars, was keenly self-aware, however. She realized that *Mildred Pierce* was likely the last, best chance to regain her lost luster.

To helm the picture, Wald briefly fantasized about Metro's George Cukor, Hollywood's leading "woman's director." After receiving a quick return to reality from Jack Warner, he formally requested Curtiz in a memo to Trilling on July 7, 1944. Curtiz was interested but wary. He considered Crawford a has-been whose time (and shoulder pads) had come and gone.

Before he convinced Jack Warner to buy the rights, Wald had engaged James M. Cain to write a treatment of his novel. Cain couldn't master it even after Wald suggested relating the story in flashback and adding a murder in order to add the dramatic climax that was missing from the novel. Wald next had a story analyst, Thames Williamson, write a treatment. Williamson incorporated Wald's flashback notion, later claiming credit for originating that idea. Williamson's treatment included a pair of changes from the novel retained in the final screenplay: Mildred doesn't have an extramarital affair with either her business partner, Wally, or her eventual second husband, Monte. Bert, her first husband, becomes less of a Caspar Milquetoast, and his affair with his neighbor Maggie Bieder-hof is diluted into a questionable friendship. Williamson also folded in Wald's desire for a murder—Mildred kills Veda after discovering her with Monte—to give the story the dramatic angle it was missing. This scene was later dropped.

Wald viewed the inclusion of a murder and its resolution as critical to successfully overcome the PCA's "compensating moral values" hurdle. Jack Warner had Williamson's treatment sent to Breen for review. The censor rejected it outright: "The story contains so many sordid and repellent elements that we feel that the finished picture would not only be highly questionable from the standpoint of the Code, but would, likewise, meet with a great deal of difficulty in its release—not only through Censor Boards, but from other public groups as well. . . . In the face of all this, we respectfully suggest that you dismiss this story from any further consideration."

Following Breen's rejection, Jack Warner wrote Wald a memo in which he suggested that the project be canceled.

Instead, Wald persevered and arranged a meeting with a representative from Breen's staff and the story editor James Geller. The producer recommended a different perspective that would place the screenplay on "a higher level, and that this approach could solve the Breen Office objections." This information was relayed to Warner, who authorized purchase of the *Mildred Pierce* rights on March 14, 1944. Roy Obringer wrote a detailed memo about the development of the shooting script that summarizes Jerry Wald's preproduction methodology:[4] "Mr. Wald does not develop a story from script to script in chronological fashion. He employs the services of a number of writers without previous acquaintance with the work of the others on the same script, in order that a full-scale contribution may be made by each writer. Mr. Wald organizes the story in his own mind on the basis of his selection and synthesizing of the work of the different writers. He must, therefore, be considered the originator and organizer of the story, regardless of a chronological line of development."

The use of different writers to develop *Casablanca* and *Mildred Pierce* was strikingly similar, with a notable exception. A significant difference between Hal Wallis and Jerry Wald was that Wallis knew what he wanted for *Casablanca* when it revealed itself to him on the page, whereas Wald knew exactly how *Mildred Pierce* should be adapted for the screen. It became a protracted struggle for him to find a writer who would do it his way.

Although he promised Williamson an opportunity to write the screenplay as a reward for his initial work, Wald instead assigned it to Catherine Turney. Turney was a skilled playwright and novelist who specialized in what Jack Warner termed "women's pictures." Even though her characters suffered through the usual soap-opera entanglements, they were talented, independent women who projected strength in crisis rather than emotively dabbing their eyes with a handkerchief. Wald thought Turney would be the perfect writer to bring *Mildred Pierce* to life onscreen.

She wrote a screenplay adapted from Cain's novel without flashback or murder. She shaded out the explicit sexual situations and revamped Veda from an operatic soprano into a nightclub chanteuse.[5] According to Turney, reducing a six-hundred-page novel to a screenplay of fewer than two hundred pages was a tough chore: "Mr. Warner was absolutely adamant about not having long movies. That meant you had to do an awful lot of maneuvering and cutting and dovetailing to fit a story of that magnitude and that many people into a comparatively small space."

Turney wrote her screenplay as a straight drama, but Wald was keen to replicate the success of *Double Indemnity* and urged her to use the murder and flashback. She ended up writing a pair of *Mildred Pierce* screenplays. The second one, dated August 11, 1944, incorporated both the murder—Veda kills Monte, and Mildred turns her in to the police while contemplating suicide—and the flashback sequence at the police station. Turney included these aspects under duress. She believed Wald's determination to turn *Mildred Pierce* into a murder mystery would spoil the dramatic aspects of Cain's novel: "That is one of the reasons why I didn't get along too well with Jerry Wald. The flashbacks took up an awful lot of footage and took away from the story itself. I thought that another murder story was not as interesting as Mildred's story."

Although much of her screenplay would be used, Turney ended up without a screen credit for ten weeks of work owing to a decision she rued for the rest of her career: "When the final script was delivered to me, the credits were reversed—I was second. It seemed a fair arrangement to me, as Randy [MacDougall] had been working closely with Curtiz . . . but my then agent thought I should remove my name. I had received nothing but solo credits and my agent objected to my being second banana, so to speak. As it turned out, it was a grievous mistake on his and my part."

Turney left *Mildred Pierce* because Bette Davis flexed her muscles and had her assigned to write *A Stolen Life*. Wald couldn't override "the fourth Warner brother" and ended searching for another writer to revise her work.

He selected Ranald MacDougall to write another original screenplay while assigning the novelist William Faulkner to do the same thing. Faulkner's 101-page draft screenplay turned melodrama into Hollywood gothic: Mildred sleepwalks with circles under her eyes that are found to be mascara, Veda swallows poison on her mother's wedding night, and Mildred's business partner and suitor, Wally, is not unlike the cigar-chomping Boss Hogg from the *Dukes of Hazzard* television series. Whether Faulkner was simply amusing himself or out of his depth remains unknown. He had a serious drinking problem and stuck to writing for the movies because he had to make a living. Like Cain, he was a gifted writer who struggled to adapt his prose style to the technique of fitting words to images.[6] His sole contribution was the addition of Lottie, the African American maid who was portrayed in the film by Butterfly McQueen.

MacDougall was the screenwriter whom Wald had been searching for. He rose from teenage usher at Radio City Music Hall to writing radio dramas and had recently scripted the Wald-produced *Objective, Burma!* His expertise in developing radio plays, in which the attention of the audience had to be maintained within the framework of a compressed three-act scenario, proved ideal for condensing an unwieldy novel into a screenplay. He dramatized Turney's adaptation and repurposed portions of the novel into a film noir motif that was part mystery and part melodrama. His creations include the discovery of Monte's body and Mildred's attempt to frame Wally by luring him to the beach house, Mildred's contemplating suicide on the fog-socked pier, and the darkened police station where the avuncular homicide dick conducted Mildred's interrogation, which is where the series of flashbacks originates. He also included a death scene of the younger daughter, Kay, that builds up Mildred's angst over her love of Veda.

MacDougall claimed afterward that he independently arrived at the notion of relating the story in flashback without being prompted by Wald. Either way, he clearly understood how to allow the story to breathe in order for Curtiz's camera to visually advance the narrative. He also fleshed out the transitional nature of Mildred's character from an apron-wearing American hausfrau selling home-baked pies to afford Veda's music lessons into Mildred Pierce Beragon, a case-hardened businesswoman adorned in mink who can toss down whiskey with her female confidante while pining for the love of her daughter from hell. Wald's objective was to have the script in the best shape possible for the start of production on December 4, 1944.

Curtiz eventually bought into Wald's vision. He and Wald had dinner with Cain at the Brown Derby and reviewed the proposed script a month before production began. Curtiz reported afterward that Cain was wildly enthusiastic. The author's feelings about the movie became less passionate, however. In November 1945 he wrote a letter to a colleague about *Mildred Pierce:* "Allowing for all the smart promotion, I still don't see in it an element to make such a smash hit. Part of the trouble is that the book wasn't really so hot—two novels in one, scrambled in a confusing way, and an idea, in addition, that I of all people ought never to have attempted, as it is something for a woman serial writer rather than a man who at least tried to work from situation. However, I should worry. It is grossing fabulously and as No. 2 smash for me, makes me quite hot in Hollywood."

The irony of the situation couldn't have escaped Cain. *Mildred Pierce* lacked much of the perverseness of *Double Indemnity* and *The Postman Always Rings Twice,* which had cost him so much money for the screen rights because of PCA censorship interference. And now Warners was adapting his novel into a feature film with the addition of a lurid murder and a more-over-the-top-than-written Veda character in order to obtain approval from the same censor.

Curtiz required more convincing about the suitability of Crawford. Wald noted that after the initial meeting between Curtiz and Crawford, "the battle of the shoulder pads began. And lipstick. And hair." By Wald's account, Curtiz's apprehension about Crawford's gilded MGM legacy was not without justification: "Mike and I wanted to deglamorize Joan, make her look like a woman who lived in a suburb and bought the cheapest dresses. At first Joan wouldn't go along, but after several lengthy meetings—filled with blood, sweat and tears—we all agreed to make the picture realistic in every aspect."

According to the producer, the first week of production was "full of fights between Curtiz and Crawford. I was the referee. Then everybody settled down and things went smoothly." Lee Patrick, who had a supporting role as Maggie Biederhof, also remembered the initial struggle: "She [Crawford] used to come on the set beautifully turned out and he [Curtiz] kept mussing up her hair and changing her makeup. 'I don't want you to look like an actress,' he kept saying."

Crawford retained a vivid recollection of a confrontation with Curtiz during wardrobe tests:

> For my early scenes, the studio designed some cotton frocks. Mr. Curtiz said *no,* they looked too smart. So I went down to Sears Roebuck on my own and bought the kind of housedresses I thought Mildred would wear. When I arrived on the set for wardrobe tests, Mr. Curtiz walked over to me shouting, "You and your damned Adrian shoulder pads! This stinks!" And he ripped the dress from neck to hem. "Mr. Curtiz," I sobbed, "I bought this dress for two dollars and 98 cents—there are no shoulder pads," and I rushed to my dressing room.

In another version of their initial dust-up, Curtiz requested Wald pay off Crawford and fire her during the first week of production. Luckily this did not occur.

Despite the preliminary fireworks, the director and star were drawn to each other's professionalism. Crawford understood that Curtiz had been testing her as part of marking his directorial territory. "He put me through a postgraduate course in humiliation," said Crawford. "Then, when he found out I could take it, he started training me." Curtiz agreed: "When I started the tests on *Mildred Pierce,* I heard my star was very deefeecult. So I say, okay Crawford, Curtiz will be *more* deefeecult. She took it. Like a trouper."

After the smoke cleared, Curtiz respected Crawford for doing what was best for the film.

Crawford approved costar credit for Jack Carson and Zachary Scott alongside her name on the screen. Her support was most notable during the casting of the key role of Veda. It was a challenge to find a young actress who could credibly portray a duplicitous bitch who transitions from carrying her schoolbooks home to seducing and murdering her stepfather. Crawford willingly participated in many of the screen tests for Veda.

Curtiz provides some sotto voce advice to Joan Crawford during *Mildred Pierce* (1945) (courtesy of the Lucas family).

Some of the twenty-odd actresses who tested for the Veda role included Maxine Cooper, Martha Vickers, Mala Powers, and Bonita Granville. At one point Wald hit on the notion of casting sixteen-year-old Shirley Temple as Veda. After appearing in *Since You Went Away* (1944), Temple had been searching for a choice role to create a new cinematic identity. Curtiz vetoed the notion without even deigning to test Temple: "And who do ve get to play Mildred's lover? Mickey Rooney?"

Ann Blyth was eventually brought in. Crawford played the scene with her while Curtiz hunkered down next to the camera. The seventeen-year-old who had started as a child actress in radio and acted on Broadway as Paul Lukas's daughter in *Watch on the Rhine* was ecstatic to have the opportunity: "Well of course, I was thrilled. Thrilled because Joan Crawford had agreed to do the test with me and that was a big plus. Rather than doing a screen test with another player. Perhaps just even doing your lines off camera with someone. So it just clicked. Everything about the scene we did, it worked."

Not only did Blyth land the part and give a memorable performance as Veda, but her successful screen test initiated an enduring friendship between the actress and director: "I sensed not only that Mike was very pleased, but that he always seemed to be in my corner. I remember we

Curtiz directs Ann Blyth in *Mildred Pierce* (1945). He became her professional champion and friend (courtesy of the Lucas family).

talked about this later on in years when I worked with him again and I wished that had happened more often. . . . He was easy, very easy, to work with. He had a wonderful way and would say all kinds of crazy things, but there was always a twinkle in his eye. . . . I was very, very fond of him."

Her confidence in Curtiz is reflected in the performances by the entire cast. Jack Carson's turn as Wally Fay is a balanced combination of unprincipled ambition and lechery. Zachary Scott's foppish villainy as Monte Beragon reinforced his subsequent typecasting as a cad. Scott wrote a letter to Wald afterward noting, "Mike did a wonderful job," and was "a truly great director." Eve Arden, playing Mildred's close confidante and a wisecracker, noted enthusiastically, "I always enjoyed working with Curtiz, who was one of the few directors who knew what he wanted and was able to express himself exactly, even in his amusing Hungarian accent."

After winning the silver medal as a shot-putter in the 1928 Olympics and making a less-than-memorable appearance as Tarzan in 1935, Herman Brix changed his name to Bruce Bennett, took acting lessons, and worked his way up from Three Stooges shorts and B Westerns. His stolid turn as Mildred's first husband resulted in a career as a Warner contract player. Bennett recalled, "Mike Curtiz . . . was very complimentary and once said that he should have pushed for an Academy Award nomination for me." Lee Patrick remembered Curtiz as a "scrupulous director I enjoyed working with . . . He was just as careful and thoughtful about my contribution as he was with Joan Crawford."

Curtiz wasn't able to get James Wong Howe to shoot the film, but Ernest Haller was superb. Supported by Haller and Anton Grot, Curtiz's mise-en-scène became cinematic artistry. The Laguna Beach tide washing away the opening credits immediately transitions to an oceanfront beach house.[7] Shots ring out and Monte Beragon collapses, gasping Mildred's name in his death rattle as the mirror behind him is pockmarked with bullet holes. After an unidentified woman drives off from the house, there is a dissolve to Mildred on the pier, contemplating suicide before deciding to lure Wally Fay to her beach house. Fay is abandoned in the beach house with Scott's corpse. The beach house becomes a nightmarish prison of spiral staircases, rippled lighting, shadowed reflections, knocked-over lamps, and a ringing telephone. The final portion of the opening takes place in the police station as Mildred encounters her first husband, Bert, who is brought in as a suspect in the murder of her second husband, Monte. As the police detective inquires, Mildred relates her story in flashback.

Curtiz added several flourishes, including the musical number that Veda performs in Wally Fay's nightclub. Wald had the good sense to allow Curtiz to direct the film unmolested while offering unstinting encouragement: "Dear Mike, Just ran last night's dailies again and I am convinced more than ever that the master is at work. My salutations Sahib! Long may you stand behind a camera."

There was some difficulty with the ending, after Veda is revealed as the murderer. According to Curtiz, it was none other than his loyal prop man, Limey Plews, who came up with the notion of having Mildred and her estranged husband, Bert, walk out of the police station into the morning sunlight.

Mildred Pierce is quintessential noir, illuminating the dark side of the American dream. But critical reaction ranged from measured praise to a distinct lack of enthusiasm. By chronicling a period perspective so cynically, the picture was ahead of its time. The *New York Sun* described the characters as "a sordid lot," and the *New York Post* noted that *Mildred Pierce* "injects a heavy shot of gall into Hollywood's milk and honeyed vision of Life in America." Howard Barnes of the *New York Herald Tribune* labeled the film "anemic," whereas the *New York Times* dinged Curtiz for letting Ann Blyth's performance as Veda go over the top.

The criticism mattered little: the release of the picture a little more than a month following the end of the war end was perfectly timed. Audiences particularly appreciated Crawford's performance. Jerry Wald primed the studio publicity department to tout her for an Academy Award even before production wrapped. As Curtiz noted about America's love for the underdog, the Crawford comeback story was tailor-made for the public. Despite his earlier disdain, Jack Warner made her the centerpiece of the film's publicity with the titillating tag line: "Please don't tell anyone what Mildred Pierce did!" The film's press book presented Crawford as a mysterious femme fatale while playing up the suspense perspective by declaring, "No One Seated during Last Seven Minutes!"

After the opening of *Mildred Pierce* on September 28, Wald wrote to Curtiz:

I would like to take my rather worn chapeau off and express my extreme gratitude for what you did with the picture. There is an old axiom which goes, "No man is a hero to his valet." The way you are treated here sometimes makes you wonder if you're appreciated, as you should be. My working with you on PIERCE taught me a lot of things, foremost being always try to do something better, despite obstacles of all kinds. Both Warners and the industry should be grateful to a man like yourself who is trying to lift pictures out of the "great train robbery flickers" to an artistic level.

The Crawford Oscar denouement had the melodrama of a Curtiz production. The star became so overwrought on the night of the ceremony that she took to her bed with a psychosomatic fever. Curtiz accepted her award and presented it to her at bedside as director and star beamed and the flashbulbs popped. *Mildred Pierce* grossed $5,674,000 against a cost of $1,453,000. In addition to Crawford, the film was nominated for five Oscars, including Best Picture. Eve Arden and Ann Blyth canceled each other out for Best Supporting Actress, allowing Anne Revere to win for *National Velvet*. Although not nominated, Curtiz was now hailed as a star reviver. An added benefit was the development of productive relationships with Wald and MacDougall that would carry over to future projects. Connie Wald, the producer's widow and a leading Hollywood hostess for decades, told me: "Jerry adored Mike, simply adored him. He so respected him as one of the truly great directors."

From the sublime results of *Mildred Pierce,* Curtiz spent the balance of the year wrestling with a film that was one of the most unpleasant experiences of his entire career. Jack Warner began negotiations with Cole Porter in May 1943 with the notion of a Technicolor musical biography about the great songwriter as a bookend to *Yankee Doodle Dandy*. The negotiations with Porter for the rights to thirty-five songs along with script approval dragged on for months. Warner Bros. eventually coughed up $300,000, to be paid to the composer over a period of nine years. The composer-producer Arthur Schwartz developed a script treatment that Porter approved. He also okayed Cary Grant to portray him. Grant agreed to a fee of $150,000 and Curtiz as the director. But when his marriage to the heiress Barbara Woolworth Hutton fell apart, the actor secluded himself and things were put off again.

Production was scheduled to start in February 1945, but now Porter was ill in the hospital and couldn't approve script changes. Cary Grant's dissatisfaction with the script resulted in his refusal to begin the picture until May. His influence over *Night and Day* would be a harbinger of significant changes in the postwar motion picture industry. On December 8, 1944, the California Court of Appeals upheld Olivia de Havilland's lawsuit against Warner Bros. The actress and her attorneys took the position that the studio's policy of suspensions violated the state's statute against indentured labor. The unanimous ruling loosened the death grip that the studios maintained on their contracted talent by adding suspension time to existing contracts. The formation of independent production companies by actors and directors loomed over the horizon. The balance of power in Hollywood was shifting away from the movie studios and toward the talent agencies that would package individual film projects for their stars.

In 1945 the studio had little alternative but to play ball with Cary Grant if it wanted to get *Night and Day* made. Grant might have exuded easygoing charm onscreen, but he became implacable when it came to deciding how he was to portray Cole Porter. Unfortunately, he was terribly miscast. As this became evident, Grant became extremely uncomfortable. It was a conundrum that could not be obscured by any script. The screenplay, eventually labored on by ten different writers, fabricated a life story of Porter so fanciful that it made Cagney's turn as George M. Cohan appear to be a documentary. Porter's life of privilege (his homosexuality cloaked by a bearded marriage could not even be hinted at) offered little in the way of an appealing story. His alleged recovery from a horseback riding accident in 1937 was used as the plot point for a fictional career comeback that included a mythical French military experience. In fact, Porter never recovered from the terrible injuries his legs sustained after his horse rolled over on him, was in constant pain, and eventually had a leg amputated in 1956. The actor Monty Woolley played himself as the composer's Yale University professor. A close friend of the songwriter, Woolley had been an English and dramatics instructor at Yale and was a contemporary of Porter's who was only three years older.

Grant became dissatisfied with nearly every aspect of the production. His insistence on having everything his own way included the usurping of directorial prerogatives such as set design, blocking, lighting, and the wardrobes of other cast members. Not surprisingly, he encountered resistance from Curtiz. Their differences became disruptive and unyielding.

At one point, the production assistant Eric Stacey observed, "I don't think there is a set in this picture that hasn't been changed by Cary." Between Grant's intransigence and Porter's authority over the script, Curtiz was the odd man out. Feeling abandoned, he handled the situation poorly. After the eleventh day of shooting, the dailies revealed that the photography of people was unbalanced because of how they were positioned in the foreground and background of the shots. Curtiz said, "I can't go on like this," and fired the respected cinematographer Bert Glennon. Arthur Schwartz, the line producer, was a Warner outsider who was essentially a composer. Steve Trilling, who had precious little expertise in either filmmaking or executive leadership, tried to keep everyone happy by avoiding decisions, while Jack Warner issued his periodic diatribes about costs and schedules. Having the company divided into two main units added to the confusion: LeRoy Prinz staged what would amount to thirty-two different musical numbers. Between filming the biography and musical numbers and the rehearsals, at one point there were eight different satellite units working on the picture simultaneously.

Six weeks into the production, Eric Stacey reported: "Regarding the rewrite and script situation *which is still extremely bad,* want you to know that even the blue pages that come out are rewritten at the suggestion of mostly Cary Grant." Grant convinced the studio to hire the screenwriter William Bowers to rewrite the script that Charles Hoffman and Leo Townsend had labored on for nearly two years. Bowers remembered: "This was one those insane things when what I wrote in the morning, I mean this literally, they shot in the afternoon and what I wrote in the afternoon, they shot the next morning."

Grant was also unhappy about how he was being photographed in his first Technicolor production, remarking that in the death scene of his grandfather, "he, himself, looks sicker than the grandfather."

Curtiz cashiered Glennon's replacement, Peverell Marley, and opted for Haller while shooting around the illnesses of Monty Woolley[8] and Selena Royle. The continual disagreements between Grant and Curtiz ended up dividing the company. Another major script revision, issued in July and originated by Grant, caused Curtiz to be, according to Stacey, "very, very depressed." On September 29—the eighty-seventh day of production—Curtiz had a meltdown while directing a scene with Grant at the ill-advised hour of 3:30 a.m. The ostensible culprit was, as usual, the sound mixer, who inadvertently created a microphone shadow, but the actual cause was the director's pent-up fury over Grant's behavior. Stacey chronicled what occurred: "After Mike got through bawling out the sound dept, he received a very large boo-o-o!! from the entire company; then Mike walked off the set and said he was going home and let the Sound Dept. direct the picture (what he meant was Cary Grant). I was successful in convincing Mike not to be foolish and go off the set—he would only be hurting himself—so he returned, resumed work and the scene was finished."

It was a measure of the director's frustration that this episode marked the only documented occasion that he walked off a film set while working. The next day Curtiz apologized to Everett Brown, the soundman, and explained that he was actually angry with Grant.

Curtiz's direction of *Night and Day* concluded when a technician's strike halted production from October 6 through 12. An assistant finished up the final scenes and retakes in November. Cary Grant bade his farewell to Curtiz: "If I'm ever stupid enough to be caught working with you again, you'll know I'm either broke or I've lost my mind." The feeling was mutual. But the passing years (and perhaps guilt) apparently mellowed Grant's feelings toward the director: the star was one of Curtiz's pallbearers in 1962.

The disharmony didn't affect the success of the picture. *Night and Day* was a hit. The most expensive picture yet produced by Warner Bros., at $4,445,000, it grossed $7,418,000 after its release in August 1946. The Technicolor photography, Grant's star power, and the Porter songbook possessed unalloyed appeal. Reviews ranged from raves to scathing diatribes. *Time* described the Warners as "inartistic penny pinchers," adding how Jack "spent years checking to make sure the lights are out at night." The review in *Life* was bannered, "Film about Cole Porter is an exemplar of what's wrong with Hollywood musicals." In response, Jack Warner barred all writers employed by *Time-Life* chairman Henry Luce from the lot. It wasn't just the critics who panned the film. Near the end of a prolifically successful Hollywood career, Bill Bowers ranked his *Night and Day* screenplay as "the worst thing I've ever done."

Viewed today, the picture is a handsome misfire. Although fiction is standard issue for Hollywood biographies, a dubbed Alexis Smith and Jane Wyman are unspectacular vocalists, and the Prinz musical numbers are no better than average. Cole Porter's musical compositions deserved better.

The end of the war was greeted as a celebratory new beginning at the studio. The contract actor Richard Erdman vividly recalled the spontaneous outburst following the announcement of V-J Day:

> We were shooting on a soundstage, down near the cafeteria, when, without warning, Jack L. Warner and his entourage entered the stage. "We will all stop shooting now, today," he announced. "We have won—the war is over!" And just as quickly, as we all began to cheer, he moved along to other stages, proud of his studio. We had played our part. We had bought our war bonds, more than any other studio. We had given our blood. We had boosted morale. We had entertained the troops. And now they were coming home. It was numbing. It was hard to believe. We stood around. We hugged one another. We gathered up our

wardrobe and our equipment and we moved out onto the streets of the lot. It was chaos and growing. Horns were honking. People were screaming, and laughing and crying. Cowboys and Indians, Mounties and Nazis, extras and executives, writers and directors, all poured out into the streets from the soundstages and the offices and the cutting rooms—then the wardrobe people, and the makeup people, and janitors and producers all from their own little kingdoms, out they came, onto the lot, jumping up and down, hugging and cheering. Mike Curtiz, ever the filmmaker, mounted a crane with a camera and operated it himself, capturing the spectacle from on high and then, most breathtaking of all, out from the music stage emerged that great studio orchestra, a ragtag ensemble led by Erich Wolfgang Korngold, pumping his baton, conducting and marching them onto the streets and onto to the lot, playing "America, the Beautiful." What a day! Glorious!

Things had never appeared better for Hollywood. The movie industry was seemingly running at peak performance, and the studio coffers were full. Curtiz was arranging a deal with Jack Warner to produce his own pictures. Only a few realized at the time that what seemed like a new beginning for the studio system was actually the beginning of the end.

27

A Michael Curtiz Production

At the end of February 1945, Jack Warner picked up the final option of Curtiz's contract, which bumped his salary up to $4,200 per week. It still wasn't enough. In addition to his profligate lifestyle, Curtiz's earnings were being devoured by taxes. President Roosevelt's wartime call for a 100 percent marginal tax rate on those fortunate enough to earn more than $25,000 per year (the present-day equivalent of $375,000) resonated with many Americans. Ann Sheridan wasn't just being cheeky when she declared, "I regret that I only have one salary to give for my country." By 1944 the top tax rate reached 94 percent. A number of wealthy Hollywood elites sought to hold on to more of their incomes. One method was to form a corporation, since the taxation rate on corporate capital gains above $50,000 was only 40 percent. Because the postwar tax rates remained sky-high, Curtiz believed that he could achieve financial security through the establishment of his own production company.

Even more than money, Curtiz sought control over his pictures. When he was asked by the *Christian Science Monitor* why he turned to independent production, there was no hesitation in his response: "Because I get my freedom. I can make pictures as I like. That will be increasingly important to Hollywood, whether it knows it or not."

After reminding Jack Warner in February 1945 that he wanted to set up his own production unit, he began negotiations that fall when his attorney, Mark Cohen, huddled with Roy Obringer. An agreement in principle was reached before the end of the year. Curtiz would own 51 percent of the company and would produce and direct two pictures per year at an annual salary of $100,000. Michael Curtiz Productions assumed 30 percent of the production cost, and Warner Bros. would pick up the remaining 70 percent. His company would garner 30 percent of the net profits, and Warner would take 70 percent. But just when it appeared to be a done deal, the agreement was put on hold. Curtiz's impatience started to spike. He wrote to Warner in March 1946 that he "would be much happier in my own unit," and he spiced up the letter by dropping in a rumor that he was considering forming a production company with Howard Hawks. There was also a report that he had received an offer to join Liberty Pictures, a production company headquartered at RKO and established by the directors Frank Capra, William Wyler, and George Stevens. Whether Warner was stalling or Curtiz wanted to finish out his contract that ended on April 10, 1946 (or both), is not clear. Despite the doubts about his future, Curtiz prepared to direct another major film at Warner Bros.

Life with Father was more than a hit Broadway play; it was a phenomenon. The 1939 Oscar Serlin production was written by Howard Lindsay and Russel Crouse and based on the serialized book by Clarence Day Jr. about the travails of his imperious stockbroker father and family in late nineteenth-century Manhattan. The stage production ran for seven years and 3,224 performances—still the longest-running nonmusical in Broadway history. It became one of the most sought-after properties for the screen. Sam Goldwyn's 1940 offer of $200,000 was turned down because Serlin had mandated a three-year clearance before the movie could be exhibited. An offer by the silent star and United Artists cofounder Mary Pickford also came up short. Jack Warner was determined to obtain the rights. In addition to doling out $500,000 and net profit percentages to Serlin, Clarence Day Jr.'s widow, Katherine,[1] and Lindsay and Crouse, Warner agreed not to release *Life with Father* until 1947. The film was a one-shot deal. Warner Bros. would have no succeeding rights to the characters or the play. Final authority resided with Katherine Day, who, with Lindsay and Crouse, was the nominal technical adviser. Robert Buckner was tapped to manage yet another challenging production: "The authors and producers of the play had been told so many times, "Don't let Hollywood ruin this picture." So they didn't give us the leeway on the script that we should have had. We were trying to get off that one set and breathe some air into it. In order to get air into it we had to change some things. [Lindsay and Crouse] . . . were very difficult to work with, particularly Lindsay."

Buckner also revealed: "It was difficult for us to persuade Lindsay and Crouse that Mike was right [as director]. They wanted somebody like George Cukor, who would have done a great job. Mike wasn't too keen about doing the picture at first. He suspected that it was out of his milieu, and he wasn't too comfortable with it. But at the same time it was a challenge for him."

Warner pushed for Curtiz, and the New York–based trio eventually agreed. Curtiz telegraphed Lindsay and Crouse, thanking them and Mrs. Day for accepting him as the director, while promising "to do everything in my power to make a picture of which we can all be very proud." Shooting began on April 11, 1946. *Life with Father* would be Curtiz's longest production at Warner Bros. It would also run a close second to *Night and Day* in terms of contentious difficulty.

Curtiz and Buckner favored William Powell to play Clarence Day. Powell was no longer a suave and romantic leading man; his years of playing Nick Charles were coming to an end. After considering Fredric March, Walter Pidgeon, Frank Morgan, and even Cary Grant, Curtiz directed a test of Ronald Colman primarily to mollify the theater-bound trio, who eventually agreed to Powell. Even though Powell seemed perfect as the officiously lovable Clarence Day, Howard Lindsay was initially dissatisfied. The playwright-actor created the Day role on Broadway and believed he himself would be the optimal choice. But Lindsay eventually bowed out; he had never appeared in a feature film and never would. His wife, the actress Dorothy Stickney, who costarred as Vinnie Day on Broadway with her husband, had film experience but no box-office value. According to Buckner, Stickney was "bitterly disappointed" that she didn't land the part. Buckner and Curtiz pretended to give the pair serious consideration by arranging screen tests as a tactical courtesy.

In order to borrow Powell from MGM, Jack Warner agreed to lend out the services of Errol Flynn for a picture to be made two years later by Metro at Flynn's salary at that time. The swap cost Warner $200,000. The choice for the role of Vinnie Day was more challenging. Myrna Loy, Rosalind Russell, Jean Arthur, and Rosemary DeCamp were considered and rejected. Mary Pickford was screen-tested after she failed in her attempt to buy the property. Pickford, who made her last film in 1933, was convinced that *Life with Father* would be her triumphant return to the screen. But she was too far along in both years and alcohol to be suitable. Buckner was tasked with delivering the bad news:

> I had the terrible job of telling Mary Pickford that she didn't get the part. She came out badly in the test, her voice was squeaky, her figure was wrong. Jack Warner and Mike Curtiz were cowards about telling her, so they told me to go to Pickfair and inform America's sweetheart that she was washed up in pictures. She made a grand entrance down a staircase and was smiling and

beaming, thinking she had the part. She just dissolved in front of my eyes when I told her the bad news. It was one of the worst moments I've ever had to face.

Pickford handled her rejection with class. She wrote a gracious letter of thanks to Buckner, noting, "As I told Mike, only the most delightful memories remain and any suggestion of a cloud has long since evaporated."

Inside the studio it was initially believed that Bette Davis was a slam-dunk for the part. The play's originators didn't agree and forced Curtiz to shoot a test of her doing a brief comedy scene. Curtiz traveled to New York to screen Davis's test for the film's triumvirate brain trust. He couldn't put her across and sent a regretful telegram:

> Dear Bette: Just returned from New York after projecting your screen test to the group that operates *Life with Father*. Bette, it was worse than the Potsdam Conference. I was not born to be diplomat so probably hurt a few people's feelings. I was and still am honestly convinced that you are the woman to play the part but I could not overcome the objections of these critics using all the technical terms of the theater such as "the characterization is too powerful," too dominating, too superior and without any naïveté, etc. etc. . . . All I can tell you is that I am heartbroken as I had looked forward to working with you and hope someday we can start on a moving picture which will not have to be approved by superior prejudiced critics of the theatre.

Despite Davis's star power, she would have been miscast as the sweetly tolerant Vinnie Day. And although Curtiz seemed sincere, she considered this one more black mark in her ledger of grievances against him.

Buckner and Warner now sought Irene Dunne. After obtaining agreement from all parties, Curtiz sent her a script, and she was eventually signed. The financially savvy Dunne inked an agreement for 10 percent of the first million gross, 5 percent of the second million, and 2 percent of all gross receipts in excess of $3 million—with a $150,000 guarantee. Dunne would earn more than $200,000. Curtiz next contacted David O. Selznick about a loan-out of Shirley Temple to play the key role of Mary Skinner, whose courtship with Clarence Jr. (played by Jimmy Lydon) was an important element of the story. In turning down the request, Selznick wrote to Curtiz: "You must know by now how highly I think of you and your talents. Also, I learned on *Casablanca* that I could rely on your word." But the producer despaired of gaining an advantage over Jack Warner: "Warners is notoriously hard to make a deal with. . . . Whenever they give another studio anything, they always get the best end of a trade."

Jack Warner decided to borrow the teenage starlet Elizabeth Taylor from MGM for $350,000, paid in ten installments. In addition, Warner Bros. conceded billing rights to Taylor on all main titles and publicity, her name to be printed at 75 percent of the size of William Powell's and Irene Dunne's. The studio's contracts with Powell and Dunne complicated the film's publicity campaign. Exactly half of all the advertising had to feature Powell's name in the first position; the other half had to favor Dunne's.

The making of the picture was no less complicated, as Eric Stacey's ominous production report on the first day of wardrobe tests indicates: "There is a terrific unpleasantness going on in this picture between Mike and Mrs. Day, and I look for a big blowup today. We ran the first day's tests that involved Powell and Dunne, and Mike and Mrs. Day went round and round verbally. Mike left and went home early and the wardrobe tests were completed by Bob Vreeland. I expect more trouble today, Monday, when we get Powell and Dunne in; who incidentally have been asking as to how much interference is to be expected from Mrs. Day, Lindsay & Crouse."

The extent of the meddling by Mrs. Day and Messrs. Lindsay and Crouse confirmed everyone's worst fears. And there was nothing that could be done about it. Their contractual agreement with Warner Bros. included this proviso: "The technical director of the photo play to advise upon matters of taste, period, characterization and general décor shall be Katherine M. Day." The trio insisted that the sets for the interior of the Day house be dimensionally representative of an 1883 New York residence, including the furniture. And of course the props had to be facsimiles of those used during the Broadway stage production. Stacey's production reports noted the difficulties:

> The progress of the company is good and the only slowness is due to the amount of time it takes to light the set. I was shown yesterday by Pev Marley *twelve* small lamps hidden around the floor to light up the dark furniture and the dark woodwork. This all takes a terrific amount of time, but apparently it is necessary and the photography is very beautiful, according to Mike.

Of course, as you know and we all know, the basic trouble with this hallway is that it is too narrow to get lights in and this fundamental situation was caused by the insistence of Day, Lindsay & Crouse for "realism" and the set becomes practically impossible to photograph because of its extreme height and extreme narrowness.

The trio's micromanagement included determining the color scheme of a milk wagon that Curtiz had to have repainted so it would photograph properly. Changing anything on the fly or improvising, as Curtiz was inclined to do, became impossible. Nearly every day brought forth a new issue that had to be adjudicated by a star chamber of strong personalities. An illustrative example was an expensive New York street scene that Buckner and Curtiz wanted to replace with something simpler. Always anxious to save a buck, Tenny Wright proactively began changing the set as Buckner attempted to head him off:

Lindsay and Crouse, who never buy any new ideas fast, want to think it over. However, they recommend strongly that we do not bring this problem to a head at once, for if we do, Mrs. Day will kill our Employment Office scene, which is even more necessary to the picture, and we already shot stuff which leads into it and follows it. You have to know Mrs. Day and her full vocal-legal authority to understand how serious this decision is. Please, pal, I've spent a year and a half in arduous diplomatic maneuvers getting this trio from New York into a fairly reasonable working relationship. They can't be finagled through the usual studio channels, by you, J.L. or anybody else—including me, half the time.

Shooting in Technicolor added another layer of complexity. It was mandated that all the actors portraying Day family members have their hair dyed red. This approach had to be refined when Powell's hair color was deemed to appear purple by the Technicolor representatives. There was also a time-consuming debate over whether Irene Dunne should wear a wig—she refused—and how changing her hair color over time would appear on film. Dunne also suffered a skin infection—she had face boils that makeup couldn't cover, which caused her to miss time on the picture.

Then there was Elizabeth Taylor. An internal memo warned of potential difficulties with the young actress: "Billy Grady [MGM casting director] tells me that Elizabeth Taylor is a nervous, high-strung youngster whose condition has caused her to absent herself fairly frequently from the pictures which she worked in for them. This has been aggravated somewhat recently by a natural condition in girls of her age."

In other words, Taylor was physically maturing at a rapid rate. In mid-May, she donned the period wardrobe that she had been fitted for seven weeks earlier, and had filled out so much in the interim that the bodice burst at the seams and had to be completely resewn.

What would be a lifelong struggle for Taylor in coping with various health maladies also manifested itself on *Life with Father*. Production files include notations of her absences owing to a variety of illnesses, including a sore throat and a severe sinus condition that required regular penicillin injections. Curtiz also had to film around her legally mandated schooling obligations and keep a teacher and social worker on the set. Even when he had her in front of the camera, the results were not always optimal, as Jimmy Lydon recalled:

Mike was a very explosive guy. He was not a clinging-vine type of director. When things went wrong, he blew his stack. He was not a mean man, but he would just lose his temper and he was funny. . . . He'd stand there in the middle of the set and he's blazing with fury. . . . Elizabeth was a lovely person, inside and out, and she was fifteen. We have this cute little scene and she sits on Father's trousers on my lap and I make her get up and everything else and she's heartbroken in the scene. Well, we started to shoot it, "Take 1," Mike says again, "Take 2, Take 3, Take 4 . . ." And it's this triple-stripe Technicolor and these big cameras, and they're very unwieldy. And I can see the bile rising in Mike, you know. "Take 5, Take 6, Take 7," and Elizabeth isn't getting it, and finally, "Take 8." And Mike blows his top. He blows up like crazy and he's hollering at Elizabeth and she starts to cry and she runs off the set. Mike follows her and he's walking up and down in front of Elizabeth's dressing room and all of us can hear him screaming at the top of his lungs, "Elizabeth, damn, don't you cry, you break my heart, you son of a bitch. Don't cry, I'm sorry," and he's screaming at her.

Although Curtiz would tab her as one of Hollywood's most promising actresses, his rapport with Taylor was further complicated by a sexual affair that he reputedly engaged in with the young star's mother. Although the fifty-year-old Sara Taylor had been cautious not to expose her daughter's career to scandal, her dalliance with Curtiz was the alleged cause of a separation from her husband that lasted for the duration of the production. The sole smoking gun was a beachside photo of Mrs. Taylor and Curtiz that turned up in a movie magazine; the MGM publicity department moved quickly to put the kibosh on the gossip. Whatever the relationship was or wasn't between Curtiz and Elizabeth Taylor's mother, it didn't endure beyond *Life with Father*.

The varied aggravations provoked Curtiz to acquire a scapegoat. The cinematographer Peverell Marley became the director's punching bag. Eric Stacey reported Curtiz complaining that Marley was not inspired and that he received very few suggestions from him. Curtiz wanted to replace Marley with Carl Guthrie, Bob Burks, or "any younger man who is more ambitious." The debonair Marley, who was married to Linda Darnell and had a distinguished career dating back to *The Ten Commandments* (1923), nearly quit the picture. As Stacey noted, "He just cannot take the rudeness and sarcasm that Mike pours on him all day long," and he also observed, "This squabble is mostly personalities and personal differences between Mike and Pev and has nothing to do with his work." The studio stood behind Marley's photography.

Curtiz became indignant when Lindsay and Crouse vetoed his notion for a snow scene on the street set. He also stepped on a nail, which resulted in an infected foot that had him hobbling around for several weeks wearing a single shoe. According to Lydon, Curtiz reacted like a mother grizzly whose cubs are threatened when anybody other than he did something that negatively affected his actors. Lydon was notified that the studio dropped his contract option during *Life with Father*. When Curtiz noticed how downcast the young actor appeared, Lydon told him what happened:

> He said, "What the matter, kid? What happened?" "Warner just dropped my option." He said, "What?" So he picks up the phone and he calls Jack Warner, yelling, "I'm coming up with Jim," and up we go. Now everybody stops working, we go into Warner's office, and Mike says, "What's the matter, Jack? This kid here, he's wonderful! You dum, dum, why would you do that?" And Mr. Warner said right in front of me, "Mike, we had to try to save some money and in order to get Jim to do the part, I had to put him under contract so I could afford his salary. And that's why

Curtiz directs William Powell in *Life with Father* (1947) (author's collection).

we dropped his option, because we don't have options any more."
. . . Mr. Warner said, "You're wonderful, Jim, but that's the way
I had to do it." And I understood and so did Mike.

The day after that incident, Lydon returned to the set after lunch and was
standing with his foot on a ladder watching Pev Marley at work: "I'm
watching him light the set and all of a sudden somebody kicked me in
the rear end and lifted me off the soundstage." Furious, the young actor
whirled around, and there was Curtiz. "He wanted to apologize for yelling at me the other day," said an astonished Lydon. "He wanted me to
turn around so he kicked me in the back."

Life with Father was a critically acclaimed hit. Seen today, it remains
charming though a bit creaky with age. The inflexibility of Mrs. Day,
Lindsay, and Crouse stifled any innovation beyond the original stage concept. Nonetheless, Curtiz's work was exemplary, as Lydon observed after
a half century of working in front of and behind the camera: "I worked

with a lot of directors and I was a director for the last part of my life-time in movies. Mike was probably one of most artistic directors I've ever known. He never picked a setup that wasn't beautifully arranged. And the cameraman didn't arrange it; Mike arranged each shot of the film he made. It was not just a close-up or a three-shot or whatever. It was always well thought out. . . . He was really an artistic man."

William Powell received his third Best Actor nomination but lost to his friend Ronald Colman for *A Double Life*. Max Steiner was nominated for his nostalgic music score and, in a slice of personal redemption, so were the cinematographers Pev Marley and William Skall. There was also a censorship issue that seems in retrospect absurd. The thematic notion throughout that Clarence Day had to be baptized in order to go to heaven was a tired gimmick even at that time. His memorable closing line, "I am going to be baptized, damn it!" was personally approved after a letter from Jack Warner to Eric Johnston requesting a waiver of the Production Code. The "damn it" was retained, though several similar expletives in the script were removed. At the last minute, after they had been shipped for distribution, Jack Warner had the final reel of every *Life with Father* print recalled and modified to excise the mild profanity. Documentation of this frantic task fills two folders of correspondence in the USC Warner archival files. Either Johnston rescinded his waiver or Warner panicked over the film's being tampered with by state and local censor boards. Either way, the omission of the final invective dilutes the effect of the last scene.

Even with the increased economies of postwar filmmaking, *Life with Father* grossed nearly $6.5 million against a cost of $4.7 million. After the premiere on August 14, 1947—a year after the production closed—Jack Warner sent Curtiz a congratulatory telegram: "Dear Mike: Just received the *Life with Father* reviews and they are tremendous. And I can't tell you what a great lift they gave me. Congratulations and thanks to you Mike for the big part you played in making this possible. Very best wishes to Bess and yourself from Ann and Jack."

Warner was feeling magnanimous. In addition to being handed a badly needed hit movie, he had also retained Curtiz, who was hard at work with his own production company on the Warner lot. After *Life with Father* wrapped on August 14, 1946, Curtiz became fed up with the stalled negotiations over his production unit and prepared to depart the studio. Was he serious? There is a September 7, 1946, internal Warner Bros. memo notifying the salary office that Curtiz was leaving. Whether this was a genuine decision or a negotiating feint, it worked. It dawned on Jack and Harry Warner that their most successful director might actually abandon the Burbank soundstages that had been his home for two decades. At the end of September, an agreement for Curtiz to produce his own movies and release them through Warner Bros. was concluded under the terms previously arrived at in December 1945.

To keep him mollified during the arduous production of *Life with Father,* Warner awarded Curtiz a $50,000 bonus. Half of the bonus was doled out during the production, and the remainder was paid after the picture was completed.

Curtiz's loyalty was further strengthened after an unpleasant episode. According to the choreographer LeRoy Prinz, the situation concerned Curtiz's daughter Kitty and a personal associate of the director named Desider Pek. Pek was one of the many Hungarians newly arrived in Hollywood to whom Curtiz extended a helping hand. The director had known Pek back in Budapest, where he wrote publicity articles about Curtiz's movies. At some point, Pek stopped by the Canoga Ranch and never left. He became Curtiz's secretary, although his exact duties are not clear since his English was worse than his employer's. He mostly sat in Curtiz's outer office and typed letters in Hungarian while chewing on cloves of garlic. As John Meredyth Lucas recalled:

> Desider Pek, in his native country, had been, at one time or another, a professional mourner, attending funerals and weeping copiously. He was ideal for the role as he vaguely resembled Boris Karloff in the *Frankenstein* makeup. He had also worked at a sanitarium for people with eating disorders—from anorexia to simple lack of appetite. His job was to sit at the head of the table and eat gigantic amounts of whatever was served, thus demonstrating the joy of food. How successful this was among Hungarians I do not know but, when Pek would accompany us to lunch, or, on a few occasions, dinner, he would wolf down his own food, then go around and clean whatever remained on anyone else's plate.

By Prinz's account, Pek's eccentricities that amused Curtiz did not wear as well on Jack Warner:

> Pek never wore a necktie and always wore a hat on the back of his head. Jack Warner didn't like the man. Later on, he told Mike he

had to get the man off the lot. That's what really brought on the whole trouble. Mike claimed he didn't have any wife, any children in Europe, but he did. His daughter [Kitty] was brought over and put into the Immaculate Heart Convent. Years later, she got expelled and turned into a notorious character, a horrible character, it's hard to describe. She was a lesbian and notorious and Mike had to get her out of the country. Then while she was out of the country, she wrote her father some terrible letters, horrible, and then Warner ordered Pek off the lot, because he was Mike's stooge and he didn't want him around. And Pek stole the letters and threatened to blackmail Warner Brothers.

Steve Trilling summoned Prinz and told him he needed to resolve the blackmail threat to protect the studio. Prinz had an unusual background. Robert Buckner said that the dancer-choreographer reminded him of a bartender. He spent time in reform school, rode the rails in freight trains as a kid, and later served with Eddie Rickenbacker as a World War I pilot. Prinz tricked the not-so-bright Pek into showing him the letters, which were stashed in a bank. The choreographer showed up for the viewing with "two friends of mine, big husky-looking guys" posing as policemen and took the letters away from Pek.

Prinz next met with Curtiz and Kitty. Although Kitty protested, "Those were just letters of a girl that was crazy about her father," the letters purportedly indicated that her 1939 suicide attempt was triggered by an aborted love affair with another woman. She launched into a tirade after Prinz related what Pek had attempted to do. Curtiz was extremely relieved and wanted the letters returned, but Prinz said he had burned them. The choreographer said that after the incident, "I was a fair-haired boy. I had a life contract at Warner Bros. if I wanted it. Jack Warner swore by me." In addition to being a backdoor troubleshooter for Warner Bros., Prinz was the choreographer on ten films directed by Curtiz and didn't leave the studio until after *The Helen Morgan Story*, in 1957.

A letter from Desider Pek to Curtiz tangentially supports Prinz's account. Dated February 18, 1946, it was written during the period cited by Prinz when Curtiz was in the midst of *Life with Father*. Written in Hungarian, it is a rambling discourse paraphrasing Curtiz and referring to himself in first person. It is composed in the imploring tone of someone whose access had recently been cut off: "You may think I'm going to ask you to invest money in my play. No, sir! That's not what I want to talk about." "I know," says Curtiz with the self-assurance of the successful man who's usually right. "Pek wants to gently remind me of my promise to give him a good job with good pay in my new corporation."

As Curtiz rid himself of Pek, he was thinking about how to build his production company. He had a definite vision of what he wanted to do: "I am going to try and build my own stock company and make stars of unknowns. It is impossible to sign up the big stars because they are all tied up for the next two years."

In addition to searching for newcomers, Curtiz surrounded himself with people he trusted. He began with his family. After moving into Marion Davies's former bungalow on the Warner lot, he installed Bess as his story editor and his stepson, John, as script supervisor. His younger brother David was brought in as a montage and second-unit director. Curtiz also hired Robert Vreeland as his assistant director and Alexina Bruner to assist Bess. Bess engaged Frances Marion (the first Hollywood screenwriter to win a pair of Academy Awards) to create original stories. Curtiz also hired George Amy, an editor, as his associate producer. Amy started at Warners as a seventeen-year-old apprentice editor and became one of the best cutters in Hollywood. He won the Academy Award for editing *Air Force* (1943) and was nominated for *Yankee Doodle Dandy* (1942) and *Objective, Burma!* (1945).

Curtiz needed someone to help him manage the production side of his company. Experienced pros such as Henry Blanke, Robert Lord, and Robert Buckner were beyond both his inclination and financial reach, so he hired Charles Hoffman, a former novelist and Warner staff screenwriter, as the titular producer for his first film production. Hoffman produced several features and eventually was the showrunner for the Warner Bros. television series *Hawaiian Eye*.

Curtiz might have finally had his own company, but it was on the Warner Bros. lot. Jack Warner continued to view him as an employee, even though they were contractual partners. Hiring a veteran colleague with a legitimate résumé as a producer might have assisted Curtiz in managing his former boss. Most critically, Curtiz needed someone with the abilities that he lacked. Even though he brought on someone named Jacques Leslie to hold the title of vice president, treasurer, and general manager, astute financial management was an absent attribute at Michael Curtiz Productions.

Curtiz would have been hard-pressed to choose a more challenging period to start his own company. The numerous problems that wracked postwar Hollywood began with prolonged labor unrest among the different unions representing the moviemaking crafts. A protracted battle between the formerly gangster-affiliated International Alliance of Theatrical Stage Employees (IATSE) and the leftist Conference of Studio Unions (CSU) began to disrupt film production shortly before the end of the war. Ostensibly the dispute was over which group would represent a breakaway cluster of set decorators and, later, who would control the carpenters who built the sets and the grips who moved them. The labor strife was an elemental power struggle that could have only one winner.

A CSU strike begun in March culminated with a riot outside the Warner Bros. main gate on October 5, 1945. Warner obtained a preemptive court order limiting the number of picketers. The CSU leader Herbert Sorrell ignored it and focused all his resources in Burbank in an attempt to shut down the studio. A free-for-all ensued: Warner security personnel, assisted by Burbank and Glendale city police, beat up the strikers, who were fighting the IATSE sluggers and scabs attempting to cross their picket lines. Both sides later exchanged charges of hiring lead-pipe goon squads. The Warner fire department, which had saved Curtiz's house a decade earlier, unleashed its hoses on the CSU strikers as cars were overturned on Olive Avenue. Security guards hefting rifles flanked Jack Warner and his retinue as they observed the mayhem from a soundstage roof. Julius Epstein memorably quipped that the studio should change its motto to "Combining good picture making with good marksmanship." Sorrell was bailed out when the National Labor Relations Board ruled that the CSU could represent the set decorators who had broken away from IATSE.

Sorrell called another strike in 1946. This time Roy Brewer, the Red-baiting head of the IATSE, was ready for him. He contrived with the studios—with the tacit support of the Screen Actors Guild and twenty-four other Hollywood unions—to cross CSU picket lines. The strike was eventually crushed. The Hollywood labor wars contributed to the passage of the 1947 Taft-Hartley Act, which significantly curtailed the power of labor unions. The unrest also provided added impetus to the House Un-American Activities Committee to renew its probing of the motion picture industry.

After the Republicans took control of the Senate and the House in 1946, HUAC, under the dubious leadership of Congressman J. Parnell Thomas, prepared to hold hearings about alleged Communist infiltration of the motion picture industry. Dalton Trumbo later applied Emile Zola's condemnation of public apathy over the Dreyfus case to this shameful period by terming it "the time of the toad." No witness called before the HUAC more aptly displayed the characteristics of an amphibian than Jack Warner. In May 1947, during a closed executive session at Los Angeles's Biltmore Hotel, Warner denied under oath that any White House pressure had been brought to bear on his studio to produce *Mission to Moscow*. The studio chief then rattled off a list of "un-American" screenwriters employed by his studio, which included several of the soon-to-be-dubbed Hollywood Ten. For once, Jack had the unqualified support of his older brother. Harry Warner hated unions, particularly the Writers Guild.[2] Jack included Julius and Philip Epstein on his list of the disloyal with nary a mention of the patriotic *Casablanca* and *Yankee Doodle Dandy*.[3]

Summoned to Washington, D.C., later that year for public testimony, Warner became flummoxed under the committee's bright lights. He read this statement into the record on October 20, 1947: "Ideological termites have burrowed into many American industries, organizations, and societies. Wherever they may be, I say let us dig them out and get rid of them. My brothers and I will be happy to subscribe generously to a pest-removal fund. We are willing to establish such a fund to ship to Russia the people who don't like our American system of government and prefer the communistic system to ours."

The studio chief's testimony became so incoherent that one committee member, Richard Nixon, had to prompt him to clarify whether he was in favor of a free press and freedom of speech. The MPAA hired the New Deal political operative–cum–attorney Paul McNutt as a legal representative for the studio brass. McNutt later remarked, "I've spent all day reviewing his testimony in an effort to have Warner appear in a less idiotic light." In truth, the Warners, Louis B. Mayer, and the other mostly Jewish studio executives were frightened. With members of Congress, including the virulent racist John E. Rankin, sitting on the committee, the stench of anti-Semitism wafted over HUAC's political inquisition. Only Harry Cohn remained in character. When the editor Robert Parrish told the Columbia mogul that his agent wanted to know if Parrish was a Communist, Cohn growled, "Tell him to go fuck himself."

The studio heads issued their so-called Waldorf statement, whereby they refused to employ the Hollywood Ten after they were cited for contempt of Congress. Loyalty oaths from the various guilds followed. It was the beginning of the blacklist that polluted the entertainment industry for more than a decade. In addition to finding some of their best talent banished, the studios were threatened with the loss of their theater chains.

The federal government's 1938 lawsuit against the studios for viola-tion of the Sherman Anti-Trust Act had been settled with a 1940 consent decree with the vertically integrated "Big Five" (Warner Bros., Paramount, Columbia, RKO, and Twentieth Century-Fox) that included the cessation of "block-booking" movies into their theater chains. Perceiving the decree as suicidal to their business model, the studios refused to enforce it, and the government reinstated the lawsuit in 1945. As the case worked its way up to the Supreme Court, it was evident that the major studios were going to be forced to divest themselves of their theaters.

Adding to their concern was the fact that the number of television stations mushroomed from a mere dozen to more than forty by 1948, as the FCC became swamped with broadcast license requests. Regardless of who owned movie theaters, it would soon be possible to relax at home and watch movies and other entertainment without purchasing a ticket.

Topping off the overall gloom, revenue projections by the major stu-dios in 1947 were universally pessimistic as the postwar box-office swoon took hold. To close a $3 million budget gap, Jack and Harry Warner began cutting employees, which included the release of contracted talent. They also rented or sold real estate to keep their studio in the black. The original Warner Bros. Sunset Boulevard studio had already been leased to a recre-ation firm that converted the soundstages into a roller rink and a badmin-ton court; Stage 1—site of *The Jazz Singer*—became the country's largest bowling alley. The "30 Acres" land, near Cordova Street in Burbank, where Curtiz sought to deploy an alligator during *The Sea Hawk,* was sold off.

Curtiz was well aware of the industry's predicament. He told a re-porter in early 1947 that "the box office is off nearly 25 percent, while the cost of making pictures is nearly double that and salaries have risen as much as 150 percent." Harking back to his European days with Count Kolowrat, he believed he had the solution: better pictures made by film-makers unhindered by meddlesome studio bosses:

> After [World War I], all Europe flocked to Hollywood to make pictures. But now Europe is building its own studios. While Brit-ish pictures are received generously in this country, it is almost impossible to get a favorable review for an American picture in Britain. Add to this the government decree making the selling of pictures obligatory and doing away with blockbooking, and you realize that Hollywood is facing a new day. Quality and quality alone will sell pictures in the future. With a condition such as

that facing him, the producer can't any longer chance interference with his picture making from studio heads who may be influenced by factors unknown to him. He must be able to make his own decisions and to stand and fall by them.

In addition to these tectonic shifts, Curtiz made a major personal transition when he and Bess sold the Canoga Ranch in 1946. Factoring into their decision was the commute to Burbank combined with the cost of managing the sprawling property, which, according to one estimate, had grown to 265 acres. The ranch, including the Tudor house, orange groves, polo field, skeet range, and Bess's poolside office, was bought for the then-enormous sum of $300,000. Over the next two decades, the ranch was eventually subdivided into thirty-five lots to accommodate the San Fernando Valley's suburban sprawl.

Curtiz and Bess's new digs were on an Encino hillside at 4300 Noeline Drive. It amounted to a smaller version of the previous ranch with a beautifully appointed main house, a pool, a horse stable, and livestock. John Meredyth Lucas's eldest daughter, Liz MacGillicuddy Lucas, remembered her early years at what would be named "The Cove":

It was what you would call a Hollywood ranch. The main house had an awful lot of space for the help, and at the end of the wing where the housekeeper, butler, and cook had their space was another wing, which my parents had. And they added a nursery and then a second nursery [for Liz's sister and brother]. The main part of the house on the ground floor was Mike's library-office, a big living room, and the huge dining room. Upstairs, Mike had his own set of rooms. Bess had her own set of rooms, and then some. It was like a throne room. . . . Mike kept a string of polo ponies and his riding horse. We were not allowed to go near the horse corral, as Mike's horse was, as they say, an "intact" stallion named Snow White without a sense of humor. I remember they had tons of chickens, so it was always fresh eggs and fresh chickens. . . . So it was not exactly self-sufficient, but it was Hollywood's idea of a working ranch.

Comfortably ensconced, Curtiz concentrated all his energies on making his new company a success. By the end of October 1946, he already had a slate of five prospective projects: *The Unsuspected, Victoria Gran-*

dolet, Romance in High C, Winter Kill (a new mystery by Steve Fisher), and James M. Cain's *Serenade. The Unsuspected* became Curtiz's initial production. From an economic perspective, he wanted to begin with a picture that was budgeted at under $2 million and used a mixture of established performers and new talent. Although Curtiz would bring in his first production at a cost of $1,720,807, he discovered that the postwar movie environment was more challenging than even he had believed.

On November 25, 1946, Michael Curtiz Productions (MCP) purchased the rights to Charlotte Armstrong's novel *The Unsuspected* for $26,250 from Warner Bros., which had bought them for $6,250. The sale of the literary property to Curtiz at more than a 400 percent markup was an ominous indicator of how Jack Warner was going to treat his new partner. MCP ended up transferring the rights to the story to the New York Trust Company in order to obtain the final portion of the financing required for *The Unsuspected.* In all, Curtiz borrowed $535,039.20 to cofinance his first picture; Warner put up the rest of the budget.

By choosing *The Unsuspected,* Curtiz sought to further exploit the postwar noir phenomenon. In 1946 nobody labeled movies such as *The Killers, The Big Sleep,* and *The Strange Love of Martha Ivers* film noirs; rather, they were tabbed "mysteries," "suspensers," "thrillers," or the catchall "melodramas." Curtiz admired what his former colleague Mark Hellinger had done with *The Killers* (1946) at Universal International, so he hired the *Killers* cinematographer, Elwood "Woody" Bredell, to shoot his initial production. Curtiz didn't want to merely replicate the shaded brilliance of Bredell's work; he intended to exceed it.

Curtiz understood that he lacked the financial capacity to recruit prominent stars, but he was resolute in pursuing the best talent. For the lead role of the suave but murderous radio host, Victor Grandison, he sought Orson Welles. Although Welles had lost much of his luster after being let go by RKO in late 1942, he remained a formidable talent who hadn't yet burned all his Hollywood bridges. Curtiz began wooing Welles in August 1946, before his production deal with Warner was finalized. He wired him at the Adelphi Theatre in New York City, where Welles's musical extravaganza *Around the World* was closing after seventy-five performances: "The part is written to your personality and I am sure you would enjoy doing it. I have wanted for many years to do a picture with you and I feel now that I have the story that would make a successful picture for both of us. . . . If there are any changes in the story which you think would improve it, I am sure we can work it out."

After receiving further entreaties from Curtiz, Welles eventually read the script and had no interest in *The Unsuspected*. He apparently also didn't need the money, an unusual state of affairs for the perpetually cash-strapped high flier. Curtiz had also sent a copy of the script to Claude Rains, who accepted. It would be the last of eleven films that Rains made with Curtiz at Warners, and he would provide his typical exemplary turn.

For the other leads, Curtiz sought actors who would also add box-office appeal. He became livid at his agent, Charles Feldman, who apparently recommended that Ava Gardner turn down the offered role of Grandison's vixen niece, Althea. Curtiz sent an angry letter to the agent-producer accusing him of disloyalty. Feldman, who pioneered single-picture package deals for his represented talent, informed Curtiz that Gardner refused the part because "she did not want to do a picture on the outside unless it was a real starring role."

Curtiz reluctantly had to accept the fact that the proffered role *was* a secondary part and that Claude Rains was not Clark Gable. He dropped the matter and was fortunate to end up with Audrey Totter. As Grandison's promiscuous niece, few actresses have played a bad girl any better. Her Scandinavian practicality dovetailed nicely with Curtiz's no-nonsense demeanor, and they got along famously. "He liked my work and wanted to put me under personal contract," Totter told the author Eddie Muller, "but Metro wouldn't let him have me."

For the young couple that is the romantic crux of the film, Curtiz fixated on Dana Andrews and Joan Fontaine. Fontaine was out of his price range, but he obtained an agreement from Sam Goldwyn for a loan-out of Andrews, another Feldman client.[4] The actor initially agreed to *The Unsuspected* so long as Curtiz accepted Virginia Mayo as his costar in a package deal. But Andrews suddenly changed his mind and backed out. Once again, it was the scope of the role—this time as compared to that of Claude Rains—that caused a star to bow out. Virginia Mayo lost interest after Andrews dropped out, although Curtiz had thought she was wrong for the part anyway. He eventually signed the former stage actress Joan Caulfield, then a Paramount costar (with Bing Crosby) in *Welcome Stranger* (1947). Caulfield had the necessary vulnerability for the Matilda Frazier character, but she lacked demonstrative sex appeal and had difficulty projecting enough presence. For one key sequence, Curtiz reportedly had to reduce her to tears to drag the necessary emotion out of her.

Since he couldn't obtain Dana Andrews and there were no other suitable actors available at the right price, Curtiz gambled that he could

Audrey Totter has coffee with Curtiz during his first American production, *The Unsuspected* (1947) (author's collection).

pull off what he had established his reputation on: take an unknown and turn him into a star. He signed the handsome Ted North, who had been a minor Fox contract player before the war, to play Steven Howard. North's actual name was Ted Steinel. He had bounced around with small roles and, after a stint in the navy, costarred with the lethal Lawrence Tierney in the RKO noir programmer *The Devil Thumbs a Ride* (1947). North originally showed up to audition for a minor part in *The Unsuspected*. After two days of screen tests, Curtiz signed him as the male lead opposite Caulfield. The actor was renamed Michael North to accentuate the billing that would introduce him to the screen. North believed that Curtiz was "a great psychologist who is to the movie industry what Knute Rockne was to football." Unfortunately for Curtiz, his Midas touch deserted him on this occasion. Michael North was not another Flynn or Garfield, possessing a voice with the sonorous formality of a sommelier reviewing a wine list. He vanished from Hollywood's soundstages shortly thereafter.

Curtiz had better luck with the supporting players. He added a mature but still vibrant Constance Bennett, whose character as Grandison's radio director, Jane Moynihan, was an ersatz version of Eve Arden. He also discovered an exciting new actor when he spotted Fred Clark playing a detective in a Laguna Beach summer stock production. Curtiz went backstage and asked Clark if he had signed with anyone. Clark said no, and Curtiz responded, "Don't until you hear from me." The newly minted producer inked him a week later for the role of the homicide copper Richard Donovan. Clark was a genuine find who could play heavies or humorous characters with equal panache.

Motivated by his new responsibilities as producer and freed from having to listen to somebody else's opinions about his work, Curtiz tackled his first production with rapidity. He started shooting on January 20, 1947, and finished principal photography on March 15, nearly a month before the targeted date of April 12. The shooting schedule apparently became a greater point of emphasis to the director when he was burning through his own bankroll. Another reason for the quick progress was Woody Bredell, a speed demon who could rapidly light a set. While innovative with camera movement and meticulous in his setups, Curtiz relied on a limited number of different camera lenses—usually no more than four—on most of his Warner films. For scenes inside Anton Grot's expansive set of Grandison's posh house, particularly those with dolly shots, he used a thirty-two-millimeter wide-angle lens for almost all the shots with more than two people. The focal length of the lens incorporated the actors into the frame while adding the appearance of greater space.

Curtiz gloried in the employment of visual symbolism in *The Unsuspected*. The film opens with Grandison—his shadow cast on the wall—stalking his secretary, whom he strangles and strings up to a chandelier as a feigned suicide. Next we find the film's various characters listening to Grandison's radio broadcast. At one point, the camera moves from Howard's reflection in the window of a moving train down a passing street to the exterior of the fleabag Hotel Peekskill. Inside the hotel, Mr. Press's (Jack Lambert's) face is illuminated by the word "kill" from the hotel's partially obscured neon sign flashing through his room's window. The sequence concludes with Donovan's reflection on a desk, listening to the radio broadcast at Grandison's house, where a surprise birthday party contingent awaits his arrival from the radio station. Curtiz and Bredell's use of reflections and shadowed lighting throughout is an extraordinarily creative example of visual mood. The picture is a template for the chiaroscuro lighting style associated with the Eagle-Lion film noirs made by Anthony Mann and the cinematographer John Alton that began production in late 1947.

Despite the striking visual design, *The Unsuspected* wasn't as strong a picture as Curtiz believed it would be. He had striven to replicate the Fox hit *Laura* (1944), but he fell short.

The script by Ranald MacDougall was the film's Achilles' heel. Charlotte Armstrong's novel included the unusual approach of revealing the murderer at the beginning of the story. Although this literary device was innovative at the time, it didn't transfer well to the screen. Curtiz retained the plot point by using a quick reflection of Grandison's face to establish his guilt in the opening minutes. Since the revelation of the murderer dispensed with traditional deployment of red herrings, the suspense is generated by the other characters—primarily Howard—figuring out that Grandison is the murderer before he deduces that they are on to him and does them in first.

After the superbly designed opening, MacDougall's convoluted exposition has Matilda offscreen on a South American cruise, hoping to forget about losing a worthless fiancé (Hurd Hatfield) to her nymphomaniac stepsister Althea. She supposedly drowns in a shipwreck as Howard materializes at Grandison's birthday party, claiming to have wed Matilda shortly before she died. Matilda then surfaces in a Brazil hospital, notifying the family by telegram that she is alive and returning home. Howard meets her at the airport, and she claims not to remember marrying or even knowing him. The picture rights itself when Grandison murders his secretary and other cast members in order to hide his embezzlement of Matilda's inheritance. In an exciting finale, he is trapped and confesses to his crimes during a radio broadcast.

Curtiz wrote to Charles Feldman after the initial preview and zeroed in on the root problem: "I was a little disappointed and discouraged because it didn't turn out the way I visualized it. . . . It looks as though I tried to make a great picture out of a story that wasn't basically a great story." *The Unsuspected* is an enjoyable visual feast with an interesting perspective about the influence of radio shortly before the populist dawn of television.

Curtiz also realized his key limitation as an independent producer: his company had no say in the advertising or promotion of its pictures. Jack Warner continued to exercise total control over studio publicity. After the film's New York premiere in October, George Amy complained to Ben Kalmenson, the studio's New York–based distribution chief, that the studio was not properly promoting *The Unsuspected* and was underselling Michael North's debut. Kalmenson blamed the disappointing New York box-office results on "the frenzy and hysteria surrounding the World Series."[5] Eight months later, Curtiz's lawyer, Mark Cohen, wrote to Kalmenson claiming that the studio hadn't spent enough money to advertise *The Unsuspected* and asked what the plan was for subsequent runs. Jack Warner ended the discussion by responding directly to Curtiz: "The answer is that we cannot lose any more money on a picture that is a failure." Neither an abject failure nor particularly successful, *The Unsuspected* grossed $400,000 over its cost.

The disappointment weighed on Curtiz when he was the special guest star on the *Vox Pop* radio show in late 1947. After being extolled on the broadcast by a cheerleading squad that included Jack Warner, Limey Plews, Fred Clark, Michael North, Joan Crawford, Jack Carson, and his wife, Bess Meredyth, Curtiz was asked about his punishing work ethic, which made him the first to arrive on the set every morning. His answer was somber: "I'm working hard but the hard work is, and my enthusiasm, what I put forth in twenty years is really a self-protection because this art, what I can call a combination of art, is very beautiful but very cruel. A man can only stand so long as he delivers the right picture. He must keep an unbroken string of success because one or two bad pictures end his career."

It had been a long journey for the young auteur from Budapest who arrived in Hollywood two decades earlier believing he knew it all. Curtiz's singular artistry had merged into the collaborative craft of studio moviemaking. When asked what it took to make a good movie, his response undoubtedly made Hal Wallis beam with satisfaction: "A director alone can't make a picture. It's depending entirely on the organization and the cooperation, what he can get from his coworkers. Any department must be the perfect department. It should be the art department, the carpenter shop, the electrician. . . . They all should cooperate with the actors and the director together and that's the only way to make a good picture."

Curtiz believed he couldn't produce two unsuccessful films in a row. In the environment then roiling Hollywood, his next picture might well be his last. He needed to find another star so he could keep making movies.

28

Vanished Dreams

For every film produced in Hollywood, there are at least ten times as many that never get made. It remains the nature of the business and was particularly acute during the studio system era. The constant buzz about upcoming productions emanated from studio trial balloons, agenda-focused leaks, and authentic reporting.

Curtiz was no exception to this speculative merry-go-round. He was supposedly going to produce Thomas Wolfe's *Look Homeward, Angel* in late 1946, followed by other projects that fizzled out for one reason or another. *Victoria Grandolet* went nowhere because of casting difficulties. After the disappointment of *The Unsuspected*, Curtiz soured on crime melodramas and allowed his option on *Winter Kill* to expire. In February 1947 he reportedly paid $50,000 for screen rights to *Sugarfoot,* a Western novel by Clarence Budington Kelland, whose writings had spawned some thirty movies, including *Mr. Deeds Goes to Town* (1936). *Sugarfoot* would eventually surface as a routine Randolph Scott Western helmed by Edwin L. Marin at Warner Bros in 1951. Curtiz traveled to New York in June 1947 for wardrobe and makeup tests of the actor-dancer James Mitchell, whom he signed for something called *Shadow of Fear,* written by Frances Marion. It was another picture that would never get made. He also owned the rights to *Serenade,* a cherished project based on a James M. Cain novel. Two years after Curtiz left Warner Bros., the studio's Technicolor musical version of *Serenade* bore little resemblance to Cain's book. Costarring the improbable duo of Mario Lanza and Joan Fontaine, *Serenade* was the worst film ever directed by the esteemed Anthony Mann and lost over $600,000.

Curtiz and his production staff (especially Bess Meredyth) reviewed a multitude of scripts and treatments before deciding on a story that Warner Bros. had originally purchased in 1939. The Argentinean scenarists Sixto Pondal Ríos and Carlos A. Olivari wrote *Musical Romance,* and Hal

Wallis optioned it for a programmer titled *Gambling on the High Seas* (1940). George Amy directed the forgotten picture starring a young Jane Wyman and Wayne Morris. In April 1947 Warner bought the property for Curtiz and transferred it to MCP for $75,000. It was a lighthearted story about a band singer who embarks on a Caribbean cruise ship assuming the identity of a socialite who is being trailed by a private eye hired by her mistrustful husband. Curtiz and Meredyth believed the scenario was perfect for a Technicolor musical comedy. Warner agreed. The picture's working title became *Romance in High C*.

Judy Garland was the top choice as the singer but her erratic behavior during the production of *The Pirate* (1948), culminating in a nervous breakdown in April 1947, convinced Curtiz that she wasn't worth the risk. It wouldn't have made any difference. Believing that they had gotten the short end of the *Life with Father* Powell-Flynn swap, Metro wouldn't have lent out even a healthy Garland; they also denied access to Kathryn Grayson. Curtiz eventually got Paramount to agree to a loan-out of Betty Hutton for *Romance in High C*. Hutton got pregnant and didn't work again till January 1949.

Curtiz also considered Lauren Bacall, who received a summons to return to Burbank while at the San José Purua Hotel in Michoacán, Mexico, where she was staying with her husband Humphrey Bogart (he was on location for *The Treasure of the Sierra Madre*). Bacall wasn't budging. Although she had no problem with Curtiz, who wanted her to come to the studio for Technicolor tests to ensure that they would both be comfortable, Bacall distrusted any recommendation endorsed by Jack Warner: "He [Warner] put me in *Confidential Agent*, which was a disaster and almost ruined me. I had to spend the next twenty years of my life trying to prove that I was legitimate enough to have my name above the title. He not only made my life hell professionally, he never had any vision, any sense of protecting anyone. Because I allowed him to make that choice [*Confidential Agent*] for me, I never allowed him to make another choice."

After reading the script that was flown down to her in Mexico, Bacall sent Curtiz a "Dear Mike" telegram: "I was hoping with all my heart that this part would be it but after reading the script I was terribly disappointed to find that it is out. I feel that I would let you down because I don't think this is something I can do with confidence. I don't feel there is any point in wasting your time and money testing for the part. Am sure that Jack will not receive this as well so I have written him a letter trying to explain my feelings. Best regards, Betty."

Ready to pull out what was left of his hair, Curtiz tested Marion Hutton, Betty's sister. She was a big band singer originally discovered by Glenn Miller. Although she had made several film appearances as a vocalist, Marion was found wanting. Curtiz finally wrote a letter to Jack Warner stating that he had decided to look for a new face and voice for *Romance in High C*. And he indeed did have his eye on an acting neophyte who could sing.

Doris Day's hit song "Sentimental Journey," recorded with Les Brown and His Band of Renown in early 1945, became the homecoming anthem for millions of American servicemen. While touring with Brown and appearing on Bob Hope's weekly radio show, Day had a string of hit records that made her one of the best-known pop vocalists.

By early 1947 her future was uncertain. The swing era had peaked and Day's marriage to the saxophonist George Weidler had unraveled. Although the couple wouldn't divorce until 1949, Weidler left his wife when he hit the road to tour with the bandleader Stan Kenton. A depressed Day prepared to head back to her native Cincinnati to work at a local radio station. There are a few different accounts of the exact circumstances under which she came to Curtiz's attention.

Her memoir, written with A. E. Hotchner, asserts that she was introduced to Curtiz the day after she sang at a party at the composer Jule Styne's house. Both Styne and the lyricist Sammy Cahn had a vested interest in locating an actress-singer for Curtiz. The duo would compose eight songs for *Romance in High C*, including "It's Magic," which would be nominated for an Oscar. Day's agent, Al Levy, brought his reluctant client to Styne's party. Day remembered being cornered by Levy and the two composers and pitched to go to Warner Bros. the next morning to audition for Curtiz.

Nearly thirty years later, Sammy Cahn assumed credit in his memoir for bringing Day to Curtiz's attention after the unsuccessful test of Marion Hutton and for coaching her through her audition. But nobody at the audition noted Cahn's presence, and Day initially auditioned for Curtiz on April 16, whereas Marion Hutton's screen test occurred afterward, on April 29. Who might have tipped off Curtiz about Doris Day? Jack Carson appeared on the *Sweeney & March* radio show with Day and would end up being her costar and rumored lover. Years afterward, Day reportedly told her friend the actress Kaye Ballard that Carson was responsible for initiating her contact with Curtiz. In any case, it is clear that Day's invitation to audition for Curtiz was not spontaneous. Al Levy received a letter from George Amy on April 14 inviting Day for a screen test at Michael Curtiz Productions. Amy noted in the letter that Day would "receive makeup, wardrobe and a script."

She went to Warner Bros. on April 16 accompanied by Al Levy. Levy chatted with her about who Curtiz was during the car ride to Burbank, but Day was feeling blue about the end of her marriage and barely paid attention. She recalled, "Nothing mattered to me except my personal life and my personal life was a melancholy ruin." Upon their arrival, Day and Levy were presented with a letter from George Amy stating that in return for testing her, Michael Curtiz Productions would have an exclusive option for her services for seven years starting at $500 per week with yearly raises to $2,500 per week. The option was valid for execution until May 20, 1947. Day's signature is appended to the letter. In other words, for the privilege of being granted an audition, she was obligated to a seven-year contract with Curtiz's company if he chose to sign her within the next six weeks.

Greeting them in his bungalow, Curtiz asked Day, "So what you do? You stand up in front of band and sing?" Day told Curtiz that she knew nothing about acting and was unenthusiastic about being in the film. After warbling a few bars of "Embraceable You," she broke down in tears and retreated to the ladies room to compose herself. A startled Curtiz asked Levy if she was ill. He explained her marital situation and Curtiz shrugged, "Oh that. Just so she's healthy."

After Day returned and sang a bit more, she broke down again and apologized profusely to Curtiz. He was charmed by the twenty-three-year-old: "You're very sensitive girl—To be good actress is to be sensitive. . . . I sometimes like girl who is not actress. Is less pretend and more heart." According to Day, Curtiz handed over a marked-up script, instructing her to memorize several scenes and return to the studio at six the next morning to be made up for a series of screen tests.

On May 2, 1947, Curtiz directed tests of Day performing alongside Don McGuire, who was subbing for Carson. She worked from 9:00 a.m. to 6:05 p.m. and nailed her three scenes, which included a pair of songs. Curtiz knew he had his star. A letter on MCP letterhead signed by George Amy exercising the April 16 option was sent out the same day. Day's memoir notes that Carson phoned later in the day to tell her that she had the part even before Levy could notify her. She signed a seven-year contract with Michael Curtiz Productions on May 8.

Although Curtiz and Jack Carson would coach her during the filming of what was eventually titled *Romance on the High Seas,* Day was a natural.[1] As she put it, "Movie acting came to me with greater ease and naturalness than anything else I have ever done." Day became a skilled actress whose admirers included Alfred Hitchcock and James Cagney. Hitchcock introduced himself to Day at a Hollywood party and subsequently cast her in *The Man Who Knew Too Much* (1956). While filming the acclaimed biography-musical *Love Me or Leave Me* (1955), in which Day portrays the torch singer Ruth Etting, opposite Cagney as her gangster-husband, Cagney took her aside and told her: "You know girl, you have a quality that I've seen but twice before. There was a gal named Pauline Lord who created the title role in Eugene O'Neill's *Anna Christie,* and I'm also thinking of Laurette Taylor. Both these ladies could really get on there and do it with everything. They could take you apart playing a scene. Now you are the third one."

It was this singular trait that Curtiz recognized during the first few bars of "Sentimental Journey," followed by her successful screen test. Although he initially tried to shape her performance into a brassy Betty Hutton hybrid, he quickly gave it up as a bad idea. In addition to preserving Day's natural character, he was determined to protect her confidence. He flatly refused to allow her to view any of the rushes. When she asked to see how a printed scene came out, Curtiz told her, "I liked it . . . and that's good enough for you." Day began taking acting instruction from a drama coach, Sophie Rosenstein, shortly after production began on June 2, but Curtiz halted the lessons, explaining:

> Doris, I tell you about acting. Some people, the lessons are very good for them. But I tell you about you—you have very strong individual personality. No matter what you do on screen, no matter what kind of part you play, it will always be you. What I mean is, the Doris Day will always shine though the part. This [*Romance on the High Seas*] will make you big important star. You listen to me. Is very rare thing. You look Gable acting, Gary Cooper, Carole Lombard, they are playing different part but always is same personality coming through. But you take other actors, maybe better actors, who become the character they are playing and lose all of themselves. They can be fantastic but big stars, never. Because there is not that personality, always there, that the audience identify with. . . . You have very, very strong personality. Is you. Is unique. That's why I don't want you to take lessons. You have a

natural thing there in you, should no one ever disturb. You listen to me, Doris. Is very rare thing. Do not disturb.

She accepted the director's counsel and never looked back. Seven decades after her screen debut, Doris Day's respect for the man she still calls "Mr. Curtiz" remains absolute.

Curtiz promptly initiated a needless squabble with Hedda Hopper over his new discovery. He believed that the columnist misquoted him as saying he was against screen-testing Mary Martin and Lauren Bacall in lieu of Doris Day. This was undoubtedly an instance of Curtiz misinterpreting what Hopper had written or listening to someone who wanted to get his goat. "You found it necessary to misquote me and cause me such discomfiture," concluded his angry telegram to Hollywood's gossip doyenne. Hopper responded with a letter—carbon-copied to Jack Warner—that characterized his protest as "childish." Chagrined over alienating the powerful columnist for no reason, he wrote Hopper an apologetic letter thanking her for "the wonderful break you gave Doris Day in your column this morning." The episode reinforced Jack Warner's growing belief that Curtiz had lost his focus on directing because of the distractions of his production company.

The Warner musicals of the postwar era fell short in comparison to the lavish classics produced by the Arthur Freed unit at MGM. Aside from creative inequalities, Jack Warner wouldn't consider matching the budgetary resources with which Metro endowed its films. Nevertheless, *Romance on the High Seas* included some high-powered expertise behind the camera. The Epstein twins wrote the screenplay, and Billy Wilder's future collaborator I. A. L. "Izzy" Diamond polished the dialogue. Curtiz also added an authentic heavyweight when he hired Busby Berkeley to choreograph the musical numbers. The director knew that dropping the choreographer Bob Sidney in favor of Berkeley would be a boon to the picture's publicity.

The legendary director-choreographer had fallen on hard times. By 1947 Berkeley had flamed through five marriages and oceans of booze. He had recently cut his wrists after the death of his beloved mother. Even so, his self-destructiveness couldn't extinguish a beacon of unique talent and a track record of previous successes. After the abortive suicide attempt was splashed all over the newspapers, Berkeley showed up in Warner's office hat in hand. In a rare gesture of sentiment coupled with respect, Warner asked Curtiz to hire him for *Romance on the High Seas*.[2]

Curtiz welcomed back his former colleague and assigned him to arrange the dance numbers in conjunction with his brother David's second unit. Berkeley's laserlike concentration rivaled Curtiz's similar focus. His *Romance* numbers were unspectacular except for the splash finish that Curtiz asked him to dream up. In Berkeley's finale Day is singing "It's Magic" amid an array of descending balloons and sparkling confetti.

Curtiz was in complete control, as Eric Stacey noted in his daily reports to Tenny Wright: "Mike's progress on this picture is remarkable, and as you know, it's due to the fact that he is always prepared way ahead and his shots are lined up, as no other director thinks this far ahead." Having the lightning-fast Bredell shoot the picture also helped. It wrapped on August 4, a week ahead of schedule and an estimated $250,000 under budget.

In addition to Day and Carson, the cast included Janis Paige, Don DeFore, and the pianist Oscar Levant, who played Day's boyfriend. Curtiz reportedly traveled to New York to convince Levant to appear in the picture, but he inexplicably gave him little to do other than a handful of sardonic scenes. The cynical pianist-actor-wit, who liked to claim he was once thrown out of an insane asylum for making the other inhabitants depressed, could be difficult. He reportedly quarreled so vociferously with Ray Heindorf that the arranger-composer asked Curtiz to take him (Heindorf) off the picture.

Prerelease buzz focused on Doris Day. Even though the screen newcomer was fourth-billed, Curtiz and Jack Warner were convinced that she would be an instant star and *Romance on the High Seas* a major hit. They were right on the first point and more right than wrong on the second, even as the most positive critical reaction deemed the picture "agreeable summer fare." The baleful Bosley Crowther termed it "woeful banality" while ascribing the cause of Day's "noisiness" to "Michael Curtiz's direction . . . as slapdash and void of distinction as it can professionally be." One can only wonder what Crowther thought he was watching. *Romance* was a well-directed, slick picture with no goals other than entertainment. The onscreen chemistry between Doris Day and Jack Carson was captivating.

Although the foreign and domestic grosses were $692,000 over the cost of $2,530,000, there were the revenues from the film's copyrighted songs, which flowed back into the studio coffers. Curtiz's seven-year agreement with Day was skewed against the artist in a manner typical of the era. MCP had right of approval on all of her radio, stage, and personal ap-

Curtiz and Doris Day with retired Marine Corps lieutenant general Holland "Howling Mad" Smith on the set of *Romance on the High Seas* (1948) (courtesy of the Academy of Motion Picture Arts and Sciences).

pearances and received 50 percent of her earnings from these endeavors. In July Curtiz approved licensing Day's likeness on Loft Candy products for a cut of the profits and free publicity for his movie while receiving half of her thousand-dollars-per-week salary from Bob Hope's radio show. Day's recording rights were surprisingly left unfettered, and she continued cutting tunes for Columbia Records. Warner Bros. received royalties on the records and the sheet music for "It's Magic," which reached the number 2 on the Billboard chart position (it remained on the chart for twenty-one weeks) as Curtiz rushed her into another picture.

Jack Warner came up with the notion to star Day with Ray Bolger in *The Life of Marilyn Miller.* Miller was reputedly the only actress in the history of the studio with whom Warner became romantically involved. The volatile former Ziegfeld star had an abbreviated screen career, dying at the age of thirty-seven in 1936. Instead, it was June Haver who would star as Marilyn Miller in *Look for the Silver Lining* (1949), directed by

David Butler, while Day was reunited with Curtiz in *My Dream Is Yours*. The film was a repackaging of the studio's *Twenty Million Sweethearts* (1934), which had starred Pat O'Brien as a fast-talking promoter intent on elevating a singing waiter, Dick Powell, into a star crooner. The new script featured Jack Carson as the schlepping agent who is fired by an egotistical radio singer, Lee Bowman. Seeking a new star for his radio program account, Carson spots Doris Day in New York working as a turntable operator for a jukebox company. A war widow and single mother, Day arrives in Hollywood, becomes a star, and ends up being entangled in a romantic and competitive triangle with Bowman and Carson.

Curtiz used the Cocoanut Grove and Schwab's Pharmacy as the backdrop for a handsome Technicolor production. He fashioned a top-notch supporting cast, including Eve Arden, at her wisecracking best as Carson's assistant, Adolphe Menjou, S. Z. Sakall, Selena Royle, slow-burning Edgar Kennedy, Sheldon Leonard, and Franklin Pangborn.

Day was visibly more comfortable, particularly during her musical numbers. The critics enjoyed her even more the second time out and were fairly positive about the picture. At first glance, *My Dream Is Yours* is a humorous paean to the travails of a Hollywood talent agent sandwiched around Day intoning Harry Warren's musical compositions. But there was an insider perspective to be gleaned from the Carson, Bowman, and Day characters, governed as they were by their show business ambitions. Martin Scorsese recalled being profoundly affected: "*My Dream Is Yours* had all the trappings of a Doris Day vehicle produced on the Warner Bros. assembly line. It seemed to be pure escapist fare. But the comedy had a bitter edge. You saw the performers' personal relationships turning sour and being sacrificed to their careers. . . . The film makes you aware of how difficult, if not impossible, relationships are between creative people. It was a major influence on my own musical, *New York, New York*. I took that tormented romance and made it the very subject of the film."

Curtiz had to go toe-to-toe with Steve Trilling to retain a partially animated segment in the picture. The number "Freddie Gets Ready" involved a dream sequence in which Day and Carson wear bunny suits, singing and cavorting with Bugs Bunny and Tweetie Bird while Liszt's *Hungarian Rhapsody No. 2* (a favorite of the Warner animator Friz Freleng) accompanied their antics on the soundtrack. Curtiz dug in his heels, particularly after Trilling threatened to cut off funding for the number near the end of production. Curtiz knew that "let's wait and see the rushes first" was a smoke screen that would result in the sequence's being canceled. He immediately called out Trilling:

> Will you please believe my judgment in regard to the "dream" sequence (cartoon number). I feel we do not have to wait until we see the picture to decide whether we need this number or not. As you know we have a very weak story and I am doing everything I can to give the picture some production and class. . . . Do not be guided by any suggestions of trying to make this dream sequence all in cartoon as I feel this would cheapen the picture from the production standpoint. I must insist that I go into to this number immediately upon completion of the picture.

Curtiz won the argument. The sequence was shot and included in the final cut. A clever notion that had been more memorably used by MGM, the animated sequence made little difference to the overall picture. *My Dream Is Yours* was a demonstrably better film than *Romance on the High Seas,* but it did similar business.

Curtiz was disheartened by the depressing fiscal realities of his production company. With MCP little more than two years old, he discovered that he had increasingly less freedom to make movies, as he was steadily accumulating debt instead of profits. In addition to the notes held by the New York Trust Company for his first pair of films, he had to get a $586,000 advance from Warner Bros. to make *My Dream Is Yours.* Jack Warner concluded that Curtiz's company was a white elephant. He had an attorney, Ralph E. Lewis, draft a confidential letter for the studio's New York legal office:

> [J. L. Warner] has become very much disturbed over the situation with Michael Curtiz Productions. . . . Mike Curtiz himself has no administrative talent whatsoever, and . . . the corporation is falling further behind financially all the time. It owes Warners approximately $1,500,000 in advances in addition to the Warner charge of 35% for overhead and other miscellaneous items. . . . Apparently the only purpose in initiating the deal in 1946 was to protect Mike Curtiz in the future and allow him to accumulate a nest egg on a capital gains basis. It is now obvious that the nest egg will not develop and Mike is apparently sacrificing his directorial abilities to his worry about financial and administrative problems.

The letter concluded with Warner's proposed solution: "J.L. wants to give Mike some kind of nest egg with a capital gains factor. He wants to deal individually with Mike and purchase Mike's 51% of the stock for a total price of $500,000 payable in installments of $100,000 per year. He then wants Mike to cancel his existing contract with Curtiz Productions and enter into a direct employment agreement with Warners on the basis of, say $3500 per week plus 10% of the gross."

Warner was creating a way out that would be financially remunerative for Curtiz and allow him to continue making movies for the studio. The prevailing story pegs Curtiz's managerial ineptitude along with the postwar box-office slump as the chief causes of his company's downward spiral. But Curtiz and others had a different perspective.

On paper, his deal with the studio appeared reasonable, but the business realities as an appendage of Warner Bros. turned profitability into a mirage. Net profits for MCP were calculated only after 20 percent and 25 percent deductions were made to Warner for domestic and foreign distribution charges, respectively, plus additional deductions that included advertising, publicity, printing, and so on. The advances to MCP for scripts and predevelopment costs were loans carrying 4 percent interest charges. The brothers Warner apparently couldn't countenance making an interest-free investment in a company on their own lot, of which they owned nearly half. Not to mention that they were slated to receive 70 percent of the profits of the movies made by a filmmaker who had worked for them since 1926 and was responsible for some of their biggest hits. From keeping lights turned off, haranguing writers to observe a time clock, and reusing nails, the studio's ethos of thrift remained unchanged. There was also a new wrinkle. Curtiz and George Amy repeatedly complained about excessive overhead charges that ate into their balance sheet. For Warner Bros., retrenchment to the new postwar world of leaner budgets and fewer movies included the advent of creative accounting that encouraged the mischarging of production costs to Curtiz's company. Byron Haskin recalled: "When they finally gave him [Curtiz] his own company at Warner Bros., they proceeded to steal him blind. The diffusers on the lake, which had nothing to do with him, they'd charge against his pictures. Everything. He couldn't make any money at all; they were charging the capital outlay of Warner Bros. against him. How do I know this? I was in Jack Warner's office—at a time when we were not too friendly, and he had a hell of a lot of nerve telling Tenny Wright in front of me, 'Slough that stuff over to Curtiz.'"

John Meredyth Lucas believed that the studio deliberately put his stepfather's production company out of business: "All Mike's Doris Day pictures were moneymakers although the Warner books showed a loss. . . . The evil of studio bookkeeping is not a new thing. But with a combination of that and other efforts, Warners was finally able to put Mike in a position that was untenable."

There was also no doubt that while Jack Warner believed Curtiz remained a potent filmmaker, he coveted Doris Day, whose contract would revert to him after he bought out Curtiz's company.

As Curtiz believed he had been royally screwed, it wasn't surprising that his final production under the MCP banner had a contentious beginning. Jerry Wald was his usual enthusiastic self, touting the proposed production of Robert Wilder's novel *Flamingo Road*. Wilder and his wife turned his book into a play that flopped in March 1946, but Jack Warner bought the property anyway. Ann Sheridan and the director Vincent Sherman rejected the initial script, but the indefatigable Wald wanted Curtiz to direct it as a vehicle for Joan Crawford and sent him a revised script by Richard Brooks with some polishing by Ranald MacDougall. Although Jack Warner asked him to make the picture and Curtiz reluctantly agreed, he was unenthusiastic about Brooks's screenplay. He also resented being forced into making *Flamingo Road* rather than James M. Cain's *Serenade,* a property that he had purchased and believed he had a commitment from Jack Warner to produce.

Curtiz forwarded the first portion of the revised *Flamingo Road* script that Wald had sent him to Steve Trilling with a covering note: "There must be something terribly and basically wrong with a story when two fine writers like Brooks and MacDougall turn in material like this. No matter how we twist it and change it, it remains drab, synthetic and uninteresting."

After a story conference the following week, Curtiz's notes to Trilling listed twenty-one specific problems with the Brooks screenplay and summarized: "The character for Crawford is just a dumb, uninteresting, unexciting girl and I don't know how to characterize her because she has no character."

Curtiz worked on preproduction while continuing to stew. He told Trilling that he didn't understand why Edmund North's original script was discarded to start over with "the basic phony idea he [Wald] had." In a note to Jack Warner, he fretted about the screenwriting costs of *Flamingo Road*: "The reason I am writing you this letter is that I now realize how much money is involved so far in purchasing the book and working on it for so many months with expensive writers. Naturally it would not be fair for Michael Curtiz Productions Inc. to assume all of these charges. I leave it to your judgment to set a story price against Michael Curtiz Productions, Inc., dated May 4, 1948, at which time I assumed the reconstruction job."

Curtiz concluded by asking to be taken off the picture if he couldn't knock the script together in three weeks. The time came and went, the script was still unresolved, and Warner refused to remove him. The following month, MCP released a press release to the trade papers that stated in part, "The production of *Flamingo Road* is being called off, the entire project is being abandoned and Miss Crawford will probably do a different picture." After Jerry Wald rebutted the story in the *Hollywood Reporter,* Curtiz responded with a memo claiming he had nothing to do with the press release and upbraided Wald for publicly insulting him. Although Curtiz was on edge, it is likely that he made a grievous error by ranting about *Flamingo Road* to his publicist or he was trying to get even for what he believed was high-handed treatment by the studio. Either way, his actions only made matters worse.

One of Curtiz's most ardent supporters, Jerry Wald, believed the MCP release caused "incalculable damage" to the production of *Flamingo Road* and confided that the director's published statement "makes me feel like throwing up." He explained to Curtiz in a memo: "If you don't like a script that is your prerogative, but certainly it is not right for you to air your feelings on the script by announcing that the entire project is being abandoned. The fact that you can't go along with us is certainly our loss."

Jack Warner termed Curtiz's actions as "uncalled for and highly unethical." Curtiz, accompanied by his attorney, Mark Cohen, was summoned to a conference with Trilling. He was reminded of his commitment to make *Flamingo Road*. It was also noted that he was not authorized to start *Serenade* until Warner approved the budget and a successful test of Jane Wyman was completed. Trilling advised Curtiz that it would be best for all concerned to end his production deal with the studio after *Flamingo Road,* adding that the studio was dropping the notion of the stock buyout. Curtiz was left to ponder the humiliating possibility of having to file for bankruptcy. He had little choice but to make *Flamingo Road* and then reengage with Jack Warner about the fate of his company after tempers cooled.

Jerry Wald sent both scripts to Joan Crawford in July 1948, asking her to state her preference. Crawford agreed with Curtiz that the North script would make a better film, so that was that. Curtiz brought in Robert Wilder for extensive rewrites. Wilder received sole screen credit, while North was credited for additional dialogue. Curtiz might have gotten his own way with the script, but not behind the camera. Tenny Wright disapproved his request for Woody Bredell, and Ted McCord shot the picture.

All was forgiven when production began in mid-September. Jack Warner sent his usual optimistic memorandum to Curtiz, noting, "Despite all the trouble we have had, I have a hunch that it will be a great box office attraction and will rival *Mildred Pierce* for top honors." In addition to Crawford and the newcomer David Brian, who joined Curtiz's acting stable, the principal players were the contract stars Zachary Scott and Sydney Greenstreet. *Flamingo Road* repurposed the rags-to-riches theme: Crawford is a carnival grind dancer, Lane Bellamy, who ends up adrift in the small southern town of Bolden City, run with an iron hand by Greenstreet as the corrupt sheriff, Titus Semple—Greenstreet's last good role. Lane falls for a milquetoast deputy sheriff, Fielding Carlisle (Scott), who is being groomed by Semple for political office. After Carlisle is forced into a marriage of convenience and Lane is framed on a prostitution rap to get her out of town (both orchestrated by the perverse Semple), she marries the political supremo Dan Reynolds (Brian) to position herself as a mink-adorned matron on Flamingo Road. After Carlisle commits suicide and Semple outmaneuvers Reynolds, matters shape up for a juicy showdown.

The usual script compromises were necessary. A house of prostitution run by Lute Mae Sanders (Gladys George) became a roadhouse tavern; Lane had to legitimately fall in love with Reynolds to placate the Breen office with an ending borrowed from *Mildred Pierce*. Curtiz finished it two weeks ahead of schedule and under budget using the downtown Hollywood Freeway construction site at Temple and Figueroa streets for Reynolds's construction company. Downtown Pomona doubled as Bolden City, and the Los Angeles County Jail was rented to shoot the finale. *Flamingo Road* didn't match the quality of *Mildred Pierce*. The picture was a formulaic, well-made melodrama that was weakened by Crawford as a sideshow Venus whom men clambered after. At forty-five, her ability to credibly put these types of roles across was diluted. The star's close-ups reveal an aged-in-vodka maturity that could not be obscured by Perc Westmore's makeup or Ted McCord's camera filters. Greenstreet walked off with the picture by essaying one of his more delightfully repugnant turns.

Flamingo Road didn't meet Jerry Wald's over-the-top expectations (he compared its potential to that of *The Best Years of Our Lives* in one of his lengthy memos), but it was the most successful of Curtiz's four MCP productions. It realized $1,365,000 over its cost and was one of only six films released by the studio in 1949 that cleared the $1 million hurdle. Jack Warner believed that his publicity campaign, which included a "hot photo of Crawford with cigarette in mouth, gams showing, etc," was responsible for the success. It was the type of picture that Warners did better than anyone else. It was also part of an era that was coming to an end.

By the time *Flamingo Road* was released, Warner Bros. was a different studio from the one that had produced *Casablanca*. There had been a mass exodus of talent. After John Huston wrapped *Key Largo* in early 1948, he left to make films with the producer Sam Spiegel.[3] Publicly branded by Warner as disloyal, the Epstein twins departed to write a play and freelance. Barbara Stanwyck became upset at being aced out by Patricia Neal to star in *The Fountainhead* (1949). She opted out of her contract in June 1948. Zachary Scott would star in the appropriately titled *One Last Fling* before moving on. Sydney Greenstreet made one more picture (1949's *Malaya,* at MGM) and then retired because of ill health. Known as the studio's "Suspension Queen," Ann Sheridan felt trapped in roles of repetitive mediocrity. After costarring with Errol Flynn in the desultory *Silver River* (1948), she forked over $35,000 to buy herself out of her contract. Bette Davis would have a final battle royal with Jack Warner, this time over the mogul's forcing her to star in *Beyond the Forest*. She finally agreed to do the film, then asked for and received a release from her contract in July 1949.

The Warner Bros. dynamism that had pioneered sound and the populist style of the studio's pictures had become increasingly ossified. Jack Warner had become less willing to keep anyone around who didn't always agree with him. Robert Buckner, the epitome of the company man, remarked on the decline of the studio he loved: "It began to go downhill. Jack was a fine studio boss as far as the overall picture was concerned, but he was not a good selector of material. . . . Jack wasn't buying material that we wanted to make, and he wasn't listening to suggestions." Rather than reenlist aboard what he viewed was a sinking ship, Buckner accepted an offer from Universal-International. Even though none of their 1949 pictures would be nominated for a major Academy Award or was in the top twenty-five of Hollywood's moneymakers that year, both Warners refused to concede that anything might be amiss.[4] The studio belonged to them, and they would run things as they saw fit. Jack was now fifty-seven and Harry was sixty-eight. Their focus shifted to attempting to maintain what they had built.

Jack Warner eventually made a formal offer to buy out Curtiz's company. As in all matters involving the studio's financial well-being, he planned the acquisition with care. A great deal of correspondence flowed among the three brothers and their attorneys in figuring out their tax position in light of the studio's purchase of Michael Curtiz Productions.

Curtiz knew he had to redouble his efforts toward directing successful motion pictures rather than continuing to flail as a production executive. He met with Warner and received the offer and asked for a couple of days to think it over. His main concern was ensuring that his profits after Warner bought his 510 shares of company stock for $400,000 would be taxed at the capital limitations rate. His other anxiety was that his younger brother David would continue to be employed by the studio as an assistant director. Warner's sole objective was to free up Curtiz to concentrate on making pictures. As he wrote to the attorney Sam Schneider earlier in the year, while they were thrashing out the tax issues for the studio and Curtiz: "I hope this can go over as it will remove a very big thorn in the operation of the studio here as I would say that we have lost the manpower Curtiz once gave us. . . . This whole situation is important to the profitability of our company." Warner emphasized to his legal team that he wanted to handle the matter personally with Curtiz and preclude him from consulting with outside attorneys and tax experts. He also expressed the belief that Curtiz was being badly served by people in his company who were looking out for their own interests. After the tax matter was resolved in his favor, Curtiz sold his company to Warner Bros.

And in the blink of an eye, the studio swallowed his company, including his contracted talent (Doris Day, Dolores Del Rio, Fred Clark, James Mitchell, David Brian, George Amy, and David Curtiz), story options (*Serenade*, *La Otra*, *Shadow of Fear*, *The 49ers*, and *No Common Clay*), and outstanding loans ($1,016,000). Warner appointed his son-in-law William T. (Bill) Orr to clean up unfinished business. Orr's first task was paying off Dolores Del Rio, whom Curtiz had signed on August 30, 1947, for *The Sanctuary*, which was never produced. Her contract was settled for $20,000.

In negotiating the director's new contract, Jack Warner initially stuck to his position of 10 percent for the profit percentage. Curtiz considered the offer insulting. To break the impasse, Harry Warner interceded on behalf of Curtiz. The seven-year deal, finalized on December 31, 1948, awarded Curtiz a salary of $3,500 per week plus 25 percent of the net receipts on his pictures. In return for the higher profit percentage, Curtiz received $100,000 less for his stock buyout. Records indicate that the studio also paid off Curtiz's outstanding notes to First National Bank in 1949. Under his new contract, Curtiz had the right of refusal for one of every two films that were assigned to him. If he turned down both films, the studio would pick one for him or assign him to a different picture. He also had the right of choice of two scripts per film. Although Curtiz cabled his thanks to Harry Warner, his new deal didn't alter the financial realities of the time. Warner Bros shut down production during January–February 1949, while continuing to trim the payroll; this included converting contracts with Humphrey Bogart and Errol Flynn to one-picture-per-year deals. When production ramped back up, Curtiz discovered how his new contract would be honored.

Despite rejecting a pair of scripts for something called *The Octopus and Miss Smith*, Curtiz was pressured into making it without being offered an alternative film. The picture was an aimless comedy starring Jane Wyman as the head of a consumer research institute whose weekend sailing excursion abruptly ends when an undersea tractor skippered by a marine biologist, Dennis Morgan, capsizes her boat. It turns out he is an engineer working on a secret government project and has to hush up the encounter. There were some amusing comedic episodes and the verbal vitriol of Eve Arden, but how anyone believed that this movie—eventually titled *The Lady Takes a Sailor*—would be anything other than a waste of talent and money was an indication of how far the studio had slipped. Curtiz's commitment to the project was noticeably lacking. "I felt his mind was elsewhere all through it," observed the actor Allyn Joslyn. "Mike was a dynamo usually, but he seemed to slink through this one with a hangdog air, as if Jack Warner was punishing him for something or other. And the results showed it."

Inaugurating his new contract with a trifle that broke even was not what Curtiz had in mind. Fortunately, Jerry Wald continued to wage what was an increasing struggle to produce quality films with serious content. In 1948 Wald fought Jack Warner every step of the way to produce *Johnny Belinda*, starring Jane Wyman. Warner hated the story about the rape of a deaf-mute Canadian who kills her assaulter and reluctantly gave in to Wald's and the director Jean Negulesco's imploring not to include a Wyman voice-over narrative. Shortly after production closed, Warner fired Negulesco, who went on to direct a string of hit pictures for Twentieth Century-Fox. After *Johnny Belinda* was nominated for ten Oscars, Warner telephoned Negulesco and told him that he knew the picture would be a winner all along

In 1945 Warner Bros. optioned *Young Man with a Horn,* Dorothy Baker's 1938 novel inspired by the brief life and career of the jazz cornet player Leon (Bix) Beiderbecke. The option was passed to the quasi-independent United States Pictures, which was run by the producer Milton Sperling in a set-up similar to Curtiz's now-defunct MCP.[5] Wald yearned to produce a film based on the book and convinced Warner to obtain the rights from Sperling and assign it to him. After receiving the property, Wald immediately sparred with Warner, who wanted to use a script written by Stephen Longstreet and cast Dane Clark as the horn player Rick Martin. Warner backed down. *Young Man with a Horn* was intermittently postponed because of the difficulty in casting the lead role. But Wald kept the project going and asked Warner to have Curtiz direct. Wald engaged Edmund North to write the screenplay with input from Dorothy Baker.

Bix Beiderbecke was a tragic figure whose alcoholism resulted in his death at twenty-eight. Although his career had the abbreviated arc of a Roman candle, he was revered by an entire generation of musicians. His friend Hoagy Carmichael remembered that his notes sounded like "a chime struck by a mallet." Eddie Condon, a Chicago jazzman, came up with a more memorable metaphor: "Bix's sound came out like a girl saying 'yes.'" The general public had nearly forgotten about Beiderbecke's improvisational genius until Otis Ferguson authored a pair of articles for the *New Republic,* "Young Man with a Horn" (July 29, 1936), followed by "Young Man with a Horn Again" (November 18, 1940).

A friend of Ferguson, Dorothy Baker, borrowed the title of his first article for her novel and included a disclaimer that "the inspiration for the writing of this book has been the music, but not the life, of a great musician, Leon (Bix) Beiderbecke." While an obvious motivation for this proviso was a shield against possible litigation from the late musician's family, Baker created distinct differences between Beiderbecke and her Rick Martin character. Martin was cast as an orphan taken in by a teen-age aunt and uncle in Georgia. The trio moves to South Central Los Angeles, where Martin becomes a latchkey kid who teaches himself the piano from a hymnal at the All Souls Mission. Martin becomes friends with Smoke Jordan, a young African American drummer who takes him to the Cotton Club, where they listen to jazz through a window before eventually venturing inside. Martin takes up the trumpet under the veteran black horn player Art Hazzard and becomes an accomplished musician. His improvisational skills earn him a gig in a major New York band, as he becomes one of the great trumpet players of the day. Although an obsessive master of his horn, Martin remains the same social loner whose life wilts under the glare of celebrity, particularly after he marries a socialite. After his marriage hits the skids and Art Hazzard dies, he bottoms out when he fails to hit an unreachable high note during a recording session and is viewed as washed up shortly before dying. Baker's book established the legend of Bix Beiderbecke as the martyred jazz avatar of twentieth-century American popular culture.

Edmund North used most of Baker's reinterpretations of Beiderbecke's life, with the principal exceptions of changing Smoke from a young black drummer to an adult Caucasian pianist played by Hoagy Carmichael and another character, Josephine, from a black to a Caucasian singer. A Wald preproduction memo noted the "elimination of the colored angle." According to one account, Carmichael, a close friend and mentor of Beiderbecke, contacted Wald and Curtiz as soon as he discovered Warner Bros. was producing *Young Man with a Horn*. Wald already had Carmichael in mind for the role of Smoke, and the latter's influence on production would be significant.

To play Rick Martin, James Stewart and Henry Fonda had their names floated, but Kirk Douglas got the nod. Douglas had zoomed to stardom as the ruthlessly obsessed boxer in *Champion* (1949), which premiered two months before *Young Man with a Horn* began production. Although his music style was dissimilar to that of Beiderbecke, the acclaimed trumpeter and band leader Harry James was hired to ghost Douglas on the horn and coach him on aping the visual technique of playing the trumpet.[6] An eager pupil, Douglas immersed himself in the project. He wrote in his memoir that he loved doing the movie and working with Harry James. The actor was intrigued by Beiderbecke's character: "Bix was like Larry Bird—the one white guy with rhythm." He claimed afterward that he wanted to add a scene in which Rick Martin went up to Harlem and jammed with black musicians after hours, but Curtiz vetoed the notion.

To complete the romantic aspect of the story, Doris Day was cast as Josephine, the heart-of-gold singer turned white by the script, and Lauren Bacall as the passive-aggressive socialite, Amy North, who plays mind games with the hapless Martin as he falls for her. Another significant cast member was Juano Hernandez as Art Hazzard. The son of a Puerto Rican father and a Brazilian mother, Hernandez had been a merchant seaman, boxer, and circus acrobat before working in radio and silent films. He projected an aura of rectitude without servility that was unique for any actor of color in Hollywood. His first mainstream role was as a man falsely accused of murder in *Intruder in the Dust* (1950), filmed in the early spring of 1949 on location in Oxford, Mississippi. Hernandez would be nominated for a Golden Globe award for a performance praised by the film historian Donald Bogle more than a half century later: "Hernandez's performance and extraordinary presence still rank above that of almost any other black actor to appear in an American movie." His turn as Art Hazzard in *Young Man with a Horn* drew back the curtain to reveal the angst of a black jazz musician of that era. Curtiz became enamored of Hernandez's acting. Their shared circus background aside, he was impressed by the Puerto Rican native who understood that effective film work was accomplished primarily with his hugely expressive eyes while subtly gesturing with a pair of hands that were the size of hymnals.

Lauren Bacall initially caused Curtiz to double his daily lunchtime ration of aspirin tablets. After agreeing to play the part, she was having second thoughts. She arranged a private meeting with Wald, complaining that her character, Amy North, was "a bitch and unsympathetic." Carl Foreman, who was hired by Wald to write another version of the script, took it one step further by adding a subtle element of lesbianism to Amy's character. As the Rick-Amy marriage implodes during the last third of the picture, distinct inferences are made about the couple's desultory sex life. As Martin agonizes about their extinct intimacy, Amy taunts him, "Besides, how do you know about anything until you try it." Curtiz accentuated a brief but riveting scene of Amy holding hands with a coiffed female friend she is planning to accompany to Europe on a painting sojourn after she dumps Martin. Wald mollified Bacall by selling her on the psychological aspects of the character, but after production began, her objections resurfaced and she clashed with Curtiz. A concerned Wald wrote to William Orr in early July: "We must do something at once about this Bacall-Curtiz situation. Not only is Bacall acting all over the place, but if the clash continues, it must end up costing us a lot of money. . . . Mike is right in his demand that Bacall play the script the way it is written and the way Mike wants it played. If Mike has to have a debate on the set every time he shoots a scene, it has to affect the rest of the cast."

Bacall eventually worked more supportively. Humphrey Bogart

schooled her about Curtiz, whom she found "brilliant with the camera"; he lost his temper "only at those who were vulnerable."

Creation of the shooting script had been the usual contentious exercise: Wald and Foreman were arrayed against Curtiz and the North script. Curtiz made substantial changes to Foreman's script in terms of sets and dialogue. Foreman believed Curtiz diluted Rick Martin's essence as a self-obsessed loner. Wald excluded the director from a meeting between Foreman and Trilling to discuss Curtiz's script changes while Curtiz passed six pages of recommendations directly to Jack Warner. Warner eventually ended the squabbling when he wrote to Wald, "I, personally, do not want to go into a routine on this, but let's not have a repetition of *Flamingo Road* and *Serenade*. In other words, no writing contests." The inevitable compromises incorporated several of Curtiz's ideas along with some of Douglas's notions.

Eager to get to work, Curtiz became irritated when Tenny Wright stopped him from scouting locations in downtown Los Angeles with his brother David, who was directing the second unit. Wright claimed that there wasn't enough script to start the work. Curtiz disagreed and protested to Jack Warner: "We have a temp. script, which, while it is not in shape dramatically, will not differ from the new script in sets and locations. . . . I believe we are on the right track; but it will take four weeks to put the script in shape and another four weeks to prepare the picture, so you are into August with your starting date." Curtiz also included a more personal concern to Warner: "I have a faint suspicion the reason we were stopped in these important preparations is that Dave [Curtiz] would automatically go on salary. I hope my suspicion is wrong and I ask you honestly, Jack, to give me the go ahead signal with full speed to start the picture within four weeks."

Warner relented and Curtiz began shooting at the end of June. The first hour of *Young Man with a Horn* was some of Curtiz's best work since *Mildred Pierce*. After testing more than one hundred boys to play Rick Martin as a child, he chose Orley Lindgren for the role. Lindgren conveyed a realistic sense of childhood loneliness while living in a downtown walk-up with his aunt (the always-sleazy Mary Beth Hughes) and setting pins in a local bowling alley. The scenes in downtown Los Angeles locations by Curtiz and Ted McCord are exquisite, particularly the sequence in which Lindgren becomes captivated by jazz and has his initial meeting with Juano Hernandez. Hoagy Carmichael provides the voice-over narrative by relating Martin's life in flashback. His laconic characterization doesn't strike a single false note, even though his piano playing was inexplicably dubbed and he didn't do much musically. Of his twenty-odd film and television roles, Carmichael considered Smoke Willoughby as tops: "Of the movies I made, *Young Man with a Horn* was a favorite of mine because my character was well-written. . . . I honestly felt properly dedicated to the part as a musician."

After the picture wrapped, Wald thanked Carmichael for "updating the script," and Curtiz wrote him an unusually fulsome letter thanking the music virtuoso for "your help with the story, with the acting, with my work and everybody's work." The authenticity was also revealed in Kirk Douglas's performance as well. As Carmichael observed, "He, too, looked like a music man to me as we played the parts together." The transition to the adult Rick Martin is seamless, as Martin continues his mentoring relationship with Hazzard and meets Jo and Smoke during his first gig in a dance hall. He and Smoke end up playing two-man gigs in mobster-run dives until Smoke packs it in and heads home to Indiana; Martin eventually hits the big time in New York with a prestigious band (led by Jerome Cowan replicating Paul Whiteman), where he meets up with Jo once again. The second half bogs down even with Curtiz's striking use of mirrors in his compositions to reflect the varying moods of the principal characters as the romantic triangle between Martin, Jo, and Amy becomes preeminent. There is a dialogue-free sequence of Amy rebuffing Martin's advances, leaving his apartment, and taking the elevator down to the lobby before pausing and returning to the elevator—to go back and sleep with him. (The Ohio state censor board excised this before approving the picture for exhibition in the Buckeye State.) Bacall's characterization of Amy was perversely interesting. Doris Day is little better than superficial in a thankless role, enlivened only when she sings. The realism of the big band culture that inspired Carmichael and Douglas had the opposite effect on her. Referring to her two failed marriages, to a trombonist and a saxophone player, she remarked that *Young Man with a Horn* "turned out to be a very upsetting experience for me since it carried me back into the band world . . . the sets and the dialogue stirred memories I was trying to forget."

Near the end of the production, Curtiz accompanied Douglas and a second unit to New York City for two days of filming. Wald and Curtiz were intent on shooting Rick Martin's final dissolution on location. Fed up with the fake look of Warner Bros.' "ersatz New York streets" and Tenny Wright's zealous enforcement of the studio's culture of thrift, Wald wrote a heated memorandum to Trilling:

[In] thinking out the *Young Man with Horn* location problem, I find it bears a strange resemblance to what happened on *Pride of the Marines* and *Johnny Belinda* plus a few others. . . . I'm curious about the fantastic tales that are spread in different directions by the production department. I'm curious about the GESTAPO system that prevails. I'm curious why it is so tough to make pictures. Talk to men who have left Warners—the Negulescos, the Daveses, the Hustons—find out from them how the production departments operate on other lots . . . find out. Your eyes will be opened. Mine have been.

Wald got his two days of location filming in New York in much the same way Curtiz overcame an earlier wrangle with Warner over the key scene at Art Hazzard's funeral. Curtiz attended an African American church service in Los Angeles specifically to prep for this scene, which he shot with great care. Warner, already uncomfortable with the picture's depiction of racial comity in the jazz world, sought to have the scene dropped. Curtiz insisted that the scene was crucial to the overall narrative, and it remained in the picture. After Rick Martin hits bottom, lying in the gutter drunk and suffering from pneumonia as a cab crushes his trumpet, he is conveyed to a fleabag alcoholic ward. But the conclusion of the picture remained unresolved. Jack Warner was determined to have a happy ending. Kirk Douglas wrote Warner a letter in which he praised Curtiz before expressing his concern about the ending: "It is my solid conviction that to portray this movie honestly you are depicting a character in whom the seeds of self-destruction were implanted from the very beginning. To do otherwise, I feel strongly, would inject a false note into a picture which I hope will be a very honest one."

Curtiz felt that the ending should replicate Baker's book and Beiderbecke's life, with the tortured musician dying of dissipation, completing the tragic saga of a supremely talented man. Jerry Wald put meat on the bones of Curtiz's notion by suggesting a dissolve from Douglas in the hospital to a close shot of Carmichael at the piano while he narrates a brief soliloquy about the permanence of Rick Martin's musical legacy: "Three or four kids are around a record machine, listening to one of Rick's records. On the record we hear the trumpet solo or Rick and then Doris singing. After Doris's sound track is over, concentrate on just a high note of the trumpet, and the excitement of the kids' faces."

Wald's concept would have maintained the film's integrity on a note

Curtiz directs a rehearsal for *Young Man with a Horn* (1950) with Kirk
Douglas and Hoagy Carmichael (author's collection).

of optimism rather than bleakness. Warner still wasn't having it. He insisted on a finale in which a miraculously recovered Martin is back in
the recording studio joyously playing his horn and Jo is singing in the
background.

After the preview in January 1950, W. R. Wilkerson, the right-wing
editor and publisher of the *Hollywood Reporter,* wrote a letter to Jack
Warner at the urging of Wald that praised the picture, but criticized the
ending: "But Jack, why that ending? It was our impression that the ending took away about 25% of the value of the picture because it was a false
ending. . . . I'm not a picture-maker and would never write the above other
than I think it's a great show that shouldn't be spoiled with such a phony,
untrue tag."

All the entreaties simply made Warner more adamant. The film had
his name on it and he would choose how it would end. It was a shame. A
superbly crafted picture with significant dramatic attributes was made to
appear trite. Wald vented to Sammy Cahn: "Unfortunately, my stomach
is not strong enough to stand the constant pounding it has to take to get
some of these decent ideas on the screen. One of these days I'll blow this
joint and see what it's like in the outside world. It can't be too tough."

At the conclusion of the production, Curtiz wrote Jack Warner a note: "For twenty-two years, you have written me a letter at the beginning of every picture, but this is the first time that I have written to you at the close of a picture. I want to tell you that I am grateful that you assigned me to direct this story, that in spite of how I fought against making it, you, with your far-sighted judgment, believed in it and convinced me that I should do the picture. I don't know how the audience reaction will be to this film but I feel that we have made a courageous picture." Curtiz added, "I pray to God" that the film would be a box-office success. The note to Warner provides a clear insight as to how anxiously Curtiz viewed his future. More than ever before, his pictures had to be financially successful for him to be able to make another one. The agonizing possibility of not being able to direct any more films continued to fuel his relentless drive.

Young Man with a Horn was a commercial success, earning $966,000 over its $1.3 million cost, and the soundtrack record featuring Doris Day's songs and Harry James's horn also did big business. Reviews were mixed: bouquets were tossed toward Douglas's performance, Curtiz's direction, and the supporting cast, while criticism was leveled at the screenplay's romantic theme and the stupid ending.

Having what might well have been an acclaimed picture slip away from him was only momentarily disconcerting. Curtiz achieved a qualified success, and for the moment that was all that mattered. But as always, he never looked backward, particularly as he was preparing to direct one of his best films, one that few people would remember.

29

Doomed Masterpiece

In November 1949 Curtiz began an ambitious saga that would become a forgotten curiosity. *Bright Leaf* chronicles the rise and fall of a turn-of-the-century North Carolinian named Brant Royle (Gary Cooper) who ascends to entrepreneurial wealth as a cigarette magnate romantically involved with two women. Royle is smitten with a southern belle, Margaret Singleton (Patricia Neal), whose tobacco aristocrat father, Major Singleton (Donald Crisp), ruined Royle's family years earlier and ran them out of town. Seeking revenge, Royle borrows money from his true-blue girlfriend, Sonia (Lauren Bacall), who runs the town bawdy house (thinly disguised as a girls' finishing school) and establishes a cigarette factory with a snake oil salesman, Chris Malley (Jack Carson), as his business partner. He bankrupts Singleton, causing his older antagonist to commit suicide. He weds the petulant Margaret, who turns on him to avenge her father's death by selling off her preferred stock and acting as an informant to the attorney general, who is investigating Royle's monopolistic business practices.

Despite Curtiz's direction, a handsome production by Henry Blanke, and sharp photography by Karl Freund, *Bright Leaf* was deemed to be overwrought. Once the novelty of the historical backdrop of the tobacco industry wore off, what remained was a familiar Warner Bros. melodrama that didn't resonate with postwar audiences. Howard Barnes of the *New York Herald Tribune* termed the picture "an unrelenting, but somewhat top-heavy celebration of the birth of the coffin nail."

Bright Leaf is an enjoyable diversion if for nothing more than the casting against type. Cooper's portrayal of the perversely obsessed Brant Royle would be his furthest professional stretch from the heroic characters of Sergeant Alvin York, Lou Gehrig, and Marshal Will Kane. Lauren Bacall, appearing in the final picture of her Warner Bros. contract, refused to attempt a southern accent in addition to running a whorehouse. Ranald MacDougall was compelled make her character Polish.

Cooper and Pat Neal continued their torrid love affair begun on *The Fountainhead* the previous year. Curtiz experienced difficulty with both of them. Neal didn't understand why she had to film the wedding scene with Cooper following a sequence in which they argued. She also claimed that Curtiz forced her to skip lunch before shooting the wedding. When Neal asked him why she couldn't eat lunch before the scene, Curtiz advised, "Because you cannot make love on a full stomach. You will be gay, lovely and charming if you pass up the tray at noontime. Ditch diggers can eat lunch, yes; actors no. I have no use for any of them who eat." Asked to characterize her relationship with Curtiz on *Bright Leaf,* Neal provided a terse response: "Ghastly." Despite her star buildup by Warners, Curtiz treated Neal as a neophyte who simply needed to do what he told her. She was also unhappy about not being able to play Bacall's bad girl role because Cooper refused to go to bat for her with Curtiz and the studio.

Cooper was periodically late (*Bright Leaf* production records indicate that the actor was late four times during a fifty-three-day shoot that finished eleven days over schedule) and had difficulty remembering dialogue. He hadn't worked in over a year. There was also his relaxed persona, which took laconic to laid-back extremes. The quickest way for an actor to antagonize the always-intense director was to convey a lackadaisical attitude. Cooper's "aw-shucks" dissembling after repeatedly blowing his lines drove Curtiz wild. He vented his frustration in a private memo to Steve Trilling. But Curtiz didn't dare confront Cooper publicly, according to Lauren Bacall:

> One morning, he [Cooper] was late and Mike was livid—so much so that he screamed at me. He wouldn't dare let go at Coop, knowing he'd just walk off the set. Now I have never handled myself well in screaming situations. I become inarticulate, usually cry. On this occasion with his ranting and raving—"Goddamn actor bum!"—I took myself tearfully to my dressing room. Finally Coop arrived, not all that late, and Mike was all over him: "Gary dahling, how are you—how do you feel?" Coop knew that Mike was full of it, but played the game.

Curtiz had additional reasons for his dissatisfaction with Cooper. He concluded that in addition to being "temperamentally unsuited to the part," Cooper was also "a very expensive actor." In citing Cooper's hefty salary of $275,000, Curtiz had a valid point. *Bright Leaf* was close to a $2 million investment at a juncture when the studio system was in a period of confused retrenchment. Jack Warner bird-dogged all the rushes with an increased sense of urgency. After writing Curtiz a memo that praised some of his footage, Warner included a brusque reminder: "I saw seventeen takes of a bit actor at a desk, then a reverse on him with six or seven more takes. It must have taken a lot of time to get this scene, which means nothing. Concentrate on the important stuff. We cannot go over schedule on this, for as we all know, the budget is way over what we thought we would spend."

Despite its craftsmanship and trio of stars, *Bright Leaf* grossed $487,000 over its cost. By the time it was released, Curtiz had completed one of his most formidable films.

The novel *To Have and Have Not* originated as an Ernest Hemingway short story titled "One Trip Across," which was published in *Cosmopolitan* in April 1934 and introduced his Harry Morgan character. After writing a follow-up piece for *Esquire* titled "The Tradesman's Return," Hemingway decided to fashion a story with Morgan as the centerpiece. It was not a labor of love. In addition to having to generate income, Hemingway was distracted by the Spanish Civil War, which he was eager to cover as a correspondent.

The story turned out to be something less than sum of its parts. Harry Morgan is a Florida charter boat skipper with a lusty wife named Marie and two daughters. The family is being economically crushed by the Depression, and Morgan resorts to smuggling alcohol and Cubans into the Florida Keys. After double-crossing some criminals who hire him, Morgan is shot by revolutionary Cubans, and he loses an arm as the narrative segues to focus on the dissolute "haves," who include a cheating sportsman, a shady lawyer, and a boozing novelist. That last may have constituted a self-loathing portrait of the author. *To Have and Have Not* is constructed of beautifully written but disparate pieces.

Howard Hawks told Hemingway that he could fashion a movie from *To Have and Have Not* (or as he put it to the author, "that piece of junk"). Hawks and Charles Feldman bought the rights to the novel from Howard Hughes for $92,500 (Hughes had purchased it in 1939 for $10,000 from a cash-strapped Hemingway) and quickly sold it at an identical price to Jack Warner. Because of objections by the Office of the Coordinator of Inter-American Affairs about the production of a film that might inflame

U.S.–Cuban relations, the locale was moved away from Key West and Cuba to Martinique under Vichy France. The location didn't matter to Hawks. He appropriated the relationship between the Morgan and Marie characters for Humphrey Bogart and nineteen-year old Lauren Bacall, jettisoned Hemingway's social commentary, and turned it into a wartime romance-adventure. This first version, released in 1944, indelibly paired Bacall with her future husband and made her an instant star. The picture also made Jack Warner a lot of money, as it was modeled more on *Casablanca* than on Ernest Hemingway.

Ranald MacDougall believed that there was a good film to be had from a script actually adapted from the novel. The Hemingway name was also the magical elixir that convinced Jerry Wald to sign on as producer. Jack Warner, who pioneered the repetitive exploitation of already-owned literary properties, quickly green-lighted the notion. After cogitating about Errol Flynn and nearly every other male Hollywood star to play Harry Morgan, Wald narrowed the field to James Cagney, Kirk Douglas, and John Garfield. After discussing the role with William Cagney, Wald decided that James was too old, and Douglas was already committed to another picture.

Garfield was both perfect and available. After his Warner Bros. contract expired in 1946, he had cofounded Enterprise Productions Inc. with the producer David Loew, the former Warner marketing executive Charles Einfeld, and Alexander "Pam" Blumenthal. With his producer-partner Bob Roberts, Garfield starred in a pair of Enterprise pictures that solidified his screen persona. *Body and Soul* (1947) was inspired by the life of the boxer and war hero Barney Ross. Distributed by United Artists, the film was a hit that resulted in Academy Award nominations for Garfield and the screenwriter Abraham Polonsky. The next Enterprise production, *Force of Evil* (1948), was written and directed by Polonsky. It was a striking picture but a financial dud. By September 1948 Enterprise was $5 million in the red and suspended operations. It was a difficult time for Garfield. Like vultures, the Red-hunters began to hover over the actor, his wife Robbe, and many of their left-wing friends. The death of his daughter Katherine in 1945 and the actor's constantly roving eye put his marriage under additional strain. Garfield also suffered a heart attack during the summer of 1949. He was antsy for a choice screen role when he signed a two-picture deal with Warner Bros. in June 1949.

Garfield's interest was piqued when Wald approached him with what was alternately called *Winner Take Nothing* and *Harry Morgan* before Jack Warner approved the title *The Breaking Point*. After receiving a copy of Ranald MacDougall's draft screenplay, he was hooked. The locale had been changed to Balboa, California, and Morgan is a returning war vet with a loving wife and two daughters, struggling to adjust to civilian life and make ends meet. His desperation to support his family as a charter boat operator results in tragedy. MacDougall used the final third of Hemingway's book as his template. He took the Marie character and divided her in two, creating Lucy, the loyal wife, and Leona, a sexpot who tempts Morgan. Instead of a stereotypical sidekick, MacDougall created an African American character as Harry's pal who offered the antithesis to the overt racism that permeates Hemingway's novel. The alien smuggling plot point was retained, though the Cuban revolutionaries were changed into American gangsters, and the bank robbery finale was switched to a Santa Anita racetrack stickup: Warner Bros. didn't want to offend politicians or bankers.

Wald asked Garfield for his opinion about a director. According to the producer, the star's first choice was Fred Zinnemann, but he was willing to "have his arm twisted" to accept Curtiz. Garfield hoped that Curtiz would replicate for him what he had done for Joan Crawford in *Mildred Pierce*. For his part, Curtiz was invigorated by the opportunity to work with Garfield for the first time in a decade and impressed by MacDougall's script. He solicited the actor's input and invited him to the Encino ranch to discuss the screenplay. Garfield composed an insightful response:

Dear Mike:

I am most happy to have heard from you. The only reason I didn't answer sooner was because I wanted to reread the Hemingway book, which I did. I quite agree with you about doing it very realistically without the phony glamour, so that there is a real quality of honesty and truthfulness, which, by the way, I feel Randy MacDougall captured from the book.

He has followed the book quite honestly, I think, and some of the questions I would like to kind of throw out for consideration or discussion are:

The deepening of the relationship with the wife so that you get a sense of a man who although he is married for many years has a real kind of yen for her, which is rarely shown in films. As Randy indicates, very warm love scenes are played with the man and the wife. I feel, however, that these scenes can be still deeper without making it too slick.

The other girl, I feel, has to be carefully gone over in the sense that Harry should be tempted, as most men are, and almost goes through with it, but in the end kind of gets cold feet. I feel this relationship can be a little clearer.

Since Eddie is to be a Negro, I am of the opinion that the relationship between Eddie and Harry can also be gone into in a little more detail to show that Eddie has similar problems to Harry's, which Randy also indicated in the script, but not with enough detail. Their regard for each other, without being too sentimental, can be kicked up a bit more.

One of the more interesting features of the book is that Harry loses his arm. That might be a little too morbid, but it has a wonderful quality, particularly later on in the book where he makes love to his wife. This kind of a relationship, if you want to include the loss of the arm, has never been shown. It might seem a little grotesque talking about it, but I certainly think it's worth considering, as it will kick up the whole latter part of the script, purely from a characterization point of view. Of course, Mr. Warner might think it's a little too morbid. However, I feel as long as Randy has stuck so close to the original story in many respects, there is no reason why this couldn't be included.

It is indicated in the book, when Harry is in Mexico, that he buys some things for his wife and children. This kind of touch, which makes him not just a tough guy, but human, creates a fuller person.

Hemingway has a marvelous description in the book (to be specific, on page 179) with which we open and close the picture, where Harry is bleeding and unconscious, the blood kind of dripping off into the water and the fish following the blood stream.

I don't mean to go into effect shots, but this is an example of what exists in the book which you might find very useful, or not as the case may be.

The main theme, which seems to me quite simple and direct is: the struggle of a man who tries to make a living for his family and to discharge his responsibilities and finds it tough.

These suggestions are all, of course, things I have thought about for quite a long time and I am just telling them to you. Maybe it will kick off a spark in your thinking.

I, too, am anxiously looking forward to working with you again and I think with Randy and Jerry we might come up with something which will be a little off the beaten path, but also excellent entertainment and a real joy to do.

With much love and regards, Johnny G.

Garfield's observations about Harry Morgan's relationship with his family and with Eddie (the character's name would be changed to Wesley Park) were spot-on. His idea concerning Morgan making love to his wife with a missing arm and fish following ocean blood trails were sequences that could never have found their way onto a 1950 movie screen.

The two principal female characters were essential. Patricia Neal was coming off a suspension for turning down Curtiz's former property *Sugarfoot*. After missing out on being the naughty girl in *Bright Leaf*, Neal jumped at playing the saucy Leona even though she and Garfield got off on the wrong foot when he bumped into her at a Hollywood party before production began. Neal recalled: "He came up to me while I was sitting on a couch and he introduced himself, and then he began hitting me on the arm with the back of his hand, saying 'You're all whore, you know that? You're all whore.'" She understood she was going to play a flirtatious tramp, but Garfield's intense Group Theater mien was off-putting. Even though the pair never clicked socially, it didn't affect either of their performances. Their scripted flirtations tested the rigors of the Production Code: Joseph Breen sent back MacDougall's script with a lengthy list of objections. After declaring that some of the offensive language, such as "chinks" and "louse," had to be deleted, Breen claimed MacDougall's script would undermine the institution of marriage. Frustrated by the censor's prudish obtuseness, Wald explained that, contrary to Breen's belief, Harry's resistance to Leona's overtures reinforced the authenticity of his marriage: "Can't a man be in love with his wife and not be interested in the other woman? What makes *The Breaking Point* attractive to us is the freshness of having your leading man love his wife and children and not jump into the nearest bundle of hay with any dame that flops her cap in his direction."

MacDougall made several changes to accommodate the censor's dictates as Wald and Trilling launched a charm offensive that convinced Breen to compromise on some of the script's suggestiveness. What made the Leona character so sexual became less about the dialogue and more about how Neal played it. Curtiz ordered her to have blond hair that accentuated her high cheekbones. This, along with the alluring Kentucky drawl and throaty laugh as she volleyed flirtatious repartee with Garfield, created a cinematic harlot for the ages.

The most challenging decision was selecting the actress to play Harry's wife, Lucy. She had to be bowed, but not beaten down by life. Her appearance was appealing, but she was no raving beauty. There also had to be the fire of sexual attraction between her and Garfield. Impressed by her performance in *Storm Warning,* Wald pushed for Doris Day, but Curtiz demurred. After *Romance on the High Seas* and *My Dream Is Yours,* he believed her identity as a popular musical star would cancel out the realism he was seeking. He tested Betsy Blair, Ruth Roman, Anne Sargent, Ellen Drew, and Donna Reed before settling on Phyllis Thaxter. "I had just left MGM and was offered a reading for a film with Michael Curtiz," Thaxter told the writer Robert Nott. "I did a brief screen testing costume, and that's when I met Garfield. He was a wonderful man, and I'm positive that he and Curtiz had a big hand in my getting the part." Thaxter's stirring turn became the spine of the film. In one of her most poignant scenes, she becomes aware of Leona's presence and believes her husband is succumbing to the other woman. In response, Lucy bleaches her hair blond in an attempt to be more appealing to Harry. A lesser actress would have allowed this sequence to devolve into cliché rather than be genuinely touching.

Casting of Wesley Park was equally important. Curtiz immediately sought Juano Hernandez. After directing him in *Young Man with a Horn,* Curtiz knew Hernandez possessed the required dramatic presence absent any racial stereotypes. As he told an interviewer, "Hernandez is the new Negro in our movies. No longer do we have janitors and shoeshine boys. Now we have a dignified, intelligent big man." The relationship between Harry and Park is the film's most refreshing aspect. It was unlike the friendly but hierarchical rapport between Rick and Sam in *Casablanca;* at no point is it possible that Park will address Morgan as "boss." Hernandez's own experiences with racial bigotry included a confrontation with Klan members while performing onstage in Texas and being forced by a deputy sheriff to assist a chain gang in the demolition of a shack while motoring through the South. He preferred normalcy in his characterizations to convey the theme of racial justice: "The latter pictures [*Intruder in the Dust, Home of the Brave,* and *Lost Boundaries* (all 1949)] set out to deliver a message and as a result they sacrificed some of their dramatic impact. If the Negro is portrayed as a real human being on the screen, that does more than anything to make him and his problems come alive."

The other supporting characters were just as scrupulously selected. Wallace Ford's portrayal of a bottom-feeding lawyer drenched in flop sweat so thoroughly debased the legal profession that it made Jack Warner nervous. After watching Curtiz's rushes, the mogul ordered that a Garfield speech damning lawyers be toned down. The rest of the actors were the additional products of Curtiz's quest for realism.

During the first week of January 1950, Wald provided his thoughts about the story to MacDougall: "The story is the study of a little man sentenced to discover his smallness rather than a big man undone by his greatness. When he was in uniform, a great deal of the responsibility of living was taken away from him. Too many producers making pictures nowadays today have an indiscriminate craving for intellectual excitement and have lost the capacity to tell and think about simple emotions. [We need] to be hitting hard on the anvil of human emotion."

MacDougall's script emphasized Morgan's angst about being a wartime hero returning to a hardscrabble civilian existence. Curtiz added a shot of his Navy Cross citation for good measure. As the script began to take shape and Curtiz was working through tests of the actors, Wald's preproduction activities assumed the fervor of a religious crusade. He bombarded MacDougall and Curtiz with lengthy memos containing stream-of-consciousness ruminations. He sent a sixteen-page memo to Curtiz and MacDougall, followed by seven more pages the next day. Although Curtiz respected Wald, this was too much. His own memo to MacDougall reflects his concerns about the producer:

Dear Randy:

I read a copy of the letter Jerry Wald addressed to you today and I am a little confused about it. I don't know what Jerry is driving at or what he is trying to say in these paragraphs:

"There's nothing vicious about Garfield. He's weak, yes, but he is hard working in his desire to keep his home together. His major fault I think is in his trying to live by rules of war. His failure is his inability to recognize that the conflicts he faces in peacetime are much different from those in wartime. He has tragically refused to recognize this point after five years of punching against a 'sea of troubles.'"

"Garfield's story is a violent and sometimes cruel one, but from it should come great pleasure in his eventually learning something . . . that no man is an island to himself and that he must assure responsibilities that there is a right way of living in the world. The aspirations of Garfield for peace and security for his family and himself are the aspirations of all of us today. His failure, for most of your script, to realize them makes for an exciting film."

Curtiz put forth his (and Bess Meredyth's) thoughts:

I think that in this story we have a straight melodrama in which we are trying to inject just a touch of the boy's war background and his post war problems. If we are going to inject deep philosophical and psychological themes we must select different incidents from those we have in the present script. I'm scared to death that you are working on a story that Jerry's mind is set on, and one which is entirely different from the script with which we started. I'm to begin this picture in two weeks, and I'm worried that in trying to follow this altogether new approach, you will turn out a confused script. Please use own judgment and work on your own script, strengthening the characters' relationships, the incidents and the drama, rather than introducing abstract elements, which don't belong to this story.

Despite his overwrought enthusiasm, one of Wald's best attributes was leaving his director more or less alone during shooting. Indeed, the producer wished everyone in the company well and advised them to beware of defecating seagulls at Balboa, California, where Curtiz began production on March 28, 1950. He held a larger than usual number of rehearsals, primarily for the key scenes that matched Garfield with Thaxter or Neal. Garfield continued to bounce ideas off Curtiz, but there was no doubt about who the boss was. "When you do your own productions, you can do it that way," Curtiz reminded him at one point. "For me, you do it this way." He also worked much more congenially with Pat Neal. She was finally playing a part she wanted and gave it her all. Her personal investiture in the picture became evident when she objected to a scene that MacDougall added on April 15. Neal wrote a thoughtful letter to Wald, Curtiz, and MacDougall to say that she believed that the new scene diluted the characterization of Harry Morgan's being tempted by Leona, which in turn weakened their final scene together in her dockside suite. According to Neal, "In counter-action lies drama. If one counter-action is removed, the drama is weakened." She concluded: "In view of the fact that I think the above mentioned is of utmost importance for the sake of the whole picture and the relationship of the main characters, may I urge you not to shoot this new scene No. 113 on Tuesday, but to reconsider. My concern is dictated by my enthusiasm for the original story or script and the way it has been transposed to the screen so far."

Curtiz shot the scene as it was written in the original script, as Morgan philosophizes to Leona, "A man can still be in love with his wife and still want something exciting to happen." An assistant, Sherry Shourds, and the dialogue director Norman Stuart insisted that "Mike WAS NOT influenced by Neal" and simply believed the original scene was more effective. Wald left it up to Curtiz, as he was elated with the footage he was seeing. He wrote to Curtiz, "The last day's rushes at Balboa were simply sensational, stupendous and damned good too!"

Curtiz continued using his younger brother David as his second-unit director, although on *Young Man with a Horn* he had begun being credited as "David C. Gardner." It is unknown if Curtiz recommended the name change to spruce up David's career or whether David wanted a degree of separation from his famous older sibling. During the war, Curtiz had helped his younger brother gain a toehold as an assistant cutter at Warner Bros and mentored him. By 1950 David was a second-unit director and montage technician. *The Breaking Point* was the high point of the brothers' collaboration. The extensive at-sea and location sequences required the second unit to work thirty-two days separately from Curtiz and the principal cast. The pair's relationship on the picture proved seamless, although it was bemusing to those present when the two brothers lapsed into rapid-fire Hungarian.

In the climax of the picture the gangsters flee the scene of the racetrack robbery. The action culminates with a cleverly staged shipboard gunfight that leaves the gangsters dead and Morgan gravely wounded. The final fadeout from Morgan on the docked Coast Guard cutter and Lucy begging him to allow the attending physician to amputate his arm struck Curtiz as incomplete. Curtiz had previously spoken with Juano Hernandez about using his son in several scenes. Nine-year-old Juan Hernandez had previously acted with his father in the groundbreaking Broadway play *Strange Fruit* (1945). Curtiz suggested a dramatic flourish and MacDougall agreed, as he had been searching for an opportunity to heighten the effect of the elder Hernandez's character, which had abruptly exited when he was killed on Morgan's boat and thrown overboard.

The finale was a work of art: Juan Hernandez looks around for his father as the Coast Guard cutter docks, the wounded Morgan aboard. Lucy tells their children to pray for their father as they all depart with him in an ambulance. Leona views the scene on the pier with her new sugar daddy and remarks as the crowd disperses: "I hate mornings. It's the worst part of the day." The camera pulls back in a stirring elevated shot: Juan is now alone on the pier, still searching for his father as the sequence fades out.

Curtiz wrapped production five days ahead of the projected schedule. He and Wald believed they had created a critical and financial success on the order of *Casablanca*.

The Breaking Point was Curtiz's best post–World War II picture. There is no sense of studio- or censorship-imposed phoniness. Everything—script, casting, direction, and photography—is wonderfully synthesized. Contextually, the picture is a classic noir dilemma: the world-weary protagonist is forced into a series of moral compromises that result in tragedy. Curtiz's lifelong crusade to portray reality onscreen reached its somber apogee with *The Breaking Point*.

Garfield gives one of his greatest performances. He knew it, too: "I think it's the best I've done since *Body and Soul*. Better than that." Wald realized early on that the picture was special and strove to separate it in the public's mind from *To Have and Have Not*. He told the critic Ezra Goodman, "This is not a remake. They [Hawks] never made a movie about the book in the first place." Jack Warner was optimistic, writing to Curtiz after the first preview, "We ran *Breaking Point* last night and it has the makings of an important picture."

Then it all fell apart.

Until the summer of 1950, the blacklist had been confined to the indiscriminate efforts of the HUAC, the American Legion, the Motion Picture Alliance, right-wing columnists (Hedda Hopper became Hollywood's "name-above-the-title" Red-baiter), and assorted politicians. The release of *Red Channels: The Report of Communist Influence in Radio and Television* on June 22, 1950, formalized the blacklist into a targeted effort to prevent a large number of people from working in the entertainment business on the basis of their perceived political beliefs. *Red Channels* was an offshoot of the magazine *Counterattack,* which was subtitled "The Newsletter of Facts to Combat Communism" and published by an organization called American Business Consultants Inc., made up by a trio of former FBI agents with access to the bureau's files. To avoid libel suits, *Red Channels* simply listed 151 people and the so-called subversive

John Garfield and Curtiz aboard the *Sea Queen* at Newport Beach during production of *The Breaking Point* (1950) (courtesy of the Lucas family).

causes they ostensibly supported. These consisted primarily of charitable contributions, organizations joined, and petitions signed, all gleaned from public records and FBI files. Although specifically aimed at the radio and television industry, copies were circulated to the movie studios. Overnight, the destructive effects of the blacklist became focused. "All of a sudden I was Typhoid Mary. I couldn't get a job anywhere," remembered the actor Mickey Knox, who even wrote out and signed a loyalty oath in an attempt to clear himself of something he hadn't done. He was not alone. Studio, television, and radio executives, as well as sponsors and independent film producers led by Cecil B. DeMille, began using *Red Channels* as a casting litmus test for movies, radio programs, and TV shows. Nearly everyone listed in the periodical would have his or her career terminated or irreparably damaged. Some, like Edward G. Robinson, were "graylisted" and scraped along by working in programmers until they eventually reclaimed their reputations by, in certain cases, having a few names squeezed out of them. Others, including Lee J. Cobb and Lloyd Bridges, named their friends and colleagues as Communists in order to keep working. The outbreak of the Korean War three days after the publishing of *Red Channels* raised the national anti-Red hysteria to a fever pitch.

John Garfield was one of the most prominent movie stars listed in *Red Channels*. His association with liberal causes and his wife's alleged membership in the CPUSA during the heyday of the Group Theatre made him a choice target. His career immediately dried up. Mickey Knox visited him in New York in May 1952. "I saw him just before he died. We walked in Central Park and he kept repeating, 'What do they want? What did I do?' They ruined his career and it destroyed him." Garfield died of a heart attack on May 21, 1952, at the age of thirty-nine.

The Breaking Point expired two years before its star. *Red Channels* was published while it was in postproduction. Jack Warner canceled Garfield's contract, which had an outstanding obligation for another film. The studio chief remained cowed after his humiliating HUAC appearance in 1947. A major publicity campaign was scratched, and the picture was quietly released in September 1950. It received laudatory reviews during a brief theatrical run. *The Breaking Point* grossed $563,000 over its cost and was not reissued. Instead, Warner bought the rights to the serialized *I Was a Communist for the F.B.I.* in order to launch a distinctive anti-Red "documentary" production.

Curtiz's political profile during the blacklist period was fixedly vague. Despite directing the infamous *Mission to Moscow* (1943), there is no known record of his ever being contacted or investigated by HUAC, the FBI, or another governmental entity.[1] Responses to Freedom of Information Act (FOIA) requests reveal that no FBI file existed for Michael Curtiz, Michael Kertész, Mihály Kertész, or Emmanuel Kaminer. Perhaps it simply didn't occur to anyone to question the political reliability of the man who directed *Yankee Doodle Dandy, Casablanca,* and *This Is the Army*. Although Curtiz has been nebulously linked with the Motion Picture Alliance, available MPA correspondence from 1944–55, including its newsletter, the *Vigil,* contains no mention of his name.

He continued, however, to take exception to anyone who slighted America. John Meredyth Lucas recalled journeying on the Twentieth Century Limited from Chicago to New York with his stepfather and encountering Alexander Korda. The two old friends were glad to see one another, and Korda attempted to convince Curtiz to relocate to England and make films for him: "Each evening we three would have dinner served in Mike's drawing room. Korda would go on about the great opportunities and freedom for a director working in England, would denigrate the harsh commercialism of Hollywood and the uncouth American audience. Mike would defend his adopted country. 'I stay on my home,' he declared. 'I am American.' He shook his head sadly. 'How hell you stand on it?' he asked. 'The English is terrible phony.'"

On the basis of his exposure to the likes of Béla Kún, Admiral Horthy, Hitler, and Joseph Davies, Curtiz believed that the political class was a species to be avoided. Keeping quiet about his specific political leanings—if he had any—was an inconsequential sacrifice to make to safeguard his freedom to make movies.

But his directorial reign at Warner Bros. had become increasingly tangential because of the rapidly changing environment at the studio.

Knowing that movie theater divestiture would soon be a reality, the Warners aggressively reconfigured the company's business model. They arranged a distribution deal for Alfred Hitchcock's Transatlantic Pictures, releasing *Rope* (1948) and *Under Capricorn* (1949). *Stage Fright* (1950) was made under a new deal whereby Hitchcock partnered nonexclusively with Warner Bros. to produce and direct four features over six years. *Three Secrets* and *The Glass Menagerie* (both 1950) were coproduced with Charles Feldman's company; *Kiss Tomorrow Goodbye* (1950) was produced with the Cagney brothers, and *The Flame and the Arrow* (1950) through a deal with Burt Lancaster's Norma Productions.

Jack Warner was also slashing fixed costs. In April 1951 he fired 6 percent of his studio's workforce, including the entire story department. What was occurring on the Burbank lot would eventually be replicated at the other studios. Warner had already bought out Jerry Wald's contract the previous year. He began reducing salaries for those kept on; for instance, he forcibly cut Henry Blanke from $5,000 to $3,500 per week. The studio's net profits of $9.4 million in 1951—the most of any movie studio that year—were boosted by the reductions that transformed its movie assembly line into a cinematic smorgasbord offering facilities, distribution, and financing options to different partners. In the process, the studio lost much of the in-house creative capacity that it had built up over the years.

The studio system had entered its Cretaceous Period, as Curtiz lumbered along as one of the last of the contract directorial dinosaurs. Although he had been making films there for almost a quarter century and was turning sixty-four, he had lost none of his zest for work. He made an effort to revive his pet project, a movie adaptation of James M. Cain's *Serenade*. Curtiz proposed to cast the reconstituted Gloria Swanson of

Sunset Boulevard, Ruth Roman, and John Raitt, writing to Warner, "I could go to Mexico with only one assistant, hiring the cameraman and technical crew and shoot all the exteriors in ten days." Warner vetoed the notion. To renew himself, Curtiz made one of his periodic trips to New York to scout material and talent by watching plays and visiting casting offices, as well as something new: television studios. While acting in a show, a young Don Murray noticed a well-dressed older man with an ascot observing the frenetic activity of a live television production. When he was told it was Curtiz, he went over and introduced himself. According to Murray, Curtiz was gracious, saying, "I came here to learn about television, to learn from you." While Jack Warner and the other moguls were flummoxed about how to respond to television, Curtiz understood the situation, telling the columnist Earl Wilson: "The solution in one word, or ees it two words? . . . Is 'amalgamate.' De beeg studios say I am wrong. Personally, I say dey are wrong. Dey will be forced to change their minds. . . . We have meeting after meeting in Hollywood saying, 'What to do?' I am sure dey will get together some time . . . but right now, no. I see it as a beeg championship fight between television and the movies." Time would prove Curtiz correct.

His New York sojourns were a form of leisure, but Curtiz's other methods of relaxation struck those close to him as bizarre. One morning in New York, his traveling companion Henry Blanke frantically sought out John Meredyth Lucas. "Come quickly! Mike. I think he's dead." The pair went into Curtiz's bathroom and found him slumped in the shower, eyes closed, the water beating against him. Lucas explained that Curtiz did this all the time: "He would finish his shower, then turn on the cold water and nap for a minute. . . . 'He sleeps in cold water?' Blanke shook his head. 'They're right. He is crazy.'"

No amount of cold water could distract Curtiz from his latest project. He was excited about helming a major biopic of Jim Thorpe starring Burt Lancaster as the legendary athlete. Lancaster's complicated contractual status included being tied to Hal Wallis (who was milking him with loan-outs to other studios) and running Norma Productions with Harold Hecht in West Hollywood while maintaining offices at Columbia and Warner Bros.

Jim Thorpe—All American was a straight contractual deal between Warner and Lancaster, separate from the arrangement the studio had with Norma Productions. Jack Warner was adamant that the pictures made by his studio and Norma "shall not be grouped or considered as a single unit for the purpose of accounting." This distinction would later become significant in light of what would occur with Curtiz's Warner contract.

Even though he was thirty-six years old, Lancaster, a former circus acrobat, was quickly whipped into top shape by a boxing coach, Mushy Callahan, and USC's track coach Jess Hill. He was taught how to play football by UCLA's gridiron coach Bill Spaulding, and Thorpe himself, who was hired as a technical adviser. With the exception of some pole-vaulting and long-jump shots, Lancaster performed the athletic scenes with his hair dyed jet-black and skin darkened to resemble Thorpe in his prime.

For years, Hollywood had been considering filming Thorpe's life as a Native American orphan from Oklahoma Territory who attended Carlisle Indian Industrial School in Pennsylvania under the legendary football coach Glenn Scobey ("Pop") Warner. His sports career was highlighted by his renowned athletic feats on the gridiron and at the 1912 Olympics. In 1930 Thorpe's autobiography, cowritten with the publicist Russell J. Birdwell, *Red Sons of Carlisle,* was sold to MGM, where it languished for twenty years. By 1950 Jim Thorpe was a sorrowful figure. Although humble and good humored, he had frequently been taken advantage of. Decades of heavy drinking had left him dissolute and broke. He had been forced to eke out a living by playing bit parts in pictures, mostly as Indians and convicts. Campaigns were launched to raise money for the destitute hero while fruitlessly imploring the Olympic Committee to return his 1912 gold medals.[2] As Thorpe's biographer Kate Buford put it, "Jim Thorpe was not a complicated man, but what happened to him was." When it was reported in the press that Warner Bros. had offered a pittance to Thorpe (the producer Everett Freeman intended to pay no more than "five or six thousand dollars") for his story, the studio was accused of mistreating him in the same manner as the countless other entities that had ripped him off in the past. A young Robert F. Kennedy penned this angry letter to Warner Bros. "Dear Sirs: I wanted you to know how shocked I, and all those with whom I have talked of the matter were at your disrespectful treatment of Jim Thorpe. As related in the nation's newspapers and magazines and commented on particularly by Arthur Daley in the *New York Times,* we feel that your monetary arrangements with Mr. Thorpe were as an extreme case of exploitation as we have ever heard. To put it bluntly—it is disgusting. We feel your company is a natural disgrace and we are urging all our friends to boycott your movies."

The final payment amounted to $12,500. Freeman worked on the

Burt Lancaster and Jim Thorpe with Curtiz on the set of *Jim Thorpe—All American* (1951) (author's collection).

screenplay with a series of writers. He began looking for a director, discussing the project with Joseph H. Lewis, David Miller, and Allan Dwan until Steve Trilling mentioned that Curtiz was interested. Freeman mollified Mrs. Thorpe by omitting Thorpe's other pair of wives and six of his seven children. He and Curtiz portrayed Thorpe's drinking within the limited context of grieving for his dead son. Impressed with her stellar turn in *The Breaking Point,* Curtiz cast Phyllis Thaxter as Thorpe's spouse. The studio publicity department attempted to build interest with an invented press release that claimed Curtiz was a member of the Hungarian Olympic fencing team who became acquainted with Thorpe during the 1912 Olympics in Stockholm. Curtiz had actually met Thorpe on the Warner lot back in 1935 when he cast him as a pirate extra in *Captain Blood.*

After selecting the location of Bacone College in Muskogee, Oklahoma, to double as the Carlisle campus, Curtiz began shooting on location on August 25, 1950. The story of the Sac and Fox outsider who became an all-American hero before hitting the skids resonated with him.

His enthusiasm wasn't dampened after he was reunited with an old antagonist. In the two decades since Curtiz had directed him in *River's End* (1930), Charles Bickford had survived professional blackballing by MGM and near death after he was bitten in the throat and dragged into the brush by a supposedly tame lion while filming *East of Java* (1935). He forged a distinguished career as a character actor and was thrice nominated as Best Supporting Actor. Paul Picerni, a contract player, observed that the years had not mellowed the rugged actor cast as "Pop" Warner:

> Charles Bickford was like steel and the characters he played were like steel and even Mike Curtiz, who was a great director but also a bully, knew enough not to get on the bad side of Charlie Bickford. During the shooting of one simple scene, Bickford came through a door and Curtiz immediately said, "Cut, cut!" Bickford looked at him and, in his usual gruff way, asked, "What the hell was wrong?" Curtiz said, "Something wrong with the timing, Charlie, when you come through the door." With fire in his eye, Bickford snarled, "Are you trying to tell *me* about timing?"—and Curtiz immediately backed down, stammering out, "No, no, not *you*, Charlie sweetheart! Who the hell is the prop man on the door? *Fix the door!*" Curtiz would bully 90 percent of the actors, but he knew he couldn't intimidate Bickford. An actor like Bickford wouldn't take any*thing* from any*body.*

Neither would an actor named Burt Lancaster. There hadn't been a movie star quite like Lancaster, who knew before he ever set foot in Hollywood that he was going to produce and star in his own films. His mercurial temperament was not driven by personal ego or glitz; it was always about what he believed would be best for the picture—*his* picture. Four years after his smash debut in *The Killers* (1946), he had become the sole arbiter on what he should or should not do in front of the camera. Like Cagney, he had graduated to directing himself. The headstrong star and the dogmatic director butted heads during a brief scene in which Thorpe downs a shot of whiskey. Picerni, a friend of Lancaster who had a small part in the picture, observed the action:

> "Good, Burt, sweetheart—very good!" Curtiz called out. "Cut, print."
>
> "Mike, if you don't mind, I'd like to do it again," said Burt.

"No need to do it again, Burt. I see vhat you do, the dribble of the whiskey come down your chin a little bit. It was very real. I like it, I like it."

Burt, staying in place, looking up at Curtiz. "If you don't *mind*," he repeated, "I'd like to do it again."

"Burt!" "There's no need to do it again. I see what you do, eez perfect. Let's move to the next shot."

There was no mistaking the impatience in Burt's voice when he said a third time, "If you don't *mind*, I'd *like* to do it *again* . . ."

By now Curtiz was fuming. "Who the hell you think you are tell me vhat to print and not to print!" he raged. "You lousy circus acrobat turned dramatic actor, who the hell you think you are?!"

Burt turned white. He took the table, flipped it up in the air, the glass and bottle went flying. "You Hungarian cocksucker," he hollered, "I'll *kill* you!"—and with that, lunged for Curtiz! Curtiz went running for the exit and Burt was right on his tail when Russ Saunders, the assistant director, and one of the grips grabbed Burt, Russ yelling, "Burt, calm down, calm down!" Burt was like a powerhouse, but they managed to get him in his portable dressing room. And once Burt was inside, you could see the dressing room move from side to side as Burt smashed his fists against the wall and tossed chairs around. At this point, I was near Curtiz by the soundstage door and I heard him say softly, ". . . Vhat the hell I say to him that make him so mad vith me?"

Lancaster's meltdown established the mood for his impassioned performance, particularly in a key scene in which he destroys a room in a helpless rage after being stripped of his Olympic medals. In addition to clashing with his two male stars, Curtiz managed to momentarily confuse twelve-year-old Billy Gray, who portrayed Thorpe as a boy. "Something that Curtiz said while directing me in *Jim Thorpe—All American* always stuck with me," remembered Gray. "He was telling me how to play a scene, looked me in the eyes, and said, 'Don't do what I say, do what I *think*.'"

Although Thorpe's life, composed through the perspective of 1950s racial awareness, often seems dated, Lancaster's performance is solid. In one of the picture's most compelling scenes, Thorpe dons a feathered headdress and buckskins, his cheeks streaked with war paint, to earn a few bucks at a 1930s dance marathon. Lancaster's flinty stare conveys the humiliating debasement that the actual Jim Thorpe doubtlessly experienced while struggling to support himself and his family. The star's authentic yen for social justice and Curtiz's sensitive focus on the underdog made *Jim Thorpe—All American* as honest as it could have been.

The prologue and finale of the picture, in which Thorpe is feted at a banquet by Pop Warner and the actual governor of Oklahoma (flown in to Warner Bros. for the scene) fulfilled the obligatory requirement for a happy ending. The film should have concluded with a beautiful scene staged by Curtiz of a weary Thorpe rediscovering himself after running over a football while driving a truck and then coaching some kids how to play ball. Once again, Jack Warner and the front office interfered and foisted on the film a clichéd ending that lessened its dramatic effect. Curtiz obediently went along, although he knew it was wrong. He had no allies to side with him.

The picture received generally positive reviews and grossed nearly a million dollars over its cost. *Jim Thorpe—All American* was characteristic of Curtiz's postwar Warner films: a well-made, profitable picture that quickly faded from the public's memory.

His next picture, *Force of Arms,* would accrue an even lesser legacy. Warner Bros. returned to the literary well of Ernest Hemingway for a World War II–based drama with the working title *The Dawn Is Ours.* Although based on a story by the war correspondent Richard Tregaskis, the Orin Jannings script appropriates the central relationship established by Hemingway in *A Farewell to Arms.* William Holden stars as an infantry sergeant, Pete Peterson, who receives a battlefield commission fighting the Wehrmacht in the San Pietro Mountains of Italy in 1943. During a liberty sojourn, he falls in love with a WAC, Eleanor (Nancy Olson), whom he had previously rebuffed. After Peterson's superior, Major Blackford (Frank Lovejoy), is killed in action, a wounded Peterson blames himself. The couple marries but Peterson's conscience compels him to return to battle. Eleanor discovers she is pregnant, and Peterson is reported missing in action. Their reunion in a Rome military hospital as victory bells peal is as improbable as it is dramatic.

It plays better than it sounds. Holden and Olson had captured lightning in a bottle the previous year in *Sunset Boulevard* (changed from *Sunset Blvd.*) (1950). Curtiz and the producer Anthony Veiller believed the pair could repeat the process in a wartime drama. They resorted to a joint memo to convince Jack Warner to use Olson and drop his preference for the contract actor Steve Cochran: "The success of the picture cannot rest on the shoulders of either the boy or the girl. It has to rest on a combination, a relationship between *two* people. . . . We recognize that Cochran is a fine actor and a strong personality but we don't think he has the sensitivity to bring this picture to life."

Veiller and Curtiz included an odd remark in their pitch: "We have seen in *Sunset Blvd.* that Holden and Olson make an enchanting couple. Audiences did warm to them and to their story. They did want that love story to have a chance, and, had it been given that chance, the picture could have had real commercial success."

One wonders what they meant by "real commercial success." In addition to being heaped with critical acclaim, *Sunset Boulevard* reportedly grossed anywhere from $3,800,000 to $5,000,000 during its first run.

Warner was convinced, but Olson did not want to be in the picture. She eventually gave in after a great deal of pressure was brought to bear. Asked about *Force of Arms* more than sixty years later, Nancy Olson termed the experience "absolutely horrifying."

> I was pregnant for the first time and I was very, very sick in the morning. Bill [Holden] was very understanding about this, but the last thing I wanted to do was be in that movie. I was married to Alan Jay Lerner. I was twenty-one and I now found myself pregnant, and I realized intuitively, not expressly, that I was in a marriage that had a lot of troubles. . . . There was also Paramount pushing me, the agents, Jack Warner phoning my house. Put that together with a very weak script . . . and a director . . . it was hard for him [Curtiz] to communicate without being extremely emotional and upset. The saving grace was my friendship with Bill.

When Olson didn't provide Curtiz what he wanted in front of the camera, he reverted to his typical behavior when young actors frustrated him: he attempted to bully her. "I honestly could not stand him," concluded Olson. "But that was not necessarily, totally his fault. He was dealing with me at a very, very delicate moment, and I just did not know how to come through for him. I was just overwhelmed." None of her anxiety is evident onscreen: she delivers a fine performance. Though the script was certainly not the equal of the standard established by Billy Wilder, Charles Brackett, and D. M. Marshman Jr. for *Sunset Boulevard*, it was refreshingly free of clichés.

What irritated Curtiz about *Force of Arms* was the monetary restrictions. Jack Warner reduced the outlay to no more than $1,200,000 for a war movie that specified extensive pyrotechnics and large numbers of extras. Veiller wrote of "dreadful trouble" on the budget. He and Curtiz had to revamp the schedule and radically reduce the employment of extras in several scenes in a cemetery and a café. An air raid in Naples was rewritten to exclude explosions and stunt people; the same group of extras had to be recycled in several different scenes to save money. The first major battle scene was reduced to fifty German extras from the budgeted number of seventy-five.

Despite the limitations, Curtiz restaged a portion of the Battle of San Pietro on location in the nearby Santa Susana Mountains with infinite skill. He obtained the assistance of U.S. Army ordnance specialists out of Fort MacArthur and Fort Ord to complement the Warner Bros. special effects crew. As the scenes were focused on Holden and his battalion in small-scale combat, the manpower reductions were effectively disguised. No one was injured, and the photography was superb, although one shot was memorably spoiled. Holden and his platoon engage in a firefight with German soldiers replete with thundering detonations, smoke pots, and stuntmen performing falls in an orchestrated cacophony of replicated combat. After all the enemy soldiers simulated death and the explosions stopped, there was one extra in a German uniform still standing in the middle of the shot, fiddling with the bolt on his rifle. Curtiz roared, "Cut! Cut!" "Vhat the hell you are *doing?*" The extra stammered that his gun had jammed. Curtiz responded, "Vell vhen your gun jam . . . why don't you haff the sense to die vhen your gun jam?"

The *New York Times* praised *Force of Arms* as "honest romance and cynicism made adult, moving and palatable by an intelligent cast, director, writers and producer." Being lauded as a "forceful amalgam of ruggedness and romance" didn't translate into the box-office success that Curtiz and Veiller had predicted. The picture grossed $632,000 over its cost. Holden and Olson clicked again onscreen, but only the critics warmed to them. The days when a merely good black-and-white studio movie could turn a worthwhile profit seemed to be at an end.

As Curtiz prepared to begin production on *I'll See You in My Dreams* in July 1951, both his past and his future at Warner Bros. were in the forefront of his thoughts. Jack Warner sent him a personal letter on June 29, 1951: "Dear Mike: On Tuesday, July 3rd, I am giving a luncheon for a man who on that date will be celebrating twenty-five years of continuous service with our company. Besides being one of our most valued and loyal artists, this man has been a good personal friend of my brothers and mine and I want to show my appreciation for all his years of hard work and effort for honoring him at this luncheon. If by now you have not been able to guess the identity of this individual, his name is Michael Curtiz or Curtiz Michael."

Curtiz celebrated his anniversary with Harry and Jack Warner and a dwindling number of old-timers on the lot, including Tenny Wright, Henry Blanke, and Bryan Foy. While lunching in the studio's executive dining room, Curtiz undoubtedly reflected on a conversation from the previous month concerning the long-delayed Will Rogers biographical opus that he was finally going to begin. Roy Obringer asked him to reduce his contractual percentage of the picture's net from 25 percent to 10 percent. Curtiz made a counteroffer to have the studio buy out his interests on the six pictures he had already directed and reach a settlement on the remaining four years on his contract, or release him, or give him a new contract that was based on a flat fee. Of greater concern was that Curtiz had not received any profit payments from Warner Bros. and had instructed his attorney to look into the matter.

30

Nerve Ending

Curtiz initially did not think much of what was alternately titled *Wish I Had a Girl* and *The Gus Kahn Story*. After he and Bess read through the first draft of the script, he wrote to Trilling: "I have read the *Gus Kahn Story* over and over again, and I am a little discouraged about it. It's the same story we've been seeing for years and years—the struggling composer and/or lyricist and the song plugger who helps them. We see them with their families and then they become successful. This is the traditional story, which the audience has seen in different pictures from different studios in Technicolor with big production numbers."

His other complaints included the script's weak character conflicts. There were objections to Kahn's wife peddling the tune "Pretty Baby" while pregnant and a contrived Santa Claus sequence that wouldn't play because the Kahn children were too old. He summarized: "I think it would be much better if you would assign to me some other story, which is more in my line. I realize it is difficult to find one, and I hate to be a problem at a time when you boys have so many, but I wish you would show this letter to Jack Warner. I have no intention of causing unpleasantness because I would like to work and work right away, but I would like to do a story which I feel I can make into a successful picture."

Curtiz's request for a different film assignment fell on deaf ears. Jack Warner had already slated him to direct the film for $1,098,000. At a time when Hollywood musicals were all being made in Technicolor, Warner mandated that the film (which would be titled *I'll See You in My Dreams*) be shot in black and white. The studio owned the rights to many of Kahn's songs and would cast Doris Day as the musical spouse. Even though he was holding the equivalent of a pair of deuces, Curtiz was bluffing in attempting to improve clichéd material. As Warner well knew, Curtiz couldn't stomach the possibility of extended time without work.

461

Along with that of Lou Edelman ("the only lovable producer at Warner Bros.," according to the film's screenwriter Melville Shavelson) the revised script would bear his stamp. The reliance on montages was scaled back, and Curtiz added scenes of Day singing at a World War I war bond rally, an army camp, and in blackface at an army canteen show. He added five other production numbers, but he was blocked from making more extensive changes after Tenny Wright notified Jack Warner about the escalating costs:

> I am now getting a rewritten script, which to my way of thinking is going to cost a lot more money than we budgeted. I wish you and Steve would go over this carefully, as you know Mike, when he works with a writer he puts in everything but the kitchen-stove. I don't remember Eddie Foy and the Seven Little Foys but they are in the script now. . . . What else is coming in with Mr. Curtiz having a free hand I don't know, so I am sending this letter to you as a warning. Will you and Steve kindly go into this and control him—the genius, I mean.

Wright's sarcasm reflected both the fiscal realities at Warners and twenty years of dealing with Curtiz's on-the-fly changes. The compromise incorporated the new scenes of Day, but the addition of the Foy family was rejected. The major decision was who would play Gus Kahn. Curtiz believed that Trilling's notion of a young Gordon MacRae as Kahn was a bad idea and convinced him that they needed to look elsewhere: "MacRae is a good singer and it seems a shame to waste his singing ability on this character because Grace [Day] and Gloria [Patrice Wymore] do all the singing in the script."

Melville Shavelson believed that no Hollywood star would want to play the part of a blue-collar songwriter whose wife ran his life. Then Edelman remembered Danny Thomas, an actor-comedian under contract to MGM. A Lebanese American with a broad smile and a toucan-size nose, Thomas had parlayed a successful career on radio into an MGM contract. He had been third billed in several musicals, but Metro still really didn't know what to do with him. Thomas was courted by Curtiz and Edelman and was eventually escorted into Jack Warner's office. According to Thomas, Warner said to him, "Of course you'll have your beak fixed." As he had previously responded to Louis B. Mayer and Harry Cohn (who had sought him for *The Jolson Story*) on the same issue, Thomas adamantly refused to surgically alter his proboscis. He explained why he and his nose were right for the part: "If you put a good-looking man in that part, you've got no picture. This man Gus Kahn wrote hundreds and hundreds of 'I Love You' songs but could never say 'I love you'—not even to his wife except once when she was under ether and couldn't hear him. . . . It's because he was shy, but more important, because he was not handsome. He didn't believe a face like his could say 'I love you' to a face like hers and get away with it."

Warner huddled in his inner sanctum with Edelman and Curtiz while Thomas waited. Curtiz eventually stuck his head out the door and gave him the nod that he had the part. "The picture was a very pleasant experience for me," recalled Thomas. "I learned a tremendous amount from director Curtiz, one of the best in Hollywood."

Patrice Wymore, a Warner contract player, was cast in the picture as a faux Ruth Etting who sings and dances while attempting to seduce Kahn, without success. William T. Orr had spotted Wymore in the Broadway musical revue *All for Love* and flown her out to Hollywood to meet his father-in-law, who signed her after a screen test. After appearing in *Tea for Two* (1950), she was paired opposite Errol Flynn in the forgettable *Rocky Mountain* (1950). While on location in New Mexico, Flynn wooed Wymore and married her before their picture was released that November.

Well aware of her husband's animus toward Curtiz, she was apprehensive about her assignment to *I'll See You in My Dreams*. But Curtiz handled Wymore with kid gloves and won her over: "Mike Curtiz was really a genius with his handling of the camera, as well as the actors. I had great respect for him as a director." She expressed less admiration for LeRoy Prinz, again the credited choreographer on a Curtiz picture. Wymore thought that Prinz was "a big joke. He couldn't direct a dance number." According to Doris Day, "Prinz didn't dance any more than Bud Westmore, who was always given makeup credit, did the makeup." Day claimed that Prinz had a brother named Eddie who actually choreographed Curtiz's musicals.

Shavelson enjoyed working with Curtiz: "Mike was wonderful. Every conference was a pound and a half of broken English. But he had taste. Mike had a great deal of talent. I suppose if Mike had been available to direct all of the pictures I wrote, I would never have become a director." The hybrid screenplay became cleverly rendered schmaltz. Insider ripostes were sprinkled throughout. In one notable exchange the composer Johnny Martin (Julie Oshins) responded to Kahn's lament about having to sell out artistically and compose hack scores for Hollywood movies: "There's only two types of people in this town. The ones that eat at Romanoff's and the ones that serve there. Stop rehearsing for a tray and give them what they want!" The dialogue was accentuated by the verve of Danny Thomas and Doris Day playing off one another. After nine pictures, Day was a first-rate actress. When Thomas sang "Pretty Baby" to her in the hospital, Day shed authentic tears, remembering the absence of her former husband, Al Jorden, when she gave birth to her son, Terry, in 1942. The film's only false note was a miscast Frank Lovejoy as Kahn's hard-drinking composer counterpart, Walter Donaldson.

Curtiz tweaked Jack Warner's concern about Thomas's prominent nose. As Kahn, Thomas arrives at the hospital in a harried state to see his firstborn son. Curtiz had him gaze with wonderment at his new baby (held aloft by a nurse), then touch his own nose with an expression of paternal doubt; the action is neatly captured by his reflection in the maternity-ward glass. The picture made Thomas a frontline star, although television became his métier beginning in 1953. He starred in *Make Room for Daddy,* a sitcom produced by none other than Louis Edelman and written by Mel Shavelson. The program enjoyed an incredible eleven-year run.

I'll See You in My Dreams was Curtiz's last hit at Warner Bros. Although the additions to the script pushed the budget up to $1,404,000, it garnered $1,758,000 over its cost and was the studio's second-highest grosser during a bleak year of twenty-five releases. According to Shavelson, the picture was the last black-and-white musical to open at Radio City Music Hall. As far as Curtiz was concerned, its success was gratifying because it allowed him to complete a highly personal project.

Eight decades after his death, it is difficult to comprehend the depth of public reverence for Will Rogers, who met his end with the aviator Wiley Post in a 1935 Alaskan plane crash. The part-Cherokee rose from a trick-roping rodeo performer to become the top headliner of the Ziegfeld Follies, eventually becoming Hollywood's most popular star. His fame transcended the world of entertainment. Rogers's wry political commentary and humorous observations, chronicled in more than four thousand syndicated newspaper columns, endeared him to a succession of presidents along with millions of Americans. Born and bred in pre-statehood Oklahoma when it was a rambunctious territory peopled by exiled Native Americans and six-gun desperadoes, Rogers became a cultural bridge from the end of the American frontier era to the modern age of entertainment and social commentary. His death at the age of fifty-five prompted an outpouring of national mourning. His name continues to adorn a seemingly endless array of public places and structures. In Oklahoma alone, there are thirteen public schools named after him.

Both Warners and Curtiz—a Rogers companion from the days of Sunday-afternoon polo matches—were among his most fervent admirers. After Jack Warner snapped up the rights to his widow's serialized magazine story about her husband, it was only a matter of time before a film would emerge. Unfortunately, it turned out to be too much time. The studio began preproduction in late 1941; Hal Wallis was scheduled to produce and Curtiz to direct. Wallis's falling-out with Warner delayed things. Mark Hellinger and Curtiz took it up again in 1943. They obtained the blessing of Mrs. Rogers, who let it be known that Spencer Tracy was the perfect actor to portray her late husband. Tracy, who had grown extremely close to Rogers during his early days at Fox, considered the prospect of portraying his friend in a movie "horrifying."

The role was offered to Gary Cooper, another movie-colony intimate of Rogers, who likewise turned it down. Joel McCrea was next in line. McCrea told both Curtiz and Jack Warner that he didn't think he was accomplished enough for the role. Warner assumed that McCrea was another actor who wanted script approval or more money or both. McCrea went back to Curtiz and explained why he didn't want to portray Will Rogers: "You know something? If you force me to do this picture, it's gonna be all on you. Because I'm telling you before we start, I'm not qualified to do it. No one's ever accused me of being a great actor. I'm a helluva man on a horse, but no great actor." Curtiz understood: "This is the first sonuvabitch actor who admitted he wasn't good enough; they all say the part isn't good enough, the picture isn't good enough. But for an actor to come and say he isn't good enough, I've got to believe you."

The search continued. A screen test of Bing Crosby demonstrated that the famed crooner-actor was unable to channel the legendary Rogers persona. John Wayne's name was floated, in vain. He revered Rogers, who had bucked him up after finding the rangy young actor sulking on the Fox lot after flopping in *The Big Trail* (1930). "You're working, aren't you? Just keep working," Rogers told him. Wayne claimed it was the best professional advice he ever got.

Though both of them never met a man they didn't like, Will Rogers had become more difficult to cast than Jesus Christ.

The project regained traction when Curtiz decided that Will Rogers Jr., by then forty years old, could portray his famous father onscreen.

He had originally intended to have the younger Rogers play himself in a cameo role. Curtiz believed that he could mold anyone with a modicum of talent into a passable actor. His fervor to make the picture was such that he convinced Jack Warner to let him try a series of screen tests of the younger Rogers, who had never acted in his life.

Despite living in the shadow of his famous father, Rogers Jr. had created his own identity. He graduated from Stanford and published the *Beverly Hills Citizen*. The younger Rogers was elected to Congress from California's sixteenth district before resigning his seat and enlisting in the military.[1] He became a decorated World War II combat officer (he was wounded in the Battle of the Bulge) and ran unsuccessfully for the U.S. Senate after the war. In a 1988 interview, Rogers Jr.—known as Bill Rogers—remembered Curtiz as "a brilliant Hungarian who became more American than Will Rogers." He elaborated on how he came to play his father onscreen: "Mike Curtiz had a hammerlock on the script and he kept wanting me and wanting me. . . . I went up to Warner Bros. for six months before production and started to work with him and get accustomed to the lights and the camera and so forth."

Curtiz proved to be so persuasive that Bill Rogers agreed to sell his newspaper and commit himself fully to the project. He brought several perquisites to the table. His appearance and voice were astonishingly similar to his father's. And he'd grown up in Beverly Hills and Santa Monica back when they were rural, riding horses and learning to rope from his dad. After directing test sequences with him on May 16 and 17, 1951, Curtiz wrote to Trilling:

> I finished all four sequences today and my impression is that Bill is the man who should play Will Rogers. With a little work, he will be fine. It's true he was terribly nervous the first day because of many things. He didn't know his lines (half the scenes were ad-libbed), his arm was hurting from the rope tricks, the light bothered him and the make-up wasn't good. But after seeing the two sequences he did today—the railroad station and the airfield—I think that with constant rehearsal before we start the picture I will accomplish what we set out to do, and he will be more than good; I think he will be excellent.

The screenwriter Robert Arthur produced *The Story of Will Rogers* and, with Stanley Roberts, revised the existing Jack Moffitt screenplay. As

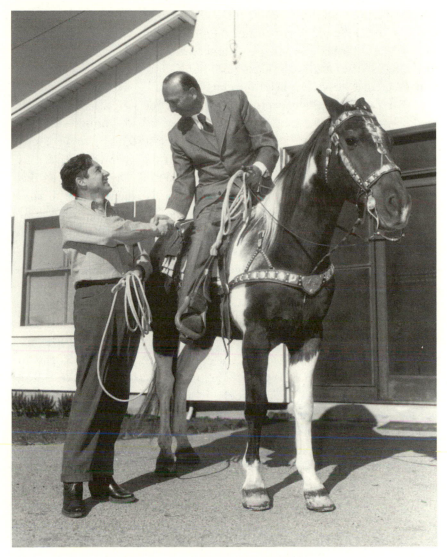

Will Rogers Jr. and Curtiz (courtesy of the Lucas family).

Bill Rogers remained a problematic acting quantity and the picture was centered on the Rogerses' marital relationship, it was crucial that Jane Wyman accept the role as Betty Rogers. It was clearly a secondary part for Wyman, who had been at Warners since 1936 and was one of their last major female stars under contract. Her Warners tenure culminated with a Best Actress Oscar for *Johnny Belinda* (1948). She calculated that the

Rogers picture could be a major hit and signed on. Wyman added box-office insurance, and, by the end of the production, Bill Rogers was eternally grateful for her easygoing assistance, which was a welcome contrast to the deadly seriousness of Curtiz. "Thank God for Jane Wyman!" he remembered. "She was so helpful to me."

Curtiz was initially concerned more about the script than Rogers Jr. He knew that he had a good first act and "a very bad, uninteresting second part," leading up the fatal plane flight. The screenwriters were leery about coloring Rogers's life with anything even slightly provocative. Curtiz demanded that Arthur provide him with Frank Davis, who worked with him on *Jim Thorpe—All American,* to revise the script in three or four weeks. It was a difficult chore to imbue conflict into a storybook life in which the principal dramatic event was the man's death. They also had to tread carefully with Bill Rogers; while personally malleable, he was resolutely protective of his father's legacy. Naturally, Curtiz was taking the revisions that he and Davis worked on and reviewing them with Bess in the evenings. It was decided to emphasize a familial rift between the easygoing son and his more severe father, Clem, played by the implacably stern Carl Benton Reid. (Will Rogers reportedly did have personal differences with his father, who died in 1911.) The exposition has the elder Rogers incessantly demanding that his young son amount to something. After Rogers becomes an entertainment success, it still isn't good enough for dear old dad, who views rope twirling and being hit with pies in Hal Roach comedy shorts as juvenile frivolity. The dramatic breakthrough, such as it is, comes after Betty Rogers urges her husband to speak out when General Billy Mitchell takes on the government over air power and is court-martialed for insubordination. As Rogers becomes an international figure and speaks at the 1932 Democratic convention as Oklahoma's anointed son, his father is moved to tears. Rudimentary Hollywood cornpone was the main ingredient of *The Story of Will Rogers,* and Curtiz ground it out as best he could.

Aware of the cost constraints, Curtiz prevailed on Robert Arthur to cut back the script. As he noted, "At the end of seventy-five pages you are at the beginning of his vaudeville career and from here on until the end, you will have a tremendous amount of material to consume time and script pages." In addition to urging the producer to obtain stock footage from *The Great Ziegfeld* (1936) for montages, Curtiz reinstituted the voice-over narration by Jane Wyman (Arthur had removed it) and replaced a number of scenes by summarizing Rogers's world travels with quick montages and brief shots of Betty receiving postcards. The reworked screenplay also incorporated many of Rogers's famous sayings—with monotonous regularity. Although he worked tirelessly with Bill Rogers, Curtiz urged Steve Trilling to up the ante to use higher-priced supporting actors such as James Gleason, who earned a hefty two thousand dollars per week. Mary Wickes, Slim Pickens, and Noah Beery Jr. (as Wiley Post) rounded out the principal cast. Eddie Cantor made a special appearance, playing himself in several of the Ziegfeld Follies scenes. Curtiz calculated that the presence of Wyman and a skilled supporting cast would relieve some of the pressure on his neophyte leading man, but it was still touch and go. To avoid being blamed for future delays, he cautioned Trilling that despite his previous endorsement, directing Bill Rogers would be a challenge: "I rehearsed with Bill Rogers on the stage today, and though I have been working with him desperately for three weeks, he is still very amateurish and awkward. He is as ill at ease as he was when we first started to rehearse. I just wanted to go on record to caution you about the schedule because it naturally will affect the budget. In the meantime, I will do my utmost to lessen the amateurish and sing-songy reading of lines."

In addition to the focused rehearsals, Curtiz was able to minimize some of his star's nervousness by emphasizing his strong points. Rogers's scenes performing rope tricks both onstage and in the saddle were well done—although he was also doubled by a stuntman—particularly a sequence based on an actual incident in Madison Square Garden when his father roped a steer that ran into the audience. As he became more comfortable in front of the camera, Bill Rogers emanated enough of his father's easygoing charm that it largely obscured his lack of acting polish. Considering the fact that Bill Rogers is onscreen for nearly the entire picture, Curtiz did a highly creditable job.

The Story of Will Rogers began production on January 21, 1952, and finished ten days over schedule on April 5, 1952. The handsome Technicolor photography accentuated a reverential paean to the legendary humorist and entertainer. Although there was little drama, the sequence of Rogers flying off with Wiley Post and circling the airfield one last time to wave good-bye to his wife before his meeting with destiny in Barrow, Alaska, was a poignant finale. Reviews were generally positive, and the director won laudatory comments from many of his colleagues. In addition to letters of praise from Mrs. Rogers, Jerry Wald, Hal Wallis, and others, Curtiz received a note from Harry Warner: "My dear Mike: I never dreamed I could be so proud of anyone as I was of you last night. Wish you would convey to everyone who participated in the making of this great picture, THE WILL ROGERS STORY, my personal thanks for making a picture that is so timely and needed in our troubled country and world of today. I am sure this picture will be helpful so that our Great Country, who so many died to create, will remain a Country and a Leader of people throughout this world and all mankind."

But Curtiz's perseverance was not a harbinger of box-office success. If *The Story of Will Rogers* had been produced a decade earlier, as originally intended, it probably would have been a smash hit. As it was, it still grossed $715,000 over its cost of $1,955,000. In a valedictory letter to Warner after he left the studio, Curtiz lamented: "The life story of Will Rogers was a tremendous undertaking. With hindsight, we can see that more money was spent on the picture than it deserved, but who could foresee that the American public was no longer interested in this great man, once their most popular hero?"

That no one in the Warner front office voiced any concern about the probable dearth of commercial appeal for a biography of Will Rogers seventeen years after his death indicates a degree of disengagement from the pulse of their business. Jack Warner was increasingly absent, enjoying the relaxing ambience of his modernist Villa Aujourd'hui at Cap d'Antibes on the French Riviera; he had purchased it in 1950 and was becoming a fixture at the Monte Carlo gaming tables. Curtiz had to deal almost exclusively with Steve Trilling, by now a worn-out shock absorber between Warner and the day-to-day operations of the studio. Harry Warner had relocated from New York to Los Angeles during the 1940s. The senior Warner's worldview remained fixated on the trifecta of family, money, and morality, but he became restless while raising Thoroughbred horses at his San Fernando Valley ranch. When the family patriarch and the youngest brother were in close proximity, their already tumultuous relationship worsened into a running series of explosive arguments. Whenever the elder Warner interjected himself into the business of moviemaking, Jack told him to butt out. Everyone at the studio knew the two brothers hated each other. The director Gordon Douglas was returning to work from the studio's private dining room one day and passed Harry Warner. "Harry said to me, 'Is my dumb brother up there?'" The elder Warner's continued presence on the lot and his visceral disapproval of his younger sibling's personal life, particularly his marriage to Ann, caused Jack to view him as someone to be gotten rid of so he could have unimpeded control of the studio. *His* studio.

Of greater concern than the familial infighting was figuring out what could be done to get people to watch movies instead of television. All the major studios were becoming increasingly desperate to compete with TV. From this anxiety emerged a belief that technical innovation could lure them back. Darryl Zanuck halted preproduction on his Technicolor epic *The Robe* at Twentieth Century-Fox to use an anamorphic camera lens that would nearly double the aspect ratio of the screened image. And the independently produced 3-D film *Bwana Devil* (1952) also created a stir that Jack Warner, among others, seized on.

Warners embraced the future while acknowledging its past. The studio began planning a 3-D horror feature that was a remake of Curtiz's *Mystery of the Wax Museum* (1933). *House of Wax* (1953), directed by his fellow Hungarian Andre de Toth became a stupendous hit.[2] Made for a modest $925,000, *House of Wax* grossed nearly $7 million.

At the same time that he reached for the 3-D life preserver, Warner tasked Curtiz with directing a Technicolor version of 1927's *The Jazz Singer*. The studio had initially considered a remake back in 1943, starring Frank Sinatra in the role originally played by Al Jolson. Danny Thomas was now the star, and there was no one more suitable to helm the remake than Curtiz, who had been directing films on the Warner Sunset lot when the history-making original was produced. The director was delighted. The overt sentimentality of Samson Raphaelson's play about the generational conflict between a Jewish cantor and his assimilated son suited the dramatic temperament of the Hungarian Jew who had so successfully integrated himself into the American fabric.

Instead of being set in turn-of-the-century New York City and focusing on Cantor Rabinowitz's son ditching the religious tradition of his devout family to become a Broadway song-and-dance man, the updated screenplay features Jerry Golding, a Korean War veteran returning to Philadelphia from overseas to celebrate Rosh Hashanah with his father. After taking in a nightclub act headlined by Judy Lane (Peggy Lee), Jerry's yen for show business lands him a gig alongside Judy, and he declines to succeed his father as cantor. The subsequent familial strife follows a well-worn path; Eduard Franz plays the uncompromising father, David (even though he was only ten years older than his "son"), and Mildred Dunnock is the evenhanded mother, Ruth.

Current events dictated how Curtiz would depict the film's Jewish characters in a contemporary American setting. At the height of the Red Scare era, highlighted by the Rosenbergs' atom bomb spy trial, there was a renewed link in the public consciousness between Communism and Jews that was originally alleged by the HUAC in 1947. *The Jazz Singer* was probably one of the few scripts that Jack Warner actually read. Assimilation had been the story of the brothers Warner dating back to when they hocked their father's gold watch to buy their first movie projector. One could also hypothesize that the struggle between the cantor and his son resembled the ongoing battle between Harry and Jack Warner, but no one cared to comment about that particular comparison.

Curtiz worked on the script with Frank Davis to ensure that it fully embodied the theme of assimilation. The casting of Thomas was not in itself unusual. Nearly every film biography about Jewish performers starred gentile actors: Larry Parks in *The Jolson Story* (1946), Tyrone Power in *The Eddy Duchin Story* (1956), Keefe Brasselle in *The Eddie Cantor Story* (1956), and Steve Allen in *The Benny Goodman Story* (1956). What made *The Jazz Singer* unique was the thematic centerpiece: a Jewish family and its faith. The picture's sole flirtation with stereotype is Alex Gerry as Uncle Louie, a warmhearted shlockmeister whose many businesses become a running gag: selling lampshades, boxes, real estate, sporting goods, and more. There are reminders placed throughout the film that Jews are prototypical Americans. The film opens with Golding arriving at his synagogue in his U.S. Army uniform as the Irish American taxi driver thanks him for the opportunity to celebrate the arrival of the New Year twice in the same year. Other cues include references to baseball when synagogue members evince a preference for the national pastime over choir practice. Tom Tully plays a friend of the cantor whose sole purpose is to engage in banter that reveals that he is a professional baseball umpire. It is also noted that George Washington visited the Mount Sinai synagogue, founded in 1790. In addition to serving as a prompt that Jews had been an integral part of America alongside the Founding Fathers, it was Curtiz's way of connecting the dots from Haym Salomon and *Sons of Liberty* (1939) to the present day.

There was a disagreement between Curtiz and Jack Warner concerning the wearing of yarmulkes during the temple sequences. Steve Trilling and Lou Edelman acted as the go-betweens during this particular tussle. Although the order from Warner was "no hats," both Curtiz and his technical adviser, Rabbi Morton A. Bauman of Temple Beth Hillel in North Hollywood, and the Sinai Temple's Rabbi David Leiber, where the scenes were filmed, protested successfully that yarmulkes should be worn. For the rabbis it was a matter of faith. For Curtiz it was a matter of realism. It was also believed that there should be no confusion about marriage outside the faith. When Judy Lane meets Golding's family for Passover, she has a line of dialogue that was dubbed in afterward: "I haven't been to a seder since I left home." Thomas believed the addition of the line was gratuitous and argued against it. As Jews who had married outside their faith, Curtiz and Warner knew it was absurd but let it go to avoid getting into a public squabble. Rested and tanned from Cap d'Antibes, Jack Warner was back watching the dailies and chided Curtiz about overshooting the temple scene. Curtiz explained that he purposely overshot the sequence so he could avoid bringing back all the extras wearing the yarmulkes. He added: "It was necessary to shoot several angles to beautify the temple atmosphere, bring out the mood and show the majestic beauty of our religion. But in spite of all this, I finished the temple sequence a day ahead of schedule."

Overshooting was the least of Curtiz's worries. He had finally settled in to direct the picture after frantically scrambling to find an actress to play Judy.

After *I'll See You in My Dreams,* Curtiz and Warner had intended to reunite Danny Thomas and Doris Day in *The Jazz Singer.* After obediently accepting every film assignment for five years, Day decided this was the moment for self-assertion. She apparently turned the part down.[3] She tried to reason with Jack Warner, who unleashed a humiliating harangue about "nickel actors who want to tell me how to run my business" that reduced Day to tears. Bess's confidante Louella Parsons wrote in her column, "My friend [Curtiz] was hurt" that Day refused to appear in the film, a charge the actress later denied in an interview on the set of *By the Light of the Silvery Moon* (1953). If Curtiz was upset with Day for declining to play second fiddle to Danny Thomas again, he quickly got over it. Casting a movie was the art of the possible, and there was nothing he enjoyed more than spotting new talent. Curtiz told Parsons that "fate must have led me by the hand into Ciro's to hear Peggy [Lee] sing," even though he was probably tipped off about Lee. It would have been difficult for anyone among the movie industry's movers and shakers to be unaware of Lee's June 1952 engagement at Ciro's on the Sunset Strip. The blond North Dakotan had hit it big with Benny Goodman's band during the war before striking out on her own. What made Lee different from other big-band singers is that she was a skilled lyricist who wrote many of her own songs. Shrewd as well as ambitious, Lee hired Mel Ferrer as her stage director. He completely repurposed the live act with new lighting and an alluring wardrobe and had Lee drop weight with a rigorous diet. The new look, combined with her alabaster skin and blonde hair, rendered Peggy Lee's live vocal stylings hypnotically stunning. She'd recently cut a hit recording of the Rodgers and Hart standard "Lover" and was warbling it nightly to sold-out crowds of glitterati in Hollywood's most prestigious nightclub.

Curtiz "sat in a dark corner" at Ciro's and watched several performances before going backstage and offering Lee a screen test. He explained afterward, "If a girl can sing a song with the warmth she can do the same thing [in a movie] on stage—if somebody will show her the technique." Curtiz had no doubt who that "somebody" was going to be. "I have no patience with anybody who has no talent," he declared. "Peggy has tremendous talent. She's a great artist in every which way." Curtiz was charmed by her low-octane personality and shyness. Initially overwhelmed, Lee hesitated. Although she had made minor appearances with her ex-husband, the bandleader Dave Barbour, in a musical short and in Bing Crosby's *Mr. Music* (1950), she knew virtually nothing about acting. But the prodigious ambition that empowered her to overcome an impoverished childhood (she was the seventh of eight children of an alcoholic railroad agent and an abusive stepmother) eventually won out.

Her screen test was nearly a disaster. She stammered and blew her lines until Curtiz advised her to treat the dialogue like the lyrics of a song. She wasn't a natural like Doris Day, but Curtiz was convinced. Soon after Lee was signed, the Warner publicity department pounced on Day's alleged refusal to appear in *The Jazz Singer* and manufactured a phony feud between her and Peggy Lee. In addition to providing buzz for the picture, Jack Warner enjoyed trying to pit his actors against each other, as he believed that it was easier to control them when they were upset with someone other than him.

Curtiz ordered Lee's hair cut short in a style that resembled Day's, but he understood the differences: "Doris is an extrovert, happy-go-lucky about every turn of fate. Peggy is an introvert—a dogged analyst, tenacious, moody, sensitive and shy almost to the neurotic stage." Lee's personality was the opposite of the Judy Lane character's, but Curtiz planned to tap into her sensitivity to extract a portrayal of an outwardly vivacious performer plagued by uncertainty. Danny Thomas believed the director pulled it off: "When [Curtiz] directed, he was great. He would sit down and talk to you, really get involved. He got very involved with Peggy. I mean, he got it out of her. In the early shootings he wasn't too happy with her *or* me. We weren't giving him exactly the emotions he wanted. . . . But he got it out of her. He got it out of all of us. At the end of the scene, he'd say, "Excellent, we do it again." And he'd cry every time, if you really moved him."

Lee was most effective during her musical numbers, which included "Lover" and her own composition "This Is a Very Special Day." During some of the dramatic scenes she found it difficult to summon emotion despite Curtiz's efforts. At one point Lee said to Curtiz, "I don't know, Michael. The way you talk and what you want . . . suddenly a door closes between us." Curtiz responded, "Now, Peggy, this time we are going to have a great scene, and we don't talk about no goddamn doors." Although Curtiz loosened her up a bit, part of Lee's reserve remained intractable.

The Jazz Singer was beautifully shot by Carl Guthrie, including some stunning montage shots of Times Square and Chicago. Ray Heindorf and Max Steiner's score was nominated for an Oscar. Reviews ranged from benignly positive to dismissive. Thomas could not project the energetic Jolson charisma necessary to elevate the film. Afterward, both stars would enjoy substantial careers in spheres other than the movies. Although Lee validated Curtiz's perception of her acting chops when she was nominated for Best Supporting Actress for *Pete Kelly's Blues* (1955), she stuck to what she did best and never cared to realize her potential as an actress. She became fond of Curtiz, though. When Lee married the actor Brad Dexter in her Beverly Hills backyard on January 1953, she asked Curtiz to give her away. Thomas never starred in another feature film. His spectacular television success grew to encompass the production of numerous hit programs, including *The Dick Van Dyke Show, The Andy Griffith Show*, and *The Mod Squad*.

From a commercial perspective, *The Jazz Singer* remake represented glossy sentiment that few people queued up to see. At $1,437,000, the budget wasn't outlandish, but it grossed less than $300,000 over its cost. Curtiz mused afterward that perhaps the Jewish theme doomed it at the box office, but it was more than that; the remake was the brainchild of older men who confused potential commercial appeal with the veneration of long-deceased icons and past triumphs. The movie business, particularly in the 1950s, wasn't for the faint of heart—or as Warner referred to them, "the stand-patters." Curtiz's *Jazz Singer* was a marginal improvement over its predecessor, but minus Al Jolson's star power, it wasn't memorable. After a forgettable adaptation for television with Jerry Lewis, the next remake, starring Neil Diamond and Sir Laurence

Olivier, surfaced in 1980. This rendition made Curtiz's version look even better.

Curtiz's quarter century at Warner Bros. was coming to an end. His dissatisfaction with the studio was caused not only by the lack of response concerning profit-sharing payments from his pictures—the studio repeatedly put off Curtiz's lawyer, Mark Cohen, when he requested accounting information—but also by his frustration about how his brother David was being treated. Curtiz offered to take less money for *The Story of Will Rogers* if the studio would continue to employ his brother. Obringer reported the details to Jack Warner: "It appears that Mike is quite steamed over his brother's not being taken care of after Mike's 25 years of service and he finally suggested that if you would give his brother a contract . . . to run for the duration of Mike's present contract . . . he would, with respect to the Rogers picture, be willing to reduce his percentage to 12½%."

David Curtiz did receive other assignments from the studio besides his brother's pictures. He ran the second unit or was an assistant director on *The Glass Menagerie* (1950), *The Enforcer* (1951), *Lightning Strikes Twice* (1951), *On Moonlight Bay* (1951), and *The Iron Mistress* (1952) before the work dried up again. Because Curtiz knew David was highly competent, he resented the demeaning process of having to ask Obringer and Warner to employ his brother.

Curtiz began directing John Wayne in *Alma Mater* during the fall of 1952. Wayne, then ranked as the country's third-biggest box-office draw, acknowledged, "It's not a standard Wayne part, but I took it anyway. It has human values." A comedic drama written and produced by Melville Shavelson, it stars Wayne as Steve Williams, a once-famous football coach who has hit the skids and is attempting to maintain custody of his young daughter, Carol (Sherry Jackson). Opportunity knocks as he strives to restore respectability to the football team of a tiny Catholic college run by the sly Father Burke (Charles Coburn). Donna Reed costars as a well-meaning social worker, Alice Singleton. Marie Windsor is Anne, Wayne's ex-wife from hell, who uses his purported parental unfitness like a blunt instrument. In a case of art imitating life, Wayne had recently separated from his volatile second wife, Chata, who was putting him through an ugly public divorce. He was also courting twenty-four-year-old Pilar Pallete Weldy, a lithe Peruvian actress who would become the third and final Mrs. Wayne. With these personal distractions, the star was not always at his best. Curtiz wrote to Trilling about Wayne's deportment: "I want you and J.L. to know I am having a lot of trouble with John Wayne. He is neurotic, nervous and irritable and, being a bad study, he often muffs his lines."

Although Curtiz tidied up his missive with "I know in the end [Wayne] will be fine," the director was essentially erecting a straw man to excuse his surplus of exposed film. What the director and star shared was a mutual passion for the movie business. Wayne respected Curtiz's expertise, dating back to his time as a twenty-year-old extra, swimming among the wrecked temple sets of *Noah's Ark* (1928). Curtiz traveled to New York to shoot some of the exteriors at the Polo Grounds and Yankee Stadium. The director initially wanted to cast Gigi Perreau as Wayne's daughter, but her price was too high. Sherry Jackson proved to be more than an effective alternative.

Buoyed by Wayne's box-office strength, the film brought in $800,000 over its cost. Credit for any success was not due to Jack Warner, who inexplicably changed the title from *Alma Mater* to *Trouble Along the Way*. Curtiz and Shavelson attempted to reason with him, but it was no use. John Wayne believed the title change was a dumb decision that hurt the picture. "[*Trouble Along the Way*] made it sound like the story of an oil truck which had busted a rear axle going up Cajon Pass. Who would buy a ticket to see that?"

Trouble Along the Way was released in February 1953, as Curtiz was beginning his final Warner feature and preparing to leave the studio. Both Paramount and Darryl F. Zanuck were seeking his services, and Obringer informed him that he would have to accept a 50 percent reduction on his contract, which still had two years to run. Jack Warner mandated that specific members of the executive staff (except him and his brothers) and other high-priced employees had to accept this salary reduction or leave. Faced with being cut from $3,500 to $1,750 per week, and his profit percentages still in limbo, Curtiz tendered his resignation.

With his departure imminent, Curtiz buckled down to make *The Boy from Oklahoma*. It amounted to little more than a dressed-up Western programmer starring Will Rogers Jr. Warner reduced the budget to $863,000, which denied Curtiz access to Janet Leigh, whom he sought as the costar. Instead, he was given Nancy Olson, who had an abnormal fear of horses. It wasn't exactly the optimum situation out of which to make a Western, but she and Curtiz managed. Olson described the experience of constantly riding horses as "agonizing" and recalled Bill Rogers as a "dear human being" who taught her how to twirl a lasso. In another instance of what had become a continuing saga, Curtiz objected to the film's clichéd

Alan Jay Lerner visits his wife, Nancy Olson, as their daughter, Liza, sits on Curtiz's lap during filming of *The Boy from Oklahoma* (1954) (author's collection).

title before beginning production in February 1953: "The title, *Boy from Oklahoma* is wrong for this picture, because several people have thought it was to be a sequel to *The Will Rogers Story*. Also, Will is too old to be termed a "boy" and besides, it's a rather conventional, unimportant title and this picture needs an unusual, colorful off-key title, which will help the box office. I'm convinced people will go see *The Naked Spur* not only because of Jimmy Stewart, but also because the title is exciting."

Curtiz suggested several alternative titles, as did Bill Rogers, who wrote to Jack Warner noting that the existing title was "bad and will harm and not help the sale of the picture." No one could tell Warner how to publicize his movies. The picture ended up making a little money, but by that time Curtiz was gone from the studio that had been his home for over a quarter century.

After months of stalling, Roy Obringer had the studio auditor generate a report on Curtiz's films. According to the report, dated September 21, 1953, all Curtiz's films made under his 1948 contract (*The Boy from Oklahoma* hadn't yet been released), except one, had lost money. The studio audit report noted that *The Lady Takes a Sailor* (1949) grew from a cost of $1,473,000 (as noted in William Schaefer's authoritative record of the costs of Warner pictures compiled during his four decades as Jack Warner's personal secretary) to $2,101,414.02 in total deductions. *Young Man with a Horn* (1950), generally regarded as a success, was reported as a $154,459.36 loss, its total deductions being $2,167,275.97. Schaefer had recorded the cost of *Young Man with a Horn* as $1,310,000—a difference of $857,275. And so it went with nine of Curtiz's films, totaling up to an aggregate loss of $4,657,832.31. Only *I'll See You in My Dreams* eked out a reported profit of $260,615.98. Although it is possible that Schaefer's figures didn't include additional costs (such as those for publicity), the differences between the two sets of figures is striking. As if this exercise in bookkeeping gymnastics wasn't enough, the studio schemed to arbitrarily group Curtiz's films together in order to deny him the money that was owed him on the sole picture it deemed profitable.

On December 1, 1953, Mark Cohen sent a telegram to the studio warning that Curtiz would be filing a declaration of relief lawsuit for an accounting of his net profits and resolution of his contract. Roy Obringer subsequently wrote to Sam Schneider, Warner Bros.' vice president in New York: "This whole question revolves around the issue as to whether or not we can group all of the pictures directed by Curtiz for the purpose of accounting or if they are to be treated as separate pictures. The contract makes no express reference to this and it is purely a matter of legal interpretation of the contract language which would govern this situation."

Bill Schaefer had written to his boss over a year before after discussing Curtiz's contract with Obringer: "Obringer states that there was never any provision in Curtiz contract whereby profits or losses of any group of pictures would be lumped together. This was not thought of or contemplated when the new deal with Mike was made as there were no specified number of pictures he was to make."

On the bottom of Schaefer's memo, Warner wrote: "rewrite clause— to group pictures from here-in." It got worse when Obringer finally negotiated with Cohen in January 1954. In addition to attempting to retroactively group the pictures to benefit the studio in a manner that was never intended, the attorney remarked to Cohen that Curtiz "should be ashamed" to have caused the studio such big financial losses by making so many unsuccessful pictures. Curtiz seethed over the insult. After he calmed down and realized this was standard treatment for anyone who left Warner Bros. and was owed money, he pulled himself together and dictated a detailed personal letter to Jack Warner. Typed on Twentieth Century-Fox letterhead—he was involved in preproduction on *The Egyptian*—he told Warner that he deeply resented Obringer's statement about his work and reminded his former boss exactly who was in charge when he was directing movies for Warner Bros.: "Yours was the final decision on the purchase and assignment of the story itself, on every important actor. You determined the balance between quality and economy, where cuts should be made and how much the picture should cost. And whatever your decisions—and I have all the budgets in front of me right now—I never went over a budget or a shooting schedule during my last eleven pictures, but devised and schemed and worked to tip the balance in the studio's favor and maintain a high level of quality within whatever restrictions were placed on me."

Although his claim about never exceeding a shooting schedule on his final pictures was debatable, Curtiz accurately pointed out, "I was always faithful to Warners in doing my very best with whatever material the studio entrusted to me." He added that he "took material that other directors would have turned down" and "often straightened out story lines, improved construction, added situations . . . [and] acted as producer on the script before directorial preparations for production ever got started." Briefly revisiting his ire, he mentioned, "For a very hard worker, I made a comfortable living. . . . I had artistic success, but never riches, so this statement of Obringer's is not only rude, but ungrateful and uncalled for."

Returning to his central theme, Curtiz continued: "If [Obringer's] statement is correct that we lost so much money, I repeat that mine wasn't the decisive voice on the price of the story, the payment of actors, etc." The content and tone of Curtiz's letter had been balanced to this point, but then he let it get away from him. He used the next page and a half for a movie-by-movie explanation of why it was always someone else's fault, or why fate or bad luck had somehow intervened to cause his pictures to be unsuccessful. This excuse-laden critique reflected his habitual finger-pointing at others to avoid responsibility, which had angered so many who worked with him over the years: "It is certainly not my fault that for *The Lady Takes a Sailor* you gave me a has-been actor as Dennis Morgan," or, "It was not my idea that a fine picture like *Force of Arms* should be cast with two people like Bill Holden and Nancy Olson whose names mean nothing at the box office."

Though he admitted, "I never dreamed I would be battling over my financial reward with Obringer or in a court action against the studio with which I spent twenty-six years and for whom I made eighty-six pictures," Curtiz specifically refuted the Obringer scenario that grouped his pictures together in determining losses: "This I emphatically deny, as the contract specifically provides that each picture stands by itself in determining profits and losses as we had agreed upon. In addition, you will recall that after the contract was signed, the studio requested me to group my pictures in groups of three, which I denied."

Curtiz concluded by stating that he wanted an independent auditor to verify the studio's financial assertions, as he did "not admit to the correctness of same." He closed with a personal plea to Jack Warner: "Don't allow these conferences to end in bitterness and spoil the wonderful association and friendship we had during our twenty-six years together. If you separate the businessman from the friend, I know we can reach a satisfactory agreement."

There is no record of a response to Curtiz's letter, but Warner informed Obringer that under no circumstances did he want this matter to be litigated. Curtiz didn't want to go to court, either. He couldn't afford to take on the studio legally, and there was no way he could refute the accounting of his films. The fact was that while several of his pictures were successful, only one of them could legitimately be classified as a box-office hit. In Warner's view, he had already bailed out Curtiz when he bought his failed production company in 1948. He wasn't going to do it again.

The matter ended on August 3, 1954. The studio paid Famous Artists Agency for its share of Curtiz's profits and awarded Curtiz $62,500 to settle his contract "without the necessity of any further payment or accounting to Curtiz under such agreement." As for the interesting bookkeeping that had swelled the deductions on each of Curtiz's films, the screenwriter Niven Busch believed that Jack Warner simply had it knocked: "Nobody came out with a sizable profit from doing any deal with Warners. They had the most foolproof, plate-steel accounting system in the world. I still don't know, and I don't think anybody else does, how they do it."

A postscript to the controversy: in 1956 John Wayne refused an offer from Jack Warner to purchase his Batjac production company because of Wayne's fear of coming out on the losing end, as did nearly everyone who dealt with the mogul. A long time afterward, Wayne and his son Michael were on the lot and ran into Warner, who greeted them with his usual enthusiasm. "You really ought to bring Batjac back to Warner Bros., Duke," he said. "You should be here, where you can be fucked by friends."

31

Only in Hollywood

Curtiz was so eager to get back to work that he harried Mark Cohen into arranging an immediate term contract for him at Paramount. Cohen mentioned Curtiz's engagement to William Wyler, for whom he was negotiating a long-term Paramount deal: "As I previously advised you, Mike Curtiz executed an exclusive term deal with Paramount as he was reluctant to wait for the protracted period of time which was necessary to conclude the proposed deal which I suggested. For that reason, I told him that it was satisfactory with me if he made a term deal with the studio."

Jack Karp, an assistant to Paramount chairman Y. Frank Freeman, had been asking Warners about borrowing Curtiz since late 1952. The studio finally had the director it sought for a musical extravaganza that had been in the offing for nearly a decade. It had been twelve years since *Holiday Inn* (1942), starring Bing Crosby and Fred Astaire, which was followed by *Blue Skies* (1946). *White Christmas* was a holiday-themed spectacular to reunite Crosby and Astaire for a third go-round. Paramount wanted Curtiz for several reasons. Though the star was the eminently bankable Crosby singing the 1942 Irving Berlin tune (the most popular record of all time), there was concern over who could best synthesize his talent with those of Astaire, Rosemary Clooney, Dean Jagger, and the dancer Vera-Ellen, along with seventeen Irving Berlin songs and assorted production numbers. The Technicolor production would also mark the debut of Paramount's new VistaVision format, a higher-resolution, wide-screen version of thirty-five millimeter that positioned the negative horizontally in the camera to allow for a larger filming area without employing the anamorphic lenses required by CinemaScope. VistaVision prints were screened in aspect ratios ranging from 1:66 to 2:1, allowing exhibitors to project wide-screen films without having to purchase new projection equipment or modify theater seating. On paper, there was no one more qualified for *White Christmas* than Curtiz. In addition to working with a myriad of actors, he had directed more Technicolor films (including four musicals) than almost anybody else. Sealing the deal was his relationship with Irving Berlin, which dated back to *Mammy* in 1930. Berlin, who was paid $250,000 for his music and a percentage of the profits for *White Christmas*, held a lot of sway over the production. He and Paramount pushed for Curtiz and convinced Crosby, who had director approval, to agree.

Curtiz had little involvement with the casting of the star players and minimal input with the development of the script. To ensure he would be ready to go, he experimented with a wide-screen Hogue lens in June 1953 to "be absolutely sure of its possibilities." He shot footage in Elysian Park from a rowboat, a traveling shot at the Long Beach Amusement Center, and a high shot of the San Pedro Fishing Harbor.

White Christmas was originally planned to costar Rita Hayworth and José Iturbi. The picture was postponed in the latter part of 1952 when Fred Astaire dropped out after reading the draft screenplay. The death of Bing Crosby's wife, Dixie Lee, in November 1952 further delayed production. Donald O'Connor was signed to replace Astaire but the hoofer-comedian came down with Q-fever. He was replaced by Danny Kaye, who leveraged a $200,000 fee and profit percentage out of Paramount. The last-minute inclusion of Kaye turned out to be an astute move. In addition to being superbly talented, his spontaneous humor loosened up the other stars, particularly the frequently taciturn Crosby, whose genial persona cloaked an often-forbidding remoteness. Kaye made everyone on the set rock with laughter when he responded to Curtiz's direction with his uproarious faux-Hungarian diction. It was one of the rare instances of the director being amused at someone publicly poking fun at him.

Bing Crosby had the final word on anything of significance on the set of *White Christmas*. As Rosemary Clooney put it, "Even though Curtiz was a celebrated director—*Casablanca*—and even though Danny Kaye had his own agenda and very strong ego, Bing was always in charge." Aside from a temporary disagreement over the selection of Loyal Griggs as the director of photography, Crosby never threw his weight around or publicly countermanded Curtiz. He occasionally disappeared to play golf, and no one, including Curtiz, uttered a peep of disapproval. Curtiz's approach to working with the world's best-selling popular singer and his costars would be conciliatory at all times. According to Clooney, "Curtiz was brilliant. He told you to do simple things and then allowed you to follow your own instincts." There were few of his customary tantrums and bullying of functionaries. His lengthy tenure at Warner Bros. now behind him, Curtiz had to become acclimated to a different world at Paramount. Limey Plews was no longer around to anticipate when the director would change his mind about where the dolly tracks should be laid or to interpret some of his utterances for the actors and crew. Clooney remembered that Curtiz "often talked to me in words, that, even though they were English, I couldn't understand." In one scene when she had to climb through a window, Curtiz provided this direction: "When we start the scene, could give me a little off from balance?" Anne Whitfield, who played Dean Jagger's granddaughter in the film, claimed the only guidance she received occurred before an emotional scene with Mary Wickes, when Curtiz advised her: "Two girl have small tear." Everybody eventually caught on. Crosby was amused when Curtiz kept calling him "Binkie."

Dance rehearsals began on July 23, 1953, and continued for thirty-five days, particular emphasis being on Rosemary Clooney and Vera-Ellen. Clooney couldn't dance well, and Vera-Ellen was not a singer. With Vera-Ellen it was simple: Clooney sang both parts for the "Sisters" number, and Trudy Stevens dubbed the rest of her songs. Clooney had to buckle down to master her dance steps while being coached by Vera-Ellen and the choreographer Bob Alton, who was assisted by Bob Fosse. After beginning production on September 21, 1953, Curtiz directed all the acting scenes and participated in some of the nineteen musical numbers, including "Love, You Didn't Do Right by Me," which Berlin wrote specifically for Rosemary Clooney. Watching the gorgeous Clooney in a stylish black Edith Head gown with a large jeweled brooch on her backside while she danced with a young George Chakiris, one can believe that the sequence might be set in a film noir nightclub. Curtiz also added his stylistic touches throughout, including the "Snow" number, which neatly transitions from Crosby, Kaye, Clooney, and Vera-Ellen singing in a Pullman club car booth to what appears to be snow-frosted cocktails being mixed at the bar. Then there was the riotous nightclub scene in which Crosby and Kaye act fey with one another while swirling oversized blue feather fans. As Kaye swatted Crosby repeatedly with his fan, the crooner broke up, and the duo resembled a giggling pair of frat boys having a pillow fight. Curtiz loved it and printed the take. Kaye was especially joyous because he had convinced Curtiz to bar his wife, Sylvia, from the set. (Danny Kaye was apparently a henpecked movie star.) Curtiz banished Mrs. Kaye and blamed it on Crosby, with "Binkie's" tacit approval. Even though he didn't cast any of the stars, he ensured that Mary Wickes, one of his favorite character players, had a significant role in the film. Clooney remembered a scene between Wickes and Crosby that featured ad-libbing. "Then Bing gave her a kiss and said, 'Wait a minute!' and went back for another kiss, which was hysterical."

Curtiz was prevented from indulging in his old habit of expanding existing sets. He wanted a large Red Cross tent added to the army camp set during the opening sequence. The producer, Robert Emmett Dolan, who was under pressure to crimp the mushrooming budget (it eventually ballooned to $3,789,000), vetoed the request. On the recommendation of Don Hartman, Dolan also had Curtiz reshoot the "Count Your Blessings" number and the general's phone call scene. Curtiz supported the need to economize by eliminating the expense of shooting Crosby and Kaye on a train observation platform by altering the scene on the fly so that they simply mounted the train steps without any supporting scenery.

Barrie Chase dropped by the *White Christmas* set to visit her friend Betty Utey, who had a small part as a dancer. Even though the twenty-year-old Chase came from a show business family (her father was the noted screenwriter Borden Chase) and she had done bits in *Scaramouche, Road to Bali,* and *Hans Christian Anderson* (all 1952), she was uncomfortable on the busy set:

> I felt out of place and took a seat on a bench by the entrance door to the soundstage, way, way back away from the action. While I was sitting there, an older man was pacing back and forth and kept glancing at me. Presently an assistant director with a clipboard came to me and said, "Mr. Curtiz would like you to come to his dressing room to read for a part." Of course, he was the older man who had been walking by and looking at me. I didn't even know who Curtiz was. I was rather green and had been sheltered by my parents. After I was escorted to his dressing room, he asked me, "Can you talk through your nose?" I gave it a try; he was delighted and sent me down to casting. The casting people were laughing and asked me if I had a party dress to wear.

Added to the cast as "Doris Lenz," Chase appeared in a party and dance scene, squeaking in a nasal tone, "Mutual, I'm sure." "They paid me two hundred dollars for the part," she recalled "and it was improvised [by Curtiz] as they shot it." The serendipitous casting selection wasn't the end of her experience with Curtiz. "He phoned my house and asked to take me out to lunch. Although it sounded all right, my mother was concerned. Mother and I eventually decided that I should go but I dressed down as much as possible. He took me to the Hamburger Hamlet that was owned by his friend, actor Harry Lewis." Lewis personally prepared their burgers as Curtiz conversed with the young dancer. "He was a complete gentleman and very complimentary. He told my Mother that I had a lot of ability and talent—he compared me to Doris Day. I remember he said, 'I don't have the power anymore to sign you to a contract, but I'll keep you in mind." Chase, who became Fred Astaire's featured dancer on television and appeared in *Cape Fear* (1962) and *It's a Mad, Mad, Mad, Mad World* (1963), would wait on line to see herself in *White Christmas*.

Another encounter on the *White Christmas* set was more personally gratifying. Despite their forty-six-year age difference, Curtiz captivated Jill Gerrard, a twenty-year-old model. Asked six decades afterward what attracted her to Curtiz, she replied, "I think I fell in love over the ascot. He was so charming, funny, and did spontaneous things. You just fell under his spell." Curtiz began an affair with Gerrard while simultaneously continuing a relationship with the actress Anitra Stevens. Curtiz had met Stevens in 1952 and was entranced by her statuesque beauty. A Detroit native, she was born Alice Ann Yoder in 1927. After relocation and graduation from Hollywood High, she attempted to break into the movies as Ann Stuart. She had little success until she met Curtiz at a casting call and changed her name to Anitra Stevens. Curtiz believed that, in addition to her physical charms, she had genuine potential as an actress and gave her a small part in *The Story of Will Rogers* (1952) that ended up on the cutting room floor. This was followed by the roles of Yvonne in *The Jazz Singer* (1952) and a flirtatious bar girl in *Trouble Along the Way* (1953). Gerrard and Stevens were apparently unaware of each other. Curtiz eventually told Gerrard that he was married and his wife would not give him a divorce. Bess mostly remained in her bed at the Cove in Encino, attended to by a retinue of nurses and servants. He continued to review his scripts with her and observed the familial and social niceties. Curtiz's ability to compartmentalize his relationships with his wife and a pair of mistresses along with others in his orbit while directing a series of sprawling movies was a tribute to the sixty-six-year-old's powers of concentration as well as his physical stamina.

White Christmas production correspondence shows that he drove himself as hard as ever. A typical entry reads: "Mr. Curtiz directed all day. Finished shooting at 5:15 pm. Lined up tomorrow's first shot until 5:25 pm. Camera called at 8:00 am." After printing the final musical number (the quartet of stars adorned in yuletide costumes, singing "White Christmas"), Curtiz addressed the cast and crew on a day that the king and queen of Greece were visiting Paramount. Rosemary Clooney was standing next to Crosby as the star openly rejected Curtiz's wishes for the only time during the filming: "Curtiz announced that we'd do it again. 'We will not film it, but Binkie and Danny and Vera and Rosemary will pretend to film it for their majesties, the king and queen of Greece.' Bing leaned over to me. 'Cover for me. I'm going over the wall.' So we did the scene without him, lip-synching to the playback, trying to pretend that Bing wasn't supposed to appear in the number, even though his voice, singing 'White Christmas' was coming out of my mouth."

Curtiz wrapped *White Christmas* on December 10, 1953. Despite the high-octane writing talent of Norman Krasna, who wrote the original screenplay, which would be rewritten by the team of Norman Panama and Melvin Frank with contributions by Melville Shavelson, Barney Dean, and Jack Rose, the dramatic results were unspectacular. Crosby later said the script was weak and should have been better. The notion of the Crosby-Kaye stage act partnering with Clooney and Vera-Ellen as sisters in song and dance to produce a variety show to rescue their former World War II commanding general's Vermont inn from bankruptcy was a tenuous premise. Much of the dialogue was languid rather than crisp. It didn't make the slightest bit of difference to audiences, who ate up the Berlin songs amid the holiday motif. *White Christmas* was instantly beloved. Just as Berlin's tune became a standard, its cinematic namesake created a singular identity, as it appealed to the emotions that millions felt each December: family, friends, snow, and yuletide cheer—and Crosby crooning the holiday songs.

The overt sentiment of Curtiz's personality, which had topped off *Four Daughters* and *Yankee Doodle Dandy,* overflowed into *White Christmas.* It was his most financially successful movie. After opening in Radio City Music Hall on October 14, 1954, the film raked in $12 million, the most successful picture of the year. The adoration became seasonally permanent; receipts eventually exceeded $30 million in 1954 dollars. Those who had profit percentage deals with Paramount (including Crosby, Berlin, and Kaye) made fortunes. Curtiz didn't. He was paid $135,833. The present-day equivalent of $1.2 million seems a parsimonious amount of compensation by modern standards. His pay for *White Christmas,* however, was

Curtiz enjoys a laugh on the set of *White Christmas* (1954) with Danny Kaye, Bing Crosby, and a visiting Danny Thomas (courtesy of the Academy of Motion Picture Arts and Sciences).

only slightly less than what he made during forty weeks of toiling for Jack Warner. Not only enjoying the adulation of helming the season's top box-office hit, he had also been concurrently working on what was ballyhooed as the biggest Hollywood period spectacle during what had become *the* era of wide-screen Technicolor extravaganzas.

Curtiz had remained close to Darryl Zanuck during the two decades since the powerhouse producer left Warner Bros. and cofounded Twentieth Century-Fox. Along with the other big-five studios, Fox was forced to shed its theater chain, as mandated by the government antitrust divestiture. With box-office receipts wilting under the glare of television, Fox's president, Spyros Skouras, purchased the rights for an anamorphic camera lens invented by Henri Chrétien, a French cinematic specialist. They barely aced out Jack Warner, whose representative arrived in Paris a day too late. Fox poured money into perfecting a system that could use the specially configured lens to film and project a new widescreen image with four-track sound using a single projection machine instead of the three-camera, three-film, and three-projector system required for Cinerama. Zanuck premiered the first CinemaScope film, *The Robe,* in September 1953.[1] It grossed $26.1 million in its first year. CinemaScope was Fox's proprietary process that would be leased to other studios. By November 1953 every other major Hollywood studio was licensed to make CinemaScope pictures, except for Paramount, which had VistaVision. Even though theater owners complained about installing new screens and projector lenses, the money rolled in, and for the time being Zanuck was redeemed. *Demetrius and the Gladiators* (1954) was a follow-on hit sequel to *The Robe.* But Zanuck was working on a bigger project.

The mogul fast-tracked the production of the mammoth historical novel *The Egyptian,* which he had purchased in 1952. Written by Mika Waltari, a prolific Finnish author of everything from historical novels to cartoons, *The Egyptian* became an international best seller after its abridged English publication in 1949. Its protagonist is the fictional character of Sinuhe, who relates his life in flashback from his birth as a foundling who becomes the royal physician to Pharaoh Akhnaton of Egypt circa 1352 B.C. His life becomes a search for meaning against the backdrop of intrigue fomented by Akhnaton's family and his own love of a Babylonian courtesan. Zanuck was convinced *The Egyptian* was the source material for a motion picture that would top *The Robe* and every other Hollywood spectacle since *Intolerance* (1916).

Zanuck offered direction of his latest epic to Curtiz, whose services he had coveted for years. There were few people in Hollywood whom Curtiz respected more than Zanuck. In a December 1958 interview, Curtiz remarked: "But my four severest critics to who I am so grateful were Jack Warner, Hal Wallis, Darryl Zanuck and Henry Blanke. They were often so brutal with me that they left me in tears, but there was always a wise teaching behind their cruel words."

Within a month after he left Warner, Curtiz was in meetings with Zanuck and Casey Robinson, his screenwriting colleague from *Captain Blood* and other Warner films. Zanuck had hired Robinson to write *The Egyptian,* but Curtiz immediately objected to his former cohort's flowery language. After reviewing Robinson's third draft with Bess, Curtiz prepared a detailed memo for Zanuck and Robinson. He believed more character development was needed for Sinuhe. "I realize this thoughtful, analytical man, who carefully considers before taking action, is a realistic and well-drawn character, but don't you feel his beliefs should be clarified so the audience will know where he stands at all times?" Curtiz provided a scene-by-scene breakdown that condensed what was a sprawling story with dubious appeal to a mass audience. A month later, he submitted a detailed compendium to Zanuck. He specified various wardrobe and prop requirements for distribution to the various Fox departments. Curtiz included a requirement for all the royal priests to have shaved heads and the lions in a key hunting sequence to be "large, black-maned males" of a type that had roamed ancient Egypt. Although he had legitimate concerns about directing such an abstract picture, his faith in Zanuck was absolute as he wrote, "But with the great work you have already done, I know it will not be difficult to perfect this script." During the debacle that followed, Curtiz's loyalty to his friend remained unbounded. John Meredyth Lucas, assessing the aftermath of *The Egyptian,* offered a telling perspective: "Friendship was a fault of Mike's."

Early on, Zanuck showed Curtiz a screen test of a sultry European actress. If her thick accent wasn't enough, she had an unchanging expression that made her look as if she were suffering from a migraine. Zanuck's wife, Virginia, was present in the screening room and wondered why the actress looked as though she were in pain. Curtiz chimed in with his usual tactlessness: "Do you know what that girl is suffering from? Deprivation. What she needs is a lover. Any volunteers?" After an awkward silence, Curtiz chuckled and added, "Line up behind *me* in the queue!" More silence. What no one in the room except Zanuck knew at the time was that the mogul had already staked out bedroom privileges with the actress whom he and his wife had christened Bella Darvi. Although Zanuck later attempted to deny it, the newly minted surname of "Darvi" was specifically designed to represent Darryl and Virginia. Zanuck decided that he would cast his paramour in *The Egyptian* as Nefer, the Babylonian temptress. The fact that the studio's hottest star, Marilyn Monroe, begged to play the part and even offered to test for the role didn't dissuade him in the slightest.

Zanuck and his wife met Bella Wegier in 1952 at a sidewalk café on the Champs Élysées. The sexy ex of a rich businessman, she was a regular at Cannes and attended the best parties along the French Riviera. Bella was socially engaging and knew how to advance her own interests. She was also a compulsive gambler in hock up to her ears. A Polish Jew whose parents immigrated to France in the 1930s, she was reportedly deported by the Nazis and survived internment in a concentration camp. The Zanucks believed they had discovered a startling new talent. Zanuck, who had already slept with Darvi in Europe while paying off her gambling debts, eventually put her in a couple of films, including Sam Fuller's *Hell and High Water*. Few people who observed Bella Darvi onscreen believed that Zanuck's latest discovery was or would be appropriate for any significant movie role. The personal magnetism that allowed her to captivate so many people was tellingly absent in front of the camera. Virginia Zanuck, who considered Darvi almost as a niece, installed her in their household, and her husband renewed clandestine trysts with their protégé after late-night screenings at the studio.

Sex was as essential to Zanuck as it was to Curtiz. The fifty-year-old Fox chieftain had been coping with a midlife crisis, as he perceived that his legendary virility was fading. He later admitted to being "absolutely besotted" with Darvi. He endeavored to persuade Curtiz that he could coax a convincing performance out of her. Curtiz didn't need much convincing. Hadn't he made newcomers into actors time and again? At some point, Curtiz casually mentioned that he intended to cast Anitra Stevens as Queen Nefertiti. This was fine with Zanuck: the Nefertiti role required little more than being elegantly swathed in beautiful Egyptian costumes. Curtiz simply wanted to do for his girlfriend what Zanuck was already doing for his. It was a literal state of affairs that could have occurred only in Hollywood. *The Egyptian* would feature the mistresses of the notably married Darryl F. Zanuck and Michael Curtiz.

Preproduction delays quickly accumulated. Casey Robinson became fed up with Darvi and her Svengali-like control over Zanuck. He described a situation that had become bizarre: "This girl was an amateur; she spoke with an accent, which made her scarcely understandable, and she assumed in the studio an importance that was unbelievable. She attended with Darryl all of the rushes and openly boasted that she ran the

Curtiz directs his mistress Anitra Stevens (Ann Stuart) in *The Egyptian* (1954) while Michael Wilding and Victor Mature chat (courtesy of the Lucas family).

studio, that she could hire anyone, fire anyone, and was quite flagrant with these boasts."

Robinson ended up quitting the picture because of Zanuck's obsession with Darvi:

> There was a breakup happening between Darryl and his children over this girl, and the kids were close to me, and on one occasion one of them came to my office in tears to speak of it. I was immediately sent for by Zanuck. I knew from the speed of the summons that my office was bugged. I said to Darryl, "Look, let's quit while we are still friends." His reply broke my heart because he said he had no friends. That he had decided that it was better to do without friends; that the people that were friends were spongers who demanded of him all sorts of favors. In short, the man's mind was deteriorating.

Richard Zanuck later spoke about his father's state of mind concerning Darvi and the other women who would follow in her footsteps: "He was normally so level-headed, such a shrewd judge of what would sell in the movie houses. But when he fell for one of these girls, this great ability he had to get people enthused about a film or someone in it would betray him. . . . He actually believed, and made *them* [his girlfriends] believe, they were the greatest discoveries of all time."

Zanuck had become so delusional that he rationalized that audiences would accept Darvi's thick accent because she was playing a "foreign" Babylonian. But Zanuck's girlfriend wasn't the chief casting challenge on *The Egyptian*.

Zanuck pulled off a major coup when he signed Marlon Brando to play Sinuhe. It lasted only until after the first read-through of the script. Philip Dunne was brought in to replace Robinson and revise the script with Zanuck. According to Dunne, "Brando was driven off the picture by Curtiz." During an initial reading by Brando, Curtiz reportedly mused out loud, "How can I, with all my genius, make you play this man who is one moment hero, the next moment villain?" Brando stared at Curtiz, realizing that this thick-accented older man was assuredly not Elia Kazan. Brando read from the script with Darvi, Jean Simmons, Victor Mature, and Gene Tierney as Curtiz coached them through it. After Brando left Hollywood, his MCA agent telephoned Zanuck and told him that the actor didn't want to be in *The Egyptian* because "Marlon didn't like Mike Curtiz. He doesn't like the role. And he can't stand Bella Darvi." A furious Zanuck filed a multimillion dollar suit against Brando, who hid out in New York attempting to duck the process servers.[2]

Zanuck now had to find another Sinuhe. After being unable to sign Dirk Bogarde, he was turned down by Farley Granger. He also rejected John Cassavetes, among others. Zanuck had a hard commitment to premiere the film by September 1954. The delays meant that he would have to cut the film as it was shot, and the other postproduction work would also have to be accelerated. Zanuck defaulted to Edmund Purdom, an English actor whom few people had heard of. Although Purdom was not without acting ability, his casting as Sinuhe meant that there was not a legitimate star in the title role. To play Akhnaton, Zanuck tapped another English actor, Michael Wilding. The screenwriter Philip Dunne later claimed that Zanuck possessed an unshakeable belief that English actors should always play nobility roles. Gene Tierney, who was beginning to suffer from clinical depression, would play Akhnaton's ambitious sister, Baketamon.

After considering Kirk Douglas as Horemheb, Sinuhe's boyhood friend who ends up becoming his adversary, Zanuck played it safe by freeing up Victor Mature from a Universal commitment. Peter Ustinov, who would dine out on Curtiz anecdotes for decades, was Sinuhe's loyal one-eyed slave Kaptah in a warm-up for his Oscar-winning turn in *Spartacus* (1960). Curtiz added one of his personal favorites, Henry Daniell, as the duplicitous high priest Mekere.

Dunne thought the breathtakingly beautiful Dana Wynter should play Nefertiti but was blocked by Curtiz. Dunne later told the author Lee Server that Curtiz "cast some lumpish girlfriend who looked about as much as Nefertiti as you or I do." Anitra Stevens might not have resembled an Egyptian princess, but she was far from dowdy. Dunne detested Curtiz, considering him to be "a classic yes man" in his dealings with Zanuck. Curtiz viewed Dunne as just another in a long line of interferers. Their relationship became tense after Zanuck, familiar with the director's habit of script changes, anointed the screenwriter as his on-set emissary. Dunne claimed afterward that instead of simply being Zanuck's factotum to control Curtiz, he had obtained unofficial status as producer of the film.

No expense was spared to make every detail as authentic as possible. Zanuck hired a noted Egyptologist, Elizabeth Titzel Riefstahl, as technical adviser. Everything was mapped out for each scene: the wall hieroglyphics reproduced from the Valley of the Kings, the exquisitely detailed and accurate wardrobe, artwork, and props, a facsimile of an actual ancient Egyptian market, even an exact replica of the crown found on the famed Nefertiti bust, which would be worn by Anitra Stevens. Over a million different props were reputedly catalogued for the film; many of them were eventually sold to Cecil B. DeMille for *The Ten Commandments* (1956). From a pictorial perspective, *The Egyptian* is probably one of the most historically accurate movies ever made.

Curtiz began filming on March 3, 1954. The pressure to finish quickly became immediate: Zanuck wrote a "Dear Mike" note detailing why he would be cutting the film sequence by sequence:

> Even on my personal productions I do not make a habit of screening without the director being present, but I am sure you know in the case of *The Egyptian,* we *confidentially* face a difficult situation. Two rival companies are trying to beat us out with stories in an Egyptian background. Jack Warner has given orders on *Land*

Zanuck and Curtiz in the mid-1950s (courtesy of the Lucas family).

of the Pharaohs to cut and score the film as they go along, and as you know it is a story with our background dealing with the building of the pyramids. We probably cannot beat out [MGM's] *Valley of the Kings* but I do not care about this so much as it is a modern story, but the Warner picture disturbs me as they have their own color process and can make prints much quicker than we can. Therefore in this case, I have to gamble and disregard protocol and have the picture cut so that we can get it into music shortly after you have finished final photography. I know you will

495

bear with me as I think you remember I am a pretty good cutter.
. . . If there is anything that I have done that you violently object
to I will either "argue you" out of it or let you "argue me" out
of it.

To make up more time, Zanuck asked Fox's music director, Alfred
Newman, to assign the music score to the composer Franz Waxman.
Waxman was unavailable, so Newman engaged the great Bernard Herrmann. With Newman and Herrmann working tight deadlines on other
projects, it was impossible for a single composer to deliver a score for the
entire film within the constraints of the compressed schedule. Accordingly, the two composers divided up *The Egyptian,* composing and conducting separately. According to Herrmann's biographer Steven C. Smith:
"Herrmann chose to score the film's darker sequences and characters; the
cruel seductress Nefer-Nefer, the scheming princess Baketamon. Newman scored the more conventional love scenes, as well as the platitudinous religious scenes at the film's end. Nearly all the rest of the score was
Herrmann: the prelude and opening scenes, the town music of Thebes, the
lion-hunt sequence and the film's finale."

The flawlessly integrated music score of *The Egyptian* remains one of
the movie's strongest attributes.

Curtiz's principal technical challenge was CinemaScope. Most directors hated the visual compositions resulting from squeezing the proportions of actors into an elongated frame while constricting camera
movement and reducing close-ups. George Stevens dryly observed, "CinemaScope is fine, if you want a system that shows a boa constrictor to
better advantage than a man." Curtiz had no choice, but he did have a leg
up. His cinematographer was Leon Shamroy, who had used the original
lens manufactured by Henri Chrétien to shoot *The Robe.* These initial
lenses caused image distortion and softness, particularly at the edges of
the frame. Incredibly, Fox filmed its first two CinemaScope pictures—
How to Marry a Millionaire and *The Robe*—using the original French
lenses. Before *The Egyptian* began, Bausch & Lomb had delivered improved lenses that removed most of the distortion and improved the visual
quality. Nonetheless, it remained a daunting artistic challenge. Shamroy
would term this period of his long career at Fox as "the terrible days of
CinemaScope." He remembered: "Those early Bausch and Lomb lenses
were hell; and the films became very granulated. We've never had the
sharpness we had in the old technically wonderful days of three-color

Technicolor. . . . It nearly drove me out of my mind, seeing what happened to my work when it was spread out all over the screen."

CinemaScope was ideal for pictures with spectacular outdoor vistas like *River of No Return* (1954) and action epics such as *20,000 Leagues under the Sea* (1954). Principally filmed on studio sets that had to be specially made for horizontal presentation, *The Egyptian* exudes a beautiful but antiseptic sheen. Shamroy self-deprecatingly observed, "One drawback in my many years at 20th was that I became too slick, too polished; everything started to look like magazine illustrations." Although Curtiz's blocking within the frame kept the full screen occupied and there are several memos from Zanuck praising his footage, there was minimal camera movement during the innumerable static scenes of actors reciting dialogue. Only in the few action sequences, including the lion hunt and the rebellion battle, did a modicum of Curtiz's visual style emerge. He also created several virtuoso lighting and art effects. One of the seduction scenes with Purdom and Darvi has an alluring bluish-purple background. Visual presentation, however, was the least of the picture's problems. In addition to being baffled when Curtiz inexplicably rehearsed stand-ins instead of the principal actors, Dunne differed with the director over the theme of religion being imbued in the film. He claimed to have corrected Curtiz after a scene of Egyptian sun worshipers concluded with a group of extras crossing themselves as though they had just observed the Crucifixion on Golgotha. The screenwriter wrote a memo to Zanuck, reporting that Curtiz appeared to be remaking *Moon of Israel*: "In scenes of soldiers persecuting people, the great majority of the persecuted seemed to be dressed in Jewish or Syrian costumes. . . . Apparently Mike is under the impression that only Jews are ever persecuted and when I try to suggest otherwise, I am told I have no understanding of such matters. . . . We should be as *Egyptian* as we possibly can and avoid the familiar stereotype of people in beards and robes being chased by the Gestapo."

Zanuck appended in type at the bottom of Dunne's memo: "I agree with you completely. . . . This is not a story of Jewish persecution. It was never intended to be. We have already made that story." One can't help wondering if Zanuck and Curtiz reminisced about *Noah's Ark* during the making of *The Egyptian*.

While revisionists might ascribe this disagreement to a gentile film mogul and screenwriter ganging up on a Jewish director, the dispute can be traced to Curtiz's memos about the original script. The director was insistent that Akhnaton's monotheistic belief in a solar deity be presented as the forerunner of Judeo-Christianity in order to make the film more appealing to a mass audience. He believed the pharaoh had to be more than an ineffectual sun-worshipping mystic who loses his throne. There are religious implications throughout the movie, including the overt symbolism of the ankh accompanied by the intermittent but unctuous voiceover narration by Purdom. However clumsily executed, most of these references were the work of Curtiz. He knew that *The Egyptian* lacked a singular theme that would resonate with a mass audience and wanted to correct this deficiency by inserting a religious motif. At one point he wrote to Zanuck, "Akhnaton is as important to this story as Jesus is to *The Robe*." Although Zanuck permitted Curtiz some leeway in portraying Akhnaton as a self-believing deity, the producer also had to water down this perspective to placate Joseph Breen, who was troubled by Akhnaton's resemblance "to an early day prototype of Christ."

Zanuck got away with more than the usual amount of sexual frankness because of the period nature of the material. Censorship in the movies was finally beginning to change. Before an ill Joseph Breen retired as the head of the Production Code Authority in 1954, one of his last official acts was writing an exception to the archaic production code that granted special dispensation for Marlon Brando to tell Karl Malden to "go to hell" in *On the Waterfront* (1954). Supporting a movie featuring a crusading Catholic priest was Breen's symbolic finale after two decades spent safeguarding American morality from the perceived excesses of Hollywood.

Curtiz was correct about the lack of thematic continuity in *The Egyptian,* but his efforts only further muddled the picture, which completed principal photography on May 7, 1954. There are three different stories within the overarching saga, and they are not unified effectively. Zanuck's vaunted editorial talent was noticeably lacking in cutting a picture to a final running time of two hours and twenty minutes. Curtiz conversely believed too much footage was removed and that Zanuck's editing hurt the movie. His long-standing frustration with others cutting his films dated back to his angst over the mutilation of *Sodom und Gomorrha* (1922).

Philip Dunne and Casey Robinson would defend their screenplay and blame the film's failure on the presence of Darvi and Wilding and the absence of Brando. The cineaste mind does boggle over the possibility of the seduction scenes between Purdom and Darvi being played by Brando and Monroe. The casting problems were contributory causes, but the principal failure of *The Egyptian* was the inability of the script to translate the sensuous power of the novel to the screen. Watching the picture six decades later, one is impressed by the lavish beauty of the production and intrigued by the nuances of the various narratives. Adherents argue that it was a misunderstood film, but audiences in 1954 were bored beyond measure. Although Purdom did his best, he was trapped inside a dull character. There was no hero to root for, hardly any action, and little drama. Peter Ustinov said the film seemed so profoundly silly while he was making it that he never bothered to watch it. He added, "It was like playing *Aida* without the music." *The Egyptian* was released to scathing reviews. Bosley Crowther disparaged Darvi and Wilding in the *New York Times*: "Bella Darvi as the heartless gold digger smiles and postures without magnetism or charm. Michael Wilding is ridiculous as the Pharaoh—a prissy Englishman in funny looking clothes. . . . Michael Curtiz has directed a few fierce and frantic crowd scenes, such as the slaughter of worshipers of the one god, and his reach for personal drama is plain. But the script and that excavated décor are a little too heavy for him to move."

Variety, usually kind to major studio productions, also pilloried Darvi: "A weak spot in the talent line-up is Bella Darvi who contributes little more than an attractive figure. Her thesping as the seductive temptress who drives Sinuhe to ruin is something less than believable or skilled."

The Egyptian was reckoned to cost $5 million and lost at least a half a million during its first run. It was quickly banished to the Fox vault as an embarrassing instance of excess. Zanuck took it badly, attempting to soothe Darvi, whom he obdurately believed had the talent to become a major movie star. A humiliated Virginia Zanuck kicked Darvi out after learning that her husband was carrying on with their protégée inside their house. Darvi returned to the gaming tables of Monaco. Zanuck followed her there, abandoning his wife and family after leaving his studio to become an independent producer for Fox in 1956. It was an ignominious exit for Hollywood's most talented studio head. He eventually broke it off with Darvi when he discovered she was having an affair behind his back—with a woman. Bella Darvi would end up a suicide in 1971.

Zanuck was also burned out from years of continuous toil and couldn't countenance what moviemaking had become: "Actors have taken over Hollywood completely with their agents. They want approval of everything—script, stars, still pictures. The producer hasn't got a chance to exercise any authority. . . . What the hell, I'm not going to work for them!" Zanuck would prove to be far from finished as a filmmaker, but his lengthy creative period at the tiller of Twentieth Century-Fox was over.

Although it was never good to be associated with a flop, Curtiz's professional reputation suffered minimal damage: everyone in the business knew who the creative guru of *The Egyptian* was. He also didn't have to travel as far as Zanuck to console his mistress. After the picture wrapped, Curtiz bought Anitra Stevens a North Hollywood house. His relationship with Stevens caused John Meredyth Lucas and his family some discomfiture after he gave his stepson's wife, Joan Winfield, a small part as a nurse to the pharaoh's children. Winfield was extremely close to Bess and was dismayed by the situation with Curtiz's mistress, which was common knowledge to the cast and crew. "Was Joan being disloyal to Mother by working with that girl?" wondered John Meredyth Lucas.

There was little time for reflection, as there was another VistaVision assignment at Paramount. *We're No Angels* (1955) was adapted from Albert Husson's play *La Cuisine des anges*. It was curious that the movie credited the Husson play but did not mention the Broadway hit play *My Three Angels*, written by Bella and Sam Spewack and directed by José Ferrer. The *New York Times* claimed that the film "stalks the Spewacks almost scene by scene."

The lighthearted story concerns three Devil's Island escapees who become involved with a shopkeeper (Leo G. Carroll) and his family (Joan Bennett and Gloria Talbott) in French Guiana on Christmas Eve in 1895. Instead of the Broadway trio of Walter Slezak, Jerome Cowan, and Robert Carroll, Curtiz had Humphrey Bogart, Aldo Ray, and Peter Ustinov. Basil Rathbone and John Baer provide the villainy that is ultimately foiled by the convicts. Curtiz was directing a play that relied on several standing sets. Only in the opening sequence, in which the trio improbably arise in a downtown Cayenne bustling with food vendors, shoppers, livestock, and soldiers, with an added diversion of a tropical rainstorm, does the picture awake as well. Curtiz's camera was becoming increasingly static. The fluid movements that incorporated long dolly shots and innovative angles became rare in his later films. For those who wonder why many of his post-Warner pictures are lacking his impressive visual repertoire, the era of wide-screen movies during the 1950s had a lot to do with it. Of fifteen features he made after *The Boy from Oklahoma* (1954), eleven were filmed in CinemaScope or VistaVision. He struggled to adapt his cinematic style to the elongated constriction of the new wide-screen format.

As for the comedic aspect of *We're No Angels,* Bogart reminded Ustinov, "You gotta remember, he's [Curtiz] got no sense of humor. So we'll have to take things into our own hands without letting him know what we're doing." As it had been at Warner Bros., Bogie's method of stress relief included needling Curtiz to the maximum extent possible. Verita Thompson, Bogart's hairdresser, recalled a creative practical joke that the star played on Curtiz:

> Curtiz was constantly complaining about his portable dressing room. He was always after the cleaning crew, nagging them about the dirtiness of the floor. . . . Bogie tired of hearing him complain about the alleged dirt, so he got a rubber or plastic dog turd from somewhere, and . . . Bogie slipped into his dressing room and placed the fake dog turd on an overstuffed beige chair that Curtiz always used—his "dirty" couch had yet to be cleaned or replaced. . . . The door suddenly burst open and Curtiz propelled himself from it like a rocket, shouting, "Where is cleaning person? I want immediately person who cleans!" Bogart grabbed him and asked what was wrong. . . . "My chair!" Curtiz said, trying to wrench from Bogie's grasp. "Boogie, a dog he has shit in my chair!" . . . Bogart walked over to the chair, picked up the fake turd and put it in his pocket. I thought Curtiz was going to faint. Then Bogie rubbed his hands together and inspected them as though to see if any traces remained on his hands. . . . Curtiz stared at Bogie with revulsion and when Bogie lifted his hand to give him a friendly pat on the shoulder, Curtiz jerked back as though he didn't want to associate with someone who would put dog turds in his pocket, let alone be touched by him. Bogart had been deadly serious all along, but he finally broke up, took the fake turd from his pocket and waved it at Curtiz, telling him, "By the way, Mike, this is a prop." Curtiz glared at him for a long moment, then shouted, "Boogie, you son of a beech!" And he slammed the door.

According to Gloria Talbott, Basil Rathbone was the originator of the fake dog shit gag and played it on Bogart who immediately co-opted it for Curtiz.

Even though Curtiz loved Peter Ustinov and let him add his own lines and bits of business, *We're No Angels* evoked chuckles rather than guffaws. It certainly was an unusual holiday picture; it featured a pet cobra

Curtiz with Aldo Ray, Peter Ustinov, and Bogart on the set of *We're No Angels* (1955) (courtesy of the Academy of Motion Picture Arts and Sciences).

named Adolph that Aldo Ray employed to do away with Rathbone and Baer. The picture was definitely offbeat: Bogart was sardonic, Ray subdued, and Ustinov irrepressible. It garnered some positive reviews and made money despite Bogart's hefty $200,000 salary. Curtiz's next picture turned out to be something entirely different.

The Vagabond King was a venerable Rudolf Friml operetta based on the novel and play *If I Were King*. There had been three previous movies about the poet François Villon saving Paris from the Burgundians circa 1463. John Barrymore essayed one of his most memorable turns as Villon in *The Beloved Rogue* (1927). Dennis King and Jeanette MacDonald starred in Paramount's early two-strip Technicolor production *The Vagabond King* (1930). The nonmusical *If I Were King* (1938), starring Ronald Colman as Villon and Basil Rathbone as King Louis XI, was nominated for four Oscars.

Paramount wanted to revisit the Friml operetta as a musical in 1951 with Tony Martin and Jean Simmons. The studio settled on Kathryn Grayson opposite Mario Lanza. Lanza's self-destructive behavior at MGM had approached the point of mental illness; he was eventually suspended and then sued for breach of contract. A wary Paramount insisted that Lanza undergo a psychiatric examination and a recording session to verify the quality of his voice before signing him to a contract. The great tenor refused. The best alternative that Paramount could manage was Oreste Kirkop, a Maltese tenor. He was billed simply as "Oreste," and his casting in the title role presented two principal challenges: he possessed virtually no acting ability and he couldn't speak English. Kirkop's facial expressions were limited to a grin that displayed most of his teeth as he opened his eyes wide enough to resemble someone experiencing a severe electrical shock. All the principal actors had to perform with a titled star whose every word was dubbed. "He couldn't speak English, so the director, Mike Curtiz, told me to speak his lines," remembered Grayson.

With the exception of Oreste, the cast was worthy of a top-notch production. In addition to Grayson, the gorgeous star of *Show Boat* (1951) and *Kiss Me Kate* (1953), there was seventy-five-year-old Walter Hampden as King Louis XI (he passed away before the film was released in August 1956). Rita Moreno brought her energetic talent to the role of the tavern wench, Huguette, who gives her life for Villon. Two newcomers, Jack Lord and Leslie Nielsen, reaffirmed Curtiz's continued ability to spot new talent. Sir Cedric Hardwicke, who had memorably played Hampden's evil brother in *The Hunchback of Notre Dame* (1939), was given virtually nothing to do except glower like an unhappy bulldog. With the exception of Moreno, much of the cast seemed uninspired. Rudolf Friml composed several new songs that made little difference.

The production exudes a tired appearance of greasepaint and artificial sets. Paramount reduced the original budget by nearly 30 percent, and the preproduction story conference notes show Curtiz arguing with the producer Pat Duggan and the rest of the team in an attempt to preserve the integrity of the picture. "Just what is this meeting about?" Curtiz asked at one point. "If you are so extreme on money and should not hurt quality, I think it is a waste of time talking about it." There is also an endless array of ornate Edith Head costumes for the principal actors that change with each scene. Several of the players, particularly Jack Lord, appear as though they were attending a masquerade ball. The use of the VistaVision camera is lackluster, even with the assignment of Hitchcock's favorite cinematographer, Robert Burks. Despite the presence of the ace fencing coach Fred Cavens, the sword fights are poorly staged. Grayson was the nominal star, but her role appears to be an afterthought. The film's script supervisor, May Wale Brown, remembered, "Confusion and chaos reigned throughout the picture." Although the press book trumpeted Oreste's screen debut as "one that will be long remembered," both he and the film were quickly forgotten. Oreste Kirkop never appeared in another movie, and after a few television appearances, he returned to sing at Covent Garden in England and retired in 1960.

Paramount's decision to drop $3 million into a Technicolor wide-screen remake of a shopworn relic during an era of transitional films that included *The Blackboard Jungle* (1955), *Giant* (1956), and *Baby Doll* (1956) seems brainless in retrospect. Kathryn Grayson, who retired from movies after this disaster, believed the entire picture was a mistake. "It never should have been made. Rudolf Friml was so upset about it that he told Paramount that he was going out of town for the weekend. He went to Hong Kong."

After such an embarrassment, Curtiz's relationship with Paramount entered a different phase. He was still under contract, and if he couldn't helm a moneymaker, then the studio wanted him to develop new talent, or it could rent him out to direct elsewhere. He ended up producing and directing a crime drama that he cast with fresh actors, including a trio of new discoveries. It was an attempt to leverage his reputation as a star-maker that was trumpeted in every press interview and publicity release. Alternately titled *Too Late My Love* and *The Kiss-Off*, the script included overtones of *Double Indemnity* with a couple of novel twists. The screenplay was jointly attributed to Frank Tashlin, Alford "Rip" Van Ronkel, and Curtiz's stepson John Meredyth Lucas. Curtiz cast Carol Ohmart (who had been an understudy as a slave girl in the Broadway production of *Kismet*) as a restless vixen, Pauline, married to a wealthy building contractor, Ralph Nevins (James Gregory) while having an affair with his assistant, Marsh Marshall (Tom Tryon). When the two lovers overhear a trio of crooks planning a jewel heist, Pauline convinces a sporadically conscience-stricken Marshall that they can cash in by robbing the thieves and disappearing with the loot. It all falls apart when a suspicious Nevins decides to follow his wife to what he thinks is a tryst.

Ohmart received a big buildup from the studio for a part that seemed tailor-made for Barbara Stanwyck.[3] She projected an enjoyable feral presence and carried off several of her scenes with femme-fatale panache. She discovered, however, that in spite of all the ballyhoo, a film debut as a backstabbing adulteress who kills her husband was not the ticket to stardom in mid-1950s Hollywood. She also needed a more facile actor to play opposite her. Tryon was a handsome six-foot-plus-tall actor who delivered a performance akin to an airline seat in the upright and locked position. His baptism by fire under Curtiz was merely a warm-up for the title role in Otto Preminger's *The Cardinal* (1963). Preminger was so sadistically abusive toward him—"Otto simply destroyed Tom," remembered his costar Carol Lynley—that Tryon eventually quit acting and became a successful novelist. Ohmart's experience with Curtiz on what was eventually titled *The Scarlet Hour* was not as bad, but manifestly unpleasant. She fought back tears after Curtiz yelled at her over a camera cue: "Leave your two damn feet here and take two steps back." The next day, "a veritable who's who" of movie stars visited the set, including Humphrey Bogart, David Niven, Yul Brynner, Cary Grant, Bob Hope, and Bing Crosby. All had either observed or were familiar with Curtiz's conduct with new actors and came to offer their support. Ohmart recalled the moment in 1989 interview: "Bogart, the spokesman, told the producer-director firmly, 'We didn't come to see you—we came to see her.' Bogey then whispered to Paramount's new discovery, 'We're with you, babe.'"

Afterward, Curtiz took her aside for some tough love: "It doesn't matter what you think of me or what I think of you. You're going to be up there in that film all by yourself. You can't take the credits off the picture."[4]

John Meredyth Lucas summarized Curtiz's dilemma on *The Scarlet Hour*: "He [Curtiz] was indeed a starmaker but to make a star you need some sort of quality, not necessarily acting ability but beauty, personality or some special attribute. None was forthcoming in this cast."

It was with the supporting players that Curtiz scored by selecting a talented ensemble, mostly from stage and television: James Gregory, Elaine Stritch, Edward Binns, and David Lewis. Rounding out the principal players was E. G. Marshall as the police lieutenant who investigates the bollixed robbery-murder.

Long afterward, Elaine Stritch responded to the author's query about *The Scarlet Hour* with the same gusto of her delightful character from the film of over fifty years earlier: "My God! I wore a *bathing suit* in that movie, that's how long ago that was. Look, Curtiz might have been an S.O.B., but he was *Michael Curtiz,* for goodness sake. *Casablanca* and all of that! What was I going to say to him?"

According to Ohmart, Stritch and Gregory walked off the set at one point to express their disapproval about her treatment by Curtiz. The dis-

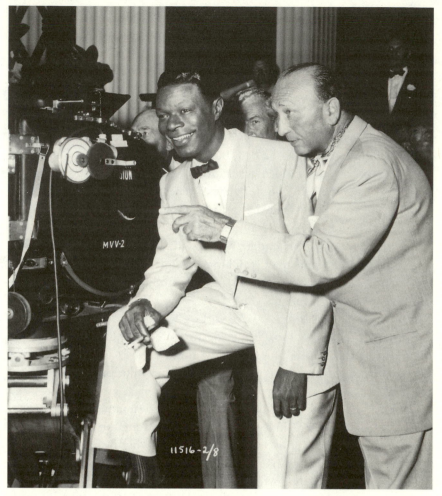

Masters of their respective crafts: Nat King Cole and Curtiz during filming of *The Scarlet Hour* (1956) (courtesy of the Academy of Motion Picture Arts and Sciences).

sent didn't improve matters, even when Nat "King" Cole sang "Never Let Me Go," a scene that Curtiz filmed in the Crystal Room at the Beverly Hills Hotel. Although *The Scarlet Hour* remains an interesting black-and-white diversion near the end of the classic film noir era, the dialogue delivers an intermittent pop rather than a consistent sizzle. The picture created a minimal stir and less profit. It was a perfect opportunity to exploit interesting camera possibilities. But VistaVision and an extremely tight schedule (the film was shot at LA locations) seemingly foiled Curtiz. There was much made of his use of a revolutionary new Fujinon camera lens, which allowed greater clarity in reduced lighting. But one can no longer judge how the film looks. *The Scarlet Hour* remains entombed in Paramount's vault, awaiting retrieval, restoration, and reassessment by a growing population of film noir enthusiasts.

Despite his out-of-wedlock children, multiple mistresses, and innumerable trysts, Curtiz had managed to avoid any scandalous reportage about his personal life for decades. While his sexual antics were generally known or rumored about, he had been left alone by an insular media long controlled by the studios and their own self-interest. Like so many things in Hollywood, compliant press coverage was becoming a thing of the past. Curtiz discovered how much the world had changed when he was arrested shortly after *The Scarlet Hour* wrapped.

Curtiz was taken into custody at a sleazy Los Angeles Skid Row hotel. The Richard was located at 815 Fifth Avenue and served as a transient house of prostitution. Although an October 5, 1955, newspaper squib noted that he was fined two hundred dollars for disorderly conduct in Los Angeles Municipal Court, *Confidential* magazine got hold of the arrest report. Along with wide-screen epics and stereophonic sound, the scandal-mongering publication became a prominent feature of 1950s Hollywood.[5] Curtiz's arrest merited a splashy spread in the March 1956 issue of *Confidential* titled "When Director Mike Curtiz Learned Two Is Company and Three Is a Crime!" that included a faux mug shot of the director. On a nearby street, where "bronze prostitutes strut the sidewalk offering themselves to any man who'll rent a room," he purportedly hired an African American couple to have sex while he sat and watched. After a pair of vice cops burst into the room, he initially protested that he was scouting film locations. The article claimed he eventually fessed up to paying the couple ten dollars for their exhibition. Even those familiar with his back-set reputation were startled. A man in his late sixties with a wife and a pair of young mistresses whose carnal interests now segued into voyeurism was unsettling, but perhaps this was another aspect of Curtiz's personal life that he had kept under wraps. Although he brushed off the incident and never issued a public statement, Curtiz hoped his latest film would put his recent pair of unsuccessful movies along with this distasteful episode in the figurative rearview mirror.

He obtained a measure of redemption with the release of Fox's *The Best Things in Life Are Free* (1956). His assignment was a final gesture from Darryl Zanuck, who had originally developed the production. It began filming less than a month after the Fox mogul retreated to Europe. The musical biography chronicled the Tin Pan Alley triumvirate of Buddy De Sylva, Lew Brown, and Ray Henderson. John O'Hara's story was brought to life by a lively script by Phoebe Ephron and William Bowers. Curtiz could have done far worse than getting Gordon MacRae, Ernest Borgnine, and Dan Dailey to play the 1920s songwriting team. Also adding verve to the film was Sheree North. North was originally signed by Fox as an alternative to Marilyn Monroe, who turned every assignment after *Gentlemen Prefer Blondes* (1953) into a teeth-gnashing ordeal for Zanuck and his staff. North was a talented dancer-actress to whom Curtiz had previously given a boost. She was grateful, remembering:

> [He] once gave me a job in a Bill Holden picture [*Force of Arms* (1951)]. Brunette girls were called and I'd just dyed my hair red hoping to change my luck. Curtiz asked me about myself. I told him I was supporting my mother and daughter—so he hired me; just for publicity stills, but we ate for three weeks. Another time, he gave me a bit in *The Jazz Singer*. I nearly got fired that time. I had managed to get a dancing job at Charlie Foy's at $10 a week and was trying to hold down both jobs at once, but fell asleep on the set. An assistant yelled, "Fire that girl!," but Mr. Curtiz said, "Let the poor kid sleep—she needs it."

Several of the choreographer Rod Alexander's musical numbers are superb, particularly "Birth of the Blues" and "Black Bottom," which paired North with the dancer Jacques d'Amboise. The sentimental content that Curtiz was an expert at navigating included the usual fictional biography and invented conflict that pits the solid family man Henderson (Dailey) and the quick-to-anger lyricist Brown (Borgnine) against the ambitious De Sylva (MacRae), who becomes a Hollywood movie producer and high-hats his partners. In reality, the partnership between the three, which spawned a clutch of hit songs, was mostly uneventful. There was also a semi-invented scene of the trio composing a song over the telephone for Al Jolson (cleverly imitated by the Canadian performer Norman Brooks) in blackface; it doesn't hold up well. Curtiz obtained greater mileage out of a couple of Runyonesque gangster characters by casting Murvyn Vye and "Two Ton" Tony Galento. Galento, a former boxer who memorably played a dock walloper in *On the Waterfront* (1954), was so colorful that Curtiz changed his striped suit to a black one. "His personality is flamboyant enough. We don't need to embroider him," he said. He also remembered Barrie Chase: he cast her as a dancer and provided a line of dialogue along with a close-up.

Curtiz appeared more comfortable with CinemaScope. With Leon Shamroy behind the camera, the entire film, particularly the wonderfully staged opening at a theatrical rehearsal, showed off some of his old timing and movement. Ernest Borgnine, who had received his Best Actor Oscar for *Marty* several weeks before the start of production, also contributed fresh energy. "I loved Mike Curtiz," Borgnine declared over lunch in 2010. "He was the reason I took the picture. What actor wouldn't want to work with the director of *Casablanca* and *The Adventures of Robin Hood*? He wore lifts on his shoes and was eccentric as hell, but he was brilliant." The feeling was mutual. After the picture wrapped, Curtiz presented Borgnine with a gold money clip engraved, "To one of the finest actors I have ever worked with. Lovingly, Mike Curtiz." According to Borgnine, Curtiz was "one of the truly great film directors."

The Best Things in Life Are Free did good business, pulling in $4 million on an investment of $2.5 million. Curtiz retained his professional reputation, but he realized that continued success in a changed Hollywood was a problematic proposition.

32

Dégringolade

In September 1956 Warner Bros. borrowed Curtiz from Paramount to direct *The Helen Morgan Story*. He wrote to Steve Trilling, "I have felt very sentimental, being back on the job at Warner's again." His compensation would total $110,000 for a maximum of twenty weeks to helm a project that had been languishing at the studio since the famed torch singer had died in 1941.

The sense of nostalgia generated by his return quickly faded as Curtiz encountered more than the usual amount of difficulty in casting the title role. Most of the bankable Hollywood stars were selecting their own material or committed to other pictures. Marilyn Monroe, Grace Kelly, and June Allyson were not lining up for what was alternately titled *Why I Was Born* and *The Jazz Age*. (It simply wouldn't be a Warner Bros. picture without multiple title changes before Jack Warner made the final selection.) Curtiz had lunch with Jane Russell, who told him she was committed to *The Fuzzy Pink Nightgown* (1957). A draft script reportedly delighted Kim Novak, but a deal with Harry Cohn at Columbia couldn't be worked out.

Love Me or Leave Me and *I'll Cry Tomorrow* (both 1955) detailed the respective travails of Ruth Etting and Lillian Roth and popularized the theme of torch chanteuses–as–tragedians. The stars of both films were approached by Curtiz, but neither wanted anything to do with Helen Morgan. Doris Day, who had won critical acclaim for *Love Me or Leave Me*, was wary about what the darker aspects of Morgan's life story might do to her image. Also declining was Susan Hayward, who believed the role was too similar to the one she'd played in *I'll Cry Tomorrow*. Curtiz had a conference with David Selznick and Jennifer Jones "until one o'clock in the morning." He wrote to Trilling afterward: "They both like the story idea very much, but they won't commit themselves. . . . I think we should protect ourselves and look farther for 'Helen' in case this Jones deal falls through." The notion of Jennifer Jones as Helen Morgan never got off the ground. Jack Warner had no intention of enduring Selznick as an ipso facto producer. Curtiz next tried out a series of singer-actresses including Patti Page, Keely Smith, and Peggy Lee, but none of them could pass muster. Curtiz decided to fall back on his starmaking reputation, saying, "If you have a good script it doesn't make any difference whether the star is known or unknown." Harking back to his recent experience on *The Scarlet Hour,* he added, "You are in trouble when you try to put an unknown in a bad script. I got too egotistical once and tried that, but I learned my lesson." He then considered and rejected Julie London and Anne Bancroft, along with just about every other up-and-coming actress in town. Curtiz's hunt for Helen Morgan was eventually dubbed Hollywood's "biggest casting search since Scarlett O'Hara." This merry-go-round began spinning around concurrently with the *Confidential* magazine piece detailing his previous year's arrest. According to the columnist James Bacon, Curtiz invited him to the Mocambo to watch "a great Irish singer" who might be "our Helen Morgan." Bacon disabused him of that notion by advising him that Ella Fitzgerald was currently headlining at the Mocambo. Curtiz was grateful for the heads-up and replied to Bacon: "Thank God you told me, Jeem. If I hired a black girl, people might get the wrong idea from that god-damn magazine."

What is revealing about his eventual decision to cast Ann Blyth is a pair of memos that Curtiz sent to Steve Trilling. On November 1, 1956, he wrote, "Three people are after me to make tests which I am trying to avoid—Linda Darnell, Jane Powell and Ann Blyth." Eleven days later he sent another note to Trilling: "Just finished the test with Ann Blyth. She is excellent." Curtiz evidently had several people pushing him to test Blyth. One of them was Hedda Hopper, who immediately assumed public credit for recommending Blyth for the part. Concerning her selection for the role, Blyth told me: "After looking back on it years later, I thought, isn't that strange. Here's Mike who did the first test [*Mildred Pierce*] all those years before and I still have to test. Not necessarily because he wanted me to test, but obviously the higher-ups, I'm sure, insisted on it." As he was when she tested for *Mildred,* Curtiz was an immediate convert. She added: "I remember after the test, his exact words to me: 'Don't worry, Annie, you've got the part.'" Blyth won the role after a six-month search that included thirty-two contenders.

For the actor to portray Larry Maddux—an amalgam of the different men with whom Morgan was involved—Curtiz sought Paul Newman, who impressed him as prizefighter Rocky Graziano in *Somebody Up There Likes Me* (1956). Newman eventually agreed to *The Helen Morgan Story* after the script was rewritten to his satisfaction. "Rewritten" is an inexact description for a screenplay that reflected the efforts of twenty different writers dating back over a decade.

Even though censorship had loosened up a bit, it remained impossible to accurately portray Morgan's dissolute life onscreen. Labeling his version of Helen Morgan "glorified," Curtiz observed that the censor's office "wouldn't have allowed" the unvarnished Morgan biography to be produced because "she always selected the wrong man—and she selected many." Although Morgan was married three times, the script portrays her as a single woman. There was also no mention of a baby girl that she gave up for adoption in 1926. This omission was a condition of the studio's agreement with Morgan's mother, Lulu, to whom Warner Bros. paid five thousand dollars to borrow her daughter's scrapbooks and other career memorabilia. Curtiz definitely captured the spirit of the singer's downfall, even though he had to omit Morgan's untimely death as a penniless alcoholic. Instead, there would be a typical cornball finale. Freshly dried out and released from the alky ward, Blyth's Morgan is escorted by Maddux to her shuttered nightclub for a surprise tribute from a sold-out crowd of show-biz swells. Walter Winchell offers a staccato summation of the Roaring Twenties as an era of mistakes, adding that Morgan "made some of the biggest." He escorts her to the stage, where Morgan hops onto a Steinway to lip-synch the movie's final number.

There was murkiness over the decision to use Gogi Grant (who also received screen credit) as Helen Morgan's unique voice instead of Blyth, who was an accomplished singer. Although neither could exactly replicate Morgan's high-pitched technique, which Curtiz thought was "outmoded" for contemporary audiences, the rationale for using Grant remains curious. A philosophical Blyth accepted the decision gracefully, but the disappointment of playing such a potent role with another singer dubbing her voice was evident:

> If you know the voice of Helen Morgan was certainly more like mine or mine would be more like hers. . . . Gogi was very popular at the time. I believe they [the studio higher-ups] felt it might be a good boost for the movie. . . . I couldn't understand it, but at the same time, I thought the meat [the part of Helen Morgan]

still was there. And I thought, "Well, I guess I will have to compromise." But I was taken aback by it for a long time, as they had
me trying to be a bit more of a blues singer, and I would go into
the studio and I guess, as I say, behind closed doors they were
thinking of something quite different. But that is still Hollywood.

Replete with guest stars, jazz age nostalgia, and period musical standards, the picture was shot in black and white by Ted McCord in a style
reminiscent of Curtiz's earlier work. Providing a stark contrast to the
era of wonderful nonsense was the grim dramatic content. To accentuate the story of her downward spiral, Morgan was volleyed between the
fast-talking hustler, Maddux, and rich, married attorney Russell Wade
(Richard Carlson). The suicide of a friend, Sue (Virginia Vincent), was
thrown in for good measure. Blyth brings it off credibly, particularly
after hitting bottom and suffering the DTs. It is a film thematically reminiscent of an earlier era. One cannot help thinking that Warner erred
by not having Curtiz make this film in 1943 with Ida Lupino and Jack
Carson.

Warner Bros. was now an altogether different studio. Jack had finally
pushed Harry Warner out in a duplicitous stock-purchase deal that left
him in sole control. The two brothers never spoke to one another again.
Curtiz would be a pallbearer at Harry's funeral in 1958. Jack Warner remained at the gaming tables in Monte Carlo and didn't bother to attend
his older brother's services.

Curtiz's return reunited him with some of the holdovers from his
glory days who still remained on the Warner lot. In addition to a final
collaboration with LeRoy Prinz, who staged the *Helen Morgan* musical
numbers, he got to butt heads once more with Tenny Wright, who would
retire at the end of the year. Wright couldn't resist a final attempt to pre-
empt what he viewed as Curtiz's budgetary excesses. The veteran production manager wrote to Trilling and Warner: "There are lot of moves in
this script which cost time and money. Some of the scenes are underwrit-
ten. If some cuts could be made, I think it would be better and not hurt the
story. It is very interesting and should be a moneymaker, but you know
Mike, he likes to enlarge scenes."

Blyth thought Curtiz hadn't changed appreciatively since *Mildred
Pierce*: "I think he had a formula and he knew that it worked." Richard Whorf was originally assigned as the producer, but he was working
on three other projects and couldn't do much to assist Curtiz. The di-

rector asked Trilling for Martin Rackin, a rising Warner screenwriter. Rackin was duly assigned as producer, but Paul Helmick, the assistant director, claimed that Curtiz developed an inexplicable dislike for Rackin and practically had him barred from the set. Helmick also observed Curtiz browbeating Ted McCord to such an extent that he was startled to learn they had worked on many pictures together (and there were more to come). Paul Newman later told the film critic Leonard Maltin that his relationship with the director was "a long rocky road."

"Curtiz had a lot of definition," remembered Newman. "He knew pretty much what he wanted, I don't always think it was the right thing, but he was very, very determined. And of course, I kidded him unmercifully, which he couldn't handle." Virginia Vincent remembered shooting a scene one freezing night on the back lot: "It was so cold our teeth were chattering." Someone in the crew slipped her and the others some brandy to keep warm. "We got too warm!" laughed Vincent. "We started to blow our lines and began giggling. Curtiz got angry with us!" During a visit to the *Helen Morgan* set, Rudy Behlmer observed Curtiz in action. A functionary was speaking with the director and remarked, "When we cut the picture . . ." Curtiz fixed the miscreant with a baleful stare. "*I* will cut the picture!" thundered the director as the offender slunk away.

Jack Warner wrote Curtiz a note after principal photography finished three days ahead of schedule on March 22, 1957: "Just returned from New York and was very happy to find the *Helen Morgan Story* completed. Cannot tell you how delighted I was to have you back here to do this picture. I feel you will be here again and again." Curtiz responded with a "Dear Jack" note that included his intent to "supervise the editing . . . and to do anything either of you [Warner and Trilling] feels is necessary—retakes or added scenes—on my own time." *The Helen Morgan Story* was critically panned as a slushy musical soap opera; the *New York Times* dismissed it as "heartwarming as an electric pad." Produced for slightly over $2 million, the picture lost at least half a million dollars. Blyth quit making pictures to devote herself to raising a family while continuing her singing career and occasional television appearances.

Trilling and Warner attempted to lure Curtiz back again for a biopic of Diana Barrymore based on her memoir, *Too Much, Too Soon*. After reading the book, he questioned Trilling about the rationale for making a film about "an ordinary tramp—sleeping with every man who comes her way . . . becoming an alcoholic. Why? How can I explain to an audience why she [Barrymore] drank and became a tramp and still get their sympathy? If we can answer this question we can have a dramatically interesting story." After reading a draft screenplay in July 1957, he concluded that Diana Barrymore led "an entire life that was distasteful," and he turned the project down. He was proved correct when the end product was a sordid picture starring a visibly ill Errol Flynn playing Flynn's former idol and fellow dissipate, John Barrymore.

After *The Vagabond King, The Scarlet Hour,* and now *The Helen Morgan Story,* Curtiz couldn't afford another disappointment. He shared his feelings with Trilling, which were accompanied by his usual self-absolution of any responsibility for movies gone wrong: "You are probably aware of the state of my career since I left Warner. I tried to cooperate with Paramount and did whatever bad stories they asked me to take on. The resulting weak pictures reflected only on me. My future pictures have to be important and successful. I can't run the risk of an 'interesting' failure." Curtiz nonetheless hoped that Warner would "not hold it [his refusal] against me in the future." But another picture for Jack L. was not in the cards. *The Helen Morgan Story* would be the last movie that Curtiz directed at Warner Bros. The rejection of the Barrymore picture and the commercial failure of *Helen Morgan* apparently convinced his old boss that Curtiz's magic touch was gone forever.

Curtiz returned to Paramount, but the studio had nothing for him. The prospect of unemployment triggered the frantic anxiety that engulfed him when he couldn't work. He also needed the money. The maintenance of his lifestyle, including the upkeep of the Encino ranch, was a big monthly nut. Bess continued to spend, and there were new expenses. Jill Gerrard had become pregnant and he had to whisk her out of Hollywood. According to Gerrard, Curtiz rented her a house on Mesquite Avenue in Palm Springs. After Curtiz's daughter Debra Candace Curtiz was born, Gerrard and the baby relocated to Apple Valley. She would periodically visit Curtiz and stay at the Ambassador Hotel, and the director footed the bills. Curtiz was proud of his new daughter. When he spent time with Gerrard and the baby, he was tender and gentle. He reacted to his final experience with fatherhood, however, much as he had to his earlier ones.

Curtiz's seeming indifference toward his own kids while spending his life bringing fictional characters to life onscreen was paradoxically consistent. Even late in life, he viewed children as things to be managed at a distance with money so that they would not interfere with his life of filmmaking. There is little doubt that a large measure of his ambivalence can be ascribed to the scandal that he believed public acknowledgment of out-of-wedlock progeny would cause. Two of Curtiz's children remained in Europe to be raised by their mothers, so there was also an "out of sight, out of mind" perspective that combined with his renowned ability to compartmentalize. This rationalization doesn't fully explain the fobbing off of his daughter Kitty to a succession of nannies and boarding schools and his treatment of Mathilde Foerster and his first son, Michael.

It was another aspect of the enigmatic director who instilled genuine empathy for the underdog in so many of his films while simultaneously venting his spleen on sound mixers and other low-level functionaries who didn't have the power to fight back. Curtiz genuinely loved Bess Meredyth and consistently acknowledged how much she contributed to his success. He could genuinely feel this way and then ignore her has he had his children, accelerating her decline into a bedridden, depressed woman whom he cheated on continually. Although paying the bills doubtlessly helped him assuage his guilt, the addition of another child at this point in his career made him much more anxious about his finances. Gerrard and her daughter eventually relocated to Arizona. "I would not raise Candy in Hollywood," she told me.

Curtiz remained dependent on an offer from the studios in part because he couldn't get his own projects off the ground. He optioned the Stephen Longstreet novel *The Promoters* before it was published in January 1957, but he couldn't obtain financing. Hedda Hopper reported he would be adapting the life of Jimmy Durante for the screen from Gene Fowler's biography *Schnozzola*. The project, ostensibly starring Danny Thomas and Ann Blyth, went nowhere. Curtiz had previously attempted to break into television back in 1952 when he reportedly approached Lee Duncan, the owner of the original Rin Tin Tin, with a treatment he had developed for a television pilot starring the heroic hound that rescued Warner Bros. in the early 1920s. Either Curtiz didn't have the money or Duncan rejected the idea. Other suitors more flush quickly lined up. *The Adventures of Rin Tin Tin* debuted on ABC in 1954 and remained on the air for five years. Curtiz eventually abandoned any notion of directing television, as John Frankenheimer remembered when he was helming a production of *The Snows of Kilimanjaro* in 1960:

> This was the time that the CBS executives brought in Michael Curtiz, whom they were trying to get to be a television director. Michael Curtiz, of course, had won the Academy Award for *Casablanca,* he'd done all my favorite movies, he'd done these

great Errol Flynn movies, and the whole thing. And he came in, and they introduced him to me just as I was blocking this show. And he was very gracious, he was beautifully dressed and so forth and so on, he had a very thick Hungarian accent. And he said, "Ah yes, good." He said, "I'm going into the, what do you call it, 'control room.'" He says, "I'm going to look." So he went in the control room. And the madness in trying to block this thing, I mean, I cannot describe it to you. Because we had cameras coming from here, and I was on the floor with a monitor, you know, so that I could see what was happening. And it's, cameras would come crashing through and just missing people, and so forth and so on, and booms coming and going through the paper, and we'd knock them down and put 'em up again. And we went in and we did kind of a stagger-through of this, I mean, you couldn't call it a run-through, because it was just, it was insane. And everybody was kind of going about their business. And suddenly I looked at Michael Curtiz, who had come in, you know, impeccably dressed. His tie was askew, and he was sweating. And he walked up to me, he said, "You are crazy!" And he walked out, and we never saw him again! Never saw him again!

Pushing seventy and older than nearly all his directorial contemporaries, including Ford, Hawks, Stevens, and Wyler, Curtiz found his career was in twilight.

Sam Goldwyn Jr. provided temporary respite with a property that he had purchased for his recently founded Formosa Productions. The son of the legendary producer met Curtiz while vacationing: "Actually, he was my next-door neighbor down in Malibu. My wife and I had just been married and we rented a house for the summer and Mike had one next door. We got to know each other and I became very fond of him, and then I had this picture I was going to make called *The Proud Rebel*. I gave him the script to read. He liked it and had some very good suggestions about the casting."

Goldwyn's property was a short story titled "Journal of Linett Moore," written by James Edward Grant, John Wayne's favorite scenarist. The story concerned John Chandler, a former Confederate officer who takes his ten-year-old son to an Illinois town to consult a doctor. The boy was traumatized into muteness after he saw his mother burned to death in the family home during Sherman's march through Georgia. The youth's only friend is his loyal border collie, a natural sheepdog. Chandler and his son become allied with a woman rancher against a ruthless sheepherder and his two sons. The dog becomes a possible cure for the boy and forces a dramatic showdown in what becomes a small-scale range war.

Goldwyn's famous father had never worked with Curtiz, but he was familiar with his reputation. "My father said to me, 'Are you sure you know what you're doing?'" remembered Sam Jr. 'Do you really think he [Curtiz] is okay? You know he's a handful.'" Goldwyn Jr. was comfortable. "I had the feeling I could get along with him, and I learned a lot from him. There were so many things he would do. And he would say and do incredible, wonderful things."

Despite his admiration, Sam Jr. knew he had to establish his control over the director. He had hired a young Joseph Petracca to write the screenplay. During an initial story meeting, Curtiz flung the script on the floor, yelling at the screenwriter, "Why you give him shit, shit, shit?" Goldwyn remembered, "I knew my moment had come. I looked at Mike and said, 'Mike, pick up the script.' I said, 'You're twice my age, you cannot act this way.' He picked up the script, handed it back to the writer, and said, 'I am very emotional man, I love script. Last little detail. But I shoot script. I shoot every word." According to Goldwyn, his authority was established. "I never, probably only one other time, had another problem. I'd just be very firm with him." The producer laughed: "And he didn't mind if there was a public confrontation."

Curtiz was stricken with appendicitis during the wee hours of August 26, 1957, just before the start of production. He was taken from the Encino ranch to St. John's Hospital in Santa Monica, where his gangrenous appendix was removed. According to John Meredyth Lucas, Curtiz had been suffering for days but concealed his condition because he was worried about delaying the picture. "He adamantly refused to go to the hospital until I had called Sam Goldwyn, Jr., my friend and producer of the picture, in the middle of the night and got his dazed assurance that the production would be pushed back. Only then did Mike allow the waiting ambulance to take him." While Curtiz was undergoing his appendectomy, he was discovered to have a nodule on his prostate gland. According to Lucas, it was biopsied, and Curtiz was informed by his doctor and Bess that the growth was benign. Although Curtiz quickly rebounded from his abdominal surgery and was back at work within a week, his rocklike constitution had developed definite cracks. According to Goldwyn, "He had a tiny stroke on the picture and he would get very tired in the late afternoon."

The Proud Rebel centered on the father and son characters, John and David Chandler. Although there was a rumor that Goldwyn was considering Dean Martin as the father, he declared that he never thought of anyone other than Alan Ladd and his son David. The elder Ladd remained a major movie star although he had begun to slip after a succession of indifferent films. Goldwyn had to convince Ladd's wife and agent, Sue Carol, "who ran the show, the Ladd show, that is." Carol expressed misgivings about Curtiz, saying, "I had only one dealing with the man and he yelled all the time." Goldwyn assured her that Curtiz was "a very sensitive guy." Ladd was enthusiastic. The star had overcome an impoverished background, and, at one point during the Depression, he had worked as a grip at Warner Bros. "Alan was delighted because he had begun as a grip on *Captain Blood*, which was one of Mike's pictures," remembered Goldwyn. "And he watched Errol Flynn and Mike go at it, and he said, 'Gee, I'd like to be in that guy's [Flynn's] shoes.' Alan told me all this." Because each man needed the other at this juncture in their careers, Curtiz and Ladd bonded.

Familial concern about how Curtiz would interact with David Ladd evaporated. The director exerted himself to develop a rapport with the younger Ladd by radiating his considerable charm. "He couldn't have been sweeter and lovelier to me," recalled David Ladd. "Our relationship basically started with him going to school with me. And then we went to UCLA to learn sign language. And Mike attended all those lessons and I also kind of remember going out to his house to rehearse sign language with him. But he was very fastidious about it. He was so kind and sweet to me throughout. And he was very kind and sweet with my father as well."

It had been seventeen years since Curtiz had worked with Olivia de Havilland. Despite their differences during nine movies together, he believed she was the optimal choice to play Linett Moore, the farmer who becomes emotionally involved with the former Confederate officer and his son. Times had changed since she won her lawsuit against Jack Warner and left the soundstages of Burbank. De Havilland was now a two-time Oscar winner and mother of two residing in France. She loved that her character was a strong, independent woman and was charmed by Goldwyn Jr. and both of the Ladds. She knew Alan Ladd was a proud and sensitive man. "*Very* sensitive." she said. "Because Mike Curtiz could be quite harsh with people, Alan was afraid that Mike would be rough on David." But Goldwyn Jr. termed the bond formed between Curtiz and the Ladds "a love affair." The sole moment of tension between David and

Curtiz occurred in a scene in which a barn caught fire. "And to burn a barn, especially in those days, you burned the barn," remembered David. "He had given me direction to get the hell out of the frame, and because he was maybe speaking in that language that I couldn't understand, I didn't. And behind the scenes, he was yelling and screaming, 'Get out! Get out of the shot!' I didn't know what the hell I was doing, so I just stayed there. But, that is the one day of conflict that I can remember where you saw the legendary Curtiz." There was another episode that was reminiscent of Curtiz's tenure at Warner Bros. Instead of using a stunt double, Curtiz insisted de Havilland drive a horse-drawn wagon that had to stop short in front of David. No one checked to see if the star was wearing a safety belt. She fell forward when the wagon stopped and landed between the horses. Bruised, but unbowed, she brushed herself off and continued working.

The relationship between Curtiz and de Havilland remained tense. "They had absolutely nothing in common," observed Sam Goldwyn Jr. "There was volatility between him and Olivia, and it would flare up sometimes," said David Ladd, remembering the anxiety between star and director; he added, "And she's a very gentle woman." Goldwyn recalled when they were shooting the interior scenes in Hollywood: "Olivia de Havilland called me up one night and said 'I have got to see you.' And I go over to the Beverly Hills Hotel, where she was staying, and she's sitting in a booth crying, and she said, 'He's still very cruel to me. . . . Why did you get involved with this very cruel man?' And then when she saw the picture, she said, 'Well, you know, I always knew he was the right director.'" In another story that Goldwyn Jr. related to Aljean Harmetz, an infuriated de Havilland phoned him in the middle of the night about Curtiz: "He was a son of a bitch when I was seventeen and he's still a son of a bitch."

Shortly after the company arrived on location in Cedar City, Utah, Curtiz's irascibility was more noticeable than any signs of fatigue from his recent surgery. Although he had Ted McCord behind the camera and Paul Helmick as his assistant director, he was working with a new crew that was not used to his explosive temperament. In his usual manner, Curtiz began excoriating members of the company when things didn't go right. A major confrontation occurred after he berated the Technicolor representative, who became fed up and called Curtiz a has-been in front of the crew. According to Helmick, an overall mutiny was brewing, and he had to remind the director that times had changed: "Mike, you just can't treat these people like they were morons! When you blow up and yell at them, they don't like it *or you*. Right now, they're lined up at the only available telephone, looking for another job, and we can't afford to lose any of them."

Curtiz reacted with shock, genuinely oblivious to the consequences of his outbursts. The next morning he apologized to the crew: "My assistant tells me I have been son of a bitch to some of you and I should be better to you; so I want to tell you that if I haven't been so good to you, I will be better and I'm sorry. That's all, thank you."

The director's truce lasted several hours before he blew up again over something trivial. Helmick remembered, "We all started to laugh at him and he realized what an ass he was making of himself." Bill Hamilton, a soundman, shared his perceptions about the picture in a series of letters to his wartime comrade the director George Stevens: "Mike started out trying to create a mood and Alan Ladd hasn't been giving out anything. He deadpans everything and acts like everything is a tremendous effort. Olivia is very good as an unmarried woman of 35. But when she has a scene with Alan, she tries to make it play and Alan deadpans and gives nothing in return, hence a bad scene." Hamilton also claimed that Goldwyn Jr. was unhappy with Curtiz, who was "going in four directions and getting no place."

The ship was righted as Goldwyn reasserted himself and Curtiz calmed down. By the second week, Hamilton reported, "Mike Curtiz and the producer have ironed out their difficulties, and so the picture is coming along fine now."

Curtiz incorporated the sweeping panoramas of the Utah locations into a story that gave audiences, as the director would put it, "a tear in the eye." In addition to Alan Ladd and de Havilland effectively playing off one another, there was a peerless supporting cast. Dean Jagger was the villainous, one-armed rancher with a pair of noxious sons (a young Harry Dean Stanton and Tom Pittman). Curtiz stocked the film with veteran character actors: Cecil Kellaway, Henry Hull, James Westerfield, John Carradine, Percy Helton, and Mary Wickes. David Ladd's superb performance elevates the picture into something truly memorable. His four-legged costar was equally credible. "Actually, it was two dogs," remembered David. "One was named King, the wonder dog [an actual champion border collie], who was the dog who did all of the action, the great maneuvering with the sheep. There was another dog, named Sam [for close-ups and interactive people scenes], and he had freckles on his snout. I remember they had to white out all the freckles on his snout." Curtiz artfully deploys the maudlin themes of a boy and his dog, a father's love for his son, and their mutual bonding with the farmwoman in a straightforward style that avoids syrupy sentiment.

The reviews were excellent. The *New York Times* hailed the film as an "honestly heartwarming drama." Alan Ladd's performance was "exceptionally expressive," and de Havilland was a "the picture of hardy womanhood." Highest praise went to David Ladd for "an astonishingly professional and sympathetic stint" alongside King, the wonder dog. Ladd won a special Golden Globe award that helped jump-start his career. Budgeted at around $1,600,000 and released by Walt Disney's Buena Vista distribution company, *The Proud Rebel* was, according to Goldwyn, "highly successful." Its box-office potential was partially diluted by the ceaseless promotion of *Old Yeller* (1957), which had been released five months earlier. What became personally enriching for Sam Goldwyn Jr. was the establishment of a close friendship with Olivia de Havilland and David Ladd that endured until his death in January 2015. There was also his relationship with Curtiz, which would be sustained through another movie. Asked for his recollections about Curtiz as a director, Goldwyn retained several impressions:

> He was very fast, very budget-conscious, not so much because he wanted to save money, because the picture was a job of work. It was his job was to see that [the actors and the crew] got to work and got it done. I'll never forget this: He'd get fanatical on the subject of getting that first shot by nine a.m. And he had a very clear idea about what he wanted the picture to look like. And he didn't play a game like it was a secret. He'd be very clear with the actors about what he wanted them to do. Mike was in complete charge and he knew everything about the picture. He remembered every take and every shot he made. We had a very good editor [Aaron Stell], and while we were cutting the film, there was a scene that didn't quite work. Mike said, "Good scene, but something missing here, I shot take such and such." The editor said, "Mike, that doesn't exist." He said, "It exists," and it turned out to be something that he shot on the third day. He had such a sense of confidence. Now that doesn't mean he couldn't be difficult.

The man who gave Curtiz his habit of completing that initial morning shot at Warner Bros. now summoned him to direct a film starring the country's newest singing sensation. Hal Wallis had prospered since leaving Warners in 1945. After producing a series of successful melodramas while amassing a stable of actors, including Burt Lancaster, Kirk Douglas, Lizabeth Scott, and Wendell Corey, he hit the jackpot in 1949 by signing the riotous nightclub duo of Dean Martin and Jerry Lewis. The success of the Martin and Lewis comedies allowed him to produce prestige pictures like *Come Back, Little Sheba* (1952), *The Rose Tattoo* (1955), and *The Rainmaker* (1956).

Wallis's gravy train was halted when the comedy team split up after sixteen films in July 1956. But he had already hooked show biz's next big fish after he spotted Elvis Presley on the Dorsey Brothers CBS television show earlier that same year. "Elvis was an original," recalled Wallis. "When he started to sing, twisting his legs, bumping and grinding, shaking his shoulders, he was electrifying." The following day, when he phoned Elvis's manager, Colonel Tom Parker, to discuss a movie contract, Wallis discovered he was matched against a worthy adversary. Parker, born Andreas Cornelis van Kuijk in Breda, Netherlands, in 1909, was a tough customer. He reportedly fled Holland ahead of a murder investigation and entered the United States as a twenty-year-old merchant sailor by jumping ship. After being drummed out of the army for desertion plus a stay in a psychiatric hospital, he worked as a carnival tout and dog catcher. He then became a music promoter and positioned himself first as Elvis's adviser and then as his manager. Wallis finally came to terms with Parker—"one of the toughest bargaining sessions of my career"—and inked Elvis to a nonexclusive three-picture deal. After 60 million Americans watched Presley perform on *The Ed Sullivan Show*, Wallis's coup became the envy of every production executive in Hollywood.

Wallis lent Elvis to Fox for his screen debut. *Love Me Tender* (1956) was a Civil War story notable for Elvis's title song, which went platinum. Next was Wallis's *Loving You* (1957). Elvis portrays a Texas-based deliveryman discovered by a publicist (Lizabeth Scott) and her bandleader beau (Wendell Corey). Neither picture was extraordinary, but it didn't matter. Elvis was a sensation and people queued up to watch him onscreen. Wallis and Colonel Parker didn't dawdle. Elvis was lent out again, this time to MGM for *Jailhouse Rock* (1957), in which he becomes a rock star after doing a stretch for manslaughter. The picture grossed ten times its cost.

Presley yearned for something more than superfluous roles that kept the money rolling in. He asked Wallis about the possibility of attending the Actors Studio. Dolores Hart, his costar in *Loving You,* told me that Elvis "wanted to be the next Jimmy Dean." Wallis had a more serious property in mind for Presley, one that he had been nurturing with Curtiz for over a year. In 1955 he had sent Curtiz a copy of the novel *A Stone for Danny Fisher* by Harold Robbins, to which Wallis had purchased the rights for $25,000. It had been adapted into an off-Broadway play directed by Luther Adler and starring Philip Pine; it opened on October 21, 1954, and had a brief run. Curtiz was enthusiastic about the potential of the book, but he was disappointed in the subsequent draft script written by Michael V. Gazzo. He believed the screenplay should mirror the novel, which depicted the economically crushing effects of the Depression on a middle-class Jewish family in Brooklyn. Instead of Robbins's conflicted Danny Fisher, who turns to boxing to support himself and his family, Gazzo created "a conventional, unreal, dead-end kid hero." He elaborated: "I much prefer the characters and situations of the novel—the realistic, poignant relationship of the father, a small professional man who has done everything possible for his son and has big plans for him, but who is trapped in an economic upheaval; and a son who is so eager for a place in the world and so bewildered and desperate at ill fortune that he blames his father in haste."

Curtiz urged Wallis to adapt the use of voice-over narration to compress the story rather than wholesale character alterations and concluded, "If you agree with me generally on these points, I believe we can straighten out the story with Gazzo. If he doesn't see it our way, I would suggest you get another writer. But I believe this story can be put in good shape in reasonable time under your guidance."

Wallis agreed with most of Curtiz's recommendations. Five months later, Curtiz read the revised script and wrote to the producer, "I appreciate the efforts of Mr. Gazzo to cooperate with our views." But he still didn't like how the screenplay deviated from the book.

To play Danny Fisher, Wallis initially considered Paul Newman (he declined, not wanting to play a boxer again after recently starring in *Somebody Up There Likes Me*), Ben Gazzara, and Tony Curtis. The signing of Presley changed everything. Casting Elvis as a Jewish kid from Brooklyn was clearly a nonstarter. This was when Wallis demonstrated his filmmaking acumen. He took an Oscar Saul and Herbert Baker treatment called *Sing You Sinners* about the troubled son of a New Orleans minister and had the premise melded into Gazzo's Danny Fisher script. Fisher became a troubled youth living in the French Quarter who ditches high school to sing in the King Creole bar. His father is a beaten-down pharmacist who lost his business and has to kowtow to land a menial job in a drugstore. Danny vows never to grovel and becomes involved with a group of hoodlums who work for Maxie, a local gangster. After Danny becomes a singing sensation, he also becomes involved with Maxie's mistress while courting a wholesome teenage girl who works the lunch counter at the local five and dime. The scenario was perfectly suited for Elvis, giving him the opportunity to play a viable dramatic role while headlining his musical numbers.

Authentic drama was included with the depiction of Danny Fisher's relationships with two different women. Fisher's sexual attraction to the gangster's hard-luck mistress was contrasted to his more conventional relationship with a virginal hash slinger who, despite being in love, wouldn't sleep with him after accompanying him to a cheap hotel. As staged by Curtiz, this scene between Elvis and his costar Dolores Hart was one of the most sensitive portions of the film.

Curtiz sent a memorandum to Wallis's assistant Paul Nathan after reviewing the final script with the working title *Sing You Sinners* (that would be changed to the more commercial *King Creole*). He recommended a different opening, which was adapted into the shooting script: "I would prefer to open the picture with Scene Three with the Crawfish woman yelling. I think it is a more picturesque opening—it takes us right into our story and it is better than opening with scenes in the Blue Shade nightclub where we meet all of our characters and know nothing about them."

He also convinced Wallis to omit the unnecessary plot segue in which Danny buys the drugstore for his father, clarified the final confrontation between Danny and Maxie, and repurposed the ending so that it did not conclude with Danny in a clinch with the good girl, thereby avoiding the sort of canned finale that Jack Warner used to force on him. He outlined ten additional story aspects and character delineations that he believed needed to be changed. Wallis agreed to incorporate roughly half of Curtiz's recommendations.

Having gotten his way in large measure on the script, Curtiz sought to impose his will on the rest of the production. He didn't care for Dolores Hart as the smitten waitress, Nellie, or Jan Shepard, who played Danny's sister, Mimi. Wallis stopped him dead in his tracks, particularly on Hart. In addition to being Wallis's contract player who debuted with Elvis in *Loving You*, Hart enjoyed what can be termed a father-daughter relationship with the producer. She remembered a different Hal Wallis from the hard-driving, impersonal executive that many respected but few liked: "Hal was a very loving, gracious, and very sensitive friend to me. He respected my life and my wishes in ways that I never would have expected from a man in his position. He never pushed himself on me. He never demanded that I be someone I couldn't be for him. I was going to be the kind of personality and the kind of actress that I was. I didn't have to do a makeover."

Wallis let Curtiz know in no uncertain terms that his usual steam-roller approach was out. Presley would be handled with kid gloves. After watching *Jailhouse Rock,* Curtiz girded himself to endure a rock 'n' roll version of Errol Flynn at his worst. Instead, he encountered a polite young man who was the first one on the set at 7:30 a.m. with all his lines memorized. When Curtiz told him he would sing three ballads in the film without his usual twists and turns, Elvis simply nodded and said, "You're the boss, Mr. Curtiz." He also asked Presley to trim his sideburns and drop some fifteen pounds; the singer eagerly complied with both requests. Curtiz was impressed by the neophyte's initial tests on a closed set: "Instead of a gyrating rock and roller, I was watching a natural, un-actory actor, underplaying his role because he knew none of the tricks of the trade." Curtiz was exceedingly gentle with Elvis, still a shy country boy who would make occasional Bible references. He provided the twenty-one-year-old with a minimum amount of direction and allowed him to exercise his own initiative. Elvis responded enthusiastically to Curtiz: "For the first time, I know what a director is." Dolores Hart believed that after three pictures Presley wanted a director who would give him the opportunity to use his own instinct as an actor. "He would go into the hotel room and try out the different possibilities," she remembered. "He was very creative. Elvis was really a very interesting young actor. I don't think that anybody ever gave him the credit for that part of himself. I think they just wanted to get that over with so they could get to the 'rah-rah-rah' song."

The "they" Hart referred to was the redoubtable Colonel Parker, who exercised a Svengali-like control over Elvis. "I had no use for Colonel Parker," admitted Hart. "The minute that man walked on the set, Elvis's eyes never went anywhere but absolutely to the Colonel. And whatever he said, it was the colonel's call. It was almost sickening to me." If not for Parker, Elvis believed he would still be sitting on the porch with his parents in Tupelo, Mississippi. He never considered his career without the colonel.

Hal Wallis ensured that Curtiz was on his best behavior while directing Elvis Presley in *King Creole* (1958) (author's collection).

Aside from badgering Wallis for minor perks, Parker didn't interfere with the filming of *King Creole*. The collective focus was on completing the production before Elvis's pending induction into the army. Cameras began rolling on January 20, 1958. A five-day location shoot in New Orleans turned into a logistical nightmare because of the huge crowds that turned up wherever Elvis was. The New Orleans police had to have a bridge built from the roof of the hotel to the roof of an adjoining building so that Elvis could come and go unmolested. After scouting locations together, Wallis and Curtiz agreed that the film should be shot in black and white. The director of photography Russell Harlan provided a noir motif that was accentuated by the Crescent City's rain-soaked streets.

A formidable supporting cast further bolstered the young star. There was Dean Jagger as Elvis's beleaguered father; Paul Stewart was the owner of the King Creole nightclub; and Walter Matthau played the gangster Maxie Fields. Carolyn Jones was Maxie's kept girlfriend, Ronnie, who falls for Danny. She had recently scored an Oscar nomination for a ten-minute part in *The Bachelor Party* (1957) and exuded a damaged sexual vulnerability that played extremely well. Curtiz wanted to dumb-down her characterization to elicit greater audience sympathy. He told Wallis she should be more like Giulietta Masina in *La Strada* (1954). In this instance, his advice was wisely ignored. Dolores Hart's memoir (cowritten by Richard DeNeut) states that Hart and Jan Shepard found Curtiz to be "a vulgar man and a bully on the set." Although that assessment is hardly surprising, the view of Curtiz that Hart expressed to me was considerably milder: "On *King Creole,* I took [Curtiz] more or less for granted, in a way, because I was young in the industry. I wasn't thinking about a director. I was starstruck and so I wasn't trying to pin down my directors' personalities, they were gods." Her opinion of Curtiz would accrue more specificity after she worked with him again in *Francis of Assisi* (1961).

Walter Matthau was inclined to overact. "Curtiz was funny," Matthau told Leonard Maltin. "He called me 'Valty.' He called Elvis Presley 'Elvy.' Mostly he said to me, 'Valty, this is not Academy Award scene. Don't act so much.' 'I know you from stage. I was stage actor in Hungary. It's too big. When you do movie, you do slow, small. Cameras very big—you very big on screen.'"

"He taught," said Matthau. "He was a good teacher. But he never told you *how* to act, he just said, 'You're too loud, you're too big.'" Ever since Cagney had embarrassed him decades earlier for acting out a scene, Curtiz's guidance to actors was usually confined to asking for more or less. His advice to Carolyn Jones after a rehearsal of a scene in which she was supposed to be intoxicated: "Dollink, act more drunkey."

With Curtiz preparing the following day's scenes at the end of each day and Wallis managing every detail, *King Creole* closed production on March 10, 1958, four days ahead of schedule. Exactly two weeks later, Elvis was inducted into the U.S. Army. After several successful *King Creole* sneak previews, Wallis and his assistant Paul Nathan wired congratulations to Private Presley at Fort Hood, Texas: "[The film] proved you are accepted as a great dramatic star as well as singer." After the premiere in early July, the *New York Times* tacitly agreed, declaring, "Elvis Presley can act." The review also gave a tip of the hat to Curtiz as "a shrewd director." Other reviews were similarly complimentary. *King Creole* was a box-office success, and Elvis's song "Hard-Headed Woman" went gold. It was, however, less profitable than his first three pictures. The adult themes diluted some of the wild enthusiasm of his core fan base. Teenage girls didn't care for his relationship with the older Ronnie or the final scene, in which he advises Nellie to wait for him to get over the other woman, even though he sings "As Long as I Have You" while she raptly watches from the nightclub audience.

Curtiz had elicited Elvis's best screen performance. Presley knew it too. *King Creole*'s Danny remained the rock icon's favorite movie role. The nuanced sensitivity he brought to Danny Fisher would not be replicated in any of his remaining twenty-six films. Colonel Parker used the lesson of the reduced box-office receipts to guide his future selection of Elvis's movie roles.

King Creole would be a high-water mark when compared to Curtiz's subsequent films. The independent filmmaker Walter Mirisch and his brothers Marvin and Harold produced his next picture. Their company had taken wing with a United Artists distribution deal in August 1957. Walter established his reputation as a savvy head of production at Allied Artists whose successes included *Invasion of the Body Snatchers* and *Friendly Persuasion* (both 1956). When he discovered that his brother Harold's Palm Springs neighbors were Alan Ladd and Sue Carol, he became friendly with the couple and pitched a novel, *The Man in the Net* by Hugh Wheeler (using the pseudonym Patrick Quentin), as a vehicle for Ladd. It was a mystery about a small-town artist, framed for the murder of his dissolute wife (Carolyn Jones), who takes it on the lam. The fugitive is sheltered and ultimately exonerated by a group of local children. Ladd recommended Curtiz as the director in the hope of recapturing the magic of *The Proud Rebel*. The relationship between the director and actor had remained close amid discussions with Paramount about reuniting them on a western titled *The Covered Wagon*.

The Man in the Net (1959), filmed on location in Thompson, Connecticut, and Worcester, Massachusetts, and at the Goldwyn studios in Hollywood, was a bore. Reginald Rose's uncharacteristically weak screenplay was compounded by Ladd's indifferent performance. Laconic under the best of circumstances, the star was reportedly suffering from shingles and drinking heavily. Michael McGreevey, who played one of the children, remembered, "It was my first film and I was terrified of Curtiz. Alan Ladd was a sweet guy, but gave nothing to the kids; he was distant."

Walter Mirisch recalled Ladd's deportment during the production: "I've never witnessed such self-destructive behavior." He vainly attempted to get Curtiz to intercede: "[Mike] wasn't inclined to address this issue with Alan. I talked to Mike several times about what he could do about Alan's drinking and how it was affecting his performance." The production was snake-bit by bad luck. Mirisch came down with hepatitis and a member of the film crew was charged with murder after a man's death in a saloon brawl. Curtiz's temperament gave the child actors a severe case of nerves (ten-year-old McGreevey vomited before one scene). He also humiliated Charles McGraw by making him repeat upward of forty-five takes of a scene before publicly dressing him down after the tough-guy actor kept blowing his lines. Mirisch summarized the situation in his memoir: "He [Curtiz] was hardly at the height of his career and, frankly, was not very inspired."

There is film footage of Curtiz directing the movie on location in Connecticut. In one reel, he is seen striding across a suburban street laden with film equipment and vigorously gesturing while discussing matters with several assistants. He might have been unimaginative, particularly when saddled with a mediocre script, but he remained energetic. Despite all the problems, it is difficult to understand how a movie directed by Curtiz with Carolyn Jones as a nymphomaniac having an affair with Charles McGraw could be so tedious.

Curtiz returned to Paramount to helm *The Hangman* (1959), a Dudley Nichols–scribed oater that emphasized characterization over action. Mackenzie Bovard (Robert Taylor) locates a wanted robber, Johnny Bishop (Jack Lord), and discovers he is a community pillar; everyone insists he couldn't be the bad guy. The determination of Bishop's identity hinges on a curvaceous witness, Selah (Tina Louise), who arrives in town via stagecoach. *The Hangman* is an offbeat Western that concludes without a dramatic payoff. Also along for the ride is Fess Parker without his Davy Crockett coonskin cap and Lorne Greene in a brief dress rehearsal for *Bonanza,* which made its NBC debut later that same year. Tina Louise recalled: "I was just a kid who had finished my first movie [*God's Little Acre* (1958)] that I liked very much. My agent had quit and I was kind of thrown to the wolves. Curtiz was a very focused, intense director. . . . I did what I was told, but felt out of place with all of these older men. Robert Taylor was nice, but he was so much older and tired. I was a teenager, really. [She was twenty-four.] I enjoyed working with Jack Lord and previously with Aldo Ray, who I felt were my contemporaries." Curtiz emphasized her physical charms with a couple of bathing scenes that were innocuous by today's standards but were criticized in the trade papers as being licentious.

Louise, whose beauty obscured her acting talent (particularly after a three-year run on TV's *Gilligan's Island*), aptly summed up *The Hangman* as a film that was "good for what it was."

What it also meant was another payday for Curtiz, although he received less than what he was accustomed to. Of greater concern was the deterioration of his professional reputation. His on-set demeanor was no longer perceived as the eccentric behavior of a filmmaking legend. A newer generation in Hollywood increasingly viewed Curtiz as an archaic figure whose time had passed. His next picture became a debacle that called into question his continued viability as a director.

Paramount engaged him to go to Europe in June 1959 to direct a screen version of *Olympia,* a play written by his late colleague Ferenc Molnár. *Olympia* was a lesser Molnár creation. The story of a romance between an Austrian princess and a Hungarian hussar captain (changed to an American) during the pre–World War I Habsburg Empire evoked little interest in anyone living outside Hungary. Nevertheless, Molnár's name was a magical lure, and an international production was put together.

The producer Carlo Ponti sought the property as the bookend of a three-picture Paramount deal for Sophia Loren, whom he had married in 1957. Maurice Chevalier was cast as her father, and John Gavin was borrowed from Universal as the Pittsburgh mining engineer who becomes involved with Loren's princess. Angela Lansbury was added as a devious countess. Ponti's production company made numerous side distribution deals with various countries in an attempt to maximize the profits.

The interiors were filmed in Vienna and Rome. The lush Austrian locations included Schönbrunn Palace, which Curtiz had used for *Sodom und Gomorrha* and *Young Medardus.* On the basis of the material and historical setting, he seemed to be the perfect director for this project. The reality proved to be quite the opposite.

Curtiz was seventy-two and hadn't worked in Europe for decades. Directing a complex production in multiple countries with an unfamiliar foreign crew would have been a difficult assignment for a director half his age. He also had to cope with Ponti, who had his own agenda in Sophia Loren. Instead of being motivated by these challenges as he usually was, Curtiz was disengaged. According to one of the screenwriters, Walter Bernstein (who took his name off the script), he was more interested in inspecting medieval castles than in communicating in any discernable manner about the making of the picture. "I thought Mike Curtiz was senile," said Bernstein. Curtiz also didn't bother to establish any relationship with Loren or the other actors. John Gavin realized early on they were in trouble. "I said to Sophia, 'We're in a terrible picture. He [Curtiz] may have been a great director once but he doesn't know what he is doing.'" Without informing Curtiz, Ponti brought in Vittorio De Sica to work with Loren and reshoot certain scenes. De Sica worked during the wee hours, when Curtiz was off the set—as early as two o'clock in the morning, according to Gavin. Bernstein recalled that De Sica was paid each day in cash "so he could go to the casino." Curtiz was apparently oblivious to what was occurring. Gavin asked De Sica for assistance and was told, "Don't change a thing. Everything you do is so American." Curtiz still knew how to stage beautiful compositions: Sophia Loren looks ravishing in a series of sumptuous costumes, and the photography is sparkling. But there was zero chemistry between Loren and Gavin in an expensive production that was meaningless flotsam. *A Breath of Scandal,* as it ended up being titled, was accurately assessed as "flimsy, witless and tedious." Around this time, Richard Erdman encountered Curtiz while crossing Melrose Avenue outside Paramount. After greeting each other warmly, Erdman asked how things were going and gestured toward the studio. Curtiz shook his head sadly and said, "They don't understand."

Although it appeared that Curtiz's career had suffered a grievous body blow, it was just another setback to be shrugged off; Sam Goldwyn Jr. then tapped him to direct *The Adventures of Huckleberry Finn* (1960). Mark Twain's classic was originally adapted in 1920, and this was followed by a 1939 MGM release with Mickey Rooney in the title role. In 1953 Metro planned a musical remake with Gene Kelly and Danny Kaye, which never came to fruition. Four songs were repurposed for the new adaptation, which MGM coproduced with Goldwyn. The production values were relatively lavish, and the Sacramento River doubled as the Mississippi river delta. An impressive cast included Tony Randall, Patty McCormack, a dastardly Neville Brand as Pap Finn, Mickey Shaughnessy, Andy Devine, John Carradine, Judy Canova, and Sherry Jackson. An additional flourish was Buster Keaton as a lion tamer.

Signing the light-heavyweight boxing champion Archie Moore to play the key role of Jim, the runaway slave who befriends Huck Finn, was an astute bit of casting. Goldwyn sent a script to Moore, who was in Montreal, training for a rematch with the Canadian boxer Yvon Durelle. Nicknamed "The Mongoose" for his ring sagacity, Moore was an intelligent man who bore no resemblance to a Joe Palooka–like pug. His brother-in-law at the time was Sidney Poitier. He conferred with Poitier about the part and told *Ebony* magazine, "Sidney told me that I could play this role very easily and even offered to give me some pointers on how to handle some of the more delicate lines." Moore and his wife reviewed the draft script and objected

Sam Goldwyn Jr. and Archie Moore look on as Curtiz instructs Eddie Hodges in *The Adventures of Huckleberry Finn* (1960) (courtesy of the Academy of Motion Picture Arts and Sciences).

to the repetitive appearance of the n-word. "It was a common word in those days, too common," said Moore. Moore made his feelings known to Goldwyn Jr., who had the script revised to greatly reduce the redundant use of the epithet. His test of a particularly sensitive scene blew everyone away. Curtiz was observed wiping away tears, and "the professionals on the set—

electricians, stage hands, and the like—broke into spontaneous applause." Curtiz told Goldwyn, "There is no need for any further testing. This is the man to do the part." Archie Moore's ability to imbue realistic dignity in a stereotypical role spoke more about his innate acting skill than any direction he received from Curtiz. Jack Murphy, a noted San Diego sportswriter and Moore intimate, commented, "As an actor, Moore is a natural. He's been playing one role or another all his life, and boxing has never known a man who could match his flair for theatrics."

Despite Moore's stellar turn and other worthy performances, the script turned Twain's edgy adventure tale into a Disneylike family movie. Although it was well directed and handsomely produced, critics mostly damned it with faint praise. According to Goldwyn, the chief reason was the miscasting of the title role: "We made one mistake with that picture, which was that Eddie Hodges had kind of come into his own in a picture with Frank Sinatra [*A Hole in the Head* (1959)], and the studio very much wanted to use him. And I couldn't come up with a decent alternative. Eddie Hodges was really more Tom Sawyer, not Huckleberry Finn. Mike knew it too, but by that time we were into production and it was too late."

The film nearly broke even with a net loss of $99,000. Curtiz's deal with Formosa Productions included another profit-sharing agreement that would amount to nothing.

During preproduction on *Huckleberry Finn,* Curtiz experienced a poignant reminder of his past days of glory. Errol Flynn paid him a visit in an attempt to land the part of the Duke of Bilgewater, which eventually went to Mickey Shaughnessy. The former swashbuckler was broke and dying. Sam Goldwyn Jr. remembered Flynn gesturing at Curtiz saying, "This man *is* my career." The great star was so dissipated that he was barely recognizable. Curtiz was extremely sentimental about his old adversary and handled him with kindness before sending him on his way. At the end of the day, Goldwyn gave Curtiz a ride home from the studio. The director, always voluble about the progress of the film, remained silent for most of the journey. Suddenly he blurted out, "Strasberg and Actors Studio can make actor, but only God can make star!" Curtiz understood and was nurtured by the star system that had held sway during his time in Hollywood. He had fought with Flynn over the actor's lack of discipline, but he deeply admired and appreciated the singular talent that was so instrumental to his own success. On October 14, 1959, shortly after Curtiz began shooting *Huckleberry Finn,* Errol Flynn died in Vancouver, Canada, at the age of fifty.

33

Out on His Shield

As Curtiz prepared to leave for Italy to direct *Francis of Assisi* (1961), he decided to separate from Bess. Despite his continued appeals that she cut back on her extravagant lifestyle, Curtiz's wife continued to live more profligately than ever. According to John Meredyth Lucas, she maintained a house that "was bursting with servants" and routinely handed out "50 and 100 dollar tips to the hairdressers and manicurists." Bess might not have changed, but neither had her husband. That his behavior was a principal reason for his wife's predicament apparently never occurred to him. Both were strong-willed people accustomed to getting their own way. Nonetheless, the pair had made a life together. "Mike always made Bess laugh," remembered her granddaughter Victoria Lucas. Responsible or not, Curtiz could no longer rationalize living with a woman who had turned herself into a quasi invalid. As John Meredyth Lucas summarized: "Despite all the help she gave him with his scripts, her wonderful sense of humor and his repeated infidelity, he had remained married to a voluntarily bed ridden woman for 30 years."

Curtiz didn't seek a divorce but arranged a property settlement agreement on March 1, 1960. The Encino ranch, estimated at 120 acres, was sold off and eventually broken up into smaller parcels. Curtiz relocated to a comfortable apartment at the Horace Heidt Estates in nearby Sherman Oaks. He continued keeping company with Ann Stuart, whose obedient devotion appealed to him more than ever. To economize, Bess moved into a smaller house in Encino, which she promptly expanded in order to house her live-in staff. Although an era had ended, Curtiz and Bess's relationship remained essentially unchanged; they had always been more like collaborative pals than a conventional couple. The director also remained close to his stepson and grandchildren, Elizabeth, Victoria, and his namesake, Michael.

Curtiz and Bess outside their Encino house (courtesy of the Lucas family).

Francis of Assisi (1961) was a Twentieth Century-Fox production; Plato A. Skouras, the son of the soon-to-be-deposed Fox president, Spyros Skouras, served as the nominal executive producer. Curtiz met the younger Skouras when they were seated together at a Fox luncheon feting Nikita Khrushchev during the Soviet leader's visit to the United States. Their discussions about the project resulted in Curtiz's being hired to direct. After claiming that he rejected a feeler from Frank Sinatra to play Francis, Curtiz selected Bradford Dillman for the title role. Dillman, who had recently won a Best Actor award at Cannes for his performance in Richard Fleischer's *Compulsion* (1959), took a studious approach to portraying the pleasure-loving merchant's son whom God calls on to establish a religious order. His costar Stuart Whitman remembered Dillman as "a very bright guy who really tucked himself in and isolated himself from everything and concentrated on just what he was doing." Although there was no observable strife on location, Dillman confided: "My mother always told me that if you can't say anything nice about someone, don't say anything at all. Just thinking about him [Curtiz] fifty years later gets me excited in the wrong way."

The film also starred Dolores Hart as Clare Scifi, who renounces her worldly life to become a nun and ultimately is canonized as Saint Clare. In a striking case of life imitating art, Hart took holy vows in 1963 and entered the Abbey of Regina Laudis in Connecticut, where she went on to become the mother prioress.[1] After six films, Hart was an experienced actress who was more observational about her director. She described a memorable meeting that took place in the Basilica of Saint Francis of Assisi, which was constructed two years after the saint's death in 1226.

> As [cast members] all gathered in the forum of the church, Mike walked through the door, turned, and greeted us all very soundly. He took off his hat as he came in and put it on his chest. He looked up and looked all around and didn't say a word. And then he looked up and there was an enormous crucifix on the wall, and he said, "Oh my friends! Look! This is wonderful! Oh! Goddamn it, isn't that a beautiful crucifix!" We were all totally wiped out with laughter, but you couldn't laugh. You didn't know what to do. But we knew immediately who we were dealing with.

Hart had no doubt but that Curtiz's coarseness rubbed the sensitive Dillman the wrong way: "Brad was a very thoughtful and loving man. He adored his wife and he adored the truth of what he was doing. Mike thought he was being meaningful, but it was just, 'Goddamn, isn't that a beautiful crucifix,' you know? You always had the feeling that you were in the hands of a farmer that was going to plant you somewhere. I have to say that I have nothing against farmers, but he wasn't an artist. I think his wholesale value was that he approached filmmaking with his entire heart and soul. And you do learn from someone who has that capacity."

The production of *Francis* ran out of money and there were several delays. Hart recalled that she spent five months in Italy on salary. The glacial pace drove Curtiz insane. His frustration, exacerbated by the language barrier, boiled over in a memorable meltdown observed by Stuart Whitman.

> We were stationed in Rome. And we had to get up at three or three-thirty in the morning and drive out to Monte Gelato—a couple of hours' drive—where we were supposed to be shooting.

And every day was the same and this went on for about twenty-seven days straight. And we never shot. The cameraman [Piero Portalupi] was one of Italy's finest. He and Mike would get up on the peak of the hill, up in front of us, and we were all waiting in parked cars, in wardrobe, with the engines running for heat. We'd sit there for a couple of hours. And for twenty-seven days this went on. Jesus, it was a pain in the ass!

Portalupi was concerned about filming through mist on the top of the hill that didn't evaporate. And Curtiz would rage at him to set up and shoot it anyway. And nothing happened. The cameraman refused to make the shot unless conditions were perfect. According to Whitman, what occurred next stunned the entire company: "Curtiz would stamp his hand down and say, 'Now, today!' and the cameraman would say, 'No, no, no, no, no,' using his hands, as an Italian does. And we could see all this for twenty-seven days. Curtiz was freaking out. He wanted to express himself so badly; he wanted to smash him, the cameraman. Instead, what he did . . . this was the beginning of his little dementia. . . . I mean it was the most bizarre thing I'd ever seen." In a complete fury, Curtiz dropped his pants and, in full view of cast and crew, defecated in front of the cameraman.

Whether he was senile at this point is a matter of conjecture. It is more likely that it was an act of impotent rage by an old man who was unable to control himself. Curtiz's self-worth continued to be defined by his direction of motion pictures. The lack of progress was intolerable. He couldn't quit, nor could he fire or assault the cinematographer, so he expressed his frustration in the only way he knew how. The grotesque display apparently worked. There were no further attempts to make the shot, and the company packed up and moved on to Segovia, Spain, where the pace of production picked up considerably. According to Whitman, Curtiz "was fine after that. The rest of the picture went smoothly." It wasn't physically easy for the director, who toward the end of production felt more fatigued than he could remember ever having been in his life. No one in the cast really noticed (Dolores Hart termed his energy level "completely unbeatable"), but he looked old and felt worse.

The picture reflected a number of attributes that characterized several of Curtiz's later films: exceptional casting, technical proficiency, indifferent writing, and lethargic tempo. Weighted down with endless talk, *Francis of Assisi* barely created a stir.

At the end of the shoot in Italy, Curtiz took Whitman aside and

A deteriorating Curtiz directs Dolores Hart and Bradford Dillman in *Francis of Assisi* (1961) (author's collection).

handed him a script for *The Comancheros,* a John Wayne picture that he was going to direct at Twentieth Century-Fox. Whitman was enthusiastic, "Of course, I read it overnight and said to him, 'Yeah, there's a perfect role for me.'" Curtiz essentially promised him the role, but when Whitman spoke with Fox, he was told that the part was already cast and nothing could be done. He called Curtiz, who told him, "Go over and talk to the Duke. He's at Paramount Studios. Work your way in there and talk to him."

Whitman caught up with Wayne as the star walked from the set to his dressing room. Wayne became conscious of being trailed by Whitman and whirled around snarling, "What the fuck do you want?" Whitman told him that he wanted to play Paul Regret in *The Comancheros*. Whitman described the part and explained in detail how he would do it and why he wanted it. The star sized him up and told Whitman he had the role. "And that was that," said Whitman. "The studio casting head got on my case about it, but who cared? If Duke wanted you, it was over."

Wayne had recently directed and produced *The Alamo* (1960), a personal dream project that left him and his Batjac production company virtually broke. He was heading for another payday with *The Comancheros*. Wayne portrayed a veteran Texas Ranger, Jake Cutter, who captures a suave gambler (Whitman) and is returning him to prison for killing the son of a Louisiana judge in a duel. The two men are forced into an alliance when Cutter goes undercover to ferret out an outlaw gang that sells whiskey and rifles to the Comanches. The outlaws' desert headquarters is run like a paramilitary family of Visigoths by a merciless, wheelchair-bound chieftain (Nehemiah Persoff).

One wonders why Wayne tapped Curtiz to direct *The Comancheros*. Although they had made *Trouble Along the Way* (1953), Curtiz was neither a Fordian father figure nor a director whom Wayne worshipped like Howard Hawks. Like Curtiz, Wayne was at his happiest while working. Although an autocrat, Wayne maintained a family atmosphere on location, surrounding himself with familiar faces. His son Patrick costarred with him in *The Comancheros,* and his five-year-old daughter, Aissa, had a small part. Wayne might have also felt that he owed Curtiz a boost, a sentiment that may have dated back to 1928, when he was a young extra, treading water in the wreckage of the *Noah's Ark* sets. The star was fanatically loyal to those who helped him on the way up. John Wayne revered every facet of the movie industry, and Curtiz had been a big part of it. In all likelihood, Wayne approved him to direct *The Comancheros* because he wanted to help out a legendary director who was past his prime and down on his uppers.

Whatever his rationale was for hiring Curtiz, Wayne soon came to regret it. Although the director began preproduction with his usual enthusiasm by casting favored cohorts, including Guinn "Big Boy" Williams (his final role), Henry Daniell, and his youngest brother, Gabriel, something was seriously amiss with his health. When the production moved to Utah and Arizona during the blazing heat of the summer, Curtiz was listless. Wayne quickly stepped into the breach. "Duke was a terrific director as long as you did what he wanted you to do," recalled Whitman.

Cast and crew quickly deduced who was in charge. Nehemiah Persoff told me: "Curtiz was very, very laid back. John Wayne really had the say about things. It was very hot, so I asked the AD [assistant director] if there was something that could be done, as we were standing around waiting in the hot sun for hours. The AD spoke to Curtiz and nothing happened. I mentioned it to Wayne, and he immediately ordered a tarpaulin set up to shade the crew. Curtiz lacked energy; he was obviously ill." Tom Mankiewicz, working on his first picture as a third assistant, remembered Curtiz being reduced to a semi-invalid by the broiling Moab heat. "Curtiz usually falls asleep in his chair by early afternoon. We protect him with umbrellas to keep the sun off and put chamois cloths filled with ice around his neck. We all take salt pills. Once Curtiz is asleep, the picture is directed by Wayne. . . . Toward the end of one particularly hot day . . . Wayne is doing a scene with Lee Marvin. We've done the 'over the shoulder' favoring Lee. I look over at Curtiz and ask, 'Turn around on Mr. Wayne now, Mr. Curtiz?' 'Yes,' he mumbles. 'Just don't turn me around.'"

Curtiz's behavior on location, never easy to endure, continued to deteriorate because of his age and infirmity. Mankiewicz thought he was "an arrogant prick." He observed Curtiz sneeze into his tablecloth during a luncheon with the mayor of Moab. He also claimed the director was nearly kicked out of the Apache Hotel for sunbathing in the nude by the pool. Matters between Mankiewicz and Curtiz came to a head after Mankiewicz attempted to warn the director not to drive Wayne's personal herd of Texas longhorns across a draw with a five-foot drop during a stampede scene. Mankiewicz screwed up his courage and asked Curtiz if they shouldn't consult with Wayne, since they were his cattle and they might be injured. In response, Curtiz grabbed an extra's six-shooter, pointed it at Mankiewicz and fired off a blank, yelling, "You're fired! Get out of here!" Mankiewicz returned to the hotel in Moab and wondered what to tell his famous father (who got him the gig), when Wayne phoned his room. The star told him, "I heard what you did out there. Thanks. I'm going out to see what that Hungarian piece of shit's doing with my cattle. See you in the morning." Mankiewicz's return to the location the next day forced a humiliated Curtiz to pretend that the incident had never occurred.

Although it doesn't measure up to Wayne's classic oaters, *The Comancheros* is a well-made film. The story takes a while to unspool. But the numerous action scenes, which were directed mostly by Wayne, helped take up the slack. The picture may have set a record for horse falls in a Western. The days of the running W were gone: two stuntmen, Cliff Lyons and Chuck Roberson, deployed horses they had painstakingly trained to fall on command. The acting was superior and included a standout turn by Lee Marvin as a partially scalped miscreant. The only burr in the saddle for the director and star was the leading lady, Ina Balin, a New York actress and an apostle of the Method. Both Curtiz and Wayne rolled their eyes as she dug down for inner motivation before each take. "Get the god-damn words out," said Wayne under his breath on at least one occasion.

Curtiz's odd behavior emerged again while directing a scene in which Whitman kisses Balin. Persoff recalled Curtiz telling Whitman, "'Don't kiss her with your mouth open. Kiss her with a closed mouth.' Stu said, 'I can't do that. I don't know any other way to kiss a woman.' Curtiz didn't argue. He simply moved the camera and shot the scene with Whitman's back facing the lens while he kissed Balin." "I'm not sure why he insisted on doing this," said Persoff. Perhaps a mentally fogged Curtiz was drift-ing back to the previous era of Joseph Breen's censorship and was at-tempting to avoid an accusatory Hal Wallis memorandum. Mercifully, his efforts didn't last much longer. As his health continued to decline, Curtiz's granitelike determination, which sustained him during nearly a half cen-tury of continual filmmaking, finally crumbled.

He fell and injured his leg while walking around the Utah location.[2] According to John Meredyth Lucas, after an X-ray at a local hospital, "his bones were found to resemble lacework." Although Curtiz was liter-ally carried off the location before finishing his last picture, most of the company was unaware that the accident had occurred. He was so obvi-ously sick that his departure was viewed as inevitable. According to Whit-man, Wayne ended up directing more than half of *The Comancheros*. Curtiz returned to Los Angeles and was admitted to St. John's Hospital. His daughter Kitty eventually broke the news to him, revealing the cause of his suffering. Curtiz's body was riddled with cancer and he had only months to live. Lucas subsequently discovered that Bess Meredyth and Curtiz's personal physician had kept the diagnosis hidden from his stepfa-ther ever since the biopsy of his prostate gland during the 1957 appendec-tomy procedure. His wife and doctor advised Curtiz at the time that there was nothing to worry about regarding the growth on his prostate. Con-trary to what they told him, the biopsy had been positive for cancer, and it had already spread through his body, precluding any surgical options. Lucas recorded the denouement of Curtiz's predicament in his memoir:

> Mother had talked to John MacDonald, the family's lifelong doc-tor and friend. They made a decision, right or wrong, not to tell Mike since there was nothing that could be done. I did not know. It remained a secret for years until Mike's estranged daughter blurted it out to him. He rushed to Dr. MacDonald and asked, "Why hell you don't told me?"

"How many pictures have made since then, Mike?" MacDonald asked.

Mike couldn't be sure of the actual count.

"How many would you have made if you'd known?"

Mike thought a moment, shook his head. "Goddamn, Mac, you're right. Is better not know."

Although Curtiz contracted cancer during an era before major breakthroughs in chemotherapy treatment, one would assume that Dr. MacDonald and Bess consulted an oncologist and explored all possible treatment options, including radiation, before condemning Curtiz to a slow and agonizing death that allowed him to direct more movies.

Realizing that his time was short, Curtiz revised and signed his last will and testament on July 26, 1961. While in the hospital, he received a final visit from John Lucas. According to Sam Goldwyn Jr., Lucas's feelings toward his stepfather remained ambivalent. He never achieved the closeness that he had always yearned for. He termed his visit with Curtiz several days before his death "a sad and frustrating meeting." Abandoning any attempt at false bonhomie, Lucas attempted to thank the man who had played such a huge part in his life, but he could not find the words to express his emotions. Curtiz couldn't either. "Well, Jick," he murmured, "I think so this is last time we see."

Curtiz was discharged from the hospital to die at his Sherman Oaks apartment on April 10, 1962, at the age of seventy-five. He wanted to be buried at Forest Lawn, near his mother. His standing as a "High Holy Day Jew" complicated matters. Rabbi Edgar Magnin, leader of the Wilshire Boulevard temple and proclaimed "Rabbi to the Stars," was out of town when Curtiz died. His associate, Rabbi Max Dubin, refused to give Curtiz a full Jewish funeral because of the director's nonobservant status. Liz MacGillicuddy Lucas related what happened next:

It turned out that one of my Dad's dearest friends was a screenwriter named Harry Kronman, who was a rabbinical student before he began writing radio plays and television shows. Rabbi Dubin was one of Kronman's old student pals when Dubin was named Moishe Dubinsky. When Harry heard that Max wasn't going to give Mike a full funeral, with the music and everything, he got on the phone and persuaded Max to do it right. He even suggested the theme for Mike's funeral: "The meaning of death to

Jews." So Mike ended up having the whole nine yards ceremony. In Hollywood, it's always whom you know.

Curtiz's funeral was sparsely attended. "So few of the people with whom he worked and who I believe had done some of their best work under his direction were there," remembered Ann Blyth. The pallbearers included Cary Grant, Alan Ladd, Danny Thomas, Jack Warner, and Steve Trilling. In attendance with Curtiz's family were Blyth, Doris Day, Horace Heidt, Wallace Ford, James Wong Howe, and Rudolf Friml, among others. Bess and Curtiz's close friend, eighty-one-year-old Louella Parsons—who had witnessed their 1929 wedding and more recently had stood as godmother at Michael Lucas's christening—could not attend because she was hospitalized for shingles and pneumonia. John Meredyth Lucas couldn't help noticing that Jack Warner attended the services "in panchromatic makeup for the photographers."

Curtiz's last rites were a prelude to the controversy that erupted after his estate entered into probate on May 28, 1962. His will made specific reference to the 1960 property settlement that he and Bess had agreed to. He left her $200,000 owed him by Paramount Pictures under his July 7, 1953, agreement with the studio. According to the will, the Paramount money was to be doled out at the rate of $1,000 per week. He also left Bess any future funds that might be realized from his profit-sharing agreement with Sam Goldwyn Jr. for *The Adventures of Huckleberry Finn* (1960). Half of his estate went to "my friend" Ann Stuart. His bequest to Stuart included 270 acres of land located in present-day Calabasas near Malibu Creek State Park (known as the "Los Virgenes Property"), along with all his household furniture and furnishings, automobile, jewelry, personal effects, and "all the rest, residue and remainder of my estate." The other half went in equal shares to his daughter Katherine (Kitty) Curtiz Eberson, his brothers David and Gabriel, and his sisters Regina and Margit.

Given his history, the lack of declarations concerning his out of wedlock children was not surprising. His will stated that he had one daughter by his first wife. There was no mention of his daughter Sonja, born to Teresa Dalla Bona, in 1923. He also made no bequests to his sons Michael Foerster and Michael Vondrak, "for the reason I have amply provided for them during my lifetime." Article 5 of the will contained the most startling declaration: "I hereby declare that a Jill Gerrard contends that I am the father of her child whom she has named Debra Curtiz. I hereby declare that I am not the father of said child and that said child is not my

Curtiz's casket being carried by Jack Warner, Cary Grant, Steve Trilling, and Alan Ladd (courtesy of the Lucas family).

issue." Curtiz claimed that his previous acknowledgment of paternity for his daughter by Jill Gerrard under signed and witnessed financial support agreements was made "under duress." Curtiz directed his Bank of America executor to rescind both agreements for the little girl "and to make no payments to or for the benefit of said child under the same or otherwise." Jill Gerrard contested the will. She knew that Curtiz was the father of her daughter and refused to accept the arbitrary revocation of the paternity and support agreements. She blamed his attorney, Mark Cohen—"an S.O.B. who hated me"—and sued the estate for support of her child. In her lawsuit filed on May 16, 1962, Gerrard requested $600 per month in support and $11,600 for medical bills and court costs. The total amount of the claim was estimated at $65,000. The trial became a minor sensation in Los Angeles; Gerrard reportedly broke down on the stand as she related the details of her romance with Curtiz, which began when the director was sixty-six and she was twenty. According to one account, she claimed that their intimacy ended after she became pregnant and discovered that Curtiz was married. She said that Curtiz initially "suggested abortion, but showed the child affection after it was born." He reputedly told the young mother that the child "had the Curtiz forehead" and (according to Gerrard) carried a photo of the little girl in his wallet and sent her money for birthdays and Christmas as well as paying her hospital bills. Lawyers for the estate called a pair of doctors who testified they doubted that Curtiz could have fathered Gerrard's child since he had had a sterility operation in 1928. Superior Court Judge James M. McRoberts didn't buy the estate's proposition of a sterile Curtiz. He ruled on August 28, 1962, that Curtiz fathered the child and ordered the estate to pay Gerrard $400 a month until the further order of the court. The case dragged on until Gerrard reportedly settled for $37,000 on March 25, 1965.

The 270 acres of land willed to Ann Stuart were sold to a real estate developer for $357,500 on August 16, 1963. (Bess Meredyth apparently retained an interest in this land because of the 1960 property settlement and reportedly sold it off to the same realtor.) Bess also reached a settlement with Paramount Pictures over the $200,000 on Curtiz's contract, which was reduced to $52,750. Stuart contested this particular agreement by asking the court to declare that if Bess received this money, she (Bess) should waive any further claim to the entire estate. The final settlement of Curtiz's estate didn't occur until October 18, 1967. Ann Stuart ended up being paid $259,084.46, including a claim for land that Curtiz was discovered to own in Hungary. Whatever was left went to Kitty and Curtiz's surviving siblings. Whether Curtiz received any undue influence from anyone concerning the disposition of his estate is unknown. The denial of paternity for his daughter by Jill Gerrard, and the omission of his out-of-wedlock children in his will, was consistent with his previous behavior. His generosity toward Ann Stuart doubtlessly reflected the closeness of their relationship during the final decade of his life.

David Curtiz succumbed to cancer on May 23, 1962, at the age of sixty-eight, only six weeks after his older brother's identical fate. Gabriel Curtiz lived until 1985, eking out a living as a character actor. Curtiz's other brother and his sisters eventually passed on, leaving his children as his surviving blood relatives.

John Meredyth Lucas enjoyed a notable career as a TV director, writer, and producer; his résumé included the original *Star Trek* series. His memoir, which chronicled his years with Curtiz, was published two years after his death in 2002 at the age of eighty-three. The Lucas children, Liz, Victoria, and Michael, retain pleasant childhood memories of Bess and "Grandpa Mike."

Kitty eventually carved out a niche as a community and political activist while living in Woodland Hills near her father's former Canoga Park ranch. A Republican, Dr. Kitty Curtiz served on the staff of Los Angeles Mayor Sam Yorty as an "international liaison." In March 1970 she was honored by the Daughters of the American Revolution for "giving unself-ishly of her time and talents in coordinating activities with Los Angeles ethnic communities." She was a staunch supporter of Mayor Tom Bradley, a Democrat, and was appointed an event coordinator for his administra-tion. The years didn't mellow Kitty regarding her parents. She remained distant from Lucy Doraine, who died in 1989 at the age of ninety-one. Years afterward, she spewed venom toward those who she believed took advantage of her father: "This woman [Stuart], who was 40 years younger and who separated him from his family, hated me from the beginning be-cause it was me who told my father he had cancer because I wanted to save his life or at least prolong it. But it was much too late. She knew what was occurring and rejected telling him because she wanted him to pass away and be able to inherit everything." She also pointed her finger at Bess and the Lucas family for "living like aristocrats and luxury while I found my-self needy and poor." Kitty passed away on December 31, 2006, also at the age of ninety-one.

After decades of feigned maladies, Bess Meredyth became seriously ill during the summer of 1969. She ran through the money that Curtiz left her and died in the Motion Picture Home at Woodland Hills on July 13, 1969, at the age of seventy-nine. Although her creative collaboration with Cur-tiz is mostly lacking any verifiable documentation, there is little doubt that Bess contributed to many, if not most, of his American films. Curtiz's ca-reer would have been very different without their partnership. In the end, it is difficult to fathom why Bess opted for a bedridden existence instead of divorcing Curtiz. By all reports, however, she wasn't outwardly morose but remained upbeat and engaged with her family and friends. Bess loved her husband, despite the emotional damage he inflicted on her. Hollywood and the movies were the glue that kept them together for three decades.

Ann Stuart spent the rest of her life in the North Hollywood house that Curtiz bought for her. Her brief heyday as Anitra Stevens portraying Queen Nefertiti in *The Egyptian* (1954) became a distant memory. She found that the money she inherited from the director—including his resid-uals and royalty payments—didn't make her happy. The actor Rick Lenz remembered his friend and neighbor as a lonely woman with "the bearing of an imprisoned aristocrat." According to Lenz, "She told me that her attitudes were based on what she picked up many years earlier from Mi-chael Curtiz." Ann Stuart never married or took up with another man. She died in 2004 and is buried in Forest Lawn, the same resting place as her long-departed lover.

Jill Gerrard eventually changed her name to Jill Gerrard Curtiz. She told me that after Curtiz died, it took eighteen years for her to marry someone else because "I loved him [Curtiz] with all my heart and soul."

After his paradoxes are pondered and all of the anecdotes retold, Curtiz's legacy is what he spent a lifetime doing. His movies continue to be savored by successive generations, even if most people can't remember who directed *Casablanca*. "I don't know what else I can tell you," said Richard Erdman, the last actor remaining from the 1940s Warner stock company. "He was the king of Warner Bros. when I was there, the absolute king of directors. There was nobody like him."

During a career retrospective shortly before his own death in 1986, the man who knew Curtiz as well as anyone deplored the present state of the film industry and offered a wistful remedy. "If only we had a Michael Curtiz today," mused Hal Wallis.

Nobody who loves the movies would disagree.

Acknowledgments

This book would not have been possible without the University of Southern California Warner Bros. Archives. Sincerest gratitude to its director, Sandra Garcia Myers, and the curators Sandra Joy Lee Aguilar and Brett Service. Kudos also to my research assistants, Lee Jameson and Roxanne Samer, who assisted me in combing through the files of more than ninety Curtiz films.

Liz MacGillicuddy Lucas, Victoria Lucas, and Michael Lucas were extremely supportive of this endeavor. Their father's memoir, *Eighty Odd Years in Hollywood,* is an invaluable resource about all things Curtiz. Michael Lucas was particularly helpful in letting me review his grandfather's photos and ephemera. He generously provided many of the photographs in this book.

László Kriston found and translated a large number of archival Hungarian theatrical and cinema magazines as well as numerous other Curtiz-related materials. László also coordinated my visit to the Hungarian film archive during a trip to Budapest, which he turned into a "Kertész before Curtiz" city tour. Köszönöm, my friend.

Balogh Gyöngyi of the Hungarian Film Archive organized all the Curtiz materials for my visit and kindly answered my follow-up questions.

David Robinson, Riccardo Costantini, and the festival organizers and staff of Le Giornate del Cinema Muto in Pordenone, Italy, invited me to participate at their 2011 festival presidium on Curtiz. I am also indebted to Lorenzo Cordelli and the festival organizers for making available several Curtiz silent films, and to Bálint Zágoni and his documentary film, *Janovics Jenő: A magyar Pathé.*

I am grateful to Michelanne Forster, Curtiz's granddaughter and author of the play *Don't Mention Casablanca,* for her candid communications about her grandmother Mathilde Foerster and her father, Michael. Another granddaughter, Ilona Ryder also corresponded with me and provided information about her family ties to Curtiz.

I am indebted to all those who took the time to communicate with me

549

about Curtiz's life and times: Walter Bernstein, Ann Blyth, the late Ernest Borgnine, Marjorie Bowers, Mary Crawford Cantarini, Barrie Chase, Jill Gerrard Curtiz, Doris Day (via her Animal Foundation Team), Bradford Dillman, Richard Erdman, Nanette Fabray, the late Sam Goldwyn Jr., Mother Dolores Hart, Marsha Hunt, Sherry Jackson, the late Sybil Jason, the late Mickey Knox, David Ladd, Rick Lenz, the late Joan Leslie, Norman Lloyd, Tina Louise, Jimmy Lydon, Carol Lynley, Dorothy Malone, Patty McCormack, Michael McGreevey, Walter Mirisch, Don Murray, the late Patricia Neal, Nancy Olson, the late Marvin Paige, the late Eleanor Parker, Nehemiah Persoff, Gene Reynolds, the late Helene Stanton Pinsky, the late Elaine Stritch, the late Virginia Vincent, the late Connie Wald, Stuart Whitman, and the late Patrice Wymore.

The renowned film historian and good friend Rudy Behlmer read over my draft chapters, offering unstinting encouragement and assistance, as well as his unfailing humor.

I have maintained my place in the SRO queue of film biographers to sing the praises of Ned Comstock, the éminence grise of the USC Cinematic Library. Ned's support was unbounded.

My thanks to the Motion Picture Academy's Margaret Herrick Library, particularly to Barbara Hall, Jenny Romero, and Stacey Behlmer. Also thanks to Barbara during her tenure at the Warner Bros. studio archive.

My appreciation goes to the UCLA Charles E. Young Research Library, Special Collections; the American Film Institute Library; the University of Texas at Austin, Harry Ransom Center; and the Los Angeles Public Library, particularly the Platt Branch.

I am also grateful to Leith Adams, Kevin Brownlow, Scott Eyman, Gary Giddins, Foster Hirsch, Scott MacQueen, Leonard Maltin, and Steven C. Smith for their specific contributions and enthusiastic support.

And thanks to Cari Beauchamp, Maggie Breitmeier, Leslie Epstein, George Feltenstein, John Gallagher, Philippe Garnier, J. R. Jones, Susan King, Edgar Krebs, Gregory Mank, John McElwee, Susan Orlean, Fred Rappaport, Gary Rhodes, Lee Server, Carol Summers, Margaret Talbot, Karl Thiede, Gina Vadnais, Mimi Vanderstraaten, Melanie Villines, Laura Wagner, Peter Walther, Marc Wanamaker, and Victoria Wilson.

Tom Weaver's editing recommendations proved to be a terrific boost, as were Cesar Mendoza's translation services and the copyediting acumen of Ann Twombly and Lindsey Westbrook. Michael Kronenberg's talent in enhancing many of the book's photographs was nothing short of phenomenal.

Patrick McGilligan's unstinting encouragement throughout a lengthy process kept me on the path to righteousness. Ditto for Anne Dean Dotson at the University Press of Kentucky.

And a bear hug for my chum Dick Erdman, who regaled me with stories of his days at Warner Bros. and urged me to write about "his champion," Michael Curtiz.

My family continues to make the journey worthwhile:

Jemma's loving forbearance sustained me along with our Patience, Lena, Haelo, and Cairo.

My brother David is a discerning cineaste whose recommendations were invariably spot-on.

And most of all for the late Jayne G. Rode (1922–2016), who lives forever in my heart.

Filmography

Directed by Michael Curtiz

1912

MA ÉS HOLNAP (Today and Tomorrow). Projectograph, 41 min. Screenplay: Iván Siklós, Imre Roboz. DOP: Raymond Pellerin. Cast: Gyula Abonyi, Jenöné Veszpréme, Endre Szegheő, Gyula Fehér, Michael Curtiz.

1913

KRAUSZ DOKTOR A VÉRPADON (Doctor Krausz on the Scaffold). Projectograph, sketch film. Screenplay: István Szomaházy. DOP: Raymond Pellerin. Cast: Gerő Mály, Gyula Szőreghy, Károly Huszár, Vilmosné Vákár, Andor K. Kovács.
GYERUNK CSAK (Come On). Sketch film directed by Curtiz for a 1913 folk opera revue. As reported in *Színházi Élet* on May 24, 1913.
HÁZASODIK AZ URAM (My Husband's Getting Married). Projectograph, sketch film. Screenplay: Nándor Korcsmáros. DOP: József Bécsi. Cast: Adél Marosi, Gyula Szőreghy, Lajos Gellért, Vilmos Sáfrány.
MOZIKIRÁLY (Movie King). Projectograph, sketch film. The operetta by Rudolf Bernauer and Rudolf Schanzer. Cast: Sári Fedák.
AZ UTOLSÓ BOHÉM (The Last Bohemian). Projectograph, sketch film. Screenplay: Zsolt Harsányi. DOP: József Bécsi. Cast: Antal Nyáray, Elemér Thury, Béla Bodonyi, Zoltán Sipos, Ilonka Bedő.
RABLÉLEK (Captive Souls). P: Ödön Uher, 99 min. Screenplay: Imre Földes. DOP: Ödön Uher Jr. Cast: Alfréd Deésy, Elemér Thury, Sári Fedák.

1914

AZ ARANYÁSÓ (The Gold Digger). P: Ödön Uher. Sketch film. Screenplay: Ferenc Molnár (Bret Harte). DOP: Ödön Uher Jr. Cast: Ilona Bedő, Lujza V. Beregi, René Sellő.

Abbreviations: DOP: Director of Photography; P: Producer; D: Director; AP: Assistant Producer; AD: Assistant Director

A HERCEGNŐ PONGYOLÁJA (The Princess in a Negligee). Kino-Riport, sketch film. Screenplay: Ferenc Ráskai. Cast: Vilma Gombócz, Kálmán Horváth, Margit Koppány, Aranka Molnár, Lajos Újváry.

AZ ÉJSZAKA RABJA (Captive of the Night). Projectograph, 45 min. Screenplay: Iván Siklós, Imre Roboz. DOP: Raymond Pellerin. Cast: Michael Curtiz.

A SZÖKÖTT KATONA (The Escaped Soldier). Miklós Pásztory (Nemzeti), 69 min. Screenplay: Miklós Pásztory (Ede Szigligeti). DOP: Dezső Polik. Cast: Béla Pogány, Mari K. Demjén, Kálmán Rózsahegyi, Sándor Szőke.

A KÖLCSÖNKÉRT CSECSEMŐK (The Borrowed Babies). Jenő Janovics (Proja), 53 min. Screenplay: Jenő Janovics (Margaret Mayo). DOP: József Bécsi. Cast: Lili Berky, Alajos Mészáros, Mariska Simon, József Berky, Mátyás Némedy.

A TOLONC (The Undesirable). Jenő Janovics (Proja), 74 min. Screenplay: Jenő Janovics, Tamás Emőd (Ede Tóth). DOP: László Fekete. Cast: Lili Berky, Victor Varconi, Mari Jászai, Andor Szakács, Gyula Nagy.

BÁNK BÁN (Bánk the Regent). Jenő Janovics (Proja), 90 min. Screenplay: Jenő Janovics (Jószef Katona). DOP: László Fekete. Cast: Mari Jászai, Tibor Kaczér, Adorján Nagy, Mihály Várkonyi, László Bakó.

1915

A PARADICSOM (The Tomato). Sketch film. Projectograph. Screenplay: Imre Földes. Cast: Jenő Faragó, Juci Lábass, Kató Berky, Emil Fenyő.

AKIT KETTEN SZERETNEK (One Who Is Loved by Two). Terrus. Sketch film. P: István Kiss. Screenplay: Arthur Földes. Cast: Michael Curtiz, László Csiky, Matild Győri.

1916

A BÁNAT ASSZONYA (Melancholy Lady). 68 min. P: Benő Moskovits. Screenplay: Michael Curtiz. DOP: János Fröchlich. Cast: Sári Vásárhelyi, Márta Szirmai.

MAKKHETES (The 7th of Acorns). Kino-Riport, 69 min. Screenplay: István Lázár. DOP: József Bécsi. Cast: Sándor Virányi.

A KARTHAUSI (The Carthusian). Star-Film, 77 min. Screenplay: Tibor Rákosi and Pál Péter (József Eötvös). DOP: Béla Zsitkovszky. Cast: Annie Góth, Alfréd Deésy, Lilla Bársony, Lajos Bónis, Pál Gajdos.

A DOKTOR ÚR (Mr. Doctor). Kino-Riport, 63 min. Screenplay: Sándor

Incze (Ferenc Molnár). DOP: József Bécsi. Cast: György Kürthy, Juci Lábass, Dezső Gyárfás, Gusztáv Vándory, Gyula Szőreghy.

AZ EZÜST KECSKE or *A MEDIKUS* (The Silver Goat or The Medical Student). Kino-Riport, 72 min. Screenplay: Aladár Fodor (Sándor Bródy). Cast: Victor Varconi, Leontine Kühnberg, Rózsi Forgács, Lajos Kemenes, Lucy Doraine, Alfréd Deésy.

A FARKAS (The Wolf). Kino-Riport, 88 min. Screenplay: László Vajda and Michael Curtiz (Ferenc Molnár). DOP: József Bécsi. Cast: Victor Varconi, Frida Gombaszögi, Lucy Doraine.

A FEKETE SZIVÁRVÁNY (The Black Rainbow). Kino-Riport, 68 min. Screenplay: László Békeffy. DOP: József Bécsi. Cast: Vilma Medgyaszay, Gusztáv Vándory, Jenő Ivánffy, Katalin Kertész (Kitty Curtiz).

A MAGYAR FÖLD EREJE (The Power of the Hungarian Soil or The Strength of the Fatherland). P: Magyar Vöröskereszt. Screenplay: Árpád Dános and Michael Curtiz. DOP: József Bécsi. Cast: Alfréd Deésy, Lucy Doraine, Gusztav Vándory, Károly Lajthay.

1917

A HALÁLCSENGŐ or *A LENGYEL ZSIDO* (The Death Bells or The Polish Jew). Star-Film, 41 min. Screenplay: László Békeffy. DOP: Vilmos Gabriel. Cast: Dezső Bánóczy, Gitta B. Gáthy, Lajos Réthey, Gyula Varsa

ZOÁRD MESTER or *ÁRVA MARISKA TÖRTÉNETE* (Master Zoárd or The Story of Orphan Mariska). Phönix-Film. Screenplay: Michael Curtiz. Cast: Gyula Hegedüs, Géza Örvössy, Lajos Réthey.

TATÁRJÁRÁS ("Tartar Invasion"). Glória-Film, 77 min. Screenplay: Michael Curtiz (Imre Kálmán and Károly Bakonyi). DOP: József Bécsi. Cast: Emmi B. Kosáry, Iván Cseh, Kamilla Hollay, Lajos Szalkay.

A KURUZSLÓ ("The Charlatan"). Phönix-Film, 54 min. Screenplay: László Vajda and Iván Siklósi (Imre Földes). DOP: József Bécsi. Cast: Gyula Csortos, Ica Lenkeffy, László Z. Molnár, Giza Báthory, Lajos Réthey.

A SENKI FIA (Mister Nobody or Nobody's Son). Phönix-Film, 78 min. Screenplay: László Vajda and Iván Siklósi. DOP: József Bécsi. Cast: Ica Lenkeffy, Gyula Csortos, Károly Lajthay, Dezső Gyárfás, Hermin Haraszti.

A SZENTJÓBI ERDŐ TITKA (The Secret of Saint Job's Forest). Phönix-Film, 86 min. Screenplay: László Vajda and Iván Siklósi. DOP: József Bécsi. Cast: Jenő Törzs, Dezső Kertész (David Curtiz), Imre Pethes, Giza Báthory, Margit T. Halmi, Lajos Réthey.

AZ UTOLSÓ HAJNAL (The Last Dawn). Phönix-Film, 81 min. Screenplay: László Vajda and Iván Siklósi (Alfred Deutsch-German). DOP: József Bécsi. Cast: Leopold Kramer, Erzsi B. Marton, Jenő Balassa, Kläry Lotto, Andor Kardos.

A FÖLD EMBERE (The Man of the Earth). Phönix-Film. Screenplay: László Vajda. DOP: József Bécsi. Cast: Oszkár Beregi, Gizella Báthory, Giza Mészáros, Ferenc Hegedűs, Dezső Pártos.

A VÖRÖS SÁMSON (The Crimson Samson). Phönix-Film, 90 min. Screenplay: László Vajda (Thomas Henry Hall Caine). DOP: József Bécsi. Cast: László Csiky, Ica Lenkeffy, János Bodnár, Gyula Csortos, Tivadar Uray, Irma F. Lányi.

A BÉKE ÚTJA or *A DIADAL ÚTJA* (The Peace Road or The Victory Road). Phönix-Film, 16 min. Screenplay: Richárd Falk. DOP: József Bécsi.

1918

TAVASZ A TÉLBEN (Spring in Winter). Phönix-Film. Screenplay: Iván Siklósi (Gaston Arman de Caillavet and Robert de Flers). DOPs: József Bécsi and István Eiben. Cast: Ica Lenkeffy, Sándor Góth, Lajos Kemenes, Károly Huszár, Erzsi B. Marton.

A CSÚNYA FIU (The Ugly Boy). Phönix-Film, 70 min. Screenplay: Iván Siklósi. DOP: József Bécsi. Cast: Leopold Kramer, Erzsi B. Marton, Jenő Balassa, Béla Bodonyi, József Sziklay.

EGY KRAJCÁR TÖRTÉNETE or *MESE EGY KRAJCÁRROL* (The Story of a Kreutzer or Tale on a Kreutzer). Phönix-Film, 46 min. Screenplay: Frigyes Karinthy. DOP: József Bécsi. Cast: Gyula Kőváry, László Z. Molnár, Böske T. Oláh, Ferkó Szécsi, Ferenc Hegedűs.

AZ ÁRENDÁS ZSIDÓ (The Jew Tenant or Jean the Tenant). Phönix-Film, 68 min. Screenplay: Richárd Falk and Iván Siklósi (Ilka Klárné Angyal). DOP: József Bécsi. Cast: Gyula Gál, Gizella Báthory, Ica Lenkeffy, Jenő Balassa, Lajos Kemenes.

AZ EZREDES (The Colonel). Phönix-Film, 87 min. Screenplay: Richárd Falk (Ferenc Herczeg). DOP: István Eiben. Cast: Béla Lugosi, Károly Huszár, Sándor Góth, Árpád Latabár, Géza Boross.

LULU. Phönix-Film, 86 min. Screenplay: Iván Siklósi (Pierre Véber). DOP: Lajos Gasser. Cast: Béla Lugosi, Rózsi Ilosvay, Sándor Góth, Kläry Lotto, Hermin Haraszti.

99 or *A 99-ES SZÁMÚ BÉRKOCSI* (The Rental Car Number 99). Phönix-Film, 81 min. Screenplay: Iván Siklósi (R. F. Foster). DOP: István

Eiben. Cast: Victor Varconi, Gyula Gál, Kläry Lotto, Béla Lugosi, Jenő Balassa.

AZ ÖRDÖG (The Devil). Phönix-Film, 92 min. Screenplay: Iván Siklósi (Ferenc Molnár). Cast: Leopold Kramer, Victor Varconi, Kläry Lotto, Erzsi B. Marton, Frigyes Tanay.

A SKORPIÓ I. (The Scorpion, Part One). Phönix-Film, 77 min. Screenplay: Iván Siklósi. DOP: József Bécsi. Cast: Victor Varconi, Kläry Lotto, Jenő Balassa, Margit T. Halmi, Lajos Réthey.

A SKORPIÓ II. (The Scorpion, Part Two). Phönix-Film, 77 min. Screenplay: Iván Siklósi. DOP: József Bécsi. Cast: Victor Varconi, Kläry Lotto, Jenő Balassa, Margit T. Halmi, Lajos Réthey.

JÚDÁS (The Judas). Phönix-Film, 99 min. Screenplay: Iván Siklósi (Max Pemberton). DOP: József Bécsi. Cast: Leopold Kramer, Gyula Gál, Juliska Németh, Kläry Lotto, Jenő Törzs.

GRÓF MONTE CHRISTO (The Count of Monte Christo). Phönix-Film. Screenplay: Iván Siklósi (Alexandre Dumas). DOP: József Bécsi. Unfinished film.

OCSKAY BRIGADÉROS (The Ocskay Brigadier). Phönix-Film. Screenplay: László Márkus (Ferenc Herczeg). DOP: József Bécsi. Cast: Victor Varconi. Unfinished film.

A NAPRAFORGÓS HÖLGY (The Sunflower Lady). Phönix-Film. Screenplay: Iván Siklósi (Ivo Vojnovic). Cast: Erzsi B. Marton, Ivo Badalic, Lucy Doraine, Lajos Kemenes, Kläry Lotto. Unfinished film.

VARÁZSKERINGŐ (The Magic Waltz). Semper-Film, 95 min. Screenplay: Michael Curtiz (Oscar Straus). DOP: Eduard Hösch. Cast: Margit Lux, Victor Varconi, Lajos Újváry, Ilona Bánhidy, Endre Boross.

LU, A KOKOTT or *EGY SZERENCSÉTLEN LÁNY TÖRTÉNETE* (Lu, the Cocotte or The Story of an Unfortunate Girl). Semper-Film, 74 min. Screenplay: Michael Curtiz (Arthur Landsberger). Cast: Margit Lux, Berta Valero, Jenő Balassa, Mária Kelemen, Ernő Tarnay.

A VÍG ÖZVEGY (The Merry Widow). Semper-Film, 77 min. Screenplay: Michael Curtiz (Franz Lehár, Victor Leon, and Leo Stein). Cast: Victor Varconi, Berta Valero, Endre Boross, Árpád Latabár, József Bánhidy.

1919

ALRAUNE. Phönix-Film, 80 min. Screenplay: Richárd Falk (Hanns Heinz Ewers). Cast: Gyula Gál, Géza Erdélyi, Kálmán Körmendy, Margit Lux, Rózsi Szöllösi.

JÖN AZ ÖCSÉM (My Brother Is Coming). 11 min. Screenplay: Iván

Siklósi (Antal Farkas). Cast: Oszkár Beregi, József Kürthy, Lucy Doraine, Ferkó Szécsi.

LILIOM. Screenwriter: László Vajda (Ferenc Molnár). Cast: Ica Lenkeffy, Lajos Réthey, Aladár Sarkadi, Nusi Somogyi, Jenő Virágh. Unfinished when Curtiz left Budapest for Vienna.

DIE DAME MIT DEM SCHWARZEN HANDSCHUH (The Lady of the Black Glove). Sascha-Film, 72 min. Screenplay: Iván Siklósi and Michael Curtiz. DOP: Gustav Ucicky. Cast: Lucy Doraine, Harry Walden.

BOCCACCIOS LIEBESNÄCHTE or *BOCCACCIO* (Boccaccio's Love Nights or Boccaccio). Sascha-Film, 81 min. Screenplay: Paul Frank and Friedrich Porges. DOP: Gustav Ucicky. Cast: Ica Lenkeffy, Paul Lukas.

1920

DIE STERN VON DAMASKUS (The Star of Damascus or The Stars of Damascus Part 1). Sascha-Film, 105 min. Screenplay: Michael Curtiz (Georges Ohnet). DOP: Gustav Ucicky. Cast: Lucy Doraine, Anton Tiller, Ivan Petrovich, Mathilde Danegger, Max-Ralf Ostermann.

DIE GOTTESGEIßEL or *DIE STERNE VON DAMASKUS, 2* (The Whip of God or The Stars of Damascus, Part 2). Sascha-Film, 116 min. Screenplay: Michael Curtiz (Georges Ohnet). DOP: Gustav Ucicky. Cast: Lucy Doraine, Anton Tiller, Ivan Petrovich, Max-Ralf Ostermann.

DIE DAME MIT DEN SONNENBLUMEN (The Sunflower Lady). Sascha-Film, 104 min. Screenplay: Michael Curtiz and Iván Siklósi (Ivo Vojnovic). DOP: Gustav Ucicky. Cast: Lucy Doraine, Erszi Marton, Ivo Badalic, Ivan Petrovich, Lajos Kemenes.

MRS. TUTTI FRUTTI. Sascha-Film, 72 min. Screenplay: Friedrich Porges. DOP: Gustav Ucicky. Cast: Lucy Doraine, Alphons Fryland, Josef König, Oskar Sachs, Armin Springer.

CHERCHEZ LA FEMME! or *HERZOGIN SATANELLA* (Look for the Woman! or Duchess Satanella). Sascha-Film, 106 min. Screenplay: Friedrich Porges. DOP: Gustav Ucicky. Cast: Lucy Doraine, Alphons Fryland, Anton Tiller, Magdalen Nagy, Max-Ralf Ostermann.

1921

FRAU DOROTHYS BEKENNTNIS (Madame Dorothy's Confession). Sascha-Film, 90 min. Screenplay: Michael Curtiz (Zsigmond Móricz). DOPs: Gustav Ucicky, Nikolaus Farkas, and Eduard von Borsody. Cast: Lucy Doraine, Alphons Fryland, Otto Tressler, Louis Salm, Kurt Lessen.

WEGE DES SCHRECKENS or *LABYRINTH DES GRAUENS* (The Terror Road or Labyrinth of Horror). Sascha-Film, 86 min. Screenplay: Fred Wallace. DOP: Gustav Ucicky. Cast: Lucy Doraine, Alphons Fryland, Max Devrient, Jean Ducret, Paul Askonas.

1922

SODOM UND GOMORRHA (Sodom and Gomorrah). Sascha-Film, 97 min. (Part 1), 82 min. (Part 2). Screenplay: László Vajda and Michael Curtiz. DOP: Gustav Ucicky. Cast: Lucy Doraine, Georg Reimers, Walter Slezak, Victor Varconi, Erika Wagner, Kurt Ehrle.

1923

DER JUNGE MEDARDUS (The Young Medardus). Sascha-Film, 153 min. Screenplay: László Vajda and Arthur Schnitzler. DOPs: Gustav Ucicky and Eduard von Borsody. Cast: Victor Varconi, Anny Hornik, Maria Hegyesi, Ágnes Esterházy, Michael Xanthos.
DIE LAWINE (The Avalanche). Sascha-Film, 125 min. Screenplay: László Vajda. DOP: Gustav Ucicky. Cast: Victor Varconi, Mary Kid, Lily Marischka, Gretl Marischka, Mathilde Danegger.
NAMENLOS or *DER SCHARLATAN* or *DER FASCHE ARZT* or *DAS MARTYRIUM EINES ARZTES* (Nameless or The Charlatan or The Fake Doctor or The Martyrdom of a Doctor). Sascha-Film, 108 min. Screenplay: László Vajda (Imre Földes). DOP: Gustav Ucicky. Cast: Victor Varconi, Mary Kid, Hans Lackner, Charles Gardener.

1924

HARUN AL RASCHID or *DER GEHEIMNISVOLLE VON MONTE CARLO* or *EIN SPIEL UMS LEBEN* (Monte Carlo's Mystery Man or A Game on Life or A Deadly Game). Sascha-Film, 104 min. Screenplay: László Vajda (Paul Frank). DOP: Gustav Ucicky. Cast: Henry Blackburn, Adolf Weisse, Mary Kid, Erich Wichl, H. Fuchs, Karl Götz.
GENERAL BABKA. Sascha-Film (no information available).
DIE SKLAVENKÖNIGIN (The King's Slave or The Queen of the Slaves or The Moon of Israel). Sascha-Film and Stoll Picture Productions Ltd., 145 min. Screenplay: László Vajda (Henry Rider Haggard). DOPs: Max Nekut, Gustav Ucicky, Hans Theyer. Cast: Maria Corda, Adelqui Migliar, Arlette Marchal, Adolf Weisse, Ferdinand Onno.

1925

DAS SPIELZEUG VON PARIS (The Toy of Paris or Red Heels). Sascha-Film, 140 min. Screenplay: Michael Curtiz (Margery Lawrence). DOP: Gustav Ucicky. Cast: Lily Damita, Hugo Thimig, Eric Barclay, Georg Tréville, Theo W. Shall.

FIAKER NR. 13 or *EINSPÄNNER NR. 13* (The Carriage Number 13 or The Horse Cart Number 13). Sascha-Film, 117 min. Screenplay: Alfred Schirokauer (Xavier de Montépin). DOPs: Gustav Ucicky and Eduard von Borsody. Cast: Lily Damita, Jack Trevor, Paul Biensfeld, Walter Rilla, Max Gülstorff.

1926

DER GOLDENE SCHMETTERLING (The Golden Butterfly). Sascha-Film, 118 min. Screenplay: Jane Bess and Adolf Lantz (P. G. Wodehouse and Fred Thompson). DOPs: Gustav Ucicky and Eduard von Borsody. Cast: Hermann Leffler, Lily Damita, Nils Asther, Curt Bois, Ferdinand Bonn.

THE THIRD DEGREE. Warner Bros., 80 min. AP & AD: Henry Blanke. Screenplay: Graham Baker (Charles Klein). DOP: Hal Mohr. Cast: Dolores Costello, Louise Dresser, Rockliffe Fellowes, Jason Robards Sr., Kate Price.

1927

A MILLION BID. Warner Bros., 70 min. P: Henry Blanke. Screenplay: Robert Dillon (George Cameron, i.e., Mrs. Sidney Drew). DOP: Hal Mohr. Cast: Dolores Costello, Warner Oland, Malcolm McGregor, Betty Blythe, William Demarest.

THE DESIRED WOMAN. Warner Bros., 70 min. Ps: Darryl Zanuck, Henry Blanke. Screenplay: Anthony Coldeway (Mark Canfield, i.e., Zanuck). Cast: Irene Rich, William Russell, William Collier Jr., Douglas Gerrard, Jack Ackroyd.

GOOD TIME CHARLEY. Warner Bros., 70 min. P: Darryl Zanuck. Screenplay: Anthony Coldeway, Ilona Fulop, Owen Francis (Darryl Zanuck). DOP: Barney McGill. Cast: Helene Costello, Warner Oland, Clyde Cook, Montagu Love, Hugh Allan.

1928

TENDERLOIN. Warner Bros., 85 min. P: Darryl Zanuck. Screenplay: Joseph Jackson, Edward T. Lowe Jr. (Darryl Zanuck). DOP: Hal Mohr. Cast: Dolores Costello, Conrad Nagel, Mitchell Lewis, Dan Wolheim, John Miljan.

NOAH'S ARK. Warner Bros., 135 min. P: Darryl Zanuck. Screenplay: Anthony Coldeway, Bess Meredyth, Michael Curtiz, Darryl Zanuck. DOPs: Hal Mohr, Barney McGill. Cast: Dolores Costello, George O'Brien, Noah Beery, Louise Fazenda, Guinn "Big Boy" Williams.

1929

GLAD RAG DOLL. Warner Bros., 70 min. P: Darryl Zanuck. Screenplay: C. Graham Baker (Harvey Gates). DOP: Byron Haskin. Cast: Dolores Costello, Ralph Graves, Audrey Ferris, Albert Gran, Maude Turner Gordon.

MADONNA OF AVENUE A. Warner Bros., 71 min. P: Darryl Zanuck. Screenplay: Ray Doyle, Francis Powers (Mark Canfield, i.e., Darryl Zanuck). DOP: Byron Haskin. Cast: Dolores Costello, Grant Withers, Douglas Gerrard, Louise Dresser, Otto Hoffman.

THE GAMBLERS. Warner Bros., 60 min. P: Darryl Zanuck. Screenplay: J. Grubb Alexander (Charles Klein). DOP: William Rees. Cast: H. B. Warner, Lois Wilson, Jason Robards Sr., George Fawcett.

HEARTS IN EXILE. Warner Bros., 82 min. P: Darryl Zanuck. Screenplay: Harvey Gates (John Oxenham). DOP: William Rees. Cast: Dolores Costello, Grant Withers, James Kirkwood, George Fawcett, David Torrence.

1930

MAMMY. Warner Bros., 84 min. P: Darryl Zanuck. Technicolor. Screenplay: Joseph Jackson, Gordon Rigby (Irving Berlin, James Gleason). DOP: Barney McGill. Cast: Al Jolson, Lois Moran, Lowell Sherman, Louise Dresser, Hobart Bosworth.

UNDER A TEXAS MOON. Warner Bros., 82 min. Technicolor. P: Darryl Zanuck. Screenplay: Gordon Rigby (Stewart Edward White). DOP: William Rees. Cast: Frank Fay, Raquel Torres, Myrna Loy, Armida, Noah Beery.

THE MATRIMONIAL BED. Warner Bros., 69 min. P: Darryl Zanuck. Screenplay: Harvey F. Thew, Seymour Hicks (Yves Mirande, André Mouézy-Éon). DOP: Dev Jennings. Cast: Frank Fay, James Gleason, Lilyan Tashman, Beryl Mercer, Florence Eldridge.

BRIGHT LIGHTS. Warner Bros., 69 min. Technicolor. P: Darryl Zanuck. Screenplay: Humphrey Pearson, Henry McCarty. DOP: Lee Garmes. Cast: Dorothy Mackaill, Frank Fay, Noah Beery, Daphne Pollard, James Murray.

RIVER'S END. Warner Bros., 75 min. P: Darryl Zanuck. Screenplay: Charles Kenyon (James Oliver Curwood). DOP: Robert Kurrie. Cast: Charles Bickford, Evelyn Knapp, J. Farrell McDonald, Zasu Pitts, Frank Coghlan Jr.

A SOLDIER'S PLAYTHING. Warner Bros., 56 min. P: Darryl Zanuck. Screenplay: Perry N. Vekroff, Arthur Caesar (Vina Delmar). DOP: Barney McGill. Cast: Ben Lyon, Harry Langdon, Lotti Loder, Noah Beery, Fred Kohler, Lee Moran.

1931

DÄMON DES MEERES (Demon of the Sea). Warner Bros., 81 min. P: Henry Blanke. Screenplay: Ulrich Steindorff, J. Grubb Alexander (Herman Melville). DOP: Sid Hickox. Cast: William Dieterle, Lissy Arna, Anton Pointer, Karl Etlinger, Carla Bartheel.

GOD'S GIFT TO WOMEN. Warner Bros., 72 min. P: Darryl Zanuck. Screenplay: Joseph Jackson, Raymond Griffith, Frederick Hazlitt Brennan (Jane Hinton). DOP: Robert Kurrie. Cast: Frank Fay, Laura La Plante, Joan Blondell, Charles Winninger, Alan Mowbray.

THE MAD GENIUS. Warner Bros., 81 min. P: Darryl Zanuck. Screenplay: J. Grubb Alexander, Harvey F. Thew (Martin Brown). DOP: Barney McGill. Cast: John Barrymore, Marian Marsh, Charles Butterworth, Donald Cook, Luis Alberni.

1932

THE WOMAN FROM MONTE CARLO. Warner Bros./First National, 65 min. P: Darryl Zanuck. Screenplay: Harvey Thew (Claude Farrère, Lucien Népoty). DOP: Ernest Haller. Cast: Lil Dagover, Walter Huston, Warren William, John Wray, George E. Stone.

ALIAS THE DOCTOR. Warner Bros./First National, 61 min. P: Darryl Zanuck. Screenplay: Houston Branch, Charles Kenyon (Imre Földes).

DOP: Barney McGill. Cast: Richard Barthelmess, Marian Marsh, Norman Foster, Adrienne Dore, Lucille La Verne.

THE STRANGE LOVE OF MOLLY LOUVAIN. Warner Bros./First National, 73 min. P: Hal Wallis. Screenplay: Erwin S. Gelsey, Brown Holmes (Maurine Dallas Watkins). DOP: Robert Kurrie. Cast: Ann Dvorak, Lee Tracy, Richard Cromwell, Guy Kibbee, Leslie Fenton.

DOCTOR X. Warner Bros./First National, 76 min. Technicolor. Ps: Darryl Zanuck, Hal Wallis. Screenplay: Robert Tasker, Earl Baldwin, George Rosener (Howard Warren Comstock, Allen C. Miller). DOP: Ray Rennahan. Cast: Lionel Atwill, Fay Wray, Lee Tracy, Preston Foster, John Wray.

THE CABIN IN THE COTTON. Warner Bros./First National, 78 min. Ps: Darryl Zanuck, Hal Wallis. Screenplay: Paul Green (Harry Harrison Kroll). DOP: Barney McGill. Cast: Richard Barthelmess, Dorothy Jordan, Bette Davis, Hardie Albright, David Landau.

20,000 YEARS IN SING SING. Warner Bros./First National, 78 min. Ps: Darryl Zanuck, Robert Lord. Screenplay: Wilson Mizner, Brown Holmes, Courtney Terrett, Robert Lord (Lewis E. Lawes). DOP: Barney McGill. Cast: Spencer Tracy, Bette Davis, Arthur Byron, Lyle Talbot, Warren Hymer.

1933

MYSTERY OF THE WAX MUSEUM. Warner Bros., 77 min. Technicolor. Ps: Hal Wallis, Henry Blanke. Screenplay: Don Mullaly, Carl Erickson (Charles Belden). DOP: Ray Rennahan. Cast: Lionel Atwill, Fay Wray, Glenda Farrell, Frank McHugh, Allen Vincent.

THE KEYHOLE. Warner Bros., 69 min. P: Hal Wallis. Screenplay: Robert Presnell Sr. (Alice Duer Miller). DOP: Barney McGill. Cast: Kay Francis, George Brent, Glenda Farrell, Monroe Owsley, Allen Jenkins.

PRIVATE DETECTIVE 62. Warner Bros., 66 min. P: Hal Wallis. Screenplay: Rian James (Raoul Whitfield). DOP: Tony Gaudio. Cast: William Powell, Margaret Lindsay, Ruth Donnelly, Gordon Westcott.

THE MAYOR OF HELL. Warner Bros., 90 min. P: Hal Wallis. D: Archie Mayo (Curtiz directed ten hours of retakes on this film). Screenplay: Edward Chodorov (Islin Auster). Cast: James Cagney, Madge Evans, Arthur Byron, Allen Jenkins, Dudley Digges.

GOODBYE AGAIN. Warner Bros./First National, 66 min. Ps: Hal Wallis, Henry Blanke. Screenplay: Ben Markson (George Haight, Alan Scott). DOP: George Barnes. Cast: Warren William, Joan Blondell, Genevieve Tobin, Hugh Herbert, Wallace Ford.

THE KENNEL MURDER CASE. Warner Bros., 73 min. P: Hal Wallis. Screenplay: Robert N. Lee, Peter Milne, Robert Presnell Sr. (S. S. Van Dine). DOP: William Rees. Cast: William Powell, Mary Astor, Eugene Pallette, Ralph Morgan, Robert McWade.
FEMALE. Warner Bros./First National, 60 min. Ps: Hal Wallis, Robert Presnell Sr. (William Wellman and Curtiz jointly directed; Curtiz was credited). Screenplay: Gene Markey, Kathryn Scola (Donald Henderson Clarke). Cast: Ruth Chatterton, George Brent, Lois Wilson, Johnny Mack Brown, Ruth Donnelly.

1934

MANDALAY. Warner Bros., 65 min. P: Hal Wallis. Screenplay: Austin Parker, Charles Kenyon (Paul Hervey Fox). DOP: Tony Gaudio. Cast: Kay Francis, Ricardo Cortez, Warner Oland, Lyle Talbot, Ruth Donnelly.
JIMMY THE GENT. Warner Bros., 67 min. Ps: Hal Wallis, Robert Lord. Screenplay: Bertram Millhouser, Laird Doyle, Ray Nazarro. DOP: Ira Morgan. Cast: James Cagney, Bette Davis, Allen Jenkins, Alan Dinehart, Alice White.
THE KEY. Warner Bros., 71 min. Ps: Hal Wallis, Robert Presnell Sr. Screenplay: Laird Doyle, (Joseph Lee Hardy, Robert Gore-Browne). DOP: Ernest Haller. Cast: William Powell, Edna Best, Colin Clive, Hobart Cavanaugh, Halliwell Hobbes.
BRITISH AGENT. Warner Bros./First National, 80 min. Ps: Hal Wallis, Henry Blanke. Screenplay: Laird Doyle (R. H. Bruce Lockhart). DOP: Ernest Haller. Cast: Leslie Howard, Kay Francis, William Gargan, Philip Reed, Irving Pichel.

1935

BLACK FURY. Warner Bros./First National, 94 min. Ps: Hal Wallis, Robert Lord. Screenplay: Abem Finkel, Carl Erickson (Michael A. Musmanno, Harry R. Irving). DOP: Byron Haskin. Cast: Paul Muni, Karen Morley, William Gargan, Barton MacLane, John Qualen.
THE CASE OF THE CURIOUS BRIDE. Warner Bros., 80 min. Ps: Hal Wallis, Harry Joe Brown. Screenplay: Tom Reed, Brown Holmes (Erle Stanley Gardner). DOP: David Abel. Cast: Warren William, Margaret Lindsay, Donald Woods, Claire Dodd, Allen Jenkins.
GO INTO YOUR DANCE. Warner Bros./First National, 89 min. Ps: Hal Wallis, Sam Bischoff. D: Archie Mayo (Curtiz directed six scenes

and retakes). Screenplay: Earl Baldwin (Bradford Ropes). Cast: Al Jolson, Ruby Keeler, Glenda Farrell, Barton MacLane, Patsy Kelly.

FRONT PAGE WOMAN. Warner Bros., 82 min. Ps: Hal Wallis, Sam Bischoff. Screenplay: Laird Doyle, Lillie Hayward, Roy Chanslor (Richard Macaulay). DOP: Tony Gaudio. Cast: Bette Davis, George Brent, Roscoe Karns, Wini Shaw, Walter Walker.

LITTLE BIG SHOT. Warner Bros., 78 min. Ps: Hal Wallis, Sam Bischoff. Screenplay: Jerry Wald, Julius Epstein, Robert Hardy Andrews (Harrison Jacobs). DOP: Tony Gaudio. Cast: Sybil Jason, Glenda Farrell, Robert Armstrong, Edward Everett Horton, Jack La Rue.

CAPTAIN BLOOD. Warner Bros., Cosmopolitan Pictures, 119 min. Ps: Hal Wallis, Harry Joe Brown. Screenplay: Casey Robinson (Rafael Sabatini). DOPs: Hal Mohr, Ernest Haller. Cast: Errol Flynn, Olivia de Havilland, Lionel Atwill, Basil Rathbone, Ross Alexander.

1936

THE WALKING DEAD. Warner Bros., 66 min. Ps: Hal Wallis, Louis Edelman. Screenplay: Ewart Anderson, Peter Milne, Robert Andrews, Lillie Hayward (Joseph Fields). DOP: Hal Mohr. Cast: Boris Karloff, Ricardo Cortez, Edmund Gwenn, Marguerite Churchill, Warren Hull.

ANTHONY ADVERSE. Warner Bros., 141 min. Ps: Hal Wallis, Henry Blanke. D: Mervyn LeRoy (Curtiz directed opening sequence). Screenplay: Sheridan Gibney, Milton Krims, Edward Chodorov (Hervey Allen). DOP: Tony Gaudio. Cast: Fredric March, Olivia de Havilland, Donald Woods, Anita Louise, Edmund Gwenn.

THE CHARGE OF THE LIGHT BRIGADE. Warner Bros., 115 min. Ps: Hal Wallis, Sam Bischoff. Screenplay: Rowland Leigh, Michel Jacoby (Alfred, Lord Tennyson). Cast: Errol Flynn, Olivia de Havilland, Patric Knowles, Henry Stephenson, Nigel Bruce.

1937

BLACK LEGION. Warner Bros., 83 min. Ps: Hal Wallis, Robert Lord. D: Archie Mayo (Curtiz directed several sequences, including the climactic courtroom scene). Screenplay: Abem Finkel, William Wister Haines (Robert Lord). DOP: George Barnes. Cast: Humphrey Bogart, Dick Foran, Erin O'Brien-Moore, Ann Sheridan.

STOLEN HOLIDAY. Warner Bros., 80 min. Ps: Hal Wallis, Harry Joe Brown. Screenplay: Casey Robinson, Warren Duff (Virginia Kellogg).

DOP: Sid Hickox. Cast: Kay Francis, Claude Rains, Ian Hunter, Alison Skipworth, Alexander D'Arcy.

MARKED WOMAN. Warner Bros., 96 min. P: Hal Wallis, Louis Edelman. D: Lloyd Bacon (Curtiz directed ten scenes). Screenplay: Robert Rossen, Abem Finkel, Seton I. Miller. DOP: George Barnes. Cast: Bette Davis, Humphrey Bogart, Lola Lane, Isabel Jewell, Mayo Methot.

MOUNTAIN JUSTICE. Warner Bros., 83 min. Ps: Hal Wallis, Henry Blanke. Screenplay: Norman Reilly Raine, Luci Ward. DOP: Ernest Haller. Cast: George Brent, Josephine Hutchinson, Guy Kibbee, Mona Barrie, Robert Barrat.

KID GALAHAD (THE BATTLING BELLHOP). Warner Bros., 102 min. Ps: Hal Wallis, Sam Bischoff. Screenplay: Seton I. Miller (Francis Wallace). DOP: Tony Gaudio. Cast: Edward G. Robinson, Bette Davis, Humphrey Bogart, Wayne Morris, Jane Bryan.

THE PERFECT SPECIMEN. Warner Bros., 88 min. Ps: Hal Wallis, Harry Joe Brown. Screenplay: Norman Reilly Raine, Lawrence Riley, Brewster Morse, Fritz Falkenstein, Julius Epstein, Jay Brennan, Lawrence Kimble, Nathaniel Curtis (Samuel Hopkins Adams). DOP: Charles Rosher. Cast: Errol Flynn, Joan Blondell, Hugh Herbert, Edward Everett Horton, Dick Foran.

1938

GOLD IS WHERE YOU FIND IT. Warner Bros., 94 min. Technicolor. Ps: Hal Wallis, Sam Bischoff. Screenplay: Robert Buckner, Warren Duff (Clement Ripley). DOP: Sol Polito. Cast: George Brent, Olivia de Havilland, Claude Rains, Margaret Lindsay, John Litel.

THE ADVENTURES OF ROBIN HOOD. Warner Bros., 102 min. Technicolor. Ps: Hal Wallis, Henry Blanke. Ds: Curtiz codirected with William Keighley. Screenplay: Norman Reilly Raine, Seton I. Miller, Rowland Leigh. DOPs: Tony Gaudio, Sol Polito. Cast: Errol Flynn, Olivia de Havilland, Basil Rathbone, Claude Rains, Patric Knowles.

FOUR'S A CROWD. Warner Bros., 92 min. Ps: Hal Wallis, David Lewis. Screenplay: Casey Robinson, Sid Herzig (Wallace Sullivan). DOP: Ernest Haller. Cast: Errol Flynn, Olivia de Havilland, Rosalind Russell, Patric Knowles, Walter Connolly.

FOUR DAUGHTERS. Warner Bros., 90 min. Ps: Hal Wallis, Henry Blanke. Screenplay: Julius Epstein, Philip Epstein, Lenore Coffee (Fannie Hurst). DOP: Ernest Haller. Cast: Claude Rains, Jeffrey Lynn, John Garfield, Frank McHugh, May Robson.

ANGELS WITH DIRTY FACES. Warner Bros., 97 min. Ps: Hal Wallis, Sam Bischoff. Screenplay: John Wexley, Warren Duff, Ben Hecht, Charles MacArthur (Rowland Brown). DOP: Sol Polito. Cast: James Cagney, Pat O'Brien, Humphrey Bogart, Ann Sheridan, George Bancroft.

1939

BLACKWELL'S ISLAND. Warner Bros., 71 min. P: Bryan Foy. D: William McGann (Curtiz directed retakes and added scenes). Screenplay: Crane Wilbur, Lee Katz. DOP: Sid Hickox. Cast: John Garfield, Rosemary Lane, Dick Purcell, Victory Jury, Stanley Fields.

DODGE CITY. Warner Bros., 104 min. Technicolor. Ps: Hal Wallis, Robert Lord. Screenplay: Robert Buckner. Cast: Errol Flynn, Olivia de Havilland, Ann Sheridan, Bruce Cabot, Frank McHugh.

SONS OF LIBERTY. Warner Bros., 20 min. Technicolor. P: Gordon Hollingshead. Screenplay: Crane Wilbur. DOPs: Sol Polito, Ray Rennahan. Cast: Claude Rains, Gale Sondergaard, Donald Crisp, Montagu Love, Henry O'Neill.

DAUGHTERS COURAGEOUS. Warner Bros., 107 min. Ps: Hal Wallis, Henry Blanke. Screenplay: Julius Epstein, Philip Epstein (Dorothy Bennett, Irving White). DOPs: James Wong Howe, Ernest Haller. Cast: John Garfield, Claude Rains, Jeffrey Lynn, Fay Bainter, Donald Crisp.

THE PRIVATE LIVES OF ELIZABETH AND ESSEX. Warner Bros., 106 min. Technicolor. Ps: Hal Wallis, Robert Lord. Screenplay: Norman Reilly Raine, Aeneas MacKenzie (Maxwell Anderson). DOP: Sol Polito. Cast: Bette Davis, Errol Flynn, Olivia de Havilland, Donald Crisp, Alan Hale.

FOUR WIVES. Warner Bros., 110 min. Ps: Hal Wallis, Henry Blanke. Screenplay: Julius Epstein, Philip Epstein, Maurice Hanline, Lenore Coffee. DOP: Sol Polito, James Wong Howe. Cast: Priscilla Lane, Rosemary Lane, Lola Lane, Gale Page, Claude Rains.

1940

VIRGINIA CITY. Warner Bros., 121 min. Ps: Hal Wallis, Robert Fellows. Screenplay: Robert Buckner, Howard Koch, Norman Reilly Raine. DOP: Sol Polito. Cast: Errol Flynn, Miriam Hopkins, Randolph Scott, Humphrey Bogart, Frank McHugh.

THE SEA HAWK. Warner Bros., 127 min. Ps: Hal Wallis, Henry Blanke.

Screenplay: Howard Koch, Seton I. Miller. DOP: Sol Polito. Cast: Errol Flynn, Brenda Marshall, Claude Rains, Donald Crisp, Flora Robson.
SANTA FE TRAIL. Warner Bros., 110 min. Ps: Hal Wallis, Robert Fellows. Screenplay: Robert Buckner. DOP: Sol Polito. Cast: Errol Flynn, Olivia de Havilland, Raymond Massey, Ronald Reagan, Alan Hale.

1941

THE SEA WOLF. Warner Bros., 100 min. Ps: Hal Wallis, Henry Blanke. Screenplay: Robert Rossen (Jack London). DOP: Sol Polito. Cast: Edward G. Robinson, Ida Lupino, John Garfield, Alexander Knox, Gene Lockhart.
DIVE BOMBER. Warner Bros., 132 min. Technicolor. Ps: Hal Wallis, Robert Lord. Screenplay: Robert Buckner, Frank Wead. DOPs: Bert Glennon, Winton C. Hoch. Cast: Errol Flynn, Fred MacMurray, Ralph Bellamy, Alexis Smith, Robert Armstrong.

1942

CAPTAINS OF THE CLOUDS. Warner Bros., 114 min. Technicolor. Ps: Hal Wallis, William Cagney. Screenplay: Arthur T. Horman, Richard Macaulay, Norman Reilly Raine (Horman and Roland Gillett). DOPs: Sol Polito, Wilfred Cline, Winton C. Hoch, Elmer Dyer. Cast: James Cagney, Dennis Morgan, Brenda Marshall, Alan Hale, George Tobias.
YANKEE DOODLE DANDY. Warner Bros., 126 min. Ps: Hal Wallis, William Cagney. Screenplay: Robert Buckner, Edmund Joseph, Julius Epstein, Philip Epstein. DOP: James Wong Howe. Cast: James Cagney, Joan Leslie, Walter Huston, Richard Whorf, Irene Manning.
CASABLANCA. Warner Bros., 102 min. P: Hal Wallis. Screenplay: Julius Epstein, Philip Epstein, Howard Koch, Casey Robinson (Murray Burnett, Joan Alison). DOP: Arthur Edeson. Cast: Humphrey Bogart, Ingrid Bergman, Paul Henried, Claude Rains, Conrad Veidt.

1943

MISSION TO MOSCOW. Warner Bros., 124 min. Ps: Jack L. Warner, Robert Buckner. Screenplay: Howard Koch (Joseph Davies). DOP: Bert Glennon. Cast: Walter Huston, Ann Harding, Oskar Homolka, George Tobias, Gene Lockhart.
THIS IS THE ARMY. Warner Bros., 121 min. Technicolor. Ps: Jack L.

Warner, Hal Wallis. Screenplay: Casey Robinson, Claude Binyon, Julius Epstein, Philip Epstein (Irving Berlin). DOPs: Bert Glennon, Sol Polito. Cast: George Murphy, Joan Leslie, George Tobias, Alan Hale, Dolores Costello.

1944

PASSAGE TO MARSEILLE. Warner Bros., 110 min. P: Hal Wallis. Screenplay: Casey Robinson, Jack Moffitt (Charles Nordhoff, James Norman Hall). DOP: James Wong Howe. Cast: Humphrey Bogart, Claude Rains, Michèle Morgan, Philip Dorn, Sydney Greenstreet.
JANIE. Warner Bros., 102 min. P: Alex Gottlieb. Screenplay: Agnes Christine Johnston, Charles Hoffman (Josephine Bentham, Herschel V. Williams Jr.). DOP: Carl Guthrie. Cast: Joyce Reynolds, Robert Hutton, Edward Arnold, Ann Harding, Richard Erdman.

1945

ROUGHLY SPEAKING. Warner Bros., 117 min. P: Henry Blanke. Screenplay: Louise Randall Pierson, Catherine Turney (Pierson). DOP: Joseph Walker. Cast: Rosalind Russell, Jack Carson, Robert Hutton, Jean Sullivan, Donald Woods.
MILDRED PIERCE. Warner Bros., 111 min. P: Jerry Wald. Screenplay: Ranald MacDougall, Catherine Turney, William Faulkner, Louise Randall Pierson, Thames Williamson. DOP: Ernest Haller. Cast: Joan Crawford, Jack Carson, Zachary Scott, Eve Arden, Ann Blyth.

1946

NIGHT AND DAY. Warner Bros., 128 min. Technicolor. P: Arthur Schwartz. Screenplay: Charles Hoffman, Leo Townsend, William Bowers, Jack Moffitt. DOPs: Peverell Marley, Bert Glennon, Ernest Haller. Cast: Cary Grant, Alexis Smith, Monty Woolley, Ginny Simms, Jane Wyman.

1947

LIFE WITH FATHER. Warner Bros., 118 min. Technicolor. P: Robert Buckner. Screenplay: David Ogden Stewart (Howard Lindsay, Russel Crouse, Clarence Day). DOPs: Peverell Marley, William V. Skall. Cast:

William Powell, Irene Dunne, Elizabeth Taylor, Edmund Gwenn, Zasu Pitts.
THE UNSUSPECTED. Michael Curtiz Productions, Warner Bros., 103 min. Ps: Curtiz, Charles Hoffman, George Amy. Screenplay: Ranald MacDougall, Bess Meredyth (Charlotte Armstrong). DOP: Elwood Bredell. Cast: Joan Caulfield, Claude Rains, Audrey Totter, Constance Bennett, Hurd Hatfield.

1948

ROMANCE ON THE HIGH SEAS. Michael Curtiz Productions, Warner Bros., 99 min. Technicolor. Ps: Curtiz, Alex Gottlieb, George Amy. (Musical sequences directed by Busby Berkeley.) Screenplay: Julius Epstein, Philip Epstein, I. A. L. Diamond (Sixto Pondal Ríos, Carlos A. Olivari). DOP: Elwood Bredell. Cast: Jack Carson, Janis Paige, Don DeFore, Doris Day, Oscar Levant.

1949

MY DREAM IS YOURS. Michael Curtiz Productions, Warner Bros., 101 min. Technicolor. Ps: Curtiz, George Amy. Screenplay: Harry Kurnitz, Dane Lussier (Allen Rivkin, Laura Kerr). DOPs: Ernest Haller, Wilfred Cline. Cast: Jack Carson, Doris Day, Lee Bowman, Adolph Menjou, Eve Arden.
FLAMINGO ROAD. Michael Curtiz Productions, Warner Bros., 94 min. Ps: Curtiz, Jerry Wald, George Amy. Screenplay: Robert Wilder, Edmund North (Wilder and Sally Wilder). DOP: Ted McCord. Cast: Joan Crawford, Zachary Scott, Sydney Greenstreet, David Brian, Gladys George.
THE LADY TAKES A SAILOR. Warner Bros., 99 min. P: Harry Kurnitz. Screenplay: Everett Freeman (Jerome Gruskin). DOP: Ted McCord. Cast: Jane Wyman, Dennis Morgan, Eve Arden, Robert Douglas, Allyn Joslyn.

1950

YOUNG MAN WITH A HORN. Warner Bros., 112 min. P: Jerry Wald. Screenplay: Carl Foreman, Edmund H. North (Dorothy Baker). DOP: Ted McCord. Cast: Kirk Douglas, Lauren Bacall, Doris Day, Hoagy Carmichael, Juano Hernandez.
BRIGHT LEAF. Warner Bros., 110 min. P: Henry Blanke. Screenplay:

Ranald MacDougall (Foster Fitzsimmons). DOP: Karl Freund. Cast: Gary Cooper, Lauren Bacall, Patricia Neal, Jack Carson, Donald Crisp.
THE BREAKING POINT. Warner Bros., 97 min. P: Jerry Wald. Screenplay: Ranald MacDougall (Ernest Hemingway). DOP: Ted McCord. Cast: John Garfield, Patricia Neal, Phyllis Thaxter, Juano Hernandez, Wallace Ford.

1951

FORCE OF ARMS (A GUY NAMED JOE). Warner Bros., 99 min. P: Anthony Veiller. Screenplay: Orin Jannings (Richard Tregaskis). DOP: Ted McCord. Cast: William Holden, Nancy Olson, Frank Lovejoy, Gene Evans, Dick Wesson.
JIM THORPE—ALL AMERICAN. Warner Bros., 107 min. P: Everett Freeman. Screenplay: Douglas Morrow, Everett Freeman (Morrow, Vincent X. Flaherty, Russell Birdwell, Jim Thorpe). DOP: Ernest Haller. Cast: Burt Lancaster, Charles Bickford, Steve Cochran, Phyllis Thaxter, Dick Wesson.
I'LL SEE YOU IN MY DREAMS. Warner Bros., 110 min. P: Louis Edelman. Screenplay: Melville Shavelson, Jack Rose (Edelman, Grace Kahn). DOP: Ted McCord. Cast: Doris Day, Danny Thomas, Frank Lovejoy, Patrice Wymore.

1952

THE STORY OF WILL ROGERS. Warner Bros., 109 min. Technicolor. P: Robert Arthur. Screenplay: Frank Davis, Stanley Roberts, Jack Moffitt (Betty Blake Rogers). DOP: Wilfred M. Cline. Cast: Will Rogers Jr., Jane Wyman, Carl Benton Reid, Eve Miller, James Gleason.
THE JAZZ SINGER. Warner Bros., 110 min. Technicolor. P: Louis Edelman. Screenplay: Frank Davis, Leonard Stern, Lewis Meltzer (Samuel Raphaelson). DOP: Carl Guthrie. Cast: Danny Thomas, Peggy Lee, Eduard Franz, Mildred Dunnock, Alex Gerry.

1953

TROUBLE ALONG THE WAY. Warner Bros., 110 min. P: Melville Shavelson. Screenplay: Shavelson, Jack Rose (Douglas Morrow, Robert Hardy Andrews). DOP: Archie Stout. Cast: John Wayne, Donna Reed, Charles Coburn, Tom Tully, Sherry Jackson.

1954

THE BOY FROM OKLAHOMA. Warner Bros., 87 min. Technicolor. P: David Weisbart. Screenplay: Frank Davis, Winston Miller (Michael Fessier). DOP: Robert Burks. Cast: Will Rogers Jr., Nancy Olson, Lon Chaney Jr., Anthony Caruso, Wallace Ford.
WHITE CHRISTMAS. Paramount, 120 min. VistaVision, Technicolor. P: Robert Emmett Dolan. Screenplay: Norman Krasna, Norman Panama, Melvin Frank, Melville Shavelson. DOP: Loyal Griggs. Cast: Bing Crosby, Danny Kaye, Rosemary Clooney, Vera-Ellen, Dean Jagger.
THE EGYPTIAN. Twentieth Century-Fox, 140 min. CinemaScope, Technicolor. P: Darryl Zanuck. Screenplay: Casey Robinson, Philip Dunne (Mika Waltari). DOP: Leon Shamroy. Cast: Jean Simmons, Victor Mature, Gene Tierney, Michael Wilding, Bella Darvi.

1955

WE'RE NO ANGELS. Paramount, 106 min. VistaVision, Technicolor. P: Pat Duggan. Screenplay: Ranald MacDougall (Albert Husson). DOP: Loyal Griggs. Cast: Humphrey Bogart, Aldo Ray, Peter Ustinov, Joan Bennett, Basil Rathbone.

1956

THE SCARLET HOUR. Paramount, 95 min. VistaVision. P: Curtiz. Screenplay: John Meredyth Lucas, Alford Von Ronkel (Frank Tashlin). Cast: Carol Ohmart, Tom Tryon, Jody Lawrance, James Gregory.
THE VAGABOND KING. Paramount, 86 min. VistaVision, Technicolor. P: Pat Duggan. Screenplay: Ken Englund, Noel Langley (Jason Huntly McCarthy, William H. Post, Rudolf Friml). DOP: Robert Burks. Cast: Kathryn Grayson, Oreste Kirkop, Rita Moreno, Cedric Hardwicke, Walter Hampden.
THE BEST THINGS IN LIFE ARE FREE. Twentieth Century-Fox, 104 min. CinemaScope, Technicolor. P: Henry Ephron. Screenplay: William Bowers, Phoebe Ephron (John O'Hara). DOP: Leon Shamroy. Cast: Gordon MacRae, Dan Dailey, Ernest Borgnine, Sheree North, Tommy Noonan.

1957

THE HELEN MORGAN STORY. Warner Bros., 118 min. P: Martin Rackin. Screenplay: Nelson Gidding, Stephen Longstreet, Dean Riesner, Oscar Saul. DOP: Ted McCord. Cast: Ann Blyth, Paul Newman, Richard Carlson, Gene Evans, Alan King.

1958

THE PROUD REBEL. Formosa Productions, Buena Vista, 103 min. Technicolor. P: Samuel Goldwyn Jr. Screenplay: Joseph Petracca, Lillie Hayward (James Edward Grant). DOP: Ted McCord. Cast: Alan Ladd, Olivia de Havilland, Dean Jagger, David Ladd, Cecil Kellaway.
KING CREOLE. Paramount, Hal Wallis Productions, 116 min. Ps: Hal Wallis, Paul Nathan. Screenplay: Michael V. Gazzo, Herbert Baker, Oscar Saul (Harold Robbins). DOP: Russell Harlan. Cast: Elvis Presley, Carolyn Jones, Walter Matthau, Dolores Hart, Dean Jagger.

1959

THE MAN IN THE NET. Mirisch-Jaguar, 97 min. Ps: Walter Mirisch, Alan Ladd. Screenplay: Reginald Rose (Hugh Wheeler). DOP: John Seitz. Cast: Alan Ladd, Carolyn Brewster, John Lupton, Charles McGraw.
THE HANGMAN. Paramount, 87 min. Technicolor. P: Frank Freeman Jr. Screenplay: Dudley Nichols, W. R. Burnett (Luke Short). DOP: Loyal Griggs. Cast: Robert Taylor, Tina Louise, Fess Parker, Jack Lord, Gene Evans.

1960

A BREATH OF SCANDAL. Titanus, Paramount, 97 min. Technicolor. P: Carlo Ponti. Screenplay: Walter Bernstein, Ring Lardner Jr., Sidney Howard, Karl Schneider (Ferenc Molnár). DOP: Mario Montuori. Cast: Sophia Loren, Maurice Chevalier, John Gavin, Angela Lansbury, Isabel Jeans.
THE ADVENTURES OF HUCKLEBERRY FINN. Formosa Productions, MGM, 107 min. Technicolor. P: Sam Goldwyn Jr. Screenplay: James Lee (Mark Twain). DOP: Ted McCord. Cast: Tony Randall, Archie Moore, Eddie Hodges, Patty McCormack, Neville Brand.

1961

FRANCIS OF ASSISI. Perseus Productions, Twentieth Century-Fox, 105 min. CinemaScope, Technicolor. P: Plato A. Skouras. Screenplay: Eugene Vale, James Forsyth, Jack Thomas (Ludwig von Wohl). DOP: Piero Portalupi. Cast: Bradford Dillman, Dolores Hart, Stuart Whitman, Cecil Kellaway, Eduard Franz.

1962

THE COMANCHEROS. Twentieth Century-Fox, 107 min. Cinema-Scope, Technicolor. P: George Sherman. (John Wayne directed half or more of Curtiz's final film.) Screenplay: James Edward Grant, Clair Huffaker (Paul Wellman). DOP: William Clothier. Cast: John Wayne, Stuart Whitman, Ina Balin, Nehemiah Persoff, Lee Marvin.

Other Work

1913

ATLANTIS. Nordisk Films, 117 min. P: Ole Olsen. D: August Blom. Screenplay: Karl-Ludwig Schröder, Axel Garde (Gerhart Hauptmann). Cast: Olaf Fønss, Ida Orloff, Ebba Thomsen, Carl Lauritzen, Frederik Jacobsen. Curtiz played a supporting role—Hans Fullenberg—and performed as an assistant director.

1914

SARGA LILIOM (Yellow Lily). 74 min. P: Magiar Színpad. D: Félix Vanyl. Screenplay: László Beöthy (Lajos Bíró). Cast: Jenő Törzs, Teréz Nagy, Mihály Papp, László Beöthy, Gusztáv Vándory. Curtiz played a minor supporting role in this early production filmed in Kolozsvár (Cluj).

1915

COX ÉS BOX (Cox and Box). Proja, 26 min. D: Márton Garas. Screenplay: Samu Sebesi (Morton Madison). DOP: József Bécsi. Cast: Andor Kardos, Michael Curtiz, Mariska Simon. Curtiz played a supporting role.

1916

KÁROLY ÉS ZITA KIRÁLYNÉ KORONÁZÁSA BUDAPESTEN (The Coronation of King Charles IV and Queen Zita in Budapest). Kino-Ripert, 109 min. This recently restored film depicting the coronation of the last Habsburg monarchs on December 30, 1916, includes a brief shot of Curtiz in front of a camera, filming a passing parade. It is probable that the film was staged and directed by Curtiz.

1921

DRAKULA HALÁLA (The Death of Dracula). Lapa Studios, Corvin Studios, 65 min. D: Károly Lajthay. Screenplay: Károly Lajthay, Michael Curtiz (Bram Stoker). DOPs: Eduard Hösch, Lajos Gasser. Cast: Paul Askonas, Margit Lux, Dezső (David) Kertész, Elemér Thury, Lajos Réthey. Curtiz cowrote the screenplay for the first known Dracula film and helped his brother David land the role as the non–blood drinking male lead.

1949

IT'S A GREAT FEELING. Warner Bros., 85 min. P: Alex Gottlieb. D: David Butler. Screenplay: Jack Rose, Melville Shavelson (I. A. L. Diamond). Cast: Doris Day, Dennis Morgan, Jack Carson, Bill Goodwin, Irving Bacon. Curtiz plays himself in a brief cameo as he is exiting his office on the Warner Bros. lot.

Notes

Prologue

1. The total number of 181 includes shorts and "sketch" films, four incomplete Hungarian films, and several Warner Bros. pictures for which he directed scenes and retakes.

Quotation Sources by Page Number

ix "many of the stars": *Daily Variety,* March 3, 1944.

x "I am here through": audio recording of 1944 Academy Awards Ceremony, Margaret Herrick Library, Academy of Motion Picture Arts and Sciences.

x "The motion picture industry": 1943 Academy Awards Official Program, Margaret Herrick Library, Academy of Motion Picture Arts and Sciences, Beverly Hills.

x "Always the bridesmaid": Aljean Harmetz, *The Making of Casablanca* (New York: Hyperion, 2002), 319–20. (Previously published as *Round Up the Usual Suspects.*)

xi "It's not enough to": Adam Biro, *One Must Also Be Hungarian* (Chicago: University of Chicago Press, 2006), 34.

xi "lunch-bums": Hal B. Wallis, SMU Oral History Collection, Dallas, no. 267, July 20, 1982, is one of many references.

xi "Curtiz eats pictures": Stephen D. Youngkin, *The Lost One: A Life of Peter Lorre* (Lexington: University Press of Kentucky, 2005), 108.

xii "I enjoyed Mike": Hal Mohr interview by Leonard Maltin in Maltin, *The Art of the Cinematographer: A Survey and Interviews with Five Masters* (New York: Dover Publications, 1978), 82.

xiii "As a director" and "Ladies and gentleman": audio recording of 1944 Academy Awards Ceremony, Margaret Herrick Library, Academy of Motion Picture Arts and Sciences.

xiv "'workhorse": see, for instance, John Wakeman, ed., *World Film Directors,* 2 vols. (New York: H. W. Wilson, 1987), 1:177; Bob Thomas, *Clown Prince of Hollywood: The Antic Life and Times of Jack L. Warner* (New York: McGraw-Hill, 1990), 82; Kate Buford, *Burt Lancaster: An American Life* (New York: Knopf, 2000), 110.

xiv "several entities in one": Frederick John, "He Arrived on the Fourth of July," *Billings (Montana) Gazette,* July 4, 1975.

xv "most of the so-called": James Bacon, *Made in Hollywood* (Chicago: Contemporary Books, 1977), 162.

xv "Of all Hungarians": undated memo from Irving Rapper, "Guide to a More Picturesque Speech, or Around the Set in Eighty Ways with Mike Curtiz"; courtesy of Liz MacGillicuddy Lucas.

xv "His command of English": Paul Henreid with Julius Fast, *Ladies Man: An Autobiography* (New York: St. Martin's Press, 1984), 122.

xvi "I don't see black": Ezra Goodman, *The Fifty-Year Decline and Fall of Hollywood* (New York: Simon and Schuster, 1961), 212.

xvi "I put all the art": Pete Martin, *Hollywood without Make-Up* (Philadelphia: J. B. Lippincott, 1948), 126.

xvii "You should be a": John Meredyth Lucas, *Eighty Odd Years in Hollywood: Memoir of a Career in Film and Television* (Jefferson, N.C.: McFarland, 2004), 102.

xviii "humiliated and furious": Hal Wallis and Charles Higham, *Starmaker: The Autobiography of Hal Wallis* (New York: Macmillan, 1980), 105.

1. A River Runs through It

Quotation Sources by Page Number

2 "Why don't you lie": Lucas, *Eighty Odd Years in Hollywood,* 75.

3 "that many times we": Martin, *Hollywood without Make-Up,* 121.

3 "foul-smelling, cramped warrens": John Lukacs, *Budapest 1900: A Historical Portrait of a City and Its Culture* (New York: Weidenfeld & Nicolson, 1988), 54.

3 "I tell my brothers then": Martin, *Hollywood without Make-Up,* 121.

4 "like a monkey": Joe Adamson and Byron Haskin, *Byron Haskin* (Metuchen, N.J.: Scarecrow Press, 1984), 121.

4 "I was good athlete": Martin, *Hollywood without Make-Up,* 121.

6 "glided through the SRO crowds": Andre de Toth, *Fragments: Portraits from the Inside* (Boston: Faber and Faber, 1994), illustration no. 2.

6 "The home of artists": ibid., illustration no. 1.

6 "Everyone knew everyone": László Kriston to the author, August 7, 2012.

7 "Who could have dared": Mihály Kertész, "Atlantis, the Filming of Gerhardt Hauptmann's Dramatized Novel," *Mozihét,* no. 1 (1913). All translations from the Hungarian are courtesy of László Kriston.

2. Actor to Director

1. At least eight of Curtiz's earliest motion pictures were "sketch films" that were complemented by a live performance.

Quotation Sources by Page Number

8 "handsome men and pretty": Victor Varconi with Ed Honeck, *It's Not Enough to Be Hungarian* (Denver: Graphic Impressions, 1976), 61.

8 "I study three languages": Martin, *Hollywood without Make-Up,* 121.

9 "I do not believe" and "I do not know": Miguel A. Fidalgo, *Michael Curtiz: Bajo la sombra de Casablanca* (Madrid: T&B Editores, 2009), 21. Translated by Cesar Mendoza.

11 "The producer signed": Martin, *Hollywood without Make-Up*, 121.

11 "The First Hungarian Dramatic": *Motion Picture News* ad, October 1912.

11 "Neither I nor my": Fidalgo, *Michael Curtiz*, 22.

12 "Kertész, the discovery": István Radó, in *A Newyorktól a Hungáriáig*, ed. Magda Konrádyné Gálos (Budapest: Minerva, 1965).

13–14 "bad memories" and "It took enormous financial": Kertész, "Atlantis, the Filming of Gerhardt Hauptmann's Dramatized Novel."

14 "It is the director": Mihály Kertész, "The Director," *Mozgófénykép Híradó* (Photo Movie News), no. 51 (1913): 70.

3. Transylvanian Idyll

Quotation Sources by Page Number

17 "My firm belief was": Jenő Janovics, in *A magyar Pathé* (dir. Bálint Zágoni, 2011).

17 "The boss wasn't": Gyöngyi Balogh and Bálint Zágoni, *An Illustrated History of the Film Production in Cluj/Kolozsvár between 1913–1920* (Cluj/Kolozsvár: Filmtett Egyesület, Magyar Nemzeti Filmarchívum, 2009).

18 "*The Borrowed Babies* adapted": Jenő Janovics, *Filmkultúra*, no. 1 (January 1936).

20 "poor visuals": Ernő Gál, *Mozihét*, no. 15 (1915).

21 "They throw money": *Újság*, July 21, 1914.

22 "No, dear Mr. Kertész": *Újság*, July 22, 1914.

24 "When we marched out": Kati Marton, *The Great Escape: Nine Jews Who Fled Hitler and Changed the World* (New York: Simon and Schuster, 2006), 22.

4. Phönix Rising

Quotation Sources by Page Number

26 "The program of our cinemas," "Good film directing requires," "A film director has to know," and "To keep the drama": Mihály Kertész, "Film Directing," *Mozgófénykép Híradó*, no. 27 (July 2, 1916).

27–28 "a film actor in": Mihály Kertész, "The Director, the Actor, the Scenarist," *Mozihét*, no. 51 (1917).

28 "In the case of": Mihály Kertész, "The Future of Hungarian Cinema," *Mozihét*, no. 53 (1916).

30 "An actor should not explain" and "I am witnessing this": Kertész, "The Director, the Actor, the Scenarist."

31 "*The Crimson Samson* was" and "The film was full": Tivadar Uray, *Theater Life* (November 3, 1935).

5. A Stirred-Up Anthill

1. *My Brother Is Coming* was restored by the Hungarian Film Archive in 1999 and can be viewed on the Internet. Composed of 26 shots and ten intertitles, the movie remains a historical template of a state-sponsored propaganda film in the Kertész style replete with waving flags, pristine horizons and a passing parade.

Quotation Sources by Page Number

35 "a huge stirred-up": S. Z. Sakall, *The Story of Cuddles: My Life under the Emperor Francis Joseph, Adolf Hitler, and the Warner Brothers,* trans. Paul Tabori (London: Cassell, 1954), 140.

36 "a noble visitor" and "stuck-up:" István Radó, in Gálos, *A Newyorktól a Hungáriáig.*

36 "Mike went home," "In the far corner," "'We've got it made," and "a detachment of": Lucas, *Eighty Odd Years in Hollywood,* 78.

38 "The soldiers of Miklós Horthy": István Nemeskürty, *Word and Image: History of the Hungarian Cinema,* trans. Zsuzsanna Horn (Budapest: Corvina Press, 1968), 55.

6. City of Film

Quotation Sources by Page Number

40 "That was because": Varconi, *It's Not Enough to Be Hungarian,* 17.

40 "It was never clear": Fidalgo, *Michael Curtiz,* 55.

42 "Mike had a European attitude": Lucas, *Eighty Odd Years in Hollywood,* 72.

42 "a sex maniac": Irving Rapper, interview by Ronald L. Davis, August 13, 1980, SMU Collection, Margaret Herrick Library.

42 "She loved to ice skate": Michelanne Forster, *Don't Mention Casablanca* (Wellington, New Zealand: Playmarket, 2010).

43 "he led quite a dissolute life": Georg Markus quoting Ilona Ryder in "Ich schau dir in die Augen, Kleines," *Neue Kronen Zeitung,* August 6, 2000, 28–29.

7. Monumental-Filme

1. *Reigen* would run the cultural gamut, from condemnation by Adolf Hitler (in 1933 the book was publicly burned in Germany) to its later adaptation into several post–World War II feature films helmed by such notable European directors as Max Ophuls, Roger Vadim, and Richard Lester.

Quotation Sources by Page Number

45 "eighty thousand extras": Nikolaus Wostry and Jan-Christopher Horak, "Sodom and Gomorrah: Notes on a Reconstruction, or Less Is More," *Moving Image* 3, no. 2 (2003): 21.

45 "Do you have any idea": Robert Von Dassanowsky, *Austrian Cinema: A History* (Jefferson, N.C.: McFarland, 2005), 27.

45 "prop madness": Walter Fritz, *Im Kino erlebe ich die Welt. 100 Jahre Kino und Film in Österreich* (Vienna: Christian Brandstätter, 1997). Translated by Lázsló Kriston.

46 "Do something with this": Varconi, *It's Not Enough to Be Hungarian,* 17.

46 "A few tables away" and "That's not good": Walter Slezak, *What Time's the Next Swan?* (Garden City, N.Y.: Doubleday, 1962), 99–100.

47 "The sight before us": Sakall, *The Story of Cuddles,* 162.

48 "At the moment": Michael Kertész interview, *Theater Life,* January 1, 1922.

48 "We were too stunned" and "A wonderful little man": Walter Slezak, *What Time's the Next Swan?* 104, 105.

49 "They fired more ammo": *Theater Life,* November 26, 1922.

50 "The film fans of the continent": *Queen of Sin* review from March 29, 1923, in *Variety Film Reviews, 1921–1925,* vol. 2 (New York: Garland Publishing, 1983).

52 "In spite of his jealousy" and "lewd, even alcoholic": *Bécsi Magyar Újság* (Vienna Hungarian Newspaper), November 11, 1922.

52 "the largest and most beautiful": Dassanowsky, *Austrian Cinema,* 21.

53 "a stylized art film": *Theater Life,* August 19, 1923.

53 "Many European cinema productions": Fidalgo, *Michael Curtiz,* 70.

8. Exodus in Red Heels

1. In Hungary's Civil Registration of Death Notices, it is recorded that Ignacz Kaminer died on March 23, 1923, of "húdéses elmezavar," that is, paralytic dementia. This cause of death opens up an interesting line of speculation in light of some of Curtiz's behavior near the end of his life.

2. The actor John Loder made his debut as an extra in a Korda film titled *Dance Extra* (1925), starring Victor Varconi and Maria Corda. He recalled observing Korda showing up late one day holding a bloodstained handkerchief to his face. Maria Corda followed him onto the set, muttering curses in Hungarian. She had found her husband talking to a young actress in his office and reacted violently.

3. A review of *The Moon of Israel* filed from London appeared in *Variety:* "In direction and production, *Moon of Israel* is strong enough to enter into competition with *The Ten Commandments* anywhere in the world, even in the United States"; *Variety,* February 4, 1925, 39.

Quotation Sources by Page Number

54 "I stay here a week": *Theater Life,* September 21, 1924.

55 "If we look at this film": *Theater Life,* March 23, 1924.

58 "Poor boy, he is working": "My Son Works with 5,000 Extras," *Theater Life,* August 17, 1924.

60 "If monkeys can have" and "she was the greatest lay": Jeffrey Meyers, *Inherited Risk* (New York: Simon and Schuster, 2002), 112–13.

62 "You can't believe what a joy": *Theater Life,* September 13, 1925.

63 "One of the two men": Martin, *Hollywood without Make-Up,* 122.

9. A Family Business

1. On July 14, 1930, a distraught man ruined by a Ponzi scheme, involving a supposed bottomless oil well, shot and killed Motley Flint in a Los Angeles Superior Courtroom. Jack L. Warner mourned the loss of one of his few close friends.

Quotation Sources by Page Number

64 "laid in the aisles" and "We've got to get": Jack L. Warner with Dean Jennings, *My First Hundred Years in Hollywood* (New York: Random House, 1964), 160.

67 "the mortgage lifter": Susan Orlean, *Rin Tin Tin: The Life and the Legend* (New York: Simon & Schuster, 2011), 81.

68 "illness, death in the family": May 10, 1926, Warner Bros. contract of Michael Curtiz, USC Warner Bros. Archives, Los Angeles.

69 "Already at age eight": Kitty Kertész Doraine interview, *Theater Life* (January [year unknown]).

10. Hungarian in the Promised Land

Quotation Sources by Page Number

71 "Harry promised Curtiz": Warner and Jennings, *My First Hundred Years in Hollywood,* 160–61.

71–73 "so that they might": P. A. Chase to S. Schneider, Warner Bros. Pictures Inc., June 24, 1926, USC Warner Bros. Archives.

73 "We have decided" and "I didn't know what": Martin, *Hollywood without Make-Up,* 123.

74 "a rather poor" and "If you think this": Michael Curtiz to Jack Warner, memo, n.d., *The Third Degree* production files, USC Warner Bros. Archives.

74 "I am up every morning": Martin, *Hollywood without Make-Up,* 123.

74 "I felt something extra": Wallis and Higham, *Starmaker,* 29.

76 "He had great artistic": Hal Mohr, interview by Leonard Maltin in Maltin, *The Art of the Cinematographer,* 82.

76 "an orgy of dissolves": Mordaunt Hall, "An Old Melodrama," *New York Times,* February 15, 1927.

77 "too much of a good thing": *Variety,* January 5, 1927, 17.

78 "Everybody is human beings": Martin, *Hollywood without Make-Up,* 124.

79 "We had a darling little baby": Hal Mohr, interview by Maltin in Maltin, *The Art of the Cinematographer,* 82.

79–80 "I am very anxious": Michael Curtiz to Harry Warner, August 20, 1927, USC Warner Bros. Archives.

80 "clever writer": Curtiz to Jack Warner, memo, n.d., *The Third Degree* production files, USC Warner Bros. Archives.

11. A Loving Collaboration

1. Curtiz's memory for birthdays and anniversaries was haphazard. On his Declaration of Intention to become a U.S. citizen dated May 24, 1931, he provided a marriage date to Bess Meredyth of December 18, 1928. On his Petition of Naturalization, filed five years later, his appended marriage date was December 8, 1930. His birth dates on similar documents also varied.

2. Curtiz never mentioned his out-of-wedlock children and omitted them entirely from his Declaration of Intention for U.S. Citizenship in 1931; he declared under oath that Kitty was his only child.

Quotation Sources by Page Number

81 "Ah, you couldn't forget": *Vox Pop* radio show audio recording, late 1947; courtesy of Rudy Behlmer.

84 "I was speaking English," István Székely, *Hypollittól a lila ákácig* (The Purple Acacia: A Memoir) (Budapest: Gondolat, 1978).

84 "Mother said, 'It would be simpler'": Lucas, *Eighty Odd Years in Hollywood,* 52.

85 "Mike made an effort": ibid, 53.

86 "Miss Bess Meredyth": *Theater Life,* January 15, 1928.

87 "the first feature-length": Warner Bros. ad for *Tenderloin* in *Variety,* March 28, 1928.

88 "being virtually the first try": *Variety,* March 28, 1928.

88 "sound bums": Richard Erdman to the author, February 10, 2012.

12. Hollywood's Great Deluge

1. There was a future return on investment when Jack Warner had the producer Robert Youngson cut the film to seven reels and re-release it in 1957 as a seventy-five-minute silent with stock music and stentorian narration. The butchered re-release fortunately spurred the creation of an acetate duplicate negative of the original version, which became integral to the one-hundred-minute restoration of *Noah's Ark* in 1989—including the dubbing-in of the original Vitaphone tracks—by the UCLA Film and Television Archive.

Quotation Sources by Page Number

91 "Send to Darryl": Curtiz's undated *Noah's Ark* treatment, USC Warner Bros. Archive.

92 "We had just a name" and "Yes, of course": Darryl Zanuck interview, *Los Angeles Times,* November 18, 1928.

94 "The police officer raises his hand," "*Noah's Ark* is a long-held dream," and "Go on!": *Theater Life,* September 9, 1928.

95–96 "I talk of my own": George O'Brien interview, *Los Angeles Times,* November 4, 1928.

96 "When I was to be blinded" and "The spear was supposed to disappear": David W. Menefee, *George O'Brien: A Man's Man in Hollywood* (Albany, Ga.: BearManor Media, 2012), chap. 7.

96–97 "Curtiz fixed the poor recumbent wretch": Cass Warner Sperling and Cork Milner with Jack Warner Jr., *Hollywood Be Thy Name: The Warner Brothers Story* (Rocklin, Calif.: Prima Publishing, 1994), 151.

97 "I knew . . . that Jackman" and "I said, 'Jesus'": Hal Mohr interview by Leonard Maltin in Maltin, *The Art of the Cinematographer,* 84.

98 "brutal," "mud, blood, and flood," and "Mr. Curtiz had been told": *Hollywood: A Celebration of the American Silent Film,* episode 1, *The Pioneers,* TV documentary miniseries (Thames Television, 1980).

98 "screaming at the extras," "a freak," "a loser," "a masochist," and "a weirdo": Adamson and Haskin, *Byron Haskin,* 96, 97.

98 "I found a man": *Hollywood: A Celebration of the American Silent Film,* episode 1, *The Pioneers.*

98 "a couple of people": Hal Mohr interview by Leonard Maltin in Maltin, *The Art of the Cinematographer,* 85.

98 "It is generally believed": Anthony Slide, *Hollywood Unknowns: A History of Extras, Bit Players, and Stand-Ins* (Jackson: University Press of Mississippi, 2012), 42.

99 "A miracle of concentrated energy": Robbin Coons, "Spell of the Game," *Oakland Tribune,* July 31, 1929.

99 "little need for the services": Warner Bros. *Noah's Ark* press book, 1928.

99–100 "Hollywood was like Liechtenstein": Budd Schulberg, interview by Kurt Vonnegut, *Paris Review,* no. 169 (Winter 2001).

100 "You know, in Chicago": Paul Lieberman, *Gangster Squad: Covert Cops, the Mob, and the Battle for Los Angeles* (New York: Thomas Dunne Books/St. Martin's Griffin, 2012), 48.

100 "the silent custodian": Stuart Jerome, *Those Crazy Wonderful Years When We Ran Warner Bros.* (Secaucus, N.J.: Lyle Stuart, 1983), 204.

100 "If any alligator gets you": John Baxter, *Stunt: The Story of the Great Movie Stunt Men* (Garden City, N.Y.: Doubleday, 1974), 155.

101 "the goddamn murderous bastards": Hal Mohr interview by Leonard Maltin in Maltin, *The Art of the Cinematographer,* 85.

101 "an idiotic super-spectacle": quoted in George F. Custen, *Twentieth Century's Fox: Darryl F. Zanuck and the Culture of Hollywood* (New York: Basic Books, 1997), 125.

101 "a film of triumph" and "ridiculous": unidentified 1929 British newspaper review of *Noah's Ark;* courtesy of Kevin Brownlow.

101 "wearisome," "inept," and "frequently border[ed] on the ridiculous": Mordaunt Hall, "The Screen: The War and the Flood," *New York Times,* March 13, 1929.

102 "taking a book": Custen, *Twentieth Century's Fox,* 125.

102 "surrounded as usual": Grace Kingsley, "A Hollywood Party!" *Los Angeles Times,* November 2, 1928.

13. General Foreman

1. An unregenerate bigot to the end, Fay was feted by a group of fascist white supremacists at Madison Square Garden in January 1946 during an evening titled "A Tribute to Frank Fay," where Hitler, Mussolini, and General Franco were also extolled.

Quotation Sources by Page Number

103 "It would have made": Bob Thomas, *Clown Prince of Hollywood,* 65.

104 "Is too much hammy": Richard Erdman to the author, April 10, 2012.

106 "expertly directed": Mordaunt Hall, "The Screen: Bankers and the Law," *New York Times,* August 24, 1929.

106 "made egregious blunders" and "leaves much to be desired": N.B.B., "The New Week's Bills," *Washington Post,* September 30, 1929.

106 "Because he's so big": "Versatility of Curtiz Amazes," *Los Angeles Times,* April 27, 1930, B11.

111 "fuck you," "burdened by a terrible," and "sadistic weightlifter": Charles Bickford, *Bull, Balls, Bicycles and Actors* (New York: Paul S. Eriksson, 1965), 269, 254, 256.

111 "as tender as any director" and "God, that kid is good": Frank Coghlan, *They Still Call Me Junior: Autobiography of a Child Star* (Jefferson, N.C.: McFarland, 1993), 77–78.

112 "great fun" and "If a director wasn't fast enough": Tom Flinn, "William Dieterle, the Plutarch of Hollywood," *Velvet Light Trap* 15 (Fall 1975): 25–26.

14. Pre-Code in Synthetic Flesh

1. There was a shot of a leering John Wray presenting a flustered Fay Wray with an illustrated *Kama Sutra* manual that was cut before the picture's release.

Quotation Sources by Page Number

115 "Warners was the greatest": Casey Robinson, oral history interview by Joel Greenberg, 1974, American Film Institute, Los Angeles.

115 "schmucks with Underwoods": Max Wilk, *Schmucks with Underwoods: Conversations with Hollywood's Classic Screenwriters* (New York: Applause Theatre and Cinema Books, 2004), xii.

116 "was charming too": Gregory William Mank, *Women in Horror Films, 1930s* (Jefferson, N.C.: McFarland, 1999), 36. Emphasis in original.

117 "an opulent orgy": Thornton Delehanty, *New York Post,* October 26, 1931.

117 "brilliant": Mordaunt Hall, *New York Times,* October 24, 1931.

118 "had a face-lift": Patrick McGilligan, *Backstory: Interviews with Screenwriters of Hollywood's Golden Age* (Berkeley: University of California Press, 1985), 92.

122 "was a machine of a person": Jeffrey Meyers, *Gary Cooper: American Hero* (New York: Morrow, 1998), 222.

123 "Looking through the finder" and "Why should they eat?": Fay Wray, *On the Other Hand: A Life Story* (New York: St. Martin's Press, 1989), 133. Emphasis in original.

123 "We design a set": from the *Doctor X* press book, as quoted in Donald Deschner, "Anton Grot: Warners Art Director, 1927–1948," *Velvet Light Trap* 15 (Fall 1975): 19.

123 "the curious camera": *Doctor X* press book, as quoted ibid.

124 "'Frankenstein' seem tame": Mordaunt Hall, "Lionel Atwill and Lee Tracy in an Exciting Murder Mastery at Warners' Strand," *New York Times,* August 4, 1932.

124 You think Cagney's gonna": John McCabe, *Cagney* (New York: Carroll & Graf, 1997), 264.

125 "Put a nigger" and "behave like Southern peasants": Lucas, *Eighty Odd Years in Hollywood,* 117, 101.

125 "Mike instructed them": ibid., 101.

126 "To me, the Negro": Phil Carter, "Michael Curtiz Says Race Unimportant in Film Making," *Los Angeles Tribune,* July 2, 1945.

126 "God-damned-nothing-no-good" and "My director made my life hell": Bette Davis, *The Lonely Life: An Autobiography* (New York: G. P. Putnam's Sons, 1962), 164–65.

127 "Mike must have hated": Margaret Talbot, *The Entertainer: Movies, Magic, and My Father's Twentieth Century* (New York: Riverhead Books, 2012), 268.

127 "I'll walk out": James Curtis, *Spencer Tracy: A Biography* (New York: Knopf, 2011), 180.

15. Regime Change

1. A programmer is a shorter, more modestly budged film that was often produced to be shown as the second, or "B," feature on a double bill.

Quotation Sources by Page Number

130 "The country is in chaos": Ian Hamilton, *Writers in Hollywood, 1915–1951* (London: Heinemann, 1990), 112.

132 "There were two Hal Wallises" and "Hal Wallis at the office": Harmetz, *The Making of Casablanca,* 31.

132 "If Hal respects you": James R. Silke, *Here's Looking at You, Kid: 50 Years of Fighting, Working, and Dreaming at Warner Bros.* (Boston: Little, Brown, 1976), 123.

134–135 "Michael Curtiz was very—exacting": Glenda Farrell as quoted by Scott MacQueen, "The Mystery of the Wax Museum," *American Cinematographer* 71, no. 4 (1990): 47.

135 "Odd, unusual camera angles": from *Mystery of the Wax Museum* press book, as quoted in Richard Koszarski's introduction to *Mystery of the Wax Museum* (Madison: University of Wisconsin Press, 1979), 28.

136 "He was like part of the camera": and "You should have kept hitting": Fay Wray as quoted in MacQueen, "The Mystery of the Wax Museum," 47–48.

136 "will pass as the reporter": Edwin Schallert, "'Wax Museum' Thriller," *Los Angeles Times,* February 11, 1933.

137 "too ghastly for comfort": Mordaunt Hall, "Lionel Atwill and Fay Wray in a Gruesome Narrative about a Mad Modeler of Wax Figures," *New York Times,* February 18, 1933.

137–138 "As Mr. Michael Curtiz": Mathilde Foerster to Jack L. Warner, July 15, 1933, USC Warner Bros. Archive.

140 "About 30 days after leaving" and "One day in a Thrifty's": undated entries from Michael Foerster's journal; courtesy of Michelanne Forster.

140 "I think you can": Michelanne Forster, email to the author, December 18, 2013.

141 "That happiness all but dissipated": Kitty Kertesz Doraine interview, *Theater Life* (n.d., ca. 1933–34).

142 "War on Paramount": *New York Times,* January 16, 1931, 27.

144 "My sole objection": Curtiz to Hal Wallis, Warner Bros. interoffice communication, June 24, 1933, USC Warner Bros. Archives.

145 "Perfect for audiences": *Variety,* September 1, 1933.

145 "If I don't follow": Lucas, *Eighty Odd Years in Hollywood,* 69.

16. Home on the Range

1. Upon Cagney's return to the studio in 1932 after a six-month suspension, he starred in a Mervyn LeRoy picture titled *Hard to Handle.* "The very definition of *that* son of a bitch," said Jack Warner.

Quotation Sources by Page Number

147 "In my memory": Lucas, *Eighty Odd Years in Hollywood,* 84.

148 "watch us make asses" and "Now of course": Niven Busch as quoted by Steve Hulett, "Darryl Zanuck, Walt Disney and Hollywood Polo," The Animation Guild (TAG) blog, June 21, 2006, http://animationguildblog.blogspot.com/2006/06/darryl-zanuck-walt-disney-and.html.

149 "It is a hell of a good" and "the usual speeding-up": J. L. Warner to Hal Wallis, Warner Bros. interoffice communication, December 13, 1933, USC Warner Bros. Archives.

150 "Your stuff is beautiful": Hal Wallis to Curtiz, Warner Bros. interoffice communication, October 21, 1933, USC Warner Bros. Archives.

151 "lowest bunch we have": Thomas Patrick Doherty, *Hollywood's Censor: Joseph I. Breen & the Production Code Administration* (New York: Columbia University Press, 2007), 53.

152 "This picture also has": J. Breen to J. L. Warner, AMPPA letter, September 3, 1936, USC Warner Bros. Archives.

152 "A cheap low-tone picture": Doherty, *Hollywood's Censor,* 53.

152–153 "Mike was a pompous," "the shvontz," and "natural-born asshole": McCabe, *Cagney,* 119, 89, 194.

153 "trying too hard" and "in the typical Cagney manner": Hal Wallis to Curtiz, Warner Bros. interoffice communication, December 1, 1933, USC Warner Bros. Archive.

154 "I want you to stop": Hal Wallis to Robert Presnell, Warner Bros. interoffice communication, February 14, 1934, USC Warner Bros. Archives.

156 "As soon as Mike" and "Is not bad trip": Lucas, *Eighty Odd Years in Hollywood,* 75–76.

158 "He buys her very expensive jewelry": ibid., 80.

158 "Hungarians!": ibid., 81.

159 "We could not deliberately": Hal Wallis to Robert Lord, Warner Bros. interoffice communication, September 13, 1934, USC Warner Bros. Archives.

159 "So an unnamed agency": Adamson and Haskin, *Byron Haskin,* 123.

160 "After all, I know" and "That is the trouble": George Frazier, "The Machine with a Rage," *True,* October 1947, 138.

160 "light as whipped cream": Jerome Lawrence, *Actor: The Life and Times of Paul Muni* (New York: Putnam, 1974), 201.

160 "He yelled, 'Bunnie!'": Adamson and Haskin, *Byron Haskin,* 121, 122.

161 "I know you are not satisfied": Robert Lord to J. L. Warner, Warner Bros. interoffice communication, November 15, 1934, USC Warner Bros. Archives.

162 "I saw *Black Fury*": J. L. Warner to Hal Wallis, Warner Bros. interoffice communication, January 16, 1935, USC Warner Bros. Archives.

163 "It is a far more subtle": "*Black Fury* Rates High Praise for Both Maker and Star," *San Francisco News,* May 11, 1935.

163 "the most notable American": Andre Sennwald, "Paul Muni in the Coal-Mine Melodrama 'Black Fury,' at the Strand—'Four Hours to Kill,'" *New York Times,* April 11, 1935.

17. The Dream Team

1. According to Errol Flynn's biographer Gerry Connelly, Flynn voiced fascination for Damita while a young man in Australia, meaning that he would probably have seen one or more of her silent Curtiz films. When Flynn arrived in Paris in June 1933, he got himself invited to a party that she attended, first introducing himself there. In February 1934, while a member of the Northampton Repertory, Flynn traveled to London and met her again backstage during her run at the Saville Theatre. Therefore, their chance meeting on the S.S. *Paris* to America in November 1934 was their third meeting.

2. Roy Obringer was a Warner Bros. attorney who rose to become the chief studio counsel. He dealt with contracted talent and (in Warner's view) their perfidious agents.

3. Olivia de Havilland's opportunity to portray Hermia in the stage production of *A Midsummer Night's Dream,* which resulted in her discovery by Warner Bros., was due to a set of fortuitous circumstances. Originally the second understudy, de Havilland ascended to the role after the lead actress, Jean Rouverol, and her understudy, Gloria Stuart, sequentially left the play to accept roles in Hollywood movies.

4. Korngold's son Ernst witnessed a memorable exchange between the pair: "One day, Steiner said to him, 'Tell me something, Korngold. We've both been at Warner's for ten years now, and in that time your music has gotten progressively worse and worse and mine has been getting better and better. Why do you suppose that is?' And without missing a beat my father answered, 'I tell vy dat is, Steiner; dat iss because you are stealing from me and I am stealing from you.'" Peter Wegele, *Max Steiner: Composing Casablanca and the Golden Age of Film Music* (Lanham, Md.: Rowman and Littlefield, 2014), 212.

Quotation Sources by Page Number

164 "My mother, just like my father" and "Dear Kitty, I am glad": Andor Váró, *Theater Life,* January 14, 1934.

165 "I got tired," "And the minute," "sleeping drug," and "Kitty, the pathetic career-seeker": "One 'Hollywood Daughter's' Tragic Fight to Save Her Soul," *Spokesman-Review* (Spokane, Wash.), July 1, 1934.

166 "Curtiz goes in for more" and "really needs what Mr. Curtiz": Harry Joe Brown to Hal Wallis, Warner Bros. interoffice communication, November 23, 1934, USC Warner Bros. Archives.

168 "Will you tell him": Hal Wallis to Harry Joe Brown, Warner Bros. interoffice communication, February 12, 1934, USC Warner Bros. Archives.

168 "swing that blackjack around": Hal Wallis to Curtiz, Harry Joe Brown, Warner Bros. interoffice communication, February 20, 1934, USC Warner Bros. Archives.

168–169 "Signed today" and "He seemed self-conscious": Tony Thomas, Rudy Behlmer, and Clifford McCarty, *The Films of Errol Flynn* (New York: Citadel Press, 1969), 23, 25.

169 "hired him on impulse": Warner and Jennings, *My First Hundred Years in Hollywood,* 125.

169 "I overheard a typical": Jack L. Warner to Hal Wallis, Warner Bros. interoffice communication, January 11, 1935, USC Warner Bros. Archives.

171 "Tenny Wright was a very reasonable": David Lewis, *The Creative Producer,* ed. James Curtis (Metuchen, N.J.: Scarecrow Press, 1993), 135.

171 "Tenny was a good Irishman": A. M. Sperber and Eric Lax, *Humphrey Bogart* (New York: William Morrow, 1997), 101.

171 "the studio was marvelously organized": Lewis, *The Creative Producer,* 135.

172–173 "Michael Curtiz was probably," "The veins in his forehead," "So much so did he," and "Instead of being hurt": Sybil Jason, *My Fifteen Minutes: An Autobiography of a Child Star of the Golden Era of Hollywood* (Boalsburg, Pa.: BearManor Media, 2005), 27, 29, 100.

174 "First, I want to thank you": Jack Warner to Irving Asher, December 10, 1934, USC Warner Bros. Archives.

175 "Annie says, 'Leave it'": Casey Robinson, oral history interview by Joel Greenberg, 1974, American Film Institute.

176 "Please let's not": Hal Wallis to Harry Joe Brown and Curtiz, Warner Bros. interoffice communication, June 20, 1935, USC Warner Bros. Archives.

176 "However we have placed": Jack Warner to Irving Asher, July 8, 1935, USC Warner Bros. Archives.

177 "Your last two days": Hal Wallis to Curtiz, Warner Bros. interoffice communication, August 15, 1935, USC Warner Bros. Archives.

177 "I worked as hard": Errol Flynn, *My Wicked, Wicked Ways* (1959; repr., New York: Cooper Square Press, 2003), 203.

177 "You are thrilled, excited": Rapper, "Guide to More Picturesque Speech."

177–178 "He wanted to be": Silke, *Here's Looking at You, Kid,* 148.

179–180 "I have talked to you" and "why it is that you": Hal Wallis to Curtiz, Warner Bros. interoffice communication, September 30, 1935, USC Warner Bros. Archives.

181 "Why do you have": Robert Lord to Hal Wallis, Warner Bros. interoffice communication, December 10, 1935, USC Warner Bros. Archives.

18. The Reason Why

1. The major studios used dialogue directors as a transitional bridge from silent to sound movies to assist actors with their line readings. The dialogue director would rehearse the company, review the script and run lines with the actors.

2. During the production of *Ben-Hur* (1925) in Rome, an estimated 100 to 150

horses died during Breezy Eason's direction of the chariot race action scenes. Rather than deal with the inconvenience and cost of treating injured horses in Italy, they were simply shot dead and sold by the wranglers for horsemeat. Some of the dead animals were used in posed publicity shots and lobby cards by Metro. The production of *Ben-Hur* became a chaotic mess; none of the Rome chariot footage was usable. When Eason staged the sequence again in Culver City, a disastrous collision killed four horses.

3. *Light Brigade*'s reputation has suffered because of the altered public perception about the treatment of animals. Horses were still viewed from a frontier and agrarian perspective in 1936. Popular sentiment concerning horses and other animals has changed radically since then. It is difficult for many modern viewers to watch the thrilling battle scenes in the picture without averting their eyes as horses and their riders tumble wildly.

Quotation Sources by Page Number

184 "The reason I called": Stephen Jacobs, *Boris Karloff: More Than a Monster* (Sheffield, U.K.: Tomahawk Press, 2011), 80.

184 "Horror pictures are a staple": Frank S. Nugent, "Karloff Is Brought Back Alive in 'The Walking Dead' at the Strand," *New York Times,* March 2, 1936.

185–186 "He came into the office": Irving Rapper interview by Ronald L. Davis, August 13, 1980, SMU Collection and Margaret Herrick Library.

186 "I have developed cauliflower": Irving Rapper, "Dialogue Director Explains His Job," *New York Herald Tribune,* September 16, 1940, 26.

186 "Michael Curtiz was the most": Irving Rapper interview by Ronald L. Davis, August 13, 1980, SMU Collection and Margaret Herrick Library.

186 "Read it? I can't": Thomas, *Clown Prince of Hollywood,* 119.

187 "If we are to save": Hal Wallis to Sam Bischoff, Warner Bros. interoffice communication, February 13, 1936, USC Warner Bros. Archive.

188 "All he talked about": Jack Warner to Hal Wallis, Warner Bros. interoffice communication, March 10, 1936, USC Warner Bros. Archive.

189 "I know in my heart": Curtiz to Hal Wallis, memo, April 17, 1936, USC Warner Bros. Archive.

189 "our bitter rancor, gentlemen": proposed new ending for *The Charge of the Light Brigade* written by Curtiz, April 17, 1936, USC Warner Bros. Archive.

189 "I'm not going to suffer": Hal Wallis to Sam Bischoff, Warner Bros. interoffice communication, April 11, 1936, USC Warner Bros. Archive.

190 "I have to go": Hal Wallis to Curtiz, Warner Bros. interoffice communication, April 13, 1936, USC Warner Bros. Archive.

190 "I remember about four months ago": Hal Wallis to Curtiz, Warner Bros. interoffice communication, April 17, 1936, USC Warner Bros. Archive.

191 "The wind was like a knife": Flynn, *My Wicked, Wicked Ways,* 211.

191 "Curtiz was a Hungarian": Rochelle Reed, ed., *Olivia de Havilland* (Beverly Hills, Calif.: American Film Institute, 1974), 20.

191 "source of joy," "'Okay,' he yelled," and "Curtiz ordered the use": David Niven, *Bring on the Empty Horses* (New York: Putnam, 1975), 117–18.

192 "I know Errol was": Patrice Wymore Flynn to the author, May 24, 2011.

192–193 "It was something that" and "It was generally understood": Yakima Canutt with Oliver Drake, *Stunt Man: The Autobiography of Yakima Canutt* (New York: Walker, 1979), 130–31.

193 "a crazy, drunk Irish-American": Baxter, *Stunt,* 207.

193 "I sincerely admired him": Canutt and Drake, *Stunt Man,* 102.

195 "three or four hundred": R. J. Obringer to D. E. Griffiths, September 29, 1936, USC Warner Bros. Archive.

196 "More smoke up here": Sheilah Graham, "Miss Graham Sees Films in Making: Director Michael Curtiz Has Trying Time 'Shooting' 'The Charge of the Light Brigade,'" *Hartford Courant,* May 1, 1936.

196 "unsafe to live with," "he did not love," and "in danger of": "Writer Wife Sues Curtiz," *Los Angeles Times,* September 6, 1936.

197 "Whatever her drive had been": Lucas, *Eighty Odd Years in Hollywood,* 72.

198 "Soon the divorce lawyers": ibid., 93.

199 "He can certainly do everything": Jack Warner to Hal Wallis, memo, July 16, 1936, USC Warner Bros. Archive.

199 "If you don't like a script": Hal Wallis to Curtiz, Warner Bros. interoffice communication, June 30, 1936, USC Warner Bros. Archive.

199 "It just seems useless": Hal Wallis to Curtiz, Warner Bros. interoffice communication, August 20, 1936, USC Warner Bros. Archive.

200 "relating to fraudulent nature": Index to Correspondence and Case Files of the Immigration and Naturalization Service, 1903–1959, for Michael Kertesz.

200 "Ah, that was an awful time": *Vox Pop* radio show audio recording, late 1947; courtesy of Rudy Behlmar.

200 "Goddamn, why hell,": Lucas, *Eighty Odd Years in Hollywood,* 74.

19. Falling Fruit

1. Wallis was critical of de Havilland's acting at one point during the production of *Robin Hood:* "She seems to have gone elegant on us and her reading of lines is reminiscent of the leading lady in high school plays"; Hal Wallis to William Keighley, telegram, November 1, 1937, USC Warner Bros. Archive.

2. Buster Wiles later revealed that Hill used a specially designed arrowhead on a concealed wire to split the arrow. Wiles also claimed to have shot the trick arrow.

3. Korngold overheard his wife being told about the Anschluss over the telephone by the actress Helene Thimig, Max Reinhardt's wife.

4. The Motion Picture Academy, embarrassed by the *Anthony Adverse* debacle, changed its procedure by recognizing the composers of the nominated and winning music scores rather than the heads of the studio music departments.

Quotation Sources by Page Number

201 "Dear Mike, I saw the stuff": Hal Wallis to Curtiz, Warner Bros. interoffice communication, January 3, 1936, USC Warner Bros. Archive.

202 "authenticity in speech": *Mountain Justice* press book, Warner Bros. Archive, USC.

203 "We got the giggles": Mank, *Women in Horror Films, 1930s,* 375.

203 "cold": Hal Wallis to Curtiz, Warner Bros. interoffice communication, September 24, 1936, USC Warner Bros. Archive.

203 "Mike is making this": Frank Mattison to Tenny Wright and Hal Wallis, Warner Bros. interoffice communication, October 22, 1936, USC Warner Bros. Archive.

203 "a solid forearm": William McPeak, undated IMDb mini-biography of Robert Barrat.

203 "Barrat had been a boxer": Mank, *Women in Horror Films, 1930s,* 375.

203 "Miss Hutchinson passed out": Frank Mattison to Tenny Wright and Hal Wallis, Warner Bros. interoffice communication, October 21, 1936, USC Warner Bros. Archive.

204 "closer to the taste": Frank S. Nugent, "'Mountain Justice,' a Hill-Billy Anthology, Is Shown at the Rialto," *New York Times,* May 13, 1937.

205 "When he came to my house": Edward G. Robinson with Leonard Spigelgass, *All My Yesterdays: An Autobiography* (New York: Hawthorn Books, 1973), 177.

205–206 "consolidating my position" and "Fake fight, retake!": Davis, *The Lonely Life,* 212.

206 "the best fight picture": James Spada, *More Than a Woman: An Intimate Biography of Bette Davis* (New York: Bantam Books, 1993), 131.

206 "Michael Curtiz has directed": *San Francisco Examiner,* May 21, 1937.

206 "the Warners' latest astronomical discovery" and "lively, suspenseful and positively echoing": Frank S. Nugent, "'Kid Galahad,' a Crisp Prize-Ring Film, Comes to the Strand and, with It, a New Star, Wayne Morris," *New York Times,* May 27, 1937.

206 "the best find": Howard Barnes, "The Screen," *New York Herald Tribune,* May 30, 1937.

208 "A huge tent city": Lucas, *Eighty Odd Years in Hollywood,* 107.

208 "atrocious dialogue": Hal Wallis to Curtiz, Warner Bros. interoffice communication, October 13, 1937, USC Warner Bros. Archive.

208 "the most amateurish thing": Hal Wallis to Sam Bischoff, Warner Bros. interoffice communication, September 17, 1937, USC Warner Bros. Archive.

208 "Hey, Technicolor bums": *Lucas, Eighty Odd Years in Hollywood,* 108.

208 "Mike was told": ibid.

209 "ornamental rather than engrossing" and "Michael Curtiz had directed": Howard Barnes, "On the Screen," *New York Herald-Tribune,* February 14, 1938.

209 "The tempo is okay": Rapper, "Guide to a More Picturesque Speech."

209 "like school children": Hal Wallis to Curtiz, Warner Bros. interoffice communication, October 21, 1937, USC Warner Bros. Archive.

209 "cinematic genius" and "Mike could make": Ronald L. Davis, *The Glamour Factory: Inside Hollywood's Big Studio System* (Dallas: Southern Methodist University Press, 1993), 167.

210 "swell Robin Hood": Dwight Franklin to J. L. Warner, Warner Bros. interoffice communication, July 19, 1935, USC Warner Bros. Archive.

210 "publicize this now": Hal Wallis to Jack L. Warner, telegram, January 8, 1936, USC Warner Bros. Archive.

210 "milking": Nicholas Nayfack, MGM, to R. G. Obringer, December 15, 1937, USC Warner Bros. Archive.

213 *Robin Hood* will not start": T. C. Wright to Hal Wallis, Warner Bros. interoffice communication, September 7, 1937, USC Warner Bros. Archive.

214 "by hook or by crook": deposition of Ward Hamilton, notarized by R. G. Obringer, November 24, 1937, USC Warner Bros. Archive.

215 "Keighley does not know": Hal Wallis to Henry Blanke, Warner Bros. interoffice communication, November 3, 1937, USC Warner Bros. Archive.

215 "I imagine that we": Hal Wallis to Henry Blanke, Warner Bros. interoffice communication, November 10, 1937, USC Warner Bros. Archive.

215 "following a disagreement": "News of the Screen: Curtiz Replaces Keighley in Direction of 'Robin Hood' Film—Chester Morris Gets Old Role," *New York Times*, December 1, 1937, 27.

215 "Unfortunately the action sequences": Wallis and Higham, *Starmaker*, 59.

216 "I found that I had": Philip K. Scheuer, "Ace Director Curtiz Defers to Judgment of Prop Man," *Los Angeles Times*, October 17, 1948.

216 "Curtiz looked over the Castle set": Al Alleborn to T. C. Wright, Warner Bros. interoffice communication, December 1, 1937, USC Warner Bros. Archive.

216 "I think this company": Al Alleborn to T. C. Wright, Warner Bros. interoffice communication, December 3, 1937, USC Warner Bros. Archive.

216 "There is one thing": Hal Wallis to Henry Blanke, Warner Bros. interoffice communication, December 3, 1937, USC Warner Bros. Archive.

217 "The boys should fall": Rapper, "Guide to a More Picturesque Speech."

217 "That kiss—she would": William R. Meyer, *Warner Brothers Directors: The Hard-Boiled, the Comic, and the Weepers* (New Rochelle, N.Y.: Arlington House, 1978), 87.

218 "He has excellent form": Rudy Behlmar, "Swordplay on the Screen," *Films in Review* 16, no. 6 (1965): 366.

219 "Singing Marie, you pretend": Buster Wiles and William Donati, *My Days with Errol Flynn: The Autobiography of Stuntman Buster Wiles* (Santa Monica: Roundtable Publishing, 1988), 77.

219 "When we exercise": Jack Warner to R. G. Obringer, memo, January 19, 1938, USC Warner Bros. Archive.

220 *Robin Hood* is no picture": Erich Wolfgang Korngold to Hal Wallis, February 11, 1938, USC Warner Bros. Archive.

220 "My father was on the verge": Brendan G. Carroll, *The Last Prodigy: A Biography of Erich Wolfgang Korngold* (Portland, Ore.: Amadeus Press, 1997), 272.

221 "Absolutely sensational": Hal Wallis to Warner Bros. New York office, telegram, April 25, 1938, USC Warner Bros. Archive.

223 "I had no idea" and "Oh, he was a villain": Reed, *Olivia de Havilland*, 15, 20.

20. Cash Cow

1. Sam Goldwyn brought the Dead End Kids to Hollywood from the original Broadway cast of *Dead End*, which he produced for the screen in 1937. Their initial

Warner Bros. picture was *Crime School* (1938), which was released six months before *Angels with Dirty Faces*.

2. Flynn also aspired to be a writer. His novel *Beam Ends,* published in 1937, is a lively adventure of three men on a boat trip between Australia and New Guinea that was based on Flynn's own youthful exploits.

Quotation Sources by Page Number

224 "Curtiz wants no question": Jack M. Clark, "Two-Gun Drama," *Cinema Progress* (January 1939): 5.

224 "With Curtiz, I must say": Casey Robinson, oral history interview by Joel Greenberg, 1974, American Film Institute.

225 "Mike's problem": Lucas, *Eighty Odd Years in Hollywood,* 142.

225 "a program comedy": Casey Robinson, oral history interview by Joel Greenberg, 1974, American Film Institute.

225 "It was terrible": Richard Erdman to the author, February 14, 2012.

225 "Light comedy requires" Hal Wallis interview, 1958, Columbia University.

226 "What Mike regarded" Casey Robinson to Hal Wallis, Warner Bros. interoffice communication, January 31, 1938, USC Warner Bros. Archive.

226 "walked off the set": Lou Baum to Tenny Wright, Warner Bros. interoffice communication, February 28, 1938, USC Warner Bros. Archive.

226 "All of those pieces": Hal Wallis to Curtiz, Warner Bros. interoffice communication, March 9, 1938, USC Warner Bros. Archive.

227 "What in the world": Hal Wallis to Henry Blanke, Warner Bros. interoffice communication, January 13, 1938, USC Warner Bros. Archive.

228 "People are gonna find out" and "Remember, they shot him": Leslie Epstein, "Duel in the Sun," *American Prospect* 11, no. 16 (2001), http://prospect.org/article/duel-sun.

228 "I also got to see": Robert Nott, *He Ran All the Way: The Life of John Garfield* (New York: Limelight, 2003), 81.

228 "Mike discovered me": Garfield quoted in Philip K. Scheuer "John Garfield Likes 'Flexible' Career," *Los Angeles Times,* April 16, 1950.

229 "was one of the very best": Harmetz, *The Making of Casablanca,* 183.

229 "We must pick up time": Hal Wallis to Henry Blanke, Warner Bros. interoffice communication, May 6, 1938, USC Warner Bros. Archive.

230 "what not to do": Harmetz, *The Making of Casablanca,* 190.

230 "Remember that scene": Nott, *He Ran All the Way,* 90.

230 "A charming, at times heartbreakingly human": B. R. Crisler, "Four Daughters," *New York Times,* August 19, 1938.

230 "Michael Curtiz's direction": *Chicago Herald and Examiner,* September 4, 1938.

233 "I gave Gorcey" and "cut out the goddamned nonsense": McCabe, *Cagney,* 165.

233 "urging Mike along": Frank Mattison to Tenny Wright, Warner Bros. interoffice communication, July 9, 1938, USC Warner Bros. Archive.

234 "the girl": Hal Wallis to Curtiz, Warner Bros. interoffice communication, July 5, 1938, USC Warner Bros. Archive.

235 "gutty": Hal Wallis to Sam Bischoff and Curtiz, Warner Bros. interoffice communication, June 28, 1938, USC Warner Bros. Archive.

235 "While the shots he has added": Frank Mattison to Tenny Wright, Warner Bros. interoffice communication, July 29, 1938, USC Warner Bros. Archive.

236 "The train barely missed" and "How do you get realism": Pat O'Brien, *The Wind at My Back: The Life and Times of Pat O'Brien by Himself* (Garden City, N.Y.: Doubleday, 1964), 253.

237 "technicality": Darryl Zanuck to Curtiz, telegram, February 14, 1939; courtesy of the Lucas family.

237 "We would really have": Jack L. Warner to Hal Wallis, memo, February 1, 1938, USC Warner Bros. Archive.

238 "Nobody wants to see": Lawrence, *Actor: The Life and Times of Paul Muni*, 209.

238 "He seems a little dubious": Noll Gurney to Jack L. Warner, September 1, 1938, USC Warner Bros. Archive.

239 "Last night I found": Hal Wallis to Tenny Wright, Warner Bros. interoffice communication, November 17, 1938, USC Warner Bros. Archive.

239 "an awful experience" and "I was in such a depressed state": Reed, *Olivia de Havilland*, 19.

241 "Was it your idea": Hal Wallis to Robert Lord, Warner Bros. interoffice communication, November 18, 1938, USC Warner Bros. Archive.

241 "Very happy over progress": Hal Wallis to Curtiz, telegram, November 21, 1938, USC Warner Bros. Archive.

242 "I hope that Mike": Hal Wallis to Robert Lord, Warner Bros. interoffice communication November 15, 1938, USC Warner Bros. Archive.

242 "I am sorry to trouble you": Robert Lord to Hal Wallis, Warner Bros. interoffice communication, November 1, 1938, USC Warner Bros. Archive.

242 "Please level with me": Hal Wallis to Curtiz, Warner Bros. interoffice communication, January 10, 1939, USC Warner Bros. Archive.

243 "Within half an hour": Lucas, *Eighty Odd Years in Hollywood*, 85.

243 "Dear Mike, Congratulations again": ibid.

244 "While she had retired": Frances Marion, *Off with Their Heads: A Serio-Comic Tale of Hollywood* (New York: Macmillan, 1972), 291.

21. Reaching Their Majority

1. There was some free publicity for *Blackwell's Island* when the New York State Board of Censors temporarily halted the premiere at the Globe Theatre in Manhattan. The censors, who apparently existed in a Twilight Zone of alternative reality, were irked because the picture depicted "things that couldn't happen such as police and prison guards accepting bribes." *New York Post*, February 27, 1939.

2. *Sons of Liberty* was matched against the less than rigorous competition of *Drunk Driving*, an MGM *Crime Does Not Pay* series entry, and *Five Times Five*, a filmed celebration of the Dionne quintuplets' fifth birthday party.

3. *Andy Hardy Comes Home*, a moribund 1958 attempt by MGM to revive the

successful series, provided definitive evidence that the studio system was circling the drain.

4. James Bacon, a columnist and friend, elaborated on the nature of Curtiz's calorie-free lunches: "Sometimes he would take an aspirin for lunch but mostly he liked to have his cock sucked." Bacon, *Made in Hollywood,* 162.

5. "Blue pages" are those script pages added to the screenplay as the film is being filmed.

Quotation Sources by Page Number

249 "I thought he was wonderful": James Wong Howe, interview by Frank Mc-Geary, 1974, Margaret Herrick Library.

250 "Curtiz had more energy": Silke, *Here's Looking at You, Kid,* 148.

250 "hand-held toy": Todd Rainsberger, *James Wong Howe, Cinematographer* (San Diego: A. S. Barnes, 1981), 190.

251 "I must agree with Mike": Henry Blanke to Hal Wallis, Warner Bros. interoffice communication, March 3, 1939, USC Warner Bros. Archive.

251 "I wish you would send": Frank Mattison to Tenny Wright, Warner Bros. interoffice communication, September 13, 1939, USC Warner Bros. Archive.

251 "I think when you see": Hal Wallis to Jack Warner, memo, February 17, 1939, USC Warner Bros. Archive.

252 "You force me to refuse": Bette Davis to Jack Warner, April 28, 1939, USC Warner Bros. Archive.

252 "you cannot call a Queen": Jack L. Warner to Gradwell Sears, July 14, 1939, USC Warner Bros. Archive.

252 "that dainty little hand" and "It wasn't a very pleasant picture": Flynn, *My Wicked, Wicked Ways,* 260, 265.

253 "She said, 'Whom would you suggest'": Irving Rapper, interview by Ronald L. Davis, August 13, 1980, Margaret Herrick Library and SMU Collection.

253 "When you work with me": Silke, *Here's Looking at You, Kid,* 150.

253 "Shut up, Mike": Spada, *More Than a Woman,* 161.

253 "jaunts on his boat": Hal Wallis to Tenny Wright, Warner Bros. interoffice communication, April 4, 1939, USC Warner Bros. Archive.

253 "We lost considerable time": Frank Mattison to Tenny Wright, Warner Bros. daily production report, July 5, 1939, USC Warner Bros. Archive.

253 "It seems as though": Frank Mattison to Tenny Wright, Warner Bros. interoffice communication, June 19, 1939, USC Warner Bros. Archive.

254 "most incredible": Silke, *Here's Looking at You, Kid,* 150.

255 "I had another display": Frank Mattison to Tenny Wright, Warner Bros. interoffice communication, June 12, 1939, USC Warner Bros. Archive.

255 "a certain person" and "a certain man who means well": Olivia de Havilland to Jack L. Warner, July 18, 1939, USC Warner Bros. Archive.

255 "I lost my cool": Olivia de Havilland, interview by Glenn Kenny, *Premiere,* October 2004, 70.

256 "I should want you" and "Please, please, make me": Elmer Sunfield, "English Broken Here," *Hollywood Magazine,* July 1940, 50.

256 "You speak too much": Frazier, "The Machine with a Rage," 136.

256 "Vot are those wires": Nanette Fabray to the author, March 14, 2011.

256 "Damn, he's good.": Olivia de Havilland, interview by Glenn Kenny, *Premiere*, 68.

257 "The reaction to the title": Gradwell Sears to Jack Warner, August 14, 1939, USC Warner Bros. Archive.

258 "I was so lonely": "Daughter of Michael Curtiz, Film Director, Tries Suicide," *Los Angeles Times,* July 23, 1939.

258 "I tried to kill myself": UPI, *Oakland Tribune,* July 24, 1939.

258 "highly nervous and highly strung": "Daughter of Michael Curtiz, Film Director, Tries Suicide," *Los Angeles Times,* July 23, 1939.

258 "Tell my father": UPI, *Oakland Tribune,* July 24, 1939.

258 "Once a journalist told my Father": Fidalgo, *Michael Curtiz,* 274–75.

260 "a frail, stooped woman": Lucas, *Eighty Odd Years in Hollywood,* 120.

260 "It was after the": László Kriston to the author, January 16, 2015.

262 "the only studio with any guts": *Hollywood Reporter,* December 8, 1938.

263 "We are routed out": Joe McNeill, *Arizona's Little Hollywood: Sedona and Northern Arizona's Forgotten Film History, 1923–1973* (Sedona, Ariz.: Northedge & Sons, 2010), 222.

263–264 "Yucca, I have a good gag," "Well, you are doubling for Flynn," "I was amazed at him," and "This was a good gag": Canutt and Drake, *Stunt Man,* 129.

264 "They're still here": McNeill, *Arizona's Little Hollywood,* 232.

264 "It is quite impossible": Errol Flynn to Hal Wallis, telegram, November 11, 1939, USC Warner Bros. Archive.

265 "If this isn't double-talking": Tenny Wright to Hal Wallis, Warner Bros. interoffice communication, November 24, 1939, USC Warner Bros. Archive.

265 "When we started out" and "It is a simple scene": Hal Wallis to Curtiz, Warner Bros. interoffice communication, December 1, 1939, USC Warner Bros. Archive.

265 "In general, Mike doesn't feel": Robert Fellows to Hal Wallis, interoffice communication, December 3, 1939, USC Warner Bros. Archive.

265 "This is the little number": Robert Buckner to Robert Fellows, Warner Bros. interoffice communication, December 18, 1939, USC Warner Bros. Archive.

266 "How much will it cost?": Robert Fellows to Hal Wallis, Warner Bros interoffice communication, December 8, 1939, USC Warner Bros. Archive.

266 "Hal is quite sick": Robert Fellows to Curtiz, Warner Bros. interoffice communication, December 13, 1939, USC Warner Bros. Archive.

267 "Because you must be" and "Anybody who should talk": Sunfield, "English Broken Here," 49–50.

268 "if you look at the script": Frank Mattison to Tenny Wright, Warner Bros. interoffice communication, January 4, 1940, USC Warner Bros. Archive.

22. The Swash and the Buckler

1. The action shots used in *The Sea Hawk* included footage originally purloined for *Captain Blood* from *The Divine Lady* (1929). *The Sea Hawk* included a few of these stock shots.

2. Warner Bros. reissued new Technicolor prints of *The Adventures of Robin Hood* that did extraordinary business after a 1948 re-release. An edited version of *Captain Blood* and a black-and-white double bill of *Dodge City* and *Virginia City* followed in 1951.

3. George Raft, who signed with Warner Bros. in 1939, exercised a self-destructive judgment in his selection of movie roles. He turned down *High Sierra, The Maltese Falcon,* and *Double Indemnity* while perpetuating the enduring myth that he refused the lead in *Casablanca* (it was never offered to him).

4. A former member of the Communist Party USA (CPUSA), Robert Rossen was one of the original "Hollywood Nineteen" subpoenaed by Congress in 1947. He was blacklisted and eventually named over 50 colleagues in 1953 in order to reclaim his career.

5. There is no record of anybody other than Raoul Walsh and Breezy Eason directing *They Died with Their Boots On.* Although Curtiz was initially tapped to direct the Custer biopic, an examination of the production files indicates that he was reassigned during preproduction after Flynn met with Jack Warner.

Quotation Sources by Page Number

270 "a complete, thorough test": Hal Wallis to Curtiz, interoffice communication, July 10, 1939, USC Warner Bros. Archive.

271 "What are you going to do": Hal Wallis to Curtiz, Warner Bros. interoffice communication, February 2, 1940, USC Warner Bros. Archive.

271 "It sounds instead": Hal Wallis to Henry Blanke, Warner Bros. interoffice communication, February 5, 1940, USC Warner Bros. Archive.

271 "beautiful," "everything is going along," and "I have been able": Hal Wallis to Curtiz, Warner Bros. interoffice communication, February 8, 1940, USC Warner Bros. Archive.

272 "unless I okay it": Hal Wallis to Henry Blanke, Warner Bros. interoffice communication, March 14, 1940, USC Warner Bros. Archive.

272 "But when the ruthless ambitions": *The Sea Hawk* shooting script, scene 267, January 23, 1940.

272 "What's the matter with you": Rudy Behlmer, ed., *The Sea Hawk* (Madison: University of Wisconsin Press, 1982), 32.

272 "Mr. Daniell is absolutely helpless": Frank Mattison to Tenny Wright, interoffice communication, February 17, 1940, USC Warner Bros. Archive.

274 "pull a gun" and "Errol, you worked hard": Sidney Skolsky, syndicated column, *Hollywood,* March 5, 1940.

274 "Mr. Curtiz is very anxious": Frank Mattison to Tenny Wright, Warner Bros. interoffice communication, April 15, 1940, USC Warner Bros. Archive.

274 "It seemed to me": Hal Wallis to Henry Blanke, Warner Bros. interoffice communication, March 7, 1940, USC Warner Bros. Archive.

275 "Get me another minister": Peter Bogdanovich, *Who the Hell's in It: Portraits and Conversations* (New York: Knopf, 2004), 370.

275 "Before he hit bottom": Raymond Massey, *A Hundred Different Lives: An Autobiography* (Boston: Little, Brown, 1979), 260.

275 "Mike walked across": Ronald Reagan with Richard G. Hubler, *Where's the Rest of Me?* (New York: Duell, Sloan and Pearce, 1965), 97.

275 "a mean streak": Massey, *A Hundred Different Lives*, 260.

276 "For Hungarian director Michael Curtiz": "Cinema: The New Pictures," *Time,* August 19, 1940.

276–277 "That list is only," "I have also been," "The 20 percent," "I compromise": Theodore Strauss, "The Blitzkrieg of Michael Curtiz," *New York Times,* May 19, 1940.

277 "Fine, go ahead": Massey, *A Hundred Different Lives*, 260.

278 "I realize that you": United States Military Academy to Herman Lissauer, Warner Bros. Research Department, July 8, 1940, USC Warner Bros. Archive.

278 "For God's sake": Gene Reynolds to the author, December 7, 2010.

279 "What's the matter?": Harrison Carroll, "Michael Curtiz Is Traditional Movie Director," *Herald Star* (Steubenville, Ohio), August 14, 1940.

279 "I was in a wagon": Gene Reynolds to the author, December 7, 2010.

279 "Errol was a strange person": Reagan and Hubler, *Where's the Rest of Me?* 96.

280 "He precedes every statement": Bob Fellows to Tenny Wright, Warner Bros. interoffice communication, September 10, 1940, USC Warner Bros. Archive.

280 "How'd you like those bums," "Heet's all propaganda," and "You're a loveable bum": Mary Louise Walliser, "Michael Curtiz Can Murder King's English but Reviewer Finds Him A Phenomenon as Director," *San Antonio Evening News,* January 1941.

280 "They get up and start singing": Hal Wallis to Curtiz, Warner Bros. interoffice communication, August 16, 1940, USC Warner Bros. Archive.

281 "What *is Santa Fe Trail*": Robert Buckner to Hal Wallis, Warner Bros. interoffice communication, November 28, 1940, USC Warner Bros. Archive. Emphases in original.

281 "graduating them en masse": Bosley Crowther, "'Santa Fe Trail,' Which Is Chiefly a Picture about Something Else, Opens at the Strand" *New York Times,* December 21, 1940.

281 "I have always said": Robert S. Taplinger, director of publicity, production notes: "The Sea Wolf," n.d., USC Warner Bros. Archive.

281 "No actor could ask" and "in everything but name": Robinson and Spigelgass, *All My Yesterdays*, 218.

281 "When we worked together": Ida Lupino with Mary Ann Anderson, *Ida Lupino: Beyond the Camera* (Albany, Ga.: BearManor Media, 2011), 52.

282 "little better than a bit": George Raft to Hal Wallis, October 23, 1940, USC Warner Bros. Archive.

285 "Curtiz would come over": Silke, *Here's Looking at You, Kid,* 148.

285 "Whenever Robinson gets into these": Hal Wallis to Henry Blanke, Warner Bros. interoffice communication, November 20, 1940, USC Warner Bros. Archive.

287 "We got all the long shots" and "In his own special dialect": Ralph Bellamy, *When the Smoke Hit the Fan* (Garden City, N.Y.: Doubleday, 1979), 162.

288 "Curtiz had to be": Tony Thomas, *Errol Flynn: The Spy Who Never Was* (New York: Carol Publishing, 1990), 122.

288 "make a two-reel short": Hal Wallis to Curtiz, Warner Bros. interoffice communication, March 28, 1941, USC Warner Bros. Archive.

288 "never misses a day," "The dialogue director," and "Flynn . . . does not like his part": Robert Lord to Hal Wallis, Warner Bros. interoffice communication, March 14, 1941, USC Warner Bros. Archive.

288 "Errol sulked quite a bit": Lucas, *Eighty Odd Years in Hollywood*, 118.

289 "I know you could not" and "If the attached note": J. L. Warner to Curtiz, memo, April 23, 1941, USC Warner Bros. Archive.

289 "Please, everybody sweat now": Charles Tranberg, *Fred MacMurray: A Biography* (Albany, Ga.: BearManor Media, 2007), 82.

290 "a lethal, lethal scene": Robert Matzen, *Errol & Olivia: Ego and Obsession in Golden Era Hollywood* (Pittsburgh: GoodKnight Books, 2010), 154.

290 "I deemed it wiser": Flynn, *My Wicked, Wicked Ways*, 297.

290 "Oh Mike. Lovely, lovely": Ann Doran, interview by Ronald L. Davis, August 10, 1983, Margaret Herrick Library and SMU Collection.

291 "Why hell I talk foreign?": Lucas, *Eighty Odd Years in Hollywood*, 120.

23. The "Pinochle" of His Career

Quotation Sources by Page Number

292 "The plot was the same" and "He gave one of the actors": McCabe, *Cagney*, 197, 211.

293 "They'd bounce him around": Adamson and Haskin, *Byron Haskin*, 96.

293 "thankless": "The New Pictures" *Time*, March 2, 1942.

295 "[Warner] told me" and "We're going to have to": Patrick McGilligan, *Cagney: The Actor as Auteur* (South Brunswick, N.J.: A. S. Barnes & Co., 1975), 146, 147–48.

295 "He and I never": Wallis and Higham, *Starmaker*, 55.

296 "Four-fifths of the people": George M. Cohan to Robert Buckner and Hal Wallis, April 15, 1941, USC Warner Bros. Archive.

296 "This is our main plea": Hal Wallis, Robert Buckner, and William Cagney to George M. Cohan, August 29, 1941, USC Warner Bros. Archive.

297 "I read it with incredulity": McCabe, *Cagney*, 202.

297 "That's the kind of life": Ward Morehouse, *George M. Cohan: Prince of the American Theater* (Philadelphia: J. B. Lippincott, 1943), 229.

297 "I spent seven months": Robert Buckner to Hal Wallis, Warner Bros. interoffice communication, January 13, 1942, USC Warner Bros. Archive.

298 "I was reading": Lucas, *Eighty Odd Years in Hollywood*, 128.

298 "The crew was standing" and "worked in a kind of": Rosemary DeCamp, *Tigers in My Lap* (Baltimore: Midnight Marquee Press, 2000), 105, 106.

299 "Mike was so happy": Joan Leslie to the author, August 5, 2011.

300 "If a man is born": Ezra Goodman, "Yankee Doodle Curtiz," *Los Angeles Daily News*, August 17, 1942.

300 "Dear Mike, As always": Hal Wallis to Curtiz, memo, December 5, 1941, USC Warner Bros. Archive.

300 "Vunderful. This time I work": *Chicago Daily Tribune,* January 18, 1942.

300 "He was a ruthless": DeCamp, *Tigers in My Lap,* 108.

300 "He would take it": Joan Leslie to the author, August 5, 2011.

300 "I didn't have to": James Cagney, *Cagney by Cagney* (Garden City, N.Y.: Doubleday, 1976)

300 "Jim doesn't sing": Joan Leslie to the author, August 5, 2011.

301 "We all tried to": DeCamp, *Tigers in My Lap,* 106.

302 "He knew almost nothing": Charles Higham, *Hollywood Cameramen: Sources of Light* (Bloomington: Indiana University Press, 1970), 88.

302 "Suppose he makes a scene": Martin, *Hollywood without Make-Up,* 119.

302 "He was absolutely both": Joan Leslie to the author, August 5, 2011.

302 "I am not at all satisfied": Jack Warner to Curtiz, memo, December 17, 1941, USC Warner Bros. Archive.

302 "Mike Curtiz came on the set": Frank Mattison to Tenny Wright, Warner Bros. interoffice communication, February 2, 1942, USC Warner Bros. Archive.

303 "This seems to me": Curtiz to Hal Wallis, Warner Bros. interoffice communication, December 12, 1941, USC Warner Bros. Archive.

303 "give me the tear" and "So we wrote the death scene": Patrick McGilligan, ed., *Yankee Doodle Dandy* (Madison: University of Wisconsin Press, 1981), 44.

303 "I stood at the door": Joan Leslie to the author, August 5, 2011.

304 "Cheeses Chrisdt, Jimmy, beautiful": Cagney, *Cagney by Cagney,* 214.

304 "I would be most grateful": William Cagney to Hal Wallis, Warner Bros. interoffice communication, November 14, 1941, USC Warner Bros. Archive.

304 "Mike, this scene": McCabe, *Cagney,* 212.

305 "All that we need": Hal Wallis to Curtiz, Warner Bros. interoffice communication, November 27, 1941, USC Warner Bros. Archive.

305 "For your information": Robert Buckner to Hal Wallis, Warner Bros. interoffice communication, January 22, 1942, USC Warner Bros. Archive.

306 "There is so much": Bosley Crowther, "'Yankee Doodle Dandy,' with James Cagney as George M. Cohan, Opens at Hollywood," *New York Times,* May 30, 1942.

306 "If *Yankee Doodle Dandy* is the best": Virginia Wright, *Los Angeles Daily News,* September 13, 1942.

306 "the pinochle of my career": McCabe, *Cagney,* 209.

306 "The most inspirational opening": Jack L. Warner to George M. Cohan, telegram, August 13, 1942, USC Warner Bros. Archive.

306 "Dear Jim, How's my double?": McGilligan, *Yankee Doodle Dandy,* 63.

308 "and the unforgettable Michael Curtiz": "AFI Life Achievement Award: A Tribute to James Cagney," televised March 18, 1974.

24. Fundamental Things

1. Julius Epstein spoke extensively with Aljean Harmetz for *Round Up the Usual Suspects* (re-released as *The Making of Casablanca: Bogart, Berman, and World*

War II). About Koch's claim of collaboration he said: "We never sat in the same room with him. We never had one conference with him. And we never asked to be taken off the picture. But Howard is a nice man, and I think he really believed what he wrote." According to Epstein, Koch later wrote him a letter of apology for his faulty memory.

2. Vincent Sherman had no quarrel with Wallis's selection of Curtiz for *Casablanca*: "I couldn't get sore because Mike was a marvelous director. I used to watch Mike's pictures to learn how to direct." Harmetz, *The Making of Casablanca*, 75.

3. Koch's work on *The Sea Hawk* for Curtiz and *The Letter* for William Wyler (both 1940) had been well received. He had been a playwright before being hired by John Houseman to write scripts for the Mercury Theatre radio company. Koch reportedly cowrote the infamous 1938 *War of the Worlds* broadcast by Orson Welles before he went to work at Warner Bros.

4. Madeleine LeBeau's weeping in a memorable close-up during the "Marseillaise" scene was probably genuine. She and her husband, Marcel Dalio (who played Rick's croupier), made it out of France just ahead of the Nazis but had to leave Dalio's mother hidden in a Paris cellar. During the production, she and Dalio were divorced. The last known surviving *Casablanca* performer, LeBeau died in 2016.

5. The director Richard Brooks claimed Bogart pulled this stunt during the filming of *Deadline U.S.A.* (1952).

Quotation Sources by Page Number

309 "We started out to make": Hal Wallis, AFI Seminar, April 10, 1974, in George Stevens Jr., ed., *Conversations with the Great Moviemakers of Hollywood's Golden Age at the American Film Institute* (New York: Knopf, 2006), 601.

309 "Excellent melodrama": Stephen Karnot, synopsis of *Everybody Comes to Rick's*, December 11, 1941, USC Warner Bros. Archives.

310 "That's what you're here for": Harmetz, *The Making of Casablanca*, 18.

312 "[Raft] knows we're going": Jack L. Warner to Hal Wallis, memo, April 2, 1942, USC Warner Bros. Archive.

312 "I have thought over": Hal Wallis to Jack L. Warner, memo, April 13, 1942, USC Warner Bros. Archive.

312 "Humphrey Bogart never study": Martin, *Hollywood without Make-Up*, 119.

313 "got the idea to use" and "my picture": Casey Robinson, oral history interview by Joel Greenberg, 1974, American Film Institute.

313 "While we handle": Julius and Philip Epstein to Hal Wallis, n.d. (early March 1942), USC Warner Bros. Archive.

313 "So I said, 'Oh'": Harmetz, *The Making of Casablanca*, 93.

314 "I greatly enjoyed Mike," "Christmas baby": Harmetz, *The Making of Casablanca*, 126.

314 "I am very critical": Martin, *Hollywood without Make-Up*, 119.

314–315 "I have been going over": Hal Wallis to Curtiz, Warner Bros. interoffice communication, April 22, 1942, USC Warner Bros. Archive.

316 "marvelous for the part": Hal Wallis to Steve Trilling, Warner Bros. interoffice communication, February 5, 1942, USC Warner Bros. Archive.

316 "pretty good": Hal Wallis to Curtiz, Warner Bros. interoffice communication, April 22, 1942, USC Warner Bros. Archive.

318 "Curtiz was marvelous": Rudy Behlmer, *Behind the Scenes: The Making of* — (Hollywood: Samuel French, 1989), 169.

318 "Goddamn, I don't remember": Lucas, *Eighty Odd Years in Hollywood,* 142.

318 "I think Mike was one of the great": Casey Robinson, oral history interview by Joel Greenberg, 1974, American Film Institute.

319 "my impression about *Casablanca*" and "Now you're really set": Casey Robinson to Hal Wallis, "Notes on Screenplay Casablanca," Warner Bros. interoffice communication, May 20, 1942, USC Warner Bros. Archive.

320 "These are turbulent days": Jack L. Warner to Curtiz, memo, May 23, 1942, USC Warner Bros. Archive.

320 "a miserable bastard," "I told him," and "He got red in the face": Harmetz, *The Making of Casablanca,* 126, 128.

321 "My question to you": Hal Wallis to George Groves, Warner Bros. interoffice communication, May 26, 1942, USC Warner Bros. Archive.

321 "I'm sorry you got mad": Harmetz, *The Making of Casablanca,* 129.

321 "Edeson and Mike are": Al Alleborn to Tenny Wright, Warner Bros. interoffice communication, June 17, 1942, USC Warner Bros. Archive.

321 "You were present": Hal Wallis to Arthur Edeson, Warner Bros. interoffice communication, May 26, 1942, USC Warner Bros. Archive.

322 "Without them, we cannot": *Warner Club News* (March 1942), USC Cinematic Arts Library, Los Angeles.

322 "Waste Is More Deadly": Harry B. Warner speech, Jack L. Warner Collection, USC Cinematic Arts Library, Los Angeles.

322 Dear Mike: I can't understand" Jack Warner to Curtiz, memo, July 15, 1942, USC Warner Bros. Archive.

322 "We are building": Hal Wallis to Curtiz, Warner Bros. interoffice communication, May 15, 1942, USC Warner Bros. Archive.

323 "I want to again ask": Hal Wallis to Arthur Edeson, Warner Bros. interoffice communication, June 2, 1942, USC Warner Bros. Archive.

323 "Again I want to say": Hal Wallis to Curtiz, Warner Bros. interoffice communication, June 4, 1942, USC Warner Bros. Archive.

325 "I suddenly realized": Harmetz, *The Making of Casablanca,* 213.

325 "I am going over": Hal Wallis to Curtiz, Warner Bros. interoffice communication, May 25, 1942, USC Warner Bros. Archive.

325 "If Sakall will do the part": Hal Wallis to Curtiz, Warner Bros. interoffice communication, June 2, 1942, USC Warner Bros. Archive.

326 "Maybe it's because": Hedda Hopper, "Home of the Freeze," *Washington Post,* July 10, 1942.

326 "We could both hear" and "We don't want to hear": Henreid and Fast, *Ladies Man,* 124.

326–327 "I see tomorrow" and "One more thing": Hal Wallis to Curtiz, Warner Bros. interoffice communication, July 6, 1942, USC Warner Bros. Archive.

328 "Only one line remained" and "One cannot give all": Harmetz, *The Making of Casablanca,* 179.

328 "shut up": Sperber and Lax, *Humphrey Bogart,* 203.

329 "every lunchtime, Curtiz argued" and "Every morning we said": Doug Mc-Clelland, *Forties Film Talk: Oral Histories of Hollywood, with 120 Lobby Posters* (Jefferson, N.C.: McFarland, 1992), 321.

329 "Round up the usual": Harmetz, *The Making of Casablanca,* 230.

330 "During the day": Al Alleborn to Tenny Wright, Warner Bros. interoffice communication, July 18, 1942, USC Warner Bros. Archive.

331 "They have the lousiest" and "The work is hard": Wegele, *Max Steiner,* 94, 10.

332 "a fast-talking, hypersensitive gnome": Wallis and Higham, *Starmaker,* 41.

332 "Dear Max: We previewed": Curtiz to Max Steiner, telegraph, Max Steiner Collection, Harold Lee Library, Brigham Young University, Provo, Utah (as cited in Wegele, *Max Steiner,* 93.

333 "Dear Hugo: Thanks for everything": Wegele, *Max Steiner,* insert.

333 "He told me it was": Hal Wallis to Charles Einfeld, Warner Bros. interdepartmental communication, August 28, 1942, USC Warner Bros. Archive.

333 "was a big flop" and "Thereafter, he kept that memo": Harmetz, *The Making of Casablanca,* 272.

333–334 "There will be a retake": Hal Wallis to Tenny Wright, Warner Bros. interdepartmental communication, November 11, 1942, USC Warner Bros. Archive.

334 "Dear Hal: Saw *Casablanca*": David O. Selznick to Hal Wallis, telegram, November 12, 1942, USC Warner Bros. Archive.

334 "Will definitely not touch": Jack L. Warner, Warner Bros., to Major Bernhard, Schneider, Kalmenson, Blumenstock, Schless, Hummel, telegraph, November 12, 1942, USC Warner Bros. Archive.

335 "Yes, indeed, the Warners": Bosley Crowther, "Movie Review: *Casablanca,*" *New York Times,* November 27, 1942.

337 "a happy accident": Andrew Sarris, *The American Cinema: Directors and Directions, 1929–1968* (1968; repr., New York: Da Capo Press, 1996), 176.

25. "Those fine patriotic citizens, the Warner Brothers"

1. In 2003 the *New York Times* hired Mark Von Hagen, professor of Russian history at Columbia University, to review Duranty's work relating to his award of the Pulitzer Prize for distinguished reporting in 1932. Von Hagen found that Duranty's reporting "gave voice to Stalinist propaganda" and "for the sake of the *New York Times* honor, they should take the prize away." The *Times*'s publisher, Arthur Ochs Sulzberger, labeled Duranty's work "slovenly" and said it should have been recognized for what it was by his editors and the Pulitzer judges. The Pulitzer board administrator at the time, Sig Gissler, refused to rescind Duranty's Pulitzer.

2. For all Jack Warner's disparagement of screenwriters, it is interesting to note

the number of writers from the Warner Bros. stable who ascended to the ranks of successful film producers. The writer-to-producer ranks would eventually include Buckner, Robert Lord, Casey Robinson, the Epstein brothers, and Delmer Daves.

3. One of the more respected historical estimates of the death toll in the Soviet Union caused by the Great Terror during 1936–38 is 3 million.

4. Koch claimed in his memoir *As Time Goes By* that he thought up the opening of *Mission to Moscow* when he "suddenly remembered" Selassie's 1936 speech while driving through Needles, Calif.

5. The Soviet Union invaded Finland on November 30, 1939, three months after the Soviet-Nazi nonaggression pact and two years before Hitler attacked Russia. The Finns held off the numerically superior Red Army for months until finally ceding for peace, along with 11 percent of its territory, on March 13, 1940.

6. Leigh Whipper (1876–1975) was the first African American actor to join Actor's Equity. Whipper received a special award from the Ethiopian government for portraying Haile Selassie in *Mission to Moscow.*

7. Koch's script included a sequence of a couple of U.S. senators discussing the benefits of an alliance with Nazi Germany in which one says, "Not only can we do business with Hitler, but we can make a nice profit doing so."

8. Arthur Upham Pope (1881–1969) was an archaeologist, pianist, museum designer, and political activist who was the biographer of Maxim Litvinov and an unabashed admirer of the Soviet Union.

Quotation Sources by Page Number

338 "The Motherland has been attacked!": Nancy Lynn Schwartz and Sheila Schwartz, *The Hollywood Writers' War* (New York: Knopf, 1982), 173.

340 "riddled with such political bias": Colin Shindler, *Hollywood Goes to War: Films and American Society, 1939–1952* (Boston: Routledge & K. Paul, 1979), 58.

340 "Joe is anxious," "an order," and "we simply couldn't lose": Warner and Jennings, *My First Hundred Years in Hollywood*, 291.

340 "Trotskyite": Ronald Radosh and Allis Radosh, *Red Star over Hollywood: The Film Colony's Long Romance with the Left* (San Francisco: Encounter Books, 2005), 96.

341 "Our people know almost nothing": Howard Koch, *As Time Goes By: Memoirs of a Writer* (New York: Harcourt Brace Jovanovich, 1979), 101.

341 "I knew that F.D.R.": David Culbert, ed., *Mission to Moscow* (Madison: University of Wisconsin Press, 1980), 16.

342 "a great leader," "insisted on the liberalism," "projecting actual secret," "To assume that this proceeding," and "had cleansed the country": Joseph Edward Davies, *Mission to Moscow* (New York: Simon and Schuster, 1941), 68, 106, 121, 43, 280.

342 "every change was at the personal request": Culbert, *Mission to Moscow,* 17.

343 "But you know": "The Cover Story: Michael Curtiz—One of the Giants," *Hollywood Close-Up,* December 25, 1958, 5.

343 "Today you start": Jack Warner to Curtiz, telegraph, November 9, 1942, USC Warner Bros. Archive.

343 "a valuable ally" and "sympathetic to the Soviet system": Koch, *As Time Goes By*, 116–17.

344 "positive accomplishments . . . fortify me": Jay Leyda to Joseph Freeman, February 3, 1943, quoted in Radosh and Radosh, *Red Star over Hollywood*, 101.

344 "Let the Soviet-haters scream," "miscast for a film," and "had been involved": Koch, *As Time Goes By*, 106, 111, 112.

345 "reluctantly accepted": *Hollywood Close-Up*, December 25, 1958, 5.

345 "leading his people down": Paul Johnson, *Modern Times: The World from the Twenties to the Eighties* (New York: Harper & Row, 1983), 276.

345 "even after the script": Culbert, *Mission to Moscow*, 23.

346 "Russia knew she was": ibid., 240.

346 "privileged knowledge," "often prone to pulling," and "Davies insisted upon the guilt": ibid., 24.

347 "Mike Curtiz had a reputation": Eleanor Parker to the author, May 15, 2010.

347 "There is no man": *Hollywood Reporter*, January 11, 1943.

347 "That, Mr. Davies": *New York Post*, September 22, 1943.

348 "I consider my stupidity": Lucas, *Eighty Odd Years in Hollywood*, 146.

348 "Mike is raising hell": Al Alleborn to Tenny Wright, Warner Bros. production report, November 23, 1942, USC Warner Bros. Archive.

349 "a conductor leading a symphony" and "When the Negus speak": "Mike Curtiz Runs the 'League of Nations' as He Jolly Well Wants," *Miami News*, December 25, 1942.

349 "Henry Victor could not remember": Al Alleborn to Tenny Wright, Warner Bros. interoffice communication, November 14, 1942, USC Warner Bros. Archive.

349 "You cannot shoot 10 takes": Jack Warner to Curtiz, November 11, 1942, USC Warner Bros. Archive. Emphasis in original.

349 "Please Mr. Curtiz,": Jack Warner to Curtiz, November 19, 1942, USC Warner Bros. Archive.

349 "Dear Jack—Believe me": Curtiz to Jack Warner, November 30, 1942, USC Warner Bros. Archive.

349 "will make a great contribution": Culbert, *Mission to Moscow*, 30.

351 "the first instance" and "the Soviet dictatorship": John Dewey and Suzanne La Follette, "Several Faults Are Found in 'Mission to Moscow' Film," *New York Times*, May 6, 1943.

351 "the booby prize" and "made up its own facts": Manny Farber, "Mishmash," *New Republic*, May 10, 1943, 636.

351 "to convey a realistic impression" and "briefly, but effectively played": Bosley Crowther, "Movie Review: *Mission to Moscow*," *New York Times*, April 30, 1943.

351 "hasten and intensify" and "the first Soviet production": James Agee, "Films," *Nation*, May 22, 1943.

351 "We would hate to be known": *Hollywood Reporter*, May 20, 1943.

351 "the interest of fairness": Jack Warner to W. R. Hearst, telegram, May 17, 1943, USC Warner Bros. Archive.

351–352 "Your film, Mr. Warner": W. R. Hearst to Jack Warner, telegram, May 20, 1943, USC Warner Bros. Archive.

352 "not a disaster" and "never broke even": Culbert, *Mission to Moscow,* 34.

352 "It was hilarious": Ronald L. Davis, *Words into Images: Screenwriters on the Studio System* (Jackson: University Press of Mississippi, 2007), 144.

353 "Mike Curtiz is very upset": Robert Buckner to Jack Warner, May 20, 1943, USC Warner Bros. Archive.

353 "Songs make history": Laurence Bergreen, "Irving Berlin: *This Is the Army,*" *Prologue* 28, no. 2 (1996), www.archives.gov/publications/prologue/1996/summer/ irving-berlin-1.html.

354 "I personally want": Jack Warner to Hal Wallis, October 15, 1942, USC Warner Bros. Archive.

354 "I understand Mike Curtiz": Irving Berlin to Jack Warner, August 29, 1942, USC Warner Bros. Archive.

354 "It is true that": Jack Warner to Irving Berlin, September 2, 1942, USC Warner Bros. Archive.

355 "if you saw a colonel": Max Wilk, *Every Day's a Matinee: Memoirs Scribbled on a Dressing Room Door* (New York: W. W. Norton, 1975), 121.

355 "If the fellow": Bergreen, "Irving Berlin: *This Is the Army.*"

355 "It's very possible": McClelland, *Forties Film Talk,* 391.

356 "female impersonators do not exist": Carl Schaefer to J. L. Warner, Warner Bros. interoffice communication, December 17, 1942, USC Warner Bros. Archive.

357 "We will be very wise": Jack Warner to Hal Wallis and Irving Berlin, telegram, July 2, 1943, USC Warner Bros. Archive.

357 "We had acquired," "would turn out to be," "a veritable Mount Everest," "Ve got to fill": Wilk, *Every Day's a Matinee,* 112, 124, 126.

358 "Mr. Curtiz has agreed": Freston & Files (attorneys for Warner Bros. Pictures Inc.) to Hugh L. Ducker, regional head, Salary Stabilization Board, n.d., USC Warner Bros. Archive.

358 "Please charge Mike Curtiz's salary": Roy Obringer to Wilder, Warner Bros. interoffice communication, February 23, 1943, USC Warner Bros. Archive.

358–359 "the peculiar manner": Hal Wallis to Johnny Hughes, Warner Bros. interoffice communication, March 10, 1943, USC Warner Bros. Archive.

359 "It was a simple little scene": Joan Leslie to the author, August 5, 2011.

361 "If you can get": Jack L. Warner to Hal Wallis, May 6, 1943, USC Warner Bros. Archive.

361 "Within hours, he proves" and "nothing but morose neutrality": Michèle Morgan and Marcelle Routier, *Avec ces yeux-là* (Paris: Éditions Robert Laffont, 1977). Translated for the author by Philippe Garnier.

361 "the rest of delays": Eric Stacey to Tenny Wright, Warner Bros. interoffice communication, September 22, 1943, USC Warner Bros. Archive.

362–363 "Considerable trouble caused today": Eric Stacey to Tenny Wright, Warner Bros. interoffice communication, October 2, 1943, USC Warner Bros. Archive.

363 "The actor is going," "Nobody is going to trigger": Leith Adams to the author, April 15, 2016.

363 "Stop giving me double talk": Jack L. Warner to Hal Wallis, telegram, November 30, 1943, USC Warner Bros. Archive.

364 "Sick and tired": Jack L. Warner to Charles Einfeld, telegram, November 30, 1943, USC Warner Bros. Archive.

364–365 "If there was a god": Richard Erdman to the author, July 21, 2011.

365 "Saw *Janie* last night": Al Jolson to Jack Warner, telegram, July 26, 1944, USC Warner Bros. Archive.

26. Victory Garden

1. Frank Pierson (1925–2012) became a distinguished screenwriter and director and served as president of the Writers Guild of America and the Motion Picture Academy.

2. Cain's two credited screenplays, which also included a host of collaborators, were *Stand Up and Fight* (1939), a Metro Western, and *Gypsy Wildcat* (1944), a Universal costume adventure starring Maria Montez.

3. The Stanwyck quote about *Mildred Pierce* surfaced in Axel Madsen's biography *Stanwyck* (1994). Madsen inexplicably attributed it to a 1973 interview that he conducted with Wald, who had died eleven years earlier, in 1962. The quote first saw print in a 1987 AFI magazine article written in tribute to Stanwyck after she received an AFI Life Achievement Award. The late Larry Kleno, Stanwyck's publicist and close friend, told Stanwyck's biographer Victoria Wilson that the renowned actress neither wanted nor sought the part of Mildred Pierce.

4. Obringer generated the memorandum in 1949 in response to a lawsuit filed by Mae Caro, who claimed that her story *Nothing to Live For* was submitted to James M. Cain in 1937 and was subsequently appropriated by the novelist for *Mildred Pierce* sans credit or payment. Warner Bros. was added to the suit, and the studio's lawyers noted that there were "very few elements" of Caro's story that did not appear in Cain's novel, deeming the merits to be "very alarming to say the least." Cain denied ever receiving the Caro manuscript, and the matter was eventually resolved in 1951, when Caro settled for $750.

5. James M. Cain was obsessed with opera. It seeped into several of his novels, particularly *Serenade,* and his fourth wife was a retired opera singer.

6. William Faulkner did his best work in Hollywood for the director Howard Hawks (*The Big Sleep, To Have and Have Not, Air Force*) but never became a highly regarded screenwriter.

7. The beach house used in *Mildred Pierce* was located at 26600 Roosevelt Highway, by Latigo Cove, just north of Malibu. Curtiz did not own the house, as has been claimed by several sources. The May K. Rindge estate owned the house, which was reportedly leased by the director Anatole Litvak. The street address changed to Latigo Shore Drive after the realignment of the highway to the bluff above the original road. The house washed away during a winter storm in 1983.

8. Monty Woolley was noted in the *Night and Day* production reports as arriving on the set late and intoxicated on several occasions.

Quotation Sources by Page Number

366 "the war had gotten Mother": Lucas, *Eighty Odd Years in Hollywood,* 142.

366 "Mike watched, horror-stricken": ibid., 144.

367–368 "My dear Jack": Darryl F. Zanuck, *Memo from Darryl F. Zanuck: The Golden Years at Twentieth Century-Fox,* ed. Rudy Behlmer (New York: Grove Press, 1993), 78–79.

368 "Steve Trilling was Jack": Martin Jurow and Philip Wuntch, *Marty Jurow Seein' Stars: A Show Biz Odyssey* (Dallas: Southern Methodist University Press, 2001), 4.

368 "I have continued to read": Curtiz to Jack Warner, Warner Bros. interoffice communication, February 25, 1944, USC Warner Bros. Archive.

368 "But we don't," "How much better," "She was ecstatic," and "Blanke would come on": Ann Doran, interview by Ronald L. Davis, August 10, 1983, SMU Collection and Margaret Herrick Library.

370 "I don't know if anyone" and "He could do everything": Joan Leslie to the author, January 25, 2008.

371 "But don't think" and "It's just that some": "Carson at Last Wins the Girl," *Medicine Hat (Alberta) Daily News,* February 11, 1946, 6.

371 "For Mr. Curtiz, I worked up," "I have to toast," and "My God, it's Frankie": McClelland, *Forties Film Talk,* 4.

373 "Jerry Wald's enthusiasm": Curtis Bernhardt and Mary Kiersch, *Curtis Bernhardt: A Directors Guild of America Oral History* (Hollywood: Directors Guild of America, 1986), 85.

373 "That has-been": Jurow and Wuntch, *Marty Jurow Seein' Stars,* 1.

374 "I desperately wanted the part": Axel Madsen, *Stanwyck* (New York: HarperCollins, 1994), 223.

374 "I didn't want to": Whitney Stine, *"I'd Love to Kiss You—": Conversations with Bette Davis* (New York: Pocket Books, 1990), 211.

374 "I didn't like the story": Shaun Considine, *Bette & Joan: The Divine Feud* (New York: E. P. Dutton, 1989), Kindle edition, loc. 3246.

374 "As I have two": "The Role I Liked Best," *Saturday Evening Post,* November 2, 1946, 76.

375 "The story contains": Joseph Breen to Jack L. Warner, February 2, 1944, USC Warner Bros. Archive.

375–376 "a higher level" and "Mr. Wald does not develop": Roy Obringer to Tom Chapman, "Genesis and Development of 'Mildred Pierce,'" November 8, 1949, USC Warner Bros. Archive.

376 "Mr. Warner was absolutely adamant" and "That is one of the reasons": Lee Server, *Screenwriter: Words Become Pictures* (Pittstown, N.J.: Main Street Press, 1987), 234, 235.

377 "When the final script": Tom Vallance, "Obituary: Catherine Turney," *Independent* (London), September 16, 1998.

378 "Allowing for all the smart promotion": Roy Hoopes, *Cain* (New York: Holt, Rinehart and Winston, 1980), 373.

378–379 "The battle of the shoulder pads," "Mike and I wanted," and "full of fights": McClelland, *Forties Film Talk,* 361.

379 "She used to come on the set": ibid., 347.

379 "For my early scenes": McClelland, *Forties Film Talk,* 328.

379 "He put me through": Considine, *Bette & Joan,* loc. 3302.

379 "When I started the tests": McClelland, *Forties Film Talk,* 329.

380 "And who do ve get": Considine, *Bette & Joan,* loc. 3283.

380–381 "Well of course, I was thrilled" and "I sensed not only": Ann Blyth to the author, December 20, 2010.

382 "Mike did a wonderful job" and "a truly great director": Ronald L. Davis, *Zachary Scott: Hollywood's Sophisticated Cad* (Jackson: University Press of Mississippi, 2006), 99.

382 "I always enjoyed working": Eve Arden, *Three Phases of Eve: An Autobiography* (New York: St. Martin's Press, 1985), 65.

382 "Mike Curtiz . . . was very": Mike Chapman, *Please Don't Call Me Tarzan* (Newton, Iowa: Culture House Books, 2001), 73.

382 "scrupulous director I enjoyed": McClelland, *Forties Film Talk,* 347.

382–383 "Dear Mike, Just ran last night's dailies": Jerry Wald to Curtiz, Warner Bros. interoffice communication, December 20, 1944, USC Warner Bros. Archive.

383 "a sordid lot": Eileen Creelman, "Joan Crawford in 'Mildred Pierce,'" *New York Sun,* September 29, 1945.

383 "injects a heavy shot of gall": Archer Winsten, "'Mildred Pierce,' a Mystery Short on Pleasant People," *New York Post,* September 29, 1945.

383 "anemic": Howard Barnes, "Mildred Pierce," *New York Herald Tribune,* September 29, 1945.

383 "I would like to take": Jerry Wald to Curtiz, September 28, 1945, USC Warner Bros. Archive.

384 "Jerry adored Mike": Connie Wald to the author, November 20, 2011.

385 "I don't think there is a set": Eric Stacey to Tenny Wright, Warner Bros. interoffice communication, September 5, 1945, USC Warner Bros. Archive.

385 "I can't go on": Eric Stacey to Tenny Wright, Warner Bros. interoffice communication, June 27, 1945, USC Warner Bros. Archive.

386 "Regarding the rewrite": Eric Stacey to Tenny Wright, Warner Bros. interoffice communication, August 9, 1945, USC Warner Bros. Archive. Emphasis in original.

386 "This was one of those": William Bowers, interview by William Froug, in Froug, *The Screenwriter Looks at the Screenwriter* (1972; repr., Los Angeles: Silman-James Press, 1991), 46.

386 "he, himself, looks sicker": Eric Stacey to Tenny Wright, Warner Bros. interoffice communication, July 6, 1945, USC Warner Bros. Archive.

386 "very, very depressed": Eric Stacey to Tenny Wright, Warner Bros. interoffice communication, July 13, 1945, USC Warner Bros. Archive.

386 "After Mike got through": Eric Stacey to Tenny Wright, Warner Bros. interoffice communication, September 29, 1945, USC Warner Bros. Archive.

387 "If I'm ever stupid enough": Warren G. Harris, *Cary Grant: A Touch of Elegance* (Garden City, N.Y.: Doubleday, 1987), 195.

387 "inartistic penny pinchers," "spent years checking," and "Film about Cole Porter": "Warner Bars Luce Mags for Panning Movie," Associated Press, August 15, 1946.

387 "the worst thing I've ever done": Bowers interview in Froug, *The Screenwriter Looks at the Screenwriter,* 45.

387–388 "We were shooting": Richard Erdman to the author, July 21, 2011.

27. A Michael Curtiz Production

1. Clarence Day Jr. died in 1935 and did not live to see his book become an entertainment powerhouse.

2. During negotiations between the Writers Guild and the movie studios, an enraged Harry Warner reportedly screamed, "They want blood. They want to take my goddamn studio. . . . You goddamn Communist bastards! You dirty sons of bitches! All you'll get from me is shit!" Hamilton, *Writers in Hollywood, 1915–1951,* 113–14.

3. Jack Warner also named the following screenwriters: Dalton Trumbo, Alvah Bessie, Ring Lardner Jr., Albert Maltz, Robert Rossen, Irwin Shaw, John Wexley, Guy Endore, Gordon Kahn, Sheridan Gibney, Howard Koch, and Clifford Odets.

4. Dana Andrews renewed a split contract with Goldwyn and Twentieth Century-Fox in 1945.

5. Kalmenson's assessment that the World Series was degrading the box-office receipts of *The Unsuspected* in New York was not without foundation. The 1947 subway series between the New York Yankees and the Brooklyn Dodgers was the first major televised sporting event in the New York metropolitan area broadcast by NBC. The fall classic between the pair of crosstown rivals dominated the attention of a mass audience in the tristate region.

Quotation Sources by Page Number

389 "I regret that I": Sam Pizzigati, "How about a Maximum Wage? Taxation: F.D.R. Wanted to Cap the Incomes of the Wealthy, an Idea Whose Time Might Have Come Again," *Los Angeles Times,* April 8, 1992.

389 "Because I get my freedom": Frank Daugherty, "Michael Curtiz Launching His Own Production Unit," *Christian Science Monitor,* March 21, 1947.

390 "would be much happier": Curtiz to Jack L. Warner, March 12, 1946, USC Warner Bros. Archive.

390 "The authors and producers" and "It was difficult for us": Davis, *Words into Images,* 151, 152.

391 "to do everything in my power": Curtiz to Howard Lindsay and Russel Crouse, telegram, November 10, 1945, USC Warner Bros. Archive.

391–392 "bitterly disappointed" and "I had the terrible job": Davis, *Words into Images,* 151.

392 "As I told Mike": Mary Pickford to Robert Buckner, February 16, 1946, USC Warner Bros. Archive.

392 "Dear Bette: Just returned from New York": Curtiz to Bette Davis, telegram, December 14, 1945, USC Warner Bros. Archive.

392–393 "You must know by now" and "Warners is notoriously hard": David O. Selznick to Curtiz, telegram, January 17, 1946, USC Warner Bros. Archive.

393 "There is a terrific unpleasantness": Eric Stacey to Tenny Wright, Warner Bros. interoffice communication, April 8, 1946, USC Warner Bros. Archive.

393 "The technical director": Contract between Warner Bros. and Katherine M. Day Trust & Messrs Lindsay and Crouse, November 30, 1944, USC Warner Bros. Archive.

393–394 "The progress of the company": Eric Stacey to Tenny Wright, Warner Bros. interoffice communication, May 1, 1946, USC Warner Bros. Archive. Emphasis in original.

394 "Lindsay and Crouse, who never buy": Robert Buckner to Tenny Wright, Warner Bros. interoffice communication, June 6, 1946, USC Warner Bros. Archive.

394–395 "Billy Grady tells me": Irving Kumin to Phil Friedman, memo, May 29, 1946, USC Warner Bros. Archive.

395 "Mike was a very explosive guy": Jimmy Lydon to the author, April 11, 2011.

396 "any younger man": Eric Stacey to Tenny Wright, Warner Bros. interoffice communication, April 15, 1946, USC Warner Bros. Archive.

396 "He just cannot take the rudeness": Eric Stacey to Tenny Wright, Warner Bros. interoffice communication, June 19, 1946, USC Warner Bros. Archive.

396 "This squabble is mostly personalities": Eric Stacey to Tenny Wright, Warner Bros. interoffice communication, April 15, 1946, USC Warner Bros. Archive.

396–397 "He said, 'What the matter,'" "I'm watching him light the set," and "He wanted to apologize": Jimmy Lydon to the author, April 11, 2011.

397–398 "I worked with a lot of directors": ibid.

398 "Dear Mike: Just received": Jack L. Warner to Curtiz, telegram, August 15, 1947, USC Warner Bros. Archive.

399 "Desider Pek, in his native country": Lucas, *Eighty Odd years in Hollywood*, 102.

399–400 "Pek never wore a necktie," "two friends of mine," "Those were just letters," and "I was a fair-haired boy": Irene Kahn Atkins, *Leroy Prinz* (Hollywood: Directors Guild of America, 1979).

400–401 "You may think": Desider Pek to Michael Curtiz, February 18, 1946; courtesy of Liz MacGillicuddy Lucas.

401 "I am going to try": Sheilah Graham, "When I Look for New Stars I Don't Look at Looks," *Boston Sunday Globe,* September 22, 1946.

402 "Combining good picture making": Leslie Epstein, "Duel in the Sun," *American Prospect,* November 16, 2001.

403 "the time of the toad": Dalton Trumbo, *The Time of the Toad: A Study of Inquisition in America* (New York: Harper & Row, 1972).

403 "Ideological termites have burrowed" and "Un-American": text of hearings before the Committee on Un-American Activities, Eightieth Congress, Regarding Communist Infiltration of the Motion Picture Industry, October 20, 1947.

403 "I've spent all day": Thomas, *Clown Prince of Hollywood*, 165.

403 "Tell him to go": Neal Gabler, *An Empire of Their Own: How the Jews Invented Hollywood* (New York: Crown, 1988), 385.

404 "the box office is off": Frank Daugherty, "Michael Curtiz Launching His Own Production Unit," *Christian Science Monitor*, March 21, 1947.

404–405 "After [World War I], all Europe": ibid.

405 "It was what you would call": Liz MacGillicuddy Lucas to the author, July 23, 2011.

406 "The part is written": Curtiz to Orson Welles, telegram, August 3, 1946, USC Warner Bros. Archive.

407 "she did not want": Charles Feldman to Curtiz, January 21, 1947, USC Warner Bros. Archive.

407 "He liked my work": Eddie Muller, *Dark City Dames: The Wicked Women of Film Noir* (New York: Regan Books, 2001), 47.

408–409 "a great psychologist" and "Don't until you hear from me": *Vox Pop* radio show audio broadcast, 1947; courtesy of Rudy Behlmer.

410 "I was a little disappointed": Curtiz to Charles Feldman, June 16, 1947, USC Warner Bros. Archive.

411 "the frenzy and hysteria": Ben Kalmenson to Curtiz, October 7, 1947, USC Warner Bros. Archive.

411 "The answer is that": Jack L. Warner to Curtiz, June 16, 1948, USC Warner Bros. Archive.

411 "I'm working hard" and "A director alone can't make": *Vox Pop* radio show audio broadcast, 1947; courtesy of Rudy Behlmer.

28. Vanished Dreams

1. Day considered Jack Carson an invaluable friend and mentor. She credits him enormously for her development into a successful film actress.

2. In addition to standing up for Berkeley at one of his weddings, Jack Warner put the full weight of the studio behind him, hiring the legendary attorney Jerry Geisler when the director was sensationally charged with second-degree murder in 1935. Despite being obviously drunk behind the wheel and causing a head-on crash that killed two people, Berkeley survived two hung juries and was acquitted after a third trial. Warner eventually wearied of his erratic behavior and, as the grosses of his movies decreased, let him go.

3. Huston noted in his memoir that he was dismayed by Warner's mistreatment of Henry Blanke, his mentor at Warner Bros, because of the producer's reluctance to accept a mandated salary reduction.

4. The Warner Bros. nominees for the 1950 Academy Awards consisted of Richard Todd for Best Actor in *The Hasty Heart* and "It's a Great Feeling" for Best Song. The studio's only other nominee was *The Adventures of Don Juan,* which won for Best Costume Design, Color.

5. Milton Sperling's production company lasted considerably longer than Curtiz's. Being Harry Warner's son-in-law didn't hurt his opportunities.

6. Harry James (1916–1983) provides an interesting comparison to the Rick Martin character. James was a trumpet player of extraordinary ability who opted for a pleasing commercial style. He had numerous hit records, a famed band that still carries his name, and piles of cash. During a tempestuous twenty-two-year marriage with the actress Betty Grable, he became a philandering alcoholic who blew most of their money on a life of excess. In an observation applicable to Rick Martin, the band singer Marion Morgan remarked that James "gave all of his warmth and love through his trumpet."

Quotation Sources by Page Number

413 "He put me in *Confidential Agent*": Thomas, *Clown Prince of Hollywood*, 150.

413 "I was hoping": Lauren Bacall to Curtiz, telegram, April 24, 1947, Jack L. Warner Collection, USC Cinematic Arts Library.

415 "receive makeup, wardrobe and script": George Amy, MCP, to Al Levy, April 14, 1947, USC Warner Bros. Archive.

415 "Nothing mattered to me," "So what you do," "Oh, that. Just so," and "You're very sensitive girl": Doris Day and A. E. Hotchner, *Doris Day: Her Own Story* (New York: William Morrow, 1976), 92–93.

416 "Movie acting came to me": Day and Hotchner, *Doris Day*, 98.

416 "You know girl": McCabe, *Cagney*, 280–81.

416 "I liked it . . .": David Kaufman, *Doris Day: The Untold Story of the Girl Next Door* (New York: Virgin Books USA, 2008), 56.

416 "Doris, I tell you": Day and Hotchner, *Doris Day*, 98.

417 "You found it necessary": Curtiz to Hedda Hopper, telegram, May 10, 1947, Hedda Hopper Papers, Margaret Herrick Library.

417 "childish": Hedda Hopper to Curtiz, May 12, 1947, Hedda Hopper Papers, Margaret Herrick Library.

417 "the wonderful break": Curtiz to Hedda Hopper, May 23, 1947, Hedda Hopper Papers, Margaret Herrick Library.

418 "Mike's progress on this picture": Eric Stacey to Tenny Wright, Warner Bros. production report, July 2, 1947, USC Warner Bros. Archive.

418 "agreeable summer fare": Seymour Beck, "To Havana—On One of Those Cruises," *New York Star*, June 26, 1948.

418 "woeful banality," "noisiness," and "Michael Curtiz's direction": Bosley Crowther, "Warners Introduce Doris Day in 'Romance on High Seas,' New Feature at Strand," *New York Times*, June 26, 1948.

420 "*My Dream Is Yours* had all the trappings": Martin Scorsese and Michael Henry Wilson, *A Personal Journey with Martin Scorsese through American Movies* (New York: Hyperion, 1997), 63.

421 "Will you please believe my judgment": Curtiz to Steve Trilling, Michael Curtiz Productions interoffice communication, May 18, 1948, USC Warner Bros. Archive.

421 "[J. L. Warner] has become very much disturbed" and "J. L. wants to give Mike": Ralph E. Lewis to R. W. Perkins, Warner Bros. Legal Department, April 19, 1948, reprinted in Behlmer, *Inside Warner Bros.*, 304–5.

422 "When they finally gave him": Adamson and Haskin. *Byron Haskin,* 97.

423 "All Mike's Doris Day pictures": Lucas, *Eighty Odd years in Hollywood,* 195.

423 "There must be something": Curtiz to Steve Trilling, Michael Curtiz Productions interoffice communication, June 21, 1948, USC Warner Bros. Archive.

423 "The character for Crawford": Curtiz to Steve Trilling, Michael Curtiz Productions interoffice communication, June 29, 1948, USC Warner Bros. Archive.

423 "the basic phony idea": Curtiz to Steve Trilling, Michael Curtiz Productions interoffice communication, June 20, 1948, USC Warner Bros. Archive.

423–424 "The reason I am": Curtiz to J. L. Warner, Michael Curtiz Productions interoffice communication, June 5, 1948, USC Warner Bros. Archive.

424 "the production of *Flamingo*": Frank Pope, editor of the *Hollywood Reporter,* as quoted by Jerry Wald to Curtiz, Warner Bros. interoffice communication, July 16, 1948, USC Warner Bros. Archive.

424 "incalculable damage": Jerry Wald to Curtiz, Warner Bros. interoffice communication, July 16, 1948, USC Warner Bros. Archive.

424 "makes me feel like": Jerry Wald memo to Alex Evelove, July 16, 1948, USC Warner Bros. Archive.

424 "If you don't like a script": Jerry Wald to Curtiz, Warner Bros. interoffice communication, July 16, 1948, USC Warner Bros. Archive.

424 "uncalled for and highly unethical": record of conversation with Marc Cohen, Mike Curtiz, and Mr. Trilling, July 27, 1948, Jack L. Warner Collection, USC Cinematic Arts Library.

425 "Despite all the trouble": Jack Warner memo to Curtiz, September 16, 1948, USC Warner Bros. Archive.

426 "hot photo of Crawford": Jack L. Warner to Mort Blumenstock, memo, July 13, 1949, USC Warner Bros. Archive.

426 "It began to go downhill": Davis, *Words into Images,* 150.

427 "I hope this can": Jack Warner to Sam Schneider, May 11, 1948, USC Warner Bros. Archive.

428 "I felt his mind was elsewhere," and "Mike was a dynamo": Lawrence J. Quirk, *Jane Wyman: The Actress and the Woman: An Illustrated Biography* (New York: Dembner Books, 1986), 127.

429 "a chime struck by a mallet": Robin H. Smiley, "Books into Film: Young Man with a Horn," *Firsts: The Book Collector's Magazine* (February 2006), 57.

429 "Bix's sound came out": Peter J. Levinson, *Tommy Dorsey: Livin' in a Great Big Way: A Biography* (Cambridge, Mass.: Da Capo Press, 2005), 16.

429 "the inspiration for the writing": Dorothy Baker, *Young Man with a Horn* (Boston: Houghton Mifflin, 1938), dedication page.

430 "elimination of the colored angle": Jerry Wald to Steve Trilling, Warner Bros. interoffice communication, November 15, 1946, USC Warner Bros. Archive.

430 "Bix was like Larry": Kirk Douglas, *The Ragman's Son: An Autobiography* (New York: Simon & Schuster, 1988), 442.

431 "Hernandez's performance": Donald Bogle, *Toms, Coons, Mulattoes, Mam-*

mies, and Bucks: An Interpretive History of Blacks in American Films, 4th ed. (New York: Continuum, 2001), 154.

431 "a bitch and unsympathetic": Jerry Wald to Curtiz, Warner Bros. interoffice communication, June 21, 1949, USC Warner Bros. Archive.

431 "We must do something": Jerry Wald to Bill Orr, Warner Bros. interoffice communication, July 2, 1949, USC Warner Bros. Archive.

432 "brilliant with the camera" and "only at those who were vulnerable": Lauren Bacall, *By Myself and Then Some* (New York: HarperEntertainment, 2005), 194.

432 "I, personally, do not want": Jack Warner to Jerry Wald, memo, April 16, 1949, USC Warner Bros. Archive.

432 "We have a temp. script" and "I have a faint suspicion": Curtiz to Jack L. Warner, Warner Bros. interoffice communication, May 23, 1949, USC Warner Bros. Archive.

433 "Of the movies I made": Hoagy Carmichael with Stephen Longstreet, *Sometimes I Wonder: The Story of Hoagy Carmichael* (New York: Farrar, Straus and Giroux, 1965), 273.

433 "updating the script" and "your help with the story": Richard M. Sudhalter, *Stardust Melody: The Life and Music of Hoagy Carmichael* (New York: Oxford University Press, 2002), 273.

433 "He, too, looked like a music man": Carmichael, *Sometimes I Wonder,* 273.

433 "turned out to be": Day and Hotchner, *Doris Day,* 127.

433–434 "ersatz New York streets" and "[In] thinking out": Jerry Wald to Steve Trilling, Warner Bros. interoffice communication, August 24, 1949, USC Warner Bros. Archive.

434 "It is my solid conviction": Kirk Douglas to Jack L. Warner, September 29, 1949, USC Warner Bros. Archive.

434 "Three or four kids": Jerry Wald to Steve Trilling, Warner Bros. interoffice communication, January 12, 1950, USC Warner Bros. Archive.

435 "But Jack, why that ending?": W. R. Wilkerson to Jack L. Warner, January 10, 1950, USC Warner Bros. Archive.

435 "Unfortunately, my stomach": Jerry Wald to Sammy Cahn, December 16, 1949, USC Warner Bros. Archive.

436 "For twenty-two years" and "I pray to God": Curtiz to Jack L. Warner, memo, August 26, 1949, USC Warner Bros. Archive.

29. Doomed Masterpiece

1. HUAC apparently didn't recall *British Agent* (1934) and the long-ago *My Brother Is Coming* (1919).

2. Jim Thorpe's Olympic medals were taken from him because he played semipro baseball. The medals were presented to his family in 1983, thirty years after Thorpe's death, in 1953. Avery Brundage, the long-serving International Olympic Committee president who competed unsuccessfully against Thorpe in the 1912 games, stonewalled initiatives to return Thorpe's medals for decades. Thorpe's daughter observed that her father was the only Olympian who had to win his medals twice.

Notes

Quotation Sources by Page Number

437 "an unrelenting, but somewhat top-heavy": Howard Barnes, "On the Screen," *New York Herald Tribune,* June 17, 1950.

438 "Because you cannot make love": Stephen Michael Shearer, *Patricia Neal: An Unquiet Life* (Lexington: University Press of Kentucky, 2006), 93.

438 "Ghastly." Patricia Neal to the author, February 18, 2010.

438 "One morning, he was late": Bacall, *By Myself and Then Some,* 199.

438–439 "temperamentally unsuited" and "a very expensive actor": Curtiz to Jack L. Warner, January 14, 1954, Jack L. Warner Collection, USC Cinematic Arts Library.

439 "I saw seventeen takes": Jack Warner to Curtiz, memo, December 5, 1949, Jack L. Warner Collection, USC Cinematic Arts Library.

439 "that piece of junk": Todd McCarthy, *Howard Hawks: The Grey Fox of Hollywood* (New York: Grove Press, 1997), 291.

441 "have his arm twisted": Jerry Wald to Steve Trilling, Warner Bros. interoffice communication, December 14, 1949, USC Warner Bros. Archive.

441–443 "Dear Mike: I am most happy": John Garfield to Curtiz, January 16, 1950, USC Warner Bros. Archive.

443 "He came up to me": Nott, *He Ran All the Way,* 255.

443 "Can't a man be in love": Jerry Wald to Steve Trilling, Warner Bros. interdepartmental communication, January 5, 1950, USC Warner Bros. Archive. Emphasis in original.

444 "I had just left" and "I did a brief": Nott, *He Ran All the Way,* 255.

444 "Hernandez is the new" and "The latter pictures set": *Ebony,* August 1950.

445 "The story is the study": Jerry Wald to Ranald MacDougall, Warner Bros. interoffice communication, January 17, 1950, USC Warner Bros. Archive.

445–446 "Dear Randy: I read a copy" and "I think that in this story": Curtiz to Ranald MacDougall, Warner Bros. interoffice communication, February 10, 1950, USC Warner Bros. Archive.

446 "When you do your own productions": John Garfield, interview by Darr Smith, *Los Angeles Daily News,* July 4, 1950, USC Warner Bros. Archive.

446–447 "In counter-action lies drama" and "In view of the fact": Patricia Neal to Steve Trilling, Curtiz, and Ranald MacDougall, April 16, 1950, USC Warner Bros. Archive.

447 "Mike WAS NOT influenced": Jerry Wald to Steve Trilling, Warner Bros. interoffice communication, April 18, 1950, USC Warner Bros. Archive.

447 "The last day's rushes": Jerry Wald to Curtiz, Warner Bros. interoffice communication, April 20, 1950, USC Warner Bros. Archive.

448 "I think it's the best": John Garfield, interview by Darr Smith, *Los Angeles Daily News,* July 4, 1950, USC Warner Bros. Archive.

448 "This is not a remake": Jerry Wald, interview by Ezra Goodman, *New York Herald Tribune,* May 7, 1950.

448 "We ran *Breaking Point*": Jack Warner to Curtiz, May 7, 1950, USC Warner Bros. Archive.

449–450 "All of a sudden" and "I saw him just before he died": Mickey Knox to the author, February 20, 2010.

450 "Each evening we three": Lucas, *Eighty Odd Years in Hollywood,* 148–49.

452 "I could go to Mexico": Curtiz to Jack Warner, Warner Bros. interoffice communication, May 26, 1950, USC Warner Bros. Archive.

452 "I came here to learn": Don Murray to the author, October 1, 2011.

452 "The solution in one word": Earl Wilson, *New York Daily News,* June 12, 1950.

452 Come quickly! Mike" and "He would finish his shower": Lucas, *Eighty Odd Years in Hollywood,* 149–50.

452–453 "shall not be grouped": Buford, *Burt Lancaster: An American Life,* 103.

453 "Jim Thorpe was not a complicated man": Kate Buford, *Native American Son: The Life and Sporting Legend of Jim Thorpe* (New York: Knopf, 2010), 3.

453 "five or six thousand dollars": Everett Freeman to Steve Trilling, Warner Bros. interoffice communication, June 14, 1949, USC Warner Bros. Archive.

453 "Dear Sirs: I wanted you to know": Robert F. Kennedy to Warner Bros., n.d., USC Warner Bros. Archive.

455–456 "Charles Bickford was like steel" and "Good, Burt, sweetheart": Paul Picerni with Tom Weaver, *Steps to Stardom* (Albany, Ga.: BearManor Media, 2007), 99.

456 "Something that Curtiz said": Billy Gray to the author, November 25, 2010.

457–458 "The success of the picture" and "We have seen in *Sunset Blvd.*": Curtiz and Anthony Veiller to J. L. Warner, Warner Bros. interoffice communication, February 22, 1951, USC Warner Bros. Archive.

458 "absolutely horrifying," "I was pregnant," "I honestly could not": Nancy Olson to the author, July 18, 2011.

459 "dreadful trouble": Anthony Veiller to Sherry Shourds, Warner Bros. interoffice communication, March 19, 1951, USC Warner Bros. Archive.

459 "Cut! Cut! Vhat the hell" and "Vell ven your gun jam": Picerni and Weaver, *Steps to Stardom,* 113–14.

459 "honest romance and cynicism" and "forceful amalgam of ruggedness": "The Screen in Review: 'Force of Arms,' Stirring War Drama, Opens at Warner," *New York Times,* August 14, 1951.

459–460 "Dear Mike, On Tuesday": Jack Warner to Curtiz, June 29, 1951, Jack L. Warner Collection, USC Cinematic Arts Library.

30. Nerve Ending

1. The brief congressional tenure of Will Rogers Jr. was distinctive for his introduction of a resolution that called on President Roosevelt to establish a commission to rescue European Jewry from extermination by the Nazis. It was the first formal action by any arm of the American government that acknowledged the Holocaust and America's moral responsibility to take action.

2. Industry wags observed that only Jack Warner would select the one-eyed Andre de Toth to direct a 3-D film. De Toth suggests in his memoir that he got the

House of Wax assignment after Curtiz turned it down, but this is neither entirely clear nor documented elsewhere.

3. Queried about this matter by the author, Day advised through her representative that she did not recall the title of the specific script that she rejected.

Quotation Sources by Page Number

461 "I have read" and "I think it would": Curtiz to Steve Trilling, Warner Bros. interoffice communication, May 29, 1951, USC Warner Bros. Archive.

462 "the only lovable producer": Melville Shavelson, *How to Succeed in Hollywood without Really Trying: P.S.—You Can't!* (Albany, Ga.: BearManor Media, 2007), 54.

462 "I am now getting": Tenny Wright to Col. J. L. Warner, Warner Bros. interoffice communication, July 5, 1951, USC Warner Bros. Archive.

462 "MacRae is a good singer": Curtiz to Steve Trilling, Warner Bros. interoffice communication, May 29, 1951, USC Warner Bros. Archive.

462–463 "Of course you'll have," "If you put a good-looking man," and "The picture was,": Danny Thomas with Bill Davidson, *Make Room for Danny* (New York: Putnam, 1991), 144, 145.

463 "Mike Curtiz was really a genius," and "a big joke": Patrice Wymore to the author, May 24, 2011.

463 "Prinz didn't dance": Day and Hotchner, *Doris Day,* 145.

463 "Mike was wonderful": Davis, *Words into Images,* 140.

465 "horrifying": Curtis, *Spencer Tracy,* 479.

465 "You know something?" and "This is the first": Patrick McGilligan, *Film Crazy: Interviews with Hollywood Legends* (New York: St. Martin's Press, 2000), 123.

465 "You're working, aren't you?": Scott Eyman, *John Wayne: The Life and Legend* (New York: Simon & Schuster, 2014), 60.

466 "a brilliant Hungarian" and "Mike Curtiz had a hammerlock": Will Rogers Jr., video interview by Phyllis Lerner, Beverly Hills Historical Society, July 1988.

466 "I finished all four": Curtiz to Steve Trilling, Warner Bros. interoffice communication, May 17, 1951, USC Warner Bros. Archive.

468 "Thank God for Jane": Will Rogers Jr., video interview by Phyllis Lerner, July 1988.

468 "a very bad, uninteresting second part": Curtiz to Steve Trilling, Warner Bros. interoffice communication, May 17, 1951, USC Warner Bros. Archive.

468 "At the end of seventy-five pages": Curtiz to Robert Arthur, Warner Bros. interoffice communication, November 20, 1950, USC Warner Bros. Archive.

469 "I rehearsed with Bill": Curtiz to Steve Trilling, Warner Bros. interoffice communication, January 14, 1952, Jack L. Warner Collection, USC Cinematic Arts Library.

469–470 "My dear Mike: I never dreamed": Harry Warner to Curtiz, July 11, 1952, USC Warner Bros. Archive.

470 "The life story of Will Rogers": Curtiz to Jack L. Warner, January 15, 1954, USC Warner Bros. Archive.

470 "Harry said to me": Ronald L. Davis, *Just Making Movies: Company Directors on the Studio System* (Jackson: University Press of Mississippi, 2005), 196.

472 "no hats": Jack Warner to Steve Trilling, Warner Bros. interoffice communication, August 10, 1952, Jack L. Warner Collection, USC Cinematic Arts Library.

473 "It was necessary to shoot": Curtiz to Col. J. L. Warner, Warner Bros. interoffice communication, August 10, 1952, USC Warner Bros. Archive.

473 "nickel actors who want": Day and Hotchner, *Doris Day,* 129.

473 "my friend was hurt" and "fate must have led me": Louella O. Parsons, "Curtiz Pleased with Peggy Lee's Signing for 'The Jazz Singer,'" *Albuquerque Journal,* July 4, 1952, 3.

474 "sat in a dark corner" "If a girl can sing" "I have no patience" "Peggy has tremendous talent": Gene Handsaker, "Peggy Lee, Top Singer, Is Given Dramatic Role," *Albert Lea (Minn.) Sunday Tribune,* October 19, 1952.

474 "Doris is an extrovert": Mike Connolly, *Hollywood Reporter,* August 1, 1952.

474–475 "When [Curtiz] directed," "I don't know Michael," and "Now Peggy, this time": Peggy Lee, *Miss Peggy Lee: An Autobiography* (New York: Donald I. Fine, 1989), 155.

475 "the stand-patters": Sperling and Milner with Warner, *Hollywood Be Thy Name,* 225.

476 "It appears that Mike": R. J. Obringer to J. L. Warner, Warner Bros. interoffice communication, May 21, 1951, USC Warner Bros. Archives.

476 "It's not a standard Wayne part": Frank Quinn, *New York Mirror,* May 3, 1953.

476–477 "I want you and J.L." and "I know in the end": Curtiz to Steve Trilling, Warner Bros. interoffice communication, October 20, 1952, USC Warner Bros. Archives.

477 "[*Trouble Along the Way*] made it sound": Eyman, *John Wayne,* 228.

477 "agonizing" and "dear human being": Nancy Olson to the author, July 18, 2011.

477–478 "The title, *Boy from Oklahoma*": Curtiz to Steve Trilling, Warner Bros. interoffice communication, February 10, 1953, USC Warner Bros. Archive.

478 "bad and will harm": Will Rogers Jr. to Jack Warner, April 10, 1953, USC Warner Bros. Archive.

479 "This whole question revolves around": Roy Obringer to Sam Schneider, December 23, 1953, USC Warner Bros. Archive.

479 "Obringer states that" and "rewrite clause—to group pictures": William Schaefer to Jack L. Warner, memo, May 14, 1952, USC Warner Bros. Archive.

479–481 "should be ashamed" through "Don't allow these conferences": Curtiz to Jack L. Warner, January 15, 1954, USC Warner Bros. Archive.

481 "without the necessity": R. J. Obringer to F. W. Witt, Warner Bros. interoffice communication, August 23, 1954, USC Warner Bros. Archive.

481 "Nobody came out," and "You really ought to bring,": Eyman, *John Wayne,* 284, 285.

31. Only in Hollywood

1. *How to Marry a Millionaire* (1953) was the first film shot in CinemaScope but it was released after *The Robe.*

2. The lawsuit was eventually settled when Brando appeared as Napoleon in the Fox production of *Désirée* (1954).

3. Ohmart claimed that Frank Tashlin told her that Stanwyck originally refused the part.

4. Carol Ohmart went on to forge an interesting acting career highlighted by a memorable turn in *House on Haunted Hill* (1958). In this film her character was married to Vincent Price's, and he was smarter than Nevins (Gregory). Instead of letting his wife murder him, he arranged to have her tumble into a vat of acid.

5. *Confidential* pioneered in salacious revelations, particularly by outing gay actors and by highlighting the taboo subject of sex between the races. Robert Mitchum, Maureen O'Hara, Lizabeth Scott, Sammy Davis Jr., José Ferrer, Dorothy Dandridge, and many other celebrities were victimized (not always inaccurately), while the studios did nothing to protect stars who were no longer their contracted assets. Lawsuits by several of the libeled—notably Maureen O'Hara—and political pressure exercised by California's Governor Edmund Brown eventually knocked the magazine off its sensationalist pedestal.

Quotation Sources by Page Number

482 "As I previously advised": Mark M. Cohen to William Wyler, July 6, 1953, Margaret Herrick Library.

483 "be absolutely sure": Curtiz to D. A., Paramount Pictures interoffice communication, June 2, 1953, Margaret Herrick Library.

483 "Even though Curtiz was": Rosemary Clooney with Joan Barthel, *Girl Singer: An Autobiography* (New York: Doubleday, 1999), 111.

483–484 "Curtiz was brilliant": *White Christmas: A Look Back with Rosemary Clooney,* Paramount DVD featurette, 2000.

484 "often talked to me" and "When we start the scene": Clooney and Barthel, *Girl Singer,* 111.

484 "Two girl have small tear": Steve Taravella, *Mary Wickes: I Know I've Seen That Face Before* (Jackson: University Press of Mississippi, 2013), 200.

485 "Then Bing gave her a kiss": Clooney and Barthel, *Girl Singer,* 111.

485–486 "I felt out of place," "They paid me $200," "He phoned my house," and "He was a complete gentleman": Barrie Chase to the author, April 25, 2011.

486 "I think I fell in love": Jill Gerrard to the author, June 23, 2012.

486–487 "Mr. Curtiz directed all day": *White Christmas* daily production report, November 12, 1953, Margaret Herrick Library.

487 "Curtiz announced": Clooney and Barthel, *Girl Singer,* 111.

489–490 "But my four severest critics": "Michael Curtiz: One of the Giants," *Hollywood Close-Up,* December 25, 1958.

490 "I realize this thoughtful, analytical man": Curtiz to Darryl Zanuck and Casey Robinson, memo, "Re: The Egyptian," July 15, 1953, Margaret Herrick Library.

490 "large, black-maned males" and "but with the great work": Curtiz to Darryl Zanuck, memo, August 5, 1953, Margaret Herrick Library.

490 "Friendship was a fault": Lucas, *Eighty Odd Years in Hollywood,* 204.

490 "Do you know what" and "Line up behind *me*": Leonard Mosley, *Zanuck: The Rise and Fall of Hollywood's Last Tycoon* (Boston: Little, Brown, 1984), 260. Emphasis in original.

491 "absolutely besotted": ibid., 262.

491 "This girl was an amateur" and "There was a breakup": Casey Robinson, oral history interview by Joel Greenberg, 1974, American Film Institute.

493 "He was normally": Mosley, *Zanuck,* 261, 263. Emphasis in original.

493 "Brando was driven off" and "How can I": McGilligan, *Backstory,* 164.

493 "Marlon didn't like Mike": Bob Thomas, *Marlon: Portrait of the Rebel as an Artist* (New York: Random House, 1973), 95–96.

494 "cast some lumpish girlfriend": Server, *Screenwriter,* 107.

494 "a classic yes man": Philip Dunne, *Take Two: A Life in Movies and Politics* (New York: McGraw-Hill, 1980), 66.

494–496 "Even on my personal productions": Zanuck, *Memo from Darryl F. Zanuck,* 242. Emphasis in original.

496 "Herrmann chose to score": Steven C. Smith, *A Heart at Fire's Center: The Life and Music of Bernard Herrmann* (Berkeley: University of California Press, 1991), 182.

496 "CinemaScope is fine": Davis, *The Glamour Factory,* 373.

496–497 "the terrible days," "Those early Bausch and Lomb," and "one drawback in my many years": Higham, *Hollywood Cameramen,* 28, 30.

497 "In scenes of soldiers" and "I agree with you": Philip Dunne to Darryl F. Zanuck, memo, Twentieth Century-Fox interoffice correspondence, April 26, 1954, Philip Dunne Collection, USC Cinematic Arts Library. Emphasis in original.

498 "Akhnaton is as important": Curtiz to Darryl Zanuck and Casey Robinson, memo, July 15, 1953, USC Cinematic Arts Library.

498 "to an early day prototype": Joseph I. Breen, PCA, to Frank McCarthy, Twentieth Century-Fox, July 17, 1953, Margaret Herrick Library.

499 "It was like playing *Aida*": John Miller, *Peter Ustinov: The Gift of Laughter* (London: Weidenfeld & Nicholson, 2002), 84.

499 "Bella Darvi as the heartless gold digger": Bosley Crowther, "The Screen in Review: 'The Egyptian' at Roxy Is Based on the Novel," *New York Times,* August 25, 1954.

499 "A weak spot": *Variety,* August 25, 1954.

499–500 "Actors have taken over": Zanuck, *Memo from Darryl F. Zanuck,* 259.

500 "Was Joan being disloyal": Lucas, *Eighty Odd Years in Hollywood,* 205.

500 "stalks the Spewacks": H.H.T. "'We're No Angels' Bows," *New York Times,* July 8, 1955.

501 "You gotta remember": Miller, *Peter Ustinov,* 84.

501 "Curtiz was constantly complaining": Verita Thompson with Donald Shepherd, *Bogie and Me: A Love Story* (New York: St. Martin's Press, 1982), 207–8.

503 "He couldn't speak English": Bob Thomas, "Music Legend Kathryn Grayson Dies at 88," *USA Today*, February 18, 2010.

503 "Just what is this meeting" and "If you are so": *Vagabond King* story conference notes, September 29, 1954, Margaret Herrick Library.

504 "Confusion and chaos reigned": May Wale Brown, *Reel Life on Hollywood Movie Sets* (Riverside, Calif.: Ariadne Press, 1995), 19–20.

504 "one that will be long remembered": press book, *The Vagabond King*, in author's possession.

504 "It never should have been made": Thomas, "Music Legend Kathryn Grayson Dies at 88."

505 "Otto simply destroyed Tom": Carol Lynley to the author, May 30, 2008.

505 "Leave your two damn feet," "a veritable who's who," "Bogart, the spokesman," "It doesn't matter what": Gregg Barrios, "Rediscovering the Last Starlet: A Mysterious Phone Call Leads to Carol Ohmart," *Los Angeles Times,* January 8, 1989.

505 "He was indeed a starmaker": Lucas, *Eighty Odd Years in Hollywood,* 202.

505 "My God! I wore": Elaine Stritch to the author, September 30, 2011. Emphases in original.

507 "bronze prostitutes strut": Marty Mechlin, "When Director Mike Curtiz Learned Two Is Company and Three Is a Crime!" *Confidential,* March 1956, 29.

507 "[He] once gave me a job": press book: *The Best Things in Life Are Free,* in author's possession.

508–509 "His personality is flamboyant": press book: *The Best Things in Life Are Free.*

509 "I loved Mike Curtiz" through "one of the truly great": Ernest Borgnine to the author, May 13, 2010.

32. Dégringolade

Quotation Sources by Page Number

Quotations by Ann Blyth, Sam Goldwyn Jr., David Ladd and, Mother Dolores Hart, Michael McGreevey, Walter Mirisch, Tina Louise, Walter Bernstein, and Richard Erdman are, except as noted, from interviews with the author.

510 "I have felt very sentimental": Curtiz letter to Steve Trilling and Warner, February 8, 1957, USC Warner Bros. Archive.

510 "until one o'clock": Curtiz to Steve Trilling, Warner Bros. interoffice communication, September 7, 1956, USC Warner Bros. Archive.

510–511 "They both like": Curtiz to Steve Trilling, Warner Bros. interoffice communication, October 18, 1956, USC Warner Bros. Archive.

511 "If you have" "You are in trouble" "biggest casting search": James Bacon, "Mike Curtiz Having Hard Time Filling Helen Morgan Film Role," Associated Press, October 21, 1956.

511 "a great Irish singer," "our Helen Morgan," and "Thank God you told me": Bacon, *Made in Hollywood,* 162.

511 "Three people are after me": Curtiz to Steve Trilling, Warner Bros. interoffice communication, November 1, 1956, USC Warner Bros. Archive.

511 "Just finished the test": Curtiz to Steve Trilling, Warner Bros. interoffice communication, November 12, 1956, USC Warner Bros. Archive.

512 "glorified," "wouldn't have allowed," "she always selected," and "outmoded": Philip K. Scheuer, "Curtiz Defends Glorified Film Version of Helen Morgan," *Los Angeles Times,* March 3, 1957.

513 "There are lot of moves": T. C. Wright to Steve Trilling and Jack L. Warner, Warner Bros. interoffice communication, February 8, 1957, USC Warner Bros. Archive.

514 "a long rocky road," "Curtiz had a lot of definition," and "He knew pretty much": Paul Newman, interview by Leonard Maltin, February 13, 1993; courtesy of Leonard Maltin.

514 "It was so cold," "We got too warm," and "We started to blow our lines": Virginia Vincent to the author, May 17, 2010.

514 "When we cut the picture" and "*I* will cut the picture!": Rudy Behlmer to the author, July 15, 2015. Emphasis in original.

514 "Just returned from New York": Jack Warner to Curtiz, March 22, 1957, USC Warner Bros. Archive.

514 "supervise the editing": Curtiz to Jack Warner, March 22, 1957, USC Warner Bros. Archive.

514 "heartwarming as an electric pad": A. H. Weiler, "Screen: 'Helen Morgan'; Ann Blyth Stars in Singer's Biography," *New York Times,* October 3, 1957.

514–515 "an ordinary tramp" and "an entire life": Curtiz to Steve Trilling, June 26, 1957, Jack L. Warner Collection, USC Cinematic Arts Library.

515 "You are probably aware" and "not hold it against me": Curtiz to Steve Trilling, July 3, 1957, Jack L. Warner Collection, USC Cinematic Arts Library.

516 "I would not raise": Jill Gerrard to the author, September 17, 2013.

516 "This was the time": Museum of Television & Radio Seminar Series: *A Conversation with John Frankenheimer,* September 24, 1997.

518 "He adamantly refused": Lucas, *Eighty Odd Years in Hollywood,* 202.

519 "*Very* sensitive," "Because Mike Curtiz could be," and "a love affair": Beverly Linet, *Ladd: The Life, the Legend, the Legacy of Alan Ladd: A Biography* (New York: Arbor House, 1979), 217.

520 "He was a son": Harmetz, *The Making of Casablanca,* 332.

520–521 "Mike, you just can't," "My assistant tells me," and "We all started to laugh": Paul A. Helmick, *Cut, Print, and That's a Wrap! A Hollywood Memoir* (Jefferson, N.C.: McFarland, 2001), 106–7.

521 "Mike started out trying" and "going in four directions": Bill Hamilton to George Stevens, September 18 and 29, 1957, George Stevens Collection, Margaret Herrick Library.

521 "Mike Curtiz and the producer": ibid.

522 "honestly heartwarming drama" through "an astonishingly professional": A. H. Weiler, "Moving Sentiment," *New York Times,* July 2, 1958.

523 "Elvis was an original," "When he started to sing," and "one of the toughest": Wallis and Higham, *Starmaker,* 161, 162.

524 "a conventional, unreal, dead-end kid," "I much prefer," and "If you agree with me": Curtiz to Hal Wallis, Paramount Pictures interoffice communication, May 3, 1955, Hal Wallis Collection, Margaret Herrick Library.

524 "I appreciate the efforts": Curtiz to Hal Wallis, Paramount Pictures interoffice communication, September 28, 1955, Hal Wallis Collection, Margaret Herrick Library.

525 "I would prefer to": Curtiz to Paul Nathan, Paramount Pictures interoffice communication, August 6, 1957, Hal Wallis Collection, Margaret Herrick Library.

526 "You're the boss" and "Instead of a gyrating": Hazel K. Johnson, "Movie Director High on Presley's Chances" United Press International, April 10, 1958.

526 "For the first time": Jan Shepard, quoted in *Elvis in Hollywood,* a 1993 Elvis Presley Enterprises documentary film.

528 "a vulgar man": Mother Dolores Hart, OSB, and Richard DeNeut, *The Ear of the Heart: An Actress' Journey from Hollywood to Holy Vows* (San Francisco: Ignatius Press, 2013), 72.

528 "Curtiz was funny" through "He was a good teacher": Walter Matthau, interview by Leonard Maltin, May 22, 1997; courtesy of Leonard Maltin.

528 "Dollink, act more drunkey": Paramount publicity release, *King Creole,* 1958, Margaret Herrick Library.

528 "[The film] proved": Paul Nathan to Pvt. Elvis Presley, telegram, May 5, 1958, Hal Wallis Collection, Margaret Herrick Library.

528 "Elvis Presley can act" and "A shrewd director": Howard Thompson, "Actor with Guitar," *New York Times,* July 4, 1958.

530 "He was hardly": Walter Mirisch, *I Thought We Were Making Movies, Not History* (Madison: University of Wisconsin Press, 2008), 98.

531 "I said to Sophia": Tom Donnelly, "John Gavin: One for the 'Seesaw,'" *Washington Post,* July 28, 1974.

532 "Don't change a thing": ibid.

532 "flimsy, witless and tedious": Bosley Crowther, "Sophia Loren Starred with John Gavin," *New York Times,* December 17, 1960.

532 "Sidney told me that": Archie Moore, "Why I Played Jim, the Slave," *Ebony,* September 1960, 43–44.

533 "It was a common word": Mike Fitzgerald, *The Ageless Warrior: The Life of Boxing Legend Archie Moore* (Champaign, Ill.: Sports Publishing, 2004), 164.

533–534 "the professionals on the set" "There is no need": Moore, "Why I Played Jim, the Slave."

534 "As an actor, Moore": Jack Murphy, "Now Archie Will Do His Acting before the Hollywood Cameras," *San Diego Union,* September 9, 1959.

33. Out on His Shield

1. Asked if her role in *Francis of Assisi* inspired her religious commitment, Mother Dolores told me that she met Pope John XXIII in Rome during the extended production, adding, "I think the film allowed me to come into a very wonderful relationship with the Church."

2. A *Los Angeles Times* obituary dated April 12, 1962, claimed that Curtiz's

cancer was discovered when he fell and broke a rib during the filming of *The Comancheros*.

Quotation Sources by Page Number

Quotations by Stuart Whitman, Bradford Dillman, Mother Dolores Hart, Nehemiah Persoff, Liz MacGillicuddy Lucas, Ann Blyth, Jill Gerrard, and Richard Erdman are, except as noted, from interviews with the author.

535 "was bursting with servants" and "50 and 100 dollar tips": Lucas, *Eighty Odd Years in Hollywood*, 208.

535 "Mike always made Bess laugh": Victoria Lucas to author, August 8, 2011.

535 "Despite all the help": Lucas, *Eighty Odd Years in Hollywood*, 222.32 and 33.

540 "Duke was a terrific": Eyman, *John Wayne*, 355.

541 "Curtiz usually falls asleep": Tom Mankiewicz and Robert David Crane, *My Life As a Mankiewicz: An Insider's Journey through Hollywood* (Lexington: University Press of Kentucky, 2012), 52.

541 "an arrogant prick," "You're fired! Get out," and "I heard what you did": Mankiewicz and Crane, *My Life as a Mankiewicz*, 52, 55.

542 "Get the goddamn words out": Eyman, *John Wayne*, 355.

542 "his bones were found": Lucas, *Eighty Odd Years in Hollywood*, 226.

542 "Mother had talked": ibid.

542 "a sad and frustrating meeting" and "Well, Jick": ibid., 227.

544 "in panchromatic makeup": ibid.

544–545 "my friend" through "and to make no payments": last will and testament of Michael Curtiz, dated July 26, 1961.

545 "an S.O.B. who hated me": Jill Gerrard, phone conversation with the author, September 17, 2013.

545 "suggested abortion" and "had the Curtiz forehead": "Curtiz Proposed Surgery, Paternity Claimant Says," *Hollywood Citizen-News*, August 17, 1962.

546–547 "international liaison" and "giving unselfishly of her time": "Yorty Sees Subversive Plot in Campus Unrest," *Van Nuys News*, March 18, 1970.

547 "This woman who was" and "living like aristocrats": Fidalgo, *Michael Curtiz*, 515.

547 "the bearing of" and "She told me that": Rick Lenz, *North of Hollywood* (North Hollywood, Calif.: Chromodroid Press, 2012), 46.

548 "If only we had": Harmetz, *The Making of Casablanca*, 331.

Bibliography

Adamson, Joe, and Byron Haskin. *Byron Haskin.* Metuchen, N.J.: Scarecrow Press, 1984.

American Film Institute. Catalog of Feature Films. www.afi.com/members/catalog/.

Anobile, Richard J. *Michael Curtiz's Casablanca.* New York: Universe Books, 1974.

Arden, Eve. *Three Phases of Eve: An Autobiography.* New York: St. Martin's Press, 1985.

Atkins, Irene Kahn. *Leroy Prinz.* Hollywood: Directors Guild of America, 1979.

Bacall, Lauren. *By Myself and Then Some.* New York: HarperEntertainment, 2005.

Bacon, James. *Made in Hollywood.* Chicago: Contemporary Books, 1977.

Baker, Dorothy. *Young Man with a Horn.* Boston: Houghton Mifflin, 1938.

Basquette, Lina, and Mary Garland Jonas. *Lina, DeMille's Godless Girl.* Fairfax, Va.: Denlinger's Publishers, 1990.

Baxter, John. *The Hollywood Exiles.* New York: Taplinger, 1976.

———. *Hollywood in the Thirties.* New York: A. S. Barnes, 1968.

———. *Stunt: The Story of the Great Movie Stunt Men.* Garden City, N.Y.: Doubleday, 1974.

Beaver, Jim. *John Garfield: His Life and Films.* South Brunswick, N.J.: A. S. Barnes, 1978.

Rudy Behlmer, ed. *The Adventures of Robin Hood.* Madison: University of Wisconsin Press, 1979.

———. *Behind the Scenes: The Making of —.* Hollywood: Samuel French, 1990.

———, ed. *Inside Warner Bros. (1935–1951).* New York: Viking, 1985.

———, ed. *The Sea Hawk.* Madison: University of Wisconsin Press, 1982.

Bellamy, Ralph. *When the Smoke Hit the Fan.* Garden City, N.Y.: Doubleday, 1979.

Bentley, Eric. *Thirty Years of Treason: Excerpts from Hearings before the House Committee on Un-American Activities, 1938–1968.* New York: Viking Press, 1971.

Berg, A. Scott. *Goldwyn: A Biography.* New York: Knopf, 1989.

Bernhardt, Curtis, and Mary Kiersch. *Curtis Bernhardt: A Directors Guild of America Oral History.* Hollywood: Directors Guild of America, 1986.

Bessette, Roland L. *Mario Lanza: Tenor in Exile.* Portland, Ore.: Amadeus Press, 1999.

Bickford, Charles. *Bulls, Balls, Bicycles and Actors.* New York: Paul S. Eriksson, 1965.

Bingen, Steven, with Marc Wanamaker. *Warner Bros.: Hollywood's Ultimate Backlot.* Lanham, Md.: Taylor, 2014.

Biro, Adam. *One Must Also Be Hungarian*. Trans. Catherine Tihanyi. Chicago: University of Chicago Press, 2006.

Bishop, Jim. *The Mark Hellinger Story: A Biography of Broadway and Hollywood*. New York: Appleton-Century-Crofts, 1952.

Bogdanovich, Peter. *Who the Hell's in It: Portraits and Conversations*. New York: Knopf, 2004.

Bogle, Donald. *Toms, Coons, Mulattoes, Mammies, and Bucks: An Interpretive History of Blacks in American Films*. 4th ed. New York: Continuum, 2001.

Bonomo, Joe. *The Strongman: A True Life, Pictorial Autobiography of the Hercules of the Screen, Joe Bonomo*. New York: Bonomo Studios, 1968.

Brodsly, David. *L.A. Freeway, an Appreciative Essay*. Berkeley: University of California Press, 1981.

Brown, May Wale. *Reel Life on Hollywood Movie Sets*. Riverside, Calif.: Ariadne Press, 1995.

Brownlow, Kevin. *Hollywood, the Pioneers*. New York: Knopf, 1979.

———. *The Parade's Gone By*. New York: Knopf, 1968.

Buford, Kate. *Burt Lancaster: An American Life*. New York: Knopf, 2000.

———. *Native American Son: The Life and Sporting Legend of Jim Thorpe*. New York: Knopf, 2010.

Burlingame, Jon. *Sound and Vision: Sixty Years of Motion Picture Soundtracks*. New York: Billboard, 2000.

Burns, Bryan. *World Cinema: Hungary*. Trowbridge, U.K.: Flicks Books, 1996.

Cagney, James. *Cagney by Cagney*. Garden City, N.Y.: Doubleday, 1976.

Cahn, Sammy. *I Should Care: The Sammy Cahn Story*. New York: Arbor House, 1974.

Calvet, Corinne. *Has Corinne Been a Good Girl?* New York: St. Martin's, 1983.

Canham, Kingsley, et al. *The Hollywood Professionals*. 7 vols. London: Tantivy Press, 1973–1980.

Canutt, Yakima, and Oliver Drake. *Stunt Man: The Autobiography of Yakima Canutt*. New York: Walker, 1979.

Carmichael, Hoagy, with Stephen Longstreet. *Sometimes I Wonder: The Story of Hoagy Carmichael*. New York: Farrar, Straus and Giroux, 1965.

Carr, Steven Alan. *Hollywood and Anti-Semitism: A Cultural History up to World War II*. Cambridge, U.K.: Cambridge University Press, 2001.

Carroll, Brendan G. *The Last Prodigy: A Biography of Erich Wolfgang Korngold*. Portland, Ore.: Amadeus Press, 1997.

Chapman, Mike. *Please Don't Call Me Tarzan*. Newton, Iowa: Culture House Books, 2001.

Clooney, Rosemary, and Joan Barthel. *Girl Singer: An Autobiography*. New York: Doubleday, 1999.

Coghlan, Frank. *They Still Call Me Junior: Autobiography of a Child Star, with a Filmography*. Jefferson, N.C.: McFarland, 1993.

Cole, Lester. *Hollywood Red: The Autobiography of Lester Cole*. Palo Alto, Calif.: Ramparts Press, 1981.

Bibliography

Considine, Shaun. *Bette & Joan: The Divine Feud.* New York: E. P. Dutton, 1989.

Cooper, Jackie, and Richard Kleiner. *Please Don't Shoot My Dog: The Autobiography of Jackie Cooper.* New York: Morrow, 1981.

Crosby, Bing. *Call Me Lucky.* New York: Simon and Schuster, 1953.

Culbert, David Holbrook, ed. *Mission to Moscow.* Madison: University of Wisconsin Press, 1980.

Cunningham, John. *Hungarian Cinema: From Coffee House to Multiplex.* London: Wallflower Press, 2004.

Curtis, James. *Spencer Tracy: A Biography.* New York: Knopf, 2011.

Custen, George F. *Twentieth Century's Fox: Darryl F. Zanuck and the Culture of Hollywood.* New York: Basic Books, 1997.

Daniel, Douglass K. *Tough as Nails: The Life and Films of Richard Brooks.* Madison: University of Wisconsin Press, 2011.

Dassanowsky, Robert. *Austrian Cinema: A History.* Jefferson, N.C.: McFarland, 2005.

Davies, Joseph Edward. *Mission to Moscow.* New York: Simon and Schuster, 1941.

Davis, Bette. *The Lonely Life: An Autobiography.* New York: G. P. Putnam's Sons, 1962.

Davis, Ronald L. *The Glamour Factory: Inside Hollywood's Big Studio System.* Dallas: Southern Methodist University Press, 1993.

———. *Just Making Movies: Company Directors on the Studio System.* Jackson: University Press of Mississippi, 2005.

———. *Words into Images: Screenwriters on the Studio System.* Jackson: University Press of Mississippi, 2007.

———. *Zachary Scott: Hollywood's Sophisticated Cad.* Jackson: University Press of Mississippi, 2006.

Day, Doris, and A. E. Hotchner. *Doris Day: Her Own Story.* New York: Morrow, 1976.

DeCamp, Rosemary. *Tigers in My Lap.* Baltimore: Midnight Marquee Press, 2000.

Decherney, Peter. *Hollywood and the Culture Elite: How the Movies Became American.* New York: Columbia University Press, 2005.

Doherty, Thomas Patrick. *Hollywood and Hitler, 1933–1939.* New York: Columbia University Press, 2013.

———. *Hollywood's Censor: Joseph I. Breen & the Production Code Administration.* New York: Columbia University Press, 2007.

Douglas, Kirk. *The Ragman's Son: An Autobiography.* New York: Simon and Schuster, 1988.

Drazin, Charles. *Korda: Britain's Only Movie Mogul.* London: Sidgwick & Jackson, 2002.

Dunne, Philip. *Take Two: A Life in Movies and Politics.* New York: McGraw-Hill, 1980.

Ephron, Henry. *We Thought We Could Do Anything: The Life of Screenwriters Phoebe and Henry Ephron.* New York: W. W. Norton, 1977.

Eyman, Scott. *Empire of Dreams: The Epic Life of Cecil B. DeMille.* New York: Simon & Schuster, 2010.

Bibliography

―――. *John Wayne: The Life and Legend.* New York: Simon & Schuster, 2014.

―――. *The Speed of Sound: Hollywood and the Talkie Revolution, 1926–1930.* New York: Simon & Schuster, 1997.

Fairbanks, Douglas. *The Salad Days.* New York: Doubleday, 1988.

Fidalgo, Miguel A. *Michael Curtiz: Bajo la sombra de Casablanca.* Madrid: T&B Editores, 2009.

Fitzgerald, Mike. *The Ageless Warrior: The Life of Boxing Legend Archie Moore.* Champaign, Ill.: Sports Publishing, 2004.

Flynn, Errol. *My Wicked, Wicked Ways.* 1959. Reprint, New York: Cooper Square Press, 2003.

Freedland, Michael. *The Warner Brothers.* New York: St. Martin's Press, 1983.

Friedrich, Otto. *City of Nets: A Portrait of Hollywood in the 1940's.* New York: Harper & Row, 1986.

Fuller, Samuel, Christa Fuller, and Jerome Rudes. *A Third Face: My Tale of Writing, Fighting, and Filmmaking.* New York: Knopf, 2002.

Gabler, Neal. *An Empire of Their Own: How the Jews Invented Hollywood.* New York: Crown, 1988.

Gálos, Magda Konrádyné. *A Newyorktól a Hungáriáig.* Budapest: Minerva, 1965.

Gansberg, Alan L. *Little Caesar: A Biography of Edward G. Robinson.* Lanham, Md.: Scarecrow Press, 2004.

Giddins, Gary. *Warning Shadows: Home Alone with Classic Cinema.* New York: W. W. Norton, 2010.

Goodman, Ezra. *The Fifty-Year Decline and Fall of Hollywood.* New York: Simon and Schuster, 1961.

Hamilton, Ian. *Writers in Hollywood, 1915–1951.* London: Heinemann, 1990.

Harmetz, Aljean. *The Making of Casablanca: Bogart, Bergman, and World War II.* New York: Hyperion, 2002. (Originally published as *Round Up the Usual Suspects.*)

Harris, Marlys J. *The Zanucks of Hollywood: The Dark Legacy of a Movie Dynasty.* New York: Crown, 1989.

Harris, Warren G. *Cary Grant: A Touch of Elegance.* Garden City, N.Y.: Doubleday, 1987.

Hart, Mother Dolores, OSB, and Richard DeNeut. *The Ear of the Heart: An Actress' Journey from Hollywood to Holy Vows.* San Francisco: Ignatius Press, 2013.

Hatfield, Sharon. *Never Seen the Moon: The Trials of Edith Maxwell.* Urbana: University of Illinois Press, 2005.

Helmick, Paul. *Cut, Print, and That's a Wrap! A Hollywood Memoir.* Jefferson, N.C.: McFarland, 2001.

Henreid, Paul, and Julius Fast. *Ladies Man: An Autobiography.* New York: St. Martin's Press, 1984.

Herzog, Peter, and Romano Tozzi. *Lya de Putti: "Loving Life and Not Fearing Death."* New York: Corvin, 1993.

Higham, Charles. *Hollywood Cameramen: Sources of Light.* Bloomington: Indiana University Press, 1970.

Hochman, Stanley. *American Film Directors: With Filmographies and Index of Critics and Films*. New York: Ungar, 1974.

Hollywood: A Celebration of the American Silent Film. 13 VHS tapes. HBO Video, 1979.

Hoopes, Roy. *Cain*. New York: Holt, Rinehart and Winston, 1980.

Hughes, Dorothy B. *Erle Stanley Gardner: The Case of the Real Perry Mason*. New York: Morrow, 1978.

IMDb. www.imdb.com/.

Jacobs, Stephen. *Boris Karloff: More Than a Monster: The Authorised Biography*. Sheffield, U.K.: Tomahawk Press, 2011.

Jason, Sybil. *My Fifteen Minutes: An Autobiography of a Child Star of the Golden Era of Hollywood*. Boalsburg, Pa.: BearManor Media, 2005.

Jerome, Stuart. *Those Crazy, Wonderful Years When We Ran Warner Bros*. Secaucus, N.J.: Lyle Stuart, 1983.

Johnson, Paul. *Modern Times: The World from the Twenties to the Eighties*. New York: Harper & Row, 1983.

Jurow, Martin, and Philip Wuntch. *Marty Jurow Seein' Stars: A Show Biz Odyssey*. Dallas: Southern Methodist University Press, 2001.

Kashner, Sam, and Nancy Schoenberger. *A Talent for Genius: The Life and Times of Oscar Levant*. New York: Villard Books, 1994.

Katz, Ephraim. *The Film Encyclopedia*. New York: HarperCollins, 1994.

Kaufman, David. *Doris Day: The Untold Story of the Girl Next Door*. New York: Virgin Books USA, 2008.

Kear, Lynn, and John Rossman. *Kay Francis: A Passionate Life and Career*. Jefferson, N.C.: McFarland, 2006.

Kinnard, Roy, and R. J. Vitone. *The American Films of Michael Curtiz*. Metuchen, N.J.: Scarecrow Press, 1986.

Kołakowski, Leszek. *Main Currents of Marxism: Its Rise, Growth, and Dissolution*. Translated by P. S. Falla. Oxford: Clarendon Press, 1978.

Koch, Howard. *As Time Goes By: Memoirs of a Writer*. New York: Harcourt Brace Jovanovich, 1979.

Koch, Howard, Philip G. Epstein, and Julius J. Epstein. *Casablanca: Script and Legend*. Woodstock, N.Y.: Overlook Press, 1992.

Koszarski, Richard, ed. *Mystery of the Wax Museum*. Madison: University of Wisconsin Press, 1979.

Kramer, Joan, and David Heeley. *In the Company of Legends*. New York: Beaufort Books, 2015.

Kroll, Harry Harrison. *The Cabin in the Cotton*. New York: R. Long & R. R. Smith, 1931.

LaValley, Albert J., ed. *Mildred Pierce*. Madison: University of Wisconsin Press, 1980.

Lawrence, Jerome. *Actor: The Life and Times of Paul Muni*. New York: Putnam, 1974.

Layton, James, and David Pierce. *The Dawn of Technicolor, 1915–1935*. New York: George Eastman House, 2015.

Lee, Peggy. *Miss Peggy Lee: An Autobiography.* New York: Donald I. Fine, 1989.

Leider, Emily W. *Myrna Loy: The Only Good Girl in Hollywood.* Berkeley: University of California Press, 2011.

Lendvai, Paul. *The Hungarians: A Thousand Years of Victory in Defeat.* Princeton: Princeton University Press, 2003.

Lennig, Arthur. *The Count: The Life and Films of Bela "Dracula" Lugosi.* New York: Putnam, 1974.

Lenz, Rick. *North of Hollywood.* North Hollywood, Calif.: Chromodroid Press, 2012.

LeRoy, Mervyn. *Mervyn LeRoy: Take One.* New York: Hawthorn Books, 1971.

Levinson, Peter J. *Tommy Dorsey, Livin' in a Great Big Way: A Biography.* Cambridge, Mass.: Da Capo Press, 2005.

———. *Trumpet Blues: The Life of Harry James.* New York: Oxford University Press, 1999.

Lewis, David. *The Creative Producer.* Edited by James Curtis. Metuchen, N.J.: Scarecrow Press, 1993.

Linet, Beverly. *Ladd: The Life, the Legend, the Legacy of Alan Ladd: A Biography.* New York: Arbor House, 1979.

Lucas, John Meredyth. *Eighty Odd Years in Hollywood: Memoir of a Career in Film and Television.* Jefferson, N.C.: McFarland, 2004.

Lukacs, John. *Budapest 1900: A Historical Portrait of a City and Its Culture.* New York: Weindenfeld & Nicolson, 1988.

Lupino, Ida, with Mary Ann Anderson. *Ida Lupino: Beyond the Camera.* Albany, Ga.: BearManor Media, 2011.

Madsen, Axel. *Stanwyck.* New York: HarperCollins, 1994.

Maltin, Leonard. *The Art of the Cinematographer: A Survey and Interviews with Five Masters.* New York: Dover Publications, 1978.

Mank, Gregory William. *Women in Horror Films, 1930s.* Jefferson, N.C.: McFarland, 1999.

Mankiewicz, Tom, and Robert Crane. *My Life as a Mankiewicz: An Insider's Journey through Hollywood.* Lexington: University Press of Kentucky, 2012.

Marcus, Ben, and Marc Wanamaker. *Malibu.* Charleston, S.C.: Arcadia Pub., 2011.

Marion, Frances. *Off with Their Heads: A Serio-Comic Tale of Hollywood.* New York: Macmillan, 1972.

Martin, Pete. *Hollywood without Make-Up.* Philadelphia: J. B. Lippincott, 1948.

Marton, Kati. *The Great Escape: Nine Jews Who Fled Hitler and Changed the World.* New York: Simon & Schuster, 2006.

Marx, Samuel, and Joyce Vanderveen. *Deadly Illusions: Jean Harlow and the Murder of Paul Bern.* New York: Random House, 1990.

Massey, Raymond. *A Hundred Different Lives: An Autobiography.* Boston: Little, Brown, 1979.

Matzen, Robert D. *Errol & Olivia: Ego & Obsession in Golden Era Hollywood.* Pittsburgh: GoodKnight Books, 2010.

Matzen, Robert, and Michael Mazzone. *Errol Flynn Slept Here: The Flynns, the*

Hamblens, Ricky Nelson, and the Most Notorious House in Hollywood. Pittsburgh: GoodKnight Books, 2009.

McCabe, John. *Cagney.* New York: Carroll & Graf, 1997.

McCarthy, Todd. *Howard Hawks: The Grey Fox of Hollywood.* New York: Grove Press, 1997.

McClelland, Doug. *Forties Film Talk: Oral Histories of Hollywood, with 120 Lobby Posters.* Jefferson, N.C.: McFarland, 1992.

McGilligan, Patrick. *Backstory: Interviews with Screenwriters of Hollywood's Golden Age.* Berkeley: University of California Press, 1986.

———. *Cagney: The Actor as Auteur.* South Brunswick, N.J.: A. S. Barnes, 1975.

———. *Film Crazy: Interviews with Hollywood Legends.* New York: St. Martin's Press, 2000.

———, ed. *Yankee Doodle Dandy.* Madison: University of Wisconsin Press, 1981.

McGrath, Patrick J. *John Garfield: The Illustrated Career in Films and on Stage.* Jefferson, N.C.: McFarland, 1993.

McNeill, Joe. *Arizona's Little Hollywood: Sedona and Northern Arizona's Forgotten Film History, 1923–1973.* Sedona, Ariz.: Northedge & Sons, 2010.

Menefee, David W. *George O'Brien: A Man's Man in Hollywood.* Albany, Ga.: BearManor Media, 2009.

Meyer, William R. *Warner Brothers Directors: The Hard-Boiled, the Comic, and the Weepers.* New Rochelle, N.Y.: Arlington House, 1978.

Meyers, Jeffrey. *Gary Cooper: American Hero.* New York: Morrow, 1998.

———. *Inherited Risk: Errol and Sean Flynn in Hollywood and Vietnam.* New York: Simon & Schuster, 2002.

Miller, John. *Peter Ustinov: The Gift of Laughter.* London: Weidenfeld & Nicolson, 2002.

Mirisch, Walter. *I Thought We Were Making Movies, Not History.* Madison: University of Wisconsin Press, 2008.

Molnár, Miklós. *A Concise History of Hungary.* Cambridge, U.K.: Cambridge University Press, 2001.

Monush, Barry. *The Encyclopedia of Hollywood Film Actors.* New York: Applause Theatre and Cinema Books, 2003.

Morehouse, Ward. *George M. Cohan: Prince of the American Theater.* Philadelphia: J. B. Lippincott, 1943.

Morgan, Michèle, and Marcelle Routier. *Avec ces yeux-là.* Paris: Éditions Robert Laffont, 1977.

Morley, Sheridan. *The Other Side of the Moon: The Life of David Niven.* New York: Harper & Row, 1985.

Mosley, Leonard. *Zanuck: The Rise and Fall of Hollywood's Last Tycoon.* Boston: Little, Brown, 1984.

Muller, Eddie. *Dark City Dames: The Wicked Women of Film Noir.* New York: Regan Books, 2001.

Murphy, George, and Victor Lasky. *"Say . . . Didn't You Used to Be George Murphy?"* New York: Bartholomew House, 1970.

Murray, Edward. *The Cinematic Imagination: Writers and the Motion Pictures.* New York: Ungar, 1972.

Negulesco, Jean. *Things I Did and Things I Think I Did.* New York: Linden Press/ Simon & Schuster, 1984.

Nemeskürty, István. *Word and Image: History of the Hungarian Cinema.* Translated by Zsuzsanna Horn. Budapest: Corvina Press, 1968.

Newquist, Roy, and Joan Crawford. *Conversations with Joan Crawford.* Secaucus, N.J.: Citadel Press, 1980.

Niven, David. *Bring on the Empty Horses.* New York: Putnam, 1975.

Nordhoff, Charles, and James Norman Hall. *Men without Country.* Boston: Little, Brown, 1942.

Nott, Robert. *He Ran All the Way: The Life of John Garfield.* New York: Limelight, 2003.

Oberfirst, Robert. *Al Jolson: You Ain't Heard Nothin' Yet.* San Diego: A. S. Barnes, 1982.

O'Brien, Pat. *The Wind at My Back: The Life and Times of Pat O'Brien by Himself.* Garden City, N.Y.: Doubleday, 1964.

O'Brien, Scott. *Kay Francis: I Can't Wait to Be Forgotten: Her Life on Film & Stage.* Albany, Ga.: BearManor Media, 2007.

———. *Ruth Chatterton, Actress, Aviator, Author.* Albany, Ga.: BearManor Media, 2013.

Orlean, Susan. *Rin Tin Tin: The Life and the Legend.* New York: Simon & Schuster, 2011.

Osborne, Richard E. *The Casablanca Companion: The Movie Classic and Its Place in History.* Indianapolis: Riebel-Roque, 1997.

Osborne, Robert. *80 Years of the Oscar: The Official History of the Academy Awards.* New York: Abbeville Press, 2008.

Parish, James Robert. *The Tough Guys.* New Rochelle, N.Y.: Arlington House Publishers, 1976.

Parsons, Louella O. *Tell It to Louella.* New York: Putnam, 1961.

Peary, Gerald, and Roger Shatzkin. *The Classic American Novel and the Movies.* New York: Ungar, 1977.

Picerni, Paul, with Tom Weaver. *Steps to Stardom: My Story.* Albany, Ga.: BearManor Media, 2007.

Quirk, Lawrence J. *Jane Wyman, the Actress and the Woman: An Illustrated Biography.* New York: Dembner Books, 1986.

Radosh, Ronald, and Allis Radosh. *Red Star over Hollywood: The Film Colony's Long Romance with the Left.* San Francisco: Encounter Books, 2005.

Rainsberger, Todd. *James Wong Howe, Cinematographer.* San Diego: A. S. Barnes, 1981.

Reagan, Ronald, with Richard G. Hubler. *Where's the Rest of Me?* New York: Duell, Sloan and Pearce, 1965.

Reed, Rochelle, ed. *Olivia de Havilland.* Beverly Hills, Calif.: American Film Institute, 1974.

Robertson, James C. *The Casablanca Man: The Cinema of Michael Curtiz*. London: Routledge, 1993.

Robinson, Edward G., and Leonard Spigelgass. *All My Yesterdays: An Autobiography*. New York: Hawthorn Books, 1973.

Roddick, Nick. *A New Deal in Entertainment: Warner Brothers in the 1930s*. London: British Film Institute, 1983.

Roderick, Kevin. *The San Fernando Valley: America's Suburb*. Los Angeles: Los Angeles Times Books, 2001.

Rose, Frank. *The Agency: William Morris and the Hidden History of Show Business*. New York: HarperBusiness, 1995.

Sakall, S. Z. *The Story of Cuddles: My Life under the Emperor Francis Joseph, Adolf Hitler, and the Warner Brothers*. Translated by Paul Tabori. London: Cassell, 1954.

Sarris, Andrew. *The American Cinema; Directors and Directions, 1929–1968*. 1968. Reprint, New York: Da Capo Press, 1968.

———. *You Ain't Heard Nothin' Yet: The American Talking Film: History & Memory, 1927–1949*. New York: Oxford University Press, 1998.

Schatz, Thomas. *Boom and Bust: The American Cinema in the 1940s*. New York: Scribner, 1997.

———. *The Genius of the System: Hollywood Filmmaking in the Studio Era*. New York: Pantheon Books, 1988.

Schwartz, Nancy Lynn, and Sheila Schwartz. *The Hollywood Writers' Wars*. New York: Knopf, 1982.

Scorsese, Martin, and Michael Henry Wilson. *A Personal Journey with Martin Scorsese through American Movies*. New York: Hyperion, 1997.

Sennett, Ted. *Masters of Menace: Greenstreet and Lorre*. New York: Dutton, 1979.

———. *Warner Brothers Presents: The Most Exciting Years—from the Jazz Singer to White Heat*. Secaucus, N.J.: Castle Books, 1971.

Server, Lee. *Screenwriter: Words Become Pictures*. Pittstown, N.J.: Main Street Press, 1987.

Shales, Tom, et al. *The American Film Heritage: Impressions from the American Film Institute Archives*. Washington, D.C.: Acropolis Book, 1972.

Sharp, Kathleen. *Mr. & Mrs. Hollywood: Edie and Lew Wasserman and Their Entertainment Empire*. New York: Carroll & Graf, 2003.

Shavelson, Melville. *How to Succeed in Hollywood without Really Trying: P.S. You Can't!* Albany, Ga.: BearManor Media, 2007.

Shearer, Stephen Michael. *Patricia Neal: An Unquiet Life*. Lexington: University Press of Kentucky, 2006.

Shindler, Colin. *Hollywood Goes to War: Films and American Society, 1939–1952*. Boston: Routledge & K. Paul, 1979.

Siegel, Don. *A Siegel Film: An Autobiography*. Boston: Faber and Faber, 1993.

Silke, James R. *Here's Looking at You, Kid: 50 Years of Fighting, Working, and Dreaming at Warner Bros*. Boston: Little, Brown, 1976.

Skal, David J., and Jessica Rains. *Claude Rains: An Actor's Voice*. Lexington: University Press of Kentucky, 2008.

Sklar, Robert. *City Boys: Cagney, Bogart, Garfield.* Princeton: Princeton University Press, 1992.

————. *Movie-Made America: A Social History of American Movies.* New York: Random House, 1975.

Slezak, Walter. *What Time's the Next Swan?* Garden City, N.Y.: Doubleday, 1962.

Slide, Anthony. *Hollywood Unknowns: A History of Extras, Bit Players, and Stand-Ins.* Jackson: University Press of Mississippi, 2012.

Smith, Steven C. *A Heart at Fire's Center: The Life and Music of Bernard Herrmann.* Berkeley: University of California Press, 1991.

Soren, David, with Meredith Banasiak and Bob Thomas et al. *Vera-Ellen: The Magic and the Mystery.* Baltimore: Luminary Press, 2003.

Spada, James. *More Than a Woman: An Intimate Biography of Bette Davis.* New York: Bantam Books, 1993.

Sperber, A. M., and Eric Lax. *Humphrey Bogart.* New York: William Morrow, 1997.

Sperling, Cass Warner, and Cork Millner with Jack Warner. *Hollywood Be Thy Name: The Warner Brothers Story.* Rocklin, Calif.: Prima Publishing, 1994.

Stack, Robert, and Mark Evans. *Straight Shooting.* New York: Macmillan, 1980.

Stevens, George, ed. *Conversations with the Great Moviemakers of Hollywood's Golden Age at the American Film Institute.* New York: Knopf, 2006.

Stine, Whitney. *"I'd Love to Kiss You"—: Conversations with Bette Davis.* New York: Pocket Books, 1990.

Sudhalter, Richard M. *Stardust Melody: The Life and Music of Hoagy Carmichael.* New York: Oxford University Press, 2002.

Surowiec, Catherine A., ed. *Le Giornate del Cinema Muto, 1–8 Ottobre 2011, 30th Pordenone Silent Film Festival.* Pordenone: N.p., 2011.

Talbot, Margaret. *The Entertainer: Movies, Magic, and My Father's Twentieth Century.* New York: Riverhead Books, 2012.

Taravella, Steve. *Mary Wickes: I Know I've Seen That Face Before.* Jackson: University Press of Mississippi, 2013.

Taves, Brian. *Robert Florey: The French Expressionist.* Metuchen, N.J.: Scarecrow Press, 1987.

Taylor, S. J. *Stalin's Apologist: Walter Duranty, the* New York Times*'s Man in Moscow.* New York: Oxford University Press, 1990.

Temple, Shirley. *Child Star: An Autobiography.* New York: McGraw-Hill, 1988.

Thomas, Bob. *Clown Prince of Hollywood: The Antic Life and Times of Jack L. Warner.* New York: McGraw-Hill, 1990.

————. *Joan Crawford: A Biography.* London: Weidenfeld and Nicolson, 1979.

————. *Marlon: Portrait of the Rebel as an Artist.* New York: Random House, 1973.

Thomas, Danny, and Bill Davidson. *Make Room for Danny.* New York: Putnam, 1991.

Thomas, Tony. *Errol Flynn: The Spy Who Never Was.* New York: Carol Publishing, 1990.

————. *The Films of Marlon Brando.* Secaucus, N.J.: Citadel Press, 1973.

Thomas, Tony, Rudy Behlmer, and Clifford McCarty. *The Films of Errol Flynn*. New York: Citadel Press, 1969.

Thompson, Verita, with Donald Shepherd. *Bogie and Me: A Love Story*. New York: St. Martin's Press, 1982.

Toth, Andre de. *Fragments: Portraits from the Inside*. Boston: Faber and Faber, 1994.

Tranberg, Charles. *Fred MacMurray: A Biography*. Albany, Ga.: BearManor Media, 2007.

Ungváry, Krisztián. *The Siege of Budapest: One Hundred Days in World War II*. Translated by Ladislaus Löb. New Haven: Yale University Press, 2005.

Varconi, Victor, and Ed Honeck. *It's Not Enough to Be Hungarian*. Denver: Graphic Impressions, 1976.

Variety Film Reviews, 1921–1925, vol. 2. New York: Garland, 1983.

Vogel, Michelle. *Olive Borden: The Life and Films of Hollywood's "Joy Girl."* Jefferson, N.C.: McFarland, 2010.

Wakeman, John. *World Film Directors*. 2 vols. New York: H. W. Wilson, 1987.

Wallis, Hal B., and Charles Higham. *Starmaker: The Autobiography of Hal Wallis*. New York: Macmillan, 1980.

Wanamaker, Marc. *San Fernando Valley*. Charleston, S.C.: Arcadia Pub., 2011.

Warner, Jack L., and Dean Jennings. *My First Hundred Years in Hollywood*. New York: Random House, 1965.

Wegele, Peter. *Max Steiner: Composing, Casablanca, and the Golden Age of Film Music*. Lanham, Md.: Rowman & Littlefield, 2014.

Wiles, Buster, and William Donati. *My Days with Errol Flynn: The Autobiography of Stuntman Buster Wiles: With a Special Appendix, the Flynn Controversy*. Santa Monica: Roundtable Publishing, 1988.

Wilk, Max. *Every Day's a Matinee: Memoirs Scribbled on a Dressing Room Door*. New York: W. W. Norton, 1975.

———. *Schmucks with Underwoods: Conversations with Hollywood's Classic Screenwriters*. New York: Applause Theatre and Cinema Books, 2004.

Wilson, Arthur. *The Warner Bros. Golden Anniversary Book: The First Complete Feature Filmography*. New York: Film and Venture, 1973.

Wilson, Victoria. *A Life of Barbara Stanwyck*. New York: Simon & Schuster, 2013.

Winters, Ben. *Erich Wolfgang Korngold's The Adventures of Robin Hood: A Film Score Guide*. Lanham, Md.: Scarecrow Press, 2007.

Wray, Fay. *On the Other Hand: A Life Story*. New York: St. Martin's Press, 1989.

Youngkin, Stephen D. *The Lost One: A Life of Peter Lorre*. Lexington: University Press of Kentucky, 2005.

Zanuck, Darryl Francis. *Memo from Darryl F. Zanuck: The Golden Years at Twentieth Century-Fox*. Edited by Rudy Behlmer. New York: Grove Press, 1993.

Index

SCREEN CLASSICS

Screen Classics is a series of critical biographies, film histories, and analytical studies focusing on neglected filmmakers and important screen artists and subjects, from the era of silent cinema to the golden age of Hollywood to the international generation of today. Books in the Screen Classics series are intended for scholars and general readers alike. The contributing authors are established figures in their respective fields. This series also serves the purpose of advancing scholarship on film personalities and themes with ties to Kentucky.

SERIES EDITOR: Patrick McGilligan